W9-BHY-672

THE ENCYCLOPEDIA OF SUICIDE

THE ENCYCLOPEDIA OF SUICIDE

Glen Evans
and
Norman L. Farberow, PhD

Facts On File®
New York • Oxford

The man who kills a man kills a man.
The man who kills himself kills all men.
As far as he is concerned, he wipes out the world.
G.K. Chesterton

The great tragedy of life is not death,
but what dies inside of us while we live.
Norman Cousins

That life is worth living is the most
necessary of assumptions, and were it not
assumed, the most impossible of conclusions.
George Santayana

The Encyclopedia of Suicide

Library of Congress Cataloging-in-Publication Data

Evans, Glen.
The encyclopedia of suicide.

Bibliography: p.
Includes index.
1. Suicide—Dictionaries. 2. Suicide—United States—Dictionaries. I. Farberow, Norman L. II. Title.
HV6545.E87 1988 362.2 88-11173
ISBN 0-8160-1397-7
British CIP available.

Printed in the United States of America

10 9 8 7 6 5 4 3 2

CONTENTS

PREFACE

In the United States someone commits suicide every 20 minutes. Suicide, not long ago ranked 22nd, is eighth on the list of causes of death in the United States. Tragically, the problem is worsening. The teen and young adult suicide rate has increased dramatically in the last three decades, and the high incidence of suicide among the elderly has reached disturbing proportions. The number of adolescent suicides has tripled in only 20 years, and more than 10,000 persons over age 60 will take their own lives this year.

The most frightening aspect about suicide is that we still do not know why a given individual chooses to end his or her life. There are myriad theories—the literature of speculation and research is vast—but they are just theories. Research to date indicates that reasons are many, complex and, as yet, inconclusive. Suicide does not discriminate; it is committed by all kinds of people from every walk of life.

At one time or another, it seems, almost everyone contemplates suicide.

It is because this problem continues to spread that *The Encyclopedia of Suicide* has been published as a companion reference to two of Facts On File's earlier books on social problems, *The Encyclopedia of Alcoholism*, edited by the late Robert O'Brien and Dr. Morris Chafetz, and *The Encyclopedia of Drug Abuse*, edited by Mr. O'Brien and Dr. Sidney Cohen.

This work is, to the best of the authors' knowledge, the first A-to-Z volume, the first encyclopedic reference, to appear in the field of suicidology. The book is designed to provide an overall view of the suicide phenomenon, including an introductory article, "The History of Suicide" by Dr. Norman L. Farberow, and entries that cover every aspect of the subject from psychological concerns to political and legal factors, from socioeconomic aspects to educational and religious considerations. In addition, there are appendixes of tabular material providing suicide rates by age groups, methods of suicide, listings of suicide prevention and crisis centers, and other key sources of information, plus a comprehensive bibliography.

The Encyclopedia of Suicide is intended for both the professional and the lay person. We have kept the language concise and comprehensible, so that the volume can be used by members of the various professional disciplines as well as by individuals who, for whatever reasons, want to know more about the problem of suicide. We have tried to define terms as simply as possible and explain complex theories clearly, free of confusing jargon.

Suicide is an intensely complicated subject, more so perhaps than people realize. Because of this and because of the format and space limitations, we could not begin to include all the information we would have liked. Thus, a bibliography is provided for readers who seek additional sources of information.

Ongoing research into the various aspects of suicide and self-destructive behavior—and the extent of the problem—turns up new and exciting information almost daily. For that reason, *The Encyclopedia of Suicide*, much like the volumes on alcoholism and drug abuse, should be considered a "work in progress." Future editions will keep readers updated on key aspects of development, theory and treatment relating to this spiraling worldwide problem.

Glen Evans
Stamford, Conn.

Norman L. Farberow, PhD
Los Angeles, Calif.

ACKNOWLEDGMENTS

We trust *The Encyclopedia of Suicide* has value as a work of reference as well as one of general interest to lay readers. If it does, we are greatly indebted to many people. Kate Kelly, who had the idea for this project and its presentation, is an editor for the publisher, Facts On File, Inc. She suggested certain listings, assisted in the final selection and edited the entire manuscript.

All works such as this are in no small part the product of pilferage from authorities in various professional fields. While we have given attribution to those whose published material we have used, we have tried to stop considerably short of pillage. We are especially grateful for some exceptionally fine pieces of work that have provided us with valuable insight and information. These include writings by Seymour Perlin, MD, Edwin Shneidman, PhD, Norman L. Farberow, PhD, Cynthia R. Pfeffer, MD, Shervert H. Frazier, MD, John L. McIntosh, PhD, Ronald Maris, PhD, Mary Giffin, MD, Richard Brandt, PhD, Jean LaFontaine, PhD, Mary Monk, PhD, George Rosen, MD, PhD, MPH, Peter Sainsbury, MD, Chester W. Schmidt, Jr., MD, Solomon H. Snyder, MD, George Vlasak, MD, Sidney Cohen, MD, Mark L. Rosenberg, MD, MPH, Dennis D. Tolsma, MPH, Lucy Davidson, MD, David Shaffer, MD, Ann Garland, MA (research scientist), John P. Myers, PhD, Julie Perlman, MSW (executive officer, AAS), Samuel C. Klagsbrun, MD, Michael Peck, PhD, Robert E. Litman, MD, Charlotte P. Ross (president and executive director, Youth Suicide National Center), Otis R. Bowen, MD (secretary, Department of Health and Human Services), Dodie Livingston (Administration for Children, Youth and Families, Department of Health and Human Services), James O. Mason, MD (director, Centers for Disease Control), Donald Ian Macdonald, MD, Alfred B. DelBello (chairperson, National Committee on Youth Suicide Prevention).

Others include Francine Klagsbrun, Rabbi Earl A. Grollman, Arnold Madison, Carol Felsenthal, Derek Humphry, Ann Wickett, Doris Portwood, Stephen C. Scheiber, MD, Brian B. Doyle, MD, Alfred Alvarez, Robert O'Brien, Morris Chafetz, MD, Herbert Hendin, MD, Richard Seiden, MD, John Langone, Clifton Fadiman and Isaac Asimov, PhD.

Mention should be made, too, of the staffs of the following agencies and organizations: National Institute on Drug Abuse, Centers for Disease Control, U.S. Department of Health and Human Services, World Health Organization, National Institute on Alcohol Abuse and Alcoholism, National Council on Alcoholism, Alcoholics Anonymous, National Self-Help Clearinghouse, Youth Suicide National Center, Information Center (San Diego, California), National Committee on Youth Suicide Prevention, Suicide Information and Education Centre (Calgary, Alberta, Canada), National Clearinghouse for Drug Abuse Information, Los Angeles Suicide Prevention Center, and San Francisco Suicide Prevention and Crisis Center and American Association of Suicidology.

On the less formal side, I wish to thank personally Christina Fortunato, my tireless typist who not only typed but also helped tighten the manuscript, and Karen Kiddey, efficient information officer at Canada's Suicide Information and Education Centre. My thanks always to my wife, Margie, and my daughter, Lisa, who never fail to extend confidence, encouragement and support.

—Glen Evans

I want to express my appreciation for the ever ready assistance of the libraries at the Brentwood Veterans Administration Hospital, the Arthur A. Mirsky Medical Library, and at the University of

California Medical School Biomedical Library. I give personal thanks to Nancy Taylor, my secretary, for her inexhaustible patience in deciphering my handwriting and typing my contributions to this work. My greatest debt, as usual, is to my wife, Pearl, who gives constantly of her love and unflagging support, and makes what is for me the difficult task of writing bearable.

—Norman L. Farberow

INTRODUCTION: THE HISTORY OF SUICIDE

Suicide has been a part of man's history since recorded time. It is not universal, for there are some places throughout the world where suicide does not occur, but such places are quite rare.

The word *suicide* is of relatively recent origin. It does not appear in the Old Testament, nor early Christian writings, nor even in the text of John Donne's *Biathanatos* (1644), one of the earliest English-language works defending suicide. Although the word seems to come from and sounds Latin, there was evidently no original single Latin word for the act; the Romans always used phrases to express the thought (Fedden, 1938). The expressions used most often were *sibi mortem consciscere* ("to procure his own death"), *vim sibi inferre* ("to cause violence to himself"), or *sua manu cadere* ("to fall by his own hand"). The word is reported by Fedden to have first appeared in 1662, when Edward Philips, in his *New World of Words*, calls suicide "a barbarous word, more appropriately derived from *sus*, a sow, than from the pronoun *sui*, as if it were a swinish part for a man to kill himself" (Fedden, 1938). The Oxford English Dictionary, however, states that suicide was first used in English in 1651 and was derived from the modern Latin word *suicidium*, which in turn had been produced by combining the Latin pronoun for self and the verb to kill. Almost a hundred years later, in 1752, the word appeared in France, in the *Dictionnaire de Trevoux*.

At one time, it was thought that suicide was a by-product of civilization and therefore unknown in primitive societies. To some extent this belief was influenced by the notion of the "happy savage" advanced by Jean-Jacques Rousseau (1761). Reliable evidence, however, indicates that suicide has existed in numerous primitive tribes around the globe (de Catanzaro, 1980). Steinmetz (1894), for example, reported finding suicide among such people as the North and South American Indians, polar people, Bedouins, people of the Caucasus, native races of British India, Melanesians, Micronesians, Polynesians and Indonesians. Malinowski (1926) described two ways the Trobriand islanders killed themselves: by jumping from the top of a palm tree and by taking fatal poison from the gallbladder of a globe fish. Firth (1961) reported a relatively high suicide rate in Tikopia, a Polynesian community in the western Pacific; Elwin (1943) reported on suicide in the Maria and other aboriginal tribes of central India; Devereux (1961) and Webb and Willard (1975) found various rates of suicide among the American Indians; Rasmussen (1931), Weyer (1932) and Leighton and Hughes (1955) found suicide among the Netsilik Eskimos of Greenland; Bohannan (1960), Fallers and Fallers (1960) and LaFontaine (1960) have reported different rates of suicide among the Africans. De Catanzaro (1981) concludes that suicide is not restricted to modern developed countries and may be said to occur with some frequency among primitive tribes and less technologically developed societies.

On the other hand, Westermarck (1908) found that suicide was unknown among the Yahgans of Tierra del Fuego, the Andaman islanders and various Australian aborigine tribes.

Attitudes toward suicide have varied greatly, in general reflecting the psychocultural history of the society in which suicide has occurred. Those societies that strongly condemned suicide most often associated the act with superstition and magic and reacted to it with horror and antagonism (Fedden, 1938). Taboos on suicide were developed in order to ward off the evils that were thought to accompany self-inflicted death or to keep the spirit of the suicide in prison so that it could not return to haunt the living.

Suicide usually took two forms: social, or institutional, suicide and individual, or personal, suicide. Each of these varied in degree and import in successive eras, but both generally could be found to some degree in all great civilizations and major religions. Institutional suicide was generally the self-destruction demanded by a society of an individual as a price for being a member of that society. An example would be sacrificing one's life for another, a practice found in some Eskimo tribes in which the old and sick were expected to sacrifice themselves to help ensure the survival of their group. In some primitive cultures, suicide was also a way of expressing anger and revenge but in a rigidly prescribed way, as when a Trobriander was accused of transgressing a tribal taboo he could climb to the top of a palm tree, name his accuser and then jump head first from the tree (Malinowski, 1926). Personal suicide, on the other hand, usually occurred out of motives of preservation of honor, expiation of cowardice, termination of pain, preservation of chastity, escape from personal disgrace by falling into the hands of an enemy, or intense despair from separation or loss of loved ones.

Suicide in Ancient Times

In ancient Egypt the attitude toward suicide was very neutral, inasmuch as death was seen as merely a passage from one form of existence to another and suicide as a humane method of escaping from intolerable hardship and injustice (McCormick, 1969). The dead were considered abstract co-equals with the living and with the Gods and thus had the same physical and emotional needs (Hankoff, 1979).

The first known writing about suicide is an Egyptian papyrus entitled *A Dispute over Suicide* (also known as *The Dialogue of a Misanthrope with His Own Soul*), written by an unidentified author during Egypt's First Intermediate Period (2280–2000 B.C.). A dialogue occurs between the soul and the self in which the man, tired of life, tries to convince his soul to accompany him into death. Many of the arguments address the question of whether a person has a right to take his life under any circumstance, reflecting the conflict between individual freedom and social responsibility. The soul hesitates, afraid the man will be deprived of a proper funeral if he commits suicide and thus the soul's chances for a blissful afterlife will be lost. The soul argues that death is accompanied by separation and grief, but the suicidal man contends that death for him would be a cure and a vacation.

Ambivalence toward the choice between life and death is the central theme of this discourse. The soul argues that death is no respecter of social position. But the suicidal self is motivated by other forces: the dishonor of his name, the loss of personal worth, the injustice and depravity of society, the reversal of value and honor, the absence of the good, the severance of friendship, a general mistrust of the world, and a fantasy with death. In death he expects to achieve the triumph of immortality and to be a god who will punish the unjust. The soul's advice, however, is to cling to life, to assume religious responsibilities and to approach death gradually in old age (Lum, 1974).

The Egyptians allowed a person condemned to death to take his own life—execution by suicide. Later, the Romans also followed this practice. Further evidence of the acceptance and tolerance of suicide by the Egyptians is reported by Hankoff (1979), who points out that among the 42 questions concerning sinful acts ritualistically asked of a dead person as a Negative Confession or a Declaration of Innocence, there was no question indicating a prohibition against suicide, even though there were questions about violence, bloodshed, and vicious or cruel acts.

Among the ancient Hebrews suicide was infrequent, apparently for several reasons. One was their strong attachment to life and a positive attitude toward the world, which, according to their teachings, God had made good especially for them, his chosen people. Man should not, therefore, find fault with God's work and those who did commit suicide were usually considered insane or temporarily deranged. As a result, sanctions were not usually imposed against their suicides; their bodies were not desecrated and they were not refused major funeral rights (Choron, 1972). Nevertheless, suicide was clearly prohibited by Judaism, which underscored the sacredness of life as well as the dignity of man and the value of the individual. It was considered an affront to God to end one's life. Life was to be preserved except when a person was guilty of murder, sexual immorality or idolatry. To commit suicide even under the most trying circumstances was to give up hope in God. The value of life, however, was not absolute; life could be sacrificed for the sake of goodness, morality and God. Exceptions to the prohibition of suicide were made specifically for extreme conditions, such as when a Jew was forced to betray his faith, when he had committed a grave sin or when he faced capture and disgrace in war.

The Old Testament and related books neither condemn nor condone suicide. The Old Testament matter-of-factly relates seven instances of self-destructive behavior: Abimelech's skull was crushed by a stone thrown from a tower, reportedly by a woman, and he had one of his soldiers kill him with his sword so that it could not be said he had been slain by a woman (Judges 9:54). When Samson's hair grew long again, and his strength returned he pulled down the pillars of a Philistine temple, crushing himself to death as well as the multitude gathered there to mock and taunt him (Judges 16:28-31). Ahitophel, foreseeing military defeat with his coconspirator Absalom in the revolt against King David, hanged himself (II Samuel 17:23). Saul, the first king of Israel, led his army in a battle against the Philistines on Mount Gilboa. Against overwhelming odds Saul fought as long as he could and then killed himself only after three of his sons had been killed and he had been severely wounded. Seeing his sovereign dead, Saul's armor bearer also fell on his sword and died with him. Saul took his own life so as not to fall into the hands of his enemies, who would have tortured him and desecrated God (I Samuel 31:4; II Samuel 1:6; I Chronicles 10:4). Zimri killed himself by burning the king's house over him when the city of Tirzah in which he was besieged was captured and he became aware of the hopelessness of the situation (I Kings 16:18). Razis, a patriotic elder of Jerusalem, also chose to commit suicide rather than be slain by his enemies (II Maccabees 14:46).

The New Testament also neither specifically prohibits suicide nor condemns suicidal behavior. The suicides of Judas Iscariot (Matthew 17:5), who hangs himself after betraying Jesus, and the suicide attempt of Paul's jailer (Acts 16:27) are reported factually and briefly.

Hankoff (1979c) relates the deaths of Saul and his armor bearer to one of the most important Hebrew taboos of that era—a strong prohibition against human bloodshed. Suicide was abhorrent to the ancient Hebrews because it exposed the community to the possibilities of uncontrolled bloodshed and an unattended corpse. Saul's suicide was a breach of the suicide prohibition and therefore required much justification, such as the inevitability of his death and the degradation that would have followed had he lived as a captive of the Philistines. The Old Testament states that he was beheaded by the Philistines and his body hung on the wall of the city. The Jews of a nearby town are reported to have courageously taken the body down in the middle of the night and carried it back to their town for a dignified burial under a sacred tree. Before the burial they burned the body as an act of reverence and as a way of undoing the illegal spilling of Saul's blood.

Siegel (1979) points out that the Torah does not explicitly forbid suicide. It is only in the accumulated body of rabbinical literature that prohibitions against suicides and the exceptions to them are provided. The example of Saul is seen as a taking of one's own life in order to avoid the greater sin of profaning God's name. Suicides were permissible if committed to prevent dishonor to God's name.

There was some question concerning burial rituals for persons who committed suicide. Burial was generally accompanied by an elaborate set of ritual acts. The specific rule was that there would be no rending of clothes and no eulogizing in the case of a suicide. However, the general rule was that the public should participate out of respect for the living rather than for the dead and should say the mourner's blessing. For all practical purposes, suicides have been treated as individuals who destroyed themselves unwillfully, so the honors and rights have usually been granted.

Two instances of the acceptability of suicide in war by the ancient Jews involved Flavius Josephus, one directly and another indirectly. Josephus, born Joseph Ben Matthias, was originally a priest and a general in the army of the Jews. He was captured by the Romans and lived the rest of his life as a Roman citizen in a time when great change was taking place in the lives of the Jewish people. He wrote the history of the time in four books, *The Jewish War*, *Antiquities of the Jews*, *His Life* and *Against Apion*.

Josephus was involved in a mass suicide when, in A.D. 68, he commanded a detachment of Jewish troops at Jotopata. Surrounded by the Roman army led by Vespasian, his soldiers wanted to kill themselves to avoid surrender, but Josephus argued against it. He argued that "for those who have laid mad hands upon themselves, the darker regions of the netherworld receives their souls, and God, their father, visits upon their posterity the outrageous acts of the parents. That is why this crime, so hateful to God, is punished also by the sagest of legislators. With us it is ordained that the body of a suicide should be exposed, unburied until sunset . . . ." He was, however, accused of cowardice and threatened with death. Josephus finally agreed that this was a situation in which they were defending the Torah and sanctifying the holy name, and therefore even suicide was justified. He proposed the usual solution in such circumstances—"that they commit mutual slaughter by lot"—and they agreed. "By chance or by the providence of God" he and one soldier remained as the last survivors, and Josephus was able to persuade the soldier to surrender with him to the Romans.

The most spectacular mass suicide occurred in A.D. 74 and was reported by Josephus. Pursued by the Romans, a group of Zealots and their families, led by Eleazar Ben Jair, took refuge on a high plateau at Masada. By this time, the Second Temple had been destroyed by the Romans, and belief in the hereafter among the Jews had become widespread. After three years of siege Ben Jair realized their stores were low and that they could not hold out much longer against the siege. Eleazar called his troops and the people together, reminded his troops of their promise never to become slaves of the Romans and persuaded them to die by their own hand. He argued that "death affords our souls their liberty and sends them to their own place of purity where they are to be insensible to all sorts of miseries." The soldiers then killed their wives and children, and followed this by killing each other, a total of 960 people. Even the battle-hardened Roman veterans were reported to have been awed by the discipline, pride and contempt for life shown by the people. The only survivors were two women and five children who had hidden in a cave.

In his books Josephus lists a number of individual suicides, some of them concerned with Herod and members of his family. For example, he reports the suicide of Herod's younger brother, Phasael, who had been captured by King Antigones. Phasael, thinking Herod to be dead, had killed himself by hitting his head against a large rock while he was in chains awaiting execution. A year later, Herod conquered Antigones and executed him in revenge for Phasael's death. The suicides described by Josephus ranged all the way from Abimelech, in 1200 B.C., through the mass suicide by the Jews at Masada in 73 A.D. He also described two suicide attempts by Herod, one in 41 B.C. by sword and the second in 4 B.C. by knife (Hankoff, 1979d).

The Greeks and Romans

The attitude toward suicide among the Greeks and the Romans varied widely over time. Despite assertions that suicide was approved in the Greco-Roman world, this was not completely true. Plato comdemned suicide in general, although he outlined a few exceptions. Aristotle condemned suicide as an act of cowardice and an offense against the state. The Epicureans and Stoics considered it a reasonable expression of human freedom, but their beliefs remained in the minority throughout that period.

Honor and its various aspects were important concerns among the Greeks and Romans. Suicide was considered an appropriate solution to dishonor during the period of Homer. One of the first examples given is that of Jocasta, the mother of Oedipus who was unaware that he was her son, and married him after he had killed his own father, again in ignorance. Another example is that of Ajax, the Greater, who was able to retrieve the body of Achilles after the latter had been killed by Paris, the Trojan, with an arrow to his only vulnerable spot, his heel. However, the armor of Achilles was given to Odysseus rather than to Ajax, who felt so dishonored as a result that he killed himself.

Suicide to maintain one's honor was highly approved. On example is that of Charondas, a prominent citizen who helped to formulate the laws in Catania, a Greek colony in Sicily. One of the laws he formulated was that no man who was armed was to enter the town assembly, on pain of death. When he inadvertently entered without removing his dagger and realized what he had done, he drew it and used it to kill himself.

Suicides of honor, to avoid capture and humiliation, were frequent in the wars among the Greeks and Romans. Examples are Demosthenes, who took poison when he was about to be captured by the leader of the Macedonians; Vulteius and all his troops, who killed themselves when they were surrounded by soldiers of Pompey and escape was impossible; and many of Otho's soldiers, who killed themselves when they learned that their emperor had killed himself rather than continue further slaughter of his men in his war against Vitellius (Rosen, 1975). Many suicides during the Roman Republic were of the heroic type. Among the more famous are those of P. Decius Mus, 337 B.C., who raced ahead of his troops to certain death in a battle near Vesuvius; Decius the Younger, son of the above, in 295 B.C., who also invited his death in a fight against the Gauls; and Cato the Younger of Utica, who killed himself in Africa when his troops were defeated by Caesar. Another heroic suicide was that of Regulus, the consul who was captured by the Carthaginians and sent back to Rome to propose peace. He gave his pledge to return no matter what happened. When in Rome, however, he argued strongly against peace and then returned to Carthage knowing that he would be killed.

Unrequited love and the death of a loved one were also considered reasonable bases for suicide. Dido was queen of Carthage when Aeneas landed there on his flight from Troy. Dido fell in love with him and killed herself when he continued on his journey. The Aegean Sea is named after the father of Theseus who forgot to raise the white sail that indicated victory as he returned from his voyage to slay the Minotaur in Crete. When Aegeus saw the black sail he assumed his son was dead, and drowned himself in the sea, which from then on bore his name. Another story involving loss of love is that of the suicide of Hero, whose lover, Leander, used to swim the Dardanelles nightly from Abydos to the Hellespont, where she lived. One night, however, the wind blew out the light that Hero set out to guide Leander and he drowned. When Leander's body washed ashore the next morning, Hero was beside herself with grief—and drowned herself as well.

Greek history also relates heroic mass suicides of some Greek soldiers after they were captured. Thucydides recounts two incidents, both taking place at Corcyra two years apart, in 427 B.C. and 425 B.C. The first involved 50 men, who, taken prisoner and condemned to death, escaped execution by killing one another or hanging themselves. Two years later, when another group was again taken prisoner in large numbers, the prisoners realized their fellow men were being taken out and executed, so they killed themselves by thrusting arrows into their throats or by hanging themselves (Choron, 1972).

According to Choron (1972), the period between the seventh and fourth centuries B.C. was filled with much pessimism and disenchantment with life and a number of philosophers, such as Theognis of Megara, Sophocles, Euripides, Herodotus and Democritus, advocated suicide, stating that it was "best to leave this world as quickly as possible." It was at this time, in 403 B.C., that hemlock was introduced. Though not readily available, it was given to Socrates as a special favor. The possibility of a quick and painless death may have been a major reason that the 70-year-old Socrates made the decision to end his own life. Later, when the Greek senate was convinced that any committed crime deserved death, the individual who wished to commit suicide was allowed to do so by choosing to drink hemlock.

Despite his choice of suicide, Socrates is known to have disapproved of ending one's life before God had decided it was time to die. "Man is situated in this life as if he were on a post or station which he must not quit without leave; because the Gods exert a providential care over us on which account we are a part (as it were) of their property and possessions; and because we should think it unjust and punishable (if it were in our power to punish) for any slave of our own to kill himself without our permission" (quoted in Williams, 1968, p. 251).

Seneca in *Epistles* and *De Ira* defended suicide as a last defense against intolerable suffering. Two examples of his conviction are "The eternal law has done nothing better than this, that it has given us only one entrance into life, but a thousand ways of escape out of it. . . . Does life please you? Live on. Does it not? Go from whence you came." Also, "Wherever you look there is the end of evils. You see that yawning precipice—there you may descend to liberty. You see that sea, that river, that well—liberty sits at the bottom. . . . Do you seek the way to freedom? You may find it in every vein of your body" (quoted in Williams, 1968, p. 253).

Epictetus, a noted Greek Stoic philosopher, stated "live as long as it is agreeable; if the game does not please you, go; if you stay do not complain." However, he urged restraint and felt the suicide should have good reason before he kills himself.

In general, the Romans did not encourage suicide and the government officially opposed it. Nevertheless, there was a permissive attitude toward it, and in some of the municipal senates, free poison containing hemlock was supplied to anyone who could give valid reasons for wanting to commit suicide. Suicide was frequent under the first Roman emperors, with whole families sometimes committing suicide in public. Most often these were families under threat of prosecution for treason. By committing suicide, a condemned person avoided forfeiture of property. Also, the suicide was permitted customary burial, otherwise denied for those who were executed for a crime. It was not until later that Roman law was changed to forbid suicide committed in order to avoid forfeiture of property. It was still possible, however, for the heirs to bring to trial the question of the guilt of the deceased. If innocence was proved, the heirs were then entitled to the deceased's effects.

Suicide in Rome was also punished primarily when the interests of the state were involved, as when soldiers or slaves killed themselves. If the soldier who committed suicide did so for no adequate reason (sickness or disease would suffice) or to avoid military duty, he was considered guilty of desertion. If the attempt was unsuccessful he was then punished with death. If his act was because of depression, sorrow or madness, however, his punishment was less severe.

Under Roman law those whose crimes merited execution would have their property officially confiscated and would also be deprived of proper burial. Therefore, when Nero ordered Seneca to commit sucide because he suspected his former teacher of having plotted against him, the order was actually viewed as a kindness. Nero also caused the death of Seneca's nephew, the poet Lucan, and of Petronius, considered the most witty, elegant and sophisticated Roman of his time (Choron, 1968). The fear of dishonor brought on the suicide of Cassius, who, rather than kill himself, ordered his slave to stab him.

One of the more striking suicides was that of Arria, the wife of Caecina Paetus, a senator who was involved in plotting against Emperor Claudius. She is reported to have plunged a sword in her breast to show her husband how and then handed the sword to him, assuring him that it did not hurt.

There is also the story of Lucrece. She committed suicide after being raped by Sextus Tarquinius, a Roman general who threatened to kill her unless she yielded to him, saying that he would tell everyone he had killed her because he had found her with a slave who was her lover. The next morning Lucrece summoned her family and her husband, told them what had happened and then killed herself. This story has been immortalized in one of Shakespeare's poems.

Stoicism accepted and, under certain conditions, even recommended suicide. Zeno, the founder of Stoicism, wrote that a wise man could accept suicide if it provided escape from intolerable pain, mutilation or incurable disease, or if it was for his country's safety or the sake of his friends. Zeno is reported to have taken his own life because, feeling advanced in age, he did not wish to endure the discomfort of a broken toe. Cleanthes, Zeno's successor, is reported to have fasted because of a boil on his gum. When the boil disappeared, Cheanthes decided he had gone so far toward death he might as well go the rest of the way.

The Middle Ages

Suicide in general was tolerated and even approved in the Roman Empire until Christian views began to influence social and legal attitudes. At the very beginning of Christianity, however, suicide was highly attractive to many Christians because it offered them martyrdom and, according to their beliefs, the opportunity to enter heaven. In addition, the church undertook care of the surviving family, thus relieving the suicide of any guilt or anxiety about abandoning them. This attitude persisted well into the fourth century.

The early Christians were morbidly obsessed with death (Williams, 1968). For them, life on earth was important only in preparation for the hereafter, so that men studied how to die rather than how to live. The primary objective became the avoidance of sin, because to engage in sin would result in perpetual punishment. Suicide was committed out of fear of falling before temptation, at times indirectly by provoking nonbelievers to kill them, at other times directly, as by jumping off cliffs in large numbers. According to St. Augustine, the heretical Donatists and Circumcelliones in North Africa killed themselves in vast numbers by leaping from cliffs with "paroxysms of frantic joy . . . till the rocks below were reddened with their blood."

Finally, St. Augustine in the *City of God* vigorously condemned suicide, stating that no private person could take upon himself the right to kill a guilty person—this right rested with the church and state; that suicide precluded the possibility of repentance, and that it violated the sixth commandment, Thou shalt not kill. It was, therefore, a greater sin than the sin one might wish to avoid by killing oneself. St. Augustine had to account for accepted suicides and sacrifices in the Old Testament, such as that by Samson and Abraham's willingness to sacrifice his son, Isaac. His answer was that in such instances divine authority had been granted for the death. St. Augustine's stand against suicide was probably a necessary corollary of the church's teaching about the importance of the hereafter (Williams, 1968). If man's life on earth was merely a period of waiting for divine glory the true believer was naturally tempted to hasten the time when he would enter eternal bliss.

In addition to St. Augustine, other early fathers of the church who contributed to the development of the church's attitude toward suicide were St. Cyprian, St. Ambrose, St. Irenaeus and St. Athanasius.

The first Christian prohibition of suicide is sometimes attributed to the Council of Arles in 452. However, the measure was directed only against the suicide of servants and it described the suicidal person as being possessed by the devil. The second Council of Orleans in 533 indirectly expressed disapproval of suicide by allowing the church to receive offerings from those killed in the commission of a crime provided that they had not laid violent hands on themselves. In other words, suicide was regarded as worse than any other crime.

The 15th canon of the Council of Braga in 563 took the decisive step of imposing penalties on all suicides and their families by denying them the usual funeral rights with the eucharist and the singing of psalms. The Council of Auxerre in 578 decreed that no oblation (mass) would be received from any person who had killed himself, and it also reaffirmed the penalties and the principle of indiscriminate condemnation for suicide. The Antisidor Council in 590 invalidated the offerings of a suicide as a means of expiation for sin. The canon of the Council of Braga denying suicides the usual funeral rights was adopted in England by the Council of Hereford in 673, bringing England into line with the practices on the Continent. The Capitula of Theodore, archbishop of Canterbury, decreed that neither mass nor Christian burial was to be performed for suicides unless they had been insane, but that prayers and psalms could be offered.

In the seventh century, there were reportedly a number of cases of persons condemned to church penance who could not face the severities involved and attempted to kill themselves in desperation. The 16th Council of Toledo, in 693, punished a person who attempted suicide with exclusion from the fellowship of the church for two months.

The church relaxed its attitude toward suicide briefly and provided in the texts of the Penitentials in 829 that masses and prayers could be said for the insane who committed suicide. In addition, the Council of Troyes (878) modified the strictness of previous legislation and allowed certain rituals for suicidal deaths. In 855, however, the Third Council of Valence denied Christian burial to those who died in tournaments, jousts and other forbidden contests considered similar to suicidal deaths.

Finally, after King Edgar's canon, in 967, accepted the ecclesiastical dictum denying burial rights to suicides, the Synod of Nimes in 1204 reaffirmed all the previous council decisions against suicide and then extended their judgments by refusing suicides even the right of interment in holy ground. While it did not go so far as to demand punishment for the dead, the severe penalty of depriving burial rights suggested a reemergence of some of the earlier pagan horror against such deaths and the practice of dishonoring the corpses (Fedden, 1938). Bodies were buried at crossroads with a stake through their heart to prevent the soul from wandering. This practice continued as late as 1811 and did not actually stop until 1823, when a suicide named Griffith was buried at the crossroads formed by Eaton Street, Grosvenor Place and King's Road. The following month a statute was passed to abolish the practice.

In France the body of a suicide was dragged through the streets head downward and then hanged on a gallows. In England properties of suicides were confiscated until 1870, and, as late as 1882, by law the suicide had to be buried at night (McCormick, 1964). The service of the Church of England still cannot be used for a suicide. However, other Protestant denominations do provide for a service (Williams, 1968). In Danzig, now a part of Poland, the body of a suicide was not permitted to be taken out through the door but had to be passed through a window, even if a hole had to be knocked in the wall when there was no window.

Two main groups continued to commit suicide frequently during the Middle Ages: heretics and Jews. Pogroms were conducted against Jews in England, especially in the early years of Richard the Lionhearted, bringing about a number of instances of mass suicides, such as the one that occurred at York in 1190, when 600 Jews killed themselves to escape oppression. Another group of suicide martyrs was the Albigenses in southern France, 5,000 of whom reportedly were put to death as heretics in 1218. The Albigenses believed in the Catharic heresy that substituted belief in a dualism—God versus Satan—for the belief in the Christian idea of a unitary God. The main tenets of their doctrine favored suicide because they included detachment from worldly concerns, rejection of private property and abolition of marriage, inasmuch as it led to the perpetuation of the human species. Their favorite methods of suicide were by fire, by jumping and by the *endura*, a voluntary fast.

Another group in which large numbers of suicides commonly occurred was the Russian Raskolniki, who, early in the 17th century, clung to the old faith in the form of the Russian Orthodox Church. Also, a number of incidents of mass suicide by immolation are reported to have occurred in crowded churches and remote monasteries. Suicide in great numbers was also reported to have occurred among wives of priests after celibacy for the priesthood was decreed in the 11th century. There were also reports of numerous suicides occurring during epidemics, particularly when the Black Plague swept Europe in the 14th century.

In the 13th century St. Thomas Aquinas formulated an authoritative church position on sucide in his *Summa Theologica*. He set forth three arguments against suicide: self-destruction is contrary to man's natural inclinations; man has no right to deprive society of his presence and activity; and man is God's property and it is up to God, not man, to decide on our life and death. Williams (1968) states that Aquinas' argument that suicide is antisocial can be easily refuted. One need only point to all the altruistic suicides, where dying for fellow men was a highly praised and honorable act. Landsberg (1933) mentions that in reality people often kill themselves because the very imperfect societies in which they are condemned to live prevent them from leading any form of creative life. Fedden (1938) points out that when individuals who feel they are misfits voluntarily remove themselves and their misery by suicide society directly benefits by their actions. The strongest argument in favor of the popular condemnation of suicide is that it strengthens the will to live. If momentary impulse is resisted, the unfortunate, discouraged person may enjoy many years of productivity and contribution to his society.

The years between St. Augustine and St. Thomas Aquinas were thus, for the most part, filled with continual expressions of rejection of and resistance to suicide, with increasingly harsh edicts both against the corpse of the suicide and his surviving family. Dante's *Inferno* appeared early in the 14th century and illustrated the strong element of fear in man's reaction to deliberate self-destruction. In his *Divine Comedy*, Dante described the souls of suicides as being encased in thorny, withered trees on which Harpies fed and inflicted severe wounds, drawing hideous cries of lamentation and pain from the trees.

Cassidy and Russo (1984) state that the Augustinian-Thomistic view regarding suicide remains essentially the position of the Roman Catholic Church. Today the church acknowledges two kinds of suicide: the illicit act of taking one's life and the licit sacrifice of one's life. In the former, an individual may cause his or her own death by doing something that is positively self-destructive or by refusing to do something that is necessary for survival; either is a positive act of self-destruction. In general, Catholic theologians agree that direct suicide is intrinsically evil. It is permissible, however, if it is committed in response to an inspiration from God, an explanation used to justify the deaths of martyrs who have sacrificed their lives in defense of their virtue or their faith. However, current thinking among Catholic theologians is that an individual's faith can be defended by means other than direct self-murder.

Sacrifice is deemed licit when the person does not desire death, or when death is not the specific aim but rather a consequence of an otherwise legitimate action that is performed. The important criterion used in judging the act is that the greater the risk to one's life the greater must be the compensating good to be obtained. Formerly the church denied ecclesiastical burial to a suicide unless signs of repentance had been shown before death. However, for many years now the church has not applied this rule and generally grants the benefit of the doubt to the victim. It is now assumed that a physical or emotional misfortune has caused a psychic disturbance severe enough to make the person not responsible for the act and therefore incapable of sin.

Eastern Attitudes

Among Oriental sacred writings, suicide was viewed with many contradictions, with encouragement in some and vigorous condemnation in others. In Japan suicide was a way in which warriors could expiate their crimes, apologize for error, escape from disgrace, redeem their friends or prove their sincerity (McCormick, 1964). In China suicide was so commonplace that it was accepted as a normal feature of everyday life. The wretchedness of people's lives in the Far East made suicide seem logical and with typical Oriental fatalism it was accepted without condemnation.

The Hindu attitude is also ambiguous, condemning it in most instances but approving it in special cases. Thus, suicide is considered justified when the person has lived a full life or has acquired a high measure of ascetic power. Hinduism institutionalized and sanctioned suttee, a ceremonial sacrifice of widows, which persisted in India for over 2,000 years. This suicide by self-immolation was demanded of the widow after the death of her husband, and she was highly praised when the tradition was followed and severely condemned when there was a failure to carry it out. Pregnant women and mothers of minors were excused from the traditional requirement. Today suttee is forbidden but may still be practiced in some of the rural provinces of India.

The Brahman doctrine was sympathetic to suicide in that it incorporated denial of the flesh, which the philosophies of the Orient constantly sought to attain. One goal of Oriental mysticism was to divorce the body from the soul, extinguishing craving and passion and allowing life's chief purpose to prevail, the acquisition of knowledge. Both Brahmanism and Buddhism are considered religions of resignation and despair.

Islam has condemned suicide with the utmost severity, following the cardinal teaching of Mohammed that the divine will was expressed in different ways and that man must submit himself to it at all times.

The Renaissance and the Reformation

The Renaissance saw the emergence of a radical change in attitudes toward suicide, with a shift toward and the awareness of the world and its beauty and a euphoric feeling that life was wonderful. This attitude lasted throughout much of the 14th and 15th centuries. The individual became important as man became aware that he was the master of his own destiny. Values and religion began to change. Luther became the representative of orthodox Protestantism, with a shift in principles from absolutism and obedience to personal inquiry and personal responsibility. Inevitably, as questions, doubts and challenges arose to what had always been taken for granted, and, additionally, the Industrial Revolution caused sweeping social and economic disruption, there came a sense of self-consciousness and isolation. A marked increase in melancholy appeared along with recognition of life's transiency. Death became an escape from the disappointments of life, and suicide began to appear much more often.

Calvinism appeared in the middle of the 16th century, starting first in Switzerland and sweeping across France (in the person of the Huguenots) to reach England, while Lutheranism became firmly entrenched in Scandinavia. The exaltation of God in Calvin's theology tended to minimize man and make man feel even more humble, raising indirectly the question of the value of the individual human. Italy saw a revival of learning and a resurrection of ideas which began to diminish the strong feeling of suicide-horror. Erasmus in his "Praise of Folly" (1509), Sir Thomas More in "Utopia" (1516) and Montaigne in his "Essais" (1580-88) show the absolute condemnation of suicide disappearing, with suicide justified albeit under still strictly defined circumstances. Erasmus took the position that God meant death to be an agony in order to keep men from committing suicide. Nevertheless, in one of his books he commends those who voluntarily kill themselves in order to leave a miserable and troublesome world, considering them wiser than those who are unwilling to die and who insist on living longer. Montaigne extolled voluntary death but later came to a more moderate practical position, concluding only that unsupportable pain, or a worse form of dying, were acceptable justifications for suicide (Rosen, 1975).

With the spreading of the Renaissance the economic conditions became more and more oppressive as man realized his poverty and lack of a future. "The Anatomy of Melancholy" by Burton (1621) condemned suicide but also pleaded for a charitable attitude towards it, asserting that it was up to God to judge. John Donne wrote "Biathanatos" in 1608, the first defense of suicide in English up to that point, but it was not published until 1644, after Donne's death. Donne, like Burton, felt that the power and the mercy of God were great enough that the sin of suicide could be forgiven. In his words it was "not so naturally a sin that it could never be otherwise and suicide was not incompatible with the laws of God, reason and nature." Burton felt that eternal damnation was not necessarily the punishment for every suicide because of the possible presence of mitigating circumstances, such as madness.

The preoccupation with death that characterized this era resulted in many new editions of the "Danse Macabre" which were illustrated by the presence of a skeleton. Rowlandson, a prominent graphic artist of that time, drew a number of the scenes. In "The Gamester's Exit," for example, a man is shown shooting himself in the head while holding a wine glass aloft in his other hand. In the doorway stands a woman vainly attempting to stop him while on the other side of the table a skeleton watches grimly (Farberow, 1972). We also find Shakespeare producing psychological studies in depth, with suicide appearing no less than 14 times in his eight tragedies.

John Sym, an English clergyman of this period, identified suicides as those who were sick in mind. His textbook (1637) was the first to show a concern for understanding and prevention, listing premonitory signs and giving suggestions on how to protect the suicide (Morgan, 1979). Sym divides suicides into direct and indirect, condemning especially the indirect type. Among the premonitory and diagnostic signs of suicide he lists "unusual solitariness, neglect of the necessary duties of a man's calling, change in manifest behavior, a distracted countenance in courage, speaking and talking to and with themselves in solitary places and dumps, reasoning and resolving with themselves about that fact and their motives to it in a perplexed, disturbed manner" (Rosen, 1985).

Johannes Neser (1613) wrote that those who committed suicide when sane and with premeditation were damned, while those who killed themselves in a state of madness were not damned because they were mentally deranged and were not responsible. Like Burton, he felt that God could decide whether salvation was appropriate in those cases where the circumstances were unclear (Rosen 1975).

The Industrial World

Throughout Renaissance and post-Renaissance periods suicide had become more and more tolerated by the educated people both on the Continent and in England, but the church still remained powerful in its condemnation of suicide, which it now branded not merely as murder but also as high treason and heresy. An important, additional cultural element was added in this era, the stigma of poverty. Up to this time being poor had not been associated with any moral position. With the rise of commercialism, the development of the Industrial Revolution, and the appearance of Protestantism a drastic change in the attitude of society toward the poor appeared. Social relationships began to be evaluated from purely economic standards. Good was now rewarded by prosperity and evil by poverty; economic failure was an indication of sinfulness. Most of the condemnation was directed toward those persons who suffered a decline in their fortune, from prosperity to poverty, and it was this change rather than the fact of poverty itself which accounted for many suicides at that time. The impact of poverty was illustrated in 1732 when Richard Smith and his wife killed their infant daughter, hanged themselves and left a long letter addressed to the public describing the hopelessness of poverty and complaining that life was not worth living.

The 18th century saw many additional changes in the attitudes toward suicide, such as opposition against the penalties imposed on suicide. During this period of Enlightenment, prominent French literary giants, such as Voltaire, D'Holbach, Rousseau and Beccari condemned the conventional harsh treatment of suicides and encouraged the exercise of empirical observation and critical reason. Voltaire (1766) brought a reasonable approach toward suicide, Rousseau (1761) brought a romanticized approach and Montesquieu (1721) brought for the first time a criticism of suicide from the point of view of the survivors. He urged a view less prejudiced against suicide in his *Persian Letters* and opposed the traditional Christian attitude toward suicide as sinful.

One of the most significant publications in this period was one by David Hume, a Scottish philosopher, entitled "Essay on Suicide" (1783). Hume argued that if suicide were to be abhorred it had first to be proven a crime against God, neighbor or self. He argued that suicide was not a crime against God because He gave man the power to act and therefore death at one's own hand was as much under His control as if it had proceeded from any other source. Second, suicide was not a breach against neighbor and society, "for a man who retires from life does no harm to society, he only ceases to do good and which, if it is an injury, is of the lower kind." Third, Hume stated that suicide can not be a crime against self because he believed that no man ever threw away a life while it was still worth keeping.

The discussion on suicide in this era saw some writers attempting to relate it to national character. Suicide was associated particularly with the English, for example, and became known as an English symptom because England's inhabitants showed a characteristic gloominess of temperament. In George Cheyne's book, "The English Malady" (1733), Cheyne associated suicide in England with inclement weather, rich heavy food and wealthy and sedentary living in large urban centers.

At about this time (1763), Merian offered one of the important new arguments by separating suicide from morality and approaching it from a medical point of view. He suggested that suicide was not a crime but an emotional illness. The natural extension of this argument was that all suicides were mentally ill in some degree and so could not run counter to the law of nature. This rationalization eventually paved the way to the church's verdict of "suicide while of unsound mind," allowing the church to skirt its own laws against suicide.

Bishop Charles Moore continued to be critical of suicide but was not so dogmatic as other ecclesiastical writers, stating that each case of suicide had to be judged on its own merits. In his book "A Full Inquiry into the Subject of Suicide" (1790), his argument was that man did not know the importance of his own life even if it appeared to be useless and that suicide might be an interference with the design that God has fashioned for each person.

In Germany, Immanuel Kant (1797) argued that human life was sacred and had to be preserved at all costs. He also stated that each individual had a definite place in the great universe according to the laws of nature and that man's ability to reason made suicide inconsistent with the sacredness of human life.

The Romantics

The last half of the 18th century and the early part of the 19th century was an era in which the Romantic poets made a great impact on the concept of death. It was in 1770 that Thomas Chatterton at the age of 17 committed suicide by poison. Alvarez (1972) describes his death as one which the Romantics took as a vivid example of death by alienation—premature death in a blazing genius. Youth and poetry and death became synonymous, with each glorified in the writings of Novalis and Jean Paul in Germany, Chateaubriand and Lamartine in France and Keats and Shelley in England. Keats died in 1821 at the age of 25, Shelley the next year at 29 and Lord Byron, two years later, at age 36. Goethe's "Sorrows of Werther" (1774) was inspired by the suicide of a young diplomat, and set a Europe-wide pattern for the Romantic style of suffering. Alvarez feels that the Romantics thought of death and suicide, childishly, as a supreme dramatic gesture of contempt toward a dull world. Suicide was fashionable and was practiced almost as an elegant sport.

Writings nevertheless continued to appear in the early 1800's against suicide. In France, one of the most prominent efforts was that of Madame de Stael (1814) who wrote that living through pain and crisis made a person better and thus it was unnecessary to commit suicide. She argued that God never deserted man and that the individual need never feel that he was completely alone. Her strongest argument was that suicide was against the moral dignity of man, an argument directly opposed to that of the Stoics and the Epicureans, who felt that suicide helped preserve man's dignity and self-concept.

Leon Meynard (1954), a 20th-century French philosopher, reasoned that suicide was caused basically by suffering and was essentially a refusal to submit to it. In order not to kill oneself one must know how to suffer. Suffering, however, could be understood only in the religious perspective. Meynard felt that the existence of God was the supreme argument against the legitimacy of suicide and that the purpose of life was not to find happiness but to seek purification through suffering. Suffering needed neither to be accepted nor resigned to, but rather to be used as a means of salvation.

The 1880s

During the 1800s a number of significant changes appeared in society. The old religious and social groupings that had offered the strongest resistance to suicide began to lose their effectiveness. Capitalism introduced incentives for individual and personal gain, making people more interdependent economically but isolating them socially. Material values supplanted religious and social values. Suicide began to be considered a disgrace, supplementing the attitudes of the preceding century, when it had been associated with sin and crime. A strong middle class was growing in society, consistent with the development of increasingly larger urban centers where industry and business could interact. Along with this new middle class came the need for the family to maintain social status within the community, making suicide something to be hidden and denied. This was especially true for the upper class, as suicide became more frequently associated with insanity.

An increasing number of efforts were made to investigate suicide from medical and sociological points of view, according to Dahlgren (1945). One of the earliest works was by Oslander (1913) who attributed suicide to mental illness, blaming such things as diseases in the head, congestion of blood in the brain, weakening of the brain by repeated intoxication, epileptic attacks, progressive inflammation in the small intestine, cardiac aneurysm, swelling of the abdominal glands, persistent constipation and defects in the sexual organs. Oslander's study of melancholic persons led him to conclude they hanged themselves to avoid the sensation of blood sinking from the brain on account of suspended aerial electricity.

Falret's (1822) contribution was significant in that he was one of the first to use statistical data on suicide, albeit not very extensively and with very few conclusions. Falret attributed suicide to four major causes: (1) predisposing, such as heredity, temperament, climate; (2) accidental direct, such as passions and worries at home; (3) accidental indirect, such as bodily pain, disease and state of health; and (4) civilization and religious fanaticism. He equated suicide and insanity, considering the former to be a special form of insanity.

A number of investigators of this period searched for suicide's relationship to psychosis and pathoanatomical signs. Did suicide automatically mean the subject was insane? Were there neurological lesions or anatomical defects that "explained" suicide? As Rosen (1975) points out, the consideration of suicide as a special form of insanity served as a stimulus for all kinds of medical observations searching for the connection between a suicide's behavior and anatomical lesions found in autopsy. Clinical pathologists in France pursued this course earnestly in the first half of the 19th century.

Esquirol, in his chapter on suicide in his book "Mental Illness" (1838), refused to accept the doctrine that suicide was a mental disease in itself, but insisted, rather, that it was a consequence of other illnesses and only a symptom of insanity. He did not believe that pathoanatomical investigations of suicide would shed light on the suicide problem and proposed instead that suicide might depend on hereditary factors. While he urged that the individual disposition be observed very closely, he did offer some general observations: Men committed suicide more often than women and the number of suicides was greatest in the spring. However, he did not believe in the influence of climate.

Writers searching for statistical-sociological relationships viewed suicide as a social phenomenon, without getting into individual cases. Casper (1825) and Etoc-Demazy (1844) are examples of this approach. Casper's statistics were based on 500 cases in which the cause was considered more frequently to be mental aberration than alcoholism and debauchery. Etoc-Demazy made a significant contribution to the demography of suicide by using rates instead of numbers. This enabled him to show for the first time that suicide tended to increase with age rather than to decrease, as had been asserted by investigators preceding him.

Brierre de Boismont is considered the second principal investigator of this period (1856). His study was an investigation of 4,500 suicides in the Seine Department over a period of 10 years. He also reported data gathered from 265 persons who either made a suicide attempt or planned one. For de Boismont suicide causes fell into two types, predisposing and determinant. In the former could be found demographic variables, such as civil status, age, sex, religion, marital status and others. Thus, he confirmed that older people committed suicide more often than younger people and that men killed themselves in a ratio of three to one over women. He denied strongly that all suicides were insane but did indicate that an attempt at suicide was often the first indication of insanity, even where mental illness had not been suspected before. Among the behavioral and social causes, he indentified such items as trouble at home and with the family, intense worry, poverty and misery and inebriation. Among somatic diseases he found pulmonary conditions were most frequent, then blindness and then cancer. He was one of the first to mention pellagra as a disease that often seemed to lead to suicide. A number of investigations seeking to pinpoint this relationship followed. Social disorganization and alienation also were identified as strong contributors to suicide.

Lisle (1856) also used statistics in dividing the causes into two major groups, predisposing and immediate. Like de Boismont he opposed characterizing suicide as a mental disease, although suicide was often due to mental illness. He found insanity, monomania and brain fever in only about one out of every four cases of suicide.

Wagner (1864), using suicide statistics, agreed that insanity could not be equated with suicide, but he did conclude that it was by far the most common cause for suicide, occurring in about one-third of all the cases. He also concluded that suicide was 100 times more common in mentally ill individuals than in mentally healthy persons.

Siljestrom (1875) studied the increase in suicides from 1730 to 1870 in Sweden and concluded the increase was due to the political, social and industrial states of transition through which society had passed during that time.

During this period the German philosopher Schopenhauer (1851) expressed the pessimism of the era in his writing. While often considered an advocate of suicide he actually was strongly against it. He felt that moral freedom, the highest ethical ideal, could be obtained only by denying the will to live. Suicide, however, was not such a denial. For Schopenhauer the denial lay in shunning the joys not the sorrows of life. He felt the suicidal person had the will to live but was dissatisfied with the conditions under which he was forced to live.

Another important work of this period is that of Morselli (1881). Analyzing data from Italy, he concluded that suicide was primarily a result of the struggle for life and nature's evolutionary process, by which weak-brained individuals were sorted out by insanity and voluntary death. Other unhappy results included misery, disease, prostitution and insanity. That men committed suicide more often than women and adults more often than children merely illustrated the struggle of life that led to suicide. To reduce suicide one needed to reduce the number of people, which could be accomplished only by birth control. In Morselli's opinion the progress of civilization and Protestantism, which refused all external worship in favor of free discussion and individual thought, were the most powerful factors in increasing the number of suicides.

Masaryk, in "Suicide and the Meaning of Civilization" (1881), also stressed the difficulty in determining the boundary between normal and abnormal mental life. He felt that civilization and the state of semi-culture were responsible for the increasing suicide frequency in almost every country. The causes of suicide lay in both the biological and social constitution of man. Suicide could not be explained only in terms of mental illness but must be looked for in the moral disorder of modern societies. Since religion was the source of morality, the increasing secularization that characterized contemporary societies meant a loss of faith. Like Morselli, Masaryk felt that Protestantism stimulated the development of free inquiry, which in turn fostered a much higher degree of individualism than the Catholic Church. The Protestant was more easily left open to doubt and to despair, which essentially was a consequence of a decline in religious belief rather than the result of Protestant theology. Masaryk urged that what was needed was to revive the moral meaning that came from belief in a superior being. Thus, the moral crisis of modern civilization could only be resolved through a religious revival, not a reversion to the repressive control that the church had exerted in previous ages. Rehfisch (1893) also saw suicide as the final link in a chain of pathological states, with civilization the underlying cause for "mental degeneration." Alcoholism was also important in suicide, he felt.

Two of the most important events in the history of suicide studies occurred near the end of the 19th century. The first was the publication of Durkheim's "Le Suicide" in 1897. Durkheim based his work on an extensive evaluation of suicide statistics in France. He concluded that suicide was a collective phenomenon that was specifically influenced by factors characterizing the society in which it appeared. The basic factors were regulation and integration, with varying degrees of each of these factors, and their interaction, producing characteristic forms of suicide. Durkheim's basic concepts are illustrated by examples of societies that fell at the opposite extremes of each concept. Thus, at one extreme of regulation a society characterized by chaos, confusion and loss of traditional values and mores would produce "anomic" suicides. At the other extreme of regulation would be found "fatalistic" suicides, where expressive and repressive constraints would produce an extreme feeling of lack of freedom and choice. At one extreme of the integration concept would be found "egoistic" suicides where the person felt alienated and separated from the institutions and traditions that were significant in the society. At the other extreme of integration would be "altrustic" suicide in which an overidentification with the values or the causes of a society might produce a too-ready willingness to sacrifice one's life in a burst of patriotism or martyrdom. Durkheim's writings have stimulated a host of sociological-statistical investigations up through the present time.

The second most important event in 1897 was the publication of the essay "Is Life Worth Living?" by William James. James concluded that man did not commit suicide because of his religious faith, but rather because faith itself was lacking. It was faith that helped man to believe, even in deep depression, that life was still worth living. Faith leads to religion which essentially postulates the existence of an unseen order in a universe beyond our comprehension.

Early 20th Century

The interest in medical investigations in suicide that had begun in the last half of the 19th century continued strongly into the 20th. Autopsies were used as a primary source of data as investigators looked for relationships between suicide and physiological or neurological conditions. Heller (1900) evaluated the pathology autopsy findings in 300 cases of suicide and found that 48% of the women were in a physiological condition that predisposed to an abnormal mental condition. Bartel (1910 and 1922), Neste (1919), Sieveking, Koopman and Bottiger (1925), Eickhoff (1926) and Beitzke (1938) found contradictory results in their investigations of the association of the suicide problem with status thymicolymphaticus and status hypoplasticus.

Pfeiffer (1912) found essentially organic changes in three-fourths of the suicides on which autopsies were conducted. Mosdzien (1925) concluded that an anatomically visible cause was related to such motives as alcoholism, financial distress, somatic disease, morality or conflict with society in 38% of the cases that he examined. On the other hand, Elo (1931) did not see anything related to mental status in the 923 postmortems on suicides that he conducted. Changes in the central nervous system were present in only 13%.

A number of other investigators in the early 1900s explored suicide from the socio-statistical point of view. One of the most prominent was Halbwachs (1930) who collected statistics in France on both attempted suicide and committed suicide and found the ratio to be 164 to 100, respectively. This is in marked contrast to the more recent studies in the United States which found a ratio of 8 to 1 for the total population (Shneidman and Farberow, 1957) and as high as 50 to 1 and 100 to 1 in adolescents and youth. Halbwachs felt that every person is anxious at the time that he commits suicide and may actually be in a state caused by anxiety or be so emotionally distressed that his state looks psycho-pathological. Every suicide is thus the result of both organic and social factors.

Cavan (1928) and Dublin and Bunzel (1933) conducted extensive sociological analysis of data on suicide, affirming that the elderly, on the basis of rate, showed the greatest tendency to suicide in comparison to any of the other groups. Dublin and Bunzel also were able to point out that nationalities in the United States frequently showed the same rates as the populations in their respective homelands.

The most significant development in the early part of the 20th century in terms of exploring motivations and stimulating investigations of suicide dynamics, was the growth of the psychoanalysis movement in psychiatry under the leadership of its founder Sigmund Freud.

Freud's approach was a radically new conceptualization of the workings of the mind, with the concept of levels of functioning ranging from conscious through unconscious (id, ego and superego), and with remarkable insights into the variety of defenses and coping mechanisms, the failures of which may lead to severe neurosis and psychosis. Freud approached suicide first from his studies of melancholia and depression (1917), and his first theory of suicide was developed from the dynamics that characterized the two states. He used his earlier theoretical concept of introjection, in which any person in an intimate relationship with another incorporates parts of that person into his own personality, with that person becoming a "part of the self." Inevitably, all intimate relationships also develop ambivalent or contradictory feelings toward the person, evidenced by fluctuating feelings of like and dislike, love and hate. Freud thought that suicide occurred with the loss of the love object or with the experience of extreme frustration from the loved one. The rage against that introjected but lost or frustrating person is retroflexed against the self and the acting out of that rage may result in death or serious injury.

Freud was not completely satisfied with his theory since there were many suicides to whom this formulation did not seem to apply. In 1922, in *Beyond the Pleasure Principle*, Freud developed his more complicated theory in which suicide became an expression of the death instinct (Thanatos). Freud postulated two basic instincts in man, the life instinct (Eros) and the death instinct (Thanatos) and saw these in continuous conflict with each other throughout any person's life. Under conditions of extreme stress and/or emotional distress, regression occurred within the individual, more primitive ego states emerged, and the potential for self-destructive behavior was markedly increased.

Karl Menninger (1938) extended Freud's concept of the death instinct even further, hypothesizing three elements that could be found in all self-destructive behavior: (1) the wish to kill, emerging from primary aggressiveness; (2) the wish to be killed, modified from primary aggressive impulses; and (3) the wish to die, derived from primary aggressiveness and other sophisticated motives. Menninger was the first to categorize and relate to suicide the more indirect forms of self-destruction that did not end in immediate death but came out in life-threatening, life-injurious activities. Some he called "chronic suicide," such as addictive behavior and asceticism; some were "focal suicides," in which the focus is on a part, organ, or system of the body, such as in polysurgery or purposive accidents; and some were "organic suicides," in which parts of the body are used in illnesses against the health and well-being of the person.

Other psychoanalytic formulations appeared as some of Freud's disciples and colleagues broke away and developed their own theories. Alfred Adler (1937) related the pathology derived from a person's striving to overcome his innate inferiority, coming to a loss of self-esteem and then attempting to hurt others by hurting himself. Carl Jung considered the self-destructive act to be an effort at rebirth and a way of escaping intolerable conditions of the present (Klopfer, 1961).

Henry Stack Sullivan (Green, 1961) postulated that the subject evaluates himself in terms of the reactions of significant others toward him. The early integration of hostile appraisals of significant others leads to an incorporated concept of negative self frequently expressed in hostile attitudes toward others. When his situation becomes unbearable the individual transfers the "bad me" into a "not me" and redirects his hostile attitude, which has been toward other people, against the self. Karen Horney (De Rosis, 1961), considered suicide to be a "performance failure" arising from the individual's inability to meet the standards expected by society. Gregory Zilboorg (1936) felt that suicide was a way of paradoxically "living by killing oneself," of thwarting outside forces that made living impossible—while maintaining the ego, rather than destroying it, by making and carrying out one's own decision to kill oneself.

Gruhle (1940) attributed about 15 to 20% of the suicides to psychosis and felt that the role of alcoholism was overestimated. Among the factors he listed as most contributory to suicide were such social factors as financial distress, increasing density of the population, one's occupation and residence; demographic factors such as aging, being widowed or divorced, or childlessness; and psychiatric factors such as alcoholism, a psychopathic state and psychosis. Factors that helped prevent suicide included decreasing density of the population, a rural occupation, youth, marriage, children and general circumstances in which emotional stimulation was experienced.

Serin (1926, a,b) initiated a procedure that was the forerunner of the psychological autopsy method, later developed by Curphey, Farberow, Shneidman and Litman (1961). Serin sent specially trained assistants to obtain information from relatives, neighbors and others, to enquire about the lifestyle and attitudes of the suicide in the days preceding his death.

While the above investigators were evaluating deaths by suicide a number of studies were also focusing on attempted suicides. Among these Gaupt (1910) analyzed all the cases of attempted suicide brought to a psychiatric clinic in Munich during the period of his study and found that one-third were "insane," about one-fourth were drunk and one-fourth were psychopaths. Stelzner (1906) studied women treated at a psychiatric clinic in Berlin and found psychiatric symptoms in 84% of the cases. East (1913), in the first English study on attempted suicide, found alcoholism more prevalent and more of a factor in attempted suicide. He felt this contrasted with completed suicide where mental illness was more prevalent. Wassermeyer (1913) found a high occurrence of alcoholism in attempted suicides. He anticipated Stengel (1971) in his cautions that suicide and attempted suicide could not be directly compared to each other because of the differences in the populations. Schneider (1933 and 1934) found only 12% of his attempted suicides could be called mentally ill and that suicide was more likely to be a primitive reaction, an escape or non-lethal communication.

Suicide and Civil Law

In early history civil and religious (canonical) law were so intertwined that it was practically impossible to differentiate between them. This was especially true in Christianity which, after its advent, was the source of increasingly severe attitudes of condemnation that governed the civil attitudes and were incorporated into civil regulations toward suicides.

Preceding Christianity, in Athenian and Greek law the body was denied burial rights and the hand of the suicide was chopped off and buried apart. Theban law also deprived the suicide of funeral rights. Roman law, on the other hand, contained no penalties against suicide and no prohibitions relating to burial and funeral rights. Roman law, with its practical and economic approach, condemned suicide especially when committed by criminals, soldiers and slaves. The soldier was condemned because it was considered desertion, and if he were unsuccessful in his attempt he was killed afterward. The slave was condemned because he was depriving his master of his services.

In English law the ecclesiastical denial of burial rights became a civil punishment when it was adopted by King Edgar in 967 A.D. Along with this the custom of dishonoring and degrading the corpse became incorporated as part of the law and the suicide's goods were forfeited to his lord unless it was the result of an act of madness or illness.

Suicide in the middle of the 13th century was punished by forfeiture of goods and land unless, as stated by de Bracton (1968), the suicide resulted from "weariness of life or impatience of pain," which then limited the loss to goods only. In the 14th century it was declared that the intentional taking of one's own life was a felony, and in 1551, under Spain's Charles V, a law was passed that confiscated the property, both goods and land, of anyone who committed suicide while under a charge of felony.

Attempted suicide was identified as a crime and written into the statutes of English law in 1854. It continued as such until 1961 when the law was repealed. Before 1916 imprisonment was the normal punishment for attempted suicide. At that point a policy was inaugurated that did not prosecute attempted suicides but instead placed them in the charge of relatives and friends. However, criminal statistics show that although the policy of both police and courts was moderate a considerable number of persons were sent to prison for attempted suicide. From 1946 to 1955, 5,794 attempted suicide cases were tried by the courts and 5,447 were found guilty. Of these 308 were sentenced to imprisonment without the option of a fine (St. John-Stevas, 1963).

Williams (1968) noted that the practice of forfeiture of the goods of a suicide to his lord was already known to Danes before they came to England. The fact of suicide was considered equivalent to a confession of guilt for the crime of which he had been accused. In England, the goods went to the Crown instead of to the local Lord. During the 18th century the Crown limited forfeiture of goods, in cases where suicide was committed, to conviction of a felony. Later, even that was waived when the forfeiture act was abolished in 1870, giving legal effect to an already established practice (St. John Stevas, 1963).

Some of the legal statements against suicide included the argument that suicide was contrary to and an offense against nature and therefore criminal, according to Justice Brown (1563). Also it was against God as a breach of the commandment, Thou shalt not kill, and against the king in that he lost one of his subjects. Blackstone (1563) declared the suicide to be guilty of a double offense—the first was spiritual in evading the prerogative of the Almighty and rushing into his presence before called for, and the second was temporal and against the king who had an interest in the preservation of all of his subjects.

In France, the corpse of the suicide was subjected to the same kind of degradation as in England. The French criminal ordinance of August 1670 required the body of a suicide to be dragged through the streets and then thrown into a sewer or onto the town dump. In the early 18th century the law required that the suicide body be buried under the gallows. The attitude toward suicide fluctuated along with French politics. Suicides and the survivors of successful suicides were punished when the liberal legislation of the Napoleonic code was overthrown. When liberty and democratic government reappeared the rights of the suicide also reappeared and were respected.

Rosen (1975) points out that the imposition of penalties in many countries varied with the social rank of the suicide and his family as well as the circumstances of the suicidal act. Physical illness and mental and emotional disease were not punished in Prussia while poverty, dishonor, despair and debt were.

In many middle European countries, secular law continues to hold attempted suicide a crime. However, this usually results only in registration of suicide attempts. As a result, Austria, Czechoslovakia and Hungary are examples of better statistics. Registration of attempted suicide has been abolished in other European countries such as Germany, Italy and Switzerland and the Scandinavian countries.

In the United States, following English law, Massachusetts passed a statute in 1660 that the body of a suicide was to be buried at the crossroads of a highway. Again following English law, this was repealed in 1823. The view that suicide was a felony was also incorporated into the laws of the individual states. As recently as 1969, seven states still had suicide as a crime on their books, but currently (1986) there are no states that consider suicide or suicide attempts a felony (Perr, 1984). Aiding or abetting a suicide, however, is still considered a crime in 18 of the 50 states.

Norman L. Farberow, PhD
The Los Angeles Suicide Prevention Center
and
The Institute for Studies of
Self-Destructive Behaviors

A

abortion It is not known just how many expectant mothers, having decided on an abortion and had the abortion done, then found the experience so shattering that they committed suicide. However, there have been a number of reported suicides involving women who had recently gone through the abortion procedure. A recent *New York Times* poll suggests that Americans in general "do not see abortion in anything like the clear, black-and-white terms described by activists on the issue." On the whole, abortion does not appear to be a major precipitating factor in suicide.

abreaction A process by which painful, unconscious, forgotten thoughts and feelings are brought to consciousness and relived. This technique is employed in psychoanalysis. In *The Savage God: A Study of Suicide*, Alfred Alvarez refers to "abreaction" as "that crucial moment of cathartic truth when the complex is removed." Alvarez goes on to explain: "Behind that is the old belief in last-moment revelations, death-bed conversions, and all those old wives' tales of the drowning man reliving his life as he goes down for the last time."

abuse, alcohol See ABUSE, SUBSTANCE.

abuse, child As with ABORTION, authorities are not certain of the specific correlation between parental abuse and the suicidal child or adolescent. They do know that the very young—children between two and 10—are attempting suicide in increasing numbers. For example, at the 1982 convention of the American Psychiatric Association, psychiatrist Periheu Rosenthal reported on her knowledge of six suicidal children that were all under five years of age. These children had been abused emotionally and psychologically, if not physically.

Children of abusive parents generally do not completely understand the problems that cause such conduct and are confused about their responsibility for their parents' behavior. The abusive parent, e.g., in the case of an alcoholic parent, often vacillates from being overly affectionate to neglectful to abusive. Children cannot understand such shifts in treatment in terms of their own behavior, and develop with poor feelings about themselves. Too often children are used by one parent in maneuvers against the other, or they may blame themselves for their parents' fighting or, in some instances, for their parents' separation or divorce.

However, as Jolly K., co-founder of the self-help organization for abusive parents, Parents Anonymous, points out, chidren subjected to mental, emotional, or physical abuse run a high risk of developing a variety of problems, and one of those problems is severe depression, a prevalent distress signal common among suicidals. Moreover, as Robert O'Brien and Dr. Morris Chafetz say in *The Encyclopedia of Alcoholism*, "The ways in which such children have learned to adjust may eventually be the source of problems later in life." They add that, "A child who always tries to smooth over conflicts and help others in the family feel at ease may later fear and deny his or her own feelings of anger and be constantly trying to please others. The roles that seemed positive in childhood may have negative consequences in adulthood."

What is needed, according to Parents Anonymous officials, is a new direction, a new spirit, and a new climate for personal and social change. They believe that it is important that the whole family be involved in treatment. The child who is "sent away" often feels increased guilt, perhaps thinking that he or she has failed completely. Also, a parent who fears that their child will be taken away is less likely to submit to any sort of treatment.

In Jolly K.'s words "The future must involve a more effective reaching-out to more and more people who need help in overcoming their problems of wrathful abuse." Perhaps the word "present" should be substituted in the previous sentence. Psychiatrist Derek Miller, chief of the Adolescent Program at Northwestern University's Institute of Psychiatry, has said, according to Dr. Giffin, "that for adolescents, this is the worst time to be growing up since the Middle Ages when the bubonic plague created chaos."

Until something constructive is done to cope with the serious problem of child abuse, suicide will continue to be an alternative for innocent young people. And yet the National Center for Health Statistics still does not compute suicide figures for children under 10. Says Dr. Mary Giffin and co-author Carol Felsenthal in *A Cry for Help: Exploring and Exploding the Myths About Teenage Suicide—A Guide for All Parents of Adolescents*, "There is a belief—lately shown to be erroneous—that suicide in children under ten is so rare as to be unmeasurable."

abuse, drug See ABUSE, SUBSTANCE.

abuse, substance Experts agree that anyone, especially a child, who abuses drugs or alcohol is a suicide risk. Among the various warning signs, substance abuse is second only to depression as a distress signal. Almost 50% of the adolescents who commit suicide are drunk or high on something shortly before their death, and that figure soars to 75% for adolescents who attempt suicide but do not succeed.

One recent study of middle-class adolescents in treatment with a psychiatrist following a suicide attempt revealed that of 24 patients, 60% were chronic users of alcohol and/or other drugs. According to psychiatrist Frank Crumley of the University of Texas Health Science Center, they had a "notable history of substance abuse, either marijuana, other drugs, or alcohol."

DR. MARY GIFFIN puts it this way: "Drug and alcohol abuse are indications of underlying feelings of hopelessness, anxiety, or depression. It often follows that when those escape hatches fail to relieve anxieties, the troubled youngster decides on the 'final fix.' In other words, the young person can abuse drugs or alcohol for years, but when something terrible happens—so terrible that neither drugs nor alcohol can numb the pain—he may panic and try suicide."

Furthermore, young people—taking their cue from all too many adults—will mix alcohol with drugs as a direct means of self-destruction. A mix of liquor and BARTITURATES, for instance, can prove deadly. The lethal mix of alcohol or drugs, and a depressed person, can be the "final fix."

Alcohol abuse is a recognized link in the self-destruction chain (see also ALCOHOLISM). Alcohol is an addictive substance. This means, quite simply, that progressive use of alcohol leads to addiction. The daily hard drinker's body builds up a tolerance to the initial amount of alcohol and, eventually, he or she must drink more to achieve the same effect. Ultimately, the drinker's body comes to rely on the drug to the point where stopping use may lead to withdrawal symptoms. Symptoms can go from a mild irritability and vague nervousness, or the half-conscious yearning for "a little of the hair of the dog" the next morning, to delirium tremens (DTs). This indicates at the least a psychological, and probably a physical, dependency.

While alcohol reduces tension and anxiety, it also dulls the senses, reduces inhibitions, and clouds judgment. As continued use of it increases, so do the drinker's physiological problems. Usually appetite and energy levels decline; sleep often becomes restless and troubled. Insomnia often follows. Then irritability and depression both increase, thus heightening the desire to drink more. The drinker quickly finds he or she is thrust into a merry-go-round situation, a no-win addictive cycle: the urge to drink more to alleviate depression, the more depressed one becomes—and the more one *must* drink to compensate. And depressed individuals court suicide through warped judgment and high-risk actions. Consciously or unconsciously, the alcohol abuser seeks relief from depression and irritability by way of the so-called "high-rise" high. Often the risk-taking spills over into such self-destructive dimensions that the drinker appears to be out to destroy himself or herself.

While no one cause is sufficient to explain the complex suicide act, there is little doubt that self-destructive persons are considerably more likely than not to be heavy problem drinkers or drug abusers.

Experts explain that even if suicidal thoughts never seem to occur to the drug or alcohol abuser, that person is doing himself in just as surely as the individual who hangs himself. People who abuse drugs and alcohol come to hate themselves, suffer loss of self-respect and self-esteem, and are usually despondent much of the time. They deplore their lives, feel dejected and worthless, and adopt a "What's the use" attitude—much the same as suicide attempters. So, instead of opting to kill themselves directly and quickly, they choose to self-destruct slowly. DR. KARL MENNINGER calls such persons "chronic suicides," and explains they might, when confronted, consider the idea of suicide to be repugnant. In other words, denial prevents their admitting that killing themselves slowly is what they are doing. They rationalize what they do by, in Menninger's words, "claiming that they are only making life more bearable for themselves." Dr. Norman Farberow labels such behavior "indirect self-destructive behavior."

The Food and Drug Administration defines *drug use* as the "taking of a drug for its intended purpose, in the appropriate amount, frequency, strength and manner"; the FDA defines *drug misuse* as "taking a substance for its intended purpose, but not in the appropriate amount, frequency, strength and manner"; and *drug abuse* as "deliberately taking a substance for other than its intended purpose, and in a manner that can result in damage to the person's health or his ability to function." When talking about drugs, *abuse potential* is a particular drug's susceptibility to abuse or abuse patterns.

Mary Giffin, MD, and Carol Felsenthal, *A Cry for Help* (Garden City: Doubleday, 1983).

Karl Menninger, *Man Against Himself* (New York: Harcourt, Brace, 1938).

Robert O'Brien, and Sidney Cohen, MD, *The Encyclopedia of Drug Abuse* (New York: Facts On File, 1984).

Academy of Certified Social Workers Members hold a minimum of a baccalaureate degree in social work. There are 96,674 members in 55 state groups that belong to the National Association of Social Workers. Mark Battle is executive officer of the Academy, which is headquartered at: 7981 Eastern Avenue, Silver Spring, MD 20910; phone is (301) 565-0333.

accident prone Authorities speculate that many so-called accident-prone individuals are actually suicide attempters. For example, auto accidents resulting in fatalities account for roughly 37 percent of all deaths in the 15- to 24-year-old group. Some of these crashes may be suicides listed as accidents, especially single-passenger, single-car accidents. Forensic experts speculate that an estimated 25 percent of these "accidents" are deliberate. In addition, "accidental" poisonings are sometimes suicide attempts in reality. DR. MARY GIFFIN says, "Each year brings one hundred thousand cases of intentional self-poisonings among children ages five to fourteen." However, the concept of death is known to be very different for the five-year-old and the 14-year-old. Actress Mary Tyler Moore's 24-year-old son, Richard, died of a gunshot wound to the head in October 1980. Friends and family claimed his death was accidental, and it was certified as an accident by the medical examiner-coroner's office. However, the possibility of suicide was considered and then discarded, even though Richard collected guns and knew how to handle them.

acculturation In a study done by J.E. Levy and S. Kunitz (1971) to determine the effect of acculturation on Navajo Indian suicide, the authors found that suicide and homicide rates were not impacted significantly by contact with people and institutions of the dominant Euro-American cultures. In "Six American Indian Patterns of Suicide," John P. Webb, MD, and William Willard, PhD, wrote: "We have attempted to show that there is no one pattern of American Indian suicide and that the cultures of American Indian groups are not necessarily disturbed forms of the Euro-American pattern." It appears that the hypothesis that suicide results from the collapse of a particular culture—expecially among American Indian tribal groups—is not consistent with history.

J.E. Levy and S. Kunitz, "Indian Reservations, Anomic and Social Pathologies," *Southwestern Journal of Anthropology* (1971).

John P. Webb, MA, and William Willard, PhD, "Six American Indian Patterns of Suicide," in Norman L. Farberow (ed.), *Suicide in Different Cultures* (Baltimore: University Park Press, 1975), ch. 2, pp. 17-33.

act of cowardice, suicide as Certain ethnic groups, e.g., Mexican-Americans, are more likely than not to consider a suicide victim a coward. Japanese-Americans sometimes make the same judgment. Strange, in light of the long tradition within each culture of honored self-sacrifice, according to David K. Reynolds, Richard A. Kalish and Norman L. Farberow, PhD, in their paper, "A Cross-Ethnic Study of Suicide and Expectations in the United States." The above serves to illustrate that the suicidal act is complex and multi-determined, and that each act must be considered from the cultural point of view as well as from the personal and social.

acting out Term used by professionals to describe the use of behavior instead of words to express emotional conflicts. This serves as a defense against their meaning. Attempters may "act out" and show aggressive, hostile, defiant behavior. Others exhibit passive patterns that include withdrawal, melancholy, noncommunicative behavior. Sometimes attempters will switch behavior techniques from active to passive categories, going from wild, impulsive, loud behavior to quiet, gloomy, uncommunicative demeanor. Some suicidal people cannot sit still (as if they're trying to run from their problems), while others seem unable to get going and suffer a washed-out, dragged down feeling (as if nothing is worth the effort). Specific behavior patterns and changes that reflect suicidal distress signals are discussed elsewhere (see DISTRESS SIGNALS).

actuarial prediction A method of statistical calculation used traditionally in insurance research and population surveys. An insurance research project, for example, would study one million people born in the same year and be able to predict the probable death rates per year. In the suicide field, actuarial prediction methods would be used to predict such data as the probability of death rate within a particular age group.

acute suicides The LOS ANGELES SUICIDE PREVENTION CENTER distinguished between suicidal cases with a triggering factor ("acute suicides") and those where suicide, in sociologist RONALD W. MARIS'S words, "just seems to happen—if not today, then some other day (see CHRONIC SUICIDES)." Maris hypothesizes that "the lower the suicide potential of any individual or risk group, the greater the importance of a contingency factor, or factors, in causing suicide."

Ronald Maris, "Sociology," ch. 5 in *A Handbook for the Study of Suicide*, (ed.) Seymour Perlin (New York: Oxford University Press, 1975).

adolescents The age group considered to fall in the teens, that is, from 12 through 19 years of age. Available data about suicide in adolescents most often refers to the 15 to 24 age group. Suicide rates increased among young people of all ages up through 1977 and since then have levelled off. The rate is still high and is tragic in the cost of lives of our young. Every day, somewhere in America, 14 young people take their own lives—5,200 every year. Each hour that passes, an estimated 30 more make a suicide attempt. That's over 700 attempts by young people every day.

DR. MARY GIFFIN writes in *A Cry for Help* that "many more young people die of suicide than cancer. Every year, the death rate for childhood cancer falls (43 percent since 1950) and the suicide rate rises (a shocking 200 percent in the last two and a half decades)."

Today, suicide ranks only behind accidents and homicides as the third leading cause of death among young people. But because so many suicides are listed as "accidents," the number of young lives claimed by suicide may be twice what is reported. This is usually because the suicide stigma still prevails in many instances; and famililes may hide the evidence from coroners. In addition, some may certify fewer suicides than actually occur because the law requires proof that the deceased intended and was aware that his or her actions would result in death. In short, the death was a case of premeditated self-destruction. Some coroners go so far as to require a suicide note, but this would underestimate the number of suicides even more, inasmuch as notes are left by an estimated 5 to 35% of the suicides.

Inaccurate as they probably are, the official suicide statistics are what we have to work with, and they are appallingly high. And the rate of increase for young people not only exceeds that of older people (the age group with the highest actual rate of suicide), but also is over eight times the growth in the suicide rate for the population as a whole.

Giffin and Felsenthal (*A Cry for Help*) quote Dr. Beatrix Hamburg of the National Institute of Mental Health (NIMH), who warns, "Adolescence is the only age group in the country in which the death rate is rising . . . Improved health measures have prolonged life for the elderly and increased survival in early childhood, but teenagers are dying in increasing numbers."

Though the causes and motivations behind this adolescent suicide phenomenon are many, varied and complex, the single most common feeling is depression, with its symptoms of loneliness, boredom, despair, low self-esteem, loss of identity, feeling worthless, etc.

In considering this disturbing trend of adolescent suicides, it would be well to remember that suicide rates have a relationship with a host of factors—interpersonal relationships, economic conditions, health, marital status, age, race, religion—and that many of the variables often overlap. Yet, in Rabbi Earl A. Grollman's words, "it becomes apparent that society does help to direct the sentiments and activities of the individual towards life or death." (See also CHILDREN AND SUICIDE.)

Earl A. Grollman, *Suicide: Prevention, Intervention, Postvention* (Boston: Beacon Press, 1971).

N. Linzer (ed.), *Suicide: The Will to Live vs. the Will to Die* (New York: Human Sciences Press, 1984).

Africa In the introduction to the suicide mortality statistics of the WORLD HEALTH ORGANIZATION (WHO), this warning appears:

> The true incidence of suicide is hard to ascertain. Varying methods of certifying causes of death, different registration and coding procedures and other factors affect the extent and completeness of coverage, making international comparisons impracticable.

Nowhere in the world, perhaps, is this more true than in Africa, the second largest continent. With so many different nations representing such varied cultures and subcultures, comparability of even regional suicide rates in Africa would be questionable. An overview of suicide, however, makes it clear (see Norman L. Farberow, PhD, *Suicide in Different Cultures*) "that the rate of suicide has been high or low in particular eras in direct relationship with variations in social controls and different emphasis on the value of the individual in comparison with the state, such as idealization of reason, rationality, individuality, and democratic processes." In short, where controls are greatest, the rate is lower; where individuals are more free, the rate is higher.

We get some idea of the cultural history of suicide in Africa in P.J. Bohannan's *African Homicide and Suicide* (a collection of essays by various writers). Anthropological studies done among African tribes revealed that their frequency of suicides was comparable with that of European countries having moderate to low suicide rates, and that suicide among them was considered evil. In certain tribes, physical contact with the body of a suicide is thought to produce dire effects, e.g., illness or suicide among one's kin. The tree on which a person hanged himself is quickly felled or burned; ancestors are placated by sacrifices; and the spot where the suicide took place is haunted by evil spirits. In some regions, suicide is a source of dread in the community, and pressure is sometimes exerted on the family by way of a suicide threat.

In one primitive tribe described by BRONISLAW MALINOWSKI in "Suicide: A Chapter in Comparative Ethics," an individual accused of a transgression of a tribal taboo would climb to the top of a palm tree, declare his hurt at the charge, name his accuser, then plunge head first to his death.

Farberow writes of the taboos accumulated around suicide in certain primitive societies: "Thus, Baganda women were especially fearful of ghosts of suicides who might possibly 'impregnate' them, and they threw grass or sticks on the place where the suicide had been buried. The later English custom of burial at a crossroads was directly linked to the primitive custom of burying at a crossroads a child who had been born feet first, and so was considered unclean. The taboos later became rituals, practiced for the purpose of purification; the original act became a moral and religious sin."

A. ALVAREZ informs in *The Savage God: A Study of Suicide* how it was ". . . the custom once common among African tribes . . . that the warriors and slaves put themselves to death when their king dies, in order to live with him in paradise." Then there were the

Circumcelliones in North Africa who, according to Farberow, "almost seemed to enjoy killing themselves (they did in great numbers) when threatened with persecution." Revenge against one's persecutor or enemy also seems to have been strong reason for suicide in some primitive societies in the Dark Continent.

An interesting fact uncovered by Bohannon: The TIV OF NIGERIA evidently have the lowest incidence of suicide yet recorded. So few, it seems, that the researcher was unable to document any cases of Tiv suicide.

Without doubt, attitudes toward suicide in Africa, as elsewhere in the world, differed in the various tribal societies and countries, and were irrevocably tied to ideologies concerning death and after-life, plus the values and/or rules of the different social structures.

After Suicide A valuable self-help book by J.H. Hewitt. Hewitt, a Christian minister, directs his advice and suggestions to survivors of suicide and deals with learning to reconcile one's religious beliefs with the suicidal death and how best to deal with one's faith afterward.

Afterwords A quarterly newsletter for survivor victims of a suicide in the family. Compiled, edited, and distributed by Adizia Wrobleski, the publication's full title is: *Afterwords: A Letter For and About Suicide Survivors*. For information concerning subscriptions, write to Wrobleski at 5124 Grove Street, Minneapolis, MN 55436-2481 (include a self-addressed, stamped envelope).

age There are those experts who submit that some persons may be born with a predisposition to depression and, thus, are more inclined to take their own lives. These authorities, however, agree that such factors as culture, personality, and the individual situation play key roles in the individual's tendency to commit suicide. And one individual situation is that of age.

For instance, more older people in the U.S. commit suicide than younger people. But the suicide rate in the 15 to 24 age group has risen sharply in recent years. The old are deadly serious about committing suicide, too. Those over 60 represent 12% of the U.S. population and commit about 25% of suicides. Some analysts think the true figure is somewhere between 30 and 40%. The national average for all ages in the U.S. is 12.1 in a 100,000 population (1983), 19.2 for males and 5.4 for females.

The anguish that leads a person to suicide seems to follow no set path. Many observers contend there can be no single explanation for why people take their own lives. Age is simply one of the many factors that makes suicide such a complex malaise. (See also ADOLESCENTS, COLLEGE STUDENTS, MIDDLE AGE AND SUICIDE, OLD AGE AND SUICIDE).

The Age of Sensation DR. HERBERT HENDIN's book is based on interviews of Columbia University students during the decade of the 1970s; therein the noted psychiatrist explains that the language of amphetamines (e.g., speed, flying, etc.) goes beyond describing the particular high the drug produces. Hendin writes, "It also suggests how much these students seek a life in which they are moving too quickly to think about what they are doing or how they feel." As DR. MARY GIFFIN says, "They may slow down just long enough to kill themselves."

aggressive behavior A forceful physical, verbal or symbolic behavior that may be self-protective and appropriate or inappropriate. It is recognized as one of the general distress signals that, along with other cues, may predict suicidal behavior. There have been cases where suicidal young people showed wildly hostile behavior, such as threatening a teacher with a knife, terrorizing brothers or sisters, stealing a neighbor's car and narrowly missing smaller children at play, running away from home, and even displaying serious violence against parents. Teenagers who fit the aggressive pattern often abuse alcohol and drugs. Psychiatrists seem to believe this type of behavior is sometimes a cover-up to mask the suicidal person's painful, depressive feelings.

Ahitophel Supported Absalom in his revolt against David. But when he realized that Absalom would be defeated, "he saddled his ass, and went off home to his own city. And he set his house in order and hanged himself." This altruistic suicide exemplifies self-destruction to escape the consequences of political or military defeat, a common occurrence within select societies and at certain periods in history. (See also MASADA.)

Alcoholic Treatment Center (ATC) Centers are funded by the NATIONAL INSTITUTE OF ALCOHOL ABUSE AND ALCOHOLISM (NIAAA) and offer treatment in three major settings: hospital, intermediate and outpatient. Following patient de-toxification, the system provides outpatient or halfway-house care. By having different treatment modes in the same place, a center can fit the type of treatment to the client's needs.

David J. Armour, J. Michael Polich and Harriet B. Stanbul of the Rand Corporation Social Science Department divide the types of treatment into 10 major categories, as follows:

Hospital Setting

1. Inpatient hospital: traditional 24-hour service based on a medical model but often including psychotherapy.
2. Partial hospitalization: partial service that allows the patient to go home or to work at appropriate times.
3. Detoxification: a short "drying out" period for patients with serious toxic symptoms.

Intermediate Setting

4. Halfway House: living quarters and services, such as job counseling, psychotherapy, etc., for patients who need extended care but do not require hospital treatment.
5. Quarterway House: similar to a halfway house, but offering more intensive, often physical care under more structured conditions.
6. Residential Care: living quarters but little or no other therapy.

Outpatient Setting

7. Individual Counseling: treatment sessions given by a paraprofessional (someone without a graduate degree in psychology, medicine, social work or a similar relevant field).
8. Individual Therapy: treatment sessions given by a professional.
9. Group Counseling: group sessions given by a paraprofessional.
10. Group Therapy: group sessions given by a professional.

Most clients at an ATC receive a combination of treatments. Usually hospital care is quite short and intermediate care extends over a much longer period.

David J. Armour, J. Michael Polich and Harriet B. Stanbul, *Alcoholism and Treatment* (New York: John Wiley and Sons, 1978), pp. 124-126.

Alcoholics Anonymous (AA) Alcoholics Anonymous is perhaps the most successful organization in the world in combatting the disease of alcoholism. International in scope, it is a nonprofit group devoted to helping anyone with a drinking problem. AA has been called the "granddaddy" of the self-help movement in the U.S.

AA was founded by Bill W. and Doctor Bob, both hapless alcoholics themselves, in Akron, Ohio, in 1935. The mutual-aid organization defines its purpose in its preamble:

> Alcoholics Anonymous is a fellowship of men and women who share their experience, strength and hope with each other that they may solve their common problem and help others to recover from alcoholism.
>
> The only requirement for membership is a desire to stop drinking. There are no dues or fees for AA membership; we are self-supporting through our own contributions. AA is not allied with any sect, denomination, politics, organization or institution; does not wish to engage in any controversy, neither endorses nor opposes any causes. Our primary purpose is to stay sober and help other alcoholics to achieve sobriety.

Because alcohol is seen as the alcoholic's "solution" to all of life's uncomfortable problems, and because alcoholism is considered a disease, AA's approach to getting sober and staying sober is a program of total abstinence. "Doing it the AA way" involves not only regular attendance at generally informal meetings and close contact with a sponsor (an experienced AA member in whom the newcomer can confide on a continuing individual basis), but also learning to establish a relationship with a "higher power." In AA's early days, as set down in the group's famous Twelve Steps program, this higher power was identified as God ("as you understand Him"). In recent years, as AA has grown to represent several million members in over 90 countries whose religious beliefs range from fundamentalism to atheism, the higher power concept has been broadened (at least for some members). It now includes a more generalized idea of spirituality or some sense of spiritual recourse within the individual. In fact, some members interpret this newer concept of the higher power to extend to an entity outside of the normal religious organizations, such as a therapy group or, particularly, AA itself.

Other unique features of AA as a highly successful self-help organization includes: a basic mistrust of professionals and other human services people who work with alcoholics outside the organization (it is felt that professionals who aren't alcoholics do not know what alcoholism is really about—and that they tend to co-opt any lay group); the view that alcoholism is a disease that cannot be cured but only controlled; and emphasis on the AA "program" as centered around "doing the steps," i.e., the Twelve Steps.

Maintenance of one's sobriety and progress on a "day at a time" basis, from one step to another, is at the core of AA's program. The group's meetings, including "step meetings" given over to study and analysis of one of the Twelve Steps, provide members with a sense of sharing, participation and progress.

AA is not without its critics. Many professionals believe the group concentrates on the symptoms and not the causes of an individual's drinking problem. Others feel the members do not learn to cope with their disease or gain self-reliance since the program encourages dependency and discourages outside interests that might diminish the central place of AA in the life of the members. Still others criticize the very name—Alcoholics *Anonymous*—claiming it diminishes individual identity. They maintain this is just another way AA perpetuates itself—i.e., by downplaying the individual's names (members use only first names) and identities and leaving them with only the label "alcoholic," AA increases their dependence upon the organization.

AA takes the view that anonymity protects members against a society that, if not still hostile to alcoholics, nonetheless continues to discriminate against them in certain instances (particularly professionals such as doctors, lawyers, teachers). Moreover, AA says that since alcoholism is now generally accepted as a disease (and that includes most major medical and health organizations) for which there is no known cure, and since AA does not consider itself a treatment program with an eventual end, the self-help organization is, therefore, permanent and self-perpetuating. To "drop out," say most AA members, is a dangerous decision which more often than not leads to a resumption of drinking with all its dire consequences.

There are other criticisms of AA. "Meetings have been called exclusionary and their tone conventional and middle class," say O'Brien and Chafetz in *The Encyclopedia of Alcoholism*. "Some find AA meetings overly inspirational" and anti-intellectual. Some are offended by what they call "the God thing."

Such criticisms aside, however, most authorities in the field of alcoholism recognize the success that AA has had. They agree, along with O'Brien and Chafetz, that the self-help pioneering organization has helped and sustained large numbers of alcoholics who would otherwise have been without help or without hope.

An estimated 5 to 10% of the alcoholics in the U.S. use AA. The organization claims a success rate of about 75%, with 50% succeeding in their initial try with AA and half of the first-time failures succeeding on their later return to "the program." Various studies corroborate AA's claims of success for an estimated 50 to 60% of the alcoholics who use it.

As further evidence becomes available of a connection between alcoholism and suicide, and especially with recent increases in drinking by women and by adolescents, self-help organizations, such as Alcoholics Anonymous, will undoubtedly continue to play key roles in the ongoing fight against such addictive behavior.

alcoholism (addiction) The American Medical Association (in *Manual on Alcoholism*, 3rd ed., 1977) defines alcoholism thus:

> Alcoholism is an illness characterized by significant impairment that is directly associated with persistent and excessive use of alcohol. Impairment may involve physiological, psychological or social dysfunction.

Mark Keller, noted Rutgers Center of Alcohol Studies authority, offered this definition of alcoholism in the *Quarterly Journal of Studies on Alcoholism* (March 1960):

> Alcoholism is a chronic disease manifested by repeated implicative drinking so as to cause injury to the drinker's health or to his social or economic functioning.

Robert O'Brien and Morris Chafetz, MD, describe alcoholism in *The Encyclopedia of Alcoholism* as "a chronic disorder associated with excessive consumption of alcohol over a period of time."

Today most authorities recognize alcoholism as a "disease," yet some still challenge this position on the grounds that a self-inflicted condition cannot properly be designated a disease.

According to O'Brien and Chafetz, the earliest known use of the term "alcoholism" was by a Swedish scientist, Magnus Huss of Stockholm. Huss published a treatise, *Chronische Alcohols Krankheit* (*Chronic Alcohol Disease*, Sweden, 1849; Germany, 1852), in which he identified a condition involving abuse of alcohol and labeled it *Alcoholismus Chronicus*. However, the disease concept of alcoholism is much older. References to it have been found in the works of the 18th century American physician

Benjamin Rush, and in Chaucer and the Roman philosopher Seneca.

It was not until 1956 that the American Medical Association (AMA) passed a resolution that officially recognized alcoholism as a disease. This landmark resolution, plus a similar one by the American Bar Association (ABA), has since led to alcoholism-related laws at the federal, state and even local government levels. It also impacted considerably on program financing, insurance coverage and hospital admissions policies, as well as the legal status of alcoholics. (See also ABUSE, SUBSTANCE.)

allopathy The main system of Western medical practice, based on the concept of treating an illness by counteracting its symptoms. It is a method of medical treatment wherein an opposing reaction is purposely produced in order to cure the afflicting disease. It is the opposite of the *holistic* approach—the method most emphasized in the U.S. today to learn about suicide—which involves research and thinking that considers biological, psychological, social structural, and social situational factors as interacting with each other.

altruistic suicide It was EMILE DURKHEIM's theory (in *Le Suicide*) that suicide was more understandable, and more explicable, when considered as a reaction to the peculiarities of society. He said that incidence of self-destruction could be traced accurately to the social conditions of the suicide attempter . . . and that, in Rabbi Earl A. Grollman's words, "The degree of suicide is a derivative of that suicide."

Durkheim, whose work is still much quoted as a landmark of sociological research into suicide, theorized that there were four types of suicide: *egoistic*, *anomic*, *altruistic*, and *fatalistic*. The altruistic suicide is where there is excessive identification and integration of the individual with society, and the social group's authority over the individual becomes so pronounced that the individual loses his own personal identity. The captain who chose to go down with his ship is an (now more or less outmoded) example of altruistic suicide. Another example are the followers of Jones who committed suicide at Jonestown, Guyana. (See also EGOISTIC SUICIDE, ANOMIC SUICIDE and FATALISTIC SUICIDE.)

Alvarez, Alfred Author of the well-known work, *The Savage God: A Study of Suicide*. The noted English poet and critic dispels the notion held by many people that suicide is either a terrifying aberration or something to be ignored altogether. He documents and explores historically man's changing attitudes toward suicide, from the various primitive societies, through the Greek and Roman cultures and the suicidal martyrdom of the early Christian church, to the attitude of the late 19th century and the gradual shift in the responsibility of suicide from the individual to society.

Alvarez discusses various theories of suicide, explores the minds and emotional states of Dante, Cowper, Donne, and others. The author includes a personal memoir of the young American poet SYLVIA PLATH and discusses why she, and so many artists in the 20th century, chose to commit suicide. From there, the author enters into the closed world of the suicide, with its own fatal logic, providing readers with his own personal view of suicide. He chronicles with startling candor his attempt on his own life. The book's title is from W.B. YEATS'S, "After us the Savage God," noted in his room after attending the first performance of Alfred Jarry's play *Ubu Roi*, in Paris, in 1896.

amae Mamoru Iga, in "Personal Situation As a Factor in Suicide" (in Wolman's *Between Survival and Suicide*), explains that *amae* is a "core element of narcissism," and is the assumption that others exist to service one's own needs. Certain people—in Iga's writing, the famous Japanese novelist YUKIO MISHIMA, who committed suicide at age 45—possess *amae* to a degree that approaches the infantile sense of omnipotence. "Consequently," says Iga, "when his (Mishima's) *amae* was not satisfied the psychological damage would have been unusually severe." This apparently happened to Yukio Mishima several times in his last years, not to mention his failure to win after being a candidate for the Nobel Prize in Literature.

ambivalence The coexistence of opposing feelings such as love and hate, respect and contempt, sadness and joy toward the same person or thing. It is perhaps the single most important psychological concept in our understanding suicide. Ambivalence: the potential suicide who wants to kill him- or herself but doesn't want to, who simultaneously wishes to die even while fantasizing rescue, who cuts his or her throat and cries for help. The ambivalence is so strong that often suicide victims have been found dead, the telephone clutched in their hand. As DR. MARY GIFFIN says, "A suicide attempt that turns deadly is the last in a long series of cries for help."

American Association of Suicidology (AAS) A non-profit organization whose goal is to understand and prevent suicide. Founded in 1968 by EDWIN S. SHNEIDMAN, PhD, AAS promotes research, public awareness programs, training for professionals and volunteers, and other programs deemed necessary for the understanding and prevention of suicide. In addition, it serves as a national clearinghouse for information on suicide.

The organization is headquartered in Denver, Colorado, where the central office is headed up by Executive Officer Julie Perlman, MSW. Membership includes mental health professionals, researchers, suicide prevention and crisis intervention centers, school districts, crisis center volunteers, survivors of suicide and a variety of lay persons who have an interest in suicide prevention.

A primary objective of AAS is to help suicide and crisis intervention centers throughout the U.S. and Canada provide quality services. The AAS has developed recognized standards for certification of these centers which are described in the AAS Certification Standards Manual for Crisis Intervention Programs.

The AAS Journal, published quarterly, is *Suicide and Life-Threatening Behavior*. Presently edited by Ronald Maris, chairman of the department of sociology, the University of South Carolina, the journal contains research, applied articles and reviews.

Newslink, a quarterly newsletter, keeps members apprised of current activities and developments in the suicide prevention field and also is a forum for communication among AAS members.

In addition, AAS produces a number of suicide prevention pamphlets for the public as well as a *Directory of Suicide Prevention and Crisis Intervention Agencies in the U.S.*

The AAS holds an annual conference every spring in a different region of the country. The conferences offer a variety of presentations in the areas of academic and clinical research, and clinical services and training for mental health professionals and volunteers. State and regional groups affiliated with the AAS conduct periodic meetings and workshops so that networking can occur on a more localized level.

AAS also produces public service announcements and releases concerning suicide prevention. Various organizational members work with the national and regional media as consultants and participants in their reporting and presentation of suicide-related issues. For example, the first week of May is designated as National Suicide Prevention Week, during which time AAS suicide prevention and crisis intervention centers work with their local media to educate and inform the public regarding suicide prevention.

Involvement in suicide prevention legislative efforts also is a priority of AAS. Members often consult on potential or pending legislation at both the federal and state levels; many have provided expert testimony for congressional committees and subcommittees.

The AAS presents yearly awards to outstanding contributors in the field of suicidology. It assists and encourages survivor activities by maintaining information on survivor groups and a listing of available books, films, newsletters and pamphlets which focus on survivor concerns.

AAS members who are available to speak, write short articles or provide training, make up the organization's Speakers/Writers Bureau. Individuals or organizations are encouraged to contact the AAS Public Information Committee through the group's Central Office, Julie Perlman, MSW, Executive Officer, 2459 S. Ash Street, Denver, CO 80222; phone is (303) 692-0985.

American Council for Drug Education (CDE) Formerly the American Council on Marijuana and Other Psychoactive Drugs (ACM). The name was changed in 1983 to better reflect the council's aim: to educate the general public about the health hazards (including suicide risk) associated with the use of psychoactive drugs. The council, established in 1977, believes that an educated public is the best defense against drug abuse or misuse; thus, it promotes scientific findings, organizes conferences and seminars, provides media resources and publishes educational materials.

American Council on Alcohol Problems (ACAP) In operation since 1895 under various names, including the Anti-Saloon League of America, the Temperance League of America and the National Temperance League. A not-for-profit organization that provides a medium through which individuals, churches and social agencies can cooperate to find a moral and scientific solution to the alcohol problem in the U.S. and also to promote abstinence.

American Indians See NATIVE AMERICANS.

American Medical Association (AMA) An organization of physicians and surgeons with the purpose of promoting the art and science of medicine and improving public health, the AMA informs physicians on progress in clinical medicine, pertinent research and landmark evolutions. The AMA also provides advisory, interpretative and referral information on medicine, health care and science. Statistics, clipping services, brochures/pamphlets, library searches, placement on mailing lists and a newsletter are available through the AMA, and they also will supply a publications list. AMA publishes the prestigious *Journal of the American Medical Association* (JAMA). AMA is, quite naturally, interested in the medical aspects of suicide and has a special committee that studies the phenomenon. Headquarters: 535 N. Dearborn Street, Chicago, IL 60610.

American Psychiatric Association The professional medical society represents some 27,000 U.S. and Canadian psychiatrists. Goals are to improve treatment, rehabilitation and care of the mentally ill, to promote research, to advance standards of all psychiatric services and facilities, and to educate other medical professionals, scientists as well as the general public. The association provides advisory, analytical, bibliographical, historical, how-to, interpretative, referral and technical information on psychiatric care, psychiatric insurance and mental illness. Will assist in arranging interviews for writers and/or researchers. Publications include advance and post-convention articles and news releases each May concerning annual meetings and scientific proceedings; more than 400 individual papers on a wide range of topics, including suicide, are available each year. Also, periodic news releases are furnished throughout the year concerning new studies published in the APA journals. Headquarters: 1400 K Street, NW, Washington, DC 20005; phone is (202) 797-4900.

American Psychological Association This professional association has goals and services within its field of expertise similar to those of the American Psychiatric Association. Also, like other concerned medical and human service associations, the American Psychological Association encourages the general public, writers, and researchers to call for information and/or referrals. Headquarters: 1200 17th Street, NW, Washington, DC 20036; phone is (202) 833-7600.

anniversaries Survivors of suicide often find that, each year, on the anniversary of the suicide, they experience renewed grief, anger, anxiety, loneliness and depression. As with a loss by "natural" death, a process is started within the survivor's psyche that psychiatrists call the "anniversary reaction." Psychiatrists and other couselors suggest these emotions be discussed by survivors with qualified clinicians who can assist them in working through their traumatic loss. Otherwise, the pain can be needlessly prolonged.

anomic suicide One in EMILE DURKHEIM's classification of the four types of suicide, the three others being EGOISTIC, ALTRUISTIC and FATALISTIC. Anomic (*anomie*, meaning "lawlessness") suicide represents the individuals who kill themselves as the result of insufficient regulation in society. A society is regulated to the extent that it controls the motivations of individual members. When society undergoes rapid changes and regulations are in transition or a state of flux, the individual may find the lack of definitive rules, customs, laws and traditions confusing and upsetting and be unable to adjust to the social change. Psychologically it often means the individual is no longer able to adjust to or feel he or she belongs to the social group. Examples might be the loss of job and role in a serious economic depression or, conversely, finding oneself abruptly among the nouveau riche (e.g., a major lottery winner).

anorexia nervosa A disorder with severe and prolonged refusal to eat, resulting in major weight loss and physical debilitation. It is usually associated with an intense fear of becoming obese and is most frequently encountered in girls and young women. Bulimia is often associated with this condition. It is a distress signal for parents, friends and teachers to look out for, because experts believe most of the victims of anorexia nervosa (or anorectics) are potentially suicidal. In essence, they are literally starving themselves to the point of self-destruction. Anorectics, like most addictive persons, are victims of a profound sense of inadequacy, low self-esteem and self-hatred. Like bulimics (see BULIMIA), anorexia nervosa-afflicted people are killing themselves slowly and deliberately, or at the very least unconsciously. This strange malady affects teenage females for the most part (an estimated one-half million in the U.S. alone); 15% of those with severe cases of anorexia nervosa die.

antidepressants A major classification of drugs developed in recent times to improve mood medically in severely depressed patients. O'Brien and Cohen, in *The Encyclopedia of Drug Abuse*, advise: "Antidepressant drugs are rarely used recreationally because although they seem to have a stimulant effect in cases of pathologic depression, they appear to have little immediate pleasurable effect on normal mood states. In fact, amitriptyline (Elavil) is occasionally abused for its sedative effect. Antidepressants are subdivided into tricyclic antidepressants (TCA) and monoamine oxidase (MAO) inhibitors." The newest tricyclic is a drug called Asendin, used for some time in Europe and other countries before the FDA (Food and Drug Administration) approved it for use in the U.S. It apparently works faster than the older tricyclics, and is said to be virtually free of side effects.

A third type of antidepressant, lithium, is sometimes used to treat manic depressives, who account for an estimated 5% of all victims of depression. LITHIUM, a salt, is a deficiency medication. As with other antidepressants, lithium has potentially toxic side effects.

While antidepressants (recommended in combination with psychotherapy) are an option for depression, most child psychiatrists avoid their use with children and, when possible, teenagers.

The Antisidor Council "The Antisidor Council," writes Norman L. Farberow, PhD, in "Cultural History of Suicide" (in *Suicide in Different Countries*), "of 590 A.D. added for the first time a system of penalties to the condemnation of suicide, and in 1284, the Synod of Nimes invoked the Church's (Catholic) final weapon for prevention, denial of Christian burial."

Antisthenes Greek philosopher (ca. 440 B.C.-ca. 360 B.C.) who founded the Cynic School of Philosophers at Athens; he advocated a simple, austere life. In *The Little, Brown Book of Anecdotes*, the editor tells of a time when, overcome by a distaste for life, Antisthenes was offered a dagger by Diogenes, who said: "Perhaps you have need of this friend?" Antisthenes replied, "I thank you, but unfortunately, the will to live is also part of the world's evil, as it is part of our nature."

Antony, Mark (Marcus Antonius) Roman statesman and soldier (ca. 83 B.C.-30 B.C.), he served under Julius Caesar in Gaul and became his protégé. After Caesar's assassination in 44 B.C., and while on an Asian tour, Antony met Cleopatra and formed a liaison with her. Ignoring his second wife, Octavia, he settled in Alexandria and ruled from there in a luxurious court until Octavian (his wife's brother) deprived him of power. In the ensuing civil war, Octavian's forces triumphed at Actium in 31 B.C., and Antony fled to Alexandria where he committed suicide upon his brother-in-law's approach. See ALTRUISTIC SUICIDE.

Apaches, White Mountain Suicide and homicide among the White Mountain Apaches (who live on a reservation in the central mountain region of Arizona) are closely related, according to Webb and Willard ("Six American Indian Patterns of Suicide" in Farberow's *Suicide in Different Cultures*). In certain situations, it appears they believe the only options open to an individual are self-destruction or murder. The authors say that "The rise in female suicides among the Apaches over the last 10 years is part of this suicide-homicide system."

The Apache suicide rate rests at a fairly high level, 50 per 100,000 (Everett, 1972; Levy and Kunitz, 1969). Levy and Kunitz (1969) reported a homicide rate of 133 per 100,000 population. During the 1930s, the male to female rate of suicide was four to one, but by the 1960s, it had developed to six male suicides to every one female suicide.

A characteristic of Apache suicide is use of highly lethal weapons. The majority of men use guns, while women suicides use burning for the most part. Apaches have always been considered highly aggressive. The adjustment to the reservation system probably represents a turning inward of the aggression historically directed toward their enemies, i.e., outer-group aggression. Also, since aggression toward kinsmen was always unacceptable in the Apache culture, the present suicide pattern may be the result of expressing what Webb and Willard call "unacceptable aggression."

April suicides Poet T.S. Eliot said "April is the cruelest month." The spring months of March, April and May have consistently shown the highest suicide rate for the year, 4% to 6% higher than the average for the rest of the year. Contrary to myth, the committed suicide rate during the Christmas season is below average. However, a study by Arthur P. Noyes, Institute for Neuro-Psychiatric Research, reveals that New Hampshire, for instance, suffers its highest number of suicides in December, and also a sharp rise in admissions to mental hospitals. Some western European countries have more suicides occurring in late spring than in other months (Dublin, *Suicide*, 1963). And more suicides are reported to occur on certain days of the week and at certain hours of the day, writes Mary Monk in "Epidemiology," chapter 10 of SEYMOUR PERLIN's *A Handbook for the Study of Suicide*. Monk, professor of community and preventive medicines, New York Medical College, says, "these temporal associations may, however, reflect the timing of the discovery of the dead person rather than the occurrence of suicide."

Aquinas, Saint Thomas Norman L. Farberow writes in "Cultural History of Suicide" that "in the 13th century, Thomas Aquinas in his *Summa Theologica* formulated the authorititave Church position on suicide for that time. Suicide was absolutely wrong for these reasons: (1) it was unnatural, (2) every man was a member of some community, and suicide was therefore anti-social, and (3) life was a gift of God and was not at the disposal of man." Farberow adds that it was at about this time that the famed *Inferno* appeared, in which DANTE illustrated contemporary attitudes toward self-destruction by showing man condemned to eternal unrest in the woods of self-destruction.

For St. Thomas (1224-1274), all life was merely preparation for the eternal. His argument, a more refined and elaborate Augustinian concept, stressed the sacredness of human life and absolute submission to God. This, then, was the basis of his three postulates.

Argentina Chapter four of *Suicide in Different Cultures* (ed. Norman L. Farberow) is written by Nasim Yampey, MD, and is entitled "Suicide in Buenos Aires; Social and Cultural Influences." Suicide in the 1960s, says Yampey, was predominant among older people, especially for the age group between 60 and 70. This reversed a trend between 1940 and 1950, when the highest rate of incidence was for the age group between 30 and 50 years old. The greatest number of suicides, says Yampey, is registered among "housewives, pensioners, students and bondholders; that is to say, those who economically represent the least productive part of the population."

Dr. Yampey also found that the apparent reasons listed by the police files were primarily: (1) weariness of life, (2) physical suffering and, in much smaller frequencies, (3) mental alienation, (4) family disgust, (5) lack of resources and (6) love contradictions.

In the period from 1964 to 1968 (Municipalidad de Buenos Aires, 1970), the suicide rate was just over 10 per 100,000 population, determined from the death certificates by the Department of Statistics of the city government. This is fairly close to official rates of other provinces. In 1967, for example, the rate of suicide in the Argentine Republic was 9.6 per 100,000. Interestingly, of the total suicides that year, 66% were Argentines, and 34% were foreigners. Regarding sex, according to Dr. Yampey, the distribution of committed suicide is 70% men and 30% women. Suicide, it seems, has historically seen a wide fluctuation over the years. There was a very high incidence of suicide in Buenos Aires at the end of the 19th century, when it reached an annual rate of 33 per 100,000 in the years 1895 and 1896.

It is Dr. Yampey's view that the problem of suicide in Argentina presents great tasks, such as an intensive epidemiological study with an analysis of its social implications, a stronger program of prevention, and a good mental health education program. A Suicide Help Center was founded in 1967 and has proven most helpful in increasing suicide prevention possibilities.

Aristotle In his *Ethics*, Aristotle (384-322 B.C.) described suicide as a failure in courage. He wrote: "To run away from trouble is a form of cowardice and, while it is true that the suicide braves death, he does it not for some noble object, but to escape some ill."

The Ethics of Aristotle (Harmondsworth, England: Penguin Books, 1953).

Arria The wife of Roman senator Cecina Paetus, who was accused of being involved in a plot against the emperor and ordered to commit suicide. When Paetus hesitated, Arria (died A.D. 42) snatched the dagger from her husband, stabbed herself, then handed the weapon back with the words, "Paete, non dolet" (Paetus, it does not hurt). See COMPULSORY SUICIDE.

art, literature and suicide Some informative articles on various aspects in different cultures of the relationships among art, literature and the subject of suicide include: N. Schipkowensky, K. Milenkov, and A. Bogdanova, "Self-destruction in Bulgarian Folk Songs," pp. 205-213 in Farberow's *Suicide in Different Cultures*; S.S. Tayal, "The Communication of Suicidal Ideation in Art Therapy"; I. Jakab and M.D. Howard, pp. 309-324 in *Psychotherapy and Psychosomatics*, 17:5-6 (1969), which deals with art therapy with a 12-year-old girl who witnessed suicide and developed school phobia.

A good bibliographic source on the subject is J. Traufman and C. Pollard, *Literature and Medicine: An Annotated Bibliography*; see pp. 225-226, "Suicide." Their book lists novels, short stories, novellas, poems, sonnets, and dramas dealing with the topic of suicide.

See also D. Lester, B.H. Sell, and K.D. Sell, *Suicide: A Guide to Information Sources*; contains a section entitled "Suicide and Literature," pp. 113-142.

F. Cutter's *Art and the Wish to Die* includes appendixes which list artists who painted suicidal themes; also, artists who committed suicide and an historical look at suicide in art.

Another excellent source is John L. McIntosh's *Research on Suicide: A Bibliography*.

In the fields of art and literature, attitudes toward suicide remain as ambivalent and divided today as in ancient Greece and Rome. There have been apologists for suicide in both cultural fields. Eminent artists and writers have over the years proclaimed man's right to self-destruction, whereas many others have condemned suicide with equal conviction.

JOHN DONNE's *BIATHANATOS* (subtitled "A Declaration of that Paradoxe, or Thesis, that Self-Homicide is Not So Naturally Sinne, that It May Never Be Otherwise") was a classic example of a new look (at the time) at an old practice. And through the years, many other writers—both inside and outside the Church—explored the endless possibilities of the topic. MONTAIGNE, in his famous *Essais*, calls death "a very secure haven, never to be feared and often to be sought." Romantic suicide has long been used by playwrights and poets; Shakespeare's *ROMEO AND JULIET* is a popular example.

Interestingly, Donne's thesis, written early in the 17th century, was not published until 1646, 15 years after the poet-chaplain's death. Born a Catholic, Donne later took Anglican orders, recognized his thesis as a "misinterpretable" subject and asked the person to whom he had entrusted the original manuscript to "publish it not, yet burn it not; and between those, do what you will with it."

DAVID HUME'S essay, "On Suicide," was also published posthumously, in 1777, a year after his death. The essay, immediately suppressed, is today considered a convincing argument against the moral prejudice that many still hold against suicide. Hume's view was that at the worst, one does not harm society by suicide, but merely ceases to do good (if good works were what one had been doing). He says, too, that one who is tired of life often is a burden on society—and hinders the work of others.

Perhaps ALBERT CAMUS summed up neatly the ambivalence and division among artists and writers over the years with regard to suicide: "What is called a reason for living is also an excellent reason for dying."

A number of the more famous artists and writers who committed suicide are dealt with in detail elsewhere in this work.

assisted suicide In many statutes referred to as "abetted" suicide. It is to give advice on methods of suicide or actually to assist someone subsequently to end their life. While it is against the law in most states to assist another person in taking his or her own life, it is not against the law to give information to people in general, especially when said group constitutes a bona fide minority, and when information given is obtained from sources already in the public domain, such as in bookstores or shops and libraries.

This has not always been the case. Within common law—the system of legal tradition inherited by the U.S. from England—suicide was at one time a crime, a felony involving moral turpitude. It was called *Felo de se*—the felony of self-murder. Under the law, property of a suicide was forfeited and burial was "ignominious."

Moreover, anyone who assisted a suicide and was present when the suicidal act was initiated was guilty of murder. If the person assisting was not present, he or she was still considered an "accessory before the fact" and was considered guilty of murder or manslaughter. In certain jurisdictions, however, the one assisting sometimes escaped punishment(s) because the principal, being deceased, could not be convicted and, thus, the accessory could not be tried.

In the past 100 years or so, most common law provisions have been abolished in the United States. The English Suicide Act of 1961 legalized suicide in that country but still made aiding and abetting suicide a criminal offense. Although in most countries suicide is no longer a punishable offense, it is still generally frowned upon by society as a whole and causes guilt feelings to those closely involved.

If suicide is no longer a crime in the U.S., aiding a suicide remains a potentially serious offense. In a 1920 case in Michigan, *People v. Roberts*, a husband who had prepared a poison and placed it within his wife's reach was convicted of first degree murder and given a life sentence. The man had done as his wife requested (she suffered from an incurable and physically incapacitating affliction). The decision was upheld in appellate court.

Today, there remains real risk of criminal prosecution for anyone who assists a suicide, even for humanitarian and compassionate reasons—and even at the victim's request. However, prosecution under criminal law does not begin until police or other law enforcement officials believe that a crime has been committed and they can identify the person or persons responsible. If no one knows a crime has occurred, no charges are filed, of course. If, for instance, a terminally ill person's death is declared "natural" by the attending physician, because no one knew another person helped in the suicidal act, then no charges would be filed and, obviously, no prosecution would begin. This undoubtedly happens more than the public generally realizes.

Should there be some question or suspicion as to final cause of death, authorities may order an autopsy. A family can usually refuse to give permission for the autopsy, if they do not, in their refusal, arouse suspicion of "foul play." Should that happen, officials will probably order that the autopsy be performed.

Whether or not criminal proceedings are started is within the discretion and judgment of the prosecutor, usually the district attorney. A number of factors govern the prosecutor's exercising this discretion, such as: if a death causes considerable public attention; if public attention is generated by a particularly vocal group opposed to the act of suicide; if there appears to be a likelihood of significant financial gain or other selfish motive on the part of the person assisting the suicide; or, if the person helping happens to be a total stranger to the suicide victim.

Once it has been determined to prosecute, a request by the victim for help in the taking of his or her life is almost certain not to be considered a valid legal defense. The risks, it seems, for aiding and abetting in the suicidal act are both real and serious. Still, there is considerable room for argument under certain circumstances (e.g., providing information only, to a terminally ill patient, about the lethality of various drugs). Then the focus in a criminal case usually becomes one of *intent* of the person to *cause*—or assist in—the death. In today's society, by way of books, movies, magazines, and television, lethality of drugs, especially if combined with alcohol, is fairly common knowledge. Thus, the closer the person who assists is to a terminally ill person (and the more specific the response to a request for help in the suicide act), the more likely is the chance of criminal prosecution.

In addition, as Richard Stanley Scott, MD, JD, points out in "Legal Risks: Potential Consequences for Those Who Aid in Active Voluntary Euthanasia," Appendix B in Humphrey's *Let Me Die Before I Wake*, there are the laws of conspiracy to consider. Scott explains: "the laws of conspiracy (agreement among two or more persons to commit a criminal act and some action by at least one of them toward further preparation) form an additional and separate basis for prosecution of those providing information on specific request."

Therefore, even for advocates of euthanasia who support the option of active voluntary "self-deliverance" for the terminally ill, the risk of criminal charges is real and serious for those persons who would assist someone in taking his or her own life.

All this concerns only criminal law. Of concern to professionals, such as physicians, psychologists, psychiatrists, nurses, social workers, attorneys and others licensed to practice a particular profession, is the potential jeopardy to their licenses should their participation in assisting another's self-destruction become known. The revocation or suspension of professional licenses comes under administrative law, which is complicated and involves a formal administrative proceeding, the accused professional's procedural rights of "due process," a specification of charges, and the right to an impartial hearing on the charges, with opportunity to cross-examine adverse witnesses and produce evidence refuting the charges. Clearly, this involved process is but one important reason why professional people are generally very reluctant to offer or provide active assistance even to tragic victims of painful terminal illnesses.

Finally, in contrast to criminal law, there is civil law which involves one citizen or more bringing a lawsuit against another or others, alleging injuries to themselves or one of their recognized "interests." A typical case in civil law might be one concerning alleged direct bodily injury to the plaintiff (the one bringing a lawsuit) as a result of medical malpractice (against the defendant physician).

The required elements for having grounds to file a civil suit include: liability, damages and causation. In the context of those who have chosen to assist a suicide, Scott says there are at least three potential areas of "exposure" to civil litigation: (1) dissent by survivors (some family member learns of the helper's role and actively disagrees with actions taken); (2) unsuccessful attempt (perhaps brought about by the potential suicide himself against the helper who either withdrew or who inadvertently botched the suicide attempt); (3) wrong person dies (when someone other than the suicide, perhaps a child, comes into possession of the drug(s), ingests them, and fatal results are misdirected).

Indeed, it is clearly established that legal risks for anyone who might agree to assist someone in suicide are present—and will continue to be present until the attitude of society, not to mention its laws, are changed. That is why voluntary euthanasia groups (see British Voluntary Euthanasia Society [see EXIT], THE HEMLOCK SOCIETY, and Concerns for Dying) are diligent in advising followers always to proceed with great care and caution when considering assistance to a terminally ill patient in "self-deliverance."

In a recent, publicized matter of suicide involving the terminally ill, former television reporter and writer BETTY ROLLIN admitted in her book *Last Wish* that she secretly helped her mother take her own life in 1983. Rollin was careful to point out to interviewers that she "did not directly help my mother commit suicide. If I did, I would not have written a book about it. I did research, and I gave my mother information."

Rollin wrote that after many conversations with evasive and fearful physicians, she contacted an elderly American doctor living in the Netherlands. The doctor, who is not identified, suggested a combination of pills for Rollin's mother, Ida, age 75, who suffered from an inoperable cancer. He told Rollin to stay with her mother for two hours after she took the pills, but to leave the apartment at that point and arrange for the body to be found by someone else.

Rollin said that before writing the book, she consulted a lawyer, who told her she had done nothing illegal. A book reviewer in *The Washington Post* said some "legal authorities . . . could see Rollin's book as a confession of murder." Rollin explained that she never brought up suicide, never encouraged it, and that all she did was provide information. "It was her (mother's) act, her wish."

Under New York State law, "promoting suicide" is a felony punishable by up to four years in prison. Joseph Jaffe, vice chairman of the New York State Bar Association's Criminal Law Committee, has said that such cases pose difficult problems.

Assisting a person whose personal choice it is to end their life is not to be confused here with the so-called "mercy killing." Whereas voluntary self-destruction involves personal decision and self-control, the mercy killing is the *unrequested* taking of another's life in order to save that person further suffering.

Mercy killing is usually an act of desperation and despair, and often the life-taker is near emotional collapse caused by the stress that comes from caring for and watching someone terminally ill. Pushed to such limits, the life-taker at some point feels compelled to hasten death—by whatever means—because no one else will.

Mercy killers are usually confronted with the criminal charge of murder or manslaughter. Up until the 1960s, "mercy killers" in Western society often were sentenced to death, later commuted to life imprisonment. In the U.S., in the past 10 years, there have been several cases where juries refused to indict or convict "mercy killers," though all evidence weighed against such a decision.

In March 1986, the American Medical Association decided that it would be ethical for their member doctors to withhold "all means of life prolonging medical treatment," including food and water, from patients that are in irreversible comas. The AMA's judicial council, meeting in New Orleans, decided unanimously that withholding treatment in such cases, even when death is not imminent, would be ethically appropriate. The council made clear its decision does not oblige any physician to stop therapy, and that each case should be decided individually. The decision will probably, at least in the long run, make the withholding of treatment more socially acceptable.

At present, there are an estimated 10,000 people who are in irreversible comas in institutions in the U.S., according to *The New York Times*. In such cases, doctors in the past have often refused to withhold or withdraw treatments (e.g., respirators, artificial feeding), citing ethical standards and fear of criminal prosecution or malpractice suits—this despite the requests of family members and the previously expressed wishes of the patients to have such treatments withdrawn.

The opinion of AMA's judicial council has no legal standing, however. Still, as an indication of a shifting of broad social opinion, it is all but certain to give prosecutors and plaintiffs pause. Today, an estimated 80% of the 5,500 Americans who die each day are wired and incubated and in institutions.

The crux of AMA's new policy—the key change—lies in the stipulation that the patient need *not* be terminally ill for halting of treatment to be acceptable. Such decisions to remove life-support systems will probably be difficult for many doctors. The recent AMA decision is but one more cautious step in the evolution of a social policy in the complex, delicate and shadowy area of dying and death.

attempted suicide Refers to behavior directed against the self which results in injury or self-harm or has strong potential for injury. Intention in the behavior may or may not be to die, or may or may not be to inflict injury or pain on oneself. Authorities are still divided as to whether attempted suicide and completed suicide are the same or different kinds of behavior. There is no question, however, that there is considerable overlap in many of the types of behavior. Yet it is also true that there are marked differences in typical age, sex, marital status and other demographic characteristics. Although only 10 to 15% of attempters go on to kill themselves, it is estimated that between 30 and 40% of suicides make at least one nonfatal attempt.

It is believed that most suicide attempts, for whatever reasons, are essentially a cry for help. However, as Edwin M. Lemert notes, it is sometimes difficult to determine whether an attempt is genuine or little more than a dramatic gesture toward self-destruction. For instance, there are reported cases where the person took a small number of sleeping pills and called a physician. There, the probability of death hardly existed. But, according to DR. MARY GIFFIN, "A suicide attempt that turns deadly is the last in a long series of cries for help." Yet another myth that persists today, despite statistics to the contrary, is that once a person tries to kill himself and fails, the pain and shame will prevent his or her trying again.

Some interesting statistics concerning suicide attempts:

- In the U.S., the ratio of suicides is about three males to one female, although women usually make two-thirds of the unsuccessful attempts at suicide.
- In most countries, attempted suicide is no longer a punishable offense, though it is still frowned upon by many segments of society and causes guilt feelings to those closely involved.
- A study carried out in Sheffield, Yorkshire, England (pop. est. 500,000), revealed that in 1960 and 1961, the number of attempted suicides was about 10 times higher than the number of suicides registered in the same period. A similar survey in Los Angeles revealed comparable results. But a Swiss survey suggested a ratio of 15 to one in nonfatal to fatal acts. (Note: These surveys included only suicide attempts where a doctor intervened; otherwise, the numbers would surely be higher.)
- The peak age for suicides lies between 55 and 64; for attempted suicides, between 24 and 44.
- Nine out of 10 teenage suicide attempts take place in the home, and take place between the hours of three in the afternoon and midnight, when their parents are home and, significantly, when they can be seen, stopped and saved. (See Giffin-Felsenthal, *A Cry for Help*, p. 16.)
- Best estimates indicate that there are between 300,000 and 400,000 suicide attempts each year in the U.S. alone and that between five to six million individuals in all have made suicide attempts.
- Follow-up studies show that roughly 10% of an attempted suicide population go on to kill themselves within a 10-year period. Other studies in this country reveal that between 20% and 65% of those who kill themselves have a history of prior attempts.
- The more lethal and violent methods (guns, explosives, hanging) are used less frequently, of course, in the nonfatal attempts than in the successful (fatal) suicidal acts. Analgesics and narcotics appear to be favorites among attempters. (See also E. Robins, et al., "The Communications of Suicidal Intent: A Study of 134 Consecutive Cases of Successful (Completed) Suicides," *American Journal of Psychiatry*, 115(1959): 724-33; and N. Farberow and E. Shneidman, "Attempted, Threatened and Completed Suicide," *Journal of Abnormal Social Psychiatry* 50 (1955): 230.)

T. Dorpat and H. Ripley, "The Relationship between Attempted Suicide and Committed Suicide," *Comprehensive Psychiatry* 8(1967): 74-77.

J. Motto, "Suicide Attempts: A Longitudinal View," *Archives of General Psychiatry*, 13(1965): 516-20.

attitudes (toward suicide and the suicidal) Suicide and suicidal behavior have been with us since ancient man first realized he could kill himself. Still, the act of self-destruction is often considered, even today, a taboo subject which stigmatizes not only the victims but the survivors as well. The word "suicide," however, is a relatively recent term, first used in 1651 and taken from the Latin *sui*, "of oneself," and *cide*, "a killing"—literally, to kill oneself.

Attitudes concerning suicide and those who try it have varied widely in societies and the groups within those societies over the centuries. These attitudes run the spectrum of feelings and emotions from revulsion, condemnation and total disapproval, to pity, benign acceptance and reluctant recognition of the right to die voluntarily at one's own hand under certain circumstances. Views have gone from taking extreme sanctions against the act of suicide to, in John McIntosh's words, "ambiguity or no clear condemnation and even to encouraging the act."

Down through the years, philosophers have pondered the problem: Plato strongly condemned suicide, along with Virgil, Cicero and Ovid. IMMANUEL KANT called suicide "an insult to humanity." The Roman Stoics accepted the option, or alternative of suicide, as did the EPICUREANS who considered that one's destiny was a matter of individual choice. Cato, Pliny and Seneca all considered suicide to be acceptable.

On the whole, however, with certain exceptions society began to take a hostile attitude toward self-destruction or "unnatural deaths." As Grollman points out, "Some felt that the manner in which one departs from life reflects not only one's own philosophy of life, but a possible contempt for one's group as well."

Suicide became taboo and superstitions and myths grew up surrrounding the abhorrent act. The law began to deal with suicide in punishing terms, even going so far as to enact statutes against the suicide's survivors . . . and as a deterrent for future offenders. In England, suicide attempters were imprisoned until 1916; then, instead of prison, the suicidal person was placed in custody of relatives or friends. In fact, not until 1961 did the British Parliament abolish the criminality of suicide and declare that the act of self-destruction was not "A Species of Felony."

Today legal restrictions have been abolished in most countries. As research in mental health increased and improved, legislation changed (if only gradually). In India, attempted suicide is still an indictable offense. For many years, nine states in the U.S. still considered attempted suicide "illegal, constituting a misdemeanor or felony." But even in those states—Alabama, Kentucky, New Jersey, South Carolina, North Carolina, North Dakota, Oklahoma, South Dakota and Washington—such laws were seldom enforced.

The various religions have profoundly influenced the American legal stance regarding suicide, because laws in America are based on English common law, which, in turn, was impacted by the Church and the synagogues.

The three denominations of modern Judaism take what Rabbi Grollman calls an "enlightened point of view" which considers the act of suicide a crime against God, but an act that can sometimes be explained away, understood and forgiven. But in Judaism, as in other religions, there has never been universal agreement. Grollman writes: "with the growth of the socio-psychological sciences, it is realized that one cannot legislate against self-destruction by religious fiat."

When Christianity came into being, suicide was commonplace in Greece and Rome. Early Christians seemed to accept the attitudes prevailing at the time. The Apostles did not denounce suicide, and the New Testament mentioned the matter only indirectly, in the report of Judas' suicide. For centuries, church leaders did not condemn suicide, despite the widespread practice.

Then Augustine denounced suicide as a sin that precluded the possibility of repentance, calling the act "a form of homicide, and thus a violation of the DECALOGUE ARTICLE, 'Thou shalt not kill.'" But earliest institutional disapproval didn't come until 533, as expressed by the Second Council of Orleans. Suicide, it was determined, became the most serious and heinous of transgressions. Grollman explains that "In 563, the Fifteenth Canon of the Council of Braga denied the suicide funeral rites of the Eucharist and the singing of psalms. The Council of Hereford of 673 withheld burial rites to those who died of self-destruction. In 1284, the Synod of Nimes refused self-murderers even the quiet interment in holy ground."

SAINT THOMAS AQUINAS refined and elaborated on Augustine's concept, opposing suicide on the basis of three postulates. His opposition was predicated on the sacredness of human life and absolute submission to God.

The philosophical and religious stances have changed over time and brought new attitudes regarding suicide. JOHN DONNE, dean of St. Paul's Cathedral, London, reacted against the Church's view of suicide. He admitted it was contrary to the law of self-preservation, but saw it as neither a violation of the law nor against reason. His position was supported in time by secular writers and philosophers, including HUME, MONTESQUIEU, VOLTAIRE and ROUSSEAU.

Among other religions, Brahmanism tolerates suicide, whereas the attitude of Buddhism is ambiguous, though it encourages suicide in the service of religion and country. Hindus consider suicide an ultimate death, thus leading to an earthbound, ghostly existence. In Japan, compulsory hara-kiri was declared illegal in 1868, though voluntary hara-kiri occurs occasionally even today.

In modern times, Dietrich Bonhoeffer considered suicide a sin because it represented a denial of God. Yet he suspended that judgment for prisoners of war, for the obvious reasons. Perhaps Bishop John Robinson best sums it up: "Truth finds expression in different ages. Times change and even Christians change with them." Overall, it appears that society's attitude toward suicidal behavior is less moralistic and punitive than it was a generation ago. Increasingly, suicide is recognized not only as a philosophical, religious, legal and cultural question, but also as a psycho-socio-biological problem. This may be another reason why there is a greater readiness today to understand rather than condemn.

Earl A. Grollman, *Suicide: Prevention, Intervention, Postvention* (Boston: Beacon Press, 1971).

John L. McIntosh, *Research On Suicide: A Bibliography* (Westport, Connecticut: Greenwood Press, 1985).

Augustine of Hippo, Saint North African theologian (354-430) and one of the fathers and doctors of the Church. Son of Saint Monica, a Christian, Augustine had been influenced by the pagan philosophers until his conversion. After a dissolute youth, he returned to his native town following his baptism at age 32 on Easter Sunday, 387. He lived a monastic life after that, was ordained in 391, and then was consecrated a bishop of Hippo in 396. His *City of God* and *Confessions* are among the greatest Christian documents. In *Confessions*, Augustine recounts how even his youthful insincerity was reflected in prayers for repentance: "Da mihi castitateur et continentiam, sed noli modo" (Give me chastity and continence, but not yet.)

As noted previously (see ATTITUDES TOWARD SUICIDE AND THE SUICIDAL), Augustine's denouncement of suicide as a sin greatly influenced thinking at the time. He espoused four arguments to justify the Church's anti-suicide position: (1) no private individual may assume the right to kill a guilty person; (2) the suicide who takes his own life has killed a man; (3) the truly noble soul will bear all suffering from which the effort to escape is an admission of weakness; and, (4) the suicide dies the worst of sinners because he is not only running away from the fear of temptation, but also any possibilities of absolution. According to Farberow, writing in *Suicide in Different Cultures*, "St. Augustine's arguments were used to prevent the rush of women to kill themselves to preserve their chastity by arguing that no woman can lose her chastity by violation, since real virginity was an attribute of the soul and not of the body."

Australia As previously noted, suicide rates vary widely between countries and between regions within a single country. For example, the rate in Australia in the late 1960s stood at 12.7 per 100,000 population, slightly above the U.S., and just below Japan. This gave Australia the 12th position in a comparison rate picture that involved 20 countries. Lowest for the selected countries was Ireland, 2.5 per 100,000 population; highest was Hungary with a rate of 33.7. Within the Australian island continent, suicide rates have varied—and will probably continue to vary—among the five continental states (Queensland, New South Wales, Victoria, South Australia and West Australia)—almost as widely as among the countries of the world.

In Australia at present there are three autonomous chapters or groups representing the right-to-die issues as set forth by THE HEMLOCK SOCIETY and other active and/or passive euthanasia organizations. Even as the euthanasia movement works to broaden its base, however, there is an ever-growing number of suicide prevention and crisis centers in the country.

Austria Has a relatively high incidence of suicide, unlike such other predominantly Catholic countries as Ireland, Italy and Spain. The suicide rate rose from 22.8 per 100,000 population in 1965 to 24.8 in the 1975-78 period. Male suicides rose from 14.9 in 1965 to 17.2 in 1975-78; female statistics showed a rate decrease, dropping from 7.8 in 1965 to 7.6 in the 1975-78 period. (Source: WHO, *World Health Statistics Annual*, 1965 and 1980).

In 1930, Austria suffered an enormously high rate of suicide, 30 per 100,000 population. In a study done in late 1965 and early 1966, the most suicides in Vienna were revealed to have occurred on Friday and Saturday (in Los Angeles at the same time, the fewest number of suicides occurred on those same two days). Norman L. Farberow and M.D. Simon ("Suicide in Los Angeles and Vienna," in *Suicide in Different Cultures*) noted that, "In general, the Viennese seemed socially alienated and isolated and in poor communication with spouses, relatives and close friends." They discovered that the Viennese primarily use domestic gas to kill themselves and that the cause was more often attributed to physical illness. Alcohol was a serious problem for about one-third of the Austrian suicides in the study.

authoritarianism Mamoru Iga and Kichinosuke Tatai, writing about suicide in Japan, point to two independent variables in the historically high suicide rates in that country: authoritarianism and culture conflict. They indicate that Japanese society is still highly authoritarian in various senses. First, people there are strongly conscious of status differences, which according to the authors provide the basic frames of reference to the Japanese mind. Both authoritarian aggressiveness and submissiveness are marked. To the Japanese, social relations are perceived as power relations, producing an intense desire for success (*shusse*). They morally condemn the person who fails in performing to role expectations. Under their patriarchal authoritarianism, the young, female and poor people suffer most.

Why does authoritarianism produce a high suicide rate? According to Iga and Tatai, "External regulations in an authoritarian social structure produce fatalistic suicides . . ." They add: "Thus, authoritarianism affects goal-means discrepancy, self-concept, and the perception of the general public's attitude toward the victim, producing a suicidogenic definition of the situation."

Mamoru Iga and Kichinosuke Tatai, "Characteristics of Suicide and Attitudes Toward Suicide in Japan," in *Suicide in Different Cultures," ed. Norman L. Farberow (Baltimore: University Park Press, 1975).*

autocide Suicides disguised as automobile "accidents." Forensic experts and highway transportation safety officials say that auto fatalities (which, in any given year, account for about 37% of deaths in the 15- to 24-year-old group) are "accidents" that are probably deliberate in roughly one-fourth of reported cases. Some reports indicated emotional stress may be present, but the conditions of the road, traffic flow, weather and status of the car are pointed out most of the time as the "culprits" in auto accidents. These fatalities probably represent the biggest block of suicides disguised as accidents (see Giffin and Felsenthal, *A Cry for Help*). If you add these so-called "autocides" to known suicides, argue authorities, they would make suicide the number one killer in the 15 to 24 age group.

Actor JAMES DEAN died at age 24 in a car accident that many still suspect was actually a suicide.

autoerotic asphyxiation A report in the *Journal of the American Academy of Child Psychiatry* defines autoerotic asphyxiation as "self-hanging while masturbating to achieve sexual gratification." The supply of oxygen to the brain is restricted, usually by a rope around the neck, as a way to heighten the pleasure of masturbation. Jerry Johnston writes in *Why Suicide?*: "Of course, a teenager engaging in this practice is not intending to kill himself. Instead a crazy pleasure is the object." Johnston adds that research indicates that victims are heterosexual males, most of them under 20 years of age. He also notes that the FBI "estimates that 500 to 1,000 deaths of this nature occur every year in the United States."

Jerry Johnston, *Why Suicide?: What Parents & Teachers Must Know to Save Our Kids* (Nashville, Atlanta, Camden & New York: Oliver Nelson, a Division of Thomas Nelson Publishers, 1987).

autopsy, psychological Method to collect data on completed suicide cases. Initially conceived as a device by which to investigate equivocal cases of suicide on behalf of the Los Angeles County coroner's office. An "autopsy" that consists of interviewing significant friends and relatives of the deceased to learn about suicidal communications, current and previous stresses, psychiatric and medical history, and general "life style" of the victim (Litman *et al*, "The Psychological Autopsy of Equivocal Deaths" in *The Psychology of Suicide*). These data, generally not investigated by the medical examiner and police investigation team, are considered useful for a more valid certification of death. Also, data from the psychological autopsy permits intercultural comparisons to be made on numerous variables that relate to the act of suicide and the developmental history of the decedent.

B

Bach, Richard American author of the best-seller *Jonathan Livingston Seagull*. DR. MARY GIFFIN and Carol Felsenthal, writing in *A Cry for Help*, cite a case involving two teenagers, a boy and a girl, who become obsessed with the possibility of reincarnation. Friends reported, say the co-authors, that after the pair read Richard Bach's *Illusions*, a book that had as its theme reincarnation, they began leading school lunchroom discussions of suicide and rebirth. Sometime later, the two teens crashed their car into their old junior high school building at 5 a.m. The boy was killed instantly; the girl, who reportedly had last-second doubts about reincarnation, just barely survived, after diving under the car dashboard.

Baechler, Jean French moral philosopher and author of *Suicides*, described in his highly regarded work the suicidal motive of *transfiguration*. Baechler uses an example from a newspaper report that read: "A pair of young people drove off the cliffs at Treport (Seine-Maritime) in a car on August 26th. Miss M.L., 21, employed in a restaurant, and Mr. P.K., 19, a student, left a letter in which they explained that they killed themselves 'to preserve their love.'" This report was evidently sufficient for Jean Baechler to classify the case as a suicide of "transfiguration," which he defined as one undertaken by the suicide victim(s) to achieve a state infinitely more desirable.

Most suicidologists are skeptical of young couple SUICIDE PACTS as transfiguration, because motives often involve anger, coercion, even revenge in such cases. HERBERT HENDIN maintains that "suicide notes in cases like this, as in most others, are designed to conceal—not reveal—motivation."

Baldwin, James American author who explores the racial significance of suicide, violence and male homosexuality in his critically praised novel *Another Country*, all the while indicating the importance of the white male to the black homosexual. Also, in his book *The Fire Next Time*, Baldwin shows that homosexuality for blacks is an alternative to drugs, crime and religiosity in coping with pain, frustration and the violence found in the ghetto. For homosexual blacks who are also suicidal, however, the rage and bitterness caused by rejection may either be expressed in their homosexual relationships and elsewhere or contained by depression and suicide.

Herbert Hendin, *Suicide in America* (New York: W.W. Norton, 1982), pp. 113-114.

Balzac, Honore de French novelist (1799-1850) who agreed with the Romantic dogma that the intense, true life of feeling does not—in fact, cannot—survive into middle age. Balzac wrote concerning the alternatives in *La Peau de Chagrin*: "To kill the emotions and so live on to old age, or to accept the martyrdom of our passions and die young, is our fate." As A. ALVAREZ notes: The "Romantics believed that 'the visionary powers' vanished inexorably, like youth and with youth . . ."

barbiturates Any one of a class of drugs, such as phenobarbital or seconal, which act as central nervous system depresssants, inducing drowsiness and muscular relaxation. They can make an already depressed person even more depressed.

In recent years, hospital admissions for narcotic poisonings have increased steadily. In England and in Wales, for instance, their number tripled between 1957 and 1964. The same phenomenon is reported in other European countries. Yet, oddly, the suicide rates have not increased substantially in these countries. Experts say this apparent paradox can be explained by the relatively low lethality of narcotic poisoning under conditions of modern treatment. Also, suicidologists believe most coroners and/or medical examiners in other countries, and in some areas of the U.S., appear to be more inclined to give an accident verdict or declare the cause of death "undetermined" in cases of narcotic poisoning than in other cases of self-inflicted death.

Mixing barbiturates with alcohol, however, can prove deadly serious. Actress Marilyn Monroe evidently overdosed on tranquilizers, barbiturates and alcohol. Indeed, the favored method of suicide or suicide attempts in the U.S. among women is analgesics and narcotics; in England and Wales, analgesics and narcotics run a distant second to domestic gas as a method of suicide.

Suicidal individuals are considerably more prone than otherwise comparable nonsuicidals to be alcoholics, drug users and abusers, and to be violent or homosexual. And within our American society today, there is a tendency on the part of young people (especially teenagers) to experiment with various forms of drugs, including the mixing of alcohol and barbiturates. People *do* kill themselves by a simple overdose of barbiturates; mixing them with alcohol (the organ most immediately affected by alcohol is the brain) produces a synergistic effect that only enhances the possibility of lethality. (See also ALCOHOLISM; ABUSE, SUBSTANCE.)

Barnard, Dr., Christiaan Internationally acclaimed physician recognized for his pioneering work in heart transplant surgery. A professor of cardiac surgery at the University of Cape Town Medical School in South Africa, in addition to his medical practice and teaching duties, he regularly lectures throughout the world. Barnard is a strong advocate of euthanasia and candidly supports the doctor's right to participate in euthanasia—as a humane and compassionate end to human suffering.

behavior modification The changing of human behavior by the application of conditioning or other learning techniques. The term is often used as a synonym for behavior therapy and involves the systematic application of learning principles and techniques to the treatment of behavior disorders, e.g., in the treatment of the alcoholic or overeater—in fact, in the treatment of many self-destructive behaviors.

For example, the two main goals in the treatment of alcoholism by behavior therapy are: first, to eliminate excessive alcohol consumption as a primary response to stress or other uncomfortable situations; and second, to establish alternative methods of coping with stressful situations. First, the addiction cycle must be broken, then new habits must be established.

Best known among the several behavior modification techniques is that of *aversion therapy*, whereby a negative value is associated with the consumption of alcohol. Another method or technique is blood alcohol discrimination training, based on internal cues, although this type of training is being questioned because of doubts about the ability of alcoholics to estimate their blood alcohol level. Other behavior modification therapy techniques include assertiveness training and biofeedback; some therapies employ a number of techniques.

A recent trend in behavior modification is that of attempting to teach controlled drinking as an alternative to alcoholic drinking. The approach is highly controversial since it contradicts the traditional "loss of control" model of alcoholism. O'Brien and Chafetz explain: "Because excessive consumption is viewed as a learned behavior rather than an irreversible process, controlled drinking is seen as a viable alternative for some alcoholics. This is flatly denied by most opponents of controlled drinking."

Opponents of behavior modification therapy maintain that it is a superficial treatment which does not really solve the problem, that its record to date is not all that impressive and that symptoms frequently reappear. For the past few years, since 1982, the methods and validity of the publicized Sobell research have especially been under increasing attack.

Robert O'Brien and Morris Chafetz, MD, *The Encyclopedia of Alcoholism* (New York: Facts On File, 1982), pp. 43-49.

M.B. Sobell and L.C. Sobell, *Behavioral Treatment of Alcohol Problems* (New York: Plenum Press, 1978), passim.

behavior therapy See BEHAVIOR MODIFICATION.

Bell Jar, The Widely read novel that deals with the subject of youth suicide. Written by Sylvia Plath, the book was pseudonymously published in England in 1962, only a few weeks before Plath killed herself. *The Bell Jar* is based closely on the events of the poet's 20th year—a year that ended ignobly in an unsuccessful suicide attempt. In his book *The Savage God: A Study of Suicide*, A. ALVAREZ subtitled part one, "Prologue: Sylvia Plath." Alvarez, who once attempted suicide himself, writes: "According to the official statistics, there would have been at least ninety-nine other suicides in Great Britain the week Sylvia died." Then he poses the rhetorical questions: "Why do these things happen? Is there any way in which such waste can be explained, since it can hardly ever be justified? Is there, for someone creative like Sylvia, a tradition of suicide, or were there quasi-literary forces leading her to it?" (See also PLATH, SYLVIA.)

bereavement, survivors of suicide There are a number of self-help or mutual aid organizations for families and friends struggling to come to terms with the loss of loved ones due to suicide. A listing of these groups is included among the appendixes of this book. One such group is L.O.S.S. (Loving Outreach to Survivors of Suicide). Another is Seasons; Suicide Bereavement is a Maryland-based mutual help group. Such groups' goals in assisting families, friends and close associates of the suicide are similar to the goals of those helping anyone who faces bereavement. In Eric Lindemann's words, "Grief work is emancipation from the bondage to the deceased, readjustment to the environment in which the deceased is missing, and the formation of new relationships."

Even in these modern times, survivors of suicide are too often forced to carry the stigma for years, if not for life. It is both unfortunate and regrettable that in all too many instances, suicide of a family member or close friend is never completely forgotten and forgiven. It becomes uppermost in importance, during the time of bereavement, for the survivor of a suicide to remember that competent professional as well as mutual aid assistance is available from many sources. This includes support from the clergy, support groups, and mental health professionals.

Berryman, John American poet (1914-1972) whose major theme was mourning. His work ranged from the public, literary work of *Homage to Mistress Bradstreet* to the more intimate cycle of *Dream Songs*. He wrote of poetic mourning for the suicide of his father, the premature deaths of friends and his own prevalent suicidal despair. Most literary authorities agree that Berryman, like Welsh poet DYLAN THOMAS, was drinking himself to death even before he took his life. DR. KARL MENNINGER called such cases CHRONIC SUICIDES.

Bettelheim, Dr. Bruno In his book *The Uses of Enchantment: The Meaning and Importance of Fairy Tales*, Dr. Bettelheim discusses the power that fairy tales and myths have over children, contending that children love them so because they embody their strongest hopes and fears. One prevalent fear that is virtually universal in fairy tales is fear of being separated from one's parents. Many suicidologists generalize that the "typical" suicidal adolescent is likely to be a teenager who early in life was literally separated from vital relationships or who never truly experienced a trusting family relationship. Thus, he or she is a victim of what psychoanalysts call "separation anxiety" and remains alone to deal with the stresses of growing up. "The young person who hasn't had sufficient nurturing to develop a sense of self has nothing when he separates from his parents," says psychiatrist DR. MARY GIFFIN. Of course, not every person separated early in life from his parents becomes suicidal. Other vital relationships may occur which help blunt the impact of such separation.

Biathanatos Poet and later the dean of St. Paul's Cathedral, John Donne wrote *Biathanatos* in 1608. It was the first defense of suicide written in English and was originally circulated in manuscript form and only published posthumously, in 1644. According to Dr. George Rosen, professor of the history of medicine, epidemiology and public health, School of Medicine, Yale University, Donne "proposed to demonstrate that suicide is not incompatible with the laws of God, reason and nature. Moreover, inherent in the condition and dignity of being a man is the right to end one's life. As Donne expressed it, 'methinks I have the keys of my prison in mine own hand, and no remedy presents itself so soone to my heart, as mine own sword.'"

Biathanatos was the model of thought on the subject of suicide for almost a century and a half. During that period, the Rationalists, such as Voltaire and Hume, openly and persistently attacked the suicide taboos and superstitions and the primitive punishments still being executed. This resulted in the laws being gradually changed as they caught up with a parallel shift in the public's emotional attitudes toward suicide.

biblical suicides It appears that biblical suicides are rare. There are only seven instances reported in the Hebrew Bible and but one in the New Testament. The instances mentioned in the Old Testament are those of Samson (Judges 16:28-31), Saul (I Samuel 31:1-6), Saul's armor bearer (Chronicles 10), Abimelech (Judges 9:54), Ahitophel (II Samuel 17:23), Zimri (I Kings 16:9), and Razis (II Maccabees 14:46).

Neither the Hebrew Bible nor the New Testament specifically prohibits suicide. Suicidal behavior is not condemned, nor is the word used; in fact, it is of recent vintage. According to medical historian George Rosen, "Each instance (of suicide) is reported factually and generally briefly. Even of Judas Iscariot, we are told simply that 'he went and hanged himself'" (Matthew 27-5).

bibliographies A fairly extensive bibliography on suicide is included in the back of this work. One of the first extensive bibliographies was published by Hans Rost, *Bibliographie des Selbst Mordes* (Augsburg; Hass & Grabherr: 1927); it contains approximately 3,800 items. One of the best and most recent bibliographies on the subject is: *Research on Suicide: A Bibliography*, compiled by John L. McIntosh (Greenwood Press: Bibliographies and Indexes in Psychology, Number 2); the press is a division of Congressional Information Services, Inc. An extensive bibliography was compiled by Norman L. Farberow, covering two periods (1897-1957 and 1958-1967), *Bibliography on Suicide and Suicide Prevention* (Washington, D.C.: U.S. Government Printing Office, 1969), P.H.S. Publication No. 1979; it contains 3,300 references. In 1974, Ann E. Prentice compiled a selective bibliography of over 2,200 items in *Suicide* (Metuchen, New Jersey: Scarecrow Press). The most complete reference source for selected bibliographies at this time is the SUICIDE INFORMATION AND EDUCATION CENTER (SIEC) at 1615 10th Avenue, S.W., #201, Calgary, Alberta T3C 0J7, Canada; phone is (403) 245-3900.

binge and purge See BULIMIA.

biological aspects Dr. Solomon H. Snyder, professor of pharmacology and psychiatry, School of Medicine, The Johns Hopkins University, Baltimore, Maryland, writing in *A Handbook for the Study of Suicide* (ed., Seymour Perlin), says that "Many biological factors may be construed as 'relevant' to the study of suicide." Dr. Snyder focuses upon a narrow range, the so-called "reward" centers in the brain, the role of norepinephrine as a neurotransmitter in these centers, and the interaction with brain catecholamines of drugs that affect mood. According to Snyder: "If there is a unique biological substratum of that state of mind that eventuates in a person taking his own life, our present knowledge of brain function might elect a possible alteration in catecholamine disposition as the major candidate."

Despite numerous reservations, Dr. Snyder believes that "investigation of the catecholamines as well as serotonin, histamine, and as yet unidentified neurotransmitters in emotional areas of the brain are likely to bear fruit in the quest to elucidate brain mechanisms whose alterations underlie suicidal and other aberrant behavior."

Solomon H. Snyder, "Biology," in Seymour Perlin, MD, ed., *A Handbook for the Study of Suicide* (New York: Oxford University Press, 1975), ch. 6., pp. 113-120.

birthdays, month of birth and suicide While there are some instances of suicides on an individual's birthday, the incidence of self-destruction does not necessarily correlate with the birthdate. Although a potentially suicidal person may suffer symptoms of loneliness, despair and loss of self-esteem on such an occasion, the suicide rates have been found to correlate posivitely with factors such as: male sex, increasing age, widowhood, single and/or divorced states, childlessness, high density of population, residence in urban centers, a high standard of living, economic crisis, drug and alcohol consumption, history of a broken home in childhood, mental disorder and physical illness.

As for month of birth and suicide, the act is consummated more in the spring than in the winter, with March, April and May the months, generally speaking, when more suicides take place. Sometimes suicidal people attach particular significance to birthdays, e.g., if a parent committed suicide on, say, the 40th birthday, the child might feel destined to die before or on that day. Or the potential suicide might arbitrarily set his or her next birthday as the very last day he or she can remain alive and will commit suicide either before or on that day. The rescue task is to keep him or her alive beyond that day. If that is successful, the suicide potential practically vanishes.

Black Americans The suicide rate in the U.S. (1980 statistics) among blacks is 6.0 per 100,000 population, whites 12.7. Black males are 10.3 compared to 19.9. Within age groups, the highest rate was for those between ages 25 and 34 (21.8%). The most noticeable difference bewteen black and white males was in the 65 and over age group, with black men showing 11.4 per 100,000 against the white male figure of 37.5—a startling 26.1 point difference in the suicide rates. Ages 5 to 14 revealed the lowest age group rate for males among both blacks and whites, .3 percent for the former and .7 for the latter group.

Black females presently show a relatively low suicide rate of only 2.2 per 100,000 population. That compares to 5.5 per 100,000 for white females (overall age figure). For black women the 35 to 44 age group had the highest rate at 4.6 per 100,000. Highest rate for white women fell to the 45 to 54 age group, 10.2 per 100,000. Black females in the 5 to 14 age group had a very low .1 per

100,000 rate, this compared to the equally low .2 for white females.

A high 50% of the black American suicides in New York City are by jumping, according to DR. HERBERT HENDIN. Hendin concludes the reason is because life in Harlem and other sections of the city where the black population is concentrated in block-after-block of tenements, five stories high and up. Sexual experience, fighting and drug usage frequently take place on the Harlem rooftops. Says Hendin: "In this context, it is not surprising that jumping from the top floors or roofs of such buildings is a very common method among black suicides."

In Hendin's well-known study of black suicide, four out of 12 seriously suicidal black males were homosexuals. This proportion greatly exceeds the rate of male homosexuals among the entire black population, which, as in the case of the white male population, is an estimated 5 to 10%. This finding suggests a link between suicide and homosexuality within the black male population. Figures for black suicidal women, according to the Hendin study, are less conclusive; one out of 13 such women (included in the study) were found to be homosexual.

Another interesting and revealing statistic: Hendin found that a breakdown of New York City figures revealed surprisingly that, among blacks of both sexes between the ages of 20 and 35, suicide was twice as frequent as it was among white men of the same age group.

Finally, the Hendin study reveals that the high frequency of suicide among older whites has led to the misconception that suicide is a "white" problem. Only after age 45 does the incidence of suicide among whites become so much greater than that among blacks of the same age, that it causes the white suicide rate to rise to a total level much higher than that of the black rate.

Herbert Hendin, *Black Suicide* (New York: Harper & Row, 1971).

bonding The strong attachment of mother to infant and infant to mother that develops shortly after birth. Many authorities in the suicidology field see a direct correlation between bonding deprivation and ultimate potential suicidal persons. The theory put simply is: The infant whose physical and psychological needs are satisfied develops a sense of well-being. Bonding, then, is literally the foundation of a child's life. Proponents of this theory maintain that the suicidal impulse can be ingrained within the first months of life. DR. MARY GIFFIN, in *A Cry for Help* (Co-author, Carol Felsenthal) says: "Breaking up with a girl friend, failing chemistry, any problem in the child's life may precipitate a suicide try, but the underlying cause frequently can be traced to emotional scars inflicted during infancy."

Plato said, "And the first step, as you know, is always what matters most, particularly when we are dealing with those who are young and tender. That is the time when they are taking shape and when any impression we choose to make leaves a permanent mark." Freud, writing some 2,000 years later, made the same point: "The very impressions we have forgotten have nevertheless left the deepest traces in our psychic life, and acted as determinants for our whole future development."

Bonding, say supporters of this theory, is the key to good mental health.

Brahmanism and suicide Norman L. Farberow points out in *Suicide in Different Cultures* that "Among the earliest of the great cultures, Oriental sacred writings contained many contradictions about suicide. Although it was encouraged in some parts, it was vigorously condemned in others. Brahmanism institutionalized and sanctioned suttee, a ceremonial sacrifice of widows that was as common in China as in India. The Brahman doctrine was sympathetic to suicide, for it was consonant with the denial of the flesh, a common objective in philosophies of the Orient."

Brahmanism is the religious and social system of the orthodox Hindus, interpreted and enforced by the Brahmans (the highest or priestly caste). Their system of doctrine and religious observances was codified c. 550 B.C., but has long since been simplified or modified in both theology and ritual, borrowing freely from newer sects of the Vedic religions (the Vedanta), e.g., Buddhism and Jainism, to create the philosophical basis for modern Hinduism in the Bhagavad-Gita and commentaries on the Upanishads.

Both Brahmanism and Buddhism are religions of resignation and despair.

Brazelton, Dr. T. Berry Considered by many to be the Dr. Spock of this generation, pediatrician Brazelton is a pioneer in neonatal research and associate professor of pediatrics, Harvard Medical School. Dr. Brazelton is a minority voice among his peers in support of working women and shared child care, which is ironic when one considers that he has pioneered and done perhaps the most extensive research in the U.S. on the subject of bonding deprivation. In Dr. Brazelton's view, only the first four months are "sacred," that is, "the most critical time for parents to begin to feel attached to the child . . . If the parents have to share (with a housekeeper, day-care center, etc.) their babies before that time, I think it's really dangerous in terms of the development of their relationships with the child" (from Giffin-Felsenthal, *A Cry for Help*, ch. 9, p. 202). For Brazelton, the ideal situation is for the mother and father to share in the baby care duties and, one hopes, for the baby to bond with both parents.

British Voluntary Euthansia Society See EXIT.

broken homes and suicide Children who are victims of broken homes through either divorce or death will frequently begin to see themselves as either guilty or unloved, sometimes both. They can become increasingly despairing, angry, anxious and depressed. The irony is that the more confused, the more depressed they become, the more need they have for the parent or parents who may no longer be there. It is all but impossible for young children to accept the fact that their parents don't love them. As a mechanism for survival, they often twist reality to blame themselves rather than their parents. They grow into adolescence at one and the same time furious with their predicament but feeling guilty. Such children too often are potential suicides.

Many experts in the field of suicidology see broken homes, latchkey kids, the overall, shifting state of the American family as among the several major reasons for the rising suicide rate among children.

Bronfenbrenner, Urie Noted child development authority from Cornell University and author of numerous articles and books related to child care and development. Dr. Bronfenbrenner is a strong advocate of the importance in the child's life of bonding. In a controversial article in the magazine *Psychology Today*, Bronfenbrenner asked, "Who is caring for America's children?" He wrote: "There has to be at least one person who has an irrational involvement with that child, someone who thinks that kid is more important than other people's kids, someone who's in love with him and whom he loves in return." Dr. Bronfenbrenner adds that a child "needs somebody who will not just be there certain hours and then say, 'I'm off now. I work nine to five.'"

Urie Bronfenbrenner, "Nobody Home: The Erosion of the American Family," *Psychology Today* (May 1977).

Bruce, Lenny Noted comedian (1925-1966) who died on August 3, 1966, at the age of 41 of "acute morphine poisoning" in Hollywood. His lifelong involvement with drugs and his lifestyle in general prompted many authorities to classify his behavior as that of a CHRONIC SUICIDE.

Buddhism In *Suicide in Different Cultures*, Norman L. Farberow writes that "one goal in Oriental mysticism was to divorce the body from the soul so that the soul might occupy itself only with supersensual realities. Buddhism emphasized that through extinction of craving or passion, life's chief purpose of acquisition of knowledge could be achieved." Both Brahmanism and Buddhism are religions of resignation and despair. "Buddhists," explains Dr. Hsieu Rin, in the same anthology, "think that suicide occurs because of one's lack of tolerance or patience toward stress." Dr. Rin notes that, although there is some sanction against suicidal behavior in Buddhistic concepts, it is nevertheless accompanied with sympathy, regret, and "a feeling of mercy to the client . . ." Buddhists believe human life is a life of stress and that the individual who kills himself is destined to remain in a hundred-year-hell and cannot expect reincarnation in any form.

Buddhism is a religion founded by the Buddha (Sanskrit: "The Enlightened One") in the sixth century B.C., based essentially on the doctrines that life is intrinsically full of suffering and that supreme felicity is to be striven for by psychological and ethical self-culture. Buddhism's distinctive character as one of the world's great religions derives from its high ethical tone and stress on self-denial and ascetic disciplines (for the laity as well as the dedicated). There are a number of more or less distorted forms of Buddhism, collectively known as *Mahayana*, that have developed outside of India, generally marked by proliferation of local deities (buddhas, bodhisattvas), and religious observances drawn from local cults. In its various forms, *Mahayana* now claims almost half a billion adherents, especially in China, Tibet, Korea, Japan and Mongolia.

Bulgaria In chapter 13 of *Suicide in Different Cultures* (ed., Norman L. Farberow), N. Schipkowensky, MD, K. Milenkov and A. Bogdanova write on the matter of "Self-destruction in Bulgarian Folk-Songs." While the authors admit that the epidemiology of self-destruction cannot be studied through such folk songs, they do contend "that the number of songs referring to various suicides can give a good idea about the frequency and the motivational structure of the act of suicide."

The authors conclude that self-destruction must have been a relatively rare phenomenon, because they could uncover reference to it only in some 200 out of the several thousand folk songs published in Bulgarian collections between 1889 and 1963. The Bulgarian folk songs, however, do depict a great variety of methods of suicide. And those that do describe self-destruction have, say the authors, "remained close to the people until the present day. Their spirit is still in conformity with the attitudes and with the authentic ideals of the people."

bulimia Another distress signal that may be one of many signs of trouble in suicidal children, anorexia bulimia—a malady that affects mostly teenage girls—is the cycle of gorging on food and then purging by inducing vomiting or taking unrealistic quantities of laxatives. Often called the "binge-purge" syndrome, bulimia (like ANOREXIA NERVOSA) is thought to be a disorder with emotional, not physical, roots. Bulimia victims are about 95 to 98% female, usually single, white, ambitious, educated and middle- or upper-class. They are college-age generally, 18 being the average age at onset, according to psychiatrist MARY GIFFIN, though there are instances of girls much younger being bulimics. Victims gorge and purge in secret and, says Giffin, "Theirs is a solitary and lonely pursuit—engaged in by terribly depressed, potentially suicidal, young women." They do it as many as eight to 10 times per day.

Experts believe that there is a relationship between bulimia and depression. One survey on eating disorders showed 60% of the women studied in the project reported feeling depressed most of the time. Twenty percent had tried suicide at least once. Bulimics also subject themselves to other serious side effects that range from ulcers to hernias, dehydration, stomach rupture and disturbance of the blood's chemical balance (which could result in heart attacks). The obsession with food is similar to an addiction to alcohol and generally ends in dominating the young person's life.

burial (for suicides) At the Council of Braga in 563, the Church condemned suicide as an act. George Rosen writes, "This position was subsequently confirmed by the councils of Auxerre (578) and Antisidor (590) and remained as canon law in 1284, when the Synod of Nimes refused burial in consecrated ground to suicides." According to Rosen, the one exception was made of the insane, judging from the *Penitentials* of Egbert, Archbishop of York, which appeared in the mid-eighth century.

The *Carolina*, the Criminal Constitution of Charles V of Spain, in 1551 confiscated all property of suicides who took their lives while under accusation of a felony. More severe, according to George Rosen, writing in *A Handbook for the Study of Suicide*, was the punishment meted out on the corpse of a suicide. "The cadaver was subjected to various indignities and degradations. A common practice in England was to bury the suicide at a crossroad by night with a stake driven through the heart." Rosen tells of a suicide buried in this manner as late as 1811, at the corner of Commercial Road and Cannon Street in East London. The bizarre practice was not discontinued until 1823.

TACITUS, the Roman historian and a distinguished lawyer, reports on so-called "bog burials," the practice of pinning down the body with a stake. This practice, confirmed by numerous authorities, seems to antedate Christianity among the Germanic peoples of Europe. The purpose was to ensure that the spirit of the dead person would not return to haunt or otherwise do harm to the living.

Attitudes toward the act of suicide remained conservative well into the 18th century. "In fact, suicide was then equated with murder in many parts of Europe, and the corpse was treated accordingly," says Dr. Rosen. For example, in France and England, the suicide's body was dragged through the streets, head downward on a hurdle (a type of frame or sledge on which criminals were dragged to their place of execution), and then strung up to hang from public gallows. The French Criminal Ordinance of August 1670 still decreed that the suicide's body be dragged through the streets, then thrown into a sewer or onto the town dump. Because of spectator reaction against the practice of dragging the corpse, the penalty was not carried out after 1768. But burial in consecrated ground was frequently denied suicides; in Prussia, early 18th century law required that a suicide be buried under the gallows.

The degree to which such burial restrictions and/or penalties were applied varied from time to time and place to place, according to Dr. Rosen. "In general," he writes, "the penalties against the body of a suicide tended to lapse by the latter part of the seventeenth century, and even the sanction of confiscation was handled more leniently. Important factors in such cases were the social rank of the suicide and his family, as well as the circumstances of the suicidal act."

Rabbi Earl A. Grollman, author of *Suicide: Prevention, Intervention, Postvention*, explains the Jewish position: "In Talmudic times (200-500 A.D.) an increasing number of suicides is recorded . . . partly due to spiritual and social crises, partly to a growing Great Roman influence. Now that the act had become more frequent, a condemnatory tone is introduced for the first time." Grollman adds that a "self-homicide" forfeited his share of the world-to-come and was denied burial honors. The Talmud decreed that suicides could not receive a eulogy or public mourning. They were buried apart, in community cemeteries.

There was never universal agreement, however. Various scholars and legal authorities disagreed on the matter, pointing out that extenuating circumstances generally accompanied any suicide. The big question: How to be certain that a death was truly a suicide? Then, too, there was the dilemma posed by a minor. Did they do the deed unwittingly? The problem was also considered from the standpoint of mental illness. If the act was prompted by madness, ought not the suicide to be treated as an ordinary deceased person? Joseph Caro (1488-1575), outstanding legal expert of the time, concluded that suicide, although considered a crime against God, could sometimes be explained rationally, understood and forgiven. Grollman says Caro's enlightened view has been incorporated into the approach of the three denominations of modern Judaism. The generally-accepted custom is to give burial and last rites in a manner similar to any other deceased.

In most Christian groups today, the question of suicide is viewed from the theological level, consideration of the psychic concerns and also the sociological implications. Suicide is recognized not only as an ethical-religious-social sciences question, but also as a major medical problem. Many, if not most, groups have revised the harsh religious laws governing suicides. For example, the Anglican Church and the Lutheran Church do not deny the victim of suicide a Christian burial.

In the Catholic Church, the *Code of Canon Law*, Canon 1240, forbids Christian burial to "persons guilty of deliberate suicide." The late Richard Cardinal Cushing of Boston's archdiocese interpreted this to mean that "The element of notoriety must be present in a suicide for the penalty to be incurred. Hence, no matter how culpable it may have been, if it is not publicly known that the act was fully deliberate, burial is not to be denied. Ordinarily, there is not too great a difficulty in granting Christian burial to a suicide, since most people these days consider the fact of suicide to be a sign of at least temporary insanity." Authorities state they cannot recall any recent cases in Massachusetts of Christian burial being denied a suicide.

In general, the funeral rites accorded to the suicide differ only in a relatively few instances from the rites accorded those who have died a natural death. Exemption from sanctions on the grounds of mental disturbance or "temporary insanity" is usually more frequently granted than in the past. (See also BURNETT V. PEOPLE.)

Burnett v. People Leading U.S. case regarding suicide. The 1903 case of *Burnett v. People* states: "We have never seen fit to define what character of burial our citizens shall enjoy; we have never regarded the English law as to suicide as applicable to the spirit of our institutions" (*Burnett v. People*, 68 N.E. 505 [Sup. Ct. IL, 1905]). It should be stressed that the U.S. *never* adopted the English commonlaw dealing with suicide or suicide victims. In English commonlaw, suicide was a felony and attempted suicide a misdemeanor until 1961, when both laws were abolished.

In another famous American case, the 1908 Texas case of *Sanders v. State*, it was declared: "Whatever may have been the law in England . . . so far as our law is concerned, the suicide is innocent of criminality" (*Sanders vs. State*, 112 S.W. 68 [Ct. Crimm App. TX, 1908]).

Burton, Robert English writer (1577-1640), Oxford-educated, author of *The Anatomy of Melancholy*, first published in 1621. The famed book is a voluminous and curious compendium of all sorts of esoteric knowledge with reference to melancholy: its definition and causes; its various types; the life of man and the institutions of society, all written in a style characterized by high fancy, extravagance, outlandish imagination, whimsy and affectation and far-fetched figures of speech.

Burton's contribution to the debate on suicide, at least in the views of A. ALVAREZ, (*The Savage God: A Study of Suicide*) "is single and simple: sympathy." Burton wrote: "These unhappy men are born to misery, past all hope of recovery, incurably sick; the longer they live, the worse they are; and death alone must ease them." Burton's views were considered courageous for the times. As Alvarez notes, "Human misery moved most of the preachers of his day to self-righteousness; it moved him to pity." Like JOHN DONNE, Burton provided a new look to what had been generally a cut-and-dried question. In Alvarez's words, "Once the suicide had been cast out as unclean, damned and degraded in sheer horror, now he began, at least, to seem human . . ."

Robert Burton, ironically, is said to have hanged himself to fulfill his own astrological prophecies about the date of his death. In Burton's own words, "Every man is the greatest enemy unto himself . . ."

business cycle In their book, *Suicide and Homicide*, authors Andrew F. Henry and James F. Short, Jr., relate the suicide rate to economic cycles. Their essential premise is that suicidal behavior is determined by both external and internal forces operating cojointly. They see aggression as often, though certainly not always, a consequence of frustration, and in RONALD MARIS's view, "that business cycles produce variation in the hierarchial ranking of persons and groups, and that frustrations are generated by interferences with the 'goal response' of maintaining a constant or rising position in a status hierarchy relative to the status position of others in the same system."

Henry and Short postulate that people in high-status categories experience greater frustration during downswings in business and less frustration during upswings in business than do those considered "low-status" categories. Contrarily, Albert Pierce, in "The Economic Cycle and the Social Suicide Rate," correlated the index of common stock prices and the male suicide rate from 1919 to 1939 and found that the suicide rate varies directly with business anomie, whatever the direction of economic change. Professor Maris reports that Albert Pierce "suggests that Henry and Short got different results because they used different and less appropriate indices of economic change."

When the Stock Market crash occurred on October 29, 1929, and stock prices plummeted (stock losses for 1929-31 were estimated at $50 billion), a number of businessmen committed suicide as a consequence of their financial losses. These suicides would appear to support the concept of "hope" as the basis of suicide theory. According to this theory, suicide occurs when the individual's life outlook (for whatever reason or reasons) is one of despairing hopelessness. Whether or not one commits suicide in such a situation depends upon a personality factor experts call "the sense of competence," which is related inversely to the potential for suicide.

C

Camus, Albert Winner of the Nobel Prize for Literature, 1957, author (1913-1960) of such well-known works as *The Fall, The Stranger, The Plague*, plus *The Myth of Sisyphus and Other Essays*. In the latter work, Camus states at the opening: "There is but one truly serious philosophical problem, and that is suicide. Judging whether life is or is not worth living amounts to answering the fundamental question of philosophy." Camus ultimately affirmed the value of life, though he also wrote, "if one denies that there are grounds for suicide, one cannot claim them for murder. One cannot be a part-time nihilist." In his famous *Notebooks*, Camus determined that "There is only one liberty, to come to terms with death. After which, everything is possible."

Albert Camus died in an automobile crash near Sens as he was returning to Paris from the southern part of France. He was only 47 at the time.

Canada Death rates from suicide in the country have continued to rise for several years. In 1980, for example, the total rate per 100,000 population was 14.0 per 100,000 (21.3 for males, 6.8 for females). By 1983, Canada's suicide rate had jumped to 15.1 per 100,000 (23.4 males, 6.9 females). The age group showing the highest death rate from suicide was the 55 to 64 group (up from 14.6 per 100,000 in 1980). For males, the group age 75 and over showed the highest death rate from suicide, 39.0 per 100,000; females aged 45 to 54 showed the highest suicide rate at 12.4 per 100,000. (Source: WHO, World Health Organization, Geneva, Switzerland, Dr. Alan D. Lopez, GES, 1986.)

Home of the SUICIDE INFORMATION AND EDUCATION CENTRE (SIEC), established in 1982 so that researchers, professionals, and other interested individuals throughout the world could have convenient access to a comprehensive collection of articles and other related data on the topic of suicide and suicidal behavior. The SIEC is a non-profit organization under the umbrella of the Canadian Mental Health Association and is supported by the Suicide Prevention Provincial Advisory Committee. It is located in Calgary, Alberta. (For additional information, see SUICIDE INFORMATION AND EDUCATION CENTRE.)

Canadian Mental Health Association (CMHA) Provides a wide range of suicide prevention data and services and has branches throughout the country, including the remote Northwest Territories and the Yukon Territory. Though Canada does not have a nationwide system of county mental health clinics (as in the U.S.), it does provide Universal Health Insurance. The government pays for treatment of both physical and mental illness. The CMHA has been instrumental in working closely with those groups operating a vast nationwide network of suicide hotlines and distress centers. In Canada, the Salvation Army also operates several suicide prevention agencies. The country has branches of the SAMARITANS and CONTACT USA (in Canada called TELE-CARE). Interested persons should check the phone book or the white pages for the number of the local branch of the Canadian Mental Heatlh Association.

cancer Cancer is a malignant tumor of any type. As it relates to suicide, it is used as a general diagnostic term for an illness which can be a condition, sometimes terminal, predisposing a person to suicidal thoughts or behavior. No figures are available that would tell us the percentage of cancer victims who kill themselves.

Among older people, diseases such as cancer still claim many more lives than suicide, though suicide kills far more teenagers and young adults than does cancer. Interestingly, in 1983 there were more than 3,300 federal grants supporting projects under the aegis of the National Cancer Institute. In the same year, there were only three federal grants backing suicide research.

The relative U.S. death rate statistics show that in 1980, malignancies (cancer) resulted in 416,500 fatalities, or 183.9 people per 100,000 population. The suicide death rate the same year was 11.9 per 100,000, or 26,900 persons.

Some professionals have done studies that led them to theorize that cancer might literally be caused by grief, simply because any strong emotional stress brings about chemical changes in the body. In *The Way We Die*, author David Dempsey (a member of the professional advisory board of the Foundation of Thanatology), writes: "An overproduction of corticosteroids reduces our natural immunity to disease, especially those triggered by viruses, and many forms of cancer are suspected to be viral in origin."

Grief, then, by whatever cause, produces feelings of panic, loneliness, despair and even guilt. And grief-exacerbated illnesses are thought by some in the medical ranks to result in cancer which, in turn, sometimes may lead to suicidal behavior or even suicide.

More research on the exact relationship between suicide incidence and cancer is needed. Many of the factors that research has indentified as putting a person at risk for suicide are things that cannot be changed, such as being a man, or having tried suicide previously. But depression or hopelessness, resulting from a particular illness, can be changed and experts say should be a central focus of therapy with anyone who is suicidal.

Cape Verde (Cap-Vert) A republic, Cape Verde (which is a bit larger than Rhode Island in square mileage) is located off the western tip of Africa. The islands are 15 in number and volcanic in origin. Total population (1982 est.) is 340,000. The capital city is Praia.

Cape Verde is one of the few countries located within or near Africa that discloses mortality data, including suicide. According to World Health Organization data, Cape Verde's 1980 (most recent figures) suicide rate totaled seven people. Six of the suicides were male, the other one female. The greatest number of suicides were in the 15 to 24 age group (3 total; 2 male, 1 female). The remaining four suicides were in the 45 and over age range. (Note: WHO data on suicide deaths are absolute numbers and rates.)

Cardano, Girolamo This Italian mathematician and astrologer (1501-1576) was well known throughout Europe and even visited England to cast the horoscope of the young king, Edward VI. An arch-believer in the accuracy of his so-called science, Cardano predicted the hour of his own death. The day dawned and found him in excellent health and safe from any harm. Rather than bear the humiliation of having his horoscope falsified publicly, Cardano killed himself.

Case Against Suicide, The Book by W.V. Rauscher, published in 1981 by St. Martin's Press, New York. The author presents chapters on various ethical issues, including "The Case For Suicide?," "The Case Against Suicide," "The Philosophers and Theologians" and "The Case Against Rational Suicide."

case registers See DATABANKS.

Cassius Longinus, Gaius Died 42 B.C., a Roman soldier who was pardoned by

Caesar though he had been a supporter of Pompey. Cassius was made peregrine praetor and promised a governorship of Syria. Nonetheless, he plotted Caesar's death, ostensibly to revive the republic. His conspiracy, involving some 60 to 80 prominent men, culminated in Caesar's assassination in the Senate, March 15 (the Ides of March), 44 B.C. Mark Antony aroused the populace against Caesar's murderers and defeated them at Philippi, where Cassius committed suicide following the first engagement. In doing so, he joined Marcus Junius Brutus, ex-governor of Cisalpine Gaul and later urban praetor, who had foolishly joined Cassius in killing Caesar. Oddly enough, Mark Antony (Marcus Antonius) later committed suicide himself, in Alexandria (30 B.C.).

Cato the Younger A tribune of the people, Marcus Porcius Cato (95-46 B.C.) had a reputation for unimpeachable honesty. He denounced political corruption, tried to implicate Julius Caesar in Catiline's conspiracy. He supported Pompey, and continued the fight against Caesar in Africa until Caesar's crushing defeat of Scipio at Thapsus. Cato is said to have read Plato's *Phaedo* twice on the night before he killed himself by falling on his own sword. (The Greek philosopher Cleombrotus is said to have been inspired by the same book to drown himself.)

cause of death See CORONERS.

celebrity suicides Studies done in the past have shown that suicide rates do rise after the suicide of a prominent person or celebrity has been heavily publicized. A prime example: The youth suicide rate went up briefly after 23-year-old actor-comedian Freddie Prinze shot himself to death. Prinze, who skyrocketed to fame as co-star of the television series "Chico and the Man," died in a Los Angeles hospital on January 29, 1977, 36 hours after shooting himself in the head with a revolver. Prinze left a note in his apartment that read: "I cannot go on any longer."

Another and perhaps more celebrated case in point is that of actress Marilyn Monroe. In the calendar month after she overdosed on sleeping pills, the suicide rate in the U.S. rose by 12%. Several of the suicides left behind notes that linked their lethal acts to the movie star's presumed suicide.

And though Beatles member John Lennon was a murder victim, not a suicide, the youth suicide rate increased noticeably after his death on December 8, 1980. As Hendin notes in *Suicide in America*: "A sense of sharing the tragic death or suicide of someone famous, or of identifying suicide with a cause, enables some people to feel that their death has a meaning it would otherwise lack."

Studies conducted by the psychiatrist Jerome Motto and the sociologist David Phillips offer some evidence that sensational media coverage of suicide and other tragic deaths results in an increase in suicide immediately afterward. These independent studies measured the increase in suicides following the sensational publicity given a particular suicide, and the drop in suicide in certain cities where there were extended newspaper "blackouts." Hendin theorizes that the suggestive or "socially 'contagious' element in suicide is likely to be magnified if suicide is given social sanction."

Herbert Hendin, MD, *Suicide in America* (New York: W.W. Norton & Co., 1982), 223-24.

Jerome Motto, "Newspaper Influence on Suicide: A Controlled Study," *Archives of General Psychiatry*, 23(1970): 143-48.

David Phillips, "The Influence of Suggestions on Suicide: Substantive and Theoretical Implications of the Werther Effect." *American Sociological Review*, 39(1974): 340-54.

Charondas Lawgiver (sixth century B.C.) of Catana, a Greek colony in Sicily, committed suicide after discovering that he had broken one of his own laws. The particular law forbade citizens to carry weapons into the public assembly. Charondas momentarily forgot this, wore his sword into the public meeting one day, and was reproached by a fellow citizen for violating one of his own laws. "By Zeus," said Charondas, "I will confirm it." He then drew his sword and killed himself.

Chatterton, Thomas British poet (1752-70) born in Bristol. As a boy, he composed poems which he pretended were the work of the medieval poet monk, Thomas Rowley, sending them to such prominent people as Horace Walpole, who at first thought them to be genuine. The best of the poems, e.g., *An Excelente Balade of Charitie* and *The Bristowe Tragedie*, were original and showed talent but were, understandably, immature. Chatterton later moved to London, where he lived in poverty doing some hack work. At age 17, he committed suicide by poison.

Thomas Chatterton—perhaps the most famous of literary suicides, at least among the poets—is said by A. ALVAREZ in *The Savage God* to have "poisoned himself not out of any excess of feeling, but because he was unable to keep himself alive by writing." Sometime later, the Romantics and others transformed Chatterton into a symbol of the doomed poet. Says Alvarez, "In fact, he was a victim of Grub Street and snobbery."

On the afternoon of August 25, 1770, Thomas Chatterton's lodging house neighbors found the young man lying on his bed. According to a surgeon named Barrett, he was "a horrible spectacle, with features distorted, as if from convulsions." He had swallowed arsenic; he was three months short of his 18th birthday. To the poet Shelley, Chatterton was one of "the inheritors of unfulfilled renown." Today he remains a symbol of the misunderstood poet; he is the subject of Vigny's tragedy, *Chatterton* (1835).

child abuse No national data are available regarding the frequency or severity with which child abuse victims are associated with suicide. Suicide appears to involve too many variables, too many factors—sociological and psychological—for any definitive answers.

Despite not having any simple, straightforward answers concerning this serious problem of abuse, both physical and emotional, experts do know that social factors, such as family breakups, reduction of the emotional availability of working parents, and family deaths, seem to be associated with potential suicidal tendencies. Children want to communicate satisfactorily with parents and feel despairing, hopeless and worthless when they fail. They often blame themselves for family problems that sometimes lead to child abuse by parents. This can cause feelings of rootlessness and low self-esteem, which can cause depression, and authorities know that depression is very much associated with suicidal behavior. And certainly repeated abuse can cause great stress that, added to the everyday stress a child experiences by competition and concerns about school and/or job, can trigger anger, irritability, or merely withdrawal—all risk factors that are often associated with suicides or suicide attempters.

As DR. MARY GIFFIN says in *A Cry for Help*, "Children need nurturing and love and they'll kill—themselves—to get it."

The suicidologists seem to agree that adolescent suicides and suicide attempts often occur in a disorganized or unhappy home where there has been a breakdown of family structure—whatever the cause—and the abused child frequently feels loneliness and isolation (even rage) because of a loss of love, or feeling they are unwanted. Then, as Allen and Peck suggest, "Facing a world of increased tensions, competitiveness, pressures and demands from parents, teachers and peers is for some too much to cope with—and self-destructive behavior results." (See also ABUSE, CHILD.)

children The suicide rate among teenagers in the U.S. has tripled since 1958. Every year, more than 5,000 young people take their own lives and another estimated two million try. The suicide rate among 15-to 24-year olds has more than doubled in the past two decades. On a given day, 14 young Americans kill themselves. Every *hour* some 30 children and adolescents in the U.S. attempt to commit suicide—well over 700 suicide attempts every day.

According to Nancy H. Allen, MPH, and Michael L. Peck, PhD, writing in "Suicide in Young People" (a booklet prepared by the AMERICAN ASSOCIATION OF SUICIDOLOGY), in most countries throughout the world suicide in adolescence rose through the 1970s and in most countries has shown a drop since. Yet suicide now ranks third among the leading causes of death during teenage to young adult years. "To some degree," say Allen and Peck, "this increase may be due to better and more accurate reporting on the part of coroners on death certificates." But better record-keeping cannot possibly account for the startling increase in suicides among the world's young people. The authors, in fact, point out that, "Many suicidologists feel that even more adolescent suicides are not reported as suicides but as accidental or undetermined deaths because of stigma to the family."

Experts have long been aware of the extent to which the adolescent lives in a constant state of turmoil. Developmental psychologists, for instance, have indicated that the internal, not to mention external, pressures in adolescence are probably greater than in any other period of human development.

Allen and Peck explain:

> Today, we recognize that young people live under a great variety of pressures, including the stresses that result from the phenomena of adolescence, from the high expectancies of early adulthood and from those strains of competition and achievement that are unique to young people. Only in recent years has the seriousness of the problem of suicides in youth begun to appear in the professional literature. The studies of suicidal behavior on the college campus, for example, have led to the conclusion that suicide is a serious public health problem and, in the college setting, ranks as the second or third leading cause of death.

Charlotte P. Ross, president/executive director, the YOUTH SUICIDE NATIONAL CENTER in Washington, D.C., says in *Youth Suicide: And What You Can Do About It* (a booklet produced and distributed in connection with the broadcast of "Silence of the Heart," October 30, 1984, on the CBS television network):

> Youth suicide is a phenomenon which is at once perplexing, contradictory, frightening and troubling. It is so troubling that we avoid talking about it. As individuals and as a nation we do not want to believe that a young person just emerging from childhood can feel that degree of sadness and despair.
>
> Yet, as we know, walls of silence serve as barriers—not pathways—to solutions. As caring people, and as citizens concerned for the future of our youth, we want to help.
>
> A most important first step is to increase our awareness and understanding of the problem.
>
> What factors motivate the teenager to put an end to his life? Why is suicide among the young occurring with such increasing frequency? What can be done to recognize youngsters at risk and prevent their deaths?
>
> Although we cannot pinpoint the exact causes of our youngsters' suicidal thoughts and actions, we do know that for any in-

dividual despairing child, they may include feelings of loss, of failure, of unimportance in the family and community, of separateness and lack of confidence in the future. We suspect the breakdown of the family unit—through divorce, both parents who work, frequent moving—deprives youngsters of the traditional support systems associated with home, family and community. Other factors, such as unrealistically high expectations by parents, teachers or by the child himself, and even the threat of nuclear war, may play a part.

Ross, whose Youth Suicide National Center co-sponsored with the U.S. Department of Health and Human Services a national conference on youth suicide in Washington, D.C., June 19-20, 1985, suggests that youth suicide strikes at every level of society in all countries of the world. Those young people we have lost through suicide include the best and brightest of their generations. Such a serious national problem, she maintains, can be solved only if we combine the efforts of individuals, organizations and government.

What can be done? Charlotte P. Ross offers this advice:

> The needs of adolescents can indeed be great, but so can the motivation, resources and willingness to help of a concerned community. Today, a number of mental health specialists, educators, government leaders, parents and concerned citizens are working together to alleviate the problem. As individuals, we can support these efforts, and most importantly, we can learn to understand and help youngsters who are depressed and who may believe that death is the only relief for their pain.
>
> You can help by becoming aware and informed . . .
>
> You can help others to become aware and informed.
>
> You can help by becoming active in organizations which deal with the problem on local and national levels, and which need your help. Your participation will support efforts to bring about change through national action for youth suicide prevention, assist local and state youth suicide prevention activities, and provide for the wide dissemination of information which can—literally—mean the difference between life and death.

In recognition of the increase in suicide among America's youth and its consequences for our society, the Congress, by Senate Joint Resolution 53, designated the month of June 1985 as "Youth Suicide Prevention Month" and authorized and requested President Ronald Reagan to issue a special proclamation in observance of that month. The President did so, and then called upon the governors of the several states, the chief officials of local governments, all health care providers, educators, the media, public and private organizations, and the people of the United States to observe June 1985 with appropriate programs and activities.

In addition, during 1985, several bills were put forth in both the U.S. House of Representatives and in the U.S. Senate that would: make grants available for teenage suicide prevention programs (H.R. 1099); establish a commission to conduct a study of the problems of youth suicide for the purpose of providing guidance in developing national policy (H.R. 1894); and require the director of the National Institute of Mental Health to develop, publish and distribute information on suicide prevention (H.R. 1243). The state of New Jersey also introduced an act in its senate and general assembly that would establish a State Suicide Prevention Advisory Council and a pilot program for the prevention of teenage suicide in the state's Department of Human Services (Assembly, No. 2286). (See also ADOLESCENTS, YOUTHS, YOUTH AND THE VERY YOUNG.)

The following statistical data and charts show the seriousness of suicide rates among children, youths and young adults in the U.S. today:

Rise in Suicide Rates Among the Young, Ages 15-24, United States, 1959-1982

Source: Division of Vital Statistics, U.S. Public Health Service

Year *Suicide Rates per 100,000 population in each group*

Year	TOTAL			WHITE			OTHER RACES		
	Both Sexes	Male	Female	Both Sexes	Male	Female	Both Sexes	Male	Female
1982	12.1	19.8	4.2	13.0	21.2	4.5	7.6	12.3	2.9
1981	12.3	19.7	4.6	13.1	21.1	4.9	7.8	12.6	3.0
1980	12.3	20.2	4.3	13.1	21.4	4.6	8.2	13.8	2.7
1979	12.4	19.8	4.8	12.8	20.5	4.9	9.8	16.0	3.8
1978	12.1	19.5	4.6	12.8	20.4	4.9	8.6	14.4	3.1
1977	13.6	21.8	5.3	14.3	22.9	5.5	9.6	15.5	4.0
1976	11.7	18.5	4.8	12.1	19.2	4.9	9.3	14.7	4.0
1975	11.8	18.9	4.8	12.3	19.6	4.9	9.1	14.4	3.9
1974	10.9	17.1	4.6	11.4	17.8	4.8	8.3	12.9	3.9
1973	10.6	17.0	4.3	10.9	17.4	4.3	8.9	14.0	4.1
1972	10.2	15.7	4.7	10.1	15.5	4.6	10.0	16.7	5.6
1971	9.4	14.1	4.7	9.6	14.5	4.6	8.4	11.5	5.3
1970	8.8	13.5	4.2	9.0	13.9	4.3	7.6	11.3	4.1
1969	8.0	12.3	3.8	8.1	12.6	3.8	6.9	9.9	4.1
1968	7.1	10.9	3.4	7.3	11.3	3.4	5.6	8.2	3.1
1967	7.0	10.5	3.5	7.1	10.8	3.4	6.1	8.2	4.0
1966	6.4	9.7	3.1	6.5	9.9	3.2	5.7	8.6	2.9
1965	6.2	9.4	3.0	6.3	9.6	3.0	5.8	8.5	3.1
1964	6.0	9.2	2.8	6.1	9.3	2.9	4.9	8.0	2.0
1963	6.0	9.0	3.1	6.2	9.2	3.1	5.0	7.5	2.6
1962	5.7	8.5	2.9	5.8	8.7	2.9	5.2	7.5	3.0
1961	5.1	7.9	2.3	5.1	7.9	2.3	4.7	7.6	2.0
1960	5.2	8.2	2.2	5.4	8.6	2.3	3.4	5.3	1.5
1959	4.9	7.7	2.1	5.0	7.9	2.1	4.3	6.6	2.2

Death from suicide, by age: United States, 1958-82

Year	All ages	5-14	15-24 Total	15-24: 15-19	15-24: 20-24	25-34	35-44	45-54	55-64	65-74	75-84	85 and over
1982	28,242	200	5,025	1,730	3,295	6,316	4,315	3,710	3,741	2,812	1,678	429
1981	27,596	167	5,161	1,770	3,391	6,343	4,207	3,629	3,589	2,574	1,487	417
1980	26,869	142	5,239	1,797	3,442	5,920	3,935	3,623	3,456	2,630	1,477	430
1979	27,206	152	5,246	1,788	3,458	5,857	3,876	3,789	3,568	2,730	1,577	394
1978	27,294	153	5,115	1,686	3,429	5,650	3,853	3,976	3,748	2,812	1,561	410
1977	28,681	190	5,565	1,871	3,694	5,827	3,955	4,417	3,951	2,931	1,472	360
1976	26,832	163	4,747	1,556	3,191	5,064	3,759	4,541	4,005	2,772	1,406	371
1975	27,063	170	4,736	1,594	3,142	5,041	3,950	4,766	3,963	2,729	1,368	339
1974	25,683	188	4,285	1,489	2,796	4,658	3,823	4,657	3,845	2,548	1,368	305
1973	25,118	157	4,098	1,427	2,671	4,237	3,739	4,634	3,921	2,617	1,385	324
1972[1]	25,004	120	3,858	1,384	2,474	4,016	3,816	4,716	4,090	2,638	1,424	320
1971	24,092	141	3,479	1,279	2,200	3,535	3,904	4,664	4,064	2,653	1,361	284
1970	23,480	132	3,128	1,123	2,005	3,516	3,897	4,638	3,984	2,585	1,299	287
1969	22,364	136	2,731	1,045	1,686	3,155	3,847	4,490	3,875	2,478	1,378	267
1968	21,372	118	2,357	916	1,441	2,855	3,809	4,477	3,897	2,311	1,267	274
1967	21,325	121	2,244	836	1,408	2,819	3,961	4,412	3,935	2,315	1,246	267
1966	21,281	116	2,010	765	1,245	2,757	3,812	4,463	3,955	2,494	1,400	267
1965	21,507	104	1,876	685	1,191	2,721	4,064	4,554	4,040	2,525	1,353	262
1964	20,588	92	1,736	652	1,084	2,623	3,806	4,466	3,779	2,519	1,297	262
1963	20,825	104	1,663	617	1,046	2,621	3,924	4,530	3,864	2,534	1,329	246
1962	20,207	103	1,502	556	946	2,509	3,670	4,448	3,820	2,504	1,378	262
1961	18,999	76	1,258	467	791	2,306	3,489	4,232	3,665	2,458	1,267	241
1960	19,041	93	1,239	475	764	2,284	3,416	4,250	3,690	2,524	1,293	242
1959	18,633	86	1,152	433	719	2,255	3,236	3,992	3,733	2,681	1,257	231
1958	18,519	77	1,088	367	721	2,273	3,236	4,115	3,645	2,648	1,209	222

Age (years)

Sources: National Center for Health Statistics. Published and unpublished data from the Division of Vital Statistics, including *Vital Statistics of the United States, Volume II—Mortality*. Specified annual issues. Hyattsville, Md.: the Center.

Notes: Beginning with 1970, data exclude deaths of nonresidents of the United States. Deaths are those assigned to the following category numbers of the indicated revisions of the *International Classification of Diseases*:

Numbers	*Year*	*Revision*	*Adopted*
E950-E959	1968-82	8th/9th	1965/75
E963/E970-E979	1958-67	7th	1955

[1] Based on a 50-percent sample of deaths.

Death from suicide, by race and sex: United States, 1958-82

Year	All races			White			Black			Other		
	Total	Male	Female	Total	Male	Female	Total	Male	Female	Total	Male	Female
1982	28,242	21,625	6,617	26,141	19,965	6,176	1,639	1,327	312	462	333	129
1981	27,596	20,809	6,787	25,452	19,166	6,286	1,658	1,315	343	486	328	158
1980	26,869	20,505	6,364	24,829	18,901	5,928	1,607	1,297	310	433	307	126
1979	27,206	20,256	6,950	24,945	18,504	6,441	1,812	1,428	384	449	324	125
1978	27,294	20,188	7,106	25,250	18,619	6,631	1.677	1,309	368	367	260	107
1977	28,681	21,109	7,572	26,579	19,531	7,048	1,673	1,275	398	429	303	126
1976	26,832	19,493	7,339	24,854	17,996	6,858	1,614	1,234	380	364	263	101
1975	27,063	19,622	7,441	25,173	18,206	6,967	1,512	1,165	347	378	251	127
1974	25,683	18,595	7,088	23,923	17,263	6,660	1,442	1,120	322	318	212	106
1973	25,118	18,108	7,010	23,412	16,823	6,589	1,383	1,075	308	323	210	113
1972[1]	25,004	17,768	7,236	23,264	16,476	6,788	1,412	1,058	354	328	234	94
1971	24,092	16,860	7,232	22,577	15,802	6,775	1,220	861	359	295	197	98
1970	23,480	16,629	6,851	22,059	15,591	6,468	1,167	863	304	254	175	79
1969	22,364	15,857	6,507	21,038	14,886	6,152	1,090	804	286	236	167	69
1968	21,372	15,379	5,993	20,212	14,520	5,692	954	722	232	206	137	69
1967	21,325	15,187	6,138	20,116	14,307	5,809	982	712	270	227	168	59
1966	21,281	15,416	5,865	20,100	14,527	5,573	956	731	225	225	158	67
1965	21,507	15,490	6,017	20,342	14,624	5,718	958	732	226	207	134	73
1964	20,588	15,092	5,496	19,545	14,300	5,245	880	669	211	163	123	40
1963	20,825	15,276	5,549	19,168[2]	14,051[2]	5,117[2]	844[2]	653[2]	191[2]	229[2]	176[2]	53[2]
1962	20,207	15,062	5,145	18,677[2]	13,933[2]	4,744[2]	786[2]	592[2]	194[2]	195[2]	146[2]	49[2]
1961	18,999	14,460	4,539	18,012	13,677	4,335	781	622	159	206	161	45
1960	19,041	14,539	4,502	18,121	13,825	4,296	741	584	157	179	130	49
1959	18,633	14,441	4,192	17,719	13,724	3,995	779	605	174	135	112	23
1958	18,519	14,366	4,153	17,684	13,707	3,977	686	543	143	149	116	33

Sources: National Center for Health Statistics. Published and unpublished data from the Division of Vital Statistics, including *Vital Statistics of the United States, Volume II–Mortality*. Specified annual issues. Hyattsville, Md.: the Center.

Notes: Beginning with 1970, data exclude deaths of nonresidents of the United States. Deaths are those assigned to the following category numbers of the indicated revisions of the *International Classification of Diseases*:

Numbers	*Year*	*Revision*	*Adopted*
E950-E959	1968-82	8th/9th	1965/75
E963/E970-E979	1958-67	7th	1955

[1] Based on a 50-percent sample of deaths.

[2] Figures by race exclude data for residents of New Jersey, which did not require reporting of the item for these years.

Death rates for suicide, by age, race, and sex: United States, 1958-82 (continued)

Year, race, and sex	All ages	Age (years)										
		5-14	15-24			25-34	35-44	45-54	55-64	65-74	75-84	85 and over
			Total	15-19	20-24							
White, male												
1982	20.7	0.9	21.2	15.5	26.4	26.1	23.6	25.8	27.9	33.1	48.5	53.9
1981	20.0	0.8	21.1	14.9	26.8	26.2	24.3	23.9	26.3	30.3	43.8	53.6
1980	19.9	0.7	21.4	15.0	27.8	25.6	23.5	24.2	25.8	32.5	45.5	52.8
1979	19.6	0.6	20.5	14.3	26.8	25.4	22.4	24.0	26.3	33.4	48.0	50.2
1978	19.9	0.7	20.4	13.6	27.4	25.1	22.4	24.8	29.0	35.3	48.3	54.5
1977	21.0	0.9	22.4	15.1	30.2	26.1	24.7	27.4	30.6	37.4	46.2	51.0
1976	19.5	0.7	18.9	11.8	26.5	23.2	23.5	27.7	31.3	36.1	43.8	50.8
1975	19.9	0.8	19.3	12.9	26.3	24.0	24.4	29.7	31.9	36.0	43.2	51.1
1974	19.0	0.8	17.6	11.7	24.2	23.0	23.8	28.3	31.9	34.8	44.7	48.9
1973	18.7	0.7	17.3	11.3	24.0	21.5	22.8	28.4	32.3	36.9	45.3	54.9
1972[2]	18.4	0.5	15.4	11.0	20.4	20.7	22.9	29.7	33.4	38.4	47.2	54.7
1971	17.9	0.5	14.4	10.3	18.9	19.3	23.2	28.6	34.5	37.8	46.6	52.1
1970	18.0	0.5	13.9	9.4	19.3	19.9	23.3	29.5	35.0	38.7	45.5	45.8
1969	17.3	0.5	12.5	8.9	17.0	18.4	22.5	28.8	34.7	36.8	48.0	54.0
1968	17.0	0.5	11.3	8.3	15.1	17.4	23.2	29.0	35.8	35.8	45.5	58.9
1967	16.9	0.5	10.8	7.4	15.0	17.2	23.8	29.4	36.2	34.1	45.1	57.6
1966	17.2	0.5	9.9	6.7	14.1	17.2	22.8	30.3	38.2	38.0	52.4	60.9
1965	17.5	0.5	9.5	6.2	13.8	17.7	23.5	31.1	39.5	38.5	50.8	59.0
1964	17.3	0.5	9.3	6.6	12.7	17.0	22.3	32.1	38.4	38.3	51.6	66.2
1963[3]	17.8	0.5	9.2	6.4	12.8	16.9	23.6	33.2	40.2	39.6	53.4	60.4
1962[3]	17.9	0.5	8.7	5.8	12.5	16.5	22.9	33.5	40.5	40.9	57.7	62.3
1961	17.1	0.4	7.9	5.5	10.9	14.7	22.4	32.8	39.7	39.7	53.5	60.8
1960	17.6	0.5	8.6	5.9	11.9	14.9	21.9	33.7	40.2	42.0	55.7	61.3
1959	17.7	0.5	7.9	5.4	11.0	14.4	21.5	32.8	41.8	45.0	56.6	63.8
1958	18.0	0.4	7.6	4.7	11.2	14.3	22.1	34.0	41.9	45.8	58.3	58.5

See notes at end of table.

Death rates for suicide, by age, race, and sex: United States, 1958-82 (continued)

Year, race, and sex	Age (years)											
			15-24									
	All ages	5-14	Total	15-19	20-24	25-34	35-44	45-54	55-64	65-74	75-84	85 and over
White, female												
1982	6.1	0.3	4.5	3.4	5.4	7.5	9.2	10.4	9.5	7.4	6.1	3.9
1981	6.2	0.3	4.9	3.8	5.9	7.7	9.5	11.1	9.4	7.3	5.5	3.7
1980	5.9	0.2	4.6	3.3	5.9	7.5	9.1	10.2	9.1	7.0	5.7	5.8
1979	6.5	0.3	4.9	3.4	6.5	7.8	10.1	11.6	9.9	7.8	6.7	5.0
1978	6.7	0.2	4.9	3.3	6.6	8.2	11.0	12.1	10.1	8.4	7.3	5.4
1977	7.2	0.2	5.4	3.5	7.4	9.1	11.2	13.5	10.9	9.4	7.1	4.5
1976	7.1	0.2	4.8	3.3	6.4	8.5	11.1	13.8	11.8	8.9	7.4	6.0
1975	7.3	0.2	4.9	3.1	6.8	8.8	12.6	13.8	11.5	9.4	7.5	4.8
1974	7.0	0.2	4.7	3.2	6.3	8.6	12.1	14.1	10.9	8.5	7.0	4.1
1973	7.0	0.2	4.3	3.2	5.5	8.4	12.2	13.7	11.8	9.0	7.5	4.4
1972[2]	7.3	0.2	4.5	2.7	6.6	9.2	12.6	13.4	13.2	9.2	7.6	5.9
1971	7.3	0.2	4.5	3.0	6.2	8.8	13.0	14.5	12.5	10.2	7.2	3.7
1970	7.1	0.1	4.2	2.9	5.7	9.0	13.0	13.5	12.3	9.6	7.2	5.8
1969	6.8	0.2	3.7	2.6	5.0	8.1	12.7	13.3	11.8	9.6	7.6	4.1
1968	6.4	0.1	3.4	2.2	4.7	7.5	11.5	13.5	11.5	7.9	6.6	4.6
1967	6.5	0.1	3.4	2.2	4.8	7.9	11.5	13.1	12.2	9.6	7.0	5.4
1966	6.3	0.1	3.1	2.1	4.5	7.8	11.3	13.1	11.4	9.5	7.5	4.1
1965	6.6	0.1	2.9	1.8	4.3	7.6	12.0	13.8	12.2	9.8	8.0	6.5
1964	6.1	0.1	2.9	1.7	4.4	7.3	10.9	12.7	10.8	10.1	6.8	4.3
1963[3]	6.3	0.1	3.1	1.9	4.5	7.5	10.9	13.0	11.6	9.3	7.8	5.0
1962[3]	5.9	0.1	2.9	2.0	4.1	7.2	9.5	12.4	11.1	8.6	7.6	7.5
1961	5.3	0.1	2.3	1.6	3.2	6.1	8.3	10.8	10.4	9.0	7.6	4.9
1960	5.3	0.1	2.3	1.6	3.1	5.8	8.1	10.9	10.9	8.8	9.2	6.1
1959	5.0	0.0	2.1	1.6	2.8	5.7	7.5	9.5	10.6	9.8	7.6	3.8
1958	5.1	0.1	2.4	1.8	3.1	5.9	7.1	10.4	10.0	9.6	6.6	6.7

See notes at end of table.

Death rates for suicide, by age, race, and sex: United States, 1958-82 (continued)

Year, race, and sex	All ages	5-14	15-24 Total	15-19	20-24	25-34	35-44	45-54	55-64	65-74	75-84	85 and over
Black, male												
1982	10.1	0.8	11.0	6.2	16.0	20.3	15.6	11.8	11.9	12.1	12.2	16.1
1981	10.2	0.2	11.1	5.5	17.1	21.8	15.5	12.3	12.5	9.7	18.0	12.7
1980	10.3	0.3	12.3	5.6	20.0	21.8	15.6	12.0	11.7	11.1	10.5	18.9
1979	11.5	0.2	14.0	6.7	22.5	24.9	16.9	13.8	12.8	13.5	10.5	15.4
1978	10.7	0.3	13.0	5.5	21.9	23.1	16.9	14.5	10.1	11.6	11.7	9.8
1977	10.6	0.3	13.0	6.0	21.6	25.1	14.8	12.1	12.5	10.8	10.6	14.3
1976	10.4	0.3	13.0	7.0	20.6	22.1	16.4	14.0	11.1	13.5	9.4	29.8
1975	9.9	0.1	12.7	6.1	21.1	23.4	16.0	12.4	10.7	11.6	11.7	4.3
1974	9.7	0.4	11.1	4.9	19.1	22.8	16.1	12.7	11.7	13.2	12.9	7.0
1973	9.4	0.3	12.7	5.7	21.9	21.9	13.6	13.4	11.4	11.3	12.3	9.8
1972[2]	9.4	—	14.7	8.1	23.5	20.3	15.0	12.9	11.1	11.1	8.1	5.0
1971	7.8	0.4	9.7	5.0	16.1	16.6	14.6	10.0	10.8	14.3	7.0	7.5
1970	8.0	0.1	10.5	4.7	18.7	19.2	12.6	13.8	10.6	8.7	8.9	8.7
1969	7.6	0.1	9.2	4.4	16.0	16.6	15.8	11.1	9.5	11.2	12.6	5.4
1968	6.9	0.2	7.2	3.8	12.3	15.4	11.8	12.1	11.5	11.7	12.1	2.9
1967	6.9	0.1	7.1	3.1	13.0	16.2	13.9	10.9	10.6	10.5	10.4	5.9
1966	7.1	0.1	7.8	4.3	13.0	17.1	10.7	13.6	12.0	10.3	11.9	18.8
1965	7.3	0.2	8.1	5.1	12.3	13.4	14.4	13.0	12.8	11.4	13.4	10.0
1964	6.7	0.2	7.5	3.6	12.9	14.7	12.3	11.4	11.5	10.9	9.7	3.6
1963	N.A.	N.A.	N.A.	N.A.	N.A.	N.A.	N.A.	N.A.	N.A.	N.A.	N.A.	N.A.
1962	N.A.	N.A.	N.A.	N.A.	N.A.	N.A.	N.A.	N.A.	N.A.	N.A.	N.A.	N.A.
1961	6.7	0.0	6.8	3.6	10.9	14.1	10.2	13.6	13.2	9.5	10.3	3.7
1960	6.4	0.1	4.1	2.9	5.8	12.4	12.8	10.8	16.2	11.3	6.6	6.9
1959	N.A.	N.A.	N.A.	N.A.	N.A.	N.A.	N.A.	N.A.	N.A.	N.A.	N.A.	N.A.
1958	N.A.	N.A.	N.A.	N.A.	N.A.	N.A.	N.A.	N.A.	N.A.	N.A.	N.A.	N.A.

See notes at end of table.

Death rates for suicide, by age, race, and sex: United States, 1958-82 (continued)

Year, race, and sex	All ages	5-14	15-24 Total	15-24 15-19	15-24 20-24	25-34	35-44	45-54	55-64	65-74	75-84	85 and over
Black, female												
1982	2.1	0.1	2.2	1.5	2.9	3.7	4.0	3.1	2.2	2.1	1.3	0.9
1981	2.4	0.1	2.4	1.6	3.2	4.6	4.2	2.5	2.9	3.0	1.0	1.8
1980	2.2	0.1	2.3	1.6	3.1	4.1	4.6	2.8	2.3	1.7	1.4	—
1979	2.8	0.1	3.3	2.1	4.6	5.4	4.1	2.9	3.8	2.6	2.5	1.0
1978	2.7	0.2	2.7	1.3	4.1	5.4	4.6	4.2	3.0	2.3	2.5	1.0
1977	3.0	0.2	3.7	2.4	5.3	6.0	4.8	4.0	3.4	1.5	1.7	1.1
1976	2.9	0.3	3.7	2.5	5.1	5.9	4.1	4.0	2.7	3.5	0.9	1.1
1975	2.7	0.1	3.2	1.5	5.2	5.4	4.0	4.0	3.4	3.0	1.2	—
1974	2.5	0.2	3.4	2.5	4.5	5.4	3.8	3.4	3.1	2.0	0.6	1.3
1973	2.5	0.1	3.3	2.1	4.7	5.0	4.5	3.2	3.2	1.6	0.7	1.4
1972[2]	2.9	0.1	4.7	3.0	6.7	5.5	4.7	4.1	3.3	1.0	1.4	—
1971	3.0	0.1	4.8	3.4	6.5	6.0	5.1	3.6	2.8	2.4	1.5	1.5
1970	2.6	0.2	3.8	2.9	4.9	5.7	3.7	3.7	2.0	2.9	1.7	2.8
1969	2.4	0.3	4.1	3.0	5.6	4.8	4.2	3.5	1.6	1.7	1.8	1.7
1968	2.0	0.1	2.9	1.8	4.2	4.0	3.7	3.2	2.4	2.0	1.4	—
1967	2.4	0.1	3.8	3.3	4.4	5.1	4.1	3.2	2.6	2.0	1.4	1.9
1966	2.0	0.2	2.3	1.9	2.9	5.4	2.6	3.3	2.8	2.2	1.0	2.0
1965	2.1	0.1	2.7	2.2	3.5	5.1	3.1	4.2	2.0	0.9	2.0	2.2
1964	2.0	0.0	1.9	1.9	2.0	4.1	4.0	3.3	3.5	2.1	1.0	—
1963	N.A.	N.A.	N.A.	N.A.	N.A.	N.A.	N.A.	N.A.	N.A.	N.A.	N.A.	N.A.
1962	N.A.	N.A.	N.A.	N.A.	N.A.	N.A.	N.A.	N.A.	N.A.	N.A.	N.A.	N.A.
1961	1.6	0.2	1.6	1.2	2.1	3.0	3.3	2.5	2.6	1.5	0.6	2.6
1960	1.6	0.0	1.3	1.1	1.5	3.0	3.0	3.1	3.0	2.3	1.3	—
1959	N.A.	N.A.	N.A.	N.A.	N.A.	N.A.	N.A.	N.A.	N.A.	N.A.	N.A.	N.A.
1958	N.A.	N.A.	N.A.	N.A.	N.A.	N.A.	N.A.	N.A.	N.A.	N.A.	N.A.	N.A.

Sources: National Center for Health Statistics. Basic mortality data from *Vital Statistics of the United States, Volume II—Mortality,* for selected years, and other published and unpublished data from the Division of Vital Statistics. Hyattsville, Md.: the Center.

Notes: Beginning with 1970, data exclude deaths of nonresidents of the United States. Rates are per 100,000 population in specified race-sex groups, based on deaths assigned to the following category numbers of the indicated revisions of the *International Classification of Diseases:*

Numbers	*Year*	*Revision*	*Adopted*
E950-E959	1968-82	8th/9th	1965/75
E963/E970-E979	1958-67	7th	1955

[1] Includes races other than white and black.

[2] Based on a 50-percent sample of deaths.

[3] Figures by race exclude data for residents of New Jersey, which did not require reporting of the item for these years.

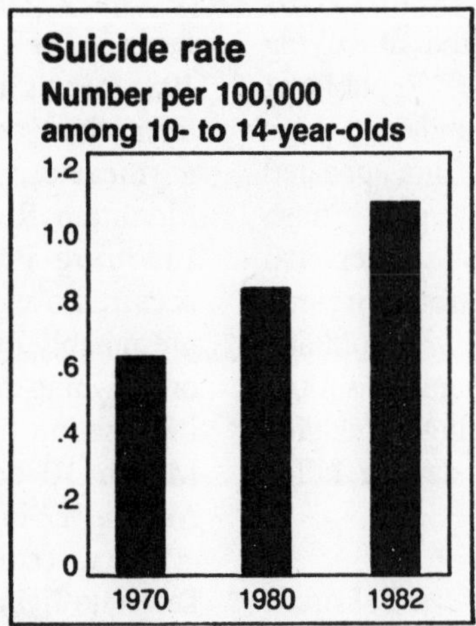
Suicide rate
Number per 100,000
among 10- to 14-year-olds
1.2
1.0
.8
.6
.4
.2
0
1970
1980
1982

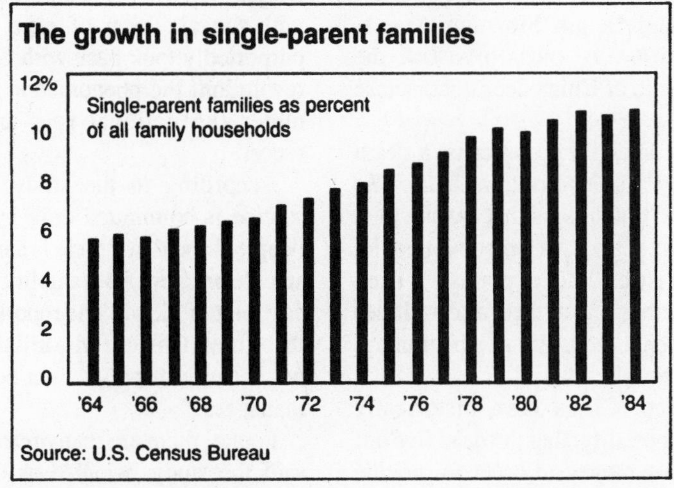
The growth in single-parent families
12%
10
8
6
4
2
0
Single-parent families as percent
of all family households
'64
'66
'68
'70
'72
'74
'76
'78
'80
'82
'84
Source: U.S. Census Bureau

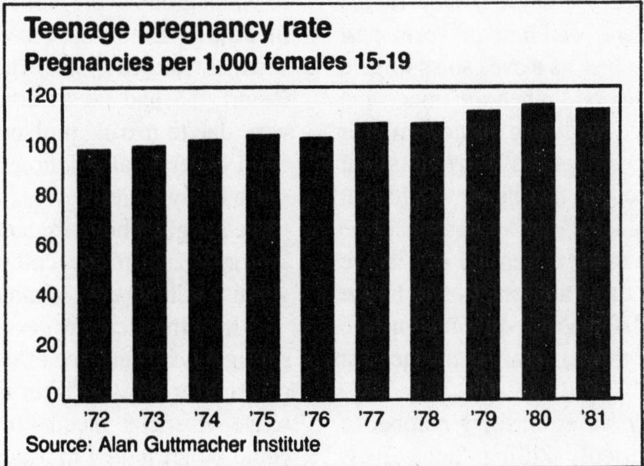
Teenage pregnancy rate
Pregnancies per 1,000 females 15-19
120
100
80
60
40
20
0
'72
'73
'74
'75
'76
'77
'78
'79
'80
'81
Source: Alan Guttmacher Institute

Chin, Larry Wu Tai Retired CIA analyst (1928-1986) convicted of spying against the U.S. for the People's Republic of China for 30 years. He was found dead in his jail cell, apparently a suicide. Chin appeared to have suffocated himself with a plastic trash bag at the Prince William-Manassas Regional Adult Detention Center in suburban Virginia. A convicted spy, Chin was 63 years old and faced two life terms in prison and fines totaling $3.3 million at his sentencing, scheduled less than a month from the day he killed himself.

China According to Dr. Alan D. Lopez, statistician, Global Epidemiological Surveillance and Health Situation Assessment, WORLD HEALTH ORGANIZATION, the People's Republic of China does not disclose mortality data.

The Chinese are, like Americans, a death denying society. Kubler-Ross, in *Death: The Final Stage of Growth*, says that despite this, the Chinese are not only a practical people, but also fatalistic. She explains, "They believe that death is one of the true certainties in life, that when there is life as a beginning, there is death as an ending."

The people of China have historically believed in immortality, that the dead live on. They burn paper money in order to provide the deceased with spending money in the "other world," and children in years past would sell themselves as slaves so as to give parents a good funeral. When the time came to cover the casket, the living would turn their backs toward the casket, so evil spirits that might hover around the dead would not follow them home. For like reasons, the Chinese wished for a patient to die in the hospital rather than at home—the house might be haunted if a mother died at home. To elderly Chinese, the hospital is still the best place to die.

In China today, an astonishing number of people are reportedly killing themselves, perhaps a greater percentage than in either Japan or the U.S. A study published in March 1986 reveals that some 63 Chinese have killed themselves at one resort, a scenic spot in northeastern China called the Thousand Mountain Resort on Liaodeng Peninsula, Liaoning Province. The suicides have occurred over the past two and a half years, presumably by the victims jumping off cliffs or drowning themselves in nearby rivers. This information from the study appeared in the March 10 edition of *Chinese Women's Newspaper* in an article bylined Li Wen.

The vast country's National Census Bureau keeps no figures on suicide. Suicide was not uncommon in pre-Communist China, but with the abolition of class inequality that purportedly took pace with Chairman Mao's revolution, the phenomenon had been swept under the national rug—until Li Wen's report.

According to the study, Li Wen says, suicide is committed only by "weak-willed people," and that "there is a need to study the suicide problem from a political and ideological point of view." The report also concluded that "most Chinese who kill themselves do so not because of politics but because of rotten marriages."

In fact, there are many reasons for suicide, said the study, which was conducted by a research group at the No. 1 People's Hospital in Fuxin, Liaoning Province. Of the 63 suicides studied at the Thousand Mountain Resort, 15 had no ascertainable cause, 33 were due to marital problems, nine stemmed from "personal relationship problems"—most likely failed love affairs—and six involved high school students who failed the all-important college entrance examinations given in China each summer.

What the researchers did emphasize strongly was that none of the 63 suicides was political or resulted from class struggle or a sense of social inequality. In short: None could be attributed to Marxian theory.

Further study of suicide in China today from a purely scientific standpoint, Li said, "cannot fail to be beneficial in preventing the reoccurrence of such cases."

As noted, suicide was common in pre-Communist China. So common, in fact, that 19th-century missionaries were appalled. Deliberate overdoses of opium and drowning were the two most preferred methods, according to H. Dyer Ball (writing in his 1892 compendium, "Things Chinese"), because they left the body undisfigured for the afterlife.

Ball wrote that committing suicide on an enemy's doorstep was the ultimate revenge because it rendered the house uninhabitable and unrentable. Everyone believed the house would be haunted by the ghost of the suicide.

(From a Peking dispatch by Michael Browning, correspondent, Knight-Ridder newspapers, March 25, 1986.)

Elisabeth Kubler-Ross, *Death: The Final Stage of Growth* (Englewood Cliffs, New Jersey: Prentice-Hall, 1975).

Christianity Self-destruction was commonplace in both Greece and Rome when Christianity came into being. Suicide at the time was tolerated and, in some instances, actually encouraged by the Stoics, the Cynics, the Cyrenaics, and the Epicureans. Early Christians seem to have accepted the prevailing attitudes of that era. According to George Rosen, MD, Yale Professor of the History of Medicine, voluntary martyrdom was frequent among the early Christians, particularly when persecution made life unbearable. Eusebius (ca. 260-ca. 340 A.D.), bishop of Caesarea, tells of Christians about to be tortured who committed suicide, "regarding death as a prize snatched from the wickedness of evil men." In fact, writes Rosen, there was virtually a pathological element present in the craving for martyrdom as expressed by Ignatius of Antioch in his letters, such as that written to Rome's Christian community. "I beseech you . . ." he wrote, "Suffer me to be eaten by the beasts that I may be found pure bread of Christ. Rather entice the wild beasts that they may become my tomb, and leave no trace of my body, that where I fall asleep I be not burdensome to any. Then shall I be truly a disciple of Jesus Christ, when the world shall not even see my body. Beseech Christ on my behalf, that I may be found a sacrifice through these instruments."

The Christians, then, saw their religion as offering a chance of martyrdom and an opportunity to die as a blood-witness to Jesus Christ. As Rosen notes, "Small wonder that with such a prospect there should have been an excessive eagerness to attain this aim by a premature voluntary death." However, Christians in general did not accept the pagan's tendency toward suicide. Yet martyrdom, with its exalted emotionalism, characterized large groups in the Roman Empire between the reigns of Nero and Julian (i.e., 54-363 A.D.).

It should be noted that the Apostles did not denounce suicide; the New Testament touched on the question of self-destruction only indirectly, in the report of Judas' death. So, as Earl A. Grollman says in *Suicide*, "For several centuries, the leaders of the church did not condemn this wide-spread practice."

Augustine (see also, AUGUSTINE, SAINT) was first to denounce suicide as a sin. Until then, there was no official church position against it. Then, in 533, the Second Council of Orleans expressed the initial organizational disapproval of self-destruction. In 563, the Fifteenth Canon of the Council of Braga denied suicides the funeral rites of the Eucharist and the signing of psalms. In 673, the Council of Hereford withheld burial rites to any who committed suicide. And in 1284 the Synod of Nimes refused suicides burial in holy ground.

For an explanation of Thomas Aquinas' refined elaboration of the Augustinian con-

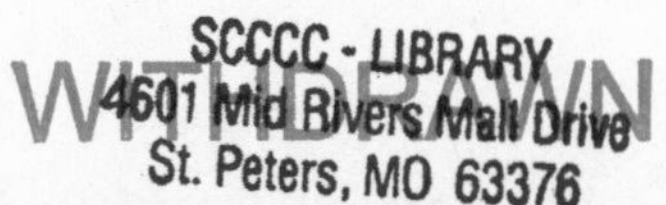

cept, see also AQUINAS, SAINT THOMAS. He opposed suicide on the basis of three postulates, stating a belief that all life was a preparation for the eternal. Aquinas stressed the sacredness of life and absolute submission to God.

Four centuries later, John Donne, then dean of St. Paul's Cathedral, reacted to the Church's existing strict attitudes toward self-destruction. He believed suicide was neither a violation of church law nor against reason. His position was soon supported by such secular philosophers as Hume, Montesquieu, Voltaire, and Rousseau. They insisted on greater freedom of the individual against Church authorities.

"In modern times," writes Rabbi Grollman in *Suicide*, "Dietrich Bonhoeffer viewed suicide as a sin in that it represented a denial of God." Yet Bonhoeffer, the German Lutheran theologian who was hanged by the Nazis in 1945 at age 39, qualified his position to accommodate prisoners of war who might commit suicide rather than give out classified information that could injure or destroy the lives of others.

Modern-day views and attitudes by Christians toward suicide are just as confused and controversial as were those of earlier times. Even with the arrival and application of sociology, psychology, psychiatry and anthropology to the problem, Christian attitudes still vary widely. Suicide is no longer a crime in any of our states; but aiding and abetting a suicide is against existing laws in 25 states. (States having specific penal laws regarding assisting suicide are: Alaska, Arizona, California, Connecticut, Delaware, Florida, Hawaii, Indiana, Kansas, Maine, Minnesota, Mississippi, Montana, Nebraska, New Hampshire, New Jersey, New Mexico, New York, Oklahoma, Oregon, Pennsylvania, South Dakota, Texas, Washington, and Wisconsin.) And Christian church authorities of varying faiths continue to regard it as a sin against God. Suicide is still covered up by many, whispered about, and concealed in many instances.

The Christian faith has always extolled the virtue of suffering, with its "ennobling" effects, as DORIS PORTWOOD points out in *Common-Sense Suicide: The Final Right*. Catholic spokesmen continue to often call suffering "the greatest possible source of heroism, purification and redemption." Protestant clergy continue in many cases to cite Job's rejection of suicide, despite his trials, as evidence that the Bible is opposed to self-destruction.

Portwood contends that "The analysis of Christ's death on the cross also is variable." She writes that "many people, within and without the Church, consider Christ's death a premeditated suicide—a deliberate sacrifice that, given his powers, he certainly could have avoided." Others, obviously, consider such an analysis as blasphemy.

There are today a number of "progressive" Christian denominations that actually distribute study literature on the option of euthanasia. Nor is suicide consistently rejected as an alternative to life by some churchmen, even for themselves. One such instance was the now famous attempted double suicide of Dr. Henry Pitney Van Dusen and his wife in 1975. He had been head of the Union Theological Seminary and enjoyed world recognition. In 1970, Dr. Van Dusen suffered a stroke and lost the speaking facility that played such a key role in his professional life. His wife suffered from arthritis. In late January 1975, they took massive doses of sleeping pills. Mrs. Van Dusen died peacefully, but not so her husband. He was hospitalized and lived until mid-February of that year. The couple's note was released then, and public opinion—both pro and con—had a field day. The famous couple's own simple note said, "Nowadays it is difficult to die," and added, "We feel that this way we are taking will become more usual and acceptable as the years pass."

Perhaps Grollman sums it up best by noting that:

> Today, many clergymen may not only view the question of suicide from the theological level, but they also consider the deep psychic causes and also the sociological implications. Ethical-religious approaches are counter-balanced with the broader perspectives of the social sciences. Increasingly, suicide is being recognized not only as a religious question, but as a major medical problem.

Doris Portman thoughtfully writes: "Heavenly bookkeeping on who does or does not deserve an afterlife must be seriously complicated." And complicated, too, are the varied points of view regarding suicide that still prevail among Christians in the 1980s.

chronic suicides Term coined by DR. KARL MENNINGER, noted psychiatrist and perhaps the best-known proponent of Freud's theory that suicide is aggression turned upon the self or retroflexed anger. Menninger, in his 1938 book *Man Against Himself*, called "chronic suicides" those individuals who might find the idea of killing themselves to be repugnant, but who nevertheless choose to destroy themselves slowly by way of drugs, alcohol or other methods. Behind their denial syndrome they justify their actions by, in Dr. Menninger's words, "claiming that they are only making life more bearable for themselves."

classification of suicides Emile Durkheim, a 19th-century sociologist, did a pioneering study of the sociology of suicide. His detailed work, *Le Suicide*, was published in 1897. DURKHEIM maintained that suicide, still looked upon at the time as a highly individual phenomenon, was more easily understood and explained as a reaction by the suicide to the peculiarities of society. Durkheim's analysis led to his identifying four types of suicidal behavior, basically falling at the extremes of two groups. The first is characterized by the extremes of integration, and the second group by extremes of regulation.

At one extreme of the integration concept lie the "egoistic suicides" which occur, according to Durkheim, "when a person feels alienated from society and has few, if any, binding ties to such institutions as family, church, business, education or social entities." The egoistic suicide is usually lonely, unmarried and unemployed. But sometimes it's the self-destruction of a teenage girl who, as Francine Klagsbrun says, "has run away from home and finds herself alone and friendless in a strange town."

"Altruistic suicide" is at the other extreme and is just the opposite of egoistic self-destruction. It comes about with people so caught up with a particular cause of the ongoing values of their society that duty takes precedence over their own individual needs. The young Japanese KAMIKAZE PILOTS during World War II are a classic example of altruistic suicides. They sacrificed their lives to crash their planes into Allied warships. The national military authority over the kamikaze pilot was so pronounced that he lost his own personal identity and instead wished to sacrifice his life for his country.

Along the other continuum, that of regulation, at the two extremes are "anomic suicides" and "fatalistic suicides." Durkheim never fully developed the concept of fatalistic suicides, which referred to suicides as a result of excessive constraints and repressive regulations in society that limited choice and reduced opportunity.

Durkheim's category of anomic suicides, however, was expounded fully, and referred especially to the confusion and sense of loss when traditional values and mores underwent marked or rapid change. Talcott Parsons, a noted sociologist, writing in *International Encyclopedia of the Social Sciences*, says that in this state of the social system, some or many of its members reach the point where they "consider exertion for success meaningless, not because they lack capacity or opportunity to achieve what is wanted, but because they lack a clear definition of what is desirable. . . . It is a pathology of the collective nominative system."

Durkheim would likely classify the society we live in today as anomic; a society, in short, where sudden changes are resulting in great unrest. The rapid changes presently taking place are having a strong impact on teenagers and young adults, and the rising rate of sucides in those age groups reflect that impact. As a result of Durkheim's original thinking and his theory of suicide classification, sociologists today believe that suicide in the U.S. can be explained as resulting—at least partly—from the peculiarities of this culture. Suicide, say many if not most sociologists, is a "barometer of social tension."

Durkheim, Emile, *Suicide: A Study in Sociology* (Glencoe, Illinois: The Free Press, 1951; first published, 1897).

Grollman, Earl A., *Suicide: Prevention, Intervention, Postvention* (Boston: Beacon Press, 1971).

Klagsbrun, Francine, *Too Young to Die: Youth and Suicide* (New York: Pocket Books, 1981).

Cleanthes Successor to ZENO, founder of the Stoics. After Zeno hanged himself at age 98, Cleanthes (331-232 B.C.) headed the Stoics who, within 100 years of Socrates' death, had made suicide the most logical and desirable of all ways out of this life. Cleanthes developed a boil on his gum, and was advised by a doctor not to eat for two days to allow the boil to heal. After fasting, the philosopher decided, "as he had advanced so far on his journey towards death, he would not now retreat." Cleanthes determined that since he'd come this far on the road to death, he might as well go all the way—and he starved himself to death.

Cleombrotus Greek philosopher said to have been inspired by Plato's *Phaedo* to commit suicide by drowning. It was in *Phaedo* that Plato made Socrates repeat the Orphic doctrine—before he drank hemlock—that suicide was not to be tolerated if it seemed like an act of wanton disrespect to the gods. A. ALVAREZ writes that Plato ". . . used the simile—often to be repeated later—of the soldier on guard duty who must not desert his post, and also that of man as the property of the gods, who are as angry at our suicides as we would be if our chattels destroyed themselves."

Cleopatra Queen of Egypt (69?-30 B.C.), who chose a most unusual way of self-destruction by allowing a poisonous snake to bite her. Hers is considered as the classic example of romantic suicide because of her ill-fated love affair with Mark Antony. Her lover, besieged by Octavian's forces at Alexandria, had earlier killed himself after receiving a false report of Cleopatra's death. Cleopatra's fateful romances with Julius Caesar and Mark Antony have often been the subject of drama, e.g., Shakespeare's *Antony and Cleopatra*, Dryden's *All For Love*, Shaw's *Caesar and Cleopatra*.

clergy and suicide prevention Members of the clergy have been a valuable resource in the area of suicide prevention. Frequently when a parent or a teacher suspects that a young person is having problems, the pastor, priest or rabbi is the first person to whom they turn. The potential suicide will often confide in a clergyman or woman before they will anyone else—because they view them as people who understand their futility and anguish, yet won't betray their confidence.

Spread throughout the U.S. are some 250 suicide prevention and crisis centers that help suicidal people cope with life crises which threaten to overwhelm them. Many of the trained volunteers and counselors who work at such centers are members of the clergy. They provide a lifeline for those distraught people who call them on "hotlines," and, in author Francine Klagsbrun's words, "pull them in out of their immediate suicidal crises and offer them relief and some hope for the future." (For additional information on the service of suicide prevention and crisis centers, see also SUICIDE PREVENTION.) Clergy volunteers take part in the same intensive training program as others to learn how to handle emergency problems they constantly face. They do not attempt long-term therapy, but only concentrate on coping with emergencies and immediate crises. For extended therapy, the clergy volunteers usually refer callers to professional psychiatrists, psychologists, social workers, or other qualified counselors who work with particular centers.

In her book *Too Young to Die*, Klagsbrun writes that it was the clergy who developed the idea of a "community center" to help prevent suicide. In 1906, two such centers opened in different parts of the world. Baptist minister Harry M. Warren established the NATIONAL SAVE-A-LIFE LEAGUE in New York City. Today about 8,000 persons a year call this center for help; the founder's son, Harry Warren, directs the center today. The second center was set up in England by members of the SALVATION ARMY. It differed from the League in that it aimed at treating suicidal persons *after* they had tried to kill themselves rather than attempting intervention beforehand. The Salvation Army's anti-suicide department exists to this day, though much of its work has been taken over by other organizations in England.

Another major suicide prevention organization started in England, and now operating centers in 26 countries of the world, is the SAMARITANS. The Reverend CHAD VARAH started the organization in London in 1953 with the notion of "befriending" suicidal people. Today, all of the Samaritan centers, both in the Commonwealth and in the U.S., are manned by volunteers who act as substitute families or close friends to people who come to them, offering love, care, compassion and companionship. The inspiration for the various Samaritan programs is not spiritual—they gain only their name from the parable of the Good Samaritan—and their approach, according to the Reverend Varah, is always secular, pragmatic and nonsectarian.

At the time the Samaritans was founded, Chad Varah was rector of St. Stephen Walbrook, one of the City of London's historic churches. An honors degree in philosophy from Oxford University, considerable success as a professional journalist and the care of a number of Anglican parishes all helped to prepare the Reverend Varah for his work with the Samaritans.

A suicide prevention service network that has a more directly religious orientation is Contact Teleministries USA (see CONTACT USA). The organization is one that boasts over 100 telephone counseling ministries throughout the U.S. They try to listen to, help and/or befriend any suicidal person, as well as others, in distress. The New York branch is headed by Dr. Norman Vincent Peale. Contact Teleministries USA says it is a Christian ministry whose aim is "sharing the goodness of God's compassionate love with each and every person." They ask their telephone volunteers to "undertake to counsel in accordance with Christian insight." Contact is an American affiliate of Life Line International, a worldwide organization with the same mission (in Canada called TELE-CARE). Persons wishing to contact any of these various organizations should check either the front of the phone book or the white pages under those names.

In Boston, Massachusetts, Father Kenneth B. Murphy organized Rescue, Incorporated, in 1959. The non-denominational agency, located at Boston's City Hospital, uses the volunteer services of over 70 clergymen and women and also the help of medical professionals. Grollman reports that in a five-year span, Rescue, Inc., received 7,893 calls from the depressed, the chronically ill, the alcoholic and the lonely. "Rescue, Incorporated," says Rabbi Grollman, "finds that the clergyman may be helpful during the moment of crisis."

For the person who is threatening or trying to kill himself or herself, the various suicide prevention and crisis center organizations extend life-saving assistance, loving care, compassion and support. Every degree of teamwork must be employed by such organizations, the professional staff, the significant volunteers, the clergy, the police, the firemen and women, as Grollman says, "to the end that life can be saved and preserved."

Pastoral volunteers and counselors who have taken special training in social work, psychology, and suicide prevention techniques can be extremely helpful to the troubled and/or suicidal person . . . but untrained members of the clergy, or any profession for that matter, working at suicide prevention centers do not pass themselves off as substitutes for effective psychotherapists.

For further information concerning the various "hotline" services, contact the National Youth Alternatives Project (NYAP), 1830 Connecticut Avenue, N.W., Washington, DC 20009. Suicide prevention and crisis centers accredited by the American Association of Suicidology (AAS) are listed in Appendix 3 of this work. *National Save-A-Life League* is headquartered at 815 Second Avenue, Suite 498, New York, NY 10017; phone is (212) 736-6191. *The Samaritans*' U.S. headquarters address is: Shirley Karnovsky, Executive Director, 802 Boylston Street, Boston, MA 02199; phone is: (617) 247-0220.

For information on Canada's suicide prevention and crisis programs, contact: *Suicide Information and Education Centre* (SIEC), Karen Kiddey, Information Officer, #201, 1615 10th Avenue S.W., Calgary, Alberta T3C 0J7; phone is: (403) 245-3900.

Look for *Boston's Rescue, Incorporated* and all nationwide contact teleministries numbers in the front section or the white pages of your telephone book.

clues, warning signs (of suicide) Suicidologists say that most people who seriously intend suicide leave discernable clues to their planned action. At times, the warnings take the form of broad hints; at other times, there are merely subtle changes in behavior. But the suicide decision is seldom impulsive. Usually, it is premeditated. DR. EDWIN S. SHNEIDMAN, one of the nation's foremost experts in the field of suicidology and a professor of thanatology at UCLA, says that "Although it might be done on impulse, and to others appear capricious, in fact, usually suicide is a decision that is given long consideration." Shneidman adds, "It is not impossible, then, to spot a potential suicide if one only knows what to look for."

The consensus among authorities is that the following are indicative suicide clues or warning signs:

- Preoccupation with themes of death or expressing suicidal thoughts;
- Giving away prized possessions, making a will or other "final arrangements";
- Changes in sleep patterns—either too much or too little;
- Sudden and extreme changes in eating habits, losing or gaining weight;
- Withdrawal from friends and family or other major behavioral changes, accompanied by obvious depression;

- Changes in school performance, lowered grades, cutting classes, dropping out of activities;
- Personality changes, such as nervousness, outbursts of anger or apathy about appearance and health;
- Use of drugs or alcohol;
- Recent suicide of a friend or relative;
- Previous suicide attempts.

Shneidman explains that three-fourths of those who kill themselves have seen a physician within at least four months of the day on which they commit suicide. People who threaten, "I'm going to kill myself," usually mean it, at least unconsciously. They just haven't yet decided on the *how* or *when*. If conditions in that person's life fail to change, he or she will soon set a time and choose the method of self-destruction.

Dr. Shneidman maintains that "when people are suicidal, a state of mind that comes and goes, there is no single trait by which all of them can be characterized. Always, however, they are disturbed and often they are depressed." The various verbal or behavioral "hints," some obvious, others subtle, should be taken seriously, say suicidologists. A suicide attempt, no matter how feeble or unlikely to succeed, is stark testimony of the suicidal state. "She simply wanted attention," is the comment which too often follows a suicide try. That, of course, is the point; that is exactly what she wanted. And, says Shneidman, "without it, she may well succeed in her next attempt."

Four out of five persons who succeed in taking their lives have previously given clues of their imminent action. And even the less pointed clues, whether behavioral or verbal in nature, though not so readily discerned by lay persons, often predict a suicide accurately. As Shneidman observes, "Once a person has finally decided to kill himself, he begins to act 'differently.'"

Those "different" actions, both verbal and behavioral, become the clues or warning signs of a potential suicide. Occasionally, according to Dr. Shneidman, the situation itself may be the "final straw," and can be a crucial indicator of the suicidal state. People already suffering from extreme depressions, for example, often commit suicide on learning—or believing erroneously—that they have a malignant tumor. In Shneidman's words, "Singly, any of these rather unexpected acts or remarks is not particularly significant, but clustered, they predict suicide."

Though these clues to suicide are not especially difficult to recognize, it is not all that easy to determine just how close the disturbed person may actually be to a suicide attempt. Trained professionals or volunteer staff members of any suicide prevention center or service (most of which are listed elsewhere in this work) can predict a suicide with more than chance accuracy. (See also DEATH WISH; EATING HABITS; FRIENDS, LOSS OF, LACK OF; IMPULSIVENESS; INSOMNIA; IRRATIONALITY; MOOD SWINGS; RECKLESS DRIVING; WILL, LOSS OF; WITHDRAWAL.)

cluster suicides In America the phenomenon called "clustering," a name given by public health officials for teen suicides in which one person's suicide triggers another in the same locale, has increased in recent years. Cluster suicides, whether actually part of a chain or coincidental, have occurred in New Jersey, New York State, Massachusetts, Nebraska, Oklahoma, Missouri, Colorado, California, Minnesota, Montana, Utah, Illinois, Texas, Ohio, Virginia, Wisconsin, Indiana, Alaska and Wyoming. This phenomenon has been responsible for setting up prevention and intervention courses in schools and communities, state suicide awareness programs, crisis and hotline centers and other anti-suicide action programs.

According to Loren Coleman, author of *Suicide Clusters*, "In bygone times, other groups have been the targets of the waves of suicides, be they Roman circus performers, early Christian church followers, or Viking warriors. Early in 1987, south Florida was in the midst of eight elderly murder-suicides. But for a problem that has been around since at least the 4th century B.C., when a series of self-inflicted hangings took place among the young women of the Greek city of Miletus, all evidence points to the youth suicide cluster phenomenon being on a dramatic increase during the 1980s."

Coleman, editor of *The Network News*, published by the Human Services Institute, University of Southern Maine, believes that "Awareness of suicide clusters is a more widespread phenomenon than some elements of suicidology would have us believe is happening. Now is the time to take the subject seriously."

Sometimes called the "Werther syndrome," after the 1774 novel *The Sorrows of Young Werther* by JOHANN WOLFGANG VON GOETHE (which resulted in many young men committing suicide in imitation of the book's central character), clustering is thought by some authorities to be triggered by the media—i.e., news stories by reporters on radio and television, in the newspapers and in magazines. Other experts openly speculate that such TV movies as ABC's "Surviving," starring Zach Gelligan and Molly Ringwald, might also play a key role in young people's suicidal behavior. They feel, as does Coleman, that "the use of the media to model non-suicidal solutions to stressful incidents and conflictual situations could thus become an important element in youth suicide prevention."

Loren Coleman, *Suicide Clusters* (Boston & London: Faber & Faber, 1987).

cocaine Although no statistics are available to indicate a direct correlation between suicide rates and use of the illegal and addictive drug cocaine, authorities do know that drug overdoses in general claim about 7,000 lives in the U.S. annually. In 1984, the U.S. drug overdose death figure was projected at 6,994, according to federal government sources.

Cocaine in the 1980s is finding fashionable new acceptance with professionals, business executives and others of the middle- and upper-middle class. The most dangerous form of abuse is injecting cocaine, though a powerful, less expensive form now prevalent—called "crack" or "rock"—comes in stick- or cigarette-shaped form. However cocaine is used, it leads from a quick high to a crash that most users relieve by taking either heroin or more cocaine—then more and more as tolerance for the drug increases. People on this merry-go-round have become suicidal during the "down" periods following cocaine use, as they have when "crashing" from other drug use. This is usually a time of extreme depression, and some users have also become suicidal as a result of losing touch with reality and imagining themselves capable of unrealistic feats and immune from all danger.

A well-known case recently involved comedian-actor John Belushi who died of cocaine abuse (evidently mixed with other drugs and alcohol) that caused acute toxicity. Belushi, of "Saturday Night Live" television fame, was 33 years old at the time of his death in Los Angeles, March 5, 1982.

cognitive aspects and feelings of the suicidal Cognitive psychology includes the study of processes that are involved in sensing, perceiving, remembering and thinking. It represents a point of view (in psychology) that stresses the importance of purpose, knowing, understanding and reasoning in behavior. As related to suicide and the suicidal, Alfred Adler, advocate and founder of "individual psychology," met in Vienna, Austria, in 1910, with other members of the Vienna Psychoanalytical Society to discuss the mysterious causes of suicide among

Viennese high school students. Other leading lights present at the historical session included WILHELM STEKEL, educator DAVID E. OPPENHEIM and SIGMUND FREUD, founder of the then new and controversial field of psychoanalysis.

At that meeting, Adler reiterated his belief, fundamental to individual psychology, that "To be a human being means to feel inferior." The inability to solve life's problems, according to this theory, activates the individual to strive to overcome his inferiority. But some persons, when they experience failure, need to destroy those around them. Suicide, said Adler, is a veiled attack upon others. He talked at length about inferiority, revenge and antisocial aggression. By an act of self-destruction, the suicide is attempting to evoke sympathy for himself and cast reproach upon those he perceives as responsible for his lack of self-esteem. Adler described the potential suicide as an inferiority-ridden person who "hurts others by dreaming himself into injuries or by administering them to himself."

Interestingly, Adler was excommunicated from the original circle of Viennese psychoanalysis by founder Sigmund Freud for proposing that the primary human drive was nothing more primitive than social aggression. Wilhelm Stekel as well was to soon part company with Freud and go his own particular revisionist way. At the symposium on suicide, Stekel theorized that the act of suicide related to masturbation and the guilt attendant upon that. He also espoused the now-famous principle on which a great deal of subsequent theory is based: "No one kills himself who has never wanted to kill another, or at least wished the death of another."

Historically, these views represented a departure from the social determinism prevalent since Emile Durkheim had published his ground-breaking *Le Suicide* some 13 years prior to the Vienna gathering (see DURKHEIM, EMILE). To Sigmund Freud, these various explanations were unacceptable. He managed to reserve comment, however, until the end of the discussion, when he admitted that the meeting had accomplished little—and then suggested that suicide in all its complexities would not be understood until more was discovered about the various and intricate processes of mourning and melancholia.

Dr. Robert Litman, in "Sigmund Freud on Suicide" (in Shneidman's *Essays in Self-Destruction*) maintains Freud knew more about the subject than he said at the time. Litman writes that it manifested itself in his early case histories. Freud's difficulty at the synmposium was theoretical: how to reconcile the self-destructive impulse with the pleasure principle. In short, if the basic, instinctual drives in humans were libido and self-preservation, then was not suicide incomprehensible, not to mention unnatural?

In Freud's famous essay on "Mourning and Melancholia," written five years after the Vienna symposium (though not published until 1917), he appears to accept the idea that suicide is simply displaced hostility. But Dr. Litman suggests the essay amounted to an initial sketch of a much more complex picture of the intricate internal world which Sigmund Freud was subsequently to draw. In *Mourning and Melancholia*, Freud theorizes there are two kinds of drives: the life instinct, or *Eros*; and the death, destructive, aggressive drive, or *Thanatos*. He said death is more than a bodily or physical event, that death is willed. There is an ongoing shifting and changing of the balance of power between the two instincts. Eros ages whereas ageless Thanatos may assert itself "until it, at length, succeeds in doing the individual to death."

Thus, according to Freud, both suicide *and* murder are aspects of Thanatos's dread action. Murder is aggression turned upon another; suicide is aggression turned upon the self. As Earl A. Grollman says in *Suicide*: "Freud's implicit value judgment is that murder is to be disapproved and prevented because it is highly destructive. Suicide, too, is murder in the 180th degree and must also be disapproved and prevented."

college students Suicide is the third leading cause of death among young people. For those of college age, it is the second leading cause, having risen from fifth place in the early 1970s. Between 1968 and the 1980s, suicide deaths in the 20- to 24-year-old age group have more than doubled.

Authorities attribute a number of reasons to this disturbing phenomenon: living at college and away from home for the first time; stress and tension caused by academic pressures; competition for jobs upon graduation; alcohol and/or drug abuse; loss of self-esteem and self-worth; feeling of being unloved and unwanted; pessimistic outlook concerning the future; sense of failure, alienation; emotional emptiness and/or confusion; lack of self-confidence; and general feeling and attitude of despair and hopelessness.

One researcher recently studied a random sample of 792 college students (all grade levels) and found that 30% had entertained suicidal thoughts during an academic year. Freshman year is evidently toughest for students. Psychiatrist Lee Robbins Gardner of Columbia University's College of Physicians and Surgeons says one study of college freshmen shows 70% had actually experienced suicide thought(s) in a given school year. In her book *Too Young to Die*, first published in 1976 and now in a fourth revised edition (1985), Francine Klagsbrun tells of returns to a questionnaire sent to a randomly selected group of high school and college students. More than one in ten had actually attempted suicide; more than half the students said that they knew people who had attempted suicide; and almost one-third reported they had either relatives or friends who had actually killed themselves. Klagsbrun adds that she "received 113 serious, carefully thought-out responses that revealed the students' concern with the subject . . . most also presented intelligent and well-reasoned answers to a question that related to the 'right to suicide.'"

Dr. Herbert Hendin uses the term "growing up dead" to describe the lives of young people whose parents didn't want them and unconsciously wished them dead. He discovered from his study of suicidal college students that most grew up sensing that their parents felt more comfortable with a lifeless child who caused them no trouble, gave them no trouble, gave them no problems. In order to please their parents, therefore, they learned in time to have no feelings and make no unsettling demands, in other words to literally "deaden" themselves emotionally.

As Klagsbrun explains, "When these young people went off to college, they began to experience feelings of excitement and challenge for the first time. These new feelings thrilled them, but also terrified them because they threatened to disrupt the quiet non-existence that had been the backbone of the students' lives." Accordingly, many of these youngsters tried suicide in order to continue, that is, to carry the deadness they knew their parents expected of them to its logical conclusion.

Francine Klagsbrun, whose book has been the basis of several television shows as well as professional and school programs, poses the key question: Who's to blame for the young suicides? Her answer is direct and revealing:

> A complexity of causes that involve social, psychological and family interactions. Rapid changes in society have disrupted family life and created increasing numbers of disturbed and dissatisfied homes. In many of these homes, children grow up feeling unwanted, even wished dead or non-existent by their parents. Such feelings may lead to inner rage and depression, and a wish to escape life through death.

Herbert Hendin, *Suicide in America* (New York: W.W. Norton & Co., 1982).

Francine Klagsbrun, *Too Young to Die: Youth and Suicide*, 4th rev. ed. (New York: Pocket Books, May 1985).

Common Sense Suicide: The Final Right A non-fiction book by DORIS PORTWOOD. A straightforward and carefully-researched examination of what has been called "the last taboo" in our society: suicide. The book is a thought-provoking statement of the right to suicide for certain members of society. She addresses the audience of which she is herself a member: the aging. Her theme: Increased longevity has its rewards; but when the penalties get too high, the self-destruct mechanisms built into all living organisms must—or at least should—be freed for people, and it must be our choice what price we, sane and long-living, ought to pay for the time we do or *do not* linger. Published in hardcover in 1978 by Dodd, Mead, the book is now available in paperback from The Hemlock Society, for $8. Order from: The Hemlock Society, P.O. Box 66218, Los Angeles, CA 90066.

Commonalities of Suicide, The Ten DR. EDWIN SHNEIDMAN, professor of thanatology at the UCLA School of Medicine and co-founder with Dr. Norman L. Farberow of the Los Angeles Suicide Prevention Center, lists 10 commonalities (in *Definition of Suicide*) he believes to be found in suicide. They are:

1. The common purpose of suicide is to seek a solution.
2. The common goal of suicide is cessation of consciousness.
3. The common stimulus in suicide is intolerable psychological pain.
4. The common stressor in suicide is frustrated psychological needs.
5. The common emotion in suicide is hopelessness-helplessness.
6. The common internal attitude in suicide is ambivalence.
7. The common cognitive state in suicide is constriction.
8. The common action in suicide is egression.
9. The common interpersonal act in suicide is communication of intention.
10. The common consistency in suicide is with lifelong coping patterns.

communication of suicidal intent As noted in the previous discussion of suicide clues or warnings, before their death or attempted death, the suicidal person leaves a discernible trail of hints—sometimes subtle, often obvious—of his intentions. Every suicide attempt, say Shneidman and other noted suicidologists, is a serious cry for help. If the cry is heard and duly acted upon, suicide can usually be prevented. Communication, again, may reflect itself in various verbal or behavioral forms. Most obvious, of course, are the self-pitying cries of those who threaten, "I'm going to kill myself." They should be taken seriously, as should such angry asides as "I wish I were dead," or "Everyone would be better off without me." All such dejected or rage-filled remarks are real communicative clues to suicide intent. All too seldom are they taken seriously. Communication can be seen as in a four-fold table, with direct and indirect on one axis and verbal and behavioral on the other. For example:

verbal direct: "I will shoot myself if you leave me."
verbal indirect: "A life without love is a life without meaning."
behavioral direct: Hoarding pills by a chronically ill, severely disabled person.
behavioral indirect: Giving away prized possessions, loss of appetite, insomnia.

The indirect communications, both verbal and behavioral, become significant when evaluated in context; that is, they are not in and of themselves a communication of suicidal intent but become so when they occur along with other clues and communications.

In addition, "blocked communication" is a factor—sometimes *the* factor—in suicide cases. In one study, 90% of teenage suicidals admitted they could not talk with their parents. Researchers concluded "The most common factor in the continuing chaos and unhappiness in the young person's life is the lack of parental appreciation or understanding." Dr. Michael Goldstein of UCLA notes that one of the two factors that indicated serious trouble ahead for suicidal children was poor or disordered parental communication. (The other factor: "overly critical, overly involved or actively hostile parenting style.")

As DR. MARY GIFFIN says in *A Cry for Help*, "The child who can talk about his pain—and his plans—to someone who is really listening can usually work out or, at least, work on his problems. The child who can't talk is the child who may commit suicide." Giffin adds, "Remember, teens who need help don't 'grow out of it.' They become adults who need help—if they live that long." (See also CLUES, WARNING SIGNS.)

community resources in suicidal crises When psychologists Edwin Shneidman and Norman L. Farberow established the LOS ANGELES SUICIDE PREVENTION CENTER in 1958, they had an all-professional staff. They later admitted volunteers to the program. Today the center has some 150 telephone volunteers who handle around 1,000 calls per month.

The Los Angeles center has become the model for many other prevention and crisis centers that have since been set up across the U.S. Today the Denver-based AMERICAN ASSOCIATION OF SUICIDOLOGY (AAS) serves as a clearing house for information and coordinates the work of all the suicide prevention centers. The AAS (see full description under AAS) publishes a journal and newsletter and develops and oversees standards for accrediting the activities of these many prevention centers. The organization holds an annual conference for professionals and volunteers, and helps to plan publicity and educational programs that are available at the regional, state and community level.

At many centers, counselors and/or volunteers work within the community in various ways to provide the latest data and suicide prevention information. Some suicide prevention people work closely with businesses, schools, fraternal clubs and church groups; others work in conjunction with prison officials, who must cope with suicide and suicide attempts among prisoners (particularly young males who have especially high suicide rates). Francine Klagsbrun reports that "increasingly numbers of suicide prevention centers have joined forces with other crisis intervention centers and hot lines that handle such problems as rape, drug abuse and accidental poisonings."

Many countries across the world now have suicide prevention centers at the community level, not unlike those in the U.S., Canada and England. Canada has a SUICIDE INFORMATION AND EDUCATION CENTRE (SIEC) in Calgary, Alberta (see Appendix 3, also COMPULSORY SUICIDE). The SIEC operates a comprehensive data bank of articles, books, films, and other information relating to suicide. It also sponsors and helps local-level groups plan and publicize suicide prevention resources. While the centre is used primarily by professionals, scholars and researchers, the general public also has access to its wealth of information about suicide. Interested groups or individuals contact: SIEC, Suite 201, 1615 10th Avenue S.W., Calgary, Alberta, Canada T3C 0J7; phone is: (403) 245-3900. Information officer is Karen Kiddey.

Dr. Edwin S. Shneidman, co-founder of the LOS ANGELES SUICIDE PREVENTION CENTER, writes in "Suicide—It Doesn't

Have to Happen" that, despite criticism from some professionals against them, there's little doubt that carefully established suicide prevention services pay off not only in lives, but also in money saved. He explains in detail:

> Community mental health improves as a result. Each community should tailor a suicide prevention service to its own needs. It should be emphasized that there is no single pattern or organization yet proved to be better or more successful than another. A suicide prevention service can be organized to operate autonomously or as a unit of the community's mental health facilities. It can be part of an emergency hospital or tied to the local university or mental health clinic. However, it seems evident that the apparent pattern for the future is that many suicide prevention services will be an integral part of the community's comprehensive mental health center—a logical site for them.
>
> Ideally, any new service will be staffed with at least one, and hopefully two, professional persons such as psychiatrists, psychologists, or psychiatric social workers. A professional psychiatric consultant should be available to the service at least for a few hours each week.
>
> The rest of the staff many be nonprofessional volunteers. Experience has proved that lay volunteers can be very effective staff members *if* they are *carefully selected* and *rigorously trained*. Generally, housewives who are mature, usually over 40, and have weathered psychological storms within their own lives, are potentially good members. For example, women who have lost children through accident or disease and have since adjusted to these personal tragedies often are compassionate, resilient and unafraid staff members. As a rule, it may be a good idea not to select people who have suffered psychotic breakdowns or who themselves at one time attempted suicide, or who appear overzealously interested in suicide.
>
> A suicide prevention service cannot open shop all at once like a supermarket. Rather, the entire process, if it would be successful, must be gradually and tactfully woven into the community. From the beginning, the organizers must solicit help—at the very least, cooperation—from the city or county medical authorities. The hospitals, the coroner's office, and the police chief should know about the beginning of any suicide prevention service. In fact, suicide prevention needs their help. The local press, radio and television should be informed about what's afoot and asked to cooperate. If a story breaks before the building suicide prevention service is ready, this premature news could be disastrous.
>
> Of course, the city government must know what plans are being made. If city officials are not the initial sponsors of such a community service, certainly their endorsement should be heartily pursued. Without local cooperation, successful suicide prevention is practically impossible.
>
> Well before the service is ready to take calls, local community sources should be informed. Local physicians, clergymen, police, government officials, and businessmen's clubs should be told. At the same time, the science writers for large newspapers or the city editors for smaller papers should be informed. The public will learn quickly about the new service.

Today's newly operating suicide prevention services are helping to explain why men kill themselves. Combined with biochemical advances toward eliminating depression, suicide prevention has begun to take effect. All of these activities aim at reducing the suicide rate in the U.S. Before that happens, the nation's suicide rate may very well appear to rise. As suicide prevention takes hold across the country, more accurate and standard methods of reporting suicides will become the practice. *Reported* suicide totals will rise for a while.

Active, increasingly effective suicide prevention services offer the suicidal person a fresh grasp on life. They promise no panacea. Life's burdens will continue.

But troubled men can persevere. The services now spreading across the country can show him that life is not so narrow—and, more importantly, that death is not the answer. Suicide is tragic and unnecessary waste. Fortunately now, it can, with appropriate measures, be prevented.

(See also HELP and PREVENTION.)

Edwin S. Shneidman, PhD, & Philip Mandelkorn, "Suicide—It Doesn't Have to Happen," American Association of Suicidology in cooperation with MSD-Health Information Services, Merck, Sharp & Dohme, West Point, Pennsylvania. (Material originally appeared in Public Affairs Pamphlet No. 406, called *How to Prevent Suicide*, by the same authors, New York City, 1967.)

Another excellent source of information relating to community resources in suicidal crisis is the Youth Suicide National Center, Charlotte P. Ross, Executive Vice President and co-Chairperson, National Committee For Youth Suicide Prevention, 1825 I Street, N.W., Suite 400, Washington, DC 20006; phone is: (202) 420-2016. For a complete description of organization's full services and activities, see listing for YOUTH SUICIDE NATIONAL CENTER(YSNC).

Editor's Note: Appendix 3 includes a complete listing of suicide prevention/crisis intervention agencies in the United States as compiled by AAS, the American Association of Suicidology.

Compassionate Friends A mutual-aid and self-help group the purpose of which is to offer support and understanding to any bereaved parent. These are sharing groups where members both talk and listen. Members find new strength, hope and the courage for living after loss of a child by suicide or other cause of death. There are branches throughout the U.S. National headquarters is in Florida. Write: Compassionate Friends, Box 3247, Hialeah, FL 33013.

competition In Japan particularly, where cultural tradition has come to mean that a family's prestige hinges on a child's academic performance, both grade and career competition is extremely fierce. Tokyo newspapers and other media have recently editorialized about the "annual slaughter of innocents" as that country's children jump off buildings, hang and gas themselves, and leap in front of speeding trains—because of failure to achieve a certain rung on the academic ladder. Children in Japan do not get a second or third chance; in fact, they must even pass a written examination to enter a "good" kindergarten. The latter is a must to enter into a good primary school which, in turn, becomes a prerequisite for a good high school and ultimately on to a good university.

Thus, it isn't surprising that the suicide rate in Japan rises every February as students write their various entrance examinations. Failure to get through "examination hell," so called by the youngsters, means shame for the student *and* his or her family because chances for later-life success are thereby greatly reduced.

Suicide rates for young people run higher in Japan than in the U.S., but the rate for young males in the U.S. has lately surpassed Japan's rate. In 1964, there were 9.2 suicides per 100,000 males in the 15 to 24 age group in the U.S. The rate in Japan was 19.2. But in 1977, the Japanese rate was unchanged while the U.S. rate had soared to 21.8. In 1982—the last year for which data are available for both countries—the Japanese rate was 14.5 compared to the higher U.S. rate of 19.8 suicides per 100,000 males in the same 15 to 24 age grouping. Experts see this as an indication that career and grade competition is becoming more intense in America.

West Germany also has a high youth suicide rate, as well as educational competition similar to that in Japan. In 1982, the suicide rate for males in the 15 to 24 group was 20.9; the rate dropped slightly to 19.4 in

1984. For females, ages 15 to 24, the 1982 suicide rate per 100,000 was 6.3; that was reduced to 5.2 in 1984.

According to DR. MARY GIFFIN, writing in *A Cry for Help* (co-authored by syndicated columnist Carol Felsenthal), for West German students under 18, the suicide rate is 50% higher than for the U.S. Giffin explains: "The country has a punishing system of preselection for higher education, which means that the student who doesn't do well from the start will have no academic future."

Business experts in the U.S. report that the phenomenon called "winner depression"—a feeling that despite great competitive success, professional accomplishments are somehow inadequate—is appearing with greater frequency in the world of business and commerce. It appears that mergers, acquisitions, the introduction of new technology, plus rising competiton from abroad—all are placing new pressure on and causing greater tension for managers and executives. Particularly vulnerable, say authorities, are the nearly 500,000 managers who have lost jobs since 1980 as a result of corporate restructuring and reorganization.

These same experts see winner depression—which has sometimes led to suicides—cropping up more often in tradition-bound fields where competition is now intense. Fields such as education, finance, hospital administration and others are pressured in ways previously of little or no concern. In many companies or organizations, baby-boom climbers breed insecurity and depression because they generally take more and greater risks than their predecessors did and often know more about new technology than their superiors.

A recent case that typifies the pattern of victims of the phenomenon of winner depression: a major university's general counsel, who directed a staff of 33 attorneys and the nine-campus institution, committed suicide by jumping off the Golden Gate Bridge. The attorney was 52 years old and had enjoyed great success. His colleagues say they had had no idea he was suffering any inner torment.

Until recently, depression was a taboo subject in the fiercely competitive business world. Today, however, as a result of the victims of winner depression, many firms take a more constructive view. Companies such as General Foods, American Broadcasting Company and Goldman Sachs use outside consulting firms to help staff people experiencing psychological and emotional problems. The consulting services say such employee-assistance programs are effective and have a high recovery rate. As one official reports, "Anxiety, stress and depression are considered by professionals to be treatable illnesses—the trick is to get employees to go."

Still the 1982 suicide rate for age group 35 to 44 in the U.S. is a high 15.4% (males rate, 22.5, females, 8.5), up from 15.2% in 1980. For age group 45 to 54, the suicide rate total in 1982 was 16.6 (24.2 males, 9.5 females,), up from the 15.9 total in 1980.

It appears that the intense competition factor affects the suicide rate of every age group in many countries, including the U.S.

compulsory suicide Compulsory seppuku or hara-kiri in Japan was declared illegal in 1868. The custom used to be reserved for the nobility and members of the military caste. It was generally commanded by the government to certain disgraced officials as a form of sanctioned punishment whereby the individual should die by his own hand rather than be beheaded. The word SEPPUKU is the only Japanese rendering of the Chinese reading of two characters, 切腹 meaning "cutting the stomach." The same two characters in reverse order can also be pronounced "hara kiri," and the latter is more common in spoken Japanese.

There have been other societies where suicide was compulsory—as a part of crime and punishment. Two good references that discuss this phenomenon are *African Homicide and Suicide*, edited by P.J. Bohannan, and *Crime and Custom in Savage Society*, by Bronislaw Malinowski.

Today, self-destruction as a military, paramilitary, or political act, though not always compulsory, brings veneration in Iran, Libya and among some members of the Palestine Liberation Organization (PLO) as well as certain splinter factions in Lebanon. This despite the fact that for Islam, suicide is the gravest sin. Suicide is expressly forbidden in the KORAN.

computers (use in suicide prevention and prediction) There have been several articles and papers published in various professional journals describing the use of computers in suicide prevention, risk prediction and identifying suicide attempters. In *Research on Suicide: A Bibliography*, John L. McIntosh lists the following references:

J.H. Greist, D.H. Gustafson, F.F. Strauss, G.L. Rowse, T.P. Laughren and J.A. Chiles, "A Computer Interview for Suicide-risk Prediction," *American Journal of Psychiatry* (130: 1973), 1327-1332.

———, "Suicide Risk Prediction: A New Approach," *Life Threatening Behavior* (4: 1974), 212-223.

D.H. Gustafson, H.J. Greist, F.F. Strauss, H. Erdman and T.P. Laughren, "A Probabilistic System for Identifying Suicide Attempters," *Computers and Biomedical Research* (10: 1977), 83-89.

D.H. Gustafson, T. Tisner, and J.H. Griest, "A Computer-based System for Identifying Suicide Attempters," *Computers and Biomedical Research* (14: 1981), 144-157.

McIntosh, an assistant professor of psychology at Indiana University at South Bend, reports that the above references describe the use of computers in suicide prevention and especially in prediction.

THE SUICIDE INFORMATION AND EDUCATION CENTRE (SIEC), Calgary, Alberta, Canada, has produced an offline bibliographic citation list (called *Thesaurus of Subject Terms*) generated by their database. There is a fee of $5 charged to out-of-province users for printouts requested through their computerized interactive retrieval service. A photo duplication service is also available for most items in the retrieval service. Cost is $2 for each item up to 10 pages and 20 cents for each subsequent page (out-of-province users only).

Any person interested in suicide or suicidal behavior is welcome to access the information available at SIEC. Users of the database will find that the computer-assisted resource library contains written and audiovisual materials specific to the topic of suicidal behaviors. Users of the database include: researchers, students, educators, health care professionals, social service agency staff, volunteers in the helping professions, librarians and members of the general public. SIEC's collection of material includes: periodical articles, books and book chapters, pamphlets, video tapes and films, conference papers and proceedings, cassettes, theses, newspaper clippings, reports, reviews, unpublished speeches and manuscripts, teaching materials, program outlines and promotional materials (e.g., brochures, posters). As of February 1985, the SIEC database contained 7,020 items.

For further information about the Suicide Information and Education Centre, write: Karen Kiddey, Information Officer, Suite 201, 1615 10th Avenue S.W., Calgary, Alberta, Canada T3C 0J7; phone is: (403) 245-3900.

Other computer search sources include:

National Clearing House for Mental Health Information Computer Search, write: National Clearinghouse for Mental Health Information, attention: Computer Search, National Institute of Mental Health, 5600 Fishers Lane, Rockville, MD 20857; phone is: (301) 443-4517.

National Library of Medicine Computerized Searches, write: National Library of Medicine, Library Search Program, Reference Section, 8600 Rockville Pike, Bethesda, MD 20209; phone is: (301) 496-4000 or (301) 496-4840.

PASAR Computerized Literature Search, write: Psychological Abstracts Information Service, 1200 17th Street, N.W., Washington, DC 20036; phone is: (202) 833-5908 or (800) 336-4980. Forms and guidelines are included in the back of each monthly issue of *Psychological Abstracts*.

The expansive increase in suicide literature—particularly increases in data on specific sub-topics in the general field of suicide—makes general computer searches both expensive and difficult. Also, as McIntosh notes in his comprehensive bibliography (1985), searches for specialized topics and sub-topics often yield relatively few references from a single database or from a single index source.

concentration, loss of, as a distress signal Loss of concentration is considered one of the several warning signs or distress signals given out by potentially suicidal persons. Sometimes the signal is hard to detect at first, then it grows progressively more apparent. Any sudden change in a person's personality is usually a warning sign. Ordinary daily tasks become difficult to carry out. There is often lassitude and lack of energy. Decisions—even the simplest kind—become difficult to make. And, with lack of concentration, depression usually begins gradually. The person often talks less, prefers to be alone, and there is a marked decline in his level of interest as well as concentration.

Contact USA Many suicide prevention services have a religious orientation. Contact Teleministries USA is such an organization. It has almost 200 centers worldwide, 104 in the U.S., that try to listen to, help and befriend the suicidal, as well as others in distress. The New York branch of the telephone counseling ministries is headed by Dr. Norman Vincent Peale of "positive thinking" fame. According to officials (and the group's informational literature) the organization is a Christian ministry that strives to share "the goodness of God's compassionate love with each and every person" and instructs its telephone volunteer workers to "undertake to counsel in accordance with Christian insights." Contact USA is the American affiliate of Life Line International, which operates worldwide. For a list of Contact centers, write: Contact USA, 900 South Arlington Avenue, Harrisburg, PA 17109. (You can also check your local telephone book in the Yellow pages under either "Suicide," "Crisis," "Mental Health," or "Counseling." In some areas, the inside front cover or first page of the phone book lists a variety of emergency services, including suicide prevention. Also, most police stations have such telephone numbers and locations.)

conversation without words Bonding has been called conversation without words between parent and child—a consistent, predictable, synchronized process, what DR. MARY GIFFIN, medical director, North Shore (Illinois) Mental Health Association, calls "a turn-taking sequence in which each partner first acts and then attends to the activity of the other." Giffin, along with many physicians, believes strongly in the importance of bonding for providing a baby an important emotional experience early on in life. "When the mother responds to the baby, she gives meaning to his actions and helps the child understand the world and believe in a sense of the predictable . . . Adult and infant are soon able to regulate their joint activity harmoniously and produce an adequate simulation of mature human discourse."

For more discussion on the importance of bonding for a healthy, thriving start in life for infants, see also BONDING. Also, see chapter nine of *A Cry for Help*, "The Key to Good Mental Health," by Mary Giffin, MD, and Carol Felsenthal (New York: Doubleday, 1983).

coping mechanisms Psychologists use the term "coping behavior" to describe the characteristic manner in which individuals deal with their physical and social environment, particularly as they mobilize their resources to handle stress. For example, people with healthy coping mechanisms can deal satisfactorily with the stressors of daily frustrations and even periodic tragedies. Those who have not acquired and developed healthy coping mechanisms, who do not display "normal" coping behavior, may exhibit totally inappropriate responses to stress (or a combination of stresses) that indicate warning signals or distress clues of potential self-destructive behavior. (See also CLUES, WARNING SIGNS OF SUICIDE.)

coroners The disparity between official suicide rates per 100,000 persons and the actual number of suicide victims exists for a number of reasons. Generally, coroners list suicide as a cause of death only when circumstances unequivocally justify such a determination: e.g., when a suicide note is left by the victim of sudden death; when the person has a history of suicidal tendencies and/or has perhaps tried self-destruction previously; or when cause of death simply cannot be other than suicide.

When such obvious clues are absent, most coroners admit that they are reluctant to rule the death a suicide. In fact, some coroners or medical examiners indicate that in many small towns and communities, suicide is seldom listed as such on a death certificate. This practice, they contend, is the pragmatic action for a coroner, because life pressures in a small community dictate certain unwritten rules of conduct. Many of these coroners also act as personal physicians for members of the community, and cannot afford to jeopardize their income by antagonizing patient-clients. Sometimes, insurance is a reason for not declaring a suicide as such.

Dr. Hal Wagner, a former chief pathologist, Cook County, Illinois, had this to say about coroners and suicide:

> Suicides are not really a matter of opinion with coroners, but I was always willing to give the dead guy the benefit of the doubt.
>
> I know from experience that people who slit their wrists don't just do it in one stroke. They make initial attempts and these cuts are called 'hesitation marks.' You look for these when suicide is in question.
>
> People who are drunk generally do not commit suicide. I believe that being drunk makes a person incapable of making the decision to end his own life.

(See *Kicking the Bucket*, by Kim Long and Terry Reim.)

Many traffic deaths, especially those involving one person in a single car collision with a stationary object, are suspected "autocides," or impulsive, spur-of-the-moment suicides. One estimate places such "autocide" explanations at 75% of this type of accident. Although there is no means to prove this commonly heard of theory of suicide, it is nonetheless applied as well in incidents involving alcohol abuse, drug overdoses, firearm accidents and sometimes even the violence that results in homicide or death from legal intervention. Authorities who use this interpretive theory have often set the actual number of suicides at twice the official U.S. figure.

Finally, there are also many and varied forms of self-destructive behavior (what KARL MENNINGER calls "chronic suicides") that may ultimately end in accidental death or death due to chronic health problems . . . in other words, long-term self-destruction by people who consciously or subconsciously have been killing themselves over a period of time. Such cases are never listed as suicides by coroners. Victims of such chronic suicides are more likely to be listed among the nation's mortality statistics for heart disease, cirrhosis of the liver, pneumonia, or "accidental death" due to drug overdose, drowning, automobile accident, fire, falls, poisoning or accidental gunshot wounds.

Coroners say they generally will consider the following as likely suicide: cut throat, hanging, self-immolation, crushing under a train and car exhaust poisoning. The following are given the benefit of the doubt by many coroners and/or medical examiners and considered as problematic (unless other unequivocal proof exists): fall from a height, drowning, firearms, poisoning and even drug overdose.

The question remains, of course, how best to assess a dead person's motives.

The chief method used widely today is that of the "psychological autopsy." Developed by psychologists Edwin Shneidman and Norman L. Farberow after they began the Los Angeles Suicide Prevention Center in 1958, the important research tool is a method to assist coroners and medical examiners to determine the cause of an uncertain death by gathering an amalgamation of data on the victim based on psychological status and personality characteristics.

Investigation teams interview relatives and friends, associates in the work place, teachers and anyone else who perhaps played a significant role in the deceased's life. The purpose, as Avery Weisman and Robert Kastenbaum state (*The Psychological Autopsy: A Study of the Terminal Phase of Life*), is "to reconstruct the final days and weeks of life by bringing together available observation, fact and opinion about a recently deceased person in an effort to understand the psychological components of death."

For a more complete explanation of this pioneering method for assessing completed suicide, see PSYCHOLOGICAL AUTOPSY.

(Second) Council of Orleans Held 533 A.D., the Council expressed the first institutional disapproval by the (Catholic) Church of suicide, which it determined was the most serious and heinous of transgressions. It was not, however, until 563 and the Council of Braga—the Fifteenth Canon—that there was institutional denial for suicides of funeral rites of the Eucharist and the singing of psalms. (See also ATTITUDES TOWARD SUICIDE AND THE SUICIDAL.)

counseling There are hundreds of suicide prevention and crisis centers, teleministries, and other relevant counseling institutions in the U.S., Canada, England and other countries around the world that indicate nations are well aware of the enormity of the problem of suicide. There are, today, many counseling facilities and self-help organizations designed to help all those who are victims of suicide and suicidal behavior. This includes services not only for potential suicides, but counseling for survivors of suicide. An example of the latter type group is LOSS (Loving Outreach to Survivors of Suicide), sponsored by Catholic Charities, which has autonomous groups in most areas of the country. Such self-help groups have proved valuable for suicide survivors—parents, brothers and sisters, friends—because they offer one another mutual support through shared feelings, strengths and hopes. Members are able to talk as well as listen and start to realize that they are not stigmatized monsters. They learn to live with their tragedy and can see that suicide happens to average people from average families. The sense of shared community and hope that members experience in these self-help groups usually extends beyond the meetings themselves and to the home. Many marriages are saved as a result of parents learning to start over, to begin talking to each other—in place of long periods of agonizing withdrawal or angry outbursts relating to trivial misunderstandings.

Other agencies and organizations are to be found in most cities, towns, and suburbs throughout the U.S. They include:

Family service agencies—the majority are community sponsored and have qualified social workers on staff; in addition, most such agencies have at least one psychiatrist who serves as a professional consultant. Sometimes these agencies are denominational, such as the Jewish Children's Bureau and Catholic Charities (sponsors of the LOSS groups for suicide survivors). Lutherans also support several hospitals that provide services similar to those offered by other Family Service Agencies.

The Family Service Association of America, with its chain of member agencies nationwide, offers low-cost individual and family counseling, family life education programs, special "rap" groups for teens and family advocacy activities. For further information about member agencies and available services, write or call: Family Service Association of America, 44 East 23rd Street, New York, NY 10010; phone is: (212) 674-6100. There are also several FSAs located in the various provinces of Canada (contact the Family Service Association of Metropolitan Toronto, 22 Wellesley Street East, Toronto, Ontario, Canada M4Y 1G3; phone is: (416) 922-3126).

See Appendix A for a listing of national and federal agencies and special help resources. All listed suicide prevention and crisis centers that are member agencies of the AMERICAN ASSOCIATION OF SUICIDOLOGY (AAS) are included under Appendix 3.

Look for CONTACT USA Teleministries number(s) in the white pages of your local telephone book. Many, but not all, of these centers provide full, 24-hour-a-day service. For a list of these Contact centers, write: CONTACT USA, 900 South Arlington Avenue, Harrisburg, PA 17109; phone is: (717) 652-4400.

The NATIONAL SAVE-A-LIFE LEAGUE, founded in 1906, is headquartered in New York. Write to: 4520 Fourth Avenue, Brooklyn, NY 11220; phone is: (718) 492-4067.

The SAMARITANS, one of the major suicide prevention organizations in England, now has centers in many parts of the world. For information concerning U.S. Samaritan groups, write: Samaritans of New York, 423 West 46th Street, New York, NY 10036; phone is: (212) 664-0505.

For information about counseling services for young people specifically, contact: The YOUTH SUICIDE NATIONAL CENTER, 1825 I Street, N.W., Washington, DC 20006; phone is: (202) 429-2016.

Various other special-focus self-help groups for troubled teenagers and their parents are described under their individual listings in this work, such as AL-ANON and PARENTS ANONYMOUS. (See also COMMUNITY RESOURCES IN SUICIDAL CASES; HELP; and PREVENTION.)

cowardice See ACT OF COWARDICE, SUICIDE AS.

Craig and Joan The book by Eliot Asinof deals with the true story of two New Jersey teenagers who killed themselves in 1969 to protest the Vietnam War. Joan Fox and Craig Badiali, both 17, asphyxiated themselves after leaving behind 24 suicide notes that explained their political protest of the war. Their suicide pact generated a great deal of national publicity, in addition to Asinof's book. The book was published by Viking Press (New York, 1971).

Crane, Hart (Harold) U.S. poet (1899-1932). The contents of his *White Buildings* (1926) and *The Bridge* (1930) were published with a few others in *Collected Poems* (1933), constituting a slim body of intense, sensitive, modernist poetry. Tormented by a sense of failure after these torturously produced pieces, Crane committed suicide by jumping overboard from a steamer in the Caribbean. A. ALVAREZ, writing about the poet in *The Savage God: A Study of Suicide*, says "Hart Crane devoted prodigious energy to aestheticizing his chaotic life—a desperate compound of homosexuality and alcoholism—and finally thinking (of) himself a failure . . ."

crime DR. HERBERT HENDIN, director of the Center for Psychosocial Studies at the Veteran's Administration Center, Montrose, New York, and professor of psychiatry at New York Medical College, points out in *Suicide in America* that all forms of psychosocial pathology tend to correlate with each other, if only, in his words, "because an individual in distress is likely to manifest the distress in more than one way." In America over the past two decades, there have been astonishing rises of almost 300% in both suicide rates and homicide rates among young white males aged 15 to 19. Writes the noted psychiatrist: "In fact, if we take young males as our reference point, the U.S. now ranks among the highest of countries in the world in both suicide and homicide." He notes, too, that persons (taken as a group) who kill themselves have committed homicide at a much higher rate than has the general population, and persons who have killed others have a much higher suicide rate than has the overall population.

Hendin believes the relation between the homicide-suicide actions in the U.S. is dramatized by the fact that guns, used in over 60% of the homicides, are used as well in some 55% of the suicides. Despite the impersonal nature of certain homicides, in four out of five homicides the victim is a relative, lover, friend or acquaintance of the murderer. "Murder, like suicide," he says, "is for the most part a personal or an interpersonal matter: both suicide and homicide usually have destructive consquences to a number of people involved with the perpetrator or the victim."

In a detailed study done in the late 1960s, Hendin revealed the then surprising information that in New York City, among blacks of both sexes between ages 20 and 35, suicide was more of a problem than it was among the white population of the same age. Among black men in New York in the age group 20 to 35, suicide was double the frequency it was among white males of the same age bracket. Writes Hendin: "While suicide among young blacks has been obscured or ignored, the high frequency of homicide by young blacks has not been similarly neglected. At all ages, the black homicide rate is significantly higher than the white homicide rate . . . " Black homicide, however, peaks at the same 20 to 35 age period as does black suicide. Hendin stresses, too, that these high suicide and homicide rates in the 20 to 35 age group cannot be attributed to the social changes of the 1960s alone—and the generation influenced by them—since the same pattern extends back to at least 1920.

Hendin says his study "made clear the suicide is often the outgrowth of a devastating struggle to deal with conscious rage and conscious murderous impulses. Study of these young people brings out the close connection between the disastrous individual and social circumstances that culminate in suicide." The rage and violence that had marked the lives of black suicidal men, Hendin noted, were equally characteristic of black suicidal women. He says the study of young suicide-prone blacks in the ghetto makes clear "that their consciousness is flooded with angry homicidal impulses." He theorizes that suicide can be a form of control of violent impulses by people who feel torn apart by them. The violence, whether suicidal or not, is an attempt—at least in part—to deal with underlying depression and despair.

Andrew Henry and James Short investigated the relationship between the business cycle and suicide and homicide rates. They hypothesized an inverse relationship, that homicide will rise during good times and fall during bad times, while suicide will do just the opposite: rise in bad times, and fall during prosperity. They also hypothesized, on the basis of Dollard's frustration-aggression hypothesis, that the suicide rates for whites would correlate more highly with the business cycle than for blacks, and that the reverse would be true for homicide, where the rates for blacks would correlate higher than for whites.

According to Lester (pp. 98-99), while the second hypothesis was confirmed, the first was not, for the prediction of a positive correlation between the homicide rates and the business cycle was not found for whites. (Henry and Short, *Suicide and Homicide: Some Economic, Sociological and Psychological Aspects of Aggression*; David Lester, *Why People Kill Themselves*.) Says Hendin: "Suicide among young blacks illustrates how distinctive psychosocial conditions shape the psychodynamics of suicide."

Though there are differences, the suicide-violence correlation extends to the white population, too. One such connection is evident in the instances where a murderer goes on to kill himself. There are no statistics that tell us with what frequency murder followed by suicide takes place in the U.S. Homicides and suicides are recorded separately, and accumulated national statistics do not provide a way to link the two.

However, Marvin Wolfgang's study of homicide in Philadelphia sheds some light on the matter. He discovered that whites made up one-fourth of all homicide offenders and one-half of the homicide-suicides (see Wolfgang's "An Analysis of Homicide-Suicide"). Around 8% of the homicides involving whites were murder-suicide. His figure of 8% represents a suicide rate for white murderers almost 700 times the national rate. As Hendin says, "it certainly dramatizes the point that suicide and murder are far from 'opposite types of adjustment.'"

In the Wolfgang study, men (both black and white) accounted for 83% of all homicide offenders but for over 90% of homicide-suicides. Ten of 53 husbands who killed their wives also killed themselves; only one of 47 wives did. The one form of homicide in which women outnumber men is in the killing of their children. Hendin points out that "child murder usually takes place in poor families with a history of prior child abuse involving the victim and other siblings. The assailants show prehomicidal behavior characterized by alcoholism, narcotic abuse and crime."

No national statistics are available that show the frequency with which child homicides are associated with parental suicide. One review (1969) of this phenomenon—some call it filicide—revealed that of 88 women who had committed murder, 42% did so in connection with either their own suicide or suicide attempt. This review, however, mixed cases in Europe and in the U.S. without distinguishing them, so the statistics cannot be assigned to America alone. Another study in Detroit by S. Myers ("The Child Slayer: A 25 Year Survey of Homicides Involving Preadolescent Victims") studied records of 71 people found guilty of preadolescent child murder. Twelve, or 17%, killed themselves as well. No data were given as to the sex or race of the murderers. In a survey of homicide in Denmark covering a 20-year period, Saverio Siciliano found that 35% of the killers were females; almost one-half of these women killed themselves subsequently. He discovered that 59% of those who killed their children later committed suicide. (Publ. in *La Scuola Positiva*, 4th ser. 3, 1961, 718-29.)

Hendin notes that of the few studies in the U.S. of child murder followed by a mother's suicide (or suicide attempt), most classify the mother's motive as "altruistic," that is, motivated by the perpetrator's concern for what would happen to the child when the killer is dead. He suggests that "a more complex mixture of attitudes toward children is involved."

In the expanding literature of research and speculation on the subject of suicide and homicide, some experts have chosen to combine Freud's psychological love-deprivation-and-aggression theory and Durkheim's social disorganization theory of suicide into the hypothesis that homicide and suicide are basically one and the same. This proposition holds that the two acts differ only in the object toward which the violence is directed. The theory goes like this: Where social relationships are strong, homicide rates are high and suicide rates low. Conversely, where social bonds are weak, suicide rates will usually exceed homicide rates. Some actuarial data supports this theory, some does not. Critics say the theory is flawed because it treats suicide and homicide as similar acts, and ignores differences in associated values and reactions of society, particularly the criminal aspect of homicide, which is missing in suicide.

As Hendin observes, "Suicide and violence toward others show many similarities even when they are not present in the same individual." He says hopelessness and desperation, for instance, are common to both. So, too, are difficulties in coping with frustration and loss, and in expressing aggression effectively.

Dr. Hendin sums up the complexities of the suicide-homicide correlation by explaining:

> It is necessary to understand violence in order to fully understand suicide, and necessary to understand suicide in order to fully understand violence. It is as important to see the suicidal intentions that may be hidden by homicide as to see the homicidal intentions that are concealed by suicide. Suicide can be used to check homicidal impulses that threaten to overwhelm the individual in ways more frightening than death. Suicidal intentions also may unleash and permit a homicide that would otherwise not take place.

It seems clear that no one theory, no one study or review, is sufficient as yet to explain fully the intricacies of the suicide-crime connection.

Crisis A journal published semi-annually by C.J. Hogrefe, Inc., 525 Eglinton Avenue East, Toronto, Ontario, Canada M4P 1S5. Full title is *Crisis: International Journal of Suicide and Crisis Studies*. Editor is Dr. Raymond Battegay, Psychiatrische Universitäsklinik, Kantonsspital, CH-4031 Basel. In the U.S., manuscripts may be submitted to Dr. Dan J. Lettieri, NIAAA, 5600 Fishers Lane, Rockville, MD 20857; Dr. Norman L. Farberow, Suicide Prevention Center, 1041 South Menlo, Los Angeles, CA 90025; or Dr. Robert E. Litman, 1823 Sawtelle Blvd., Los Angeles, CA 90025.

crying as communication Crying is considered a distress signal for the potentially suicidal, especially in cases where the person feels depressed and wants to be alone much of the time. Such persons will often withdraw from family and friends, lose their sense of humor, and may cry for no apparent reason—or for the most trivial reasons. Conversely, as Francine Klagsbrun points out in *Too Young to Die*, "when the depression becomes especially severe, they find themselves incapable of crying even when they want to."

Crying, then, is but another behavior trait—a clue, warning or distress signal—of the overly wrought, anxious, unhappy individual who probably exhibits a cluster of clues that may indicate the potentially suicidal. These suicide-prone persons, experts agree, need help immediately. And the help may come from understanding family and friends, from suicide prevention or crisis center personnel, or, as is often necessary, in the form of professional treatment by a trained psychiatrist, psychologist, social worker or physician aware of and sensitive to such conditions. (See also COMMUNICATION OF SUICIDAL INTENT.)

culture Dr. Jean La Fontaine, reader in social anthropology, London School of Economics and Political Science, writes in "Anthropology," chapter 4 of Perlin's *A Handbook for the Study of Suicide*:

> An important conclusion of the studies of suicide so far is the indication that the social factors involved are highly complex and involve basic cultural values: the goals held out by society as desirable and the means by which they are attained. Moreover, the social evaluation of success or failure and the degree to which responsibility for this is believed to rest with the individual are also elements in the complex. How deeply society holds the individual responsible for his own failure, either to achieve the ends expected of him or to conform to social norms, and whether there are alternative outlets and explanations available to the unconforming individual: these enter into the social situation of suicide. . . .

It would be folly, indeed, to try and understand even the simplest facts known about suicide or suicidal behavior and ignore differences in associated values, attitudes, myths and misconceptions and reactions of a particular society. For example, there are specific assumptions implicit in the way social scientists view suicide as a "social phenomenon." They contend that some suicide is "normal" in a country or a community. The TIV OF NIGERIA (believed to have the lowest incidence of suicide yet recorded), the ritualized handling of the elderly YUIT ESKIMO, the Trobriand sinners, all regard the act of suicide differently.

In the U.S., suicide is frequently associated with mental illness; in fact, it is too often considered "proof" of such derangement where, as La Fontaine notes, "none exists." Some researchers contend that roughly one-third of the suicides in America are later found to have been suffering from mental illness requiring psychiatric treatment. And most of the rest, according to this view, have unstable and vulnerable personalities.

Other societies, of course, have different and varied views. In some societies, as a case in point, madness would preclude the act of self-destruction, since only a "sane" individual is considered capable of the rational choice between life and death. As Dr. Jean La Fontaine says, "The assessment of individual suicides as victims of mental disease depends largely on the fact that our society holds and teaches certain views about it."

Moreover, similar outlooks or attitudes concerning suicide often differ within segments of a particular society. In Britain, and more recently in Australia and the U.S., there has been the gradual growth of a movement (see HEMLOCK SOCIETY) to allow legalized voluntary euthanasia for the elderly and incurably ill. This sociocultural phenomenon, along with the legalization of abortion, signifies attitude changes regarding the value of life and the individual's right to assume full responsibility for a life-ending decision of this sort. Self-immolation as a political protest (e.g., Peter Walker, a Canadian youth who had read the book *Craig and Joan*, and left a note saying, "So I guess I am like Joan and Craig and dying for peace and love") has brought veneration in some sections of certain societies from time to time. Another case in point: the suicidal acts by terrorist-fanatics in the Middle East, some of whom are Muslims—despite the KORAN decrying suicide as an act worse than homicide. Shiite Muslims believe that to die in a *Jihad*, or holy war, assures them of a place in Heaven.

As Dr. Jean La Fontaine concludes, "The collective representations through which individuals view suicide seem to have changed." The same could be said for the various world societies with their divergent cultures. Since the beginning of recorded history and man's discovery that he could kill himself as well as other living creatures, attitudes toward suicide have differed in various societies and cultures, and are generally linked with ideologies of death and afterlife. Cultural attitudes toward suicide seem to be as ambivalent and divided today as in ancient Greece and Rome. In recent times, there have been apologists for suicide even among the clergy. Prestigious philosophers and writers have defended man's right to end his own life, whereas eminent others have decried such a right with equal conviction.

Not a few authorities postulate that the "permissiveness" of modern society in general, which reflects a growing tolerance of deviant behavior, may be responsible, in part, for the rising suicide and suicide attempt rate. The various world societies appear to be less moralistic and punitive toward suicidal behavior today than, say, a generation ago. Whether or not this societal attitude implies a greater readiness to understand than condemn, a lack of value commitment, or merely general apathy, remains to be seen. Yet the tendency to conceal suicidal acts still prevails in most cultures, even though the reasons for this reaction are not the same as at those times in man's history when suicide, or even attempted suicide, was considered a crime and a sin.

Suicidal acts will continue to be committed, but the world's various societies and cultures will, it appears certain, view this peculiarly human problem in different ways and for different reasons.

Czechoslovakia The country has for some time had a high rate of suicide in spite of its predominantly Catholic population. The overall rate per 100,000 population for all ages in 1983 was 19.2%. Male suicides represented 29.5% of the total, females only 9.3%. In the various age groups, the 75 and older segment led others with a startling 54.5%. In the 25 to 34 age group, the incidence rate was 19.9% overall—32.1% male and 7.3% female. As high as the suicide rate in Czechoslovakia was in 1983, it was nowhere near the astonishing, world-leading rate in nearby Hungary, with its 45.9% rate total per 100,000 population. Asked about the fact that Hungary has for several years been the world's most suicide-prone nation, Dr. Geza Varady, director of the Institute for Mental Health in Budapest, told an interviewer: "The phenomenon reflects the Hungarian temperament, which is volatile and likes dramatic gestures." Many suicidologists contend that statistics such as the World Health Organization statistics used here do not say as much about national characteristics as they do about the way facts are gathered or covered up in the various reporting nations.

D

Dada Shortlived European literary and art movement (ca. 1916-22) that reflected disillusionment with all conventions and World War I. "Dada" is a word of French baby talk for anything to do with horses. The two founders of the movement were Richard Huelsenbeck, a German poet and medical student, and Hugo Ball, another German poet; some authorities say Tristan Tzara and the artist Hans Arp were the founders. Dada was representative of the extreme, violent and self-destructive impulse against *everything*, not simply against the establishment and the bourgeoisie which was the artists' audience, but also against art, even against Dada itself. The movement was a precursor to surrealism and subsequent radical art doctrines. Dada negated all formalism in art and produced "paintings" that were primarily collages made of such materials as newspaper bits, buttons and photographs.

A. ALVAREZ sums up the whole movement by saying that its reign "began with a suicide [Vache's], ended with one, and included others in its progress." He adds: "Like so many of the Dadaists, Dada died by its own hand." Jacques Rigaut, whose suicide in 1929 is thought by many to mark the end of the Dada era, said that "suicide is a vocation." Other Dadists who committed suicide included Arthur Craven and Jacques Vaché.

Dante Alighieri Perhaps the greatest of Italian poets (1265-1321). His chief work, one of the world's poetic masterpieces, is the *Commedia*, after his death called "Divina" (*The Divine Comedy*). For Dante, there appears to have been no recognition or acceptance of extenuating circumstances regarding suicide. In George Rosen's words: "Dante found the souls of suicides encased in thorny, withered trees on which the Harpies fed, inflicting wounds from which issued cries of lamentation and pain." Dante, indeed, put suicide in the Seventh Circle of Hell, below the heretics and the murders, to express his moralistic horror of suicide.

daredevils (as chronic suicides) Suicide is the number-three killer of young people; for those of college age, it is the second leading cause of death (having risen from fifth place in the early 1970s). Many suicidologists believe that suicide is actually the number-one killer of young people, that many homicide and accident victims are suicides "in disguise." Giffin writes of a recent study that revealed more than 25% of murder victims caused their own deaths by deliberate intimidation of another who carried a weapon. In one case, Dr. Giffin reports, a teenager who knew his gun was unloaded, brandished it at police officers, causing them to shoot him in self defense.

Dr. Karl Menninger calls them "chronic suicides": the daredevil type who shouts "Look, no hands" as he speeds on his motorcycle on a narrow road; the preteen boy, dressed in Superman cape, who jumps from the roof; or the thousands of adolescents slowly self-destructing with their dangerous abuse of drugs and alcohol.

Sigmund Freud, pioneer in the study of the unconscious mind, concluded that everyone has a desire to harm or even totally destroy him- or herself. Some people, because of their unfortunate life circumstances, are driven to suicide openly and consciously. Others seek more subtle means without comprehending why or what they are doing. Fortunately, most persons seem able to perceive the consequences of their self-destructive behavior and change direction. Most people, in fact, control these negative urges or impulses. But there are still far too many people, especially among the young, who either do not recognize their own self-destructiveness or deny it till it is too late. As one expert put it, "Their unconscious minds pump various excuses into their conscious thoughts." The latter group are the ones who drive too fast, drink excessively, smoke three packs a day, mix drugs and alcohol and play Russian Roulette with loaded guns. They are the "daredevils."

Some suicide experts suggest this as a possible cause of actor James Dean's death, at age 24, in a car accident on a lonely California highway. On September 30, 1955, Dean—a heavy drinker and drug user at the time—was driving at a reckless 85 mph in his silver Porsche on Highway 41 at Chalome, near Pasa Robles. He was en route to a sports car race at Salinas, when he smashed into another car. He was pronounced dead on arrival at the Pasa Robles Hospital. To compound the tragedy, some grief-stricken fans committed suicide. (See also CELEBRITY SUICIDES.)

databanks, bases Many, if not most, suicidologists seem to agree that all suicide theory—and even supposition—dependent upon official and suicide statistics is suspect per se. Jack Douglas, in *The Social Meanings of Suicide*, reveals five major forms of unreliability in the official statistics on suicide:

> (1) unreliability resulting from the choice of the official statistics to be used in making the test of the sociological theories; (2) unreliability resulting from subcultural differences in the attempts to hide suicide; (3) unreliability resulting from the effects of different degrees of social integration on the official statistics keeping; (4) unreliability resulting from significant variations in the social imputations of motives; (5) unreliability resulting from the more extensive and professionalized collection of statistics among certain populations.

Kurt Gorwitz, a sociologist and assistant director for research and analysis, Office of Health and Medical Affairs, the State of Michigan, in "Case Registers," a chapter of Perlin's *A Handbook for the Study of Suicide*, suggests as one answer to the problem, development of data banks on suicides and suicidal attempts and "the means of linking this information with other related systematic data collection systems."

Gorwitz notes that data banks are employed in many areas for a variety of purposes; thus terms can be defined in different ways. He explains:

> Here it is used interchangeably with case registers and refers to a record-keeping system in which certain information is submitted routinely to a central agency on each individual coming to the attention of a specified set of facilities, agencies, and professional personnel because of a defined illness, disability or action. Data on each reported episode of these individuals are linked longitudinally within this agency to form a cumulative record of their careers in this field.

Sociologist Gorwitz explains how case registers have served for years as an important resource for certain types of statistical analysis not available with traditional data collection procedures. He discusses how data banks were established in the late 19th and early 20th centuries as management tools in various communicable disease control programs. And how other health-related data banks in such fields as blindness, cancer, rheumatic fever and stroke are of more recent origin and function primarily for research purposes. He adds, "Several drug abuse registers have now been established."

Posing the question, "Must we be content with dubious suicide statistics and with even more questionable data on suicidal attempts?" Gorwitz suggests that "the level of present knowledge could be markedly improved and expanded by the maintenance of systematic data banks on suicides and suicidal attempts." He believes that:

> such case registers could provide data such as the number of persons attempting suicide in various population sub-groups during specified time periods, the probability and frequency of re-occurrence, and the proportion of suicide attempters who ultimately succeed in this endeavor. Linkage with comparable data from psychiatric case registers would provide continuing statistics on the numeric and sequential relationships between treated mental illnesses, attempted and completed suicides.

The state of Maryland has had such a register since 1961, and Gorwitz discusses it in detail, including the pluses and minuses. He then suggests sequential steps necessary to establish a suicide register. They are:

1. Administrative decision to develop such a register.
2. Key questions and decisions.
3. Contact of all possible respondents.
4. Determination of questionnaire form.
5. Development and maintenance of storage retrieval procedures.
6. Maintenance of continuing operations and goals.

In Gorwitz's view, "the Suicide Register should serve as an important research resource and as an important tool for program planning, administration and evaluation."

Kurt Gorwitz, "Case Registers," ch. 11 in *A Handbook for the Study of Suicide*, ed., Seymour Perlin (New York: Oxford University Press, 1975).

David of Augsburg During the whole of the medieval period, there was a growing recognition that mental and emotional disorder could lead to suicide. Such states, and their potential consequences, are often related to the concepts of melancholy or *acedia*, that is, spiritual sloth (to use a term of Dr. George Rosen, a medical historian). David of Augsburg, a Franciscan who lived during the middle of the 13th century, distinguished three types of *acedia*, according to Siegfried Wenzel:

> The first [he said] is a certain bitterness of the mind which cannot be pleased by anything cheerful or wholesome. It feeds upon disgust and loathes human intercourse. This is what the Apostle calls the sorrow of the world that worketh death. It inclines to despair, diffidence and suspicions, and sometimes drives its victim to suicide when he is oppressed by unreasonable grief. Such sorrow arises sometimes from previous impatience, sometimes from the fact that one's desire for some object has been delayed or frustrated, and sometimes from the abundance of melancholic humors, in which case it behooves the physician rather than the priest to prescribe a remedy.

George Rosen, "History," chapter 1 in Seymour Perlin's *A Handbook for the Study of Suicide* (New York and London: Oxford University Press, 1975).

The David of Augsburg quote is from: Siegfried Wenzel, *The Sin of Sloth, Acedia in Medieval Thought and Literature* (Chapel Hill: University of North Carolina, 1967), p. 160.

"A Day in the Life" There is little doubt that some young people who commit suicide lack a sense of their own mortality, a lack of understanding of death's finality. "In Loveland, U.S.A.: Study of Teenage Suicide," an ABC-TV "Directions" program (produced and written by Herbert Danska, December 13, 1981, second of a two-part series), the suicide of Peter Walker, a Canadian youth, is evidence of the vague notion some youngsters have concerning death.

Young Walker's suicide note, full of specific family instructions, requested that the Beatles' "A Day in the Life" be played during the funeral. The song is about a man who killed himself by blowing his brains out. It was as though Peter Walker, like Tom Sawyer, believed that he would be in attendance at his own funeral that next school day, that he'd be a hero to his classmates for staging such an "awesome" funeral. Several other young people's suicides have been tied to this Beatles' tune.

Dean, James B. As noted under DAREDEVILS (AS CHRONIC SUICIDES), the actor James Dean (1931-1955) was killed at age 24 when he was speeding along in his new silver Porsche Spyder spots car and slammed into another auto at an intersection. He died instantly. Some suicide authorities suggest that Dean's death might come under the heading of "chronic suicide," a term attributed to Dr. Karl Menninger, an ardent Freud follower and author of the book *Man Against Himself*.

Menninger interpreted most accidents to be the result of unconscious self-destructive drives. Recent studies indicate that suicidal fantasies and so-called "death wishes" do lie at the root of some traffic and other kinds of accidents. Many others appear to be related to brash, impulsive, spur-of-the-moment behavior—a "daredevil" defiance of fate that Dr. Menninger still considers as self-destructive or "chronic" suicide.

Actor James Dean, born in tiny Fairmont, Indiana, had a reputation as a sullen, unfriendly, moody person to those in power, a man who would not give ground if he thought he was right. His few close friends thought him warm and loyal. In an interview not long before his death, Dean is quoted as saying, "If a choice is in order, I'd rather have people hiss than yawn." At famed Chasen's restaurant, he often accompanied rude requests for service by table-banging and silver-clanging. He reputedly drank heavily and used drugs abusively at times. On the eve of his death, he had attended a party at Malibu, which had ended in a shouting match with another person.

Yet, Dean's sudden death touched off the greatest wave of posthumous hero worship in Hollywood since the untimely death of Rudolph Valentino. Some fans committed suicide. Many of his fans refused to accept his death. Today, over 30 years after his death, fan mail for Dean keeps arriving, mostly from teenagers across the country who identified with the troubled youngster, the man-boy anti-hero, played by the actor in *Rebel Without a Cause*.

Death by Choice Book by Roman Catholic theologian Daniel C. Maguire. He takes the position regarding the concept of death by choice that "Death by choice in a medical context is a difficult reality to the point where it must be treated and judged separately. My position is that, with suicide as with war, there are massive presumptions against its moral rightness."

Daniel C. Maguire, *Death by Choice* (Garden City: Image/Doubleday, 1984).

death certificates Some suicidologists are of the opinion that death certificates today simply do not provide enough, or the right kind of, data to be helpful to the field. Ronald Maris, writing in "Sociology," a chapter in Perlin's *A Handbook for the Study of Suicide*, says: "Even more accurate and complete death certificates do not provide enough nor the right kind of data; they do not help us to assess the development of suicide."

As an example, accurate estimates correlating suicides (and the risk of suicide) with religious affiliation cannot be easily obtained since religion is not recorded on death certificates (see Dublin's *Suicide*). Yet religious affiliation is known to affect a person's risk of suicide.

In addition, Gorwitz suggests that suicide statistics are "grossly understated based on cause-of-death certification." Suicide statistics, it seems, are much more unreliable than those for less controversial suicide, especially in small towns or communities where coroners are also personal physicians for members of the community. Dublin suggests in *Suicide: A Sociological and Statistical Study* that the recorded suicide figures are understated by as much as one-fourth to one-third. Unfortunately, suicide data are sometimes quoted without either qualification or recognition of the incomplete nature of death certificate information.

The LOS ANGELES SUICIDE PREVENTION CENTER (LASPC) and the Los Angeles Medical Examiner-Coroners' Office joined forces in 1957 to furnish coroners' death certificates the stamp of scientific authority "within the limits of practical certainties imposed by the state of the art." As a result, selected cases involving "sudden, unnatural death" that were equivocal (among suicide and other methods of death) were then referred by the medical examiner-coroner to the LASPC with a request for a "psychological autopsy." The latter is when a team from LASPC helps coroners determine the cause of death when it has not been clearly indicated. After the psychological autopsy, in joint consultation, the mode of death is decided and a proper title for the death is entered on the death certificate. (See also PSYCHOLOGICAL AUTOPSY.)

death education In the past decade schools across the country have begun to offer courses on death and dying. According to author Fergus M. Bordewich, in "Mortal Fears" (*The Atlantic*, February 1988): "Thousands of schools are involved." He adds, "However, the actual number isn't known, both because death education is a relatively new phenomenon and because it is often presented as a part of more-traditional courses."

Proponents of death education say it is beneficial and long overdue. Critics, on the other hand, claim such courses are often introduced haphazardly by unqualified teachers and point to cases of negative, damaging end results as information impacts upon young people. In fact, says Bordewich, "The suicides of former death-education students in Missouri and Illinois, and the traumatic reactions of others . . . have generated increasing criticism of death education."

Conservatives complain, according to Bordewich, that the practice "arrogates to itself the prerogatives of home and church . . ." In Oklahoma, conservative legislators tried unsuccessfully to introduce a bill that would ban death education altogether. Says Bordewich, "Less ideological critics worry that in the hands of unskilled and overenthusiastic teachers, death education may in fact inspire more anxiety, depression, and fear than it reduces."

Some schools have asked students taking such courses to write their own obituaries, their own epitaphs, or even to visit funeral homes and crematoria. Others have had students lie down in empty coffins, plan their own funeral services, and attend death education classes held in cemeteries.

There is a relatively new organization called the Association for Death Education and Counseling that offers a certification program. Only about a hundred people, according to Bordewich, have passed through the four-year-old program. He writes: "Serious thanatologists believe that if death education is to become a truly meaningful part of school curricula, it must be standardized and professionalized." Austin Kutscher, president of the Foundation of Thanatology, feels that no school should introduce a death education program until it has planned the course with help from sociologists, psychologists, or counselors and until the school's parent-teacher association has given its approval.

Finally, Fergus M. Bordewich writes, "In the classroom, death education seems often to consist in a pop-psychology approach to life and death which avoids a serious examination of its own effects."

Fergus M. Bordewich, "Mortal Fears," *The Atlantic* (February 1988), 30-34.

Death of Peregrinis, The An essay written by Greek satirist Lucian after he personally witnessed the fiery death by immolation of Peregrinis Proteus, a Cynic philosopher. Peregrinis, who early in his life left home under suspicion of having strangled his wealthy father to get his hands on the family fortune (it was never actually proven), in 165 A.D. ended his restless, wandering life before a large crowd at the Olympic festival by cremating himself on a pyre in the Indian manner. Peregrinis instructed his disciples to establish a cult in his honor after his death; this was done in his native town of Parium, on the Hellespont. It is said that the statue set up in his honor worked miracles and attracted many pilgrims.

Historian George Rosen suggests that "Perhaps his (Peregrinis's) last words provide a clue to his personality and behavior. Just before jumping into the fire, he exclaimed: 'Gods of my mother, gods of my father, receive me with favor.'"

As Dr. Rosen notes in "History," chapter one of Perlin's *A Handbook for the Study of Suicide*: "The time of Peregrinis was a period of sick souls, when many were filled with contempt for the human condition, felt themselves to be aliens in this world, and asked the question, 'What are we here for?'" SENECA (ca. 5 B.C.-65 A.D.) in his *Epistles* says that a desire possessed many, a longing for death. EPICTETUS (ca. 50-120 A.D.) also noted this death wish among young men and tried to restrain it by urging them not to commit suicide.

Epictetus, *The Discourses as Reported by Arrian, The Manual and Fragments*, 2 vols. trans. W.A. Oldfather. (Cambridge, Mass.: Loeb Classical Library/Harvard University Press [1954-64]; 2:10-11, 28-29, 288-89.)

death wish (as suicide clue) Psychiatrist DR. HERBERT HENDIN says that students he interviewed at Columbia University during the 1970s (for his book, *The Age of Sensation*) "were drawn to death as a way of life." Suicidal adolescents will often seem to have a "death wish." They amble across busy streets, speed around icy corners on motorbikes, and mix drugs and alcohol without knowledge of their synergistic effect. Other suicidal behavioral hints sometimes include repeated auto accidents, driving bicycles into stationary objects, and picking fights with bigger youngsters and sometimes even with policemen.

This kind of attitude reflects an abnormal preoccupation with death and usually means the person is trying to send parents or significant others a message. Talcott Parsons and Victor Lidz, in "Death in American Society" (see *Essays in Self-Destruction*, ed. Edwin S. Shneidman) say that:

> It has become almost commonplace that most, if not all, individuals have "death wishes" directed at both "significant others" and themselves. Hence suicide, regarded as a consciously deliberate act, must be considered as the limiting case along a common and deeply grounded range of variations—the case in which death wishes for oneself (e.g., Freud's famous *Thanatos*) gain full ascendancy over one's personality.

As Shneidman notes, "Almost everyone who seriously intends suicide leaves clues to his imminent action. Sometimes there are broad hints; sometimes only subtle changes in behavior. But the suicide decision is usually not impulsive."

death with dignity See EUTHANASIA.

Decalogue Article The Decalogue, or Ten Commandments, was the primary source for Augustine's denouncement of the act of suicide (at the time there was no official Catholic Church position on suicide). He asserted that the act could not be condoned, even in the case of a woman whose honor was endangered, because "suicide is an act which precluded the possibility of repentance, and it is a form of homicide and thus a violation of the Decalogue Article, 'Thou shalt not kill.'"

Deerhunter, The A 1981 film about Vietnam (later aired on television) that contains a realistic scene depicting U.S. soldiers and Vietnamese playing Russian roulette with a loaded pistol. There were reports of people (most were young males in their teens and early twenties) shooting themselves in the head within a few days of watching the movie. Dr. Thomas Radecki, a psychiatrist from Illinois, presented to local television station managers evidence of 27 documented cases of self-inflicted wounds (24 people died from their wounds) in an attempt to pressure the managers into either cancelling the movie or cutting the Russian roulette scene. No stations took his warning seriously and several shooting events followed in New York, Washington and Chicago.

On October 21, 1981, Dr. Radecki, testifying before a congressional committee investigating television violence, stated: "I can comfortably estimate that 25-50% of the violence in our society is coming from the culture of violence being taught by our entertainment media, most strongly by the television and movie industries. This estimate is based on solid research findings."

definition of suicide The word "suicide" translates literally from its Latin origin: *sui*, "of oneself," plus *cide*, "a killing," becomes to kill oneself. However, the many professionals—suicidologists, philosophers, researchers, medical and social scientists—who have studied and written about the phenomenon of suicide have still to satisfactorily define the term. Most of those in the field agree that, in psychologist John L. McIntosh's words, the definition of the term is more than simply "a philosophical question." For how the word itself is defined, concludes McIntosh, "has implications and large effects for statistics that are compiled on the official number of suicides, and for researchers, so that there is a clear communication regarding what and who is being studied."

In fact, scores of definitions have been employed by writers in the field of suicidology. Some definitions are determined by the individual's theoretical orientation, others by the specific phenomena being studied. Also, the term may refer not to a single action, but rather to a variety of behaviors. There are, for example, suicidal wishes, thoughts, intentions, ideation, gestures, attempts, completions, equivalents. Moreover, as McIntosh notes, the term is sometimes classified by various schemes (e.g., Edwin Shneidman's degrees of intention and Norman L. Farberow's continuum of direct-indirect). Then there are terms such as "partial," "cessation," "deliberate self-harm," "life-threatening behavior" and "self-destructive," all of which are either used originally or quoted in this and other works concerning suicide.

Thus far, as McIntosh suggests, no single term, definition or taxonomy yet serves sufficiently to represent what he deems "the complex set of behaviors that have been suggested as suicidal." Most authorities seem to agree that the definition of just what constitutes a suicidal act is a must for satisfactory suicide statistics . . . because data that rely on differing concepts and/or definitions of suicide are not strictly comparable. "A standard set of terms and definitions," says McIntosh, "are greatly needed to advance the science of suicidology and aid communication and understanding of the field."

John L. McIntosh, *Research on Suicide: A Bibliography* (Westport, Connecticut: Greenwood Press, 1985).

Definition of Suicide Written by Edwin Shneidman, PhD, professor of thanatology at the UCLA School of Medicine, and published in 1986 by John Wiley & Sons. Dr. Shneidman's book presents an original set of 10 characteristics common in suicide. He provides detailed explanations of these "Ten Commandments of Suicide" that together offer an intimate portrait of the suicidal person's emotions, thoughts, internal attitudes, desires, actions and inner stresses.

The author, cofounder and formerly co-director, with Dr. Norman L. Farberow, of the Los Angeles Suicide Prevention Center, uses examples of actual suicide to construct a deeper, clearer understanding of the driving forces behind the act itself. Dr. Shneidman draws valuable lessons from literature, philosophy, psychology and systems theory, illustrating the lessons with the classics of Herman Melville, Stephen C. Pepper, Henry A. Murray and James G. Miller.

Definition of Suicide is considered by authorities as both a major theoretical treatment of self-destruction and a practical first-aid manual and guide for preventing suicidal deaths. Shneidman, charter director of the Center for the Study of Suicide Prevention at the National Institute of Mental Health in Bethesda, Maryland, is also author of *Death of Man* (1973, nominated for a National Book Award) and *Voices of Death* (1980), plus over 150 articles and chapters on suicide in various publications, journals and essay anthologies.

"Dejection: An Ode" Written by Samuel Taylor Coleridge in 1802, this autobiographic poem resulted from his unhappy love for Wordsworth's sister-in-law, Sarah Hutchinson. It is an intensely moving confession of his poetic sterility, a recognition of the death of his creativity as a kind of suicide. A. ALVAREZ, in an essay adapted and abridged from *The Savage God: A Study of Suicide*, wrote: "That he [Coleridge] recognized this as a form of suicide, I think, certain, if for no other reason than that the passage reworks a theme from his 'Monody on the Death of Chatterton,' a poem that was apparently on his mind for years." In fact, according to Alvarez, in the last additions to the final version of "Dejection: An Ode," Coleridge admitted his own temptation to commit suicide. Alvarez adds that "Coleridge's symbolic suicide—creative death by opium—was to become one of the Romantic alternatives for those fated not to die prematurely . . ."

delle Vigne, Pier Longtime chief counselor (1190-1249) of Emperor Friedrich II Hohenstaufen. According to Dr. George Rosen, a professor of the history of medicine at Yale, Piere delle Vigne was accused of treachery by conspiring against his lord in 1247 and was imprisoned and blinded. In despair, and to avoid further torture, delle Vigne took his own life. His suicide is significant in history primarily because it is the one suicide to which DANTE (who seemed unable or unwilling to recognize any extenuating circumstances where self-destruction was involved) refers specifically. Dante, in fact, actually talked with Pier delle Vigne, quite a concession for a person who found the souls of suicides "encased in thorny, withered trees on which the Harpies fed . . ."

George Rosen, "History," in Dr. Seymour Perlin's *A Handbook for the Study of Suicide* (Oxford University Press, 1975), p. 15.

Demosthenes Athenian orator (384?-322 B.C.), one of the greatest of all time. He based his political career on enmity against the Macedonians. He was ultimately exiled (in 324) on charges of financial corruption brought by the pro-Macedonian faction in Athens. Returning in 323, after the death of Alexander the Great, Demosthenes organized an unsuccessful revolt and took poison while fleeing Antipater, who captured Athens in 322 B.C. Demosthenes's end came in the famed temple of Poseidon. In committing suicide, the great Greek orator joined the company of some of the ancient world's most distinguished men.

Denmark Dr. Mary Monk's chapter on epidemiology in Perlin's *A Handbook for the Study of Suicide* states that: "Suicide rates for many foreign countries are available in annual reports published by the World Health Organization." High rates are reported in Denmark, Sweden and Austria, lower rates in the U.S., England and France, and the lowest rates in Ireland, Italy and Spain.

Monk, professor of community and preventive medicine, New York Medical College, explains that on investigating psychodynamic reasons for high rates in Sweden and Denmark but low rates in Norway, Hendin found different dynamics emphasized in the three Scandinavian countries that he felt might be at least partly responsible.

Latest figures available (1984) from the World Health Organization on Denmark show a slight percentage increase over 1983, from 28.6 to 28.7 suicides per 100,000 population. This is down, however, from the 1980 high of 31.6 per 100,000 population. Interestingly, the female suicide rate rose between 1983 and 1984 from 20.4 to 21.0 (per 100,000) while the male rate dropped slightly from 37.0 to 36.5 per 100,000 population. Highest suicide rate by age group for males was age 75 and over (67.3), for females it was the 45 to 54 age grouping (41.1). Among the 15- to 24-year-olds, the male rate was 16.1 per 100,000 population, and for females only 4.1.

dentists As far back as the 1920s there was a widely held belief that dentists were in an unhealthy profession—too much stress—and that they were committing suicide at a rate greater than other professionals and the general population.

In 1956, the American Dental Association (ADA) did a "Study on Dentist Mortality," and reported more suicides among white male dentists than among the general white male population—though the difference was not significant statistically. But this was followed in 1963 by an article in the *New England Journal of Medicine* that provided "scientific proof" of high dentist suicide rates. The piece, "Suicide in Professional Groups," by P.H. Blachly, H.T. Osterud and R. Josslin, compared suicides in several occupations from 1950 to 1961 in Oregon. The study indicated that dentists and attorneys committed suicide at a rate three times greater than other white-collar workers. Specific average suicide rates over 100,000 persons per group per year, 1950 to 1961, were, according to the study: physicians, 30.29; dentists, 62.03; attorneys, 53.18; engineers, 28.67; male teachers, 19.50; female teachers, 4.33; white-collar workers, 15.7; and laborers, 39.0.

Another article frequently cited in support of high suicide risks for dentists appeared in 1966, F.L. Glass's *Mortality of New England Dentists 1921-1960*, published as "US Public Health Service Publication, November 999-RH-18." This study compared all white male dentists practicing in New England in the period from 1921 to 1960 with the general population, with the white male population and with white male physicians. Except for two periods (1921 to 1925 and 1931 to 1935) dentist suicides were greater than those for the entire male population. Dentist suicide rates were not, however, statistically different from those for white male physicians.

Seven years later, in 1973, a study of physician suicides in California reported that dentist suicides were exceeded only by those of chemists and pharmacists.

More recently, in 1976, G. Orner and R.D. Mumma of Temple University's School of Dentistry completed a *Mortality Study of Dentists*. In their massive and comprehensive work on dentists' suicides, the authors disagreed with and refuted the conclusions of previous studies. Orner and Mumma concluded that dentists had "lower cause-specific death rates for all causes," including suicides. Their research included dentists across the U.S. and compared this data to cohort groups in the general white male population. The study investigated both ADA and non-ADA dentists and dentist suicides over a six-year period, 1960 to 1965.

Considerable expertise is required to interpret the significance of differing dentist suicide rates reflected in the various studies done over the years. But it now seems safe to say that there is little or no basis for concluding that dentists are more likely to kill themselves than other comparable professional group members. The body of data in the Temple study incidates that dentists across the board are generally a rather healthy group.

G. Orner and R.D. Mumma, *Mortality Study of Dentists* (Philadelphia: Temple University School of Dentistry, 1976).

depression Roughly one-half of all suicides each year in the U.S. are said to be victims of depression. People have recognized the existence of the condition we now know as depression since ancient times, indeed, as far back as the early Egyptians. The Old Testament refers to this disorder; King Saul, for instance, suffered from a severe recurrent depression. While attitudes and theories have changed, medical descriptions of this universal ailment have remained somewhat the same through the years.

There was a time when suicide clinicians linked the act of self-destruction almost exclusively to depression. But this failed to explain why patients often kill themselves after depression has lifted. Yet experts estimate that the risk of a depressed person committing suicide is about 50 times higher than for a person who is not depressed. Jack D. Douglas, PhD, author of *The Social Meanings of Suicide* (1967), explains the personality theory of suicide (which stresses the differences between the suicidal and nonsuicidal person): "Motivations are the most frequently cited differences, and the desire to escape depression is the most frequently cited motivation." While he concedes that depression is common among those who commit suicide, Douglas cautions: "Disagreement exists, however, on whether the depression results from events outside the person, especially a social situation leading to loneliness or failure, or is organic in origin."

The simple truth is: No one theory can account for the many and varied forms of suicidal behavior. Certainly not all severely depressed persons commit suicide; nor do all those who kill themselves suffer from depression. But depression is a warning sign that should not be ignored. It ranks high on the list of predisposing factors for suicidal behavior. Erwin Stengel, who has specialized in the study of the social effects of suicidal attempts, perhaps sums it up best: "Among the mental disorders, depressive illness carries the highest suicidal risk. A feeling of worthlessness and despair and a wish to die belong to the clinical picture of this illness, but even in this condition, the urge to commit suicide varies."

The problem of suicide, in one way or another, seems to cut across all known diagnoses—or, more correctly, all symptoms.

Finally, since the risk of a severely depressed person committing suicide is so pronounced, it is essential to recognize the signs of depression (so as to be in a position to save someone from suffering, or even from self-destruction). Some of the many warning signals depressed people usually exhibit, admittedly in varying degrees, are: sadness (prevailing mood), glumness, apathy, expression of feeling empty and numb, inability to enjoy anything, attitude of pessimism and hopelessness, feelings of worthlessness, guilt and anxiety, indecisiveness (even on unimportant matters), difficulty in concentrating or remembering things, and, often, preoccupation with suicidal thoughts. Other warning signs include persistent sadness, withdrawal, uncommunicativeness, physical complaints such as headaches, stomachaches, insomnia, fatigue and, at times, aggressive behavior. There is more often than not a decline in sexual drive as well.

Scientists today believe that biochemical abnormalities that result in changes in a person's body chemistry play a key role in the development of depression, or may be the product of depression. Yet biochemical abnormality is but one of many variables that may be the cause of depression. It is now thought that genetic factors may also be involved and responsible to an unknown extent.

Erwin Stengel, *Suicide and Attempted Suicide*, rev. ed. (New York: Jason Aronson, 1974).
Jack D. Douglas, *The Social Meanings of Suicide* (Princeton: Princeton University Press, 1967).

derivation (of the word "suicide") Dr. Norman L. Farberow, co-author of this work and co-founder and co-director, the LOS ANGELES SUICIDE PREVENTION CENTER, writes in *Suicide in Different Cultures* that:

> one possible derivation is the word "suist," meaning a selfish man, and "suism," meaning selfishness. In 1671, the third edition of Phillips' *New World of Words* protested against the word "suicide." The index to Jackson's *Works*, published two years later in 1673, used the word "suicidium." However, the *Oxford Dictionary* states that suicide was first used in English in 1651, just six years after Donne's *BIATHANATOS*, and is derived from the modern Latin "suicidium," which in turn stems from the Latin pronoun "sui," for "self," and verb "cide," "to kill."

Thus, in a strictly etymological sense, it was not possible to commit "suicide" until about the mid-1600s. As Edwin Shneidman says in his *Definition of Suicide* (1985), "One could, of course, do harm to oneself, starve oneself to death, throw oneself upon one's sword or off one's roof or into one's well—but one could not 'commit suicide.' The word, and with it the basic concept of suicide, did not exist." (See also DEFINITION OF SUICIDE.)

despair Exactly what is despair? And how is it different from depression?

According to J.P. Chaplin's *Dictionary of Psychology*, depression is:

> 1. in the normal individual, a state of despondency characterized by feelings of inadequacy, lowered activity, and pessimism about the future. 2. in pathological cases, an extreme state of unresponsiveness to stimuli, together with self-depreciation, delusions of inadequacy, and hopelessness.

Despair, not a medical term, is defined by Webster's New World Dictionary (Prentice Hall, 1986) as "1. a despairing; loss of hope 2. a person or thing despaired of or causing despair."

Kierkegaard, in his *Journals*, wrote:

> The whole age (i.e., the Romantic period in the arts) can be divided into those who write and those who do not write. Those who write represent despair, and those who read disapprove of it and believe that they have a superior wisdom—and yet, if they were able to write, they would write the same thing. Basically they are all equally despairing, but when one does not have the opportunity to become important with his despair, then it is hardly worth the trouble to despair and show it. Is this what it is to have conquered despair?

As A. ALVAREZ has noted, despair was for Soren Kierkegaard what grace was for the Puritans, a sign of "spiritual potentiality." The Danish religious thinker and philosopher rejected all orthodox religion, philosophy and science, holding instead that truth can be attained only by a tragic, pessimistic, soul-searching individualism.

Richard Brandt, PhD, chairman of the department of philosophy, University of Michigan, in his chapter, "The Morality and

Rationality of Suicide," in Perlin's book, notes that:

> many suicides seem to occur in moments of despair. What should be clear . . . is that a moment of despair, if one is seriously contemplating suicide, ought to be a moment of reassessment of one's goals and values, a reassessment which the individual must realize is very difficult to make objectively because of the very quality of his depressed frame of mind.

If, as many experts contend, suicide is the mortality of depressive illness, certainly despair is an accompanying factor or response.

diabetes There have been cases where diabetes victims consistently "forgot" to take their medication and, as a result, became dangerously sick. Complications from such destructive behavior have even led to diabetics' death. In such situations, people seldom think to connect the self-destructive behavior directly to suicide. They are simply, tragically, examples of the kind of "uncounted suicides" described by DR. KARL MENNINGER—the so-called "chronic suicide." Menninger, in *MAN AGAINST HIMSELF* (1938), describes and interprets for readers the many self-destructive acts in which people engage. He separates suicides into three categories: chronic, organic and focal. In the case of a diabetic who deliberately "forgot" his medication, became dangerously ill and died, death would seem to fall within both the chronic and organic categories. (Organic suicide, to Menninger, results when the death wish is expressed by means of a physical illness such as diabetes.)

dialysis, self-destructive behavior in patients There have sometimes been instances of indirect self-destructive behavior in chronic hemodialysis patients, including self-mutilation (what Dr. Menninger categorizes as "focal" suicide, in which there is self-mutilation and/or multiple accidents). For further information, read: H.S. Abram, G.L. Moore and F.B. Westervalt, Jr., "Suicidal Behavior in Chronic Dialysis Patients"; also K.E. Gerber, A.M. Nehemkis, N.L. Farberow and J. Williams, "Indirect Self-destructive Behavior in Chronic Hemodialysis Patients."

DiMaio, Dr. Dominick Former medical examiner for New York City. When asked about the number of unreported suicides and the lengths to which people will go to hide a suicide, DiMaio told DR. MARY GIFFIN and Carol Felsenthal (co-authors, *A Cry for Help*, 1983): "Families sometimes will tell you all kinds of stories to make a suicide look like an accident. A kid blows his brains out with a gun, or jumps off a building. The parents come in and tell us he was playing Russian roulette, or that he slipped while playing on the roof."

Unfortunately, even in today's nearly taboo-free times, the suicide stigma is still too shattering for some families, so much so that coroners and medical examiners will frequently play the dread game and agree to disguise the truth. Most experts seem to agree that the actual number of suicides is, at the very least, twice what is reported in the U.S.

Diogenes Greek philosopher (?412 B.C.-323 B.C.), principal exponent of the Cynic school of philosophy. He held that happiness consisted in the satisfaction of one's basic needs and decried the pursuit of wealth or success. His view concerning suicide was that "the wise man will for reasonable cause make his own exit [*exagoge*] from life on his country's behalf, or for the sake of his friends, or if he suffers intolerable pain, mutilation, or incurable disease." (See Diogenes Laertius's *Lives of Eminent Philosophers*, 2:235.)

It was Diogenes who, seeing that Antisthenes was overcome by a distaste for life, offered a dagger to his friend and said:

"Perhaps you have a need of this friend?" Antisthenes replied: "I thank you, but unfortunately, the will to live is also part of the world's evil, as it is part of our nature."

direct and indirect self-destructive behavior John L. McIntosh points out in *Research on Suicide: A Bibliography* (1985) that a recently discussed comparison study in the field of suicidology involves direct vs. indirect self-destructive behavior (ISDB). For a further, insightful look at such a comparison, see *The Many Faces of Suicide: Indirect Self-Destructive Behavior*, edited by Farberow. This valuable contribution includes 26 chapters that deal with different aspects of ISDB.

Both classifications end in death, it's true, but direct suicide death is, in Professor McIntosh's words, "quick and more obviously what has traditionally been termed 'suicide.'" Whereas, with ISDB, writes McIntosh, "we consider slow forms of suicide which hasten death, but are not clearly what is usually meant by the word 'suicide.'" ISDB examples might include: overeating and chronic obesity, smoking, alcoholism or other drug overuse or abuse, risk-taking, accident proneness, and not adhering to behavior regimens that would sustain and/or prolong health and life. The various chapters in the Farberow book consider these and other ISDBs.

To date, experts have failed in their efforts to come up with a term, definition or classification that satisfactorily covers the complex grouping of behaviors that have been put forth as "suicidal." Writes McIntosh, author of a number of books on the subject, "A standard set of terms and definitions are greatly needed to advance the science of suicidology and aid communication and understanding of the field."

"Discovery" An ABC television program that focused on suicide, specifically that of a boy named Mark Cada who took his own life. The program presented several viewpoints and opinions, one of which reinforced the notion that a young person's view of death usually, if not always, includes the belief that after death, he or she will remain behind in some way, hovering about invisibly to relish the parents' grief. One of Mark's friends, who admitted to contemplating suicide, explained, "I think about really getting back at 'em. It's like you have nothing you can really hit 'em below the belt with, so go for it all." The two-part program was produced in 1981.

Disease Control, Centers For The CDC is one of six agencies of the U.S. Public Health Service. It is responsible for surveillance and control of communicable and victim-borne diseases, occupational safety and health, family planning, birth defects, lead-based paint poisoning, urban rat control, and health education. The Centers deal with programs that include tracking, combatting and publicizing epidemic and disease outbreaks, foreign travel (making health recommendations and setting forth requirements), surveillance of international health activities, training of foreign health workers, etc. The CDC will provide references, background materials and photographics on communicable diseases and other subjects, such as suicide.

Publications include *The Morbidity and Mortality Weekly Report* and *Surveillance Reports*. Mailing lists are maintained and anyone may request these publications. Lucy Davidson, MD, medical epidemiologist, Violence Epidemiology Branch, Center for Health Promotion and Education, is the person to contact on matters concerning the subject of suicide. Write to Dr. Davidson at: Centers for Disease Control, 1600 Clifton Road, N.E., 3-SSB30, Atlanta, GA 30333; telephone is: (404) 329-3521.

distress centres (Canada) Canada, like the U.S., has a nationwide network of suicide hotlines; metropolitan Toronto alone has nine in its area. Distress centres, the Canadian term for suicide hotlines, nearly always have telephone numbers listed on the inside front cover of the local phone book, along with other emergency numbers. If no phone book is available, one can simply dial "O." Operators have numbers for crisis services of all kinds, including suicide prevention. In larger population centers of Canada, as in the U.S., one can also dial 911 for emergency services.

Canada suicide prevention services are also available to anyone at Salvation Army agencies and at branches of the SAMARITANS and Contact (in Canada, called TELE-CARE). Check the front of local phone directories or the white pages under those names. In addition, there are Canadian Mental Health Association (CMHA) branches throughout the country, including the remote Northwest Territories and the Yukon Territory.

Researchers, scholars, educators and suicide professionals will find that the Suicide Information and Education Centre (SIEC), which is international in scope, has a comprehensive data bank of articles, newspaper and magazine clippings, books, films, cassettes, etc., about suicide. Contact: SIEC, Suite No. 201, Attn: Karen Kiddey, Information Officer, 1615 10th Avenue S.W., Calgary, Alberta, Canada T3C OJ7; telephone is: (403) 245-3900.

distress signals DR. EDWIN S. SHNEIDMAN contends that almost everyone who seriously intends suicide leaves clues to his or her imminent action. "Sometimes there are broad hints," says Shneidman, "sometimes only subtle changes in behavior. But the suicide decision is usually *not* impulsive. Most often, it is premeditated." Called risk factors, early-warning clues or distress signals, these changes of behavior represent very important signs to trained suicide prevention authorities. (These vital symptoms are discussed fully under the listing CLUES.) While any one of the noted symptoms probably is not critical, a combination of several requires immediate attention.

divorce The aftermath of any divorce may result in one or more individual self-images getting shattered to the point of what DR. MARY GIFFIN calls "terminal weakness." The battered person may be either or both of the adult victims of divorce, or their children.

The U.S. currently, and unfortunately, has the highest divorce rate in the world, about one divorce for every two marriages. A look at the statistics for divorce and teen suicide reveals a numbing parallel. As Giffin notes in *A Cry for Help* (co-authored with Carol Felsenthal): "In the last twenty years in the U.S., both the number of divorces granted and the number of young suicides committed have tripled."

A number of reliable studies indicate that most young suicides are children of divorce. In one recent study, reported by Dr. Giffin, 71% of young suicide "attempters" came from broken homes. Dr. Joseph D. Teicher, University of Southern California director of adolescent psychiatric services, conducted research on young suicides in Los Angeles County. He found that:

- 72% had one or both natural parents absent from home;
- 84% of those with stepparents wanted them to leave;
- 58% had a parent who had been married more than once.

Similarly, a Bellevue Hospital (New York City) study showed that of 102 teenagers who attempted suicide, two-thirds of them lived with only one (or neither) parent.

Dr. Giffin notes, too, that psychiatrist Barry Garfinkel, Hospital for Sick Children, Toronto, studied family backgrounds of 505 young suicide attempters treated over a seven-year period. Garfinkel compared their family lives with a control group of young people admitted to the same emergency room for non-suicide-related reasons. More than half of the families of the suicide attempters had an absent parent, while in one quarter of these families, *both* parents were absent.

For adolescents, many experts believe divorce is more difficult to accept than death. Says Giffin, "Death is final—an irrevocable separation. Divorce means torturous memories lingering for years, the beloved parent dropping in and out of a child's life, and the child's terrible fear that he was somehow responsible for the split; that if his parents really loved him, they would have stayed together."

As for adults, the French social philosopher EMILE DURKHEIM, in his definitive work, *Le Suicide*, concluded that the suicide rate varies inversely with the integration of social groups of which the individual forms a part. His collected data on suicide showed, among many other findings, that the suicide rates of the unmarried, and especially the divorced, exceed the rates of the married. Most general correlations seem to agree with the conclusion that the single, the divorced, and the widowed have a higher rate of suicide than married individuals. For example, the state of Nevada has the dubious distinction of ranking highest in the U.S. in both the suicide deaths and divorce rate categories (1980 federal government sources). New Jersey, on the other hand, ranks 44th among our fifty states in divorce rate and 50th in deaths by suicide.

Durkheim used the term ANOMIC SUICIDE to describe that category when a person experiences a sudden and great change in fortune or position in society. He used the term also to describe entire societies wherein social institutions, such as the family, have changed or broken down so abruptly and quickly that people affected often are confused about their positions and goals. As one might expect, suicide rates in such societies are considerably higher than in more rigid ones in which each individual knows his or her role in life.

doctors Among professional disciplines, physicians have one of the higher rates of suicide. In Great Britain, according to John May, editor of *Curious Facts*, women doctors are six times more likely to commit suicide than other women, while male doctors kill themselves at twice the average rate for men. Writes May, "The reason is thought to lie in the stress of the job combined with easy access to, and familiarity with, deadly drugs." In *Kicking the Bucket*, co-authors Kim Long and Terry Reim state that "suicide claims more than 25% of all deaths for doctors under the age of forty, with the preferred method being hanging."

Rose and Rosow, in a computerized study in California of over 200,000 deaths, showed that physicians *and* health-care workers are twice as suicide prone as the general population.

Suicide rates derived from data provided by and presented in the *Journal of the American Medical Association* (JAMA) indicate more than 100 physician suicides a year, according to Scheiber and Doyle. That is equivalent to the size of an average graduating class of medical students. The authors note, in *The Impaired Physician*, that:

> Again, these figures under-represent the true rates since they are dependent on other sources reporting the causes of death. In studying these statistics, Blachly *et al.* found that there were more deaths by suicide than by other violent means. It is well known that many coroners conceal suicides by physicians reporting only the presumed pathophysiological, e.g., cardiac arrest or pulmonary failure.

Psychiatrist-teachers Stephen C. Scheiber and Brian B. Doyle report that studies of suicide in physicians indicate the male rate is

1.15 times greater than the expected male population rate. For female physicians the rate is three times greater than the expected rate of the female population. In the over-45 age group, there is "a marked excess in expected rate." In the 25 to 39 age group, 26% of all physician deaths are attributed to suicide.

The two psychiatrists suggest that "many 'accidental' deaths, such as one-car accidents, solo-flight airplane accidents, and drownings, are suicides, but are not recognized or reported as such."

The American Medical Association, The American Medical Student Association and The American Psychiatric Association all recognize the growing seriousness of this problem and submit that suicide prevention and intervention programs are now urgently needed among physicians. These organizations have established special task forces and committees to deal with the problem of suicide and suicide attempts by member-colleagues.

Dominican Republic Latest World Health Organization (WHO) statistics available (1982) for this country show that the suicide rate in the Dominican Republic is a very low 2.3 per 100,000 population. Of that total, 3.7 is the male rate, 0.9 the rate for females. Highest rates for males appear in the 75 and over age group (27.3); for females, rates are highest (3.8) in the age group of 45 to 54.

Although contemporary attitudes toward suicide are generally more tolerant than in the past, more predominantly Catholic countries such as Ireland, Spain and the Dominican Republic exhibit low suicide rates in comparison with nations dominated by other religions or religious groups.

Donahue, Phil The popular television talk-show host conducted a two-part program on college student suicides as a segment of the NBC network's "Today Show," September 3, 1980. He interviewed both suicide attempters and parent and student survivors. The idea was to show the growing seriousness of this psychosocial problem in the U.S., and perhaps to shed light that would permit parents, educators, and therapists to help young college-age would-be suicides find ways out of their problems, seek satisfaction in new, positive options, and in so doing accept the promise of a future.

Donatists The Donatists were so extravagant in their horror of life and so desirous of martyrdom that they inspired their contemporary, St. Augustine, to the view ". . . to kill themselves out of respect for martyrdom is their daily sport." JOHN DONNE noted, with no little embarrassment "that those times were affected with a disease of this natural desire of such a death . . . for that age [the Donatists flourished in the fourth and fifth centuries] was growne so hungry and ravenous of it [i.e., martyrdom], that many were baptized only because they would be burnt, and children taught to vexe and provoke Executioners, that they might be thrown into the fire."

As A. ALVAREZ writes in *The Savage God*: "It culminated in the genuine lunacy of the Donatists, whose lust for martyrdom was so extreme that the Church eventually declared them heretics." Edward Gibbon, in his principal work, *The Decline and Fall of the Roman Empire* (6 vols., 1776-88), describes their unique glory:

> The rate of the Donatists was enflamed by a phrensy of a very extraordinary kind: and which, if it really prevailed among them in so extravagant a degree, cannot surely be paralleled in any country or in any age.

The Donatists didn't care how they perished, so long as their conduct was, in Gibbon's words, "sanctioned by the intention of devoting themselves to the glory of the true faith and the hope of eternal happiness." When all else failed, they would, in the presence of relatives and friends, plunge headlong from some lofty rock, and, writes Gibbon, "many precipices were shown, which had acquired fame by the number of these religious suicides."

Edward Gibbon, *The Decline and Fall of the Roman Empire*, vol. III.

A. Alvarez, *The Savage God* (New York: Random House, 1972).

Seymour Perlin, ed., *A Handbook for the Study of Suicide* (New York: Oxford University Press, 1975).

Donne, John English poet (1573-1631), who entered the Church in 1615 and became dean of St. Paul's, London (1621-31). As a young man, he was considered the foremost metaphysical poet in Britain, noted for his beautiful, witty love lyrics. His sermons are also distinguished.

Donne, who was chaplain to James I, removed suicide from the then exclusive realm of religion and morality, placing it in the province of the individual. To him, it was the act of a person driven by personal motives. He wrote a defense of suicide when he was young in which he candidly admitted that he had contemplated taking his own life. It was because of such extreme personal revelations that he refused to have the famed book, *Biathanatos*, published. Written in 1607 or 1608, the book was not published until 1646, 15 years after his death and nearly 40 years after it was written.

Donne's defense of suicide was one of the first reactions against the prevailing Church attitudes toward the act. He agreed that self-destruction was contrary to the law of self-preservation—but no more than that. He postulated that suicide was neither a violation of the law nor against reason. Other noted secular writers and philosophers—HUME, MONTESQUIEU, VOLTAIRE and ROUSSEAU—later echoed Donne's position, arguing that suicide was indeed defensible under certain conditions. They wrote notable essays stressing the need for greater freedom of the individual against the ecclesiastical authority.

In the end, suicide for the famed poet-preacher was not a possibility. As Alvarez points out, "Donne's Christian training and devotion, like his intellectual energy, were ultimately stronger than his despair." Alvarez concludes that what is certain is that John Donne added a new element to what had previously been thought of as a "cut and dried question."

Dostoevsky, Feodor Mikhailovich Russian novelist (1821-1881) who became involved with a semi-revolutionary group, was arrested and condemned to death, and at the last moment reprieved and sent to Siberia. There he underwent the torments reported in many of his later novels, e.g., *The House of the Dead* (1858). In his novel *The Possessed* (1871-72), Dostoevsky's graphic treatment of nihilism, the anti-hero Alexsey Nilich Kirilov kills himself, he says, to show that he is God. Secretly, however, he kills himself because he knows that he is not God. He commits, by shooting himself, what the author calls a "logical suicide," self-destructing triumphantly.

Off and on throughout 1876, Dostoevsky reportedly stewed over the suicide question, pursuing the subject in newspapers, official government reports, and in conversation with friends. In *The Diary of a Writer* he wrote: "It is clear, then, that suicide—when the idea of immortality has been lost—becomes an utter and inevitable necessity for any man who, by his mental development, has even slightly lifted himself above the level of cattle."

But Dostoevsky, in the last analysis, refuses the character Kirilov's logic and as an individual clings to his traditional beliefs in Christianity and its attendant love and charity. As Alvarez states, "Christianity was, as it were, the excuse he gave himself for writing, for continuing to celebrate the life that swarms in his books." Dostoevsky to this day remains one of the preeminent novelists of the world—in his bitter, sharp denunciation of conditions, his depiction of suffering and injustice, his psychological analysis of human beings, and finally, in his compassion.

Douglass, Jack D., PhD Author of the well-known sociological study of suicide, *The Social Meanings of Suicide*, Douglas believes that EMILE DURKHEIM's explanation of the suicide rate is flawed since it's neither operationally defined, nor based on data with a common social meaning.

In "Sociology," a chapter in Perlin's *A Handbook for the Study of Suicide*, Ronald Maris writes: "Finally, Douglas emphasizes the need to get at the 'situated meanings' of suicide rather than their abstract meanings; he advocates a basic reorientation of the sociological work in suicide in the direction of intensive observation, description, and analysis of individual cases of suicide." As Maris observes, Douglas's methodology tends toward what Harold Garfinkel calls "ethnomethodology," via, "uncovering the unstated, implicit, commonsense perceptions held and acted upon by participants in a situation."

Douglas is also known for outlining the fundamental dimensions of meanings required in the formal definition of suicide. These are:

1. The *initiation* of an act that leads to the death of the initiator.
2. The willing of an *act* that leads to the death of the willer.
3. The willing of self-destruction.
4. The loss of will.
5. The *motivation to be dead (or to die)* which leads to the initiaiton of an act that leads to the death of the initiator.
6. The *knowledge* of the actor that actions he initiates tend to produce the objective state of death.

It is Jack D. Douglas's view that "current research and thinking on suicide seem to emphasize a holistic approach—that is, one that views biological, psychological, social structural, and social situational factors as interacting with each other."

drop-in centers Name given by the Chicago area's North Shore suicide workers—volunteers, clergy, social workers—to suburban places where young people may "drop in" to listen to music, do their homework, play cards or just "rap." The important thing is that staff workers get to know the adolescents and teens, and can observe them over a period of time. "The first step is to be available," according to one social worker. "You learn a lot over a game of cards, and it gives the kids a chance to know me." The theory: Though it sometimes takes weeks, even months, if the child is troubled, he or she will in most cases eventually open up, start talking. As DR. MARY GIFFIN, coauthor of *A Cry for Help*, notes, "These drop-in centers are valuable because they tend to attract the students who feel that they have no place else to go." Drop-in centers provide a haven, a source of crisis support, for youngsters who lack caring communication and feel alienated from school, their peers, often even their own parents."

drug abuse There is no doubt that drugs and alcohol may cloud the view of the person who seeks death. Some find the solution, all too many give up. The potential for suicide is in all of us; whether or not the potential grows and rises to the surface depends on how well our individual system of checks and balances continues to function.

While there is no single explanation for suicide, certainly drugs and alcohol (which is simply a drug in liquid form) play a key role in many suicide attempts and "completed" suicides. One study of 100 young adults from New York City's Upper East Side who had tried suicide found that each suffered from some form of psychiatric illness, with depression chief among them. The most frequently given reason for attempting self-destruction was a feeling of utter hopelessness brought about by the threatened or actual loss of an important person in their lives. Some of the group blamed their attempts on alcohol and/or drug abuse; fearful of psychiatric symptoms, they became hopeless and isolate themselves.

Many suicide attempters say they often feel, "I'm not worth saving." A case in point is the young college student from Florida who tripped out on drugs and wrote, before he burned himself to death: "I have killed myself because I can no longer run my own affairs, and I can only be trouble to those who love and care for me . . . There is nothing but misery for all of us should I allow myself to deteriorate further." Speaking directly to the problem of drugs, the young man wrote, "It could be too much for your mind to handle. It could blow out all the circuits as it did with me."

Francine Klagsbrun, author of *Too Young to Die: Youth and Suicide*, asserts that drug abuse and alcoholism each have much in common with suicidal behavior, and can be related to it. She writes that:

> drug abuse and suicide are closely linked. From studies of young drug abusers, we know that these people suffer almost unbearable despondency. They hate themselves and feel useless and worthless, much the way suicide attempters do. Rather than choosing outright suicide, many drug abusers chip away at their lives, dying slowly, little by little. Others alternate between deadening themselves with drugs and seeking actual death through suicide.

Psychiatrist Herbert Hendin studied college students abusing drugs as part of a psychoanalytic study he conducted at Columbia University for his book *The Age of Sensation*. He discovered that while some drug abusers mixed the drugs they used, others favored one or another group of drugs depending upon their emotional problems and needs. For example, Hendin learned that students who got stoned on marijuana every day shared problems that related to feelings of aggressiveness and competitiveness. These students usually came from families that stressed competition and high achievements. They resented the feelings they realized their parents had instilled in them. So they used marijuana to reduce their drives, simultaneously rebelling against pressures to succeed from parents.

More seriously, LSD and other psychedelic drug abusers wanted to, in Klagsbrun's words, "escape beyond all emotions and feelings." These students grew up feeling rejected and lonely; they didn't allow themselves to get close to others because it might prove too painful. Klagsbrun reports: "They used LSD to 'blow their minds' and open up new worlds of experience. But their new worlds and their mind-blowing experiences served all the while to push away their emotions, to shelter them from the rage and despair they might feel if they permitted themselves to feel anything."

Amphetamine abusers in the Hendin study were mostly women students. Most of these users wanted desperately to please their parents, to fulfill the goals their parents had set for them. These pleasers ignored their own needs, kept themselves high on amphetamines, according to Klagsbrun, "'speeding' through their days with no time left to think about how they felt or what they wanted. Having destroyed their true selves, these young women programmed themselves to be efficient machines. But at times when the programming failed and the machinery broke down, they became openly suicidal."

Until recently, the most despairing, self-destructive drug misusers and abusers have been heroin users. This fact came across in Hendin's Columbia University study. These students had usually suffered early and deep hurt in their lives. They "did drugs" to prevent further hurt, to dull all feelings and keep everybody—parents, peers, even themselves—at a safe distance.

Now, during the mid-1980s, the most highly used and abused drug appears to be cocaine. The drug is sniffed, injected and only lately smoked in an extremely fast-food version called "crack." Crack, known as "rock" on the West Coast of the U.S., allows users to "freebase" a pure form of the dangerous drug without volatile substances like ether or special tools. All users need is a test tube to mix the powder with baking soda or ammonia and a simple butane lighter. The mixture is heated, hardens, and then is broken into chunks to be smoked, usually in a small pipe.

Crack is processed, packaged and priced—$10 to $20 for a vial, versus $60 to $70 for a gram of cocaine powder—for easy consumption. So quickly has it spread across America that authorities (medical, legal, and judicial) are calling it a new national epidemic. "Crack knows no social or economic boundaries," says Dr. Arnold M. Washton, director of addiction treatment at Regent Hospital in Manhattan and research director for the national 800-COCAINE hotline in Summit, New Jersey. "It can be thought of as an equal opportunity drug, for ghetto dwellers to boardroom executives."

Washton estimates at least one million people in the U.S. have now tried crack. There is, he contends, a new wave of cocaine addiction as a result. The hotline, in the first six months of 1986, was getting more than 200 calls a day from users in 25 states. In Manhattan and Detroit, police officials report that 90% of the cocaine trade is in crack; in Dallas, it's 60%; San Francisco, 33%. The New York Police Department's special anti-crack task force made more than 50 arrests in its first week of operation (May 1986). Seattle and Los Angeles also have task forces to combat crack's persistent spread.

Unlike the slow rush of cocaine sniffed through the nose, crack delivers an instant jolt to the user's central nervous system. It hits the brain in a highly concentrated form. After a high of five to 10 minutes, the user undergoes a wrenching crash and immediately craves more. "It's unique in drug abuse history," says Robert Stutman, special agent in charge of the New York Office, U.S. Drug Enforcement Administration, "because it's relatively inexpensive, you get an instant high . . . and it's extremely addictive."

Agent Stutman says that "rock" first surfaced in Los Angeles in 1981. Early in 1985, dealers began to make it in New York City's Harlem district and in the Bronx. They dubbed it "crack" after the chunks of plaster that fell from tenement house ceilings. Dealers often stamp their wares with brand names, such as "White Cloud," "Conan," "Super" and "Cloud Nine." They hire teenagers to peddle it on the street.

Paranoia and extreme agitation caused by the crack "high" have, in many cases, led to violent crime and suicidal behavior. Crack wrecks the user's mind and body, causing convulsions, brain seizures, heart attacks, respiratory problems and severe vitamin deficiencies. Addicts suffer depression and suicidal or homicial thoughts when they crash. "Crack is stringing out enough young people today that they're getting desperate," says Philip McCurdy, head of a Phoenix House for Adolescents in Westchester County, New York, an area that has suffered a rash of suicides in recent years. McCurdy reports users are seeking help because "they think they're going to die."

Despite its relatively low per-unit cost, addicts end up spending thousands of dollars on binges, smoking the contents of vial after vial in crack or "base" houses—not unlike modern-day opium dens—for days on end without food or sleep. Authorities say users will do anything to repeat the brief high, including robbing their parents, relatives, and friends, selling their possessions and their bodies. Says one young victim, now in a New York area treatment center, "Your head gets so light, it's like you're walking on air. When you start using crack, you don't want to do anything else but keep on smoking it."

Crack, like other addictive drugs—including some over-the-counter prescription drugs—leads all too quickly to serious trouble, from a euphoric high to a startling crash that many people relieve by taking more . . . then more and more. Users gamble with their lives again and again. And, as Francine Klagsbrun says, "when even [being] drugged to numbness cannot help them block out the emotional pain that torments their souls, they use their drug to kill themselves."

Several well-known users who gambled with various forms of drugs and lost, include rock singer Janis Joplin, John Belushi of "Saturday Night Live" fame, singer-performer Elvis Presley and comedian-actor Freddy Prinze.

Authorities report that thousands of teenagers and other young people (in the 20 to 26 age group) have plunged so deeply into the alcohol-drug abuse scene that it has cost them their lives. Unfortunately, thousands of others are now living lives where "accidental" death and/or suicide become daily occurrences. Some experience the agonizing, slow death of mental, emotional and physicial deterioration, while untold numbers die or become crippled or disfigured for life because of highway crashes caused by reckless driving or driving while in a drugged stupor.

Writes Klagsbrun in *Too Young to Die*:

> Behind them all—the drug freaks, the alcoholics, the careless drivers—hovers the specter of death. In dozens of ways, they play with death, they challenge death, and often they seek death. When they do die from their drugs or drinking or driving, their deaths are not counted into official lists of suicide statistics. But you would not be wrong to say that many of these people destroyed themselves, as surely as did those who openly committed suicide.

(See also ABUSE, SUBSTANCE and ALCOHOLISM.)

Francine Klagsbrun, *Too Young to Die: Youth and Suicide* (New York: Pocket Books, 1985).

Margaret O. Hyde and Elizabeth Held Forsyth, MD, *Suicide: The Hidden Epidemic* (New York: Franklin Watts, 1978).

Mary Giffin, MD, and Carol Felsenthal, *A Cry for Help: Exploring and Exploding the Myths About Teenage Suicide—A Guide for All Parents of Adolescents* (Garden City: Doubleday, 1983).

druids According to A. ALVAREZ, there was a druid maxim which promoted suicide as a religious principle: "There is another world, and they who kill themselves to accompany their friends thither, will live with them there." Alvarez notes that "this is not unlike a custom once common among certain African tribes: that the warriors and slaves put themselves to death when their king dies, in order to live with him in paradise." Druidism was a Celtic religion suppressed in Gaul and parts of the British Isles by the Romans, but lasting in Wales, Ireland and Scotland until the advent of Christianity. The priests, called druids, had considerable secular power. Druidism was pantheistic.

A. Alvarez, *The Savage God: A Study of Suicide* (New York: Random House, 1970), p. 55; originally published by Weidenfeld & Nicholson, London, 1970.

Du Suicide et de la Folie Suicide Medical historian George Rosen calls Brierre de Boismont "probably the most important contributor to the problem of suicide" in the mid-19th century. Writing in "History," a chapter of Perlin's *A Handbook for the Study of Suicide* (1975), Dr. Rosen notes:

> In his treatise *Du Suicide et de la Folie Suicide* . . . published in 1856, he made extensive use of statistics, but he also used information obtained by questioning 265 individuals who either had planned or attempted to commit suicide. On the basis of a detailed analysis, Brierre de Boismont denied that all suicides are due to insanity, even though a large number are caused by mental illness.

Among the more important causes he lists, according to Dr. Rosen, are insanity, alcoholism, illness, family troubles, love problems and poverty. These and other findings brought him close to a sociological explanation of suicide. He discovered, for example, a higher proportion of unmarried people, of old people and of men among the suicides studied. Brierre de Boismont, in Rosen's view, saw suicide "as a consequence of changes in society leading to social disorganization and to alienation for many people." His views were similar to those expressed by E. Lisle in a work also published in 1856.

Dr. George Rosen, professor of the history of medicine and epidemiology and public health, Yale School of Medicine, concludes that both Brierre de Boismont and Lisle, as well as other investigators of the time, were pointing to the conclusion Durkheim was to state in 1897: Suicide will not be widely prevalent in a society that is well-integrated politically, economically and socially.

George Rosen, MD, PhD, MPH, "History," ch. 1 of *A Handbook for the Study of Suicide*, Seymour Perlin, ed. (New York and London: Oxford University Press, 1975).

A. Brierre de Boismont, *Du Suicide et de la Folie Suicide Consideres dans Leurs Rapports avec la Statistique, la medecine et la philosophie* (Paris: J.B. Bailliere, 1856).

Dublin, Louis I. Author of *Suicide: A Sociological and Statistical Study, The Facts of Life From Birth to Death*, and with B. Bunzel, *To Be or Not to Be*. Durkheim's *Le Suicide* established a model for sociological investigations of suicide; there have been a number of subsequent studies of this genre. Dublin's work falls within the sociological tradition. He is considered one of the principal demographers of suicide this century. He did a valuable summary of suicide rates that showed the wide variation in those rates during the period 1900 to 1960. Dublin noted the inverse association between economic prosperity and suicide and the positive association between depression and suicide. He also suggested that recorded (i.e., cause-of-death certification) suicide figures are understated by as much as one-fourth to one-third.

Dungeons and Dragons Co-authors Kim Long and Terry Reim, writing in their 1985 book *Kicking the Bucket*, state that "the popular game 'Dungeons and Dragons' has been implicated in the motivation for at least nine suicides and murders, according to one survey."

"60 Minutes," the popular CBS television program, did a segment on this phenomenon in September 1985, and interviewed parents of young suicides, medical experts, and officials of the company (TSR Hobbies, Lake Geneva, Wisconsin) that produces the game. Although interview results were inconclusive, some authorities and survivor-parents seem to feel the game is dangerous (involving, as it does, role-playing by youngsters who are highly impressionable) and should be banned. Gary Gygax, head of TSR (Technical Studies Rules), denies any such charges and insists that to his knowledge, no deaths by either suicide or homicide have been attributed directly to *Dungeons and Dragons*.

There is a D&D Basic Set adventure game and the Advanced D&D adventure game books: *Dungeonmaster's Guide*, *Player's Handbook* and *Monster Manual*. The books draw heavily on the fantasy worlds of writers like J.R.R. Tolkein and Robert E. Howard. The firm also publishes a magazine, *The Dragon*.

During the game itself, players progress by ascending to "experience levels" and become more powerful—if they don't die. There is no board. The action occurs entirely in the player's mind, but sometimes with the help of little lead figurines for particularly complicated situations. *Dungeons and Dragons* campaigns can last for hours or years; they end when the players decide they have had enough. Nobody "wins" in the traditional sense of the word.

U.S. News and World Report, in its issue of March 31, 1986, asked Dr. Cynthia Pfeffer, 1986-87 president of the American Association of Suicidology and associate professor of clinical psychiatry at Cornell University Medical College: "Do games such as Dungeons and Dragons increase (suicide) risk?"

Dr. Pfeffer, author of *The Suicidal Child*, replied: "I wouldn't necessarily blame the game. It has very good, redeeming qualities, but it may affect those who are already vulnerable. Perhaps we need to be on the lookout for teenagers who are too intensely involved with playing the game so that peers may begin to be watchful if one of their friends goes awry. The game may serve as an early warning clue to suicide."

Durkheim, Emile French social philosopher (1858-1917) and pioneer in social psychology. His monumental book, *LE SUICIDE* (1817), in Edwin Shneidman's words, "established a model for sociological investigations of suicide." It also, adds Shneidman, "demonstrated the power of the sociological approach."

Durkheim, who also is considered a pioneer in the origins of religion, analyzed his French data on suicide and then proposed four kinds of suicide, each emphasizing the strength or weakness of the individual's relationship or ties to society. They are: "altruistic" suicides, wherein the group's authority over a person is such that the person loses his own identity and wishes to sacrifice his life for the community (e.g., the servicemen or -women who happily and willingly give their lives for their country); "egoistic" suicides, in which the person has too few ties with his community, and there is a diminution of religious, family, political and social controls; "anomic" suicides, which occur when the individual simply cannot adjust to social change and finds he has lost the customary relationship with his society (e.g., in times of business crisis, such as a depression, or in an era of unprecedented prosperity where the *noveau riche* can't adjust to new life styles and standards); and "fatalistic" suicides, which result from excessive regulation, e.g., among prisoners or slaves.

Edwin Shneidman, founder-president of the American Association of Suicidology, speculates that "Durkheim was not as interested in suicide per se as he was in the explication of the power of his general sociological method."

Emile Durkheim's classic study of the causes and nature of self-destruction continues to be important reading for any serious student of the subject. Perhaps one of the most significant contributions Durkheim made was to stimulate further research and discussion of the subject of suicide.

dysphoria Depression accompanied by anxiety; as opposed to duphia (a psychological state, often pathological, of extreme well-being, optimism in outlook and heightened motor activity). A feeling of malaise or nonspecific illness or general discomfort that often accompanies a hangover or withdrawal.

E

East, John P. U.S. senator (Republican) from the state of North Carolina for five and one-half years. East (1931-1986) was found dead on the floor of the garage of his home in Greenville, North Carolina, on the morning of June 29, 1986. The county medical examiner ruled the death a suicide. Police said the garage was sealed and full of fumes from a station wagon inside. Dr. Stan Harris, the medical examiner, said after conducting an autopsy that Senator East had asphyxiated from breathing carbon monoxide. Senator East had announced in 1985 that he would not seek a second term in office because of ill health.

Eastman, George Eastman (1854-1932) was born poor and his family could give him little chance for schooling. Despite this inauspicious start in life, thanks to the profits of the company he founded, Eastman Kodak, he was able to contribute $100 million to various educational institutions. George Eastman committed suicide rather than spend his last years in loneliness and without the prospect of further accomplishment.

eating habits, as distress signal Most authorities agree that a noticeable, often dramatic, change in a person's eating habits is a warning sign or distress signal. DR. MARY GIFFIN and Carol Felsenthal in *A Cry for Help* note that "Most suicidal children will show changes in eating habits . . . changes that will be one of many early signs of trouble. A minority of children—almost always girls—will show extreme eating disorders that usually last several years and come to monopolize their lives."

Parents, teachers, friends and counselors should consider eating disorders, especially anorexia nervosa and bulimia, as definite and urgent warning signs. Experts say such persons are, like alcoholics or drug abusers, killing themselves slowly, rather than instantly with a bullet through the brain or a rope around the neck. (See ANOREXIA NERVOSA and BULIMIA.)

Ecclesiastes From this important book of the Old Testament, one of the Hagiographa, this significant quotation:

> That which befalleth the sons of men befalleth beasts; even one thing befalleth them; as the one dieth, so dieth the other; yea, they have all one breath; so that a man hath no preeminence above a beast; for all is vanity. All go to one place; all are of the dust, and all turn to dust again. Who knoweth the spirit of man that goeth upward, and the spirit of the beast that goeth downward to the earth?

economic class One common misconception among the many fallacies one hears about suicide is that the very wealthy kill themselves at a rate higher than others on the economic scale. It's simply not true. Statistics show that suicide does not discriminate and strikes equally among rich and poor alike, adults as well as adolescents. Suicide is usually caused by a combination of forces acting on a person, and one of those forces may be economic fluctuations. But such forces affect poor people as well as wealthy people.

education about suicide In his valuable addition to the literature on the subject of suicide, John L. McIntosh, PhD, author/compiler of *Research on Suicide: A Bibliography*, entitles chapter 7, "The Need for Education About Suicide." McIntosh strongly stresses that negative ideas, various myths, false assumptions and the lingering taint of taboo—all suggest a "great need for education of the public, especially those in contact with the potentially suicidal (often called 'gatekeepers,' e.g., personnel in the medical and helping professions)."

In fact, the primary reason for this work's existence is a recognition for an increasing and, in Professor McIntosh's words, "widespread dissemination of accurate information about suicide . . ." Some basic components of such education concern: clues or distress signals of potential suicides, information that creates more positive, caring attitudes in both the professional and lay communities, methods of prevention, intervention and postvention, and the availability of resources when suicidal intentions are encountered or after a suicide has taken place (for survivor victims).

Like the tightrope walker who has conquered heights, suicidologists and others working in the field—psychiatrist and psychologist, social worker and hotline volunteer—must use their own particular knowledge and skills to combat the prejudices, disgraces and stigma that still throw a smokescreen over the serious topic of suicide in our time.

John Langone, author of *Death Is a Noun*, says it objectively and candidly:

> As our fearful attitudes toward death—particularly murder and suicide—often prevent us from learning more about it, so too can a fear of life pose a problem. "As long as there is more dread of life than fear of death," writes the distinguished psychiatrist Dr. Joost A.M. Meerloo, "death will tempt people with the promise of greater security than they can find in this lifetime—unless and until such time as we are able to teach man to accept and embrace his own destiny."

Egbert, Archbishop of York In his *Penitentials*, Egbert recognized and made burial allowances to those suicides who were judged victims of mental and emotional disorders. Even though the *Penitentials* appeared in the middle of the eighth century, Egbert made an exception for the insane concerning burial in consecrated ground. (See also CHRISTIANITY.)

For further reading, see H.R. Fedden's *Suicide: A Social and Historical Study* (London: Peter Davies, 1938), pp. 133-135, 155.

egoistic suicide In his landmark book, *Le Suicide*, EMILE DURKHEIM proposed four kinds of suicide, all pointing up the strength or weakness of the individual's relationship or ties to society. "Egoistic" suicides, Durkheim suggested, take place when one has too few ties with one's community. Most suicides, if one agrees with Durkheim's theory, are egoistic . . . the person has few community ties, at a time when institutional (i.e., family, religious, social, political) controls are lax. Suicide happens when—and because—the person is not properly integrated into his or her society but is, instead, dependent upon his or her own resources and devices.

Egypt A devout and still relatively backward country, Egypt, where suicide is considered by most people to be a mortal sin, has a correspondingly low suicide rate, the lowest in the world. World Health Organization (WHO) figures for 1980 (latest available statistics) show no suicides for Egypt. In fact, there were virtually no instances of self-inflicted injury, with a rate of only 0.1 (per 100,000). These statistics, some experts believe, say less about national character than the way facts are gathered or covered up. While highly industrialized and prosperous countries tend to have comparatively high suicide rates, they also tend to have more sophisticated methods of collecting the information on which statistics are based, and comparatively few prejudices against doing so.

Religion is a factor here, as well, since Moslems are among the most extreme of religionists in their attitudes toward self-destruction. The *Koran*, the sacred scripture of the Moslems, decries suicide as an act worse than homicide.

Elavil® The brand name for a tricyclic antidepressant, made by Merck, Sharp & Dohme, with sedative effects and which contains amitriptyline. It is one of a group of antidepressants called tricyclics (the other group, the monoamineoxidase inhibitors, is known as MAO inhibitors). The mechanism of Elavil's action is not known, though it is thought more likely to alleviate endogenous depression than other depressive states. Used with central nervous system depressants, it can have an addictive effect. Abrupt cessation can result in nausea, headache and malaise, but these withdrawal symptoms are not necessarily indicative of addiction.

"Patients who are potentially suicidal," say O'Brien and Cohen (in *The Encyclopedia of Drugs Abuse*), "should not have access to large quantities of the drug as severe overdosage can result in convulsions, congestive heart failure, coma and death." Elavil is available in 10 mg, round blue tablets; 25 mg yellow tablets; 50 mg beige tablets; 75 mg orange tablets; 100 mg mauve tablets; and 150 mg, capsule-shaped blue tablets. It is also supplied in 10 mg vials for injection.

DR. MARY GIFFIN notes in *A Cry for Help* (with co-author Carol Felsenthal) that most studies show that approximately 65% of depressed adult patients will respond to the first tricyclic they're given. "And after a course of these drugs," she adds, "many people never suffer a second bout."

The medical community is not quite sure just why antidepressants seem to work better for some people than for others. Still, the trend today is toward increased use of these drugs, and at lower and lower ages. Giffin states that "Dr. Barry Garfinkel, a Canadian authority on youth suicide, goes so far as to blame the astronomical rise in the youth suicide rate on '. . . pediatricians and family doctors (who) don't recognize depression in children and are not treating it with antidepressant drugs.'"

Anyone taking an ANTIDEPRESSANT of either type—tricyclic or MAO inhibitor—should do so only under strict care of a physician. As Dr. Mary Giffin, medical director, Irene Jossalyn Clinic of the North Shore Mental Health Association in Northfield, Illinois, says: "The key to the effectiveness of an antidepressant is the doctor who prescribes it. He must be up to date and experienced in using these drugs."

electroconvulsive therapy (ECT) Sometimes called electroshock therapy, this is a form of somatic therapy consisting of the application of a weak electric current to the head in order to produce convulsion and then unconsiousness. Introduced about 40 years ago, some 10 years before antidepressant drugs, ECT has caused a great deal of controversy in both medical and lay sectors. Many, if not most, people think it an inhuman procedure.

Yet ECT is a fairly widely used treatment for severe cases of depression. An estimated 60,000 to 100,000 persons, usually adults, undergo ECT every year. Many experts in the field consider ECT an effective treatment, but certainly not the treatment of choice for depressed young people. It is most often reserved for treating elderly patients who have received little or no relief from psychotherapy or drugs. Supporters of ECT claim studies show that the treatment is effective in 90 to 95% of cases (as opposed to 65 to 70% for drugs). In one eight-year study of ECT at the National Institute of Mental Health, only one of nine severely depressed adult patients failed to respond.

Though many psychiatrists contend that ECT results in fewer complications and side effects than the use of antidepressants, ECT does cause some memory loss of the hours and even days preceding such treatment. However, experts say the loss is, for the most part, transitory. Still, ECT frightens many people and is considered by families of patients to be too primitive and inhumane even when they realize that the patient's risk of suicide is great.

emergency rooms, help in Suicidal persons who survive a serious attempt are usually rushed by EMS or paramedic teams to a hospital emergency room where doctors and nurses work skillfully and furiously to save the person's life. Authorities urge parents and/or relatives no matter what the attitude is of the suicide attempter, to make certain the victim is seen, evaluated, and treated (where possible) by a professional therapist.

Parents or relatives must realize they cannot expect or rely on the emergency room staff of a hospital to refer a suicidal patient for psychiatric care. There are times, of course, when the staff will call in a hospital psychiatrist or psychologist for consultation on an attempted suicide victim. When this happens, the patient is often transferred, after recovering from the attempt, to a psychiatric ward. But a family cannot count on this always happening; emergency room staff personnel are simply too busy (or uninterested) to follow through with psychiatric consultations. They often see their duty as being to "patch up," to use Klagsbrun's term, a suicide attempter and then send him home.

The problem: Once the person—and especially the adolescent—checks out of the hospital, statistical studies indicate that the majority fail to seek additional professional assistance. It is up to the suicide attempter's family to make certain he or she receives therapy by a certified professional.

Empire State Building It is a fact that certain suicidal persons are attracted to specific sites. Arnold Madison, in his book *Suicide and Young People* (New York: Houghton Mifflin/Clarion Books, 1978), writes that "For many years, jumping from the observation deck atop the Empire State Building in New York City seemed the solution to many unhappy people's problems. Once an effective railing was installed, some persons did select other means by which to kill themselves. But others probably reconsidered their problems and sought help rather than death."

empirical understanding Ronald Maris, PhD, editor of *Suicide and Life-Threatening Behavior* (official publication of the American Association of Suicidology), explains that sociologist Max Weber "distinguishes between empirical or observational understanding of social behavior and motivational or subjective understanding. The former he called *Begreifen* and the latter, VERSTEHEN." For example, writes Maris, "*Begreifen* could be achieved by discovering frequency of participation of Protestants, Catholics, and Jews in business. However, *Verstehen* of these rates of participation could only be arrived at by an analysis of the values and sentiments of religious groups . . ." Maris adds that *Verstehen* "gives rise to 'meaningfully adequate' understanding."

Both of these theories of understanding, as distinguished by Weber, have been used by experts in trying to determine and explain the meaning of suicide to the persons actually involved. For further reading about Max Weber's notions of empirical understanding vs. motivational understanding, see his book *The Protestant Ethic and the Spirit of Capitalism.*

Ronald Maris, "Sociology," ch. 5 in *A Handbook for the Study of Suicide*, Seymour Perlin, ed. (New York and London: Oxford University Press, 1975).

employment LOUIS I. DUBLIN, author and demographer of suicide in the U.S., presents interesting and valuable data on suicide rates in which he points out the inverse association between economic prosperity and suicide and the positive association between depression and suicide. His summary was based on suicide rates during the period from 1900 to 1960.

Andrew F. Henry and James F. Short, trying to determine more clearly how economic cycles are related to suicide, analyzed separatedly the trend in suicide rates for whites and nonwhites, males and females, and young and old persons. Their study showed the rate increased more for high status groups (whites, males and younger individuals) during economic depressions than for low-status groups. They concluded that the data indicate high status groups are more sensitive to the frustrations produced by business cycles.

Dublin also compared suicide rates for different occupational groups and social classes. In the U.S., rates of suicide were highest among laborers, while in Great Britain both professional and laborer groups had higher rates than other occupational groups. Experts caution that occupation may be an important factor in assessing suicide rates not only because of the work involved, but also because of the lifestyle outside of work established by persons in particular occupations.

A.F. Henry and J.E. Short, Jr., co-authors of *Suicide and Homicide*, found that during rapid rises in the business index, suicides tend to fall. With only slight business index increases, during the final phase of increase, the suicide rate does increase—but primarily among females, particularly among those least involved in the machinations of the economy. Generally, business cycles are more highly correlated with male suicides than with the suicide of females. But, they've discovered, the suicide of black females is more highly associated with business fluctuations and employment than is the suicide of black males.

Ruth Shoule Cavan says that suicide rates vary in response to economic conditions. She writes that "In the U.S., for example, rates declined during the prosperous years of World Wars I and II but rose during the interwar period in the depression of the 1930s. After World War II, during a period of rising economic prosperity, the rates remained low. European countries in general showed similar trends."

One thing is certain concerning suicide and employment: it must be regarded as an important causative factor in this peculiarly human problem. The unemployed rank among the other high risk groups that research has uncovered.

Louis I. Dublin, *Suicide: A Sociological and Statistical Study* (New York: The Ronald Press, 1963).

Andrew F. Henry and James F. Short, Jr., *Suicide and Homicide* (New York: Macmillan/The Free Press, 1954).

Ruth S. Cavan, *Suicide* (New York: Russell & Russell, 1965, reprint; originally published by University of Chicago Press, 1926).

England The teachings of St. Augustine and other early church leaders became incorporated into the laws of the Roman Catholic Church and later the Anglican Church. Suicide was declared an act inspired by the devil, as church councils deemed it a mortal sin. Bodies of suicides were denied Christian burial and even suicide attempters were excommunicated. Church laws did distinguish, however, between the self-destruction of sane and insane persons, and also excluded young children from the harshly cruel penalties imposed by Anglican Church law.

When a suicide did take place, townspeople often dragged the degraded body through the streets to be spat upon or hanged from public gallows. Sometimes the victim was buried on the spot where he or she had committed suicide; at other times, the body remained unburied in the area of town reserved for public executions. Often the suicide's body was buried at a crossroads with a stake driven through its heart and a stone placed on the face to prevent the dead person's spirit from rising.

In England as recently as 1823, the body of a suicide named Griffiths was dragged through the streets of London and buried at a crossroads. Mr. Griffiths was the last suicide in England whose body was so mistreated. Parliament passed a law shortly thereafter authorizing private burial of a suicide in a churchyard or in a private burial ground. In 1961, a law was passed that repealed all previous civil rulings about suicide—rulings that had been based on early Anglican church doctrine. Today it is no longer a crime to attempt or successfully to commit suicide in England. Famed poet-preacher JOHN DONNE, who became dean of St. Paul's Cathedral in London, was highly influential in changing the people's attitudes by his defense of suicide in the book *BIATHANATOS*, published in 1644, 13 years after his death. About 100 years later, Scottish philosopher DAVID HUME argued convincingly against treating suicide as a crime in his short essay, "On Suicide." Suicide was regarded at the time as so widely prevalent that many *believed* the problem constituted a national emergency.

The World Health Organization (WHO) statistics on suicide and self-injury includes Wales's figures with England (Northern Ireland and Scotland are listed separately). Most recent statistics (1982) show a suicide rate per 100,000 population totaling 8.6, a slight drop of .3 since 1981. The male suicide rate is 11.5 as opposed to the much lower female rate of 5.9. Highest rate for specific age groupings is that for 65 to 74 years of age. For males it is the 75-plus group, 22.5 per 100,000 population. Highest female age group rate is the 65 to 74 category, where the rate is 11.7 per 100,000 population.

For an insightful discussion of the patterns of suicide in Great Britain, which reveal some curious anomalies and contradictions, read "Some Cultural Aspects of Suicide in Britain," by Maxwell Atkinson, PhD, Faculty of Economic and Social Studies, University of Manchester, Manchester, England. The piece is ch. 8 of *Suicide in Different Cultures*, ed., Norman L. Farberow (Baltimore, London, Tokyo: University Park Press, 1975). (See also GREAT BRITAIN.)

English Malady, The George Cheyne, English physician, wrote this treatise which appeared in 1733 and presented suicide as a medical problem. Doctor-medical historian George Rosen says of it, "He (Cheyne) would have had this work published posthumously had he not been urged by his friends because of 'the late frequency and daily increase of wanton and uncommon self-murderers, produced mostly by this distempter . . . to try what a little more just and solid philosophy join'd to a method of cure, and proper medicines could do, to put a stop to so universal a lunacy and madness.'" Dr. Cheyne's work carried one of the most comprehensive subtitles known to the literature of suicide. The full title: *The English Malady: Or a Treatise of Nervous Diseases of all Kinds, as Spleen, Vapours, Lowness of Spirits, Hypochondriacal, and Hysterical Distempers, Etc.* (London: G. Strahan and J. Leake, 1733), See pp. 36-37.

Enlightenment, Period of That mid-18th-century span when new, refreshing views began to cause less prejudiced, more tolerant attitudes and opinions about suicide. Leaders of the so-called "Enlightenment" included VOLATIRE, d'Holbach, ROUSSEAU, HUME and Beccaria, among others. They and their allies condemned the traditional cruel treatment of suicides and, in Dr. George Rosen's words, "assaulted the Christian interpretation through the exercise of empirical observation and critical reason, thus laying the foundation for a secular approach to the problem of suicide." For in-depth information relating to this significant period, read Lester G. Crocker's "The Discussion of Suicide in the Eighteenth Century."

environment In "History," a chapter of Perlin's *A Handbook for the Study of Suicide*, Dr. George Rosen, professor of the history of medicine, Yale University, writes that "Notions of environmental influence can be traced back to antiquity with roots in medicine and geography, both evident in the Hippocratic corpus, specifically in *Airs, Waters, Places*." Rosen says these notions were transmitted throughout the MIDDLE AGES in various ways, until they began to take on added significance in several fields of thought and practice during the 16th and 17th centuries. Thinkers, writers and medical professionals alike started to discuss the causal role of environmental factors such as air, diet, temperature, in both social and medical problems. These discussions became so frequent and widespread in the 18th century that they led to the opposing of sanctions against suicide and the urging of a more tolerant view of such acts. This era became known as the above-described PERIOD OF ENLIGHTENMENT.

Mary Monk, PhD, professor, community and preventive medicine, New York Medical College, New York City, sums up the matter of environmental factors and variations in suicide that have been studied this way: "The relation of suicide to climatic conditions such as barometric pressure, humidity, or precipitation can best be described as confused."

DR. CHRISTIAAN BARNARD, writing in *Good Life Good Death*, brings this notion to the environmental-suicide discussion:

> The evolutionary principle of natural selection—the survival of those best-fitted for the environment—would make us expect a rise in the suicide rate consistent with growth in population and increase in competitive activity.
>
> More and more persons compete for fewer and fewer resources, hence, the pressures on the individual increase dramatically. This has already been foreshadowed by comparisons of urban and rural health and crime statistics.

Henry Morselli, an Italian professor of psychological medicine, was an early researcher of the subject. In his book *Suicide: An Essay on Comparative Moral Statistics* (first published in Milan in 1879, reprinted in 1975 by Arno Press, New York), Morselli studied endless statistics and, among other things, tried to relate "cosmico-natural" influences such as climate, geological formations and so on to suicide. He also considered biological factors, social conditions of the suicidal person and individual psychological influences.

Many, if not most, of Professor Morselli's conclusions would be challenged today (e.g., the frequency of suicide in various parts of Italy generally is in a direct ratio with stature, and the inclination to self-destruction increases from South to North as the stature of Italians gradually increases). Yet, if Morselli's correlations seem strange, consider that there was a study in the Spring 1977 issue of *Suicide and Life Threatening Behavior* that attempted to correlate the rate of suicides with the moon's position. The only relationship appeared to be a slight increase in the number of suicides during the new moon phase, suggesting perhaps that a small percentage of suicide-prone people are influenced by lunar changes.

It has also been postulated by some authorities that geography may affect persons who live in isolated areas, in regions where days are short and the nights long, and/or where climate is "gloomy," i.e., rainy or cloudy. Northerly places, such as Scandinavia, show higher suicide rates than tropical regions. In the U.S., suicide frequencies are higher as one travels from east to west (Nevada has the country's highest suicide rate per 100,000 population, at 22.9 in 1980, with Arizona and Alaska close behind).

Others theorize that spring is the deadliest time of year for suicides and winter the least deadly. One researcher notes that people of slight physique tend to commit suicide in early spring, those more stockily built, toward the end of spring. More suicides are said to occur on certain days of the week—Monday is the favored day (in 1979 about 82 suicides happened nationwide every Monday). Also, suicides are said to prefer certain hours of the day, usually in late afternoon or early evening, presumably when they know other family members are at home.

Some of these environmental correlations obviously play a part in the frequency and motivation of suicidal persons, but other circumstances and statistics vary so greatly that it is impossible to draw any useful conclusions. Environments in which there is crime, violence, alcohol and/or drug abuse, divorce, unemployment, etc., appear to make some individuals especially vulnerable. In fact, it seems clear that much more needs to be learned about the myriad problems of families, and the individual people who make up those families, if we are to make any meaningful headway in understanding the enigma of suicide.

Epictetus Greek philosopher (ca. 55 A.D.-ca. 135 A.D.), an eminent exponent of stoicism. His principal doctrines are contained in his *Encheiridion*. Though the philosophy of stoicism was among several at the time that accepted and recommended suicide under certain conditions, particularly as an escape from evil, Epictetus opposed self-destruction. He noted the spread of dissatisfaction among numerous individuals, a resentment against the world which was generally associated with self-hostility, and felt obliged to restrain it, urging people not to commit suicide.

Epicureans Adherents of a philosophy that taught that pleasure was the goal of life and was attained by moderation, matching desires to possibilities. Expounded by Lucretius, the philosophy was much followed in Rome and during the Renaissance. Epicureans opposed suicide. Self-destruction simply did not fit their concept of the calm life with its primary quality of joy—free, because, writes Dr. George Rosen in S. Perlin's *A Handbook for the Study of Suicide*, "its adherents felt themselves delivered from supernatural terrors and fears of capricious divine action."

Epicurus Greek philosopher (?342 B.C.-270 B.C.) whose work was popularized by Titus Lucretius Carus, Roman poet, whose *De Rerum Natura (On the Nature of Things)* is generally considered the greatest philosophical poem of antiquity. Lucretius's poems, consisting of six books, celebrate the epicurean philosophy of a life contemplative and free of passions. It was enormously influential with the revival of the classics in the Renaissance.

Epicurus, as did the Neoplatonists of the late Empire, opposed suicide and taught his adherents accordingly.

epidemic (of young suicides) Youth suicide, the subject of national conferences, a number of books and articles, several television films, and national news coverage, rose dramatically from four suicides per 100,000 in 1954 to 13.6 in 1977, a rise of 240%. In comparison, the rate for the general population increased by only 32%. Considerable attention has been accorded the phenomenon of suicide "clusters" that crop up in certain communities, such as Omaha in the winter of 1985-86. Charlotte P. Ross, executive director, Youth Suicide National Center, Washington, D.C., estimates that the actual number of youth suicides is "at least four times greater than those reported. These numbers, however, are only the most visible 'tip of the iceberg.' Recent studies indicate that more than two million U.S. high school students attempted suicide last year [1985]."

Dr. Cynthia Pfeffer, 1986-87 immediate past-president of the AMERICAN ASSOCIATION OF SUICIDOLOGY and author of *The Suicidal Child*, says that even the number of pre-adolescents who commit suicide has increased. She concedes the number is low compared to adolescent rates, but warns: "That's not to say that the younger population shouldn't be taken seriously. I've found it relatively common for pre-adolescents to think about, threaten, or attempt suicide."

The term "epidemic" is used by many, particularly the media, to draw attention to the extraordinary number of adolescents and young adults who killed themselves in the 1970s and early 1980s. Recent trends in the youth suicide rate do show a leveling off in young suicides. At the May 1986 National Conference on Risk Factors for Youth Suicide, held in Bethesda, Maryland, and sponsored by the U.S. Department of Health and Human Services, Carol L. Huffine, PhD, director of research, California School of Professional Psychology, said: "Although there is evidence that the rate of suicide among youths is declining, it is still very high and, more importantly, we are left feeling powerless to explain the unanticipated increase or to prevent such a social tragedy from recurring."

Recent data from the Centers for Disease Control in Atlanta indicate that suicide rates for all age groupings of youths have leveled off. Adolescent suicide (ages 10 to 14) increased from 0.9 per 100,000 in 1981, but held steady at 1.1 for 1982 and 1983. The teenage (15 to 19) rate remained constant at 8.7 for 1981-83. The young-adult group (20 to 24) showed a decline from 15.6 in 1981 to 15.1 in 1982 and 14.8 in 1983. There has been virtually no evidence of an "epidemic" upswing in the suicide rate for any of these three categories during the past three years (1984 through 1986).

As for what authorities expect the mid-1980s numbers to show, Steve Stack, associate professor of sociology, Auburn University, writing in *The Wall Street Journal* (May 28, 1986), concludes: "Given the preliminary data for 1984 that indicate no change in our very high rate of divorce and final economic data that indicate a further drop in the youth unemployment rate, that year's figures should remain steady or decline somewhat." Professor Stack adds, "Either way, about 5,000 young people will have continued to take their lives annually. It may be news that the number is not getting worse. It is not very good news that it remains so high."

Charlotte P. Ross, "*Youth Suicide: And What You Can Do About It*" (Washington, DC: National Committee for Youth Suicide Prevention, 1984); Ross was co-chairperson.

Carol L. Huffine, PhD, "*Social and Cultural Risk Factors for Youth Suicide*" (Berkeley: California School of Professional Psychology, 1986).

Steven Stack, "A Leveling Off in Young Suicides," *The Wall Street Journal* (May 28, 1986); Stack is associate professor of sociology, Auburn University.

epidemiology Dr. Mary A. Monk, PhD, professor of community and preventive medicine, New York Medical College, explains the term thus: "Epidemiology is concerned with the investigation of the frequency and distribution of a disease or condition, and of the factors that influence its distribution. The data obtained may be useful in formulating programs of control or prevention; and the efficacy of such programs may be evaluated by epidemiological methods."

Epidemiological methods have long been applied to the phenomenon of suicide; Durkheim employed the tools of epidemiology in the 1890s to calculate suicide frequency rates among different groups of people and the changes in those frequencies over time. But as Dr. Monk notes: "The interpretation of epidemiological data is thus related to the training and persuasion of the interpreter."

Epistles Seneca, Roman statesman, philosopher and author, in his famous *Epistles* refers to a desire which seemed to possess many at the time—a morbid longing for death (*affectus qui multos occupavit, libide moriendi*). Seneca was tutor and trusted advisor to Emperor Nero until he fell from Nero's favor and was obliged to commit suicide in 65 A.D. (See Seneca's *Epistles*, 24:25.)

equivalents of suicide Arnold Madison, in *Suicide and Young People*, devotes chapter six to what he calls "Suicidal Equivalents." He refers to, and investigates for the reader, those actions such as drinking, smoking, drug-taking and reckless driving that may reflect an unconscious wish to die. He writes:

> Sigmund Freud, the pioneer in the study of the unconscious mind, said that everyone has a desire to harm or even totally destroy him or herself. Some people, because of the unfortunate circumstances of their lives, are driven to suicide openly and consciously. Others seek more subtle, slower means without comprehending why or what they are doing. Certain persons are able to perceive the consequences of their self-destructive urges and change their direction. As a rule, most people are able to control these negative impulses fairly well and live, normal, happy lives.

Madison categorizes suicidal equivalents by Those Who Surrender to Death, Those Who Mock Death, Those Who Hasten Death, and Those Who Seek Death by the Hands of Others. Such "suicide equivalents" are sometimes labeled by experts as a partial suicide, a subintentioned suicide, a sub-meditated suicide, indirect self-destructive behavior or a suicide equivalent, respectively. Authorities such as Norman L. Farberow have long insisted that the definition of who and what constitutes a suicide should include the numberless, diverse group of individuals engaged in life-shortening activities. While these kinds of death are not ruled "suicides," they represent cases where definite, unconscious lethal intention is involved. (See also ABUSE, SUBSTANCE and DAREDEVILS.)

Arnold Madison, *Suicide and Young People* (New York: Houghton Mifflin/Clarion Books, 1978).

Norman L. Farberow, *The Many Faces of Suicide* (New York: McGraw-Hill, 1980).

equivocal deaths A post-suicide term concerning the "PSYCHOLOGICAL AUTOPSY." An "equivocal death" is one in which the cause is uncertain or unclear. The psychological autopsy procedure often makes possible a decision as to the cause of death. This usually proves therapeutic for grieving survivors. The psychological autopsy is the brainchild of psychologists Edwin Shneidman and Norman L. Farberow, cofounders in 1958 of the Los Angeles Suicide Prevention Center.

Erasmus, Desiderius Dutch humanist scholar and writer (1466-1536). In his colloquy *Funus* ("The Funeral," 1526), he explains why God meant death to be an agony and explains further that he did this "lest men far and wide commit suicide." Yet Erasmus had said otherwise in his well-known *The Praise of Folly* (1509), wherein he commends those who would voluntarily kill themselves to be rid of a miserable and troublesome world, considering them, in medical historian Dr. George Rosen's words, "wiser than those who are unwilling to die and want to live longer." His *Encomium Moriae* ("*The Praise of Folly*") was a satire on the state of Europe in his time; it became a best-seller, sometimes called "*In* Praise of Folly."

Eros In his famous paper entitled, "Mourning and Melancholia," SIGMUND FREUD postulates his theory of suicide: There are, the founder of psychoanalysis said, two kinds of drives, one being the life instinct, or *Eros*, the other, the destructive, aggressive and death drive, or *Thanatos*. In *Suicide*, Earl A. Grollman writes: "For Freud, death is more than a bodily event. Death is willed. There is a constant shifting of the balance of power of the two polar instincts: Eros ages; but ageless Thanatos may assert itself 'until it, at length, succeeds in doing the individual to death.'"

"Thus," Rabbi Grollman adds, "suicide and murder are aspects of Thanatos' impulsive and devastating action." Murder, Freud theorizes, is no less than aggression turned upon another, while self-destruction is aggression turned upon the self. He implies that murder is highly destructive and is to be disapproved and prevented. Suicide, as Freud explains it, also becomes murder in the 180th degree and it too must be disapproved of and prevented.

Eskimos and suicide According to Arnold Madison in *Suicide and Young People*, certain Eskimo civilizations practiced suicide motivated by social concern. Because these people lived in regions where the food supply was limited, aged members of the group sometimes would deliberately "wander off and freeze to death, in order that the others might sustain themselves with whatever food was available."

The Iguliic Eskimos believed that a violent death was a guarantee the individual would end up in paradise, which they called the Land of Day. In contrast, according to A. ALVAREZ, "those who died peacefully from natural causes were consigned to eternal claustrophobia in the Narrow Land."

For further information, read E.F. Folk's "Psychological Continuities: From Dissociative States to Alcohol Use and Suicide in Arctic Populations"; also A.H. Leighton and C.C. Hughes, "Notes on Eskimo Patterns of Suicide."

Esprit des lois Charles de Secondat, Baron de Montesquieu, in the *Esprit des lois* (1748), theorized that the occurrence of suicide among different peoples was due to climatic influence combined with certain cultural factors. He maintained, for example, that the English willed themselves to die without reason, seemingly in the midst of happiness, while the Romans committed suicide as a consequence of education, closely tied as it was to their customs and way of thinking. Montesquieu concluded that English suicides were a result of a malady caused in the long run by the local climate's effects on both body and mind. He reasoned, therefore, that suicide should not be punishable.

Montesquieu's view, according to medical historian George Rosen, "reflects the trends of opinion about suicide that had been developing up to his time, and presage the directions that societal concern with suicide would take in the eighteenth and nineteenth centuries, indeed up to the present."

Esquirol, Jean Etienne In two massive volumes published in 1838 in Paris, Esquirol held that suicide was almost always a symptom of insanity. But he admitted it was not a disease per se. He emphasized hereditary factors, also the need to consider the individual's disposition. As part of his research, Esquirol talked to a number of suicide attempters. His work, published by J.B. Bailliere, carried the lengthy title: *Des Maladies mentales, considerés sous les* *rapports medieaux, hygieniques et medico-legaux.*

Essais Michel Eyquem de Montaigne, in his *Essais*, wrote that death is "not a remedy for one malady only, but for all ills. It is a very secure haven, never to be feared and often to be sought. It is all one whether man ends his life or endures it; whether he ends it before it has run its course or whether he waits for it to end; no matter whence the end comes, it is always his own; no matter where the thread snaps, it's the end of the road."

Montaigne, however, ultimately asks the question, "What situations, then, can truly justify the act of killing oneself? . . . After all, since there are so many sudden changes in human affairs, it is difficult to judge at what point we are really without hope . . . I have seen a hundred hares save themselves, even in the greyhounds' jaws." The French essayist concludes that the only acceptable justifications for suicide are unsupportable pain or a worse death. He had all but come full circle from earlier apparent approval of the views of the ancients (who extolled voluntary death) to a more moderate position.

ethics and morality of suicide The controversy concerning the ethics of suicide has long raged not only among philosophers, but among religious disciplines as well. CAMUS, in his *The Myth of Sysiphus*, wrote that: "There is but one philosophical problem: whether or not to commit suicide." Sir Thomas Browne, in *Religio Medici* (written in 1635 and published in 1642), stated that: "Herein are they not extreme that can allow a man to be his own assassin and so highly extoll the end by suicide of CATO." The linguist, David Daube, writes in *Philosophy and Public Affairs* (1972): ". . . the history of the word 'suicide'—and a strange one it is, mirroring the flow of civilizations and ideologies as well as the vagaries of the fate and fame of individual authors." Donald Attwater, in *The Penguin Dictionary of Saints* (1965), writes about Saint Pelagia (circa 304), a 15-year-old Christian girl who lived in Antioch during the persecution of Christians by Diocletian. When soldiers broke into her home to seize her, she eluded them and "in order to avoid outrage," she jumped to her death from the housetop. She is venerated by Catholics as a maiden martyr, an example of death before dishonor, despite once-harsh religious laws with regard to suicide.

As John L. McIntosh states in *Research on Suicide* (1985): "Recently, those controversies have been brought to the fore by many forces: changes in resuscitation and life-preserving technologies, longer life expectancies, publicized 'rational' suicides, and 'how-to' manuals (providing explicit and specific information regarding methods of suicide) which have been published in several countries." In addition, literature and the media have provided instances concerning easy and accepted suicide (e.g., a Kurt Vonnegut short story, "Welcome to the Monkey House," a Charlton Heston-Edward G. Robinson film, *Soylent Green*, or the 1980 PBS program, "Rational Suicide," which dealt with the late Jo Roman's suicide).

Indeed, complex ethical, moral and religious views on suicide, along with legal arguments, in McIntosh's words, deal with "topics such as the determination of the point of death and life, abortion, and euthanasia in polarity, disagreement, controversy and uncertainty." That such ethical and moral disagreements continue to rage can be seen by the fact that, existing side-by-side in modern cultures, are both suicide *prevention* agencies and suicide *assisting* groups.

Society has not been able or willing as yet to resolve—and in certain cases even consider—these sticky ethical and moral problems as they relate to the issue of suicide. This ethical-moral-religious-social ambivalence regarding suicide stands in the way of understanding fully what Albert

Camus called a "fatal game that leads from lucidity in the face of existence to flight from light." It goes without saying that both professional and public discussions of these aspects of suicide will be with us for some time to come.

ethnomethodology In his *Studies in Ethnomethodology*, Harold Garfinkel describes the term as a methodology for uncovering the unstated, implicit, commonsense perceptions held and acted upon by participants in a situation. Ronald Maris, PhD, editor of *Suicide and Life-Threatening Behavior* (official publication, the American Association of Suicidology), states that "we should recognize that sometimes sociologists are prone to forget that social institutions have their origin in individual human exchange; on the other hand, we should recognize the many questions that are raised by reliance on ethnomethodology alone." (See Maris's "Sociology," in Perlin's *A Handbook for the Study of Suicide*.) Maris notes that the following questions remain: "How does the researcher identify his subjects (i.e., suicides) for study, if he does not know what 'suicide' means; how does one locate 'suicidal statements' or a 'suicidal action'?" Maris concludes that error can occur by accepting the patient's definition re suicide or suicidal action as the *only* one.

euphoria A psychological state, often pathological, of extreme well-being, optimism in outlook and heightened motor activity. Euphoria is characteristic of manic states. This feeling of elation and extreme well-being can be achieved with a variety of psychoactive drugs. At least one drug, according to Solomon H. Snyder, professor of pharmacology and psychiatry, School of Medicine, the Johns Hopkins University, reserpine, which depletes brain norepinephrine, can produce a syndrome in man closely resembling endogenous depression in man, and is associated with a high incidence of suicide. (See Snyder's "Biology," in Perlin's *A Handbook for the Study of Suicide*.)

Europe Despite cultural differences that are striking and often large, the basic relationships of the major demographic variables noted elsewhere in this work for the U.S. are also found in most European countries. The motives and methods of suicide victims vary greatly, as do contemporary cultural attitudes toward suicide. (Attitudes in general are more tolerant toward suicide than in the past; still, many cultures and religions continue to view self-destruction as an abomination.) Among European nations, countries having the highest suicide death rates (per 100,000 population) are: Hungary 45.9; Austria 26.9; and Denmark 28.7. Countries with the lowest suicide death rates (per 100,000) are: Malta 0.3; Greece 3.7; and Ireland 6.9. (Note: Figures are for 1983-84.) (See also individual countries.)

Eusebius, Bishop of Caesarea In *The Ecclesiastical History* (trans, J.E.L. Oulton, 2 vols.; Cambridge, Massachusetts: Harvard University Press/Loeb Classical Library, 1959-64), Eusebius (ca. 260-ca. 340 A.D.), Bishop of Caesarea, relates tales of Christians about to be tortured who chose instead to commit suicide, "regarding death as a prize snatched from the wickedness of evil men." Voluntary martyrdom was frequent among the early Christians. (See 2:10-11, 28-29, 288-89.)

euthanasia The word "euthanasia," as derived from its original Greek context, means an easy or painless death. In recent years, two types of euthanasia are usually mentioned in professional discussions of termination of life. One is typed as "active" or direct—i.e., where life is ended by "direct" intervention, such as administering to a patient a lethal dose of a drug. The other is called "passive" or indirect—i.e., where death results from withdrawal of life-support or life-sustaining medications. DR. CHRISTIAAN BARNARD, who received international acclaim and recognition for pioneering work in heart transplant surgery, writes in *Good Life, Good Death: A Doctor's Case for Euthanasia and Suicide* that: "Indeed, even though many doctors will not admit it, passive euthanasia is accepted medical practice—a common occurrence in wards where patients live out their final hours."

The concept of "death with dignity" is today an ever-increasing focus of debate. Reasons for this concern are medical advances in technology that have brought about marked demographic changes in population(s) and a significant increase in the number of retired/aged persons. In fact, as Dr. Barnard points out, the issue is generating considerable legislation, much of which, he believes, "confuses rather than clarifies a salient question in euthanasia: Who will pull the plug?"

Most people's notion of euthanasia is best described by the term "mercy killing," or *active* intervention to end life. The layman has little or no concept of the possibility of a *passive* form of euthanasia. So-called mercy killings rose 10 times in the 1980s, say co-authors Derek Humphry and Ann Wickett in *The Right to Die: Understanding Euthanasia*. This, compared to any five-year period since 1920. The authors, husband and wife, are co-founders of the HEMLOCK SOCIETY in Los Angeles, California. The Humphrys' book, *Jean's Way*, is Derek's account of helping his critically ill first wife take her own life. Humphry also published the first U.S. guide to "self-deliverance," *Let Me Die Before I Wake*, in 1981; it was revised in 1984. At first its copies were available to members only.

In 1935, the British Voluntary Euthanasia Society was formed, followed by the founding in 1938 of the Euthanasia Society of America. In 1980, the World Federation of Right-to-Die Societies was founded, with 27 groups from 18 countries joining. According to Humphry & Wickett, already in the 1980s the number of pro-euthanasia groups has trebled. Prominent U.S. supporters of euthanasia have included Dr. Walter C. Alvarez, Robert Frost, Dr. Henry Sloane Coffin, Dr. Harry Emerson Fosdick and Margaret Sanger.

As Derek Humphry and Ann Wickett admit, "Perhaps one of the biggest controversies surrounding euthanasia will manifest itself in 1986-87, when efforts are made to introduce the Humane and Dignified Death Act in California." This litmus test legislation, authored by Los Angeles attorneys Robert L. Risley and Michael White with assistance from the Hemlock Society, will, if passed, allow a physician to not only switch off life-support systems, but also to take the life of the dying patient "upon a competent request."

As early as 1978, Pope John Paul II predicted that the great moral issue of the 1980s would be euthanasia. It has also proven to be a monumental medico-legal issue.

At present the Hemlock Society is working to qualify The Humane and Dignified Death Act (California Civil Code, Title 10.5) for an initiative to introduce the legislation in California. This requires 450,000 signatures of registered voters before it can qualify to come before the state's electors in November 1988. This, according to the society's executive director, Derek Humphry, "will be the first place in the world in which voters have been asked about their views on euthanasia." The Humane and Dignified Death Act will, if it becomes law, excuse *only doctors* from the crime of assistance in suicide, and then only for advanced, terminally ill cases. For further information, read *A Humane and Dignified Death: A New Law Permitting Physician Aid-in-Dying*, by Robert L. Risley (Glendale,

Calif.: Americans Against Human Suffering, 1987).

Euthanasia Conference One of the more significant views of the euthanasia concept was stated by Dr. Joseph Fletcher, one of the U.S.'s leading Protestant ethicists, in a paper delivered at a 1984 euthanasia conference in New York City. The University of Virginia professor of medical ethics put forward eight levels of attitude and opinion on the human initiatives that can be taken in the case of a patient dying of an incurable disease. They are:

1. An absolute refusal to elicit any human initiative in the death or the dying. Life must always be considered as the ultimate human value.
2. A qualified refusal, in that the doctor can refrain from employing *extraordinary means* of preserving life but would nevertheless do whatever possible by ordinary means to keep life going.
3. Declining to start treatment in a patient who has an incurable disease and is suffering from a curable intercurrent illness (for example, the terminally ill cancer patient with pneumonia). The doctor refuses to initiate treatment for the lung infection that can be cured and in this way may actually hasten death.
4. Stoppage of treatment, with consent, where it is the patient's wish not to be treated any further.
5. Stoppage of treatment, without consent, when the attending physician feels that further treatment can only prolong suffering.
6. Leaving the patient with an overdose of narcotic or sedative, thus assisting the dying person to take his own life.
7. Prior permission is given by the patient to the doctor to administer an injection, under certain circumstances, from which the patient will not recover.
8. Without consent, and on his own authority, the doctor ends the patient's life with an overdose of drugs.

In the second, third, fourth and fifth situations, the doctor does not take the initiative in ending the patient's life. Each is a gradation of "passive" euthanasia. Grade levels six, seven and eight, however, describe gradations of "active" participation or direct euthanasia.

Dr. Fletcher argued for the quality of life, the quality of death, and the right to choose. "The issue is *which kind of death*," he said, "an agonized or a peaceful one, death in personal integrity or in personal disintegration, a moral or demoralized end to mortal life."

Following the conference, however, avid opposition from medical, religious and legal quarters to any form of euthanasia continued.

Euthanasia Education Council (EEC) Established in 1969, the EEC was instrumental in distributing more than a quarter of a million copies of the Living Will in an effort to ensure a patient's right to a natural death, unencumbered by heroic efforts or unnecessary resuscitation. Indeed, as Humphry and Wickett note in *The Right to Die*, "massive distribution of the Living Will is a tribute to the dual efforts of both the Society for the Right to Die and the Euthanasia Education Council. Together, they respond to and fill a pressing need dramatized by the KAREN ANN QUINLAN case."

Until 1979, the Society for the Right to Die and the EEC operated as separate arms of the U.S. right-to-die movement. They shared the same offices in Manhattan and concentrated on passive euthanasia. According to Humphry and Wickett, the Society focused its efforts on enactment of state right-to-die laws, while the nonprofit Council stressed educational and philosophical issues of "dying with dignity." The close working relationship between the two groups ended in 1979 when the EEC stopped financial support of the Society, primarily because of EEC's disapproval of "indiscriminate or ill-conceived leglislation." EEC became convinced that such "legislation may have the unintended effect of limiting rather than broadening the individual's decision-making power." This was a departure from the position of founder Dr. Charles Potter, who embraced both active and passive euthanasia.

(Note: The Euthanasia Society of America, political arm of the Euthanasia Education Council, was called the Society for the Right To Die after 1975, its aim being to legalize the above-noted Will in individual states.)

Derek Humphrey and Ann Wickett, *The Right to Die: Understanding Euthanasia* (New York: Harper & Row, 1986).

Christiaan Barnard, *Good Life, Good Death: A Doctor's Case for Euthanasia and Suicide* (Englewood Cliffs, New Jersey: Prentice-Hall, 1980).

excommunicaton, of suicide attempters When the teachings of St. Augustine and other early church fathers were incorporated into the laws of the Roman Catholic Church (and later the Anglican Church), suicide was declared an act inspired by the devil. Church councils proclaimed it a mortal sin, and ruled that the bodies of suicides be denied Christian burial and that even suicide attempters must be excommunicated. However, church law made a distinction between the suicides of sane and insane persons, and also exempted young children from the penalties of the church laws. One could generalize and say that these religious doctrines against the act of suicide still remain in effect in the Roman Catholic Church and in many Protestant churches, but today many priests and ministers usually are more tolerant and have found ways to modify them in most circumstances.

Increasingly, church officials are coming to recognize suicide as not only a religious question, but also a major social-medical problem. Groups such as the Anglican Church have established special commissions to consider the revision of harsh religious laws concerning suicide. The Lutheran Church in America does not view suicide as an "unforgiveable sin," and a Lutheran suicide is not denied a Christian burial.

As for Islam, suicide is the gravest of sins. By the act of self-destruction, one violates his *Kismet*. Suicide is forbidden in the Koran which decries taking one's own life as an act worse than homicide. Paradoxically, we live in a time when Shiite Muslim suicide bombers are not uncommon in their zeal to die in a *Jihad*, or holy war. This, to fanaticists, assures them of a passport to heaven; never mind that the Koran contains nothing stating that killing guarantees a passport to heaven.

Judaism, too, considers suicide a sin. The Hebrew Bible did not specifically prohibit suicide; nonetheless, Jewish laws established later forbade it and denied full religious burial rites to people who took their own lives.

Jews over the years, however, have recognized and honored so-called "heroic" suicides—that is, self-destruction to avoid being murdered by enemies, forced into idol worship, sold into slavery or sexually abused. In fact, dying with honor to preserve one's beliefs and affirm one's freedom to control life and death has continued throughout Jewish history, from MASADA in A.D. 73 to the Nazi concentration camp in TREBLINKA during World War II.

The Japanese at one time ritualized suicide through the ceremonial death with honor of SEPPUKU, or *hara-kiri*. This was for the samurai, or members of the military class. *Hara-kiri* was officially outlawed in 1868, yet the tradition of suicide in the name of honor still influences certain Japanese practices. This ancient glorification of death with honor (e.g., the Japanese soldiers who died as kamikaze piltos during World War II) may be responsible, at least in part, for the high rate of suicide among young Japanese today.

Perhaps Rabbi Earl A. Grollman sums the topic up best in his book *Suicide*: "Instead of thundering pronouncements, the clergyman may better serve by delving into the person's complex physical and psychological makeup, and then sharing his religious resources of love and understanding. Say the sages: 'Do not judge your neighbor until you are in his place.'"

exile Self-imposed exile in some societies was an alternative to suicide. These voluntary exiles were socially acceptable (e.g., the Tixopia would set out to sea by canoe, a voyage likely to result in death) and would sometimes die at the hands of strange communities.

existentialism The modern philosophical movement was founded by Soren Kierkegaard and later developed in Germany by Heidegger and Jaspers. It was given wide popularity after World War II by the writings of Jean Paul Sartre and Albert Camus in France. Existentialism embraces both religious mysticism (Kierkegaard) and atheism (Sartre) and is a philosophy of "crisis." It regards the whole of human and cosmic existence as a series of critical situations, each demanding the whole inner resources of the individual for its resolution; crisis follows crisis to their ultimate end in death. Despair and disillusion are the chief characteristics of existentialism.

Erwin Stengel, the distinguished suicidologist and author of *Suicide and Attempted Suicide*, tells of a Swiss psychiatrist who described in detail the experiences of a patient whose suicide appeared to follow inevitably from her way of "being in the world." Another author, says Stengel, was strongly influenced by existentialism, and rejected the principle of suicide prevention as "a medical prejudice against death." This lay-psychotherapist advocated suicide if "death is needed by the soul." As Stengel says, "There is nothing new in these ideas."

EXIT The British Voluntary Euthanasia Society, started in 1935, was known briefly (in 1979) as EXIT. It was in 1979 that EXIT underwent a startling increase in younger members who, in early 1980, announced they intended to publish a booklet that offered explicit guidance to the dying on how to "accelerate" their death if they so chose. Membership of EXIT, according to Derek Humphry, co-founder, the HEMLOCK SOCIETY, and author of *The Right to Die*, who retained close ties with the organization, had been stagnant at around 3,000 for years, but "rocketed in months to more than 10,000."

EXIT's announcement about its self-deliverance booklet created international controversy, not to mention disagreement among its own members (some older members could not tolerate the idea of making the option available to everybody). While EXIT's officials attempted to deal with the group's inner turmoil, the newly formed Scottish EXIT brought out a guide of its own, modeled after the London organization's outline. This type of publication was easier to produce in Scotland because specific laws against assisting suicide did not apply there.

In the U.S. Derek Humphry, a former journalist who'd been investigated by the Department of Public Prosecution in London in 1978 for aiding in his cancer-stricken wife Jean's suicide, became convinced that a similar book (lengthier and less of a "suicide recipe book") should be published here. Feedback he'd received also convinced him that America's right-to-die groups should campaign openly for both active and passive euthanasia for the terminally ill in accordance with strict guidelines. This concept was a radical departure from the firm commitment to passive euthanasia held by Concern for Dying and the Society for the Right to Die.

In August 1980, Derek Humphry and his second wife, Ann Wickett, formed the Hemlock Society, an organization "supporting the option of active voluntary euthanasia for the terminally ill." Humphry also announced plans for publishing the first U.S. guide to self-deliverance, *Let Me Die Before I Wake*, which appeared in early 1981, available to members only. By year's end, no less than four books (or pamphlets) on self-deliverance for the terminally ill were available: Scottish EXIT's *How to Die with Dignity* (31 pp.), Hemlock's book (110 pp.), Holland's *Justifiable Euthanasia: A Manual for the Medical Profession* (11 pp.), and the London EXIT's *A Guide to Self Deliverance* (32 pp.). The latter included an essay by the renowned author ARTHUR KOESTLER, then a vice president of London's Voluntary Euthanasia Society. On March 3, 1983, the bodies of Koestler and his wife Cynthia were found in their home by police. They were victims of a double suicide.

The British Voluntary Euthanasia Society (formerly (EXIT) is headquartered at 13 Prince of Wales Terrace, London W8 5 PG. The Voluntary Euthanasia Society of Scotland is at 17 Hart Street, Edinburgh EHI 3RO, Scotland.

explosives (as suicide method) Most male youths who commit suicide do so with guns and explosives. Hanging is the second most common method, while taking pills and poisons is the third. Female youths who kill themselves do so most often with pills and poisons, but in recent years, guns and explosives have become the second most common method. Hanging is the third method most often employed by young female suicides. On the other hand, young males and females who attempt, with non-lethal results, generally do not use such violent methods as guns, explosives or hanging. Most attempters (without fatal results) have taken barbiturates or other drugs, poison or slashed their wrists—all methods that allow time for rescue.

About 63% of male suicides (of all ages) use firearms and explosives while roughly 38% of female suicides employ this method. (Note: Figures are for 1980.)

extended family, demise of A particular way of life, phenomenon of our early society, in which three generations and sometimes even an aunt, uncle and cousins in addition, lived under one roof. Many social scientists and suicidologists believe that the extended family served to protect each member from self-destructive impulses. Today, the nuclear family—generally with both father and mother working or perhaps more so, the single-parent family—offers less support and protection, say authorities who decry the demise of the old extended family unit. They point out, too, that no alternative institutions are replacing the extended family. Churches, schools and community neighborhood groups are actually declining in influence, at least in their capacity to complement the family. Even the familiar ethnic enclaves of big cities have begun to disintegrate.

Just how much the demise of extended families influences today's alarming rise in suicide among young people is, of course, difficult to measure. One thing seems certain, however, and that is that relationships now are negatively affected by a highly mobile population with weaker roots than in past generations. With less family and community attachment, young people admit they are wary about making permanent commitments because so many around them have disintegrated.

F

Fadlan, Ibn An Arab who, during 921-22 A.D., was secretary of an embassy from the Caliph of Baghdad to the Bulgars of the middle Volga. Ibn Fadlan describes a Rus funeral. (The Rus were Scandinavian, chiefly Swedish, traders and soldiers in Russia.) When a Rus chieftain died, his women slaves were asked who chose to die with their chief. The woman who answered "I" was subjected to a series of rituals and after 10 days was killed and cremated together with her master. This is not unlike similar forms of institutional suicide practiced among both the Thracians and the Hindus, each with customs whereby a widow or a concubine offered her life when the husband/master died.

fallacies about suicide There are many myths, misconceptions and fallacies that are associated with suicide. Unfortunately, these fallacies may often do great damage or cause inestimable harm. Here are some of the more prevalent and, as Arnold Madison says in *Suicide and Young People*, "most inaccurate fallacies about suicide."

Misconception: "Suicide is a crazy or insane act."
Fact: Psychologists view suicide as a defensive action; a problem-solving technique to preserve the integrity of the psychological system despite its devastating effect on the physical being.

Misconception: "Suicide is inherited."
Fact: Though historically there appear to be such examples, research shows that members of a certain family may develop a belief that they are "destined" to commit suicide, and therefore the result is facilitated.

Misconception: "Suicide is the rich man's curse."
Fact: People of different economic, social and intellectual levels can become suicide statistics. This misconception may have arisen because a wealthy person's suicide often seems more newsworthy than the death of a boy or a girl from the ghetto.

Misconception: "Suicides always occur in bad weather, spring or at night."
Fact: There are people who react negatively to dark, gloomy days, and research shows that low pressure systems might affect our emotions. However, the suicide figures do not bear out this statement. Spring, which to many brings the hope of blossoming new life and even love, might contribute to a suicidal person's decision, but again there is little accurate authentication to back up this belief. Most suicides in America occur during the day, as opposed to Japan where they happen at night. However, suicide prevention centers do note that they receive more calls in the evening. This may be due to the fact that many of the callers are simply lonely. During the day they had a degree of companionship at work, perhaps, but when the business day was over, they came home to empty rooms. Isolation invites mental depression.

There are many other misleading myths and misconceptions about the act of suicide. Most grew out of superstitions and fears that have been repeated over the centuries. Francine Klagsbrun, in *Too Young to Die*, notes that fallacies other than those discussed by Arnold Madison include:

"*Once she decided to commit suicide, nothing could have stopped her*." Authorities point out this is wrong on a number of counts. Most suicidal persons are ambivalent to the last seconds about wanting to die and wanting to live. They send out cries for help in the form of direct and indirect, subtle and not-so-subtle clues and/or messages that often tell others to save them (that is, if significant others are listening). Moreover, no individual is constantly suicidal; there are times when the urge to self-destruction is dominant, and still other times when the desire to cope with life's problems prevails. That is why suicidologists know that many suicides are preventable.

"*You should never talk about suicide in front of a suspected suicidal person—it may give that person ideas.*" Another wrong notion, since the person already has his or her own set of ideas. Prevention specialists say you can usually help by bringing suicidal thoughts into the open so they can be discussed freely.

"*It couldn't have been suicide because he/she left no note.*" In a now-classic study, psychologists Norman L. Farberow and Edwin Shneidman, cofounders of the Los Angeles Suicide Prevention Center, discovered among other things that only a small percentage—about 15%—of people who kill themselves bother to leave suicide notes. In fact, the mistaken idea that *all* suicides leave notes has led some coroners and medical examiners to mislabel suicidal deaths without notes as "accidents."

"*They loved each other so very much . . . they wanted to die together.*" The ill-conceived notion of the romantic suicide has been with us for centuries. As FRANCINE KLAGSBRUN notes in *Too Young to Die*, "Romanticizing suicide places it in the realm of artistry and beauty, and removes it from the grim realities of everyday life." A. ALVAREZ writes in *The Savage God* that romantic suicide, in the tradition of Shakespeare's *Romeo and Juliet*, is a tradition written deeply into Western literature. But the cold, hard fact of the matter is, there's nothing beautiful or romantic about real-life suicidal couples. They represent lives unfulfilled, and in the case of young people, a tragic end to short lives found to be without value or potential.

As Klagsbrun notes with candor: "The myths build, one on another, accepted as truths by most people. And the facts, the appalling facts and figures about young suicides, remain unknown."

Arnold Madison, *Suicide and Young People* (New York: Houghton-Mifflin/Clarion Books, 1978).

Francine Klagsbrun, *Too Young to Die: Youth and Suicide* (New York: Pocket Books, 1985).

A. Alvarez, *The Savage God* (New York: Random House, 1972).

Fallers, L.A. and M.C. Authors and anthropologists who wrote, among other things, "Homicide and Suicide in Busoga" (in ed., P.J. Bohannan, *African Homicide and Suicide*). The various chapter-essays in Bohannan's book discuss in several ways the social situations of how case histories are used to supplement information and data acquired by other means. Such writings have been important in understanding how cultural values may differ from one society to another—and how changes in the various forces acting on a given society can be seen to affect that society's suicide rates.

Falret, J.P. Published in 1822 the first study of suicide that made use of statistical data, though admittedly on a small scale. In his *De l'hypochondrie et du suicide*, Falret classified causal factors that may lead to suicide under four headings:

1. Predisposing—heredity, temperament, climate;
2. Accidental direct—passions, domestic troubles, etc.;
3. Accidental indirect—bodily pain, illness;
4. General civilization, civil disorders, religious fanaticism.

Falret's work was yet another step in helping authorities realize that suicide resulted from the interaction of many causal factors.

George Rosen, "History," ch. 1 of *A Handbook for the Study of Suicide*, ed. Seymour Perlin, MD (New York: Oxford University Press, 1975).

fame ALFRED ALVAREZ, writing in *The Savage God*, notes that during the period in

France (1830s) of the young Romantics, suicide actually became fashionable. He cites the case of one man, charged with pushing his pregnant mistress into the Seine, who defended his action by saying, "We live in an age of suicide; this woman gave herself to death." Alvarez adds: "For the young would-be poets, novelists, dramatists, painters, great lovers, and members of countless suicide clubs, to die by one's own hand was a short and sure way to fame." In a satirical novel published in 1844, *Jerome Paturot a la recherche d'une position sociale*, the protagonist observes that "a suicide establishes a man. Alive one is nothing; dead one becomes a hero . . . All suicides are successful; the papers take them up; people feel for them. I must decidedly make my preparations."

families We live in a society today that EMILE DURKHEIM would have surely classified as "anomic," that is, a society wherein sudden changes have caused confusion and unrest. He used the term (in addition to his categorizing of "anomic suicide") to describe societies in which social institutions either changed abruptly or broke down so rapidly that people felt confused and frustrated about their positions and goals.

One such institution that has undergone rapid change in a short time span is the family. Where once the extended family, in FRANCINE KLAGSBRUN's words, "served as a center for the teachings and traditions of society, today people question the very value of the family itself." People opt for non-traditional "alternate" lifestyles unheard of in other times. Single people live together for years, unmarried, because they "don't want to marry." Homosexual couples adopt children, and single women have children whom they raise alone with little or no stigma attached.

In *Too Young to Die*, Klagsbrun shows that "even when traditional families have been established, separations and divorces have become so commonplace that marriages that last any length of time have become the exception."

One out of every two marriages now ends in divorce in America, and about one million young people are affected by these divorces. Single-parent family statistics indicate that presently one out of every six children is being raised by only one parent—usually the mother. Social psychologist URIE BRONFENBRENNER says, "Never in the history of any society have we had a situation in which only one person and sometimes less than one is left with the responsibility of bringing up a child."

Dr. Bronfenbrenner, an authority on child development from Cornell University, points out that American parents spend less time with their children than parents of any other nation in the world (and especially so the American father). He did a study of small children from middle-class families to learn the amount of contact they had with their fathers. Average contact: 37 seconds per day. Another study showed fathers spent only 90 minutes per week with children aged six through 10. A third study showed that 44% of 156 preschool children said they would rather watch television than be with their fathers.

In addition, there's the phenomenon popularly called the "latch-key kids," children of the two-paycheck family in which both mother and father work. These young people literally grow up isolated from their parents, grow up alienated from family members who once represented authority figures. In fact, today's adolescents grow up in an isolating world to the extent that isolation in the guise of privacy becomes a sought-after value. They watch TV—alone; compute—alone; listen to music—alone; play video games—alone.

As a result of these chaotic and relatively quick changes in family life, our nation's young people have become increasingly vulnerable to the dynamics of suicide. Add to that the usual pressures of the age that cause stress, frustration and pain for all young people, particularly teenagers, and you have a time-bomb of social ills that range from abandoned codes of conduct to weak communication skills, from substance abuse to suicide.

Teens often blame themselves for family and parental problems, a process which sometimes leads to suicidal behavior. Divorce, for example, may lead to financial pressures, and these usually add to the stress on young people.

Steven Stack, PhD, associate professor of sociology at Auburn University, says that "the young often experience a sense of deep loss over a divorce since routine contacts with one parent are greatly reduced." Professor Stack adds: "Research on the families of teen suicide victims indicates they are more likely than other families to be characterized by recurrent yelling, less affection, a pattern of hostility, nagging parents, a symbiotic relationship between parent and child that prevents no autonomy, intolerance of crises, depressed and/or dominant mothers, neglect of children for a career, too much or too little discipline, and geographic mobility that breaks up social networks."

When one considers what has happened to the family institution since, say, World War II, it becomes much easier to understand the high incidence of suicide among America's young people. Like today's plastic possessions, our children's lives and the family bonds that once connected them to others appear to have become disposable. (See also EXTENDED FAMILY, DEMISE OF.)

family doctor See PHYSICIAN-PATIENT RELATIONSHIP.

family therapy (for suicide survivors) DR. MARY GIFFIN, writing with co-author and medical writer Carol Felsenthal, says in *A Cry for Help*, "The survivors of a suicide must accept the fact that theirs is a fight for survival and that techniques for survival are different from techniques for living. There is no alternative but to use survival techniques." The authors stress that suicide survivors can be taught that "the future can bring resolution to what seems an inextricable plight." This takes time, of course, intensive work, and usually though not always, professional help.

Another method by which the victims of a suicide in the family can move beyond survival to, in Dr. Giffin's words, "reintegration and learning to live again," is therapy provided by self-help groups. These organizations are valuable in that they offer mutual support, strength, and sharing with other parents who have suffered similar experiences and survived. Victims come to see that suicide happens to people from all walks of life, to people much like themselves from families much like their own. Survivors of a suicide discover in self-help groups the simple but successful technique of sharing common problems and solving them together.

There are many self-help groups for suicide victims throughout the country, such as Suicide Bereavement, Safe Place, and LOSS. Their goal: to provide survivors with friends who are supportive and understanding, to help victims assimilate the grief experiences and grow because of and through it.

The NATIONAL SELF-HELP CLEARINGHOUSE, headquartered in New York, keeps a complete listing of regional area self-help clearinghouses in the U.S. and Canada. For a list of self-help groups that deal with the problem of surviving a family member's suicide, write to:

California
San Francisco Self-Help Clearinghouse
Mental Health Association
2398 Pine Street
San Francisco, CA 94115
(Maria Weiss, 415/921-4401)

California Self-Help Center
UCLA School of Public Health
405 Hilgard Avenue
Los Angeles, CA 90024
(Alfred Katz, 213/825-1749)

San Diego Self-Help Clearinghouse
1172 Morena Boulevard
P.O. Box 86246
San Diego, CA 93138
(Ellen Murphy, 619/275-2344)

Canada
Self-Help Clearinghouse
CAMAC, Inc.
14 Aberdeen
Montreal, Quebec, Canada J4P 1R3
(Jocelyn Paiement)

Connecticut
Connecticut Self-Help Mutual Support Network
19 Howe Street
New Haven, CT 06511
(Vicky Smith, 203/789-7645)

Illinois
Self-Help Center
1600 Dodge Center—Suite S-122
Evanston, IL 60201
(Daryl Isenberg, 312/328-0470)

Minnesota
Community Care Unit
Wilder Center—919 Lafond Avenue
St. Paul, MN 55104
(Tom Duke, 612/642-4060)

Michigan
Berrien County Self-Help Clearinghouse
Riverwood Community MHC
2681 Morton Avenue
St. Joseph, MI 49085
(Robert Hess & Charles Livingston, 616/983-7781)

Nebraska
Self-Help Information Services
1601 Euclid Avenue
Lincoln, NE 68502
(Barbara Foy, 402/476-9668)

New Jersey
Self-Help Clearinghouse of New Jersey
St. Clare's Hospital, Pocono Road
Denville, NJ 07834
(Ed Madara, 201/625-7101 or 367-6274)

New York
Brooklyn Self-Help Clearinghouse
30 Third Avenue
Brooklyn, NY 11217
(Carol Berkvist, 718/834-7341 or 834-7332)

Long Island Self-Help Clearinghouse
New York Institute of Technology
6350 Jericho Turnpike
Commack, NY 11725
(Audrey Leif, 516/499-8500)

New York City Self-Help Clearinghouse, Inc.
186 Joralemon Street
Brooklyn, NY 11201
(Fran Dory, 718/852-4291)

Orange County Department of Mental Health
Consultation and Education Department
Harriman Drive, Drawer 471
Goshen, NY 10925
(Phyllis Chasin, 914/294-6185)

Rockland County CMHC
Sanitorium Road
Pomona, NY 10970
(Robert Page, 914/354-0200, ext. 2237)

Westchester Self-Help Clearinghouse
Westchester Community College
Academic/Arts Building
75 Grassland Roads
Valhalla, NY 10595
(Leslie Brock, 914/347-3620)

Oregon
Portland Self-Help Information Service
Regional Research Institute
Portland State University
P.O. Box 751
Portland, OR 97207
(Doreen Akkerman, 503/226-9360)

Pennsylvania
Self-Help Group Network
2839 Beechwood Boulevard
Pittsburgh, PA 15217
(Betty Hepner, 412/521-9822)

Philadelphia Self-Help Clearinghouse
John F. Kennedy CMHC/MR
112 N. Broad Street, Fifth Floor
Philadelphia, PA 19102
(Jared Hermalin, 609/429-7963)

Self-Help Information Network Exchange
Voluntary Action Center
200 Adams Avenue, Room 317
Scranton, PA 18503
(Arlene Hopkins, 717/961-1234)

Tennessee
Overlook Mental Health Center
6906 Kingston Pike
Knoxville, TN 36919
(Carole Vocher-Mayberry, 615/598-9747)

Texas
Tarrant County Self-Help Clearinghouse
Tarrant County Mental Health Association
804 West 7th Street
Fort Worth, TX 76102
(Karen Hale, 817/335-5405)

Dallas County Self-Help Clearinghouse
Dallas County Mental Health Association
2500 Maple Avenue
Dallas, TX 75206
(Carole Madison, 214/871-2420)

Washington, D.C.
Greater Washington Self-Help Coalition
Mental Health Association of Northern Virginia
100 North Washington Street, Suite 232
Falls Church, VA 22046
(Linda Figueroa, 703/536-4100)

Wisconsin
Continuing Education in Mental Health
University of Wisconsin Extension,
414 Lowell Hall
610 Langden Street
Madison, WI 53706
(Roger Williams, 608/263-4432)

Mutual Aid Self-Help Association (MASHA)
P.O. Box 09304
Milwaukee, WI 53209
(Maryann Heitl, 414/461-1466)

fantasy world, retreat into Potential suicides will sometimes, for reasons that have more to do with their fantasies than with actual causes, lose their hold of the real world altogether. When this happens and they retreat into a world of fantasy, they have been known to do such imagined things as destroy their parents, a good friend or lover, even themselves, in fact, every aspect of the life he or she could no longer tolerate. Such situations happen generally when the individual becomes incapable of handling life's pressures and pains and he or she reaches a breaking point. Although this type of illness, whether neurotic or at the psychotic stage, is serious and potentially dangerous, it can often be controlled if treated early, and a possible suicide may well be prevented.

farmers During late 1985 and throughout 1986, America's farmbelt was being described as a "time bomb" because so many farmers were committing suicide. Debt-ridden midwestern and southern farmers were starting to feel the pressures and anxieties that accompanied low crop prices, relatively high interest rates and low land values. These and other more subtle political factors began combining to force people off farms that, in many instances, had been in their families for generations. Land was being lost in forced sales and equipment and livestock was seized.

Dan Levitas, a research consultant for Prairie Fire, a rural self-help advocacy group based in Des Moines, Iowa, said this about suicides triggered by desperation over the farm economy and individual farm family financial stress: "Nobody keeps records, but I would estimate there have been more than 25 suicides among farmers in Iowa this year, including six in September (of 1985)."

As the farmers' problems continued to mount, the Middle West's suicide phenomenon spread southward and even into the eastern regions of upstate New York and central and southern New Jersey. Many small towns deteriorated as Main Street businesses and farm equipment dealerships closed their doors. And several farmers became so troubled that they killed themselves. Lucinda A. Noble, director of the Cornell University Cooperative Extension System reported to the media: "I know of five suicides in the past nine months that were people engaged in agriculture who were over-extended and decided life was not worth living."

Another bizarre aspect of the farmer suicides: Mental health experts say bankers, because of their role in making yearly loans to farmers to buy seed and long-term mortgages to buy land, have in some instances become the target when things go wrong. One 63-year-old farmer, who farmed near the tiny southeastern Iowa town of Lone Tree, apparently distraught over his financial plight, killed the president of his bank, a neighbor and his own wife before he committed suicide.

In Elk Point, South Dakota, a county director of the Farmers Home Administration (FHA), the federally chartered lender of last resort for family farms, shot and killed his wife, two children, and the family dog. He then drove to his office and turned the gun on himself. He left this handwritten note on the desk: "The job has got pressure on my mind, pain on my left side." Friends said that the man had been upset for weeks by his work, torn between his strict allegiance to the FHA rules and his feeling for farmers. The man faced some especially unpleasant tasks in coming days because the U.S. Government had just lifted a two-year moratorium on FHA foreclosures. About 20 farmers in his county were behind in their payments.

Pete Zevenbergen, director of the Community Mental Health Center in Cedar Rapids, Iowa, says of the crisis, "It's almost a combat mentality. When you're besieged, you're really feeling that you don't have alternatives and you become irrational. The guy you're shooting at isn't necessarily the enemy."

Farmers are not totally unique in such a situation, of course. There is tremendous stress and pain to persons when economic and social dislocation occurs on a large scale, whether in rural or urban areas. But the farmers' predicament—which generates an additional stress element—is the fact that in such crises they not only lose their farms, but their businesses as well. Moreover, the farmer who loses his job may lose one that was held by his father, his grandfather and other ancestors for 100 years or more.

In mid-February 1986, more than 65,000 farmers around the country received letters from the FHA notifying them that they must restructure or renegotiate their farm loan payments or face foreclosure. The federal agency, with some 2,000 field offices in the U.S., said it took the drastic action to recover $5.8 billion in deliquent loans.

fathers, distracted It has been, and continues to be well-documented, that parents' attitudes, fathers included, and the overall quality of family life play an important role in the development of children. FRANCINE KLAGSBRUN writes in *Too Young to Die*, "More than anything else, family background and experiences during the early years of life play a major role in creating suicidal wishes among young people. Study after study has found that a large proportion of young suicide attempters and completers came from disturbed or disrupted homes, lacking in stability and support." In fact, psychologists and juvenile authorities in other fields generally state that broken homes cause numerous kinds of antisocial and/or deviant behavior among young people, including drug addiction, alcoholism, juvenile delinquency and suicide. (See also FAMILIES.)

Fawcett, J.A. Along with co-author William G. Bunney, Jr., and M. Leff,

Fawcett was able to separate high- from low-risk mental patients on the basis of stated intent to die, communication of this intent only to the significant other, and attempted behavioral change just before attempted suicide. According to Dr. Seymour Perlin and Chester W. Schmidt, Jr. (in "Psychiatry," ch. 8 of Perlin's *A Handbook for the Study of Suicide*), "In addition to the specific acute features, *chronic* behavior patterns also distinguished the high-risk patients: interpersonal in capacity, marital isolation and negation or distorted communication of dependency needs." For additional information, read: J.A. Fawcett, M. Leff and William G. Bunney, Jr., "Suicide: Clues from Interpersonal Communication."

fear of punishment and/or separation, as distress signal In some young people, the fear of punishment and/or separation (often as a form of punishment), real or imagined, may cause them to think obsessively of suicide as the only solution.

In families where there is little or no communication, or communication is absurdly twisted, violence sometimes becomes the only interchange between parent and child. Children who are punished regularly (and often brutally) come to think they can do nothing right. They also discover quickly that their parents are easiest to live with after they've gotten rid of their aggression through such abuse. These child-victims sometimes become self-destructive. They anticipate their parents' abuse by punishing themselves. Then, tragically, one day they self-inflict the final, lethal punishment.

For the troubled, overly-anxious or depressed young person, fear of separation can become quite morbid and totally devastating. Routine separations experienced by most of us in life—e.g., going to kindergarten, going off to college, breaking up with a girl- or boyfriend, moving to a new neighborhood or town—are difficult enough, but for the insecure, highly sensitive child they can prove debilitating.

Sometimes the young person affected by these fears leaves clues that indicate potential self-destructive action. Such clues may be in the form of broad hints; or they may be subtle changes in behavior. Usually, as Edwin Shneidman, author of *Definition of Suicide*, says, potential suicides show attitudes reflecting themselves in various verbal or behavior "clues." For further information on the crucial indicators, or clues, of imminent or potential suicide, see CLUES, WARNING SIGNS OF SUICIDE. All, as Professor Shneidman points out, are real, and "too seldom taken as such."

female suicides Overall suicide rate per 100,000 population for females in the U.S. was 5.6 (according to 1982 figures supplied by the World Health Organization). This compares to the male rate (per 100,000) for the same year of 19.2 Age grouping with the highest rate for females was from 45 to 54; the figure, 9.5. Lowest by age group, 0.2, for those 5 to 14. White females' suicide rate was higher than was that for other races: white female rate per 100,000 was 4.5, for other races, 2.9.

The ever-changing patterns of suicide among young females—from teens into early mid-twenties—is complex. Traditionally, women (including girls) are the major attempters among suicidal persons in America. But the suicidal act ends lethally more often among men. For the U.S. population as a whole, about three times as many women as men attempt to kill themselves each year, and about three times as many men as women complete suicide. FRANCINE KLAGSBRUN, author of *Too Young to Die*, reports that "Some researchers estimate that, among young people, as many as nine times more girls than boys attempt suicide without completing it."

femme fatale As the era of Romanticism degenerated (from mid to late nineteenth century), so, too, did the idealization of death. In *The Romantic Agony*, Mario Praz explains how fatalism in time came to mean fatal sex. As ALFRED ALVAREZ notes, "the femme fatale replaced death as the supreme inspiration." Baudelaire said, "*Le satanisme a gagne. Satan s'est fait ingenu.*" Social, religious and legal taboos against suicide lost their power even as sexual taboos gained strength. Alvarez contends that homosexuality, incest and sado-masochism began to replace suicide in the cultural conscience, "if only because they seemed at the time far more shocking." Alvarez concludes that "Fatal sex also had the added advantage of being safer and slower than suicide, an enhancement rather than the contradiction of a life dedicated to art."

The idea, established by the Romantics, that one of the prices of genius was suicide, faded gradually. But nothing would ever be the same; suicide, in Alvarez's words, "has permeated Western culture like a dye that cannot be washed out."

A. Alvarez, *The Savage God: A Study of Suicide* (New York: Random House, 1972).

Fifth Commandment Organized religions were the first to condemn suicide. Christianity believed life to be a gift from God, and that only God may take life away. Moreover, self-death violated the Fifth Commandment delivered to Moses on Sinai: *Thou shalt not kill*. The Judeo-Christian tradition as well as Islam held, however, that suicide in the form of martyrdom was permissible. The Jews also believed suicide to be acceptable action if carried out to prevent torture, rape or slavery. King Saul, for example, fell on his sword after defeat in battle. The mass self-destruction of the defenders of MASADA, a Jewish fortress beseiged by Romans in A.D. 72-73, to prevent capture was also considered a heroic action. (See also DECALOGUE ARTICLE.)

Fiji Islands Early Fiji Islanders forced the many wives of a tribal chieftain to kill themselves when he died. The women would actually compete with one another in the rush to destroy themselves, believing that the first to die would become the chieftain's favorite wife in "the world of the spirits." Not a few early societies insisted that certain members commit suicide for ritual purposes. (See also SUTTEE.)

Filipino-Americans Psychologist John L. McIntosh in 1981 published a bibliography that included references for U.S. racial minorities such as Blacks, Native Americans, Asian-Americans, Hispanics, Chinese-Americans and Filipino-Americans. For results of his study based on official statistics, see J.L. McIntosh's *Suicide Among U.S. Racial Minorities: A Comprehensive Bibliography.*

Many elderly members of minority ethnic groups find it impossible to adjust to a new way of life in America and choose to die by their own hands. Others who may wish to die live on because of their family's pride, their physician's principles, their formal affiliation with a church, or an ethnic community attitude that views suicide as a blot on the record.

Finland Among the world's cultures, Finland's has historically ranked high in both homicide and suicide. World Health Organization (WHO) statistics for 1983 show the country's suicide rate per 100,000 population to be 24.4. The male suicide rate was a very high 39.8, while the female rate was only 9.9. Highest among listed age groups was 45 to 54, with a 39.7 suicide rate per 100,000 population. The 1983 suicide rate figure is slightly higher than the 1984 rate of 23.5 (*Demographic Yearbook, 1978*, published by the United Nations in 1979). The Finns, then, have the fourth highest suicide rate in the world, surpassed only by Hungary, Austria and Denmark. A. ALVAREZ notes in *The Savage God* that on non-national charts, the highest suicide rate in the world is perhaps that of West Berlin. Its rate is twice that of West Germany as a whole. "The city is," writes Alvarez, "a model of what Durkheim called 'anomic'—moral, cultural, spiritual, political and geographical alienation." In addition, a high proportion of the population is middle-aged and elderly.

firearms as suicide method In 1980, firearms were used in 57.7% of all suicides in the U.S. Among men the percentage was 63.1, while 38.6% of women lethal suicides used a firearm. Men usually kill themselves in a more violent manner (shooting, stabbing, hanging) than do women, who seem to prefer a more passive means of self-destruction (drugs, inhaling gas, swallowing poison). Women, however, have begun to use guns more frequently than, say, a decade ago (this is so particularly in the South).

HERBERT HENDIN, MD, author of *Suicide in America*, says that the method employed by the suicide often tells a great deal about the "psycho-social meaning of the act." He cautions, too, that suicidal method, as it relates to motive, includes not only the lethal means employed but also the circumstances surrounding the suicide, such as whom, if anyone, the individual "informs of his suicidal intentions and what the contents are of any suicide note that is written." Finally, the method-to-motive relationship in suicide can only be understood if one considers the cultural context in which suicide occurs.

Firth, Raymond W. In his book *Tikopia Ritual and Belief*, Firth writes of the Tikopian method of committing suicide by setting out to sea in a canoe, knowing that the voyage will probably result in death. If, however, the man survives and returns, he would not suffer loss of face, unlike a Japanese who tried suicide and failed. As Firth notes, suicide thus appears to be a means of escaping the community and its stressful pressures.

Flaubert, Gustave French writer (1821-1880) whose most famous novel, *Madame Bovary* (1857), describes Emma Bovary's attempts to escape her drab existence through adultery and finally suicide. Flaubert confessed in his letters that as a young man "I dreamed of suicide." He wrote that he and his young provincial friends, "lived in a strange world, I assure you; we swung between madness and suicide; some of them killed themselves . . . another strangled himself with his tie, several died of debauchery in order to escape boredom; it was beautiful!" (From Flaubert's *Correspondence*; Paris, 1887-1893.)

The famous novelist was once asked who the real-life Emma Bovary was. The author smiled wistfully and said, "*I* am Madame Bovary."

Flood, R.A. With C.P. Seager, compared completed suicides of psychiatric patients with two control groups. One notable finding was the "high incidence of previous suicidal attempts in the suicide group compared with the two control groups." They also noted the suicide group's high incidence of disturbed relationships with hospital staff that led to premature discharge, often against medical advice. Doctors Seymour Perlin and Charles W. Schmidt, Jr., in the former's *A Handbook for the Study of Suicide* (p. 154), conclude that aside from the issue of treatment of the suicide group, "the significance of this finding may be in the parallel disruptions with the losses of significant others before and after hospitalization." The Flood-Seager report is entitled: "A Retrospective

Examination of Psychiatric Case Records of Patients Who Subsequently Committed Suicide."

follow-up, of suicidal persons (by Suicide Prevention Centers) The primary goal of any suicide prevention worker is to stop the caller from killing himself. Edwin S. Shneidman and Norman L. Farberow, cofounders of the Los Angeles Suicide Prevention Center, agree that remaking the caller's personality, curing all his troubles, no matter how serious, is not the major intention of a suicide prevention service. In fact, the active, effective SPC has a limited goal, to provide an immediate, ready contact between the highly disturbed person calling a 24-hour "hotline" or "lifeline" and the community's helping agencies that are available.

Fortunately, as Dr. Shneidman points out, "people are not permanently suicidal." Even for the most despairing person, the suicidal mood ebbs and flows. In the majority of cases, SPC staffers can provide the tension relief needed to ease a critical suicidal situation. They can then "arrange" things for the suicidal caller; that is, set up an interview with a staff psychiatrist, psychologist, social worker or volunteer. Sometimes a meeting is arranged between the suicidal and a "significant other." (The telephone therapist determines who this might be: father, mother, wife, lover or whoever.) The idea is to avert the critical moment that will drive the caller to the brink of self-destruction, then provide the necessary follow-up help as quickly as possible.

Each Suicide Prevention Center necessarily tailors its service to its own needs. Dr. Shneidman emphasizes that "there is no single pattern or organization yet proved to be better or more successful than another." Some SPCs operate autonomously, others are a unit of the community's mental health facility. An SPC can also be part of an emergency hospital or tied to the local university.

"Active, increasingly effective suicide prevention services," says Dr. Shneidman, "offer the suicidal person a fresh grasp on life. They promise no panacea. Life's burdens will continue. But troubled men can persevere. The services now spreading across the country can show him that life is not so narrow—and more importantly, that death is not the answer."

The majority of suicidal callers want and need help, and help is what SPC workers provide. Dr. Norman L. Farberow, cofounder and co-director of the prototypical Los Angeles Suicide Prevention Center, says that follow-up studies indicate the center to be of considerable help. When questioned a short time after their calls, 87% of the people said that they had been helped. Questioned a long time after their distress calls, 80% still maintained that they had been helped. Twenty-eight% said that the SPC had saved their lives; 34% said the facility "might" have saved their lives.

Rabbi Earl A. Grollman contends that "the suicide prevention center must be thoughtfully created, properly administered, and generously supported in order to extend maximum understanding and assistance." He believes that such services are "a most important community facility for both prevention and intervention."

For a more complete discussion of SPCs and the various levels of assistance, see PREVENTION, INTERVENTION, and POSTVENTION. (Note: An updated list of Suicide Prevention Centers throughout the U.S. is provided in Appendix 3.)

forfeiture, law of According to Henry de Bracton, legal authority of his own mid-13th century in England, an ordinary suicide forfeited his goods, while a person who killed himself to avoid a felony conviction forfeited both goods and land. This so-called "law of forfeiture" remained in force throughout England into the 19th century. It was, however, often circumvented through the claim of insanity. (For further information see Henry de Bracton, *De legibus et consuetudinibus Angliae* 2:424.)

Forrestal, James Former U.S. banker and Cabinet officer in the Franklin D. Roosevelt and Harry S. Truman administrations, Forrestal (1892-1949) left banking as America's entry into World War II loomed closer. He became undersecretary of the navy (1940-42), secretary of the navy (1942-47) and first secretary of defense (1947-49). He committed suicide while a patient at Bethesda Navy Hospital in 1949 by leaping from the window of his 16th-floor room in the famed medical center.

France Official, legal and ecclesiastical attitudes toward suicide were conservative until well into the 18th century. Suicide was, in fact, equated with murder in various countries in Europe. In France, the corpse was treated accordingly; the body was dragged through the streets, head downward on a hurdle, and *then* hanged on a gallow. Medical historian Dr. George Rosen notes that the French Criminal Ordinance of August 1670 "still required that the body of a suicide be dragged through the streets and then thrown into a sewer or onto the town dump." Despite the law, however, many such cases were overlooked and such severe penalties were not carried out. In Toulouse, for example, Rosen says the punishment of dragging the corpse was imposed in 1742 and again in 1768, but "it is worth noting that the suicides occurred in jail and that the victims were either convicted of or indicted for a criminal offense." Spectator revulsion against the practice caused cessation of the penalty after 1768, although burial in consecrated ground was often denied the suicide in this predominantly Catholic nation.

In 1822, C. Lachaise studied the question of suicide in Paris. Concerning statistical data available from mortality tables, he noted that the cases reported probably understated the dimensions of the problem for two reasons: first, relatives in certain cases tried to prevent a family disgrace by having the death attributed to some other cause, such as insanity; second, reported suicides did not consider the large number of attempted suicides that for one or another reason failed. Moreover, Lachaise decided that suicide was more frequent in the laboring class (*la classe des proletaires*) primarily because of poverty.

Another extensive study concerning suicide in France was done by Brierre de Boismont, and was considered an important contribution to the problem of suicide in the mid-19th century. In his treatise *Du Suicide et de la folie suicide*, published in 1856, de Boismont not only used statistics extensively, but he also questioned 265 persons who had either planned or attempted suicide. On the basis of his comprehensive, detailed study, de Boismont denied that all suicides are due to insanity, though a large number admittedly are caused by mental illness. He listed these important causes: insanity, alcoholism, illness, family troubles, love problems, and poverty. His findings also brought him close to a sociological explanation of suicide. For instance, he discovered a higher proportion of unmarried persons, of old people, and of men. Historian Rosen writes: "More generally, he saw suicide as a consequence of changes in society leading to social disorganization and to alienation for many people." E. Lisle, in a work also published in 1856, in Paris, expressed remarkably similar views.

It is obvious that Brierre de Boismont, E. Lisle, and other 19th-century investigators of suicide were heading toward Emile Durkheim's now-famous conclusion stated in *Le Suicide* in 1897: that suicide will not be widely prevalent in a society that is well-integrated politically, economically and socially.

Recent statistics (1983, World Health Organization) show France's suicide rate to be high, relatively speaking. Using rates per 100,000 population, the 1983 total was 21.8—31.7 among males, 12.3 among females. The 75-plus age grouping shows the highest rate per 100,000 population—57.3. Interestingly, the 25 to 34 age group has exactly the same rate of suicide per 100,000 population as the nation's total, 21.8.

Emile Durkheim, *Le Suicide* (1897), trans. J.A. Spaulding and G. Simpson (Glencoe, Illinois: The Free Press, 1951).

Dr. George Rosen, "History," ch. 1, *A Handbook for the Study of Suicide*, ed. Seymour Perlin, MD (New York: Oxford University Press, 1975).

fraud DR. MARY GIFFIN and Carol Felsenthal theorize in *A Cry for Help* that some young people feel they simply don't have what it takes to succeed. Such children, pushed to succeed and achieve by parents, believe their accomplishments come only through extraordinarily hard work and that even the smallest reversal "can send them reeling." And since they are fulfilling someone else's goals instead of their own, these young people often have fragile personalities. Their sense of self is brittle. Says Dr. Giffin, "They consider themselves frauds and fear that, one day, everyone else will reach the same conclusion."

The co-authors use several case histories to illustrate their "I'm a fraud" theory. In each instance, the affected youngster's crisis grew until a suicide. In each case, their own view of self was one of fearful inadequacy.

Mary Giffin, MD, and Carol Felsenthal, *A Cry for Help: Exploring and Exploding the Myths about Teenage Suicide—A Guide for All Parents of Adolescents* (New York: Doubleday, 1983).

French Criminal Ordinance of August 1670 This infamous ordinance required, among other things, that the body of a suicide be dragged through the streets and then thrown into a sewer or onto the town dump. Despite the law, cases were sometimes ignored and the severe penalties were not applied. The penalty was last carried out in Toulouse, in 1768. (See also FRANCE.)

Freud, Sigmund Austrian psychiatrist (1856-1939) of Jewish descent, founder of modern psychoanalysis. Though much of Freud's work was controversial, particularly his theories about children's sexuality, his concept of the unconscious mind underlies most modern inquiries into human behavior and motives.

Concerning the act of suicide, Freud viewed the urge to kill oneself as essentially a problem within the individual. He believed that life and death forces are in constant conflict in every person, even though these conflicting forces are unconscious.

On April 27, 1910, the Vienna Psychoanalytic Society met for a discussion dealing with "Suicide in Children." Freud said then that in their desire to wean children from their early family life, schools often exposed the immature student too abruptly to the harshness of adult life. He added that too little was known about suicide but that perhaps the self-destructive action was actually a repudiation of life because of the craving for death. This particular remark, we now know, foreshadowed Freud's later belief in a death instinct.

Sigmund Freud's paper "Beyond the Pleasure Principle" presents his later theory of suicide. There are two distinct kinds of drives: One is the life instinct, or *Eros*; the other, the death, destructive and aggressive drive, or *Thanatos*. There is an ongoing, constant shifting of the balance of power between the two instincts. Eros ages, but ageless

Thanatos may assert itself "until it, at length, succeeds in doing the individual to death."

Suicide, as well as homicide, is an aspect of the impulsive destructive action of Thanatos. Murder, Freud believed, is aggression turned upon another, suicide is aggression turned upon oneself. His implied value judgment is that murder should be disapproved and prevented because it is highly destructive. Suicide must also be disapproved and prevented since it is nothing less than murder "in the 180th degree."

Freud's studies on suicide were far more extensive than the ideas noted here. His theories were developed between the years 1881 and 1939.

Friedman, Paul Published a well-known analysis in 1967 of 93 suicides over a seven-year period among New York City policemen. He found that "nine out of every ten individuals in this group killed themselves with revolvers." Friedman concluded that there is no relation between particular methods of suicide and suicide intent. As Dr. Herbert Hendin suggests, "the relation of method to motive in suicide cannot be understood without reference to the cultural context in which suicide occurs." For further information, read Friedman's "Suicide Among Police: A Study of 93 Suicides Among New York City Policemen, 1934-1940," in Shneidman's *Essays in Self-Destruction*, pp. 414-49.

friends, loss or lack of, as distress signal Presuicidal persons of all ages tend as they move closer to self-destruction either to drop their close friends or deliberately to make themselves so obnoxious that the friends drop them. Potential suicides will often become either very withdrawn or overly aggressive. In any case, this is an important distress signal or warning sign to parents, friends or associates. In suicidologist Edwin Shneidman's words, "Once a person has finally decided to kill himself, he begins to act 'differently.' He may withdraw to become almost monklike and contemplative."

Friendship Line, the A direct, person-to-person service in San Francisco where specially trained volunteers regularly call elderly persons to offer emotional support. An offshoot of the city's suicide prevention program, started in 1963 by Bernard Mayes, this direct, person-to-person service figures importantly in the suicide and mental health education of other minority (e.g., Chinese, blacks) peoples and groups throughout the Bay Area. Staff members offer consultation, training, and seminars to schools, universities, hospitals, and mental health agencies. San Francisco is referred to by many as the suicide capital of the U.S. (it isn't, but it does have a high suicide rate per 100,000 population), and SAN FRANCISCO SUICIDE PREVENTION has worked hard to reverse this situation. The program also includes two drug lines and a Grief Counseling Program for those who have suffered a loss by suicide or other traumatic circumstances. The entire staff at the center (which includes the Friendship Line) has between 150 to 200 volunteers.

frightening event, as cause of suicide Arnold Madison, in *Suicide and Young People*, contends that family life, especially for the very young, is a major factor in producing a sense of competence within children. He writes that, "A single frightening moment, which threatens future happiness, can prompt a young person to suicide . . ." Madison feels that the "seeds of suicide" are planted in our culture, and cultures around the world display certain similarities (e.g., the importance of family life for our children).

Frost, Robert Lee U.S. poet (1874-1963), much of whose work reflects the New

England countryside, where he spent a large part of his life. Frost's description of the family in his famous poem "The Death of a Hired Man" contains the oft-quoted line, "Home is the place where when you have to go there, they have to take you in." Suicidologists, including DR. MARY GIFFIN, medical director, the Irene Josselyn Clinic of the North Shore Mental Health Association, Northfield, Illinois, say that kind of family is increasingly rare. Today, if the family doesn't like you, you often get kicked out. We call these youngsters "throw-away children," and many have ended up as suicides. The U.S. Department of Health and Human Services estimates that each year more than one million youngsters between 10 and 17 years of age either leave home or are forced to leave. These children suffer loss of family ties that often seem to make life empty of meaning and hope, of reason to go on.

frustration In a study that illustrates the social-psychological side of suicide, Andrew Henry and James Short's *Suicide and Homicide* relates the suicide rate to economic cycles. They agree with French sociologist EMILE DURKHEIM, author of *Le Suicide*, that high social status and low external restraint are associated with high suicide rates, but they go further by postulating that the suicide's behavior is determined by both external as well as internal forces operating conjointly. Ronald Maris says that the two authors contend that aggression is often, though not always, a consequence of frustration, that business cycles produce variation in the hierarchical ranking of persons and groups, and that frustrations are generated by interference with the "goal response" of maintaining a constant or rising position in a status hierarchy relative to the status position of others in the same system.

Ronald Maris, "Sociology," ch. 5, in *A Handbook for the Study of Suicide*, ed. Seymour Perlin, MD (New York: Oxford University Press, 1975).

funerals See BURIAL (FOR SUICIDES).

"Funus" (The Funeral) In his 1526 colloquy, "Funus," ERASMUS explained why God meant death to be an agony, and said that he did this "lest men far and wide commit suicide. And since, even today, we see so many do violence to themselves, what do you suppose would happen if death weren't horrible? Whenever a servant or even a young son got a thrashing, whenever a wife fell out with her husband, whenever a man lost his money, or something else occurred that upset him, off they'd rush to noose, sword, river, cliff, poison." Yet, paradoxically, in his *The Praise of Folly* (1509), Erasmus had commended those who voluntarily killed thenselves to get rid of a miserable and troublesome world. One must remember, however, that the Dutch scholar's earlier writing, *Encomium Miriae (The Praise of Folly)*, was intended as a satire on the state of Europe in his time.

Furst, Sidney and Ostrow, Mortimer In a major psychoanalytic article concerning the relationship of suicide method versus motive, "The Psychodynamics of Suicide," Furst and Ostrow suggest that the suicidal method is an expression of a sexual wish and/or punishment for a fantasized crime. In *Suicide in America*, Herbert Hendin, MD, writes: "Without psychodynamic evidence from case material, they (the team of Furst-Ostrow) maintain that male homosexuals, if suicidal, will stab or shoot themselves or arrange to be stabbed or shot as an extreme expression of their wish to be attacked by another man's penis." Hendin concludes that if these writers were correct, homosexuality would be a far more important factor in suicide in the U.S. than elsewhere in the world, since only in America are guns the major method of suicide.

Furst and Ostrow also regard falling from heights as an expression of sexual guilt for "phallic erection under improper circumstances." Dr. Hendin's rebuttal: "Given the alternative of such unsubstantial speculation . . . psychiatry has settled for the safe but sterile statistical approach that has dominated the subject." Hendin, along with other suicidologists, believes that "Psychodynamic study of the suicidal individual can often provide evidence of the meaning of the choice of a particular method."

Furst and Ostrow, "The Psychodynamics of Suicide," in *Suicide Theory and Clinical Aspects*, ed. L. Hankoff and B. Einsidler (Littleton, Massachusetts: PSG Publishing Co., 1979), pp. 165-178.

Herbert Hendin, *Suicide in America* (New York: W.W. Norton, 1982).

G

games, psychological John H. Hewett, Christian minister and ethicist, writes in *After Suicide*: "Families play games together just as you and I do individually. We have seen that suicide doesn't happen in a vacuum. It drops like a bomb into a real, relating family. It kicks off an incredible round of negative family games that can become destructive if they're not adequately refereed."

Dr. Hewett, pastor of the Graefenburg Baptist Church, Waddy, Kentucky, lists 10 of the most common games played by families in the aftermath of suicide: scapegoating, keeping an impossible secret, the survival myth, circle the wagons, king (or queen) of the mountain, the silent treatment, who loved/was loved the most? let's grieve forever, halo and pitch fork, and head for the hills.

Hewett's premise is that most families who get caught up in such games block off all effective communication among themselves. Communication, he says, is the key to surviving together in suicide's aftermath.

It was Eric Berne, in his landmark book *Games People Play* (Grove Press, 1964), who popularized the concept of psychological "games." Berne defined a game as an ulterior behavior pattern that usually involves some kind of "con." These patterns, as Hewitt notes, are usually destructive, motivated by hidden desires to win a payoff of some kind or a desired feeling.

John H. Hewitt, *After Suicide* (Philadelphia: Westminster Press, 1980).

gas, as suicide method Women, more so than men, seem to prefer a more passive means of self-destruction. For instance, women will more likely ingest a lethal dose of drugs, swallow pills or poison, or inhale gas rather than shoot or hang themselves. Authorities conclude this may be because women don't usually want to shed their blood or disfigure themselves.

The poet Sylvia Plath, who had made several previous suicide attempts, sealed her kitchen and turned on the gas, but not before she left a note about how to reach her doctor. A series of miscalculations—her helping woman arrived late, the door was locked, a neighbor had been knocked unconscious by the escaping gas, workmen had to force the building door open—cost Plath her life. ALFRED ALVAREZ, who described his friend's death in his book *The Savage God*, wrote, "Her calculations went wrong and she lost."

More British citizens than Americans use gas as a method of suicide because of its greater availability in homes and apartments. But the fact remains that as long as society produces suicidal people, methods will be found.

Gas ranks behind firearms, poison, hanging/strangulation as a suicide method in the U.S.

gatekeepers Term used for those involved with and engaged in the educational process concerning suicide prevention, intervention and postvention—the physicians, psychiatrists, psychologists, psychotherapists, nurses, social workers, clergymen, lay volunteers and others who are most likely to know of persons about to take their lives. Many of these professionals and lay volunteer workers are generally in a strategic position to identify and do something about a potentially dangerous situation.

genetic predisposition EMILE DURKHEIM determined that his extensive data showed no significant association between suicide rates and genetic factors.

However, suicide in a particular individual's family does appear to increase this kind of action. A person (especially when young) sometimes imitates the behavior patterns of certain parents or other relatives. For example, a person close to someone who commits suicide may determine that death is a way out of extremely stressful circumstances. This may increase the chances of its future use, especially where an individual identified strongly with the deceased.

Some authorities think that suicides tend to repeat in some families because of innate or genetic predisposition to severe depression, family exposure to extreme stresses, guilt and grief resulting from the first suicide, and/or the ways in which families relate. Modern biochemical techniques of increased sophistication have begun recently to point to what EDWIN SHNEIDMAN terms "a substantial effort to reduce the reason for suicide to biological depression." Still, Dr. Shneidman, a thanatologist, concludes that "while there may be some basis for this, it is far from the whole story. Suicide and depression are not synonymous."

Interestingly, whenever one sees a listing of "those most likely to commit suicide," one of the categories always included is "a history of suicide in his/her family."

geographic factors Some authorities concede that geography may influence people who live in isolated areas, in those areas where days are short and the nights long and/or where climate is predominantly rainy or cloudy. An Italian professor of psychological medicine, Henry Morselli, in his book *Suicide: An Essay on Comparative Moral Statistics* (published in Milan in 1879 and reprinted in 1975 by the Arno Press, New York City), stated that "with respect to Italy, by comparing the geographical distribution of suicide with that of stature, the following is the formula by which their relation may be expressed. The frequency of suicide in the various parts of Italy generally is in a direct ratio with stature, and the inclination to self-destruction increases from south to north as the stature of the Italians gradually increases."

In the 18th century, there was the widespread notion that England was a "land of melancholy and suicide" (Oswald Doughty, "The English Malady of the Eighteenth Century"). Commenting on this, medical historian Dr. George Rosen says, "Natives and foreigners generally accepted the allegation that gloominess was a characteristic of the inhabitants of the British Isles, particularly the English. This melancholy was more than just a mood; it was a disease, a malady of mind and body which directly affected the imagination and was liable to end in self-destruction." The condition was linked etiologically with both the physical and social environment.

These notions of geographic (or environmental) influence have been traced back to antiquity, with roots in geography and medicine. Hippocrates perhaps started such ideas in *Airs, Waters, Places*. During the 16th and 17th centuries, increasing significance was placed on such notions in many fields of thought, study and practice. While considering questions of national character and cultural differences, writers and scholars discussed causal roles of such environmental aspects as air, diet and temperature in medical and social problems. According to Rosen, these discussions became even more frequent in the 18th century, and the use of such ideas led many writers (among them Bodin, Arbuthnot and Montesquieu) to oppose sanctions against suicide and to urge a less prejudiced and more tolerant view of suicide.

While many of the discussed conclusions are challenged today, there does seem to be a global geographical correlation. Northerly places, such as Scandinavia, show higher suicide rates than countries in the more tropical climes. However, other factors such as religion must be considered here.

There are significant geographical variations evident in America. For instance, Nevada is the state which consistently leads suicide rate statistics. The 1980 rate was 22.9 per 100,000 while the U.S. rate that year was 11.9 per 100,000. Other states that often have relatively high suicide rates are: Alaska, Arizona, California, Colorado, Florida, Montana, New Mexico, Oregon, Washington and Wyoming. In 1980, New Jersey had the lowest suicide rate, with only 7.4 per 100,000.

Highest U.S. regional rates are generally those of the Rocky Mountain and West Coast areas, with the South showing the lowest rate, with the exception of Florida.

It was once thought that the rural suicide rate was much lower than that of urban and suburban areas; however, the rural suicide rate in the U.S. in recent years is very nearly that of urban areas. (See FARMERS.)

Finally, consider the case of West Berlin, where the suicide rate is double that of West Germany. West Berlin is alienated socially, politically, culturally and geographically. Just how accurate the suicide rates are for the city no one knows, but they offer interesting evidence of Durkheim's classification of suicide described as *anomie*. The alienated city has an astounding suicide rate of 40.9 per 100,000. This contrasts with certain isolated places such as some South Sea islands and the Hindu Kush Mountains of India where suicides are not committed at all.

ghetto living Two groups with generally high suicide rates and/or reported suicide attempts are young black men and adolescent girls, black and white. Black males in their early twenties have the highest suicide rate of any black people at any age. In New York City, for example, roughly twice as many young black men as their white counterparts kill themselves. Similar trends have been noted in other large urban centers in the U.S.

Why so many young black suicidal acts? According to HERBERT HENDIN in *Black Suicide*, the causes include rage, self-hatred and the frustrations that go with ghetto living. Many black youngsters reared in big city ghettos live in fatherless homes where mothers are away at work much of the time. These children are often cared for by relatives or neighbors, and great numbers care for themselves. Because of their uncertain and stressful family life, many black children grow up filled with anger, says Hendin; and they develop a sense of hopelessness about the future. For boys without a father with whom to identify, the lack of support often produces a despair even more extreme than that experienced by girls. By the time they reach their teens and early twenties, the rage and hopelessness in black males is aggravated further by the frustrations of life in the ghetto. Finding themselves locked into the poverty and despair of the ghetto culture, they are usually unable to realize the economic security they see in society at large. This realization too often results in young black males killing themselves.

Psychologist Richard Seiden says that the young black suicide rate would perhaps be even higher if certain "victim-precipitated" murders were included among them. In such murders, the victims deliberately provoke others into killing them. This tactic is used by young blacks who consider suicide to be a weak, "feminine" solution to their problems. They equate masculinity with physical prowess and toughness. Seiden explains that these young black males will sometimes create violent situations, threatening others, often wielding guns or knives, and then getting themselves killed. This, to them, is a better way out of the dread ghetto existence than "cowardly" self-destruction.

FRANCINE KLAGSBRUN points out in *Too Young to Die* that in some urban centers, "the ratio of completed suicides for young men and women narrowed during the 1980s, with many more girls and young women actually committing suicide than in the past. In California, the highest increases in suicide rates among any group of women during the 1980s, for example, were among urban black women in their early twenties."

Klagsbrun adds that "young women about to enter the job market or undertake professional careers still find many doors closed to them. This is especially true of young black women, whose suicide rate, like those of urban black men, have risen sharply." The same can be said of Puerto Ricans and so-called ghetto white persons. In fact, the conclusion may be drawn that urban ghettos expose people to those factors that, by definition, place them in high suicide risk groups—factors such as crowding, stress, despair, money problems, lack of future, tension, violence. The list is seemingly endless.

Francine Klagsbrun, *Too Young to Die: Youth and Suicide* (New York: Pocket Books, 1985; first printing, Houghton Mifflin, 1976).

Herbert Hendin, *Black Suicide* (New York: Basic Books, 1969).

Richard H. Seiden, *Suicide Among Youth*, Public Health Service Publication No. 1971 (Chevy Chase, Maryland: U.S. Government Printing Office, 1969).

M.E. Wolfgang, "Suicide by Means of Victim-Precipitated Homicide," *Journal of Clinical and Experimental Psychopathology and Quarterly Review of Psychiatry and Neurology*, 20 (1959):345-349.

Giffin, Dr. Mary Medical director of the Irene Josselyn Clinic of the North Shore Mental Health Association in Northfield, Illinois. Dr. Giffin is co-author with Carol Felsenthal of *A Cry for Help: Exploring and Exploding the Myths About Teen Suicide—A Guide for All Parents of Adolescents.* Psychiatrist Giffin has been researching, investigating and writing about her findings into the causes of teenage suicide for many years. *People*, *Time*, *McCall's*, *Family Circle* and *The Wall Street Journal* have all written about Dr. Giffin's work in this field.

gifted children Among the many myths of suicide is that of the stereotypical "genius" who commits suicide. In reality, every type of person, Christian or Jew, rich or poor, white or black, young or old, fat or thin, tall or short, high or low I.Q, commits suicide. But, as DR. MARY GIFFIN and Carol Felsenthal note, "still, it is true that many of the young people who attempt or complete suicide fall into the category of gifted students."

The authors write that, "The mistake that parents of these children frequently make is assuming that intellectually precocious children are also emotionally precocious. They're not. The fourth-grader who reads at the twelfth-grade level is, emotionally, still in the fourth grade." Dr. Giffin and journalist Felsenthal review, among others, the case history of Dallas Egbert who shot himself to death at age 17. They explain:

> Even as a toddler, his brilliance was obvious. He knew his alphabet at age two, he could read at three, he finished high school at fourteen and he entered Michigan State University at fifteen. Intellectually, he was a genius; emotionally he was a baby. His brilliance coupled with his physical immaturity (he regularly skipped grades in school) resulted in his being shunned by his classmates.

Generally, gifted children such as Dallas Egbert simply can't relate to their classmates. They become loners, preferring books or special interests to friends. The more they retreat into themselves and their intellectual activities, the less chance they will ever make friends. Intellectually they are years above their peers; socially and emotionally they may be six-year-olds. These gifted children often end up so miserable they cannot communicate with anyone, including members of their own families. Alienated, entrapped by minds that developed so much faster than their bodies, their despair leads to hopelessness and misery—and they kill themselves.

Mrs. Jean Casey, mother of gifted 17-year-old Shaun, who killed himself, said on a recent "Phil Donahue Show," that the Los Angeles County Suicide Prevention Center officials explained that "10 percent of these gifted seniors and freshmen in college are walking around feeling suicidal . . . the difference is a coach or a counselor or somebody. Another adult who relates to them . . ." (From "Donahue" transcript #01161.)

Gisu of Uganda, the In certain societies, suicide sometimes appears to be a last resort. Dr. Jean La Fontaine, writing the chapter entitled "Anthropology" in Seymour Perlin's *A Handbook for the Study of Suicide*, says: "Among the Gisu of Uganda, it seemed that suicides of the elderly sick usually took place after a variety of other means of alleviating their condition had been tried and proved ineffective."

The Gisu consider suicide as a rational act, a deliberate and logical choice between life and death, although as La Fontaine notes, "subsidiary theories account for the fact that in the same situations, some people may choose death and others will not."

Again La Fontaine on the Gisu: "The Gisu of Uganda feel that ritual cleansing after a suicide is necessary to protect the suicide's close kin from danger and to prevent the contagion of suicide, causing the suicide of anyone passing the spot where the suicide occurred. To conceal a suicide is thus both dangerous and culpable; moreover, it is not possible to perform the necessary ritual in secret." For further information on suicide in various African societies, see *African Homicide and Suicide*, ed. P.J. Bohannan. The essays in this book include Dr. La Fontaine's on the Gisu.

"goal-gradient" phenomenon Richard Brandt, PhD, professor and chairman, department of philosophy, University of Michigan, explains the "goal-gradient" phenomenon as it applies to the consideration of suicide in "The Morality and Rationality of Suicide," chapter three of Perlin's *A Handbook for the Study of Suicide*.

Brandt writes that, "Events distant in the future feel small, just as objects distant in space look small. Their prospect does not have the effect on motivational processes that it would have if it were of an event in the immediate future." Psychologists call this the "goal-gradient" phenomenon. Brandt explains that, "In the case of a person who has suffered some misfortune, and whose situation now is an unpleasant one, this reduction of the motivational influence of events distant in time has the effect that present unpleasant states weigh far more heavily than probable future pleasant ones in any choice of world courses."

Dr. Brandt believes that it should be clear from the above that "a moment of despair, if one is seriously contemplating suicide, ought to be a moment of reassessment of one's goals and values, a reassessment which the individual must realize is very difficult to make objectively, because of the very quality of his depressed state of mind."

God Bless You, Mr. Rosewater
Novel written by Kurt Vonnegut, Jr., wherein the author includes a line that reads, "Sons of suicides seldom do well." Vonnegut could have added, "nor do daughters." In fact, children of suicides of both sexes have a higher than average suicide rate. Experts point out that this is not due to any biologically inherited tendency toward suicide, but because these children all too often grow up with what psychiatrist Robert Jay Lifton calls "survivor guilt." The latter phenomenon is a key factor in the feelings of anger and low self-esteem suffered by a young person after the suicide of a parent. Dr. Lifton explains that all children go through "little survivals" during their growing years and each painful separation from a parent—each withdrawal of love or threat of rejection—is a "death equivalent." These experiences produce feelings of guilt and blame, feelings that are compounded by a parent suicide. Such experiences, added to what Klagsbrun calls "the existing storehouse of guilt and self-doubt," place the youngster in a more vulnerable (and self-destructive) posture than an ordinary child.

Some young people try to "atone" for their painful feelings by killing themselves. And, as Klagsbrun notes, "On a more mystical level, children of suicides sometimes kill themselves in order to be reunited through death with the parent who abandoned them so abruptly."

Francine Klagsbrun, *Too Young to Die: Youth and Suicide* (New York: Pocket Books, 1985; first printing Houghton Mifflin, 1976).

Robert J. Lifton, *Death in Life: Survivors of Hiroshima* (New York: Random House, 1967).

Goering, Hermann Wilhelm
German politician (1893-1946), founder of the Nazi secret police force, the Gestapo. Goering joined the Nazi party in 1922 as a young man of 29 and held many important posts in Hitler's government before he became economic dictator (1937) and marshal of the Reich (1940). He was condemned to death for war crimes at the Nuremberg trials, but cheated the gallows by taking poison and committing suicide before his execution. On the wall of his office in Berlin, Goering, a concerned wildlife preservationist, had posted this notice: "He who tortures animals wounds the feelings of the German people."

Goethe, Johann Wolfgang von
German poet, novelist, playwright and scholar (1749-1832). With his good friend, Friedrich Schiller, Goethe was the leading spirit in the *Sturm und Drang* period of German literature. His autobiographical novel, *The Sorrows of Young Werther* (1744), was acclaimed throughout Europe. Young people everywhere read and wept over Goethe's story about a young man who commits suicide after being torn apart by uncontrollable passions. Young dandies began to dress like Werther, speak like Werther and even to destroy themselves like Werther. It became a point of status to suffer for one's genius, to struggle for art's sake, and to die young—a hero mourned by all the world. Goethe's martyr of unrequited love and unbelievably extreme sensibility created a new, idealistic, romantic style of suffering. The Romantic stance, as ALFRED ALVAREZ notes in *The Savage God*, became "suicidal." It was young Werther who, writes Alvarez, "made the act seem positively desirable to the young Romantics all over Europe."

Goethe, paradoxically, recounts how as a young man he greatly admired the Emperor Otto, who had stabbed himself. Goethe finally decided that if he were not brave enough to die in like manner, he wasn't brave enough to die at all. He wrote: "By this conviction, I saved myself from the purpose, or indeed, more properly speaking, from the whim of suicide." (Quoted by Forbes Winslow in *The Anatomy of Suicide*, London, 1840, p. 118.)

Goethe created an epidemic of romantic suicides throughout Europe with his novel, yet he was almost 83 years old when he died, asking that "more light may come in."

grades (school) as a warning sign One of the several distress signals of the young person who may be considering suicide is a slackening interest in school attendance and school work and, consequently, a decline in grades. As DR. MARY GIFFIN notes in *A Cry for Help*, "Because school is the major activity in a child's life, it is also one of the best barometers of his mental health. If a child's grades fall precipitously, chances are something is wrong. Get that child talking about what's bothering him. When a child swerves from a long-established pattern, something usually is."

Great Britain (plus Northern Ireland) Suicide rates in England and Wales dropped in 1982 (latest WHO figures available) to a total of 8.6 per 100,000 population; this from 8.9 in 1981. The male suicide rate was considerably higher than that of females, the comparison being 11.5 to 5.9. Highest rates overall were in the 65 to 74 age group, with 14.1 per 100,000.

In Northern Ireland, the 1983 suicide rate rose to 9.0 (per 100,000) from 5.9 in the previous year. The rate for men stood at 11.3, compared to 6.8 for women. The 55 to 64 age group suicide rate was highest in this category, 19.3.

Scotland's suicide rate per 100,000 population rose from 9.8 in 1983 to a total of 10.1 in 1984. Among age groupings, again it was the 55 to 64 category that was highest, with a 16.8 suicide rate per 100,000. The total male versus female comparative suicide rates were 14.5 (male) to 5.9 (female). In the 75-plus age group, the male suicide rate per 100,000 was a very high 23.2 in Scotland. (Note: All statistics are those reported to the World Health Organization [WHO], Geneva, Switzerland.)

Greece Latest WHO suicide rate figures available are for 1983. They show a rate total per 100,000 population of 3.7; for males 5.5 as compared to the low female rate of 2.0. The highest suicide rate figures are for the 75-plus age group: Rate totals here are 9.0 combined, 14.1 for males and 5.3 for females.

The ancient Greeks held no clear-cut attitudes toward suicide, with Greek city-states differing markedly in their views and laws concerning self-destruction. In Thebes, for instance, suicides were condemned, and the victim was granted no funeral rites. In Athens, the law decreed that one hand of a suicide would be cut off and buried apart from the rest of the victim's body—since it was the hand that committed the dread act.

Other Greek communities established special tribunals to hear arguments of those citizens who wished to end their lives. A magistrate who was convinced by a particularly persuasive argument from an individual could grant permission for that person to kill himself. Magistrates in some areas even supplied poison hemlock to would-be suicides. Magistrates generally considered insanity, profound physical suffering, or overwhelming grief and sorrow as grounds sufficient to permit suicide.

Greek philosophers and thinkers considered the suicide phenomenon from their own points of view, in terms of ethics and morals. Perhaps the most famed suicide of ancient times was that of the Greek philosopher Socrates, teacher of Plato. Socrates died by his own hand, drinking a cup of hemlock, though his death in 399 B.C. was actually a form of execution that had been ordered by the rulers of Athens, who had tried him on the charge of corrupting the young people of his city-state. Plato quotes his mentor as saying before his death, "No man has the right to take his own life, but he must wait until God sends some necessity upon him, as he has now sent me." Like Socrates, Plato and his own student, Aristotle, both condemned the act of suicide. The Greek Stoic philosophers who came later held a much more lenient view of suicide. Yet both Zeno, founder of the Stoic philosophy, and his successor Cleanthes, supposedly took their own lives.

grief, of suicide survivors After any death of a loved person, survivors experience what professional authorities deem a "grief process." At first there is disbelief ("I can't believe she's gone"), followed by profound grief and sorrow. Survivors often weep, suffer loss of appetite, and have endless sleepless nights. They may feel anger, bitterness, outright rage. Some wonder how they can bear life without the dead loved one. At long last, sometimes months later, survivors begin to function normally and focus their thoughts on the future. This last stage is the "healing stage" in the grief process. Survivors often feel sadness and a sense of loss for years, but they are able to continue living, and generally to enjoy their lives.

In the case of suicide survivors, however, as FRANCINE KLAGSBRUN, DR. MARY GIFFIN and others point out, grief doesn't always resolve itself in the same manner as in other forms of death. Klagsbrun writes in *Too Young to Die*, "The grief feeds on the anger and guilt and the never-to-be-answered question of 'why?' And it grows and spreads under the disapproval of society, leaving survivors dragged down by a depression that may never be closed off. Sometimes the depression leads to a cycle of suicide or self-destructive acts for the survivors themselves."

The grief process, says Klagsbrun, is especially harsh and extreme when survivors must deal with a teen or young adult suicide. Everyone involved with the suicide—parents, brothers, sisters, friends—copes with their own kind of suffering.

Freud spoke of "grief work" in which there is abnormal desire for reunion with a lost loved one. Immediately after a suicide occurs, survivors need the help and intervention of others to do what is called the "mourning work" in order to continue living meaningful lives and avoid their own self-destruction. Psychologist and thanatologist Edwin S. Shneidman describes such needed help for survivors as "postvention."

Postvention, in Klagbrun's view, means "giving survivors the support they need just after a suicide and, over a period of time, helping them come to terms with the tragedy that has struck them."

Survivors should be encouraged to seek immediate help from a professional whom they trust: a psychiatrist, psychologist, social worker, minister, priest, rabbi or physician; or, in the case of youngsters, a school psychologist, counselor, teacher or administrator. Professionals can assist survivors in getting past the first stages of shock and disbelief, and then help them through the guilt and anger phases that come next.

As Dr. Giffin says, "The survivors of a suicide must accept the fact that theirs is a fight for survival and that techniques for survival are different from techniques for living." The co-authors of *A Cry for Help* add: "But it takes time, hard work, and almost always, professional help before the bereaved can move beyond survival to reintegration and learning to live again."

Griffiths, Mr. In 1823, in England, the body of one "Mr. Griffiths," a suicide, was dragged through the streets of London and buried at a crossroads. Mr. Griffiths became the last suicide in England whose remains were so desecrated. Parliament immediately passed a law ordering that the corpse of a suicide must be buried privately in either a church yard or a designated burial ground.

group conscience EMILE DURKHEIM, among the first sociologists to collect data on suicide and to present the rates in tabular form, was convinced that the collective conscience of a group was a major source of control in all societal matters, including the phenomenon of suicide. He felt that every social group has a set of beliefs and sentiments, a totality of social likeness. As Ronald Maris, editor of *Suicide and Life-Threatening Behavior* explains, for Durkheim the suicide rate depends upon forces external to and constraining of individuals. "To the degree that the societal groups are harmonious," Maris writes, "integrated and regulated and the individual is an active, central member of those societal groups, then the individual's suicide potential will be low and a population of such individuals will have a low suicide rate."

group therapy and self-help A "postvention" treatment and technique that involves group rather than specific individual treatment as a way of stressing that a survivor-patient's problems are not unique. Usually, but not always, fewer than a dozen or so persons are involved in a group. This allows for maximum participation, and the group is generally led by a psychiatrist, a psychologist or a social worker. Members reveal their problems for the scrutiny of others and discuss them openly as a group. This popular (especially since the 1970s and early '80s) type of therapy allows all members present to benefit vicariously from the resolution of fellow members' mutual problems. The technique is not unlike that of such well-known self-help groups as ALCOHOLICS ANONYMOUS, Parents Anonymous or Gamblers Anonymous where problem people find a way up and out of their dilemma by sharing knowledge of that way with those who can use it. For a listing of self-help clearinghouses for suicide victims, look under FAMILY THERAPY (FOR SUICIDE SURVIVORS).

growing up dead Term used by DR. HERBERT HENDIN to describe the lives of young people whose parents didn't want them and unconsciously wished them dead. Also title of a book by Brenda Rabkin (*Growing Up Dead: A Hard Look at Why Adolescents Commit Suicide*), published originally in Canada. Rabkin's book focuses on the suicide of a Canadian teenager, Peter Walker, among others.

Guest, Judith Author of the best-selling novel *Ordinary People*, about the suicide attempt of a young boy, Conrad Jarrett. The fictional work was later made into a highly successful movie starring Mary Tyler Moore, Donald Sutherland and Timothy Hutton. Experts disagree about whether or not popular books and films dealing with suicide should be publicized to the extent that they are. The more enlightened view is that the subject ought to be covered more responsibly and thoroughly in popular literature, as well as in the various other modern media. Most of today's educators agree.

guns as suicide method See FIREARMS AS SUICIDE METHOD.

H

Hadrian Roman emperor (76-138) from 117 until his death by suicide in 138 A.D. His reign was considered to be a golden era of peace and prosperity for the empire. It is likely that his self-destruction was due to pathological depression after the death of Aelius Verus, but prevailing views of the time led to the definition and consideration of such cases as moral, not medical, problems.

hanging as suicide method Hanging is the second most common method among teenage boys and young men who kill themselves. It is the third most common method of suicide among girls. From 1960 to 1980, male suicides by hanging increased by 421 cases, while there were 96 fewer cases by this method among females. As Dr. Jean La Fontaine notes in Perlin's *A Handbook for the Study of Suicide*, "In many societies, it is rare to find suicide by poison or drugs. Some methods such as hanging require a steadfastness of purpose that makes the labeling of death by suicide unequivocal."

Hannibal Commander of the initially successful Carthaginian army against Rome during the Second Punic War (218-201 B.C.). Hannibal (247-183 B.C.) was forced eventually to withdraw to Africa, where he was defeated at Zama (202 B.C.). When King Antiochus III of Syria, whom he was counseling on how to conduct his war against Rome, was defeated, Hannibal fled to Crete, then to Bithynia in Asia Minor, where a detachment of Roman soldiers caught up with him and surrounded his hideout. Hannibal then took out the phial of poison that he always carried with him and drank it. "Let us relieve the Romans of the fear which has so long afflicted them," he said, "since it seems to tax their patience too hard to wait for an old man's death."

hara-kiri See SEPPUKU.

health service institutions There are hundreds upon hundreds of such institutions throughout the U.S., a complex of medico-social organizations we refer to as the "health system." There has been, and still is, a great deal of controversy as to the extent to which the suicide case fits the general institutionalized expectations of the sick role or patient role. George J. Vlasak, PhD, assistant professor, department of behavioral sciences, School of Hygiene and Public Health, the Johns Hopkins University, Baltimore, Maryland, writes in "Medical Sociology," which appears as chapter seven in Seymour Perlin's *A Handbook for the Study of Suicide*, that too often, "the competent helper, the health system, as a system of status-roles pertaining to the existing medical and allied occupations and callings, is far from being ready, able, or willing to present the suicide patient with an alternative and equally far-reaching solution, and confines its operations to its much more limited domain, resisting its redefinition by the claims of the suicide case."

Hebrew Bible Medical historian George Rosen of Yale University notes that "Biblical suicides are rare. There are only seven instances reported in the Hebrew Bible and one in the New Testament." Neither the Hebrew Bible nor the New Testament prohibits suicide. Suicidal behavior is not condemned and, in fact, there is no specific word for the act itself. Professor Rosen says that, "even of Judas Iscariot, we are told simply that 'he went and hanged himself'" (Matthew 27:5).

Edwin Shneidman, writing in *Definition of Suicide*, makes the sometimes forgotten point that, "In the Western World, the pervasive moral ideas about suicide are Christian, dating from the fourth century, A.D., enunciated by St. Augustine (354-430) for essentially non-religious reasons." St. Augustine, notes Professor Shneidman, was concerned primarily about the decimation of Christians by suicide and "against the suicide by Christians only for reasons of martyrdom (or religious zealotry, fired by the hope of immediate martyred entrance into heaven)."

The recorded suicides in the Hebrew Bible: Samson, Saul, Saul's armor bearer, Ahitophel, Zimri, Razis, and Abimelech. In the New Testament: Judas Iscariot.

(See also INTRODUCTION.)

Hegesias Lived in Alexandria under Ptolemy II and was a philosopher of the Cyrenaic school. Hegesias lectured on the miseries of life and, according to Jacques Choron in *Suicide* (New York: Scribners, 1972), his success was so profound that "many among his listeners committed suicide." Given the nickname *Peisithanatos*—the advocate of death—Hegesias was eventually forbidden to lecture. For further information, read Cicero's *Tusculanae Disputationes* (Tusculan Disputations), 1, XXXIV: 33.

help for suicides Scattered throughout the U.S., there are over 250 suicide prevention centers accredited by the AMERICAN ASSOCIATION OF SUICIDOLOGY (AAS). Almost all of these 24-hour, seven-day-a-week crisis facilities offer emergency telephone (hotline) services designed to give help quickly. Some have emergency rescue squads to assist would-be suicides *after* they have taken an overdose, slit their wrists or otherwise injured themselves. Others tie in with hospital emergency services that can get help to the distressed person as quickly as possible. An updated list of these suicide prevention and crisis centers is in Appendix 3.

In addition, there are hundreds of self-help or mutual-aid groups in both the U.S. and Canada not only to help frustrate attempted suicides but also to extend help to survivors of suicides. Key self-help clearinghouses are listed under FAMILY THERAPY (FOR SUICIDE SURVIVORS).

Help is also available from professionals in private practice, in Community Mental Health Clinics, hospital emergency rooms, several national agencies, such as the NATIONAL INSTITUTE OF MENTAL HEALTH and the NATIONAL MENTAL HEALTH ASSOCIATION, suicide-prevention "chains" (operating worldwide) such as CONTACT and the SAMARITANS, and the New York-based NATIONAL-SAVE-A-LIFE LEAGUE.

Canada, like the U.S., has a nationwide network of suicide hotlines. Because it is impossible to list a comprehensive directory of suicide prevention and crisis services for Canada—new facilities open and existing ones move or close every day and addresses and phone numbers change—the best, safest course of action is to consult an updated telephone book or dial either "0" for operator information or 911. In Canada, the SALVATION ARMY operates its own suicide prevention facilities. Canada also has branches of The Samaritans and Contact (in that country, called TELE-CARE). Again, check the front of the phone book or the white pages under those names. In non-emergency situations, help and advice is available to anyone through the facilities of the CANADIAN MENTAL HEALTH ASSOCIATION, which has branches countrywide, even in the remote Northwest Territories and the Yukon Territory. Information is also readily available to professionals and lay persons alike from the SUICIDE INFORMATION AND EDUCATION CENTRE in Alberta. This splendid organization, international in scope, is listed separately in this work, as are the AMERICAN PSYCHIATRIC ASSOCIATION, AMERICAN PSYCHOLOGICAL ASSOCIATION, the NATIONAL ASSOCIATION OF

SOCIAL WORKERS, AMERICAN ASSOCIATION OF SUICIDOLOGY, the YOUTH SUICIDE NATIONAL CENTER, and the INTERNATIONAL ASSOCIATION FOR SUICIDE PREVENTION. (See Appendix 3 for some Canadian addresses.)

A positive by-product of the gradually widening public awareness of the seriousness of the suicide problem is the introduction of suicide-prevention classes in the U.S. public school system. Such additions to the health curriculum of the nation's schools will help would-be suicides by strengthening their defenses and also assist friends, relatives and teachers of potential suicidal youngsters. Effective help and assistance can thus be enhanced for those who are seeking aid to fight self-destructive feelings and emotional stress.

Hemingway, Ernest U.S. writer (1899-1961). His longer works of fiction include *The Sun Also Rises* (1926), *For Whom the Bell Tolls* (1940) and *The Old Man and the Sea* (1952). An avowed sportsman and hunter, Hemingway extolled machoism, courage and stoicism in his short stories and novels, which were written in simple, terse style. Like his father, he was always subject to severe depression. And, also like his father, Hemingway committed suicide with a shotgun, in 1961.

hemlock Greek city-states differed considerably one from the next in their laws concerning suicide. Magistrates in some areas went so far as actually to provide would-be suicides with the poison hemlock with which to kill themselves. Generally, these magistrates considered sufficient causes for suicide to include: insanity, profound physical suffering or overwhelming sorrow.

The most famous instance involving the use of hemlock to kill oneself is that of the Greek philosopher Socrates. Tried on the charge of corrupting the young people of Athens, Socrates was sentenced to death by drinking hemlock.

Hemlock Society, The Founded in 1980, in Los Angeles, by Derek Humphry and his second wife, Ann Wickett, co-authors of *The Right to Die: Understanding Euthanasia*, and of *Jean's Way*, an account of how Humphry helped his critically ill first wife take her own life. Humphry, currently director of the Hemlock Society, was a newspaper reporter for 35 years, working for many British journals, including 14 years with London's *Sunday Times*. Ann Wickett is editor and senior writer for Hemlock and a leading authority in the field of EUTHANASIA.

The Hemlock Society is a national, nonprofit organization with an annual membership fee of $20.00. The Los Angeles-based educational organization supports "the option of active voluntary euthanasia (self-deliverance) for the advanced terminally ill mature adult, or the seriously incurably physically ill person." The group believes that, as suicide is no longer a crime, assistance in suicide should also be decriminalized where a terminally ill or seriously incurably ill person requests this help.

The Society strives to help campaign for better understanding of euthanasia and to work toward improved laws in this area. It publishes a newsletter, *Hemlock Quarterly*, that updates members on ethical, legal and operating developments. The Society address is P.O. Box 66218, Los Angeles, CA 90066; phone is (213) 391-1871.

Hendin, Herbert, MD Director of the Center for Psychosocial Studies at the Veterans Administration Center in Montrose, New York, and professor of psychiatry at New York Medical College. Dr. Hendin is the author of several landmark books, including: *Suicide in America*, *Suicide and Scandinavia*, *Black Suicide* and *The Age of Sensation*. In 1982, he received the Louis I. Dublin award of the American Association of Suicidology (AAS).

An internationally-known authority in the field, Dr. Hendin has done much to assist in the integration of psychological and social knowledge about suicide. His book, *Black Suicide*, provides what Arthur Kobler of *Contemporary Psychology* says is "a rich picture of the impact of culture on character."

hereditary factors In 1822, J.P. Falret published the first study of suicide to make use of stastical data, though admittedly on a small scale. He classified causal factors leading to suicide under four headings: (1) predisposing—heredity, temperament, climate (the last of little significance); (2) accidental direct—passions, domestic troubles and the like; (3) accidental indirect—bodily pain, illness; (4) general—civilization, civil disorders, religious fanaticism. Falret's study was published in Paris as *De l'hypochondrie et du suicide*.

Jean Etienne Esquirol, in *Des Maladies mentales, consideres sous les rapports medicaux, hygieniques et medico-legaux*, published in two volumes in Paris (1838) by J.B. Bailliere, also emphasized hereditary factors and the need to consider the individual disposition.

Brierre de Boismont, perhaps the most important contributor to the study of suicide in the 1850s, more generally concluded that suicide was a consequence of societal changes that lead to social disorganization and to alienation for many people. His treatise *Du Suicide et de la folie suicide consideres dans leurs rapports avec la statistique, la medecine et la philosophie* was published in Paris (1856) by Germer Bailliere. Similar views, according to Dr. George Rosen writing in "History in the Study of Suicide," were expressed by suicide investigator and statistician E. Lisle in his work, *Du Suicide, statistique, medecine, histoire et legislation*, published in 1856.

EMILE DURKHEIM, in his classic work *Suicide* (published in 1897) determined that his extensive data showed no significant association between suicide rates and genetic factors.

Not a few experts, however, think that suicides tend to repeat in some families because of innate or genetic predisposition to severe depression, family exposure to extreme stresses, guilt and grief resulting from the first suicide, imitation and identification and/or the ways in which families relate. (See also GENETIC PREDISPOSITION AND SUICIDE.)

Herodotus Greek historian (?484-?425 B.C.), born in Halicarnassus, Asia Minor. He lived for some time in Athens, then traveled in 443 B.C. as an Athenian colonist to Thurse in Italy. There he is supposed to have spent the rest of his life, writing *The Persian Wars*, which later earned for him from Caesar the title of Father of History.

Herodotus describes the custom among Thracians of a form of institutional suicide wherein, after a man died, his wives (the Thracians practiced polygamy) vied for the honor of being the one he had loved most. The wife accorded this honor was then slain over the grave and buried with her husband. The Greek historian also described at length the suicide of Cleomenes, king of Sparta (end of the sixth century B.C.), who was obviously mentally deranged.

heroin In her book *Too Young to Die*, FRANCINE KLAGSBRUN includes a chapter entitled "Uncounted Suicides," subtitled "How People Kill Themselves Without 'Committing Suicide.'" As Klagsbrun notes, thousands of young people in the U.S., and indeed throughout the world, have plunged deep into the drug scene (including heroin) and "live on the outskirts of death." Many of these young people spend their shortened lives in and out of jail, in and out of drug treatment facilities and hospitals, in "a revolving-door routine that leads nowhere." And, as the author notes, "many die . . . some suddenly, of an overdose or fatal combination of drugs; others experience the slow death of mental and physicial deterioration."

When drug users do die—whether from their drugs or driving under the influence or suicide—their deaths are usually not counted in official lists of suicide statistics. But, in Klagsbrun's words, "you would not be wrong to say that many of these people destroyed themselves, as surely as did those who openly committed suicide."

KARL MENNINGER, in his book *Man Against Himself*, describes and interprets the many self-destructive acts in which people engage. People do such things, Menninger points out, because they may unconsciously want to die without having to take the responsibility for killing themselves. He calls these people "chronic suicides" who destroy themselves slowly, almost always on the pretext of "making life more bearable."

Heroin is a narcotic, diacetylmorphine, derived from morphine, which it greatly resembles. It is a central nervous system depressant which also relieves pain. It was developed in 1848 by the Bayer Company in Germany. Heroin acts to depress aggression as well as appetite and sexual drive. Other effects include constipation and suppression of the coughing reflex. As O'Brien and Cohen note in *The Encyclopedia of Drug Abuse*: "Depending on the method of administration, heroin induces varying degrees of euphoria; orgasmic reactions often follow intravenous injection. After a 'fix' a sense of well-being replaces feelings of depression or low self-esteem and this is followed by sleep—'going on the nod.'"

The greatest danger of heroin use is death from what lay persons call an overdose. Street-sold heroin is usually so adulterated that the user is unlikely to get a large enough amount to suppress respiration. O'Brien and Cohen note that most deaths are due to what medical examiners call acute reactions. "These include," the authors say, "hypersensitivity with pulmonary edema, infections, complications associated with the adulterants used and the combination of heroin with alcohol or barbiturates. The death rate is high among young people under 35. Only a small percentage of addicts in the U.S. are over 40." In the mid-1980s, U.S. government authorities estimate from 400,000 to 750,000 users in this country. Southwest Asia has become the major supplier. The heroin habit can cost an estimated average of $10,000 a year. "No class, race, educational level or community is free from the problems of heroin abuse," say Robert O'Brien and Dr. Sidney Cohen.

Although studies have shown that alcoholics and other drug users are at a particularly high risk of attempting suicide, no statistics are available to indicate how many heroin users actually commit suicide. Studies do show that between 15% and 64% of those who attempt suicide and up to 80% of successful suicides were drinking at the time of the act. Combining alcohol with other drugs is responsible for a large number of suicides and "accidental deaths."

Hippocrates As late as the mid-twentieth century, medical authorities still considered the causes of depression to be psychological. Yet even in ancient times, scientists suspected that some types of depression had both a physical and a psychological origin—that there were, simply stated, some imbalances in the body chemistry. Hippocrates (460-ca. 377 B.C.), a Greek physician called "the father of medicine," blamed what he chose to call "black bile." Interestingly, scientists today now agree that a "kind of black bile," to use psychiatrist DR. MARY GIFFIN's term, is the culprit. These are delicate chemical compounds called amines; manufactured and stored in the nerve cells, they assist in sending messages from nerve cell to nerve cell in the brain. In some people, and physicians don't know why, depression is caused by the brain's inability to transmit chemical messages.

Notions of environmental influence on one's state of being, especially as relates to gloominess and melancholy, can be traced back to ancient times, with roots in both medicine and geography; both are evident in the Hippocratic corpus, according to medical historian Dr. George Rosen, specifically in *Airs, Waters, Places.*

Hispanics and suicide For suicide-related behavior among Hispanics, few statistics exist and available figures (one such example being attempted suicide) are based on either estimates or empirically collected data. Many Hispanic communities might well fall into high suicide risk categories because of such factors as: being socially isolated; experiencing interpersonal conflict or problems, including marital or family discord; lacking personal resources; high unemployment rate; mental disorders, especially depression, alcoholism, and schizophrenia; not communicating well with those around them; and physical illness. Professor John L. McIntosh of Indiana University at South Bend did a doctoral dissertation study of suicide among U.S. racial minorities (University of Notre Dame, 1980) that includes 144 pages of suicide data from many sources, predominantly for the characteristics of age and race/ethnicity. Another source of information is Norman L. Farberow's *Suicide in Different Cultures*, which includes articles on various cultures around the world. One such article is by Dr. Farberow, D.K. Reynolds and R. Kalish, a cross-ethnic study of suicide attitudes and expectations in the U.S.

Most Hispanics are of the Catholic religion, and in the U.S. Catholics appear to have suicide rates that are higher than the rates for Jews, but lower than the rates for Protestants. As for countries that are predominantly Catholic, they appear to have very low suicide rates (with Austria the exception).

In truth, suicide is one of the few facets of American life that still cuts across all classes and groups; suicide is truly democratic in scope and no one ethnic group is more susceptible to it than another.

Professor McIntosh presented a paper entitled "Hispanic Suicide in Ten U.S. States" at the Joint Meeting of American Association of Suicidology and the International Association for Suicide Prevention in San Francisco on May 24, 1987. McIntosh's study represents the largest single compilation of Hispanic suicide data to date in the United States.

The 10 states from which data were gathered included: Arizona, California, Colorado, New Mexico, Texas, Illinois, New Jersey, New York, Nevada, and Oregon. These states represent about 80% of the U.S. Hispanic population. Dr. McIntosh explains that "Hispanic data are most often not available in other states and the most glaring example with respect to Hispanics (and particularly Cuban Americans) is Florida." McIntosh adds that, "Compiling data for the ten states indicates a younger pattern of suicide and lower overall suicide rates than among white populations in the states and for the nation as a whole."

Specific results and appropriate references were included in McIntosh's conference paper. These data and McIntosh's conclusions are as follows:

The mean annual rate of suicide for Hispanics (7.7 per 100,000 population) in the 10 states of this investigation for 1979–84 was found to be lower than that for Native Americans (13.6) and whites (12.9) for the somewhat comparable period 1979–81, comparable but somewhat lower than those for

Japanese-Americans (9.1) and Chinese-Americans (8.3) in 1979–81, but slightly higher than that for blacks (5.7) and Filipino-Americans (3.6) in 1979–81. The rate for these 10 states combined was also lower than that noted for the period 1976–80 by Smith et al. for the Spanish surname population in Arizona, California, Colorado, New Mexico and Texas (9.0). The rates calculated in the present investigation are conservative ones (i.e., a high estimate) because the population figures used in the calculation of rates are for the year 1980. If population estimates for the actual mid-point of the 1979–84 period (i.e., the mean for the years 1981–82) were available they would have been larger than that for 1980 and would have resulted in slightly lower suicide rates than were produced here.

Breaking the states included into their geographic regions, a slightly lower rate was observed for 1979–84 for the five Southwestern states of Smith et al.'s study for 1976–80 (8.07 vs. 9.0, respectively) and for those five states and Nevada, the other Southwestern state in this investigation (rate = 8.08). An even lower rate was observed for the Midwestern state of Illinois and the Eastern states of New York and New Jersey (6.43), and when these three non-Southwestern states are combined with Oregon, the lowest rate of all was observed (6.37).

On a state-by-state basis, it was observed that Hispanic suicide rates varied rather widely across the 10 states but that the overall rates were generally lower than for whites in the nation as a whole. The only exception was for New Mexico where a rate of 17.0 was found, but five states were equal to or above the average rate for the 10 states combined of 7.67 (7.7) whereas five were below it.

When looking separately at suicide rates by sex, it was found that Hispanic males had considerably higher rates than Hispanic females for the 10 states combined (rates of 12.71 and 2.85, respectively), and for each of the states separately. In no case was the ratio of male to female suicide rates less than 3.1. The rates for both Hispanic males and females were approximately 50% lower than those for whites of the same sex in the nation as a whole (e.g., for 1984 rates were 19.7 and 5.4 for white males and females, respectively).

The data for Hispanics in each of the states clearly show that Hispanic suicide in general is a younger phenomenon than that for the white population as a whole. The mean age of Hispanic suicides in the Southwestern states ranged between approximately eight and 12 years younger than that for white suicides in the same state (the low 30s compared to the low to mid-40s, respectively), while the range was six to nine years younger for the states in the Midwest and Eastern regions (the mid- to upper-30s compared to the mid-40s). When comparing these mean ages to those obtained by McIntosh (1985) for ethnic/racial groups for the year 1980, it can be seen that the Hispanics in the 10 states of this investigation were younger than whites (mean age = 43.7), Chinese- (46.7), Japanese- (46.0) and Filipino-Americans (39.4), more comparable to blacks (36.0) and older than Native American suicides (28.7).

The age-specific suicide rates for Hispanics as compared to those for whites and other racial and ethnic groups in the U.S. also reveal this young pattern for Hispanics. Indeed, Hispanic suicide rates peak in the 25- to 34-year age grouping and decline slightly with increasing age; a pattern similar to that for blacks and Native Americans, but in contrast to the patterns for whites and all three Asian-American populations that peak in old age. Youth suicide rates are higher than those for Asian-Americans, similar to those for blacks, but lower than those for whites and Native Americans. At the other end of the age spectrum, however, Hispanic elderly suicide rates are lower than those for whites, Chinese- and Japanese-Americans, similar to those for Filipino-Americans, and higher than rates for elderly blacks and Native Americans.

Although the data for specific groupings within the Hispanic population are incomplete and small numbers on which to base rates often result from such a breakdown, it can tentatively be said that rates are generally lower for Mexican-Americans and Puerto Ricans than for Cuban-Americans. In addition, Puerto Rican suicides tend to be slightly younger than Mexican-Americans who are in turn generally younger than Cuban-American suicides. Clearly, some of the different geographic levels of suicide observed in this investigation may reflect the makeup of the Hispanic suicides in the various regions of the country.

Just as assuming that all nonwhite groups are homogenous was demonstrated to be fallacious in earlier studies, the white population (to which the overwhelming majority of Hispanics belong) is also not homogenous across its subgroupings. (Although data do not exist, it might even be hypothesized that other white ethnic groups may also exhibit different levels and patterns of suicide than does the white population as a whole.) In fact, when the lower suicide rates for Hispanics are included in that for all whites, the effect is to slightly lower the overall white rate and lessen the differences that exist between the non-Hispanic white population and most other racial and ethnic groupings.

Clearly, said McIntosh, many more questions than answers can be derived from this investigation. There is a great need for long-range studies of Hispanic suicide to determine trends over time more clearly. The data for such a consideration are available from this compilation but have not yet been closely scrutinized. One of the important issues of such a study is the consistency and reliability of the ethnic and Spanish surname or origin-coding in the data. One of many possible questions related to the data reliability may be whether the higher rates and larger numbers of suicides observed in the Southwestern states may partially reflect better reporting or identification of Hispanic origin in those states.

Also, a number of questions need to be addressed by studies of individual Hispanic suicides rather than by large-sample studies such as the present investigation. Such studies would provide the much-needed explanations of Hispanic suicide. The factors of family support and cohesion, Roman Catholicism, and the manner by which emotions are expressed are all possible aspects that may help to understand lower suicide rates for Hispanics. As well as blacks and Native Americans, Hispanics are a younger population than found for whites and the nation as a whole. This shows the need to target young Hispanics, especially since the highest rates of suicide are seen there. Why are Hispanic youth and particularly males at high risk for suicide? Do the similar suicide patterns by age for Hispanics, blacks and Native Americans suggest similar explanations? Why are the old and females among Hispanics at low risk for suicide? Are suggestions for black and Native American elderly appropriate here? These questions only begin to demonstrate the need for further research into Hispanic suicide and the need to scrutinize and improve the reporting and quality of suicide data by ethnicity, especially among this large minority group.

Hitler, Adolph German dictator, founder-leader of the National Socialist German Workers' (Nazi) Party. Austrian-born son (1889-1945) of a customs official, he was orphaned at 15, refused admission to a Viennese art academy, lived in abject poverty, and became a violent anti-Semite. He served in the Bavarian army during World War I, received the Iron Cross and attained the rank of corporal. Hitler wrote *Mein Kampf* (*My Struggle*) while imprisoned in Landsberg Fortress for trying, with a group of embittered malcontents, to seize power in Bavaria in a beer-hall *putsch* at Munich (November 8-9, 1923). Preaching Aryan supremacy and fanatic nationalism, he promised world conquest by the German "master race." Appointed chancellor by the aged President Hindenburg in 1933, and despite his own party being a minority in the Reichstag, Hitler managed to establish a dictatorship. He put all Germany in the Nazi grip and when Hindenburg died in 1934, Hitler combined the offices of president and chancellor in the title of *Der Führer*.

Thereafter, Hitler's militaristic, aggressive foreign policy led inexorably to World War II (1939-1945). A carefully-planned plot by leading army and civil officials to assassinate Hitler failed in July 1944, and Heinrich Himmler crushed the revolt. But when the victorious Allied armies converged on Berlin in April 1945, Hitler presumably killed himself along with his mistress-bride Eva Braun, in a bombed steel and concrete bunker on April 30. Several other high-ranking Nazi officials also committed suicide at the fall of Berlin, including Himmler and Paul Joseph Goebbels, propaganda minister.

Holland (Netherlands) Suicide rate per 100,000 population showed an increase from 10.1 in 1980 to 12.4 in 1984 (World Health Organization figures). For males, the 1984 rate per 100,000 was a relatively high 15.2; for females, the rate was 9.6 per 100,000. Highest suicide rates among age groups were for the 75 and over category, with 24.6 per 100,000 population. Males 75-plus had an astounding 42.7 suicide rate per 100,000 population. Among females, the 65 to 74 age group was highest, with a suicide rate of 21.2 per 100,000.

home, support-therapy in In DR. MARY GIFFIN's view, "Nobody is more important in determining therapy's success (note: for victims of severe depression or failed suicide attempts) or failure than the parent." Writing in *A Cry for Help*, Giffin and Carol Felsenthal make the commonsense point that parents should "assure the child that therapy is nothing to be ashamed of, that, on the contrary, it is an opportunity to get in touch with one's feelings, to become happier and more sensitive."

In fact, persons of any age undergoing psychotherapy following a suicide attempt need all the support and encouragement close relatives can give them. The person should also be allowed privacy when that is desirable. But parents and other relatives should always make themselves available to talk and especially to listen. Also, parents—as well as siblings—must learn to accept the new attitudes and behaviors that the individual wants to try out. As this relates to children, Dr. Giffin says we "should always remember that the child's problems took several years to build to the point of trouble and will take time to solve." This could also be said of adults undergoing in-home support-therapy.

homosexuals Among the groups most prone to suicidal behavior, many experts include homosexuals. These obervers have noted the frequency of homosexuality and homosexual preoccupations among many suicidal patients. Concern over homosexuality, says DR. HERBERT HENDIN in *Suicide in America*, "is often assumed to be the probable motive of suicide in such cases." A recent study by Stephen Schneider, Norman L. Farberow and Gabriel Kruks of 52 gay college men and 31 non-gay college men found that 19% of the college gays, 23% of the community gays and only 6% of the non-gay controls had made prior suicide attempts. When any kind of suicidal behavior was counted, such as suicide threats and suicide impulses, over half of each of the gay groups reported positively, 52% and 59% of the college and community gays, respectively, compared to 23% of the college non-gays. A major feature in their study, Farberow and colleagues report, was the linkage of the reported suicidal behavior with the critical points in the development of homosexuals, such as awareness of same sex attractions, becoming involved in first homosexual relationships and accepting self-identity as gay.

A team of Washington University researchers has provided evidence of a link between overt homosexuality and attempted suicide. They studied 57 homosexual women and 89 homosexual men and also saw 45 single heterosexual women and 35 heterosexual men as controls. Hendin writes: "They found that both male and female homosexuals showed only a slightly greater percentage of emotional disorders than did an unmarried heterosexual control group." Statistically, however, there was a greater incidence among the "gay" group of problem drinking, drug abuse and attempted suicide.

Concerning suicide, 23% of the female homosexual group, compared with only 5% of the female heterosexual control group, had attempted to kill themselves, a statistically significant difference. Seven percent of the male homosexuals and none of the heterosexual controls had tried suicide.

In Herbert Hendin's study of black suicide in *Archives of General Psychiatry*, four out of 12 seriously suicidal black males were homosexuals. "This proportion," says Hendin, "far exceeds the rate of male homosexuality among the entire black population, which, as in the case of the white male population, has been estimated to be between 5 and 10 percent." Hendin's finding suggests a link between suicide and homosexuality within the black male population. Only one of 13 black suicidal women was found to be homosexual. Farberow and colleagues in their study also found that a disproportionate percentage of the minority men in their two gay groups had been suicidal, 69% versus 31%. Their minorities included Hispanics, blacks, Pacific/Asians and others.

In his famous novel, *Another Country*, author JAMES BALDWIN explores the racial significance of suicide, violence and male homosexuality. He also indicates the significant importance of the white male to the black homosexual. Baldwin shows black homosexuality as an alternative to drugs, crime or religion in dealing with the extreme anxieties and stresses of the ghetto.

Hendin suggests that "unresolved separation anxiety" is a common aspect noticeable in both suicide and homosexuality. In other words, "Suicide is often an attempt to master the anxiety and rage of such rejection."

Suicidal homosexuals appear to be extremely vulnerable to rejection of any kind. Even today, the "gay life" still represents, in all too many instances, an alienated and isolated existence. In Dr. Hendin's view, "Since such [long term] relationships usually lack social or family support, rejection or disappointment signifies not merely abandonment but despair over the inability to escape emotional isolation."

honor, suicide to regain lost In many early societies, either actual suicide or suicidal activities were employed to regain an individual's lost honor. Among certain African tribes, for instance, men sought revenge against their enemies by killing themselves, a practice known as "killing oneself upon the head of another." When such a suicide occurred, custom had it that the enemy responsible must, in turn, immediately kill himself in the same way. This bizarre practice continued well into modern times.

St. Augustine formulated his prohibitions against suicide in order not only to prevent the early Christians seeking martyrdom but also to forestall young Christian maidens from killing themselves in order to preserve their chastity. Lucrece, whose story is written so beautifully in a Shakespeare poem, killed herself before her family in order to affirm her honor after she was forcibly raped by Sextus Taquinius the night before. Among the Romans, death to regain lost honor was chosen by such people as Ajax the Greater, CHARONDAS, DEMOSTHENES, CATO THE YOUNGER and many others. (See Introduction, on history of suicide.)

In North America, Cheyenne Indian warriors who had lost face for whatever reason would then place themselves in life-endangering situations. If the shamed warrior acted bravely in his risk-taking venture—perhaps a buffalo hunt, a war party against another tribe, self-inflicted pain—he won honor among his tribesmen, and thus regained lost self-esteem. If he failed and died from his actions, the tribe considered his death an honorable, face-saving one.

FRANCINE KLAGSBRUN writes in *Too Young to Die* that "lack of self-esteem without a traditional way of regaining it became a major cause for a high suicide rate among the Cheyenne in modern times." Kept on the reservation, tribesmen suffered loss of pride, of many of their traditions, and of their old means of supporting themselves. They became subservient to the white people and were dependent upon them for their welfare. With traditional buffalo hunts, war parties, and other age-old methods of handling feelings of unworthiness and dishonor forbidden to them, says Klagsbrun, "many young men turned instead to open suicide."

Among the Chinese, suicide was the accepted way for a defeated general or deposed ruler to regain lost honor. And the Japanese considered HARA-KIRI an accepted, honorable death for samurai, or members of the military class. Outlawed in 1868, the ritualized hara-kiri form of suicide continued to influence Japanese practices. For example, during World War II more than a thousand young Japanese pilots died as KAMIKAZE flyers who flew their planes at Allied warships. And in 1970, famed Japanese author YUKIO MISHIMA committed hara-kiri as a plea to his countrymen to revive old traditions and old values, including the concept of dying with honor.

"The practice of dying with honor to preserve one's beliefs has been prevalent throughout Jewish history, as Jews suffered persecutions and tortures in different countries in which they lived," says Klagsbrun. It happened in A.D. 73 at the fortress of MASADA and again during World War II in TREBLINKA, a notorious Nazi concentration camp.

hope, hopelessness There is almost always a complicated mix of feelings, attitudes and motives involved in any suicide attempt. Suicidologist-psychologist Norman L. Farberow stresses that the suicide decision is usually not impulsive; it is, in fact, premeditated. Although it is sometimes done on impulse, and may seem capricious to others, usually suicide is a decision that is given long consideration.

One prevailing attitude when people are suicidal—a state of mind that experts agree comes and goes—is the feeling of hopelessness. The victim sees no hope in the direction his or her life has taken and feels helpless to do anything about it. Yet despite this oppressive feeling of hopelessness, the would-be suicide usually still wishes for a last-minute solution to his or her problems. For many suicidal persons, there is an ambivalence, a confused tugging between loving and hating, between hope and hopelessness, between wanting to break away from family and friends while still wanting desperately to communicate with them. And all the while, there is present within the suicidal that feeling of being without any real hope, of being hopelessly entrapped in a life situation that cannot be controlled.

Hopelessness has been shown to be the critical factor in suicidal behavior—even more important than the depression factor—in a series of studies by Aaron T. Beck, professor of psychiatry at the University of Pennsylvania, and by Maria Kovacs, among others.

Doctors Farberow and Edwin S. Shneidman coined the well-known term "cry for help" essentially as it relates to suicide attempts, where help can still possibly prevent a personal tragedy.

hospitalization, involuntary Like alcoholics, drug abusers, or child beaters, many suicidals are caught in the web of denial. They deny need of help and will refuse to accept any. Often even close family members or trusted friends fail to convince them to meet with a professional therapist or to enter a psychiatric hospital. In cases of extreme denial or refusal to accept help, when critical suicidal danger exists, the victim may have to be institutionalized against their wishes by parents or other close relatives together with recognized physicians.

Involuntary hospitalization is not the ideal solution to the suicidal person's problems of course, and psychiatrists generally avoid such a measure unless they are convinced it is essential to save a life. There are, in fact, some psychiatrists that say involuntary hospitalization violates the individual's civil rights, and they will have no part in such a step. Most professionals in the mental health field maintain, however, that in certain instances suicidals must be hospitalized for their own protection and the protection of others.

A good professional therapist has one immediate goal in treating a suicidal person, as FRANCINE KLAGSBRUN notes, and that is to make the person feel that others care. "Underneath the hopelessness and despair of most suicidal people," writes Klagsbrun, "lies a devastating sense of worthlessness. Before they can cope with the causes that led to their unhappiness, they must be able to see themselves as worthwhile human beings whose lives deserve to be saved."

hospitals, help in for suicides There are usually mixed reactions among suicide attempters after they awaken in a hospital. They often deny the attempt and refuse to discuss the realities of the drastic event. Sometimes, the patient is angry at having failed and vows secretly to succeed at self-destruction the next time. And there is the group of attempters who admit a great feeling of relief at finding they are alive. For the latter, the suicide attempt often represents a turning point, and with the professional help of therapists (not to mention support from family members), the beginning of a new life.

Whatever the attempter's attitude, however, he or she must be seen, evaluated and usually treated by a professional therapist. The success of such therapy after a suicide attempt depends to a large degree on the patient's support from family, friends and associates. It has been pointed out by authorities that no suicide attempter grew up in a vacuum, and none of them in treatment returns to a vacuum-sealed existence. For this reason, therapists try to involve parents, siblings and sometimes close friends of the victim in the therapeutic process. Also, it is not uncommon for the parents of a suicidal—particularly in the case of a child or a young adult—to undergo therapy at the same time. Such therapy aims at helping parents understand just what problems and pressures perhaps led to a suicide attempt in their family . . . and to instruct them in ways to prevent future crises.

The competent therapist shows both suicidals and parents (or other relatives) the importance of opening up channels of communication within the family circle, how to talk about their fears and frustrations, their concerns and confusions, and not to have to use suicidal acts as their means of communication.

hostile behavior, as suicide clue Usually the suicidal person's attitude reflects itself in a number of verbal and behavioral "CLUES." Among the various behavioral hints or warning signs is aggressive, often hostile behavior.

DR. MARY GIFFIN and Carol Felsenthal, writing in *A Cry for Help*, cite instances where a young person's wild, angry behavior got him expelled from school: He had threatened a teacher with a knife, terrorized smaller children at an adjacent school, stolen another teacher's car and narrowly missed a pedestrian.

In a study conducted by Dr. Richard Seiden, University of California, Berkeley, 60% of those who had attempted suicide had tried such aggressive techniques as disobedience, sassiness, defiance and rebelliousness. Less than 18% of the control group of those non-suicide attempters had tried such tactics.

Other aggressive patterns among suicidal youngsters have included: shoplifting, joyriding in another's car, alcohol and other drug abuse. Some run away from home, become sexually promiscuous, fight with friends and occasionally with members of their own families. In a study of 39 disturbed children, psychiatrist Cynthia Pfeffer (immediate past president of the American Association of Suicidology) found that one-third of the subjects who were suicidal showed significantly more motor activity during the half-year preceding their evaluation.

Such hostile, aggressive behavior, including physical risk-taking, may indicate what psychiatrists call "masked depression." This is behavior that generates excitement and covers up or "masks" their real feelings, which are anxious, painful and depressive.

"How You Can Help in a Suicidal Crisis" In her book, *Too Young to Die: Youth and Suicide*, FRANCINE KLAGSBRUN provides readers with an excellent listing of things we can all do to help in a suicidal crisis. Her vital, seven-point list is used here with permission:

1. *Recognize the clues to suicide*. Look for symptoms of deep depression and signs of hopelessness and helplessness. Listen for suicide threats and words of warning, such as "I wish I were dead," or "I have nothing to live for." Watch for despairing actions and signals of loneliness; notice whether the person becomes withdrawn and isolated from others. Be alert to suicidal thoughts as a depression lifts.
2. *Trust your own judgment*. If you believe someone is in danger of suicide, act on your beliefs. Don't let others mislead you into ignoring suicidal signals.
3. *Tell others*. As quickly as possible, share your knowledge with parents, friends, teachers or other people who might help in a suicidal crisis. Don't worry about breaking a confidence if someone reveals suicidal plans to you. You may have to betray a secret to save a life.
4. *Stay with a suicidal person*. Don't leave a suicidal person alone if you think there is immediate danger. Stay with the person until help arrives or a crisis passes.
5. *Listen intelligently*. Encourage a suicidal person to talk to you. Don't give false reassurances that "everything will be okay." Listen and sympathize with what the person says. Don't judge or criticize the person for his or her feelings or actions; he or she already feels guilty enough.
6. *Be supportive*. Show the person that you care. Help the person feel worthwhile and wanted again.

Hume, David Scottish philosopher and historian (1711-1776). His *Treatise of Human Nature* (1739-40) tackles major problems in human perception and existence. Hume wrote a short essay, "On Suicide," published after his death, that was quickly suppressed. He argues against the view of considering suicide a crime. "The life of a man," Hume wrote, "is of no greater importance to the universe than that of an oyster." The implication was that a man who kills himself does not disrupt the larger order of the universe. Moreover, says Hume, he "does no harm to society; he only ceases to do good which if it is an injury, is of the lowest kind." The essay by the onetime librarian of the Advocates' Library in Edinburgh is included in collections of his works.

humor, loss of Among the cluster of symptoms noticeable in people who are clinically depressed is the loss of their sense of humor. They withdraw from family and friends, keeping to themselves; and they may cry for the most trivial reasons. They act sad and dejected and nothing appears humorous to them. As FRANCINE KLAGSBRUN notes, "Depressed people whose symptoms go unnoticed may pull further into themselves."

Humphry, Derek Co-founder with his wife, Ann Wickett, of the HEMLOCK SOCIETY in 1980 in Los Angeles, where the couple lives. Humphry, presently director of the Hemlock Society, was a newspaper reporter for 35 years, working for a number of British journals, including 14 years with the London *Sunday Times*. In 1978, he moved to the U.S. to work for the *Los Angeles Times*. The international acceptance of the book *Jean's Way*, the story of his first wife's death, as a classic account of "rational voluntary euthanasia," launched Humphrey on a career campaigning for the right of what he terms "self-deliverance." Humphrey is also author of five books on human rights issues, including *Let Me Die Before I Wake* and *The Right to Die: Understanding Euthanasia* (co-author, Ann Wickett).

Humphry's work, lectures and writing place him at the forefront of the field as a compassionate and articulate spokesman for individual choice.

Hungary According to the World Health Organization (WHO), at least 1,000 people worldwide kill themselves each day. In recent times, when countries are ranked according to their suicide rates, Hungary is at the top year in and year out. This may say less about national characteristics than about how facts are gathered, reported or covered up.

In 1984, WHO reports that Hungary's overall suicide rate was 45.9 per 100,000 population, up from 40.7 in 1977. The 1984 suicide rate among males was a very high 67.6; for females, still a high rate of 25.7 (both figures based on per 100,000 population). Among persons aged 15 to 24, Hungary's suicide rate was 17.2 per 100,000 population, 26.7 for males, 7.2 for females. Highest suicide rate among the various age groups was the 75-plus category: Overall rate per 100,000 was 124.7—196.0 for men, 85.6 for women.

The reasons for the high rate of suicide in Hungary are obscure. The country enjoys one of the highest standards of living in Eastern Europe, and has one of the least repressive regimes among Soviet-bloc nations. Dr. Ceza Varady, director of the Institute for Mental Health in Budapest, explains that "the phenomenon reflects the Hungarian temperament, which is volatile and likes dramatic gestures." (Quote from *Curious Facts* by John May.)

In the summer of 1986, Andrea Csilla Molnar, 17-year-old Miss Hungary, committed suicide by taking an overdose of heart medicine, according to the government newspaper *Magyar Hirlap*. The young winner of Hungary's first beauty contest since before World War II was found dead at her parents' home in Fonyod on Lake Belaton after taking an overdose of Lidocain. The reason for her suicide is not known.

"hurried" children Term used in the DR. MARY GIFFIN-Carol Felsenthal book *A Cry for Help* to describe children who are pushed by parents to grow up too fast. SIGMUND FREUD was, perhaps, the first psychiatrist to show concern about this phenomenon. In 1910, discussing suicide in children before the Vienna Psychoanalytic Society, Freud noted that teachers, in their attempt to wean children from early family life, often rushed the immature student too abruptly into the harsh realities of adult life.

Psychology professor David Elkind wrote in "Growing Up Faster" that hurried children today are thrown into an adult world that overwhelms, terrifies and sometimes causes them to develop self-destructive behavior patterns. Elkind, a professor of child study at Tufts University, points out that hurried adolescents frequently suffer anxiety about academic success. They then may solve this anxiety by using alcohol and other drugs; girls may get pregnant to prove they can accomplish something "adult." As these actions make things worse, suicide may become another "adult" option.

Dr. Giffin makes the point that many young people, instead of trying to match an image held up by their parents, "try to match one held up by the media." She cites the case of one girl who attempted suicide and explained, "There's a lot of pressure in the media to be like Brooke Shields. You can't get away from that face on the billboards. I'm attractive, but I'm not going to be on any billboard. It's an unattainable goal."

Many authorities agree that one result of "hurried" children is that eight in 10 boys and seven in 10 girls have sexual intercourse during their teen years. One-third of the nation's teenagers have sexual intercourse by their 15th birthday. Forty percent of the girls now 14 will be pregnant at least once during the next five years. Some of these young people will become suicide attempters or lethal suicides.

I

Iceland In an epidemiological study that served as a valuable guide to planning psychiatric care and suicide prevention in the community, T. Helgason followed for 60 years Icelanders born between 1895 and 1897. Once hundred and three (or nearly 2%) developed a manic-depressive illness; 34 of them were dead by 1960, 18 by suicide. That is, more than half of the manic-depressives' deaths were suicides and 17% of all cases of manic-depressive illness committed suicide. In short, people with this diagnosis contributed a far greater proportion of suicides than did those with other psychiatric disorders. Therefore, an easily recognized and readily treated mental disorder is high on the list of mental illnesses associated with suicide.

In 1983, Iceland's suicide rate per 100,000 population was 16.9. The gender breakdown was 27.6 for males, 5.9 for females. In the 15 to 24 age group, the suicide rate per 100,000 population was 13.5. Highest rate among age groups was for the 65- to 74-year-olds—a very high 59.3 per 100,000. Males in this age bracket had an alarming rate per 100,000 of 111.1, whereas females' rate was 13.9.

Dr. Peter Sainsbury, "Community Psychiatry," ch. 9 in *A Handbook for the Study of Suicide*, ed. Seymour Perlin (New York: Oxford University Press, 1975).

identity, loss of, and suicide As in other losses, loss of identity or self-image leads to depression. Often the depression is deep-seated and if unnoticed may push the person further into depression, and even into suicide. FRANCINE KLAGSBRUN says in *Too Young to Die* that "of all the losses teenagers might suffer, the one that affects the greatest number is a sense of lost identity. In some ways, the teen years themselves can be viewed as a time of just such a loss, a time that can lead to confused, depressive feelings."

It is during the teen years that so many things happen—voices change, bodies change, interests change, sexual feelings change drastically—and, almost overnight, the child becomes, in Klagsbrun's words, "an almost-but-not-quite adult person." These changes, exciting and desired by most young people, nonetheless produce extreme anxieties, tensions and mood alterations. Youngsters often become frightened, dejected and angry at both themselves and "the threatening outside."

Teenagers also develop a fascination with death and dying. They wonder about many aspects of life that they previously had taken for granted. And, as Klagsbrun notes, many teens and young adults have an unrealistic view of death. Most seem to think they're immortal. Even many who become suicidal usually lack a true or realistic concept of the finality of death. Klagsbrun says, "Their fascination with death along with the tensions of adolescence makes young people especially vulnerable to depression and to dark, self-destructive thoughts."

Most young people, of course, manage the horrors of adolescence and go on to live productive, mature lives. But for those who receive too little love and understanding, who feel alienated and without support, and who suffer loss of identity as a result, the option of self-destruction takes on an unreal attraction.

Loss of identity has also been identified as one of the causes of the high suicide rate among the elderly. Loss of job, loss of family, loss of lifelong friends and loss of physical health, either singly or in combination, may bring about strong feelings of loss of self-concept, loss of purpose, and feelings of meaninglessness.

Ignatius of Antioch During the period when the craving for martyrdom became almost epidemic among the early Christians, Ignatius of Antioch wrote letters, particularly those to the Christian community of Rome, that epitomized the state of zeal and mania. "I beseech you . . . ," he wrote, "Suffer me to be eaten by the beasts that I may be found pure bread of Christ. Rather entice the wild beasts that they may become my tomb, and leave no trace of my body, that when I fall asleep I be not burdensome to any. Then shall I be truly a disciple of Jesus Christ, when the world shall not even see my body. Beseech Christ on my behalf, that I may be found a sacrifice through these instruments."

Christians generally despised the tendency toward suicide among pagans, but premature, voluntary death as a martyr characterized large segments in the Roman Empire between the reigns of Nero and Julian (i.e., 54-363 A.D.).

Dr. George Rosen, "History," ch. 1 in *A Handbook for the Study of Suicide*, ed. Seymour Perlin (New York: Oxford University Press, 1975).

illness, depression as Depression is an illness that is difficult to cope with; because of the very nature of the ailment, the person suffering from depression takes little action to get better. It is an affliction that can affect all age groups; in any given year, some 15% of all adults over age 18 will experience significant depressive symptoms. The rate of depression is high among adolescents (particularly from minority groups) and women in their 30s, but the over-60 age group is the most vulnerable population segment.

"Depression is considered *the* underlying cause of suicide," say S.S. Miller, J.A. Miller and D.E. Miller in *Life Span Plus*, "since it engenders a body-mind state that makes the individual vulnerable, weary and isolated, without hope for the future."

Some 10,000 Americans over age 60 commit suicide each year. The over-65 age group suffers the highest incidence of suicide of any age group—10% of the population accounting for 25% of all suicides.

Still, depression is treatable and curable even though it has a severe debilitating effect on the individual—physically, psychologically and emotionally. Many celebrated people suffered from bouts of depression and went on to great accomplishments, among them, Abraham Lincoln, Winston Churchill, SIGMUND FREUD, Nathaniel Hawthorne, and the biblical King Saul.

Authorities indicate that there is a good chance—some say as high as 90 to 95%—of recovery from depression with proper treatment. About half of those depressed patients who fall victim to a single attack of depression never suffer a recurrent attack.

Although today we don't believe, as did the ancients, that depression is caused by too much "black bile" in the body, the old theories weren't altogether wrong. Scientists have discovered certain biochemical abnormalities in association with depressive states, which may play an important role in the development of depression—or may result from depression. Other variables responsible for the illness called depression may include genetic factors that may be involved to an unknown extent.

Symptoms of depression may include physical irritations such as sleep disturbance, loss of appetite, headaches, diminished sex drive, and general aches and pains. Psychological symptoms include nervousness, anxiety, lethargy, crying and loss of concentration. In pathological cases, individuals suffer an extreme state of unresponsiveness to stimuli, together with self-deprecation, delusions of inadequacy and hopelessness. The world seems overwhelming and incomprehensible.

Theories about the illness we call depression are often divided into four different approaches: genetic, biochemical, psychological and socio-cultural. In certain individuals one of these factors may appear to be more important to the onset of depression than the others. But all of these aspects contribute to most cases, and treatment (if it is to be successful) generally takes every one of them into account.

Treatment, depending upon the degree and type of depression, may include antidepressant drugs, psychotherapy and ECT (electro-convulsive therapy). Each of these three conventional methods by which depression is treated present certain drawbacks, especially involving suicidal patients. Drugs offer the dangers of side effects and improper dosage, interactions with other drugs or foods, and allergic and/or toxic reactions. Psychotherapy takes time, patience and money (or insurance coverage) to find the appropriate therapist. In the case of suicide-prone depressives, there often is not enough time. And this therapy is the slowest-acting. ECT (electroconvulsive therapy) is the quickest acting of the conventional treatment methods, but it is also the least understood and most controversial. Though it has a reportedly high symptom cure rate (about 60% in endogenous depression, that is, illness not triggered by any external event), it often requires repeat treatments, and the effects of this therapy upon brain function are unknown and may be harmful. Use of ECT should not be undertaken without fully understanding the nature of the treatment and its possible side effects. (See also ANTIDEPRESSANTS, ELECTROCONVULSIVE THERAPY and PSYCHOTHERAPY.)

illness, mental Mentally ill individuals—especially those suffering from depressive illnesses—are usually considered among suicidal high-risk groups. Erwin Stengel, who has specialized in the follow-up and the study of social effects of suicide attempts, says that about one-third of the people who kill themselves are found to have been suffering from mental illness requiring physical treatment. Among the mental disorders, depressive illness carries a very high suicidal risk. The clinical view of this illness pictures a feeling of worthlessness and despair and a wish to die, but even in this distraught condition, the urge to commit suicide varies.

Other major mental illnesses, such as schizophrenia, also reveal an above-average incidence of suicide. Stengel notes that abnormal personalities with aggressive tendencies show increased liability to suicide; for instance, the incidence of suicide among murderers has been found to be excessive.

This does not mean that every person who commits suicide is psychiatrically ill in the clinical sense, but in Stengel's words, "even in the absence of mental illness a suicidal act is an abnormal reaction to stress, abnormal being defined statistically—that is, not in keeping with the reactions of the large majority of persons to comparable situations."

Sociologists tend to deny the mental illness factor in the causation of suicide. But recognition of psychopathology in the causation of suicide does not do away with sociological theories. Says Stengel: "The motivations underlying suicidal acts carried out by the mentally ill are fundamentally the same as in the general population, although they are derived from disorders of mood or from such abnormal contents of thought as delusions."

In *Some Facts About Suicide*, authors Erwin J. Shneidman and Norman L. Farberow write, "Studies of hundreds of geniune suicide notes indicate that although the suicidal person is extremely unhappy, he is not necessarily mentally ill."

E.J. Shneidman and N.L. Farberow, *Some Facts About Suicide*, PHS Publication No. 852 (Washington, DC: U.S. Government Printing Office, 1961).

Erwin Stengel, *Suicide and Attempted Suicide*, rev. (New York: Jason Aronson, 1974; original work published 1964).

illness, terminal The question about the justification of suicide in the case of terminally ill people is still hotly debated in the U.S. Do these people have the choice of death rather than life? Should physicians be permitted to "pull the plug" on life-sustaining machines regardless of the quality of that life?

A unanimous decision in March 1986 by the American Medical Association (AMA) Judicial Council ruled that it would be ethical for doctors to withhold "all means of life-prolonging treatment," including food and water, from patients in irreversible comas. The policy stated that withholding treatment in such cases, even when death is not imminent, would be ethically appropriate. However, the Judicial Council of the AMA noted that its decision did not oblige any physician to stop therapy and that each case should be decided individually. The policy stemming from the Council's New Orleans meeting is expected ultimately to make withholding of treatment in the case of terminally ill patients more socially acceptable. At present, though, it will be of greatest concern to families and physicians of the estimated 10,000 people who are in irreversible comas in institutions around the country.

The opinion of the AMA's Judicial Council has no legal standing, of course, but as an indicator of shifting social opinion, it is likely to give prosecutors, plaintiffs and judges pause.

The controversy involving the terminally ill person's right to die has its roots in the recent radical changes that have taken place in American health care. In 1950 a majority of Americans died at home, with the family doctor and relatives in attendance. Now about 80% of the 5,500 Americans who die each day do so, wired and incubated, in an institution where expensive technology is arrayed and controlled by specialists who likely know little about the patient beyond the medical problem.

Dr. Sara Charles, who has written about such matters, says: "Traditionally the doctor-patient relationship was mutually trusting. With the intrusion of the law, it has become mutually mistrusting. Treatment has too often become a detached technical decision."

It is this mistrust Dr. Charles refers to that has resulted in thousands of medical malpractice suits, some ending in multi-million-dollar awards.

There exists, of course, a subtle negotiation process about death among doctors, patients and family. The process, a poorly kept secret in many hospitals, involves trying certain methods of life-prolonging treatment and then, if they have not worked, tacitly withdrawing them. In effect, removing treatment results in death, but the official cause is always given as the underlying disease. Such negotiated deaths depend (and rely) on trust between the givers and takers of health care.

The long-run implications of the 1986 AMA ruling will surely and eventually affect millions of Americans who must make such decisions for themselves or for infirm relatives. The debate will also have immense financial implications. Today, with medical costs still rising, one in nine Americans is over 65. By the year 2030, the figure will climb to an estimated one in five.

Dr. Norman Farberow says, "It is appropriate to indicate some of the research on terminal illness and suicide such as: Some illnesses are known to be fatal, such as cancer (unless diagnosed and treated early) and AIDS, today's acquired immunodeficiency syndrome. Suicide, according to research I've done on cancer patients in Veterans Administration Hospitals, was bound to occur significantly more often than expected. And today, although research on this aspect has not as yet been systematically gathered, preliminary clinical reports have linked suicide to serum-positive and AIDS-identified cases."

In July 1987, at a first-ever joint conference of the American Association of Suicidology and the International Association for Suicide Prevention, Dr. Stuart Younger chaired a panel on "AIDS and Rational Suicide" and quoted Dr. Peter Admirall of the Netherlands who said the problem wasn't between active or passive, but with voluntary and involuntary euthanasia. According to Dr. Younger, the Netherlands physician has stated that "90% of AIDS patients are killed by their doctors." (Reported by Sister Mary Frances Seeley in AAS's *NEWSLINK*.)

Illusions Book by author Richard Bach (*Jonathan Livingston Seagull*), with a theme dealing with reincarnation. Dr. Mary Giffin and Carol Felsenthal report in *A Cry for Help* that a teenage couple read *Illusions*, became obsessed with the possibility of reincarnation and planned their suicides. The two, a 16-year-old boy and a 15-year-old girl, crashed a car into a school building at 5 A.M., hoping to move to a "higher plane of existence." The boy was killed instantly. The girl, who must have had last-second doubts, just barely survived, after diving under the dashboard. The building the couple's car crashed into was their old junior high school.

imitation in suicide Dr. Cynthia Pfeffer, immediate past-President of the American Association of Suicidology and associate professor of clinical psychiatry at Cornell Medical College, says, "There is probably an element of contagion in the so-called 'clusters' of teenage suicide—mutual influencing of one adolescent by another. It's the vulnerable youngsters who seem most likely to be affected."

A series of suicides in the aerospace community of Clear Lake City, Texas, home of the Johnson Space Center, is a recent example of what public health authorities call "clustering"—the phenomenon of teenage suicides in which one person's suicide triggers another in the same locale. In a period of two months, the chain of deaths saw six teenagers in the city and neighboring areas commit suicide.

In the past 10 years other outbreaks have occurred in a growing number of widespread communities that include: New York's affluent Westchester, Rockland and Putnam counties, north of New York City (a string of 12 deaths); Plano, Texas, an upper-middle-class city of 100,000; Cheyenne, Wyoming, population 47,264; Cherry Creek School District near Denver, Colorado; and Columbus, Ohio.

Psychologists believe that many at-risk teenagers are subconsciously crying out for attention and may consider suicide the "ultimate revenge." Julie Perlman, MSW and executive officer, the American Association of Suicidology, explains: "A kid may say, 'Look, he did it, and look at all the attention it got. People really felt badly, so why don't I do it?'" Thomas Barrett, a psychologist for the Denver area's Cherry Creek School District, says, "When one suicide occurs, it brings other kids who are vulnerable to the surface."

Dr. Edwin S. Shneidman writes in *Suicide: It Doesn't Have to Happen,*

> No one knows what it is like to be dead. At best, one can only imagine what it would be like if one were alive to watch—an invisible personality—at one's own funeral. Often, such an attractive fantasy intoxicates the suicidal mind, and tips the scale to death. But until the very moment that the bullet or barbiturate finally snuffs out life's last breath—while the ground is rushing up—the suicidal person wants terribly to live.

A September 1986 report published by *The New England Journal of Medicine* says that television news coverage of suicides and TV dramas about the topic appear to cause a temporary increase in the number of teenagers who kill themselves. No comparable increase was found in adult suicide rates. Spokespersons for both the CBS and NBC networks questioned the report's validity as well as methods used in the studies.

Doctors Robert E. Litman and Norman L. Farberow of the Los Angeles Suicide Prevention Center are now conducting a survey to better identify youths susceptible to suicide. The study is part of a five-year program recently enacted by the California state legislature. This involves a random survey of 1,000 teenagers and a like number of parents. Teens are asked if they know anyone who has tried to harm or kill himself; why they did it; and what could have been done to prevent it. They are then asked if they themselves have considered or attempted suicide. Between 3 and 5% report attempts.

Meanwhile, about 5,000 young people will continue to take their lives with each passing year. As Steven Stack, associate professor of sociology, Auburn University, said recently: "It may be news that the number (of teen suicides) is not getting worse. It is *not* very good news that it remains so high." (See also CLUSTER SUICIDES.)

immaturity, of gifted children It is a fact that many of the young people who attempt or complete suicide are gifted students. It is also a fact that all kinds of young people from all kinds of backgrounds, with IQs of every level, kill themselves.

There have been many instances where an intellectually precocious child who is emotionally arrested commits suicide. One woman, Mary Connelly, a mother of seven children whose IQs ranged from 130 to 150, says that five of them had contemplated suicide. These children's minds developed so much faster than their bodies that serious social and emotional problems resulted.

Data on gifted children and suicides or suicide attempts are at best skimpy and uncertain, so it is not clear to what extent the psychological problems of "gifted" students resemble those of average IQ.

immaturity, of parents Some families are plagued by a reversal in the parent/child roles. The child is expected, unfortunately, to nurture the parent, a burden that may be fraught with danger. In *Vivienne: The Life and Suicide of an Adolescent Girl*, co-authors John E. Mack and Holly Hickler write vividly of this tragic situation. The mother of the family sought advice and help from the girl, Vivienne Loomis, who was not yet 14. The young person complained in a letter to her former teacher that among other reasons for her initial suicide attempt was the fact she could no longer tolerate trying to manage her mother's problems, her father's problems, her sister's problems and, most of all, her own problems.

Cynthia Pfeffer, 1986-87 president of the American Association of Suicidology, discovered, along with colleagues at the Albert Einstein School of Medicine, that parents of suicidal young people they studied generally possessed character traits normally associated with children. The parents were dependent, wanted instant gratification, were victims of severe mood swings, and lacked the capacity to communicate with or offer guidance to their offspring. This resulted in the immature parents failing to parent until their children felt frustrated, worthless and blamed themselves for family problems. "They often believed that they could solve the problems in the family," Dr. Pfeffer is quoted by Dr. Mary Giffin as saying, "and depreciated themselves when met with disappointment. Fantasies of escape from such disturbing circumstances were prevalent. Often death was evidenced as a means of eliminating stress and attaining peace and satisfaction."

It appears that all too many of today's parents, for whatever reason, are preoccupied with themselves and forget that children are just that—children. As Dr. Giffin says, "Children need nurturing and love and they'll kill—themselves—to get it."

immolation, self There have always been cases in recorded history of the bizarre practice of self-immolation. In 165 A.D., the Cynic philosopher Peregrinus Proteus cremated himself on a pyre in the Indian manner. SUTTEE, as practiced in India until prohibited by law in 1829 (although reportedly still practiced in remote parts of the country), required that the widow of her Indian husband immolate herself on her husband's pyre as the body was being cremated (see INDIA). And as recently as the Vietnam War, several Buddhist monks set fire to themselves in protest. In 1969, Czech student Jan Palach chose self-immolation as a political act, both as a gesture of defiance and a condemnation of the system imposed on his country by the U.S.S.R.

Self-immolation as a political act has brought veneration in some situations, such as those generated by the Nazi concentration camp horrors, the conditions of terror in Russian Gulags, and the intolerance of other perverse systems.

The above described acts of self-destruction can be traced to what Emile Durkheim typed as altruistic suicide, whereby the group's authority over the individual is so pronounced that the individual loses his or her own personal identity and wishes to sacrifice his life for his community. There is also anomic (meaning "lawlessness") suicide involved in some of these cases, i.e., suicide committed because the individual is unable to adjust to new conditions of living.

immortality Young people who attempt or successfully carry out suicide often do not have a true sense of mortality. To them, death represents a rather vague, even romantic concept. And often suicide, as an attractive fantasy that, according to Shneidman, "intoxicates the suicidal mind," becomes a realistic method for testing feelings of immortality.

Young people have always felt this way, regardless of the particular era. But, as Dr. Mary Giffin notes, "for the television generation, the sense is heightened." Most young people's (especially adolescents') experience with death is restricted to books, films or television. Sometimes a hero or heroine faces death each week a dozen times and survives, wisecracking.

Children fantasize and, like Tom Sawyer, believe they will be around to attend their own funerals. Tragically for many of these children, only the harsh reality of a suicide attempt makes them realize that they are, indeed, mortal. Suicidal young people often believe in the words of the theme song of M*A*S*H, that "SUICIDE IS PAINLESS." They see death as a sort of magical, mystical adventure. Dr. Giffin tells of one eight-year-old who jumped out of the window thinking that as soon as he cleared the frame, he would be sucked magically upward to rejoin his dead father in heaven.

Dr. William Worden, Harvard Medical School, is researching suicide at the Suicide Prevention Clinic, Massachusetts General Hospital. He speculates that the recent increase in the belief in reincarnation may be responsible, at least in part, for today's suicide rates among our young population.

Dr. Giffin writes of one 16-year-old girl who left a suicide note explaining that she was about to kill "just the bad part of myself." The implication was that the good part would somehow survive and make what she called a "new beginning." In a poem the victim left behind she talked about returning to the womb where "finally I will be protected, wrapped in water and warmth."

impulsiveness, as suicide clue Most young people who kill themselves have trouble controlling their impulses. They will often react to situations before thinking things through and/or overreact to stimuli. As Dr. Mary Giffin says, "An adolescent may be less depressed than an adult but commit suicide over some seemingly trivial event out of an inability to delay self-destructive action."

Fortunately, the young person's impulsiveness reflects itself in non-fatal ways that may be a clue to suicidal behavior. He or she might get a failing grade on an exam, for example, and drop the course then and there. He or she might have a meaningless quarrel with a girlfriend or a boyfriend and leave town without further ado. These behavioral clues, some more subtle than others, should be taken seriously. Four out of five persons who commit suicide have previously given clues—verbal, behavioral or both—of their intent. Singly, these unexpected acts of impulsiveness may not be particularly significant, but clustered with other "CLUES" they can predict potential suicide.

incest In his *Crime and Customs in Savage Society*, BRONISLAW MALINOWSKI discusses what has been referred to by some as "the best-known case in the history of anthropological theory." The case of Trobriand (off the coast of New Guinea) suicide, used by Malinowski, shows how public disapproval of a man who had committed a major sin, in this instance incest, acted as a legal mechanism by inducing the offender to take his own life. His discussion was concerned primarily with law, but subsequently led anthropologists to reconsider the nature of suicide in primitive societies. Suicide is thus forced on the Trobriand individual as the only solution to an intolerable situation. Such action, however, could not be said to earn the suicide posthumous social approval.

In modern societies, there are some cases of suicide that result directly from incest, both on the part of victim and perpetrator.

India Early societies sometimes pressured certain members into killing themselves for ritual purposes. Behind the ritual lay a strong belief in life after death. Such thinking motivated widows in ancient India who practiced SUTTEE.

Women threw themselves upon their husbands' funeral pyres or drowned themselves in the Ganges River. The practice was encouraged by Hindu priests and relatives of the widow. By self-destruction a faithful wife not only atoned for her husband's sins, but also opened the gates of paradise to him. The general populace venerated a widow who practiced suttee and condemned one who refused, sometimes actually threatening her with physical punishment. The practice of suttee continued in India for hundreds of years. It was outlawed by the British rulers of India in 1829, yet slow-changing customs saw it continue on occasion into the early 1900s.

Dr. A. Venkoba Rao writes about suicide in India in Norman Farberow's *Suicide in Different Cultures* and points out that early periods in history espoused different attitudes toward suicide. Thus the Vedic period permitted suicide on religious grounds while the Upanishads strongly condemned it. The *Dharmastra* called all suicides, except those committed for religious purposes, cardinal sins and denied suicides funeral rites and cremation. Brahmanism recommended that the person planning to kill himself must fast for three days. If the suicide attempt failed there was severe punishment. Hinduism held that life is not a term but only one of a series. Vedantic philosophy with its theory of reincarnation admitted to physical death but the soul was considered immortal. Death was an opportunity for a new life.

The custom of suttee, or *sati* in India, was not indigenous to the country. It was practiced by the Scythians and the Thracians earlier. The Kathei, an ancient Punjabi tribe, made *sati* a law to prevent the wife poisoning the husband. The practice was outlawed in 1829 by a law passed in Vice-Regent Lord Bentinck's tenure. Mass suicide in India, known as *jaubar*, was followed by the women of the Rajput class to avoid molestation by the victors in battles with other tribes. *Sallekhana*, suicide by self-denial of food, is permisslble only to ascetics, according to the Jain religion. In India today, attempted suicide continues to be an offense, so that notification of authorities is avoided. Socially, survivors are looked on as "tainted members" and marriages in such families become difficult. When suicides do occur, the most common method is ingestion of an insecticide, a wide variety of which are easily and commonly obtainable.

The World Health Organization has no reliable data on the rate of suicide in India today. Nor is the country included in the United Nations' 1978 *Demographic Yearbook* (latest published by that organization). However, Dr. Rao has reported data on suicide in India in Dr. Lee A. Headley's *Suicide in Asia and the Near East*. Government statistics for all India on completed suicide indicate that the suicide rate from 1965 to 1977 fluctuated from 6.3 to 8.1 with most of the years averaging around 7.7 per 100,000. The reliability of the data is suspect because of the wide range and willingness of the reporting persons, efficiency of police in conducting investigations, and ability of the police surgeon in determining the death was a suicide.

Among the 21 states the highest rate in 1972 was 20.5 for Kerala while the lowest was 0.70 for Jammu and Kashmir. Among the eight Union territories (administered by the government of India), the highest rate for the same year was 52.5 for Andaman and Nicobar Islands while the territory of

Lakshadweep reported none. However, Lakshadweep had a population of only 33,000 and the population in the Andaman and Nicobar Islands was only 118,000. In all of India, males generally commit suicide more often. Suicide was most commonly associated with the younger age groups. In 1972, 45.4% of the suicides were by persons 18 to 29 years of age.

indirect self-destructive behavior (ISDB) Indirect self-destructive behavior refers to the group of behaviors that, according to Norman Farberow in *The Many Faces of Suicide*, is distinguishable from direct or overt self-destructive behavior by the criteria of time and awareness. The effect of the behaviors is long-range, with the time possibly spanning many years, and the person is usually unaware of or at least does not care about the effects of his behavior. Despite knowing what the results of his continuing the behavior will be, he does not consider himself a suicide.

These behaviors have often been called unconscious suicide; EMILE DURKHEIM referred to them as a kind of embryonic suicide, while Karl A. Menninger called them "focal suicide." The activities for the most part may shorten life, bring about loss of limb or sense, cause systemic malfunctioning, destroy family, employment and friend relationships, cause loss of economic stability and generally negate effective personal and social functioning.

The behaviors include self-mutilation, polysurgery, disregard of physicians' regimen in long-term chronic illnesses, malingering, psychosomatic illnesses, substance abuse, hyperobesity, smoking, violent crime, compulsive gambling, and others. Some experts include high-risk sports, such as mountain climbing, scuba diving and hang gliding—when the participant exceeds the bounds of caution and begins to take unreasonable chances.

Among other characteristics are strong tendencies toward denial, a focus on the present and a need to obtain immediate gratification from his behaviors. There seems to be a strong flavor of excitement-seeking in the activities, as if it's the stimulation of the process rather than the achievement of the goal that is most important.

It is not fully known whether indirect and direct suicidal behavior occur more frequently in the same person or more generally substitute for each other. Some early research indicates it may be a factor of age, with the one substituting for the other more often in young and middle years, and the two occurring more frequently together in the older years.

infant, bonding Bonding is when a "mothering" figure or so-called "primary caregiver" (and this can be a father, grandmother or housekeeper) devotes himself or herself to a baby with loving care that is constant and consistent. Dr. Silvia Feldman, a psychotherapist and family counselor, wrote of bonding in *Choices in Childbirth*: "The major reason for the rapid adaptation to the routines and responsibilities of motherhood is the psychological and biological phenomenon called bonding, which transforms ordinary adults into motherly and fatherly types."

Responsiveness is the primary ingredient of bonding, says DR. MARY GIFFIN, and "Responsiveness makes the difference between a baby who grows up feeling helpless and one who grows up feeling competent and confident."

The fear among many medical and health care professionals is that with the two-paycheck family, no one is caring for America's children. Dr. URIE BRONFENBRENNER asks in "Nobody Home: The Erosion of the American Family," Just who is caring for the country's children? Others such as Dr. Giffin, Dr. Benjamin Spock and Professor John Killinger of Vanderbilt University have written on the subject.

Psychiatrist Arnold Tobin warns that a time bomb can be set ticking in a child's infancy if bonding is disturbed by a mother's returning to work too early, leaving the baby with multiple sitters or in a day-care center.

Signs of failed bonding or bonding deprivation, at least to many experts, are now being seen in today's young people (e.g., erratic actions, aggressive behavior, lack of repect for authority, chronic anxiety, violence, alcoholism, drug abuse, etc.). It is even reflected in the high rate of suicide for youngsters in America. Giffin says, "we reap what we sow," and that "bonding is the foundation of a child's life. We must realize that the suicidal impulse can be ingrained within the first few months of life . . . the underlying causes [of suicide] frequently can be traced to emotional scars inflicted during infancy."

Plato said centuries ago, "And the first step, as you know, is always what matters most, particularly when we are dealing with those who are young and tender. That is the time when they are taking shape and when any impression we choose to make leaves a permanent mark." Two thousand years later, Freud made the same point: "The very impressions we have forgotten have nevertheless left the deepest traces in our psychic life, and acted as determinants for our whole future development."

Mary Giffin, MD, and Carol Felsenthal, *A Cry for Help: Exploring and Exploding the Myths About Teenage Suicide—A Guide for All Parents of Adolescents* (Garden City: Doubleday, 1983).

information, dissemination of Widespread private and public support is at long last being mobilized to fight the suicide problem in the U.S. In California, for example, a law enacted in 1983 made funds available for development of special educational programs in the public schools to discuss and teach ways of preventing teen suicides. Since then, other states have begun programs similar in nature and purpose. On a national level, the Center for Disease Control in Atlanta undertook a study aimed at identifying possible victims and preventing suicide.

In June 1985, the Department of Health and Human Services, Administration for Children, Youth and Families, and the YOUTH SUICIDE NATIONAL CENTER cosponsored a NATIONAL CONFERENCE ON YOUTH SUICIDE in Washington, D.C. President Ronald Reagan proclaimed the month "Youth Suicide Prevention Month."

In May 1986, the Task Force on Youth Suicide (sponsored by the U.S. Department of Health and Human Services) conducted a two-day National Conference on Prevention and Intervention in Youth Suicide, held in Oakland, California. A final meeting of the Task Force, held in Bethesda, Maryland, in November 1986, discussed "Strategies for the Future: Youth Suicide."

The above-mentioned conferences were attended by public health professionals, physicians, nurses, social workers, psychiatrists, psychologists, mental health program officials, suicidologists, educators and school couselors, as well as concerned citizens. The conferences' objectives: to present and discuss multi-disciplinary findings in suicide prevention and interventions; to explore effective strategies for combating this problem; and to develop recommendations for private and public sector action.

In response to growing national concern for the suicide problem, Bill HR 4650 (Youth Suicide Prevention Act) passed the House of Representatives, July 14, 1986. It was referred to the Senate Subcommittee on Education, Arts and Humanities.

The bill would establish a grant program assisting local education agencies and private nonprofit organizations to establish and operate youth suicide prevention programs. Grants will be used to:

1. Increase awareness of youth suicide among families, students and community leaders;
2. Train school personnel and community leaders in prevention strategies;
3. Coordinate youth suicide efforts with government alcohol substance abuse programs;
4. Utilize community resources in development and implementation of youth suicide prevention programs; and
5. Cooperate with other appropriate agencies and organizations in youth suicide prevention.

One million dollars would be authorized the first year (FY'87) and "such sums as may be necessary" would be authorized the following two years. No grant, however, would exceed $100,000 per year.

Senate Bill 2551 (Youth Suicide Prevention Act) was introduced on June 12, 1986. It will further the high level of commitment of the administration to combat youth suicide and to focus the concentration of those efforts into a clearinghouse. The bill provides for no new authorization since the Department of Health and Human Services has indicated an ability to fund the clearinghouse with existing appropriations.

When and if this bill passes the Senate, both bills would go to the Conference Committee where an attempt to merge the bills would be made so that the essence of each remains intact. The Committee's finalized bill will then go for a final vote. If it is passed, it will then go to the President for his signature.

All of the above efforts are just a beginning; such efforts to inform people at every level must be broadened and spread throughout the country. For all too many people, suicide remains today what it has been in the past: a stigmatized "closet" affliction. The total subject needs to be further researched, talked and written about, and more information made available to everyone, young persons and older persons alike—and, as FRANCINE KLAGSBRUN stresses, "not by sensationalizing the facts, but with honesty."

inheritance, of depression In normal individuals, depression is a state of despondency characterized by feelings of inadequacy, lowered activity and general pessimism about the future. This described disorder is one of the distress signals for spotting possible suicidal behavior. It is not inherited, however. For various and often complex psychological reasons, one suicide in a family may lead to others. But biologically—and contrary to popular myth—suicides do not "run in families."

It should be noted, that, based on studies past and present, some psychiatrists believe a tendency or predisposition to depression *may* be passed through families. However, just what part genetics and what part environment play in producing depression, is not yet known. In November 1981, scientists at the University of Rochester Medical School reported in the *New England Journal of Medicine* the discovery of one or more genes that make people susceptible to severe depression. Other studies have underscored the physiological and genetic nature of many depressions. Still other research results indicate that a person hospitalized for depression is 30 times more likely to commit suicide than a non-depressed person.

But the illness itself remains pretty much a mystery. No one has yet come up with a comprehensive, proven theory for the cause or causes of depression. We do know, however, that it manifests itself through recognizable symptoms and, in most cases, we know how to go about treating it.

insomnia, as suicide clue One of the several symptoms of depression, which increases the individual's vulnerability to suicidal ideation, is persistent insomnia. Although mental depression, frequently a prelude to suicide, is unfortunately hard to recognize, externally, often the individual confides that he or she is experiencing insomnia. Family members notice immediately when someone is having sleep problems. The person affected awakens much earlier than usual or else has difficulty getting to sleep at night. Excessive sleep may also be a symptom of mental depression. The person tries to blot out the unhappy hours with sleep. That person may decide one day that death's eternal sleep is the only true, tranquil state.

Again, for the person contemplating suicide, insomnia—or excessive sleep patterns—may be clues to self-destruction. Suicide is most often premeditated. It may sometimes be done on impulse, and to others appear capricious, but usually killing oneself is a decision that is given long consideration.

institutional suicide Instances of suicide out of loyalty are akin to RITUAL SUICIDES (see SEPPUKU) and are frequently described among different peoples in various historical periods. For instance, Nicholas of Damascus, an historian in the time of Augustus, was a chieftain of the Sotiani, a Celtic tribe, and employed a handpicked bodyguard of some 606 men who were bound by a vow to live and/or die with him, no matter whether the chief died in glorious battle or of a fatal disease. Another instance of institutionalized suicide is the well-known practice whereby a widow or a concubine gives her life when the husband or master dies. HERODOTUS describes this custom among the Thracians, who practiced polygamy. When a man died, the wives vied for the honor of being judged favorite—and the woman accorded this honor was then slain over the grave and buried with her beloved husband. Analogous to this case of institutional suicide is the familiar Hindu custom of SUTTEE. Here the widow immolates herself with the husband's corpse. Yet another example is the altruistic (to use Durkheim's category) suicides by the Japanese KAMIKAZE PILOTS of World War II, who flew their planes at Allied warships, destroying themselves in the process. Much earlier there was the Japanese ritualized, institutional suicide in the form of hara-kiri, a ceremonial death with honor for Samurai, or members of the military class.

insurance and suicide Generally speaking, state insurance laws explicitly specify a limited number of conditions which exempt individual life insurance holders from collecting coverage. Suicide is such a condition. Although insurers are not obliged to exempt suicides, it is nevertheless an almost universal practice in the insurance business.

Rob Bier, manager of Media Information/Media & Editorial Services, the American Council of Life Insurance, Washington, D.C., explains the industry practice in the case of suicide this way:

> While virtually all life insurance policies make some exclusion for death from suicide, the exclusion is of a limited nature. After a period not to exceed two years, in most cases, death from suicide is covered on the same basis as is death from any other cause. Individual companies sometimes make the exclusionary period shorter than that permitted by law, but the ACLI is not aware of any which drop it entirely.
>
> The operative theory here is that individuals contemplating suicide should not be able to purchase life insurance benefits for their survivors. Not only would that be

bad business for insurers, but it could conceivably serve in some cases to remove some of a person's hesitations about committing the act. The presumption is that after an interval of a year or two, there is a vanishing likelihood that the person bought the policy in contemplation of suicide. Furthermore, some possibly fraudulent act of the policy's purchaser, committed in the past, should not result in the beneficiaries being denied the protection they had come to rely upon.

Life insurers are only interested in whether a death is from suicide if it occurs during the so-called 'contestable period' of the policy. In such cases, they generally rely upon the findings of the medical examiner or other local official who issues the death certificate. Reliance upon the M.E.'s determination is not absolute, however. Companies are free to make their own judgment, and from time to time you will hear of an insurer disputing the findings of an M.E. If the beneficiaries disagree (i.e., dispute a denial of benefits), the matter usually ends up in court.

A typical suicide clause such as that mentioned above reads as follows:

> If within two years following the date of issue of this policy and while it is in force, the insured, whether sane or insane, shall die by his own hand or act, the Company will be liable only for the amount of the premium paid hereunder, which shall be paid in one sum to the beneficiary herein.

At one time, life insurance contracts excluded the risk of suicide entirely. This was unfortunate, since in a given case, the whole purpose of the policy (usually, to protect dependents) could be defeated. Today, the clause is intended to protect against adverse selection, not to exclude the risk of suicide as such.

It is interesting to note, further, that the question of whether a death was by suicide or due to other causes will sometimes end up in court and be left to the jury. When this happens, the historic tendency on the part of the courts has been to lean over backwards to hold for dependents. There is a legal presumption that a person *will not* take his or her own life, and this, plus the jury's attitude noted above, makes it difficult to prove suicide even where the facts clearly point to it. Indeed, the courts have gone to extraordinary lengths at times in holding that suicide had not been proven and in deciding that the company was liable.

Following is a state-by-state summary of "suicide" provisions in individual state insurance codes, including each state's citation in the specific code (note that some states have no suicide provision in their insurance code as of this writing):

State	Citations	Period—Limitation of Liability of Insurer
Alabama	Sec. 27-15-24	2 years
Alaska	Sec. 21.45.250	2 years
Arizona	Sec. 20-1226	2 years
Arkansas	Sec. 66-3323	2 years
Colorado	Sec. 10-7-109	1 year
Delaware	Sec. 2926, T. 18	2 years
Georgia	Sec. 56-2507	2 years
Hawaii	Sec. 431-553	2 years
Idaho	Sec. 41-1925	2 years
Kentucky	Sec. 304.15-260	2 years
Louisiana	Sec. 22-170	2 years
Maine	Sec. 2525, T. 24A	2 years
Maryland	Sec. 410, Art. 48A	2 years
Missouri	Sec. 376620	Not specified
Montana	Sec. 40-3826	2 years
Nevada	Sec. 688A.260	2 years
New Mexico	Sec. 59-16-3	2 years
New York	Sec. 163(4), Ins. Code	2 years
North Dakota	Sec. 26-03-24	1 year
Oklahoma	Sec. 4024, T. 36	2 years
South Dakota	Sec. 58-15-45(5)	2 years
Tennessee	Sec. 56-1112(5)	2 years
Texas	Art. 21.35, Ins. Code	2 years
Utah	Sec. 31-22-15	2 years
Virginia	Sec. 38.1-437	2 years
Washington	Sec. 48.23.260	2 years
West Virginia	Sec. 33-13-25	2 years
Wyoming	Sec. 16-16-125	2 years
Puerto Rico	Sec. 1323, T. 26	2 years

Source: American Council of Life Insurance, Washington, D.C., 1986

integration Ronald Maris, PhD, editor of *Suicide and Life-Threatening Behavior* and head of the Center for the Study of Suicide, University of South Carolina, writes in "Sociology," Chapter 5 in Seymour Perlin's *A Handbook for the Study of Suicide*:

> Groups with high suicide rates tend to be made up of individuals who are socially isolated from significant others and who, since they do not participate in society, do not benefit from social sanctions or normative restraints on their behavior. Thus, we can refine DURKHEIM's general explanation of the suicide rate to read that the suicide rate varies inversely with external constraint *and* that external constraint has two dimensions, viz., integration (egoism) and regulation (anomie). That is, when social integration and regulation are high, egoism and anomie—and the suicide rate—are low.

Ronald Maris, writing about Emile Durkheim's hypothesis, mentions the famed French sociologist's two other minor causes of suicide: altruistic (the polar type of egoistic) and fatalistic (the polar type of anomic). Maris says, "ALTRUISTIC SUICIDE results from excessive integration as in HARA-KIRI and fatalistic suicide occurs under conditions of excessive regulation, such as black suicides in jail in repressive communities."

International Association for Suicide Prevention (IASP) The IASP is an international organization in which individuals and societies of interested disciplines can find a common platform for interchange of experiences, information and literature about suicide.

The first meeting of the IASP was in Vienna in 1960. Its constitution was written in 1963-64 by Ringel, Aigner and Norman L. Farberow, and was registered in Vienna in 1964-65. The Association aims at disseminating the fundamentals of suicide prevention among both professionals and the general public; the planning of specialized training in suicide prevention; and the encouragement and carrying out of research programs, especially those which require international cooperation.

The IASP has four classes of membership: regular, associate, supporting and honorary. All members are elected by majority vote of the executive board. Regular members are those individuals and societies regularly engaged in suicide research and/or prevention activities. Societies may become members only when two of their members are regular members of the IASP.

The association holds an International Congress for Suicide Prevention and a general assembly of the association once every two years. The congress serves to bring together members from all parts of the world for the discussion of scientific papers and for the transaction of the affairs of the association in plenary and executive sessions. At present, 40 countries are represented in the membership.

CRISIS, official bulletin of the Association, serves as a medium for the international exchange of experiences and information about suicide prevention. Annual IASP dues for individuals and societies are $50 (or the equivalent in other countries). For details on how to join or to inquire about the work of the organization, write to: Gernot Sonneck, M.D., Secretary General, International Association for Suicide Prevention, Central Administrative Office, Psychiatric University Clinic, Spitalgasse 23, A-1090 Vienna, Austria.

intervention The primary goal of every person working in the field of suicidology is, of course, prevention. When PREVENTION has failed, however, and a suicidal crisis occurs (i.e., after the suicidal person begins to act out harming himself or herself), the only answer is "intervention." The cardinal rule of suicide intervention is the same as that for prevention: *do something*. We can all do something about preventing suicides through positive intervention. if you suspect that one of your loved ones or friends—or for that matter a mere acquaintance—is contemplating suicide, you can help by intervening and following certain guidelines. The following guidelines are offered by the AMERICAN ASSOCIATION OF SUICIDOLOGY (AAS). They could help you save the life of someone you care about; they could help you prevent a suicide.

1. Take threats seriously. If someone you know threatens suicide, listen. Four out of five people who commit suicide have tried it or have threatened it previously. The old myth, "those who talk about it won't do it," is dangerously false. More than likely, by threatening suicide, the person is calling for help—trying to let you know how bad things are.
2. Watch for clues. Most people considering suicide give clues of their intent. Look for marked changes in personality, behavior and appearance. Watch for signs of depression, such as insomnia, loss of appetite, or continual exhaustion. Be alert when a person turns to destructive behavior patterns such as drug and alcohol abuse, especially when this behavior is unusual. A person feeling suicidal may start preparing for death. Making out a will, giving away beloved pets and valuable possessions, saving pills, or buying a gun could indicate that a person is contemplating suicide.
3. Answer cries for help. Once you are alerted to these clues that may constitute a "cry for help" from a loved one or friend, you can help in several ways. The most important of these is not to ignore the issue. It is better to offer help early than to regret not doing so later. The first step is to offer support, understanding and compassion, no matter what the problems may be. The suicidal person is truly hurting.
4. Confront the problem. If you suspect that a person is suicidal, begin by asking questions such as, "Are you feeling depressed?" "Have you been thinking of hurting yourself?"—leading up to the question, "Are you thinking of killing yourself?" Be direct. Don't be afraid to discuss suicide with the person. Getting him to talk about it is a positive step. Be a good listener and a good friend. Don't make moral judgments, act shocked or make light of the situation. Offering advice such as, "Be grateful for what you have . . . you're so much better off than most," may only deepen the sense of guilt the person probably already feels. Discussing it may help lead the person away from actually doing it by giving him the feeling that someone cares.
5. Tell them you care. Persons who attempt suicide most often feel alone, worthless and unloved. You can help by letting them know that they are not alone, that you are always there for them to talk to. Tell loved ones how much you care about them, and offer your support and compassion. By assuring the person that some help is available, you are literally throwing him a lifeline. Remember, although a person may think he wants to die, he has an innate will to live, and is more than likely hoping to be rescued.
6. Get professional help. The most useful thing you can do is to encourage the person who is considering suicide to get professional help. There are mental health clinics, psychiatrists, psychologists, social workers, family doctors, and members of the clergy who can help in every community. And in your community there are groups of people dedicated specifically to preventing suicide. Your ability to get professional guidance for the suicidal person may save his life.

7. Offer alternatives. Don't leave the initiative up to a suicidal person. Instead, provide him with a list of agencies in your area where he can go for help. These centers provide professional counseling to individuals and offer alternate ways to solve problems. A list of over 250 centers throughout the U.S. is in Appendix 3 of this work.

Once every minute of every day, someone in America attempts suicide. Official statistics show nearly 30,000 people take their own lives each year. Suicide victims come from all walks of life, from all kinds of economic and educational backgrounds. The presence of a good friend, a caring and loving family member, or involvement with helping professionals, can all lower suicide risk and can reduce the shocking statistics.

Iran Gives no suicide rate data to the World Health Organization offices in Geneva, nor to the Demographic Yearbook published by the United Nations. Researchers might be interested in an article by S. Irfani, "Personality Correlates of Suicidal Tendency among Iranian and Turkish Students," or a piece by H. Gharagozlov & M. Hadjmohammadi, "Report on a Three-year Follow-up of 100 Cases of Suicidal Attempts in Shiraz, Iran." Some data have been reported by Hassan Farzam, MD, writing in Lee A. Headley's *Suicide in Asia and the Near East*. The data, as might be expected, were collected before the overthrow of the Shah's government. There is no way of knowing whether similar results would prevail if current data were available. Iran is 98% Muslim, with most belonging to the Shia sect, a minority branch more conservative than the majority Sunnis. The Koran strictly prohibits suicide, promising punishment in Hell; such actions are embarrassing and bring shame to the family. During the Shah's regime, the official statistics were based on cases sent for autopsy to the Department of Legal Medicine in the Ministry of Justice. Data were for Tehran only, as the various districts and cities did not send their data to a central office. From 1964 to 1974, there was little variation in the number of suicides, which numbered between 23 and 41 per year. Most suicides were by hanging, 50%, followed by shooting, 26%. In Shiraz, a city of 300,000, the completed suicide rate was reported as 5.6 per 100,000. As Dr. Farzam states, the actual rate of completed suicides in Iran remained unclear because comprehensive data were not available.

Ireland Ranks low among countries in its suicide rate. This is perhaps due to the high number of Catholics in its population. The Catholic Church integrates people with its relatively close-knit order and its authoritarian body of common beliefs and tenets. Also, the church teaches that suicide (under most circumstances) is a mortal sin that is punishable in the hereafter.

Latest figures from the World Health Organization (WHO) for Ireland are from 1982. In that year, the total suicide rate per 100,000 population was 6.9 (male rate was 10.2, female rate 3.6, per 100,000). This shows an increase in the total rate since 1980, when the suicide rate was 6.3 per 100,000 population. The male suicide rate rose in that two-year period from 8.3 to the 1982 percentage of 10.2, while the rate for females dropped from 4.3 to 3.6 in the same period.

irrationality as suicide clue A warning sign or distress signal that could indicate a suicidal person is perhaps in danger. When a person begins to act peculiarly or irrationally, he or she may be sending out clues of severe stress or mental illness. This is especially so when the individual's behavior represents a marked and sudden change in manner. Don't be afraid to intervene; the worst you can do is to be wrong, and feel a little foolish for a time.

But better that you err on the overcautious side than to ignore a suicidal clue.

"Is Life Worth Living?" A now-famous speech delivered by the American philosopher-psychologist William James, in 1895, to the Harvard Young Men's Christian Association. James had suffered severe clinical depression as a young man, so was well qualified to discuss from first-hand knowledge the suicidal impulses that can overtake a person. In addressing the title question in his lecture, James's answer to the question was a resounding "yes." While it's true that none of us can prove God exists or that reason guides the course of the universe, anyone can make a positive decision to believe those things, said James. "Believe that your life is worth living," he advised, "and your belief will help to create the fact." The philosopher considered suicide a "religious disease," the cure for which is "religious faith."

Islam Moslems have always been strong in their condemnation of suicide. THE KORAN, holy scriptures of Islam, expressly forbids suicide as the gravest sin, a more serious crime, in fact, than homicide. Moslems believe that each individual has his or her *Kismet*, or destiny, which is preordained by God and must not be defied. The recent phenomenon of suicide missions involving Islamic terrorists would seem to contradict the historic attitude. But these are not viewed as suicide, rather as *jihad*, as a holy mission with death, should it occur, guaranteed to lead to paradise in the next life. It is also true that while the strong religious prohibitions have kept the reported suicide rates low, they have also suppressed the reporting of any such events by the family to avoid the shame and embarrassment that could follow.

isolation, or withdrawal, as suicide clue The potential suicide will sometimes retreat from life and into his own world, isolate himself from family members and friends, and become a morose loner seemingly incapable of giving or receiving love. In severe cases, such a person becomes suffocatingly depressed and suicidal, refusing to allow even parents or a spouse to intrude on their deadened, lonely world.

Whatever the reason—growing up feeling unloved, loss of a loved one, or loss of physical health—isolation or withdrawal is a highly critical clue and a crucial indicator of suicidal behavior.

Israel In 1978, Israel's suicide rate per 100,000 population was 4.9; the country ranked 44th among 68 nations listed in the United Nations' 1978 *Demographic Yearbook*. In 1983, with the latest available World Health Organization data, the suicide rate was 6.1 total (per 100,000 population). The male rate per 100,000 was 8.2, the female rate 3.9. Highest rates per 100,000 are found in the 75-plus age group: overall rate 65.5, male 79.1 and female 56.9. In the young person's grouping, age 15 to 24, the 1983 figures were: 8.3 total; 11.5 males and 5.1 females.

Although Jews worldwide have historically had low suicide rates, the suicide rates among Jews in Israel appear to be slowly increasing. Interestingly, of the three major religions in the U.S., the Jews have the lowest suicide rates. However, religious statistics are difficult to compile because religion is not shown on death certificates.

The Hebrew Holy Scriptures contain only six brief references to self-destruction. And, as Rabbi Earl A. Grollman points out in *Suicide: Prevention, Intervention, Postvention*, "In each case, there are extenuating circumstances, such as the fear of being taken captive or the possibility of suffering humiliation or unbearable pain." (See also BIBLICAL SUICIDES.)

Italy Latest World Health Organization statistics show this country with a total suicide rate per 100,000 population of 7.3, the male rate being 10.1, female rate 4.6. As with most countries, highest rates are found in the 75 and older age group, the total being 20.2 per 100,000 population. Males in the 75-plus group had a suicide rate of 37.4, females 10.2 (per 100,000 population).

In 1978, according to the United Nations' *Demographic Yearbook*, Italy ranked number 41 out of 68 nations reporting. According to U.N. criteria for data used, the suicide rate that year was 5.8 per 100,000 population. Interestingly, but not unexpectedly, Italian immigrants have rates lower than the U.S. natives but higher rates than persons in their birthplace. Such data could, of course, indicate merely that reporting of suicide in the U.S. is more uniform. As a predominantly Catholic country, Italy has always had relatively low rates of suicide, along with Ireland and Spain.

J

Jair, Eleazar ben Zealot leader of ancient Hebrews at MASADA who became known for perhaps the most heroic mass suicide in the old world. It took place in A.D. 73 at the Fortress of Masada located at the edge of the Judean Desert, overlooking the Dead Sea. The Romans had overrun Judea and destroyed the Second Temple in A.D. 70, but a garrison of some one thousand men, women and children of Eleazar ben Jair's Zealot sect held the fortress and continued to resist the Roman forces, using modern-day guerilla war tactics. When defeat appeared certain, the Hebrew leader urged his followers to kill themselves rather than become Roman slaves.

The Jewish historian, JOSEPHUS, writes that the soldiers slew their wives and children, then drew lots to determine who among them would kill their companions and then take their own lives. At slaughter's end, some 960 persons had either been killed or taken their own lives. Only two women and five children had escaped the massacre, and remained alive to tell the story as recorded by Josephus in *The Jewish War*, a contemporary account of the war with Rome (67-73 A.D.). Flavius Josephus, incidentally, was himself imprisoned in Rome by Vespasian and later adopted Roman citizenship.

James, William American philosopher and psychologist (1842-1910) who admitted to suicidal impulses as a young man while suffering severe clinical depression. In 1895, he delivered a now-famous address to the Harvard YMCA and spoke of those feelings and what he called "the nightmare view of life." Entitled "IS LIFE WORTH LIVING?" James's lecture was a classic example of positive thinking. He answered the title question with a resounding "Yes," and told his audience: "Believe that life is worth living and your belief will help to create the fact."

The brother of novelist Henry James, William taught at Harvard. Perhaps his most influential thesis was that faith, which had been eroded by the isolation accompanying advancing urbanization and by the individualism fostered by the teachings of Protestantism, had diminished to a dangerous degree. Among his books are *The Varieties of Religious Experience* (1902) and *Pragmatism* (1907).

Japan The Japanese at one time ritualized suicide in what they called "hara-kiri" or "SEPPUKU." Outlawed in 1868, this form of ceremonial death had been an integral part of the old moral code, going back to the days of the Samurai warrior. The only honorable means for a disgraced warrior to redeem himself was to commit seppuku, in which he disemboweled himself with his own sword. A samurai warrior would sometimes kill himself to show allegiance to a fallen leader. Also, an emperor might order a member of the military class to commit hara-kiri to avoid the disgrace of a public execution. The ritual of seppuku sometimes took hours to complete (it was an elaborate process). Then a second person, usually the closest friend of the suicide who considered himself honored to terminate the pain and suffering, ended the ritual by beheading the suicide with a sword.

According to Seward (1968), the ritual of seppuku was institutionalized during the feudal ages, from 1190 through 1867, and characterized *Bushido*, the moral code of the warrior class. Even though the practice has been outlawed, the tradition of suicide with honor is still in evidence from time to time in Japan. During World War II, for example, over a thousand young Japanese soldiers died as KAMIKAZE PILOTS while flying their planes at Allied warships. When defeat was inevitable in that conflict, a number of prominent, high-ranking army and navy officers committed ritual hara-kiri rather than suffer the humiliation of surrender. More recently, in 1970, the famous novelist, playwright and actor, YUKIO MISHIMA, committed ritual suicide at the age of 45. He urged his countrymen to return to old values and traditions, one of which was the ancient concept of dying with honor.

Some suicidologists speculate that the old Japanese notion of death with honor may be responsible, at least in part, for the high rate of suicide among today's young Japanese. According to Francine Klagsbrun in *Too Young to Die*, "More than twice as many Japanese young people as Americans between the ages of fifteen and twenty-four kill themselves." The author writes that "deep feelings of insecurity that develop in many Japanese homes, along with fierce competition in school and in the job market, play an important part in these suicides, according to studies that have been made." Success is very important to the Japanese people. Failure, such as failing admission to a good university, is usually traumatic and one of the most cited reasons for suicide among Japanese youths. Also, failing in performance once entry is achieved brings shame and dishonor not only to the student but also to his or her family.

Another basic belief in many Japanese is the ancient Buddhist concept of *muso-kan*, a philosophy that says the human body is merely a temporary home for the soul. Thus, biological existence is not the supreme height that one reaches—and may not have much meaning.

Recent World Health Organization statistics indicate that the Japanese suicide rate per 100,000 population is 10.3 for the 15 to 24 age group, down from 11.8 in 1983. Highest suicide rate (per 100,000) by age grouping: age 75-plus with a percentage of 65.5. For the nation as a whole, the rate is 20.4 per 100,000 population (27.6 male, 13.3 female), down from 21.0 in 1983. These rate statistics indicate that young people in the U.S. have surpassed Japan's suicide rate for those in the 15 to 24 age group (according to WHO, the total for American 15- to 24-year-olds was 12.1 in 1982).

Jack Seward, *Hara-Kiri: Japanese Ritual Suicide* (Rutland, Vermont: Charles & Tuttle, 1968).

"Jay's Journal" Daily diary of a boy who killed himself after writing, "Dear World . . . I don't want to be sad or lonely or depressed anymore, and I don't want to eat, drink, eliminate, breathe, talk, sleep, move, feel or live anymore . . . I'm not free, I feel ill, and I'm sad and I'm lonely."

Jay's Journal, Beatrice Sparks, ed., *N.Y. Times*, 1979.

Jews BIBLICAL SUICIDES are rare; only seven instances are reported in the Hebrew Bible and one in the New Testament. Neither the Hebrew Bible nor the New Testament prohibits suicide, nor is suicidal behavior condemned. Even of JUDAS ISCARIOT we are told only that "he went and hanged himself" (Matthew 27:5). The Judeo-Christian tradition (as well as ISLAM) has always held that suicide in the form of martyrdom was permissible. In fact, the most significant sanction of suicide among Jews was to avoid apostasy, the forced rejection of the Jewish faith and adoption of another religion or God. Suicide, however, was in violation of the Fifth Commandment, delivered to Moses on Sinai: Thou shalt not kill. But the Jews did look at suicide as a positive act if employed to prevent torture, rape or slavery. King Saul fell on his sword after defeat in battle. And the defenders' mass suicide at MASADA (see also ELEAZAR BEN JAIR) to prevent capture by the Romans was considered to be a heroic act.

In Talmudic times (200-500 A.D.) the number of recorded suicides shows an increase. Rabbi Earl A. Grollman writes in *Suicide* that this was due in part to spiritual and social crises, "partly to a growing Greco-Roman influence." As the act became more frequent, a condemnatory tone was introduced for the first time. The Talmud decrees that a suicide is to receive no eulogy or public mourning. He is to be buried apart, in community cemeteries, says Grollman.

There was never universal agreement on the matter of suicide, writes Rabbi Grollman. Some authorities said relatives had a duty to the deceased regardless of the circumstances of death (e.g., Rabbi Moses ben Nachman, great Talmudist scholar of the 12th century). Others questioned the action: "Are the rules valid for minors or the mentally incompetent?" "How do you know that the person really committed suicide, especially if he had not explicitly declared intent nor performed the act in front of witnesses?"

Today, though thought of as a crime against God, suicide may sometimes be explained away, understood, and forgiven, says Grollman. "This enlightened point of view has been incorporated into the approach of the three denominations of modern Judaism." With the growth and complexities of the socio-psychological sciences, Rabbi Grollman says, "it is realized that one cannot legislate against self-destruction by religious fiat. Suicide must not be simply condemned. It must be understood and prevented."

In Israel, in 1983, according to WHO figures, the overall suicide rate per 100,000 population was low: 6.1%. Males commit suicide more often than females, 8.2% to 3.9%, with highest rates per 100,000 population in the 75-plus age group (30.5 total: male 44.6, female 17.8) A study of suicide among white adults of New York City's three major religions showed the rate for Jews higher than that for Catholics, but lower than for Protestants.

Earl A. Grollman, *Suicide: Prevention, Intervention, Postvention* (Boston: Beacon Press, 1971).

Johns Hopkins University At Baltimore, Maryland, founded in 1876 on the basis of a bequest by Johns Hopkins, a Baltimore merchant. The coeducational school pioneered an excellent suicidology program in its School of Medicine, of which program Dr. Seymour Perlin, author of *A Handbook for the Study of Suicide*, was a former director. The program is no longer active at JHU.

Johnson, Barclay D. Author of "Durkheim's One Cause of Suicide," contends that empirical studies of suicide reveal ALTRUISTIC and fatalistic suicide are so infrequent that they need not be included in a general explanation of suicide. Many authorities disagree with this conclusion, however. (See also EMILE DURKHEIM.)

Joluo (of Kenya) Members of this African tribe manage, according to G.M. Wilson, writing "Homicide and Suicide Among the Joluo of Kenya" in Bohannan's *African Homicide and Suicide*, to keep knowledge of cases of suicide within the clan, lest the clan's prestige in the community suffer. Other clans, e.g., the Gisu of Uganda, believe that to conceal a suicide is not only dangerous, but also culpable.

Jones, Reverend Jim See JONESTOWN, GUYANA "MASSACRE."

Jonestown, Guyana, "Massacre" Name given by media and others to the November 18, 1978, mass suicide-execution of followers of the Reverend Jim Jones's People's Temple cult. On that date, the Rev. Jim Jones's People's Temple cult came to a tragic end as Jones led a mass suicide-execution of 911 of his followers in the jungle of the Cooperative Republic of Guyana. The earlier, Port Kaituma ambush of U.S. Representative Leo J. Ryan and others investigating mistreatment of Jones's American followers, evidently triggered one of history's biggest mass suicides.

Jong, Erica U.S. novelist and poet was so distraught over the suicide of poet ANNE SEXTON that she wrote: "I hope she knew how many people loved her and how much. I wish there had been some way to tell her and make it stick." Jong's tribute to Anne Sexton was published in *The New York Times*.

Joplin, Janis American singer-entertainer (1943-1970) who died, some say deliberately, from an overdose of heroin in the Landmark Hotel, Los Angeles. Her road manager discovered the body the next day. Remnants of the heroin were found in a wastebasket by her bed. Joplin, a homely girl from Port Arthur, Texas (where high school classmates called her names, of which "pig" was the favorite), became known as the Queen of the Hippies. In the winter of 1969, she appeared on the cover of *Newsweek* magazine.

Josephus, Flavius Jewish historian and soldier (37 -? 95 A.D.). He commanded a Jewish force in Palestine in the uprising against Rome in A.D. 66, was forced to surrender and was imprisoned in Rome by Vespasian. During the final moments of his battle with Vespasian, Josephus debated with his soldiers and offered various reasons why suicide was undesirable. He reluctantly agreed to the insistence of his soldiers that suicide was preferable to capture. Interestingly, following the Jewish custom of that time, each soldier slew one other soldier who was in turn killed by the next man. It ended with just Josephus and a fellow soldier remaining, and Josephus was easily able to convince the soldier to surrender along with him.

Later he became a follower of Titus and adopted Roman citizenship. He wrote *The Jewish War*, an account of the war with Rome (67-73 A.D.); *The Jewish Antiquities*, a history of the Jews from the beginning to the outbreak of the war; and an account of his own life, defending his conduct and emphasizing his pro-Roman sentiments. He wrote sensitively about the defenders of MASADA, who ultimately killed themselves rather than surrender to the Romans.

Josephus agreed on the obligation to uphold and defend the Torah, "to sanctify the Holy Name," under all circumstances. In this cause even suicide was justified.

Philo, *The Embassy to Gaius*, translated and edited by E.M. Smallwood (Leiden: 1961).

Flavius Josephus, *Complete Works of Flavius Josephus*, translated by William Whiston (Grand Rapids: Kregel, 1974).

Joyce, James Irish novelist (1882-1941), who left Ireland in 1902 and spent the remainder of his life on the Continent. At the beginning of the 20th century, popular opinion generally viewed suicide as a deviation from normality. Joyce presents this attitude in an episode in his famous novel *Ulysses*. On the way to a funeral, four men discuss attempted suicide and death.

> "But the worst of all," Mr. Power said, "is the man who takes his own life." Martin Cunningham drew out his watch briskly, coughed and put it back. "The greatest disgrace to have in the family," Mr. Power added. "Temporary insanity, of course," Martin Cunningham said decisively. "We must take a charitable view of it." "They say a man who does it is a coward," Mr. Dedalus said. "It is not for us to judge," Martin Cunningham said.

So, by the 20th century, suicide in England was more a social disgrace than it was a sin—at least among the middle class.

James Joyce, *Ulysses*, 2 vols. (Hamburg: Odyssey Press, 1932), 1:99-100.

Judaism and suicide (See JEWS.)

Judas Iscariot The disciple who betrayed Jesus for 30 pieces of silver. Motives given for the betrayal are greed (according to Matthew) and the power of the devil (according to John). At the Last Supper (a Passover Feast), Jesus predicted the betrayal, which Judas accomplished by leading soldiers to Jesus and identifying him with a kiss. Judas, in remorse, killed himself by hanging (Matthew 27:3-7). Aceldama, where Judas killed himself near Jerusalem, became a pauper's burial ground after it was bought by the priests with the 30 pieces of silver flung at their feet by Judas.

K

kamikaze pilots An example of ALTRUISTIC SUICIDE, as categorized by French sociologist Emile Durkheim, which occurs among people so dedicated to a cause or to certain values of their society that they place duty before personal needs, even before their lives. The Japanese kamikaze pilots of World War II flew their planes at Allied warships, destroying themselves in the process. More than a thousand young Japanese died in this manner. (See also JAPAN.)

Kant, Immanuel German transcendentalist philosopher (1724-1804). His most famous work is the *Critique of Pure Reason* (1781). Concerning suicide, Kant sided with the major religions, that it was morally wrong. But he took a different line of reasoning to reach that conclusion. Life, to Kant, is sacred because it is part of nature. As such, he said, each life has a place within the laws of nature, and each person must preserve his or her own life. To ignore this duty and end one's life is immoral. To Kant, true morality is rising above individual and personal feelings of despair, carrying out one's duties, and living one's life in the face of adversity. However, he did say, "It is not suicide to risk one's life against one's enemies, and even to sacrifice it, in order to preserve one's duties towards oneself."

Emile Durkheim seems clearly to have been influenced by Kant's notion of a "categorical imperative," viz., that it is each individual's duty to act in such a way that his or her private will could become a universal law.

Katz Adjustment Sales A rating scale including 205 items, designed to provide measures in these general areas (e.g., symptomatology and social behavior, performance of social activities, expectations regarding social activities, free-time activities, and satisfaction with free-time activities) to enhance the value of the PSYCHOLOGICAL AUTOPSY (chief method for assessing the former psychological status and personality characteristics of a recently-deceased person). The psychological autopsy is one of the most important research tools to have grown out of the famed Los Angeles Suicide Prevention Center, founded by psychologists Norman L. Farberow and Edwin Shneidman in 1958. The method has helped coroners and medical examiners determine the mode of a death when it is not clearly indicated.

Kawabata, Yasunari Japanese novelist (1900-1972) and winner of the Nobel Prize for literature in 1968. According to Mamoru Iga, in Wolman's *Between Survival and Suicide*, he "left his home in Kamakura in the afternoon of April 16, 1972, for his workroom in nearby Zushi. There was no sign of suicidal intention. That evening, he was found dead with a gas conduit in his mouth in the room, which commanded magnificent views of both oceans and mountains." Kawabata was 72 years old.

Keats, John British romantic poet (1795-1821) who had studied to be a surgeon. *Lamia and Other Poems* (1820), including his great odes and narrative poems (e.g., "The Eve of St. Agnes"), secured his reputation. Keats was seriously ill with tuberculosis, a condition exacerbated by his tormented love for Fanny Braume and which caused him to suffer deep depression and suicidal feelings. He died in Rome at age 25, convinced that true feelings cannot survive into middle age. He was idolized by the ROMANTICS of the era.

Kentucky Although suicide has never been a crime in the U.S., and the property of suicides has never been confiscated, attempted suicide was at one time regarded as a felony in a few states, among them the state of Kentucky. But even in that state, attempters were almost never prosecuted. The state now rarely prosecutes persons who help others attempt or commit suicide, although this is still regarded as a criminal offense. Still, the stigma against suicide remains in the general population. Kentucky is in the South, the region with the lowest rate for suicide in the U.S. (with the glaring exception of Florida).

Kiev, Ari New York psychiatrist and author, and director of Cornell University's Suicide Prevention Center. Kiev wrote *The Courage to Live*. In one study he conducted, Dr. Kiev found that mildly and moderately disturbed patients posed a greater risk of suicide than psychotic or schizophrenic patients.

Klagsbrun, Francine Author-researcher, she wrote the best seller, *Too Young to Die: Youth and Suicide*. With an introduction by Harold S. Kushner, author of *When Bad Things Happen to Good People*, Klagsbrun's book has been highly acclaimed as an important work on the subject of youth and suicide. She is married to Dr. Samuel C. Klagsbrun, whom she calls "a psychiatrist's psychiatrist." Dr. Klagsbrun is a board member of the NATIONAL COMMITTEE ON YOUTH SUICIDE PREVENTION, headquartered in New York City.

"Kleenex mentality" Phrase employed by Sister Delores Gartanutti of New York's Noah's Ark Shelter (for runaways). She is quoted as saying that "The whole sixties idea of 'do your own thing' has moved into the seventies and eighties with disposable relationships—if it doesn't work, if it's not perfect, I want something else." Sister Gartanutti contends that people today have this attitude toward children, that our kids become either runaway or throwaway children. (It is estimated that one million young people between 10 and 17 leave or are forced to leave home each year in the U.S.) This "Kleenex mentality" has a direct relationship to the disturbing suicide rate among young people in the U.S.

Lynn Langway, "A Nation of Runaway Kids," *Newsweek*, October 18, 1982.

Koestler, Arthur British writer (1905-83), born in Vienna. In 1940 he settled in Britain, where his anti-Stalinist novel *Darkness at Noon* (1940) was first published. In addition to several novels, he wrote a number of books on political and philosophical topics. Koestler suffered in later life from Parkinson's disease, and in 1983, he and his wife, Cynthia, committed suicide together. He was 78 and already dying (he had written a suicide note in June 1982), but Cynthia Koestler was only 55 and in good health. Koestler was a vice president of the VOLUNTARY EUTHANASIA SOCIETY in London and had written an essay for the society's booklet "A Guide to Self-Deliverance."

The Koestlers' maid found a note on March 3, 1983, instructing her to ring the police and "tell them to come to the house." Police found them sitting in their usual places, he in the armchair with an empty brandy glass in his hand; Cynthia to his left, on the sofa. They had been dead about 36 hours, from an overdose of BARBITURATES. Cynthia Koestler had typed a brief footnote to her husband's suicide note: "I should have liked to finish my account of working for Arthur—a story which began when our paths happened to cross in 1949. However, I cannot live without Arthur, despite certain inner resources."

Arthur and Cynthia Koestler, *Stranger on the Square*, with preface by Harold Harris (New York: Random House, 1984).
New York Times, March 4, 1983.

Koran, The Sacred scripture of the Moslems, comprising 114 *suras* (chapters) of unequal length, nearly all of which are supposedly of divine revelation—Allah speaking directly through the angel Gabriel to Mohammed. The holy scriptures of ISLAM expressly declared suicide to be a more serious crime than homicide. Moslem belief explains this attitude: Each person has his or her Kismet, or destiny, which is foreordained by Allah, or God, and must not be defied. Some suicides do take place in Moslem countries; however, strong religious restrictions keep rates relatively low.

Kraepelin, Emil German psychiatrist (1856-1926) and author of *Lectures on Clinical Psychiatry*, who expressed the belief that mental disturbances were a direct factor in at least one-third of all suicides. Many authorities disagree, stressing that such a relationship should be considered with great care because of the problems in defining mental health and mental illness. His relatively large rate figure is based on fact that the high incidence of mental illness among suicides had been previously pointed out by a number of investigators, according to Kurt Gorwitz, ScD, assistant director, research and analysis, Office of Health and Medical Affairs, State of Michigan, Lansing.

Kubler-Ross, Elizabeth Psychiatrist, a world-renowned leader and authority on death, and the author of *On Death and Dying, To Live Until We Say Goodbye* and *Death: The Final Stage of Growth*, Dr. Kubler-Ross practiced general medicine in Switzerland before coming to America. She began her work with the dying while teaching psychiatry at the University of Chicago. Most of her books are available on cassette tapes from Ross Medical Associates, Flossmoor, Illinois.

L

"Lady Lazarus" Poem written by Sylvia Plath in which she all but boasted of a recent suicide attempt. She concluded the poem with:

Dying
Is an art, like everything else.
I do it exceptionally well.
I do it so it feels like hell.
I do it so it feels real.
I guess you could say I've a call.

On February 11, 1963, SYLVIA PLATH committed suicide. Her suicide attempt ten years before had been, from all appearances, deadly serious.

Sylvia Plath, *The Collected Poems: Sylvia Plath* (New York: Harper & Row, 1981).

(Alan) Landsburg Productions See "TEENAGE SUICIDE: DON'T TRY IT."

Lanterman-Petrie-Short Act (LPS) Adopted in California in 1967, the act is considered a landmark in the reform of involuntary commitment, for suicidal persons in particular and for psychiatric patients in general. In that state, prior to LPS, a person could be committed indefinitely if found to be "of such mental condition that he is in need of supervision, treatment, care or restraint," or "dangerous to himself, or to the person or property of others . . ."

Under the old system, California courts committed over 1,000 persons per month to state institutions, often after only cursory psychiatric examination and court hearing. LPS, on the other hand, prohibits involuntary detention for longer than 72 hours. If, as Dr. HERBERT HENDIN notes in *Suicide in America*, either of these conditions prevails, the person can be certified for 14 days of "intensive treatment." After expiration of the 14-day certification period, suicidal persons can be confined for up to 14 additional days, if the person gives overt indication of continued danger to self or by an attempt or threat to suicide in the first 14-day period, or if he was *originally* detained for an attempt or threat and, in the judgment of the psychiatrist, continued to present that threat. (In other words, he need not have made an additional attempt or threat during the first 14 days of hospitalization.)

Unfortunately, while LPS solved one problem, it created a new one. Because inadequate provisions were made to help the suicidal, many patients discharged after the short time span have turned up quickly in municipal hospitals or worse—floundering alone on the streets of cities and towns throughout the state. As Hendin writes, "Of course, the trend in the past decade to 'deinstitutionalize' psychiatric patients has created the same problem in states that do not have laws comparable to LPS."

Latin America Generally speaking, suicide rates per 100,000 population show that Latin American countries rank lower than most reporting nations. Authorities believe that the relative low rates in most Latin American countries may be due to the prevalence of Catholicism with its authoritarian body of common beliefs and dogma concerning suicide. It should be noted that data regarding different countries are often of questionable reliability because of varying reporting methods and criteria used by the United Nations for its *Demographic Yearbook*. (See Farberow's *Suicide in Different Cultures* for an excellent reference on the various cultures of Latin America vis-a-vis aspects of suicide; also see Aponte's "Epidemiological Aspects of Suicide in Latin America.")

Law, Liberty and Psychiatry Book by right-to-suicide advocate THOMAS SZASZ, psychiatrist. Szasz writes: "In a free society, a person must have the right to injure or kill himself . . . there is no moral justification for depriving a person of his liberty in order to treat him." Dr. Szasz opposes involuntary hospitalization or forced treatment for suicidal persons under any circumstances. Intervention, he believes, should come only when a person asks for help.

law enforcement officers Generally speaking, those whose work involves giving nurturance and assistance to other persons seem to have a greater propensity toward suicide. Job-related stress is a factor in suicide among service workers, as well. Although reliable data are unavailable due to varying methods of reporting (and instances where the official death certificate lists cause of death as other than suicide), it appears that police and other law enforcement persons are also a high-risk group.

The various law enforcement agencies and departments throughout the U.S. must necessarily play a significant role in suicide prevention, and often in INTERVENTION. Theirs is a critical relationship in assisting prevention and crisis intervention centers. Many police departments in metropolitan centers have special training for officers on how to handle suicidal persons. For further information, see C.E. Martin's *Readings in Suicide for Law Enforcement Officers*.

Robert Loo, PhD, chief psychologist, Royal Canadian Mounted Police, reports that between 1960 and 1983, the average annual rate (14.1 per 100,000) of suicide in the RCMP was approximately half that of the comparable general population. The most common method of suicide was by service revolver. He compares this data to Heiman (1975) and Friedman (1968) data covering the period of 1960 to 1973 for New York City's police force. Loo reports Heiman found an annual *average* of 19.1 per 100,000. In Great Britain, the average annual suicide rate in the London metropolitan police force for 1960 to 1966 was only 7.8 per 100,000. Authorities consider differences between Great Britain and the U.S. police forces, in access to firearms and in the use of deadly force by police, as contributing factors to the marked difference in police suicide rates.

Overall, as Dr. Loo notes in "Suicide Among Police in a Federal Force," "the causal factors explaining police suicide need more explicit study; however, the literature to date suggests that both psychological and sociological factors contribute to the phenomenon of police suicide and that no single explanatory factor is sufficient."

law and the legal aspects of suicide Early legal aspects of suicide found civil and church law almost inseparably mixed. English law incorporated ecclesiastic canons when King Edgar adopted into civil law the punishments against the corpse (degradation) and estate (confiscation) of the suicide. These customs were discontinued only in 1823 when the law burying the corpse at a crossroads was repealed, and in 1870 when the law forfeiting goods was erased.

Attempted suicide became a crime in England in 1854 and continued until its repeal in 1961. While a number of countries still retain laws making attempted suicide a crime, in most the law is used to register the attempts and to provide for treatment. In the U.S., laws against committing, or attempting suicide have been repealed in each of the states. Aiding and abetting suicide remains against the law in 21 of the states.

In the courts, the attitude of the law on the case for and treatment of suicide has moved from rigid accountability for all such deaths to the principles of foreseeability and the need to take reasonable risks (within the standard of care in the community) in the treatment program in order to allow improvement.

Several authorities have written excellent essays and books concerning the legal aspects of suicide. They include: Helen Silving, Glanville Williams, Thomas Shaffer, and Margaret P. Battin.

Edwin S. Shneidman, *Definition of Suicide* (New York: John Wiley, 1985).

H. Silving, "Suicide and the Law," in E.S. Shneidman & N.L Farberow, eds., *Clues to Suicide* (New York: McGraw-Hill, 1957).

G. Williams, *The Sanctity of Life and the Criminal Law* (New York: Alfred A. Knopf, 1957).

T.L. Shaffer, "Legal Views of Suicide," in E.S. Shneidman, ed., *Suicidology: Contemporary Developments* (New York: Grune & Stratton, 1976).

M.P. Battin, *Ethical Issues in Suicide* (Englewood Cliffs, New Jersey: Prentice-Hall, 1982).

Lennon, John British rock star (1940-1980) and member of the Beatles, who died from gunshot wounds on December 8, 1980, in New York City's Upper West Side. The U.S. teen suicide rate increased noticeably after Lennon's death by an assassin. Many young people obviously felt that they had a long-standing relationship with him and his loss was like losing a family member.

Let Me Die Before I Wake Book written by DEREK HUMPHRY, founder of the HEMLOCK SOCIETY, and most recently published in 1984 by Hemlock/Grove. This controversial guide to "self-deliverance" for the dying person has been and still is widely debated in many professional circles and in the media. First editions of this 1981 book were sold only to members of the Hemlock Society. Public desire for more information about voluntary EUTHANASIA resulted in later extended editions.

Derek Humphry and Ann Wickett, his wife, have also written *The Right to Die: Understanding Euthanasia*.

Lettres Persanes In one of his *Lettres Persanes*, written in 1721 by "Usbeck" from Paris to his friend "Ibben" in Smyrna, Montesquieu ridicules the European laws on suicide and defends its practice. The French political philospher's *The Persian Letters*, published anonymously at Amsterdam in 1721, is a bitter satire on the church and the politics of France. Defending suicide, he wrote: "Life has been given to me as a gift. I can therefore return it when this is no longer the case. . ." He added, "when I am overwhelmed by pain, poverty and scorn, why does one want to prevent me from putting an end to my troubles, and to deprive me cruelly of a remedy which is in my hands?"

Charles Secondat, baron de Montesquieu, *Oeuvres completes*, 2 vols. (Paris: Gallimard, 1949-51) 1:246.

Levy, J. Author of "Navajo Suicide." He considered the different behavior required of Navajo Indians in various roles, concluding that traditional modes are inadequate to maintain the relationships that are important in modern Navajo society. Navajo men, for example, are more affected than women, since they must always undertake new roles. As Jean La Fontaine notes in "Anthropology," in Perlin's *A Handbook for the Study of Suicide*, "changes of fortune that affect the suicide rate are not a direct cause, but affect an individual's ability to grasp what is required in the changed roles and to play them satisfactorily." In the matter of suicide, Levy is saying, role situations offer a better framework than relationships.

life insurance There are certain instances where present-day suicides are victims of economic punishment. Insurance companies generally establish a one- to two-year waiting period after a policy comes into effect before the company is required to make payments to survivors of an insured suicide. Only a few companies refuse any benefits if the insured has committed suicide. (See INSURANCE AND SUICIDE.)

Life's Preservative against Self-Killing John Sym, an English country clergyman (1581?-1637), worried about an increase in suicide in his country and wrote this treatise (published the year of his death). It made available to readers his personal experiences in counseling potential suicides. Sym believed that many suicides were sick in mind and could not be held responsible for their behavior. Thus, he said, not all suicides were in a state of damnation.

He did, however, divided suicide into direct and indirect forms and condemned those types involving intemperance, gluttony, dueling and foolhardiness. Sym's main interest, though, was in the prevention of suicide, as the book's title expresses. He describes certain premonitory and diagnostic signs, such as "unusual solitariness, neglect of one's duties, change in behavior, talking to oneself, a distracted countenance and carriage, and threatening speech and action."

Lifton, Robert Jay Psychiatrist and author of *The Broken Connection.* Writing about the global suicide which threatens everyone and poisons our daily lives, Dr. Lifton stresses the fact that we are in danger—even if there's no nuclear war—of breaking our psychological connections to our own sense of continuity, generativity and fantasized immortality. These connections, says Lifton, are of vital necessity if we are to sustain our human relationships. Dr. Lifton writes: "In every age, man faces a pervasive theme which defies his engagement and yet must be engaged. In Freud's day, it was sexuality and moralism. Now it is unlimited technological violence and absurd death." Lifton is also author of *Death in Life: Survivors of Hiroshima.*

Lincoln, Mary Todd President Lincoln's wife (1818-1882) was tried for insanity before a jury after his assassination. Son Robert Lincoln tried to have his mother declared legally incompetent after she began to suffer hallucinations and phobias, but the law required a trial before a person could be institutionalized. Mrs. Lincoln attempted suicide after being judged insane by the court, and was placed in a sanitarium, where she received treatment. She improved sufficiently for yet another court to reverse the insanity verdict in 1876. She died six years later.

LINKS Actually, the Link Counseling Center in Atlanta, Georgia. Director is Iris M. Bolton. Mrs. Bolton is the author of the book *My Son, My Son,* in which she recounts the story of her son's suicide, the struggles to understand it, and the problems encountered in the need to accept and rebuild family and life afterward. Prominently mentioned in Dr. Mary Giffin's and Carol Felsenthal's book *A Cry for Help,* LINKS was started in 1972. It is not a suicide crisis center but rather a meditation or youth counseling center, manned by volunteers, counselors and social workers. Ms. Bolton, the director, is a suicidologist, however, and says that occasionally matters involving suicide are discussed at LINKS. See list of youth suicide prevention and intervention programs in appendix 3 of this work. The address is 218 Hilderbrand, N.E., Atlanta, GA 30328; phone is (404) 256-9797.

lithium Lithium, an element of the alkali-metal group, has been found in recent years to be useful in treating manic-depressive disorders. People with manic-depressive psychosis experience mood swings between great heights of exhilaration and profound depths of despair. Physicians suspect the disease originates from biochemical causes within the body. Lithium treatments appear to keep the disease in check and help the patient live a normal life. Lithium, a salt, is a deficiency medication. The manic-depressive (whose state, incidentally, represents about 5% of all depressions) has too little salt in his or her system.

However, lithium does have potentially toxic side effects which require careful monitoring of its level in the blood when it is being used.

Litman, Robert E. Co-director and chief of psychiatry, the Institute for Studies of Destructive Behaviors and the Suicide Prevention Center, Los Angeles, California. Dr. Litman is a former president, the American Association of Suicidology, and secretary general of the International Association of Suicide Prevention. He is a pioneer in the area of psychological autopsies—along with Drs. Edwin Shneidman and Norman L. Farberow—and is currently recognized as the foremost expert in suicide and the law. Dr. Litman is frequently called concerning forensic cases involving the question of suicide. Dr Litman traced the development of FREUD's thoughts on suicide from 1881 to 1939. His analysis points out that, among other things, there is more to the psychodynamics of suicide than hostility. As Dr. EDWIN SHNEIDMAN notes in *Definition of Suicide*, these factors include several emotional states (e.g., rage, guilt, anxiety, dependency) plus a great number of "specifically predisposing conditions." For instance, feelings of abandonment and of helplessness and hopelessness are vital keys. (See R.E. Litman's "Sigmund Freud on Suicide," in Shneidman's *Essays in Self-Destruction*.)

Dr. Litman has conducted many worthwhile studies relating to suicide, suicidal behavior and the prevention and intervention aspects of suicide.

The Little Prince Saint-Exupéry, expert pilot and author of many popular books about flying, wrote *The Little Prince* in 1943. The children's book (which has since become a classic for adults as well) is a fantasy that romanticizes suicide as a form of "going home." SAINT-EXUPÉRY was 44 years old when he disappeared in his plane on July 31, 1944, after leaving Bastia in Corsica on an Allied reconnaissance mission over France. He never returned—and no trace of him or his plane was ever found. Some people are convinced the pilot-author's death was a suicide, stressing that the evening before his final flight he had prepared a letter in the form of a will. Others who saw him before he left noted that he had complained of a sleepless night and appeared restless and depressed.

Locke, John British philosopher (1632-1704), regarded as the father of empiricism. He denied the existence of any inborn knowledge or innate ideas. In his *Two Treaties of Government* Locke wrote: ". . . Man being all the workmanship of one omnipotent and infinitely wise Maker; all the servants of one sovereign Master, sent into the world by His order and about His business; they are His property, whose workmanship they are made to last during His, not another's pleasure . . . Everyone . . . is bound to preserve himself, and not to quit his station wilfully . . ."

Lock's theological argument against suicide had wide support in Great Britain at the time.

London, England In his study *Suicide in London*, Peter Sainsbury revealed high suicide rates in areas with rooming houses and single-person dwelling units, and in areas with high rates of mobility and other signs of social disorganization. Such analyses of suicide rates within small, specific geographic areas have led experts to valuable clues in the etiology of the phenomenon. As a whole, England in 1982 (including Wales) had a suicide rate per 100,000 population of 8.6, down from 8.9 in 1981. The suicide rate for males was 11.5 in 1982, for females 5.9.

loneliness Loneliness is a state which exacerbates any other problem, disappointment, loss of job, death in the family, etc.

Shneidman writes in *Definition of Suicide*: "Closely-related to hopelessness-helplessness is the overpowering feeling of loneliness." Professor Kenneth Colby, in a UCLA course in "Programmed Information for Dealing with Depression and Suicide" (1984), writes: "In addition to hopelessness, people thinking of suicide often feel a terrible loneliness. They may shut one off from unfeeling others and one becomes numb, impervious to solace. Life, now grim as well as drab, loses its value and one determines to abandon it. Death seems the perfect release from troubles . . . Confusion will be ended and calm and control will finally be achieved." Philosopher Bertrand Russell wrote of loneliness in his *Autobiography* (1967), stating: "I have sought love . . . because it relieves loneliness—that terrible loneliness in which one shivering consciousness looks over the rim of the world into the cold, unfathomable lifeless abyss . . ."

Bertrand Russell, *Autobiography* (Boston: Little, Brown, 1967).

Edwin Shneidman, *Definition of Suicide* (New York: John Wiley & Sons, 1985).

The Loneliness of Children Book by Vanderbilt University professor John Killinger, who theorized that the important choice with regard to child care is, for most women, between their children's needs and their own. He argues that America's children must not be deprived of the parental attention which creates security and sound character. Lack of proper parental care and attention can create insecurity, anxiety, even fear—and sometimes leads to a despair that establishes a suicidal mind-set.

Loomis, Vivienne The authors John E. Mack and Holly Hickler wrote about the suicide of this young girl in their 1981 book, *Vivienne: The Life and Suicide of an Adolescent Girl*. The book reveals how the more Vivienne cried out for help and was ignored, the more explicit her cries became. High school teachers, administrators, even her parents failed to see her extreme misery and feelings of despair and hopelessness. In one book report, the girl explained how living in a world where everything is superficial, insipid and mean makes death seem an escape, a blessed event, a sanctuary. Mrs. Loomis recalled that the family, out of respect for her daughter's privacy, did not read any of Vivienne's journals, letters or poetry until after her death. As Dr. Mary Giffin notes, "respect for privacy is a luxury that parents of suicidal children cannot afford."

Los Angeles Suicide Prevention Center Founded in 1958 by psychologists Norman L. Farberow and Edwin S. Shneidman. They began the center with an all-professional staff but in time welcomed volunteers to the program, which includes research, prevention and intervention aspects. Today the center has about 150 volunteer workers who handle approximately 1,000 calls per month. Doctors Shneidman and Farberow, both pioneers in the field of suicidology, made the Los Angeles Center the prototype for prevention and crisis centers, not only in the U.S., but also throughout the world. Much of the research that has been done about destructive behavior, suicide and suicide prevention has been by these two authorities at the center. Among other things, they developed the vital research method called the "psychological autopsy," a means to help medical examiners and coroners determine the cause of a death when it is not clearly indicated.

The Los Angeles Suicide Prevention Center and Institute for Studies of Self-Destructive Behavior is currently directed by Norman L. Farberow, PhD, and Robert Litman, MD; chief executive officer is Sheila Halfon. Address: 1041 S. Menlo Avenue, Los Angeles, CA 90006; phone is (213) 386-

5111 (administrative), or (213) 381-5111 (24-hour crisis line).

LOSS (Loving Outreach to Survivors of a Suicide) Self-help groups, sponsored by Catholic Charities, located in cities across the country. The groups are for family members who have lost someone to suicide. The sense of community, of sharing and hope that people find in such groups usually extends beyond the meetings, to the home. For other such self-help groups, see the appendix in the back of this work.

loss, sense of, and depression Depression is often caused by a person's feeling a deep sense of loss for someone or something that has been loved. It may be triggered by the loss of a loved one, or of a job, or even the loss of a particular feeling or sense of being (e.g., loss of feeling wanted or needed). As Francine Klagsbrun notes, "the loss is so significant to the person that it leads to overwhelming sorrow along with feelings of weakness and unworthiness."

Any serious loss, according to Klagsbrun, such as loss of a child, a spouse, or loss of one's physical health, can devastate a person and thus lead to severe, unrelenting depression and, subsequently, to suicidal thoughts. Young people are especially vulnerable to crippling losses. Klagsbrun writes in *Too Young to Die*, "Of all the losses teenagers might suffer, the one that affects the greatest number is a sense of lost identity. In some ways, the teen years themselves can be viewed as a time of just such a loss, a time that can lead to confused, depressed feelings."

It is no accident that the suicide rate is higher among the unmarried, the divorced and the widowed than among the married. Similarly, those who live in anonymous urban settings are more likely candidates for suicide than those living in rural areas where the sense of community and extended family is stronger. Of Durkheim's four varieties of social conditions that cause sufficient stress for people to want to commit suicide, "anomic" is the one that applies here. The individual cannot adjust, for example, to a sudden, shocking loss—of a job, a marriage, a wife, a close friend or all of his or her money. All these losses, unless help is forthcoming, may result in an "ANOMIC" SUICIDE. In this type of suicide, the individual's society seems to have lost for the individual its familiar structure and customary guiding organization.

love During adolescence, young people experience many emotional as well as physical changes. Often intense emotions experienced in early childhood are restimulated by adolescent changes, adding to the stresses, pressures and problems ordinarily accompanying these years. For example, just as crippling as, say, the actual physical loss of a parent is the sense of love lost, a feeling of not being loved or cared for. Young people who grow up feeling unloved come to think of themselves as unworthy of love. Even adults may develop a self-image of uselessness and ineptness, and they too can and do turn against themselves and others.

Psychiatrist Samuel C. Klagsbrun, who has treated many children and young adults, says that the way youngsters experience loss of love influences their reactions. Francine Klagsbrun quotes her husband in *Too Young to Die*:

> Children who have received little love from their earliest days have, in a sense, lost love before they've even found it. These children grow up as deadened and morose adolescents and adults. They may retreat into a fantasy world, isolate themselves from others, and become "loners" incapable of giving or receiving love. In the most severe cases, they become seriously depressed and suicidal, allowing nobody to intrude on their lonely world. Children who have enjoyed some love in early life and then suffered the loss of that love—through

death, divorce or the breakup of a family--may show other forms of depression as they grow older. They may become enraged at the parents who loved them and left them and then turn that rage inward against themselves. Such young people often get into violent arguments with their parents, become disruptive in school and, in some cases, become serious juvenile delinquents. Tragically, their very anger and hurtful actions usually lead to greater rejection by parents and friends. And this rejection, in turn, pushes the person further into depression, and often into suicide.

Psychologist R.E. Gould calls young people who feel unloved by parents "expendable." He theorizes that the expendable child feels his parents don't love him, feels anger but can't express it, and feels that his parents never wanted children and, thus, would be better off without him. In an effort to gain this longed-for parental love, the child turns his anger inward, as Dr. Klagsbrun noted, incorporating the "wishes" of his parents to be without his presence, and becoming suicidal.

Freud said that all of us grow up with mixed feelings of love and hate for our parents. Some experts describe suicide as killing off a part of yourself that you don't like. The suicidal person hates some parts of himself and tries to "kill them off."

Karl Menninger, the famous analyst, summed up the complex motives for suicide thus: the wish to kill, the wish to be killed, and the wish to die. There is anger against others as well as oneself in the suicidal individual. Suicide, then, may be viewed as murder in the 180th degree.

Another idea that may trigger youth suicides is what some experts term the "Romeo and Juliet Factor." Even before Shakespeare wrote about these two star-crossed teenage lovers, romantic love in literature and drama had often been associated with death. Often, lovers planned to be "reunited in death," as noted by Sandra Gardner and Dr. Gary Rosenberg, a psychiatrist, in *Teenage Suicide*. These authors write that "though it makes a good movie, the linking of love and death can produce lethal results for romantically inclined teenagers." However, investigators have pointed out that this usually occurs only in the young person already emotionally distressed and in a "danger zone" for potential suicide. Other authorities, e.g., David Phillips, PhD, R. Gould and D. Shaffer, have done studies that show only a possible *correlation*, not a *causal* connection between books, movies, or newspaper articles and suicidal behavior. As Dr. Farberow says, "we have to be careful about assuming the latter connection." Thus, if love turns sour or suddenly isn't available for whatever reason, the so-called "love-and-death" movie or book or play can be a motivating factor for a suicidal or otherwise problem-plagued young person. These affected young people romanticize suicide as a "way out" of family and romantic problems . . . and a movie or book can sometimes be the triggering factor in a suicide or suicide attempt. As Gardner and Rosenberg write: "The reuniting-after-death concept is one of the biggest elements in the romanticization or glamorization of suicide."

Several teenagers who obviously romanticized suicide killed themselves after seeing the film *An Officer and a Gentleman* in which a secondary character commits suicide. Experts noted that there was an increase in the number of suicides after MARILYN MONROE died, after JAMES DEAN's death in an auto crash, and after JOHN LENNON was shot. However, this increase was followed by fewer suicides for a short while, "self-correcting" to the average number for that time of the year.

Lowell, Robert U.S. poet (1917-1977), also noted during the 1960s for his deep involvement in left-wing politics. Lowell suffered severe depression at times, also suffered a serious nervous breakdown and was confined to a mental facility where he later admitted to entertaining suicidal thoughts. Lowell was an alcoholic and was actually imprisoned for five months by the courts for refusing to serve in the army.

Lowry, Malcolm English novelist (1909-1957), famous primarily for his novel *Under the Volcano*, now recognized as a masterpiece. An alcoholic, he died in Ripe, Sussex, in England. Lowry confessed to thoughts of suicide to escape his isolated alcoholic hell, much like the hero of his great novel.

loyalty suicides Term sometimes used to describe suicides committed out of loyalty, e.g., soldiers who slay themselves out of a desire to either imitate their leader's example, or simply to join their leader in the afterlife they envision. In his account of Otho's death, Tacitus mentions that some of the emperor's soldiers "slew themselves near his pyre . . ." Such suicides closely parallel INSTITUTIONAL SUICIDE and RITUAL SUICIDES, such as the Hindu custom of SUTTEE, in which the widow immolated herself with the corpse of her husband. They are also related to Emile Durkheim's concept of ALTRUISTIC SUICIDE, in which the person is "overidentified" with his society and kills him or herself out of "loyalty" to its expectations or demands.

LSD Users of this drug often confessed to wanting to "blow their minds" in search of new other-world experiences. All they actually accomplished was to avoid their real emotions, or, as FRANCINE KLAGSBRUN notes, "to shelter them from the rage and despair they might feel if they permitted themselves to feel anything." Not a few young people, especially during the 1960s, committed suicide or attempted suicide while in an LSD-induced state. LSD, or lysergic acid diethylamide, is one of a group of psychomimetic drugs called hallucinogens that produce psychotic symptoms and behavior. Symptoms may include hallucinations, illusions, body and time-space distortions, and, less commonly, intense panic or mystical experience.

Lucan (Marcus Annaeus Lucanus) Roman poet (39-65 A.D.), at first a favorite of Nero, Lucan later became involved in a conspiracy against him, and upon its discovery, committed suicide. As Lucan himself said, "how simple a feat it is to escape slavery by suicide."

Lucian Greek satirist (ca. 125-ca. 190 A.D.) and teacher of rhetoric and philosophy. He became prefect at Alexandria in later life. He witnessed the fiery suicide by immolation of Peregrinus and wrote an essay, "The Death of Peregrinus," depicting the Cynic philosopher as an exhibitionist, a man with an insatiable craving for notoriety.

M

males, U.S. suicide rate and potential suicides Generally speaking, women attempt suicide about three times as often as men; however, men complete suicide about three times as often as women. According to the National Center for Health Statistics, throughout the period 1970 to 1980, white males had the highest suicide rate of any race or sex group, and in 1980, white males constituted 70% of all suicide deaths in the U.S. The highest suicide rate for males occurred in the oldest age groups (over 65 years of age), and for females, the highest suicide rates occurred in mid-life (ages 45 to 54). White males have, for the past 30 years (1950 to 1980), consistently had the highest suicide rates of any race and sex category. During this same period, black and other males had the second highest rates; white females had the third highest rates, while black and other females have consistently had the lowest rates. From 1950 to 1980, age-specific suicide rates for males increased for the three youngest age groups, but decreased for the four oldest age groups.

In 1980, of all suicides committed in this nation, 70% occurred to white males with 22% occurring to white females, 6% to black and other males and 2% to black and other females. The ratio of suicide among males to the ratio among females is higher for black and other races than for white; this ratio has shown an increase over the decade (1970-1980) for both racial categories.

White males have shown the greatest decline in median age of persons who committed suicide between 1970 and 1980 (48.8 in 1970 to 39.8 in 1980). By 1980, more than one-third (34.4%) of males who committed suicide were under age 30. By 1980, the median age of *all* persons in the four race or sex groups who committed suicide in the U.S. was 39.9 years of age.

The Centers for Disease Control, U.S. Department of Health and Human Services, considers the most striking aspect of the change in U.S. suicide rates from 1970 to 1980 to be the large percentage increase in rates for males in both the 15 to 24 and 25 to 34 age groups and the consistent percentage decrease in rates for females in all age groups *except* the youngest age group (15 to 24). Between 1970 and 1980, suicide rates for males 15 to 24 years of age increased 50%. In the 25 to 34 age group, suicide among males increased almost 30%. White males generally attain their highest suicide rates in the oldest age groups while black and other males generally attain their highest suicide rates in early adulthood.

The pattern of suicide by method varies little by race but varies greatly by sex. While the male pattern of suicide by method has changed only slightly between 1970 and 1980, the pattern of suicide by method for females has undergone a significant change. In 1970 as in 1980, firearms (and explosives) were the leading method of suicide for males (58.4% and 63.1%, respectively). There has been an increase between 1970 and 1980 in the percent of suicides in which firearms (and explosives) were used by males and females in both racial groups. (While the International Classification of Disease (ICD) category for firearms includes firearms and explosives, less than 1% of suicide deaths classified in the category "firearms and explosives" are due to explosives.)

Age-adjusted suicide rates by marital status for white males, black males, white females and black females for 1979 show that married persons in all four race and sex groups have the lowest suicide rates. The most striking feature of suicide rates by marital status is the very high rates for widowed males of both white and black races.

Males have a markedly higher risk of committing suicide than do females . . . and the differential appears to be widening even more. Between 1970 and 1980, almost three-fourths (72.8%) of suicide deaths occurred to males, and the rate for suicides increased among males while it decreased among females. There has been a marked increase in the contribution of young, white male suicide deaths to the national suicide problem since 1970. White males ages 15 to 39 represented less than one-fourth (22.6%) of all suicides in the U.S. in 1970. By 1980, suicide deaths for white males in that same age group had jumped to more than one-third, or 35.0% of all suicides in the country. Within the 15 to 24 age group, most of the increase in the suicide rate is due to an increase in the white male suicide rate. Suicide rates increased among white males 15 to 19 years of age by 60% and among white males 20 to 24 years of age by 44% in the 11 years from 1970 through 1980.

To show the magnitude of suicide as a U.S. public health problem, consider that in 1980 alone, suicide accounted for an estimated loss of some 619,533 potential years of life for persons between the ages of 1 and 65. Three-quarters of those estimated loss of potential life years were for males of all ages, either white or black. Suicide was the 10th leading cause of death for all persons in 1980—and the third leading cause of death for persons 15 to 34 years of age. Suicide ranked as the second leading cause of death for white persons 15 to 34 years of age.

Centers for Disease Control, *Suicide Surveillance, 1970-1980* (Atlanta: Department of Health and Human Services, April 1985).

Malinowski, Bronislaw Polish anthropologist (1884-1942) and author of *Crime and Custom in Savage Society*, a book presenting what has often been called "the best-known case in the history of anthropological theory," dealing with the case of Trobriand (in the southwest Pacific) suicide. Malinowski uses his collected material to show how public disapproval of a man who had committed a major sin—in this instance, incest—acted as a legal device by prompting the offender to commit suicide. Though Malinowski's argument was concerned with the field of law, the case led anthropologists to reconsider the nature of suicide in primitive societies.

Man Against Himself Definitive work by Karl Menninger, the famous psychiatrist, who agrees with Freud in the concept of the simultaneous presence in man of contradictory and conflicting drives, the life instinct (Eros) and the death instinct (Thanatos). In *Man Against Himself*, Dr. Menninger describes, analyzes and interprets the many self-destructive acts in which people engage. He writes about different kinds of deaths that result from the interplay of the life and death instincts, which take different forms and which he calls chronic, focal and organic suicides. Within the act of suicide he asserts that one may find three elements intermixed in varying proportions in each suicide: (1) the wish to kill; (2) the wish to be killed; (3) the wish to die.

Mandel, Michel R., MD Director of Somatic Therapies Consultation Service at Massachusetts General Hospital, Boston, and a member of the American Psychiatric Association. Dr. Mandel, along with many other psychiatrists, considers ECT, ELECTROCONVULSIVE THERAPY, the treatment of choice when the risk of suicide for a severely depressed patient is great. Dr. Mary Giffin, in *A Cry for Help*, quotes Dr. Mandel thus: "We're talking about a group of people for whom as a matter of fact, nothing *but* brain stimulation is really going to be of help."

manic depressives Manic-depressive disorder is a bipolar disorder in which there are swings between episodes of both mania and depression. The illness may be subdivided into manic, depressed or mixed types on the basis of the presenting symptoms. In the mixed or circular type, the person has extreme mood swings, going from the depths of despair (lowered mood, sleep disturbance, decreased appetite, intense feelings of worthlessness) to soaring heights of euphoria (excitement, expansive or irritable mood, flights of ideas, distractibility, impaired judgment and sometimes grandiosity). This disease often begins during teen years or in the early twenties and may continue throughout the patient's life. The medical community suspects that manic-depression originates from biochemical disorders within the body. Physicians usually treat the illness with LITHIUM carbonate, an alkali metal—especially for acute mania, and as a maintenance medication which helps to reduce the duration, intensity and frequency of the mood swings.

As the depression phase becomes more severe, or pronounced, the danger of suicide becomes greater. Victims often fall into a deep, dark despondency, and are inundated by oppressive thoughts of suicide. Family members, friends, and associates should be alert to the victim's symptoms, suicidal conversation and overt hints of death wishes. As Francine Klagsbrun notes: "The best you can do is be aware if a friend or relative begins to act in ways that seem disoriented or irrational to you." (See also DEPRESSION; LOSS, SENSE OF, AND DEPRESSION.)

Many Faces of Suicide, The Book edited by Norman J. Farberow, outlining the area of indirect suicide (Menninger calls it focal or organic suicide), noting its characteristics and its differentiation from direct or overt suicide, especially in terms of time (long- vs. short-term) and awareness (the role of intention). A number of experts have contributed chapters to the book on such subjects as hyperobesity, auto accidents, heart disease, psychosomatic illnesses, malingering, gambling and high risk activities.

MAO inhibitors A group of antidepressant drugs that inhibit the enzyme monoamine oxidase that breaks down serotonin and norepinephrine in the brain and increases the levels of biogenic amines. MAO inhibitors are used to relieve depression. Two other groups of antidepressants are called tricyclics and tetracyclics. These function by partially inhibiting the amount of chemical neurotransmitters that are reabsorbed, leaving more available for use in neurotransmission. The main types of MAO inhibitors are isocarboxazid (Marplan), phenelaine (Nardil) and tranylepromine (Parnate). They are extremely potent, and side effects are frequent and may be severe. Used in combination with other drugs—narcotics, stimulants, depressants—in an uncontrolled manner, the effect can be fatal. The same is true when MAO inhibitors are taken with common foods that contain tyramine, such as cheese, herring, salami and chocolate. MAO inhibitors are considered extremely dangerous drugs and are usually only administered under close medical supervision.

Marcus Aurelius Roman emperor and Stoic (121-180 A.D.); he approved of suicide only when committed on a rational basis, but not, as medical historian George Rosen notes, "to put on a show or to simply express irrational ideas." As Marcus Aurelius wrote: "How admirable is the soul which is ready and resolved, if it must this moment be released from the body, to be either extinguished or scattered or to persist. This resolve too must arise from a specific decision, not out of sheer opposition like the Christians, but after reflection and with dignity, and so as to convince others, without histrionic display."

Marcus Aurelius, *Meditations of the Emperor Marcus Aurelius*, 2 vols., ed. and trans. A.S.L. Farquarson (New York: Oxford University Press, 1944), 1:217.

marijuana The dried, flowering tops, leaves and stems of the Indian hemp plant *Cannabis sativa*, which contain the psychoactive substance tetrahydrocannabinol (THC) and are usually smoked in cigarettes ("joints") or pipes.

According to O'Brien and Cohen in their *Encyclopedia of Drug Abuse*, after caffeine, nicotine and alcohol, marijuana is the fourth most popular abused substance in the world. Despite its illegal status in the U.S., there are an estimated 16 million regular users. The number of users increased each year until 1978; since that time, surveys have shown significant drops in marijuana use. This decrease in use is attributed to a change in attitude among young people. In 1978, 35% felt that regular marijuana was associated with great risk; by 1982, this figure had risen to 60%. "In many states," say O'Brien and Cohen, "the law remains unchanged while actual enforcement policies testify to a diminishing concern among police officers with recreational users."

According to the two authors,

> The effects of marijuana are highly subjective and are affected by a number of variables, such as the quality of the drug, the dosage, the experience and expectations of the user and his environment. In very high doses, THC can produce hypnotic and psychedelic effects, including time and space distortions, enhanced sensory perceptions, euphoria and free-flowing thoughts. Adverse psychological reactions, such as anxiety and paranoia, can occur, usually in novice users.

Psychiatrist Herbert Hendin studied both men and women students abusing different kinds of drugs as part of a larger psychoanalytic study of Columbia University students he conducted for his important book, *The Age of Sensation*. Hendin theorized that students who got stoned on marijuana every day had problems that related to feelings of aggressiveness and competitiveness. These students, generally, came from families that stressed competition and high achievement. The students resented these feelings which they realized were instilled in them by their parents. They used and abused marijuana to cope with (and reduce) these aggressive, competitive drives and to revolt against pressures from their parents to succeed.

People who use marijuana are also apt to drink alcohol. When alcohol is taken with marijuana there is a greater impairment of motor and mental skills than with either drug alone. While the use of marijuana does not produce physical dependence, after long-term chronic use it does often produce psychological dependence on the euphoric and sedative effects.

O'Brien and Cohen write that "A lethal dose has never been established since no deaths directly related to the action of marijuana have been reported. Research with mice indicates that for a human weighing approximately 154 pounds, a lethal dose of marijuana containing 1% THC would be 15 pounds smoked or 30 pounds eaten—all at once."

Although no reliable data exists to prove or disprove effects of marijuana use and abuse on suicide rates, this can be misleading. People who smoke marijuana—and especially those who combine it with alcohol—forget their problems for a time and become carefree and high. But neither marijuana nor alcohol relieves depression (alcohol is a depressant itself). As Klagsbrun notes in *Too Young to Die*, after the high wears off, the user is not actually feels lower than before, only now he is weighted down with the additional feelings of guilt and remorse for having smoked and drunk too much. The old feelings are renewed and the cycle may start again. It often becomes a merry-go-round with the pattern of rebelling against pressures and depression, smoking and drinking, and more pressures and depression continuing for years. If these people continue in this cycle without getting help for their basic problem(s), they usually alienate family, friends and associates—and find themselves more isolated, alienated and depressed than ever. Overwhelmed by their situation, their judgment impaired, they may turn to suicide. (Note: the suicide rate among alcoholics alone is a shocking 58 times higher than it is among the normal population. The person who mixes alcohol with other drugs is even more vulnerable to suicide in his mind's foggy state and its concomitant loss of judgment. (See also DRUG ABUSE.)

Herbert Hendin, *The Age of Sensation* (New York: W.W. Norton, 1975).
Robert O'Brien and Sidney Cohen, MD, *The Encyclopedia of Drug Abuse (New York: Facts On File, 1984).*

Maris, Ronald W., PhD Professor and chairman, department of anthropology and sociology, University of South Carolina, Columbia. Maris is the author of *Pathways to Suicide* and serves as editor of *Suicide and Life-Threatening Behavior*, the official publication of the American Association of Suicidology (AAS), published quarterly by Guilford Publications in New York. Dr. Maris also directs the Center for the Study of Suicide, University of South Carolina. He has written many articles and essays for professional journals on the subject of suicide and other destructive and life-threatening behaviors. Dr. Maris is also the editor of *Biology of Suicide*.

marital status and suicide Suicide rates are lowest among married persons. It should be noted, however, that most people who kill themselves are married simply because the majority of adults are married (though this has been changing in recent years). In other words, even though the suicide *rates* are low for married adults, the actual *number* of suicide victims among marrieds is relatively high.

According to data from the National Center for Health Statistics, age-adjusted suicide rates by marital status for white males, black males, white females and black females for 1979 show that married persons in all four race and sex groups have the lowest suicide rates, with single persons who had never married having the second lowest suicide rates. Rates are high among widowed and divorced people in almost all age groups. (Among the widowed, a spouse's death often acts as a strong precipitating factor to take their own lives.) The most astonishing feature of suicide rates by marital status is the very high rates for widowed males of both white and black races. Only in the white female group did divorced persons have a rate that exceeded the rate for widowed persons. (See Appendix I, Figure 9.)

Factors that indicate a low suicide potential include: female, youth in or with rural occupation, religious devoutness, marriage, large number of children, membership in lower socio-economic class.

martyrdom There have been many instances in history of the phenomenon linking suicide with a desire for martyrdom. George Rosen in his "History," chapter one of Perlin's *A Handbook for the Study of Suicide*, notes that voluntary martyrdom was frequent among the early Christians. He writes: "As a youth, Origen of Alexandria (c. 185-253/54 A.D.) experienced the martyrdom of his father in 202 and was possessed by a passionate desire to suffer the same fate." Origen's mother prevented him from committing suicide, but his attitude did not change.

Other early examples include Vibia Perpetua, a young married mother of 22 who chose to die in the arena in the reign of Septimius Severus, EUSEBIUS, bishop of Caesarea, tells of Christians about to be tortured who chose instead suicide, "regarding death as a prize snatched from the wickedness of evil men." This type of pathological craving for martyrdom and its emotional climate (brought about by the desire to die as a blood-witness to Christ) characterized large groups in the Roman Empire, says Dr. Rosen, between the reigns of Nero and Julian (i.e., 54 to 363 A.D.).

Ultimately, strengthened by the increasingly important status of Christianity, both as a tolerated faith and as the state of religion, voluntary martyrdom was discouraged by church leaders, and opposition to all suicide was stiffened. It was not until 563, however, at the Council of Braga, that suicide as an act was condemned by the church. This position remained canon law until 1284 when the Synod of Nimes refused burial in consecrated ground to suicides. However, we have witnessed recent examples of voluntary martyrdom in the KAMIKAZI PILOTS of Japan in World War II and the Middle Eastern terrorists who willingly die during or as a result of their actions in behalf of *Jihad* (or holy war).

People who entertain even vague notions of martyrdom through suicide are encouraged to read Alfred Alvarez's poignant and graphic book *The Savage God*. After his own suicide attempt, Alvarez wrote:

> We all expect something of death, even if it's only damnation. But all I got was oblivion . . . I thought death would be . . . a synoptic vision of life, crisis by crisis, all suddenly explained, justified, redeemed, a Last Judgment . . . Instead all I got was a hole in the head, a round zero, nothing. I'd been swindled . . . death is simply an end, a dead end, no more, no less . . .

Masada The Jewish fortress besieged by the Romans in A.D. 72-73, where the defenders committed mass suicide to prevent capture. By the time it was ended, some 960 persons had been killed (soldiers slew their own wives and children in some instances) or had committed suicide. Their Zealot sect leader, ELEAZAR BEN JAIR, had urged them to kill themselves in a heroic act rather than become Roman slaves. Only two women and five children escaped the spectacular massacre and remained alive to relate the story as recorded by FLAVIUS JOSEPHUS, the Jewish historian and soldier.

M*A*S*H theme song See "SUICIDE IS PAINLESS."

mass suicides MASADA is perhaps the best known site of mass suicides in the ancient world. An eerie parallel to Masada occurred during World War II at TREBLINKA, one of the most terrifying Nazi concentration camps. Untold thousands of Jews, mostly from Eastern Europe, were sent to Treblinka in eastern Poland, for extermination. Over time, these heretofore benumbed people started to commit suicide one by one, rather than submit to the horrors they were experiencing and the ultimate persecution that would end in extermination at the hands of their Nazi tormentors. According to FRANCINE KLAGSBRUN, their deaths by suicide affirmed the freedom to control their own lives and deaths. These acts of suicide also led, writes Klagsbrun, "to the first signs of solidarity among them, with those who remained alive helping those who wanted to kill themselves so they would die quickly."

Klagsbrun adds, "These flickerings of friendship marked the beginning of a rebellion that later took the form of open revolt, one of the few such revolts that occurred in a Nazi concentration camp."

In 17th-century Russia, the Great Schism (The Raskol) left the dissenting religious group called the Raskolniki in such despair that many followers sought death rather than wait for the end of the world (which they had predicted would occur before the end of the century). Between 1672 and 1691, over 37 mass immolations took place in which more than 20,000 Raskolniki voluntarily burned to death. They had thought it senseless to live and risk being contaminated by heresy. (See also JAMESTOWN, GUYANA.)

materialism Chicago's *Tribune Magazine* carried an article on teen suicide written by April Olzak which began: "What can you do to prevent your child from becoming suicidally depressed and committing suicide? Don't make too much money, and don't live in certain high-status suburbs. It could kill your child." An exaggeration, but like most hyperbole, it contains an element of truth. Affluence does seem to spawn an unusually greater share of teen suicides. Psychiatric social worker Stanley A. Levis is quoted by MARY GIFFIN and Carol Felsenthal in *A Cry for Help*, "People here (Chicago's affluent North Shore) want more from their social lives, marriages and children. By the very nature of their lifestyle, they often get less."

As Dr. Giffin notes: "The deprivation here is emotional, not material. The young people have good schools, spectacular houses, designer jeans, but they lack support, love and caring parents. It's more elusive, but it's as real to these kids as the physical deprivation found in the ghetto."

Time magazine ran an article on teen suicide (September 1980) and referred to Chicago's North Shore as "the suicide belt." One teen girl who had known several suicides, is quoted as saying, "Growing up here, you're handed everything on a silver platter, but something else is missing. The one thing parents don't give is love, understanding, acceptance of you as a person."

There is, of course, a complex of causes for so many young suicides and suicide attempts, causes that involve social, economic, psychological and family interactions. But certainly materialism, the consistent pursuit of things, must take its share of the blame for the despair, dissatisfaction and disturbed feelings of many young people today.

April Olzak, "Teenage Suicide and the North Shore Connection," *Chicago Tribune Magazine* (July 27, 1980).
Editors of *Time*, "Suicide Belt: Rates Up for Affluent Teens," *Time* (September 1, 1980).
Mary Giffin, MD, Carol Felsenthal, *A Cry for Help* (Garden City: Doubleday, 1983).

Maximus Valerius Historian (42 B.C.-37 A.D.) and contemporary of Tiberius, wrote that Roman suicides were not uncommon during the rule of Caesar Augustus. He recorded that in the important port city of Marseilles, the municipal senate actually supplied free HEMLOCK-laced poison to anyone who could give valid reasons for wanting to commit suicide.

J. Choron, *Suicide*, (New York: Scribners, 1972).

McIntosh, John L. Assistant professor of psychology at Indiana University at South Bend, he is the author of *Suicide Among U.S. Racial Minorities, Suicide Among Children, Adolescents, and Students*, and *Suicide Among the Elderly*, plus articles in *Omega, Suicide and Life-Threatening Behavior*, and the *Journal of Gerontological Social Work*. He is co-editor (with Edward J. Dunne and Kaven Dunne-Maxim) of *Suicide and Its Aftermath: Understanding and Counseling the Survivors*. He also compiled *Research on Suicide: A Bibliography*, published in 1985, an important addition to the bibliographies on suicide. Professor McIntosh is a member of the American Association of Suicidology.

"Me and Bobby McGee" Hit song made famous by rock singer JANIS JOPLIN, who died at age twenty-seven of an overdose of heroin. Tragically, teenagers of the day (late 1960s and early 1970s) innately understood and empathized with a popular line from the tune which said, "Freedom's just another word for nothin' left to lose." As Dr. Mary Giffin notes, the line "can serve as an epitaph for this generation, children who are given much too much freedom too soon."

Mead, George Herbert American philosopher (1863-1931) and author of the book *Mind, Self and Society*, which influenced many sociologists to theorize that there can be no self without social experience, since the ability to communicate with oneself—taking yourself as an object—is dependent upon having communicated with others. As Ronald Maris explains, "The individual gets outside himself by seeing himself as others do (what C.H. Cooley called the 'looking-glass self') and by taking the attitudes of other individuals toward him." Mead said that the two aspects of self, which he called the "I" and the "me," differed in that the "me" represents the organized set of internalized attitudes of others toward you, while the "I" is the individual's *response* to this set and, thus, the source of novelty, creativity and uncertainty. These concepts are used in the sociological study of suicide, e.g., by Jack Douglas in his *The Social Meanings of Suicide*.

media, effects of suicide coverage A number of suicidologists and other authorities have criticized news coverage, by newspapers, magazines, television and radio, contending that reading or hearing about a suicide victim in the news is often enough to push some disturbed or impressionable people over the edge.

In 1979, sociologist David Phillips found that news stories of suicides did stimulate a wave of imitative acts. He checked Los Angeles traffic records for periods immediately following locally publicized suicides and discovered that for three days after a suicide report in the Los Angeles area, auto fatalities rose by 31%. He later found a similar jump in fatalities in Detroit, following front-page coverage of a suicide. (It would be impossible, of course, to prove that the auto deaths were suicides rather than accidents.) On the other hand, studies have revealed that a drop in suicides in cities has taken place during extended newspaper blackouts, e.g., when a strike has shut down the paper. There have been many reports of rises in the number of suicides following media coverage of a celebrity's suicide, (e.g., MARILYN MONROE).

Many, if not most, experts appear to agree that the far greater danger lies in preventing discussion and exposure of the subject of suicide. Not to report and discuss suicide simply places it back in the taboo category and promotes more myth and misinformation, which, ultimately, may cause more suicides. As Gardner and Rosenberg conclude: "The proper kind of discussion—educational, informative, factual—is the only weapon we have against teenage suicide. Sometimes the media can turn around and provide that educational and informative forum."

As Gardner and Rosenberg note, a positive example of what the media can do is one segment, called "The Breaking Point," done by the cast and writers of the TV show, *The Facts of Life*. This segment dealt with a young suicidal girl who overdoses on pills and dies. Everyone on the show felt that the subject was handled sensitively, not sensationally, and was done in good taste. They later received a letter from a teenage girl who admitted that watching the segment kept her from actually going through with her own suicide. In actress Kim Field's words, "to know that you saved a life through a TV show is a wonderful feeling."

Exposure to suicides is a possible risk factor, of course, either directly or indirectly. But as the Centers for Disease Control says in its November 1986 report, *Youth Suicide in the United States, 1970-1980*, "Research has not yet been completed to determine the effects of exposure to previous suicides on subsequent suicides."

Sandra Gardner and Dr. Gary Rosenberg, *Teenage Suicide* (New York: Julian Messner, 1985).

Sheila Mary Eby, "How Publicity Affects Violent Behavior," *Psychology Today* (January 1981).

Mary Giffin and Carol Felsenthal, *A Cry for Help: Exploring and Exploding Myths About Teenage Suicide: A Guide for All Parents of Adolescents* (Garden City: Doubleday, 1983).

medical personnel Physicians, nurses and ancillary medical therapists and technicians serve as a first line of defense against suicide. They are frequently called "gatekeepers" because they are often the first persons to learn of depression or suicidal feelings, many of which are masked or disguised in physical symptoms. Medical personnel trained in interpretation of the common physical and emotional signs of depression provide the opportunity for early identification and intervention.

Grollman notes in *Suicide* that medical personnel in hospital emergency rooms or serving in Emergency Medical Services are often called on to save the life of a suicide attempt. Often the first to be greeted by an attempter on recovery, the attitude and understanding offered the attempter is crucial for averting further suicide attempts or subsequent suicidal behavior. The medical personnel are also important in their interaction with the families of the attempters; they may be puzzled, confused or angry.

Our medical professionals—doctors, psychiatrists, psychologists, nurses, therapists, etc.—need to have more information about the suicide problem made available to them. People turn to them for help, yet they themselves sometimes feel threatened and inadequate when confronted with a suicide problem. Even so, by his or her acquired basic medical knowledge, skills, and attitudes, a medically-trained person—physician, clinical psychologist, nurse—has the disciplined capacity, in Earl A. Grollman's words, "to understand an individual's innermost feelings, demands, and expectations."

There is an ongoing need, however, for additional training of medical personnel in the problems of suicide awareness—in the areas of INTERVENTION, prevention and POSTVENTION. This country also needs additional mental health facilities (there is a noticeable lack of such facilities in urban areas where blacks reside). While public, state and federal funds are now supporting many organizations that train and instruct medical and paramedical personnel in the fighting of the suicide problem, more help is needed.

In addition to medical emergency services that offer help immediately in suicide crises, many communities now have mental health centers, crisis centers, suicide prevention centers, "hot lines" and walk-in services. Many of these prevention and crisis facilities have medical personnel as well as mental health personnel, psychiatrists, nurses, medical residents, psychologists, social workers, psychotherapists, trained volunteers and others on staff. A list of centers that deal specifically with suicide crises and are accredited by the American Association of Suicidology (AAS) are in appendix 3 of this book.

Menninger, Karl Psychiatrist (1893-), founder of the famed Menninger Institute in Topeka, Kansas. Considered by many to be one of the foremost figures in American psychiatry, he is author of many works, including the important book, *Man Against Himself*, in which he describes and interprets the many self-destructive acts in which people engage. He summed up suicide in this way: the wish to kill, the wish to be killed, the wish to die. He said there is extreme anger against others, as well as oneself in the suicidal person. Dr. Menninger extended Sigmund Freud's concept of the death instinct (self-destruction) and its role in man's functioning, especially as it interacts with the life instinct (self-preservation) in times of stress and crisis. His book *The Vital Balance* describes five levels of personality organization from high to poor at which a person can function. Suicide, because it is self-destructive and often lethal, is listed in level 5, the lowest level.

menstruation and suicide There have been theories put forth based on cases where suicide and attempted suicide happened during the menstrual cycle. There are even such notions in the fragmentary Hippocratic work *Peri parthenion* (on the diseases of maidens). Since every type of person, under almost every conceivable circumstance, commits suicide—it being one of the few facets of American life that is truly democratic—one could say the menstrual cycle sometimes brings on depression which, in turn, makes the potentially suicidal person more vulnerable. But all victims of suicide usually show signs of intense emotional stress or mental disturbance, severe depression being only one symptom. It is evident that menstruation is more likely to be a contributing or precipitating factor than a primary cause. For further information, read J. Birtchnell and S. Floyd's "Attempted Suicide and the Menstrual Cycle—A Negative Conclusion."

mental illness Most people who are diagnosed as mentally ill are not suicidal. In fact, not all victims of suicide may be said to have shown indications of severe emotional or mental disturbance at all. Earl Grollman writes in *Suicide* that "Among those who are psychotic (estimated at less than one quarter of suicidal patients), the rate among schizophrenics and manic-depressives is disproportionately high." But Edwin Shneidman cautions "the causes of suicide are multiple and layered," and mental illness is but one such precipitating factor.

Most suicides are terribly unhappy and suffer deep depression. They suffer feelings of hopelessness, isolation and despair. They may be neurotic or may have a character disorder; but the great majority are not insane. (One study of suicidal patients done by psychiatrist ARI KIEV found that mildly and moderately disturbed patients were greater suicide risks than patients who were psychotic or schizophrenic.) Some experts have suggested that psychosis may even be a substitute for, or a protection against, acting on suicidal impulses.

mercy killing See ASSISTED SUICIDE and EUTHANASIA.

methods of suicide The most commonly used method of suicide in the U.S. is firearms. The ICD (International Classification of Diseases) includes firearms and explosives in the same category, although only 1% of suicide deaths classified thus are due to "explosives." In 1970, 50.1% of the suicides in America were committed with firearms and explosives. By 1980, 57.3% of all suicides (26,869) were committed with firearms and explosives.

The pattern of suicide by method doesn't vary a great deal by race, but does vary considerably by sex. Male patterns of suicide method didn't change much between 1970 and 1980. In 1970 as in 1980, firearms and explosives were the number one method of suicide for males (58.4% and 63.1%, respectively), followed by hanging, and strangulation and suffocation (14.6% and 14.6%, respectively).

There was a noticeable shift, however, between 1970 and 1980 in the most frequent suicide method employed by females. In 1970, poisoning by solids or liquids was the most frequently used method (36.7%), followed by firearms (and explosives) (30.2%); in 1980, firearms and explosives were the methods used most frequently by females (38.6%), followed by poisoning by solids and liquids (26.9%). There was also an increase between 1970 and 1980 in the percent of suicides in which firearms and explosives were used by males and by females in both racial groups.

Centers for Disease Control, *Suicide, Surveillance, 1970-1980 (Atlanta: Department of Health & Human Services, April 1985).*

Middle Ages There were varying social attitudes and practices with respect to suicide during the Middle Ages. Dr. George Rosen, in his interesting chapter entitled "History," in Perlin's *A Handbook for the Study of Suicide*, states that, "Custom based on folk beliefs, ecclesiastical views, and medical theories preceded legal authority in dealing with suicide as a crime."

Antagonism to suicide and its eventual condemnation in the Holy Roman Empire had several sources, according to Rosen. These sources included economics, religion, philosophy, and ultimately the legal world. There was a so-called law of forfeiture that remained in force in England into the 19th century—though it was frequently bypassed through claims of insanity.

On the continent, various municipal law codes did not punish suicide. The *Carolina*, the Criminal Constitution of Charles V, in 1551 confiscated the property of a suicide while the dead victim was under accusation of a felony.

In those times, the corpse of the suicide was often subjected to bizarre indignities and degradations. Many, if not most, of these practices stemmed from religious and magical sources of long-standing. For example, the practice of pinning down the body predates Christianity among Europe's Germanic peoples.

Indeed, states Dr. Rosen, "Official, legal and ecclesiastical attitudes toward suicide remained conservative until well into the eighteenth century; suicide was equated with murder in various parts of Europe, and the corpse was treated accordingly. In France and England, the body was dragged through the streets, head downward on a hurdle, and then hanged on a gallows." The three common penalties—confiscation of property, degradation of the corpse, and refusal of burial in consecrated ground—reflect attitudes toward suicide during the Middle Ages, attitudes prevalent throughout the 18th century. New attitudes toward suicide began to develop and emerge, if only tentatively, during the Renaissance and came out into the open in the 18th century.

The complex of social, religious, economic and legal attitudes regarding suicide during the Middle Ages is discussed under appropriate title headings throughout this work and in the Introduction.

Miletus, the maidens of Miletus was an ancient Greek city in Western Asia Minor (it is now in ruins). The story is told of the maidens of Miletus, who suddenly, with no apparent reason, were seized by a desire to die, and thereupon many hanged themselves. To deal with the bizarre situation, the Milesians passed a law that all maidens who hanged themselves would be carried to the grave naked except for the rope with which they had committed suicide. Deterred by the vision of a shameful, disgraceful burial, the young women ceased in their desire to die and the epidemic was over.

military defeat History is filled with examples of self-destruction to escape the consequences of military defeat. Such examples go back to biblical times as exemplified by Ahitophel, a supporter of Absalom in his revolt against David. When Ahitopel saw that Absalom would be defeated, "he saddled his ass, and went home to his own city. And he set his house in order and hanged himself."

Vulteius, a tribune supporting Caesar in the civil war against Pompey, saw that escape was impossible and called upon his troops to die by their own hands rather than fall alive into the enemy's hands. Not one soldier survived.

The defeat of the Zealots on MASADA and the subsequent slaughter is another example, as is the defeat of FLAVIUS JOSEPHUS that resulted in the suicide of all but one of his men and himself—and his subsequent conversion to a Roman citizen.

And as recently as World War II, a number of German and Japanese military leaders chose suicide rather than surrender to Allied authorities.

Mishima, Yukio Noted Japanese novelist (1925-1970) and a candidate for the Nobel Prize for Literature. He committed HARA-KIRI on November 25, 1970, along with one of his admirers, following the traditional SAMURAI ritual. Mishima had been hailed as a writer of genius upon the publication of his first major work, the autobiographical *Confessions of a Mask* in 1949. He was also a playwright, a master of the ancient martial arts of karate and swordsmanship, and an actor in both his own stage plays and on the screen. Mishima's dramatic suicide was considered not as a rash act, but as a bold gesture planned in great detail months before by a man who envisioned violent death as the ultimate assertion of self.

Marguerite Yourcenar, *Mishima: A Vision of the Void* (New York: Farrar, Straus & Giroux, 1986).

Mithradates King of Pontus (ca. 131 B.C.-63 B.C.), he overran Roman territories throughout Asia Minor, and sent large armies into European Greece. Sulla in Greece and Timbria in Asia defeated Mithradates, and he concluded peace, ca. 84 B.C., giving up his conquests and paying tributes. War broke out again in 74 B.C., ending in his defeat by Pompey in 66 B.C. His plans for a new war miscarried, and he ordered a mercenary to kill him. Mithradates had immunized himself against poisons by years of swallowing small doses. When he finally tried to commit suicide by taking poison, he failed—and then had to order the deed done.

mobility of families Many authorities in the field of suicide believe that, along with the demise of the extended family, along with affluence, the two-paycheck phenomenon, and emphasis on materialism as a way of life, transience—parents climbing the corporate ladder, constantly uprooting the family—figures prominently among the social causes of the rise of America's suicide rate for children. Certainly, moving about every two years or so can be traumatic for young people. They never really have an opportunity to develop lasting friendships. They're asked to enter new neighborhoods, attend new schools—and they often pay a costly price for the high rate of mobility. Friendships, roots, are an important part of a child's emotional and mental health, particularly when the child cannot get along with his or her parents, or the parents are too busy to offer understanding, advice and support. Children today are in sore need of love and understanding, say the experts, not to mention good, solid values.

Monroe, Marilyn American movie actress (1926-1962). She died at age 36 from an apparent overdose of drugs and alcohol. Her death is still debated, but is generally presumed to have been a suicide. Just after the blonde movie star's death, the notes of a number of suicides linked their own deaths to Ms. Monroe's. Subsequent study noted a 12% rise in the number of suicides in both the U.S. and England following her death.

Montaigne, Michel de French writer (1533-1592), mayor of Bordeaux from 1581 to 1585, author of a remarkable series of *Essais* that were exploratory, rather than dogmatic, in character. He broke with the Christian church in its attitude toward suicide, and considered suicide to be a foolish act, but not one that was immoral. He tried to understand and explain in his essays the various situations that might lead people to commit suicide.

Montesquieu, Charles, Baron de la Brede French political philosopher (1689-1755), whose first important work,

The Persian Letters, published anonymously at Amsterdam in 1721, is a bitter satire on the church and the politics of France, including ridicule of the barbarous and unjust European laws on suicide, a practice he defended. In one of his *Lettres Persanes*, written by "Usbek" from Paris to his friend "Ibben" in Smyrna, Montesquieu said, "Life has been given to me as a gift. I can therefore, return it when this is no longer the case . . ."

Montreal Tel-Aide One of a network of Canadian suicide hotlines. Currently the address and phone number are: C.P. 205, Succursale "H," Montreal, Quebec PQ H3G 2K7; phone is (514) 935-1101 or (514) 935-1105. For up-to-date numbers of other hotlines in Canada, consult the phone book or dial 0 or 911.

mood swings as suicide clue Four out of five persons who commit suicide have previously given verbal and/or behavioral "CLUES" of their intention to do so. Among specific behavior changes are sudden mood swings, roller-coaster ups and downs that seem unpredictable. As these highs and lows persist, such behavior is a warning that the person is unhappy, unstable and is being increasingly sapped of both energy and emotional stability.

morality Richard Brandt, PhD, professor and chairman, department of philosophy, University of Michigan at Ann Arbor, writes in chapter three of Perlin's *Handbook for the Study of Suicide* that:

> From the point of view of contemporary philosophy, suicide raises the following distinct questions: whether a person who commits suicide (assuming that there is suicide if and only if there is intentional termination of one's own life) is morally blameworthy, reprehensible, sinful in all circumstances; whether suicide is objectively right or wrong, and in what circumstances it is right or wrong, from a moral point of view; and whether, or in which circumstances, suicide is the best or the rational thing to do from the point of view of the agent's personal welfare.

The question of whether suicide is morally wrong or sinful has been debated and argued since ancient times because the answer to it was thought to be relevant as to how the suicide victim would spend eternity. Today, the practical issue is not as significant, although in an occasional isolated case, a normal funeral service and burial may be denied a person who killed himself "sinfully." As Dr. Brandt notes, "The chief practical issue now seems to be that persons may disapprove of a decedent for having committed suicide, and his friends or relatives may wish to defend his memory against moral charges."

The safest statement one could make on this complex subject is that there has never been, and will probably never be, a complete agreement on the morality of suicide.

Perhaps the most forceful defense of suicide is that put forth by the Jungian analyst James Hillman. He contends that the preventive approaches of law, medicine and theology are major stumbling blocks to an adequate understanding of suicide. He says medicine has not honestly confronted the problem, since physicians are dedicated to the prolonging of life. The legal stand has been: We might kill others in ways and on grounds that do not break the law, but, hypocritically, we can never under any circumstances justify or excuse killing ourselves. And the minister opposes suicide not because it contradicts God, but by "reason" of a fallacious theological dogma.

Hillman views suicide as a meaningful, legitimate way of entering death which can "release the most profound fantasies of the human soul." He quotes David Hume: "When I fall upon my sword, therefore I receive my death equally from the hands of the Deity as if it has proceeded from a lion, a precipice, or a fever."

Sigmund Freud's implicit value judgment, according to Earl A. Grollman, "is that murder is to be disapproved and prevented because it is highly destructive. Suicide, too, is murder in the 180th degree and must also be disapproved and prevented."

Carl Jung, the Swiss psychiatrist who eventually differed from his colleague, Sigmund Freud, believed, as did James Hillman, who was trained at his institute in Switzerland, that the unconscious longing for a spiritual rebirth is crucial to a self-imposed death.

The morality of suicide will surely continue to be debated as long as people destroy themselves. To present all the arguments that convincingly shed light on this question would be a book in and of itself.

Earl A. Grollman, *Suicide: Prevention, Intervention, Postvention* (Boston: Beacon Press, 1971).

More, Sir Thomas English author and statesman (1478-1535), successful at the bar, became Lord Chancellor in 1532. On his refusal to take the oath impugning the authority of the Pope, demanded by Henry VIII, he was beheaded in 1535; for this martyrdom he was canonized in 1935. Sir Thomas More justified suicide as a form of euthanasia in his *Utopia* (written in Latin, 1515-16).

mortality statistics Statistics for a city, state, region or country that are used to establish various general associations between suicide and the personal characteristics of individuals who kill themselves (age, sex, religious or marital status), between suicide and temporal or seasonal events, and between suicide and geographic locations. It is from these general associations that experts gain clues that allow them to test specific hypotheses concerning causes. Rates of suicide are calculated by dividing the number of persons in a group committing suicide by the total number of persons in that group. One major problem in this regard is that of obtaining valid data on completed suicides. Rankings, such as those used by the U.S.'s Centers for Disease Control (CDC), are based on death certificate data and may represent a significant degree of misclassification and subsequent underreporting of suicide as a cause of death. According to officials at the CDC, in a recent survey of 200 medical examiners, more than half felt that the reported number of suicides is probably less than half the true number, CDC puts it this way:

> The limited accuracy and reliability of suicide statistics are, in part, attributable to the lack of a commonly accepted and applied definition of suicide. Judgments by physicians, coroners, and medical examiners play a part in the process by which suicides are classified, but there are no uniform criteria for the classification of suicide to guide these judgments.

(Centers for Disease Control: *Youth Suicide in the U.S., 1970-1980*, issued November 1986.)

Moslems The Moslems have always strongly condemned suicide. The KORAN, the holy scriptures of ISLAM, specifically declares that suicide is a more serious crime than homicide. In committing suicide, one violates his *Kismet*, or destiny, which is preordained by God. The faithful Moslem awaits his destiny; he does not snatch it from the hands of God. While there are some suicides in Moslem countries, strong religious prohibitions have historically kept rates relatively low, or at least kept suicides from being acknowledged and recorded when they did occur.

mothers, working There are many authorities who take the view that the relatively recent phenomenon of "working" mothers may have helped to push the youth suicide rate in the U.S., especially to its current heights. (See also BONDING.)

Mourning and Melancholia Paper written by Sigmund Freud in 1917. He looked inside the individual for the cause of suicide, postulating that people who kill themselves are actually killing the image of the love object within them—a love object they both hate and love and, importantly, identify strongly with. Freud later commented, in 1920, that he doubted that suicide could occur without the repressed desire for either matricide or patricide. Murder, he said, is aggression turned upon another. Suicide is aggression turned upon the self. Freud called suicide "murder in the 180th degree."

Earl A. Grollman, *Suicide: Prevention, Intervention, Postvention* (Boston: Beacon Hill, 1971).

murder, suicide as Dr. KARL MENNINGER, an ardent follower of Freud who built his own theories of suicide on those of the Austrian psychoanalyst, theorized that suicide is a form of murder in which both the murderer and the murdered exist within one person. Menninger said that every person who attempts or completes suicide is driven both consciously and unconsciously by three motives: the wish to kill, the wish to be killed, and the wish to die.

"murder in the 180th degree" The term Sigmund Freud applied to the act of suicide. Freud's value judgment is that murder is to be disapproved and prevented because it is highly destructive. Suicide, too, must also be disapproved and prevented since it is nothing less than "murder in the 180th degree."

Musset, Alfred de French poet, dramatist, novelist (1810-1857). His only novel is *Confessions of a Child of His Age* (1835); autobiographical in structure and content, it mirrors the disenchantment and pessimism of the young writers of the age, the *mal du siècle* ("sickness of the century"). Typical of the idealization of suicide at the time was de Musset's comment, upon seeing a lovely view in nature, "Ah! It would be a beautiful place in which to kill oneself." He was content, however, merely to posture—and write about it.

"Myth of Sisyphus, The" Famous essay by Albert Camus, French journalist, dramatist and novelist, wherein he analyzed the problems of life, such as whether or not life is worth living. Camus wrote: "There is but one truly serious philosophical problem and that is suicide." When he wrote *The Myth of Sisyphus* in 1940, France had just fallen to the Germans, and Camus had suffered a serious personal illness and depressive crisis—but he began with suicide and ended with an affirmation of individual life, in and for itself, desirable because it is "absurd," with no final meaning or metaphysical justification.

myths concerning suicide Over the years, many myths have grown about suicide. In fact, like other once-taboo subjects, fallacies, myths and misconceptions seem intrinsic to suicide. Unfortunately, they often do great damage. Here, as noted by Klagsbrun, are several of the more prevalent and *most inaccurate* myths surrounding the topic of suicide:

1. The person who talks a great deal about suicide won't actually attempt it.
2. A person who tries and fails to commit suicide probably will not attempt suicide again.
3. If a person has been very depressed for a time, says there's nothing to live for,

and wants to die, then abruptly begins to act relaxed and cheerful, one can safely assume that his or her suicidal thoughts have passed.

4. The individual who attempts suicide has got to be crazy.
5. Once someone decides to kill himself, nothing can stop him.
6. Statistics indicate that suicide strikes mostly among the very wealthy because they are so jaded and bored with life.
7. Suicide runs in one's family.
8. Mention suicide to suicidal persons and it gives them ideas.
9. It cannot be suicide, if the person didn't leave a note.
10. They loved each other so much, they wanted to die together.

None of the 10 popular myths about suicide is true, but each one is still widely believed by the majority of people. That's one reason why so few of us know the facts, the disturbing realities of suicide. These misconceptions have a way of growing, along with the suicide rates in many instances, when they are accepted as truths by all too many people. And, as Francine Klagsbrun notes in *Too Young to Die*, "the facts, the appalling facts and figures about young suicides, remain unknown." To arm yourself properly to assist someone, you should know the myths about suicide.

N

National Association of Social Workers Professional association that is a good source of recommendations for suicide information. Encourages the public to call for referrals concerning special help resources. Offers aid in social work, social welfare and social services. Arranges interviews. Supplies statistics, newsletter, and monthly newspaper *HASW News*. Issues policy statements on such issues as immigration, racism, social services, housing, lobbies for social service legislation. Write: 1425 H Street, NW, Suite 600, Washington, DC 20005; phone is (202) 628-6800.

National Center for Health Statistics Part of U.S. Department of Health and Human Services. Primary agency within HHS responsible for gathering and dissemination of data and statistics relating to major health matters in the U.S., with a view to supplying this information to researchers and other professionals concerned with the delivery and quality of health services in the country. Address: 3700 East-West Highway, Room 1-57, Hyattsville, MD 20782; phone is (301) 436-8500.

National Committee on Youth Suicide Prevention A private, nonprofit organization founded in 1984 by Alfred B. DelBello, former lieutenant governor of New York State. NCYSP is a voluntary nationwide network of concerned parents, professionals, and business leaders, with chapters in every state. It works to reduce the number of actual and attempted suicides among America's young people by establishing, funding and supporting programs for youth suicide prevention. Also supports research leading to greater specific knowledge of the problem.

Publishes a National Directory of Youth Suicide Prevention and Intervention Programs which provides a comprehensive listing of community resources available for assistance in dealing with youths suspected to be at risk of suicide. DelBello is NCYSP chairman, Linda Laventhall is the organization's executive director. Address: 67 Irving Place South, New York, NY 10003; phone is (212) 677-6666.

National Directory of Youth Suicide Prevention and Intervention Programs Prepared and edited by Ann Garland, MA, research scientist, and David Shaffer, MD, psychiatry, director, division of child psychiatry, professor of pediatrics and psychiatry, College of Physicians and Surgeons of Columbia University; New York State Psychiatric Institute. The project was supported by The Ittleson Foundation, Inc., and the New York State Office of Mental Health.

National Institute of Alcohol Abuse and Alcoholism (NIAAA) The NIAAA (established in 1971) predates the Alcohol, Drug Abuse and Mental Health Administration (ADAMHA), of which it is a component institute. It is charged with providing leadership, policies and goals for the federal effort in the prevention, control and treatment of alcohol abuse and alcoholism and the rehabilitation of affected individuals. Also publishes periodic special reports to the U.S. Congress on alcohol and health. Address: P.O. Box 2345, Rockville, MD 20852.

National Institute of Mental Health (NIMH) Active over many years in studying the multifaceted problems relating to suicide and suicide prevention; as a division it has always been the main source of funding in research into the etiology and treatment of suicide and the dissemination of information to those involved in working with suicidal persons. In 1986, participated (as cosponser and component agency of the U.S. Department of Health and Human Services) in three conferences to examine the risk factors, prevention and interventions in youth suicide. Address: 5600 Fishers Lane, Room 17-99, Rockville, MD 20857; phone is (301) 443-3673.

National Institute on Drug Abuse (NIDA) NIDA is a component institute (established in 1972) of the Alcohol, Drug Abuse and Mental Health Administration (ADAMHA), which is charged with providing leadership, policies and goals for the federal effort in the prevention, control and treatment of narcotic addiction and drug abuse, and the rehabilitation of affected individuals. Its mandate is much the same as that of the National Institute on Alcohol Abuse and Alcoholism. Address: 5600 Fishers Lane, Rockville, MD 20857.

National Mental Health Association Nonprofit, publicly supported organization serving the entire country as clearinghouse for, among other things, community mental health clinics. Address: 1800 N. Kent Street, Arlington, VA 22209; phone is (703) 528-6405.

National Save-A-Life League Founded in 1906 by Baptist minister Harry M. Warren, as a community center to help prevent suicides. The founder's son, Harry Warren, directs the center today, following many of the guidelines established by his father. The league receives about 8,000 calls per year from persons asking for help. Address: 815 Second Avenue, Suite 409, New York, NY 10017; phone is (212) 736-6191.

National Self-Help Clearinghouse Cofounded in the mid-1970s by Dr. Alan Gartner and Dr. Frank Riessman, both pioneers in the self-help field. The organization provides a complete list of self-help groups nationwide to assist persons wishing to contact such groups. Offers a variety of services, and publishes reports, papers and a newsletter. Address: Graduate School and University Center, City University of New York, 33 West 42nd Street, Room 1227, New York, NY 10036; phone is (212) 840-1259.

Native Americans It has long been believed that suicides occur at a higher rate among the Native Americans than in any other cultural subgroup of the U.S. population. John P. Webb and William Willard, writing "Six American Indian Patterns of Suicide" in Farberow's *Suicide in Different Cultures*, question this and cite two important reasons: (1) the difficulty in discerning any one common Native American suicide pattern; and (2) the absence of any report of suicide incidence in many studies of Native American groups. Say Webb and Willard: "It is curious that the pronouncement of a high suicide incidence among all American Indians has been so uncritically accepted."

The authors point out that statistics, misleading as they can be without some knowledge of the various Native American groups' cultures, do show that "some reservations have a suicide rate 10 times the national average." But they maintain it is erroneous to attribute one suicide pattern to all Native Americans. It is their view that "most works on suicide have pointed to American Indians as having a noble past, a dismal present, and no future. These observations cannot help but shape public policy and, more importantly, the beliefs of Indians concerning their self-value."

Webb and Willard conclude that there is no one pattern of suicide among the Native Americans and that the cultures of Native American groups are not necessarily "disturbed forms of the Euro-American pattern." The writers take the position that it would be much more instructive if researchers and analysts would study the creative adaptations of the Native Americans "that have allowed them to continue to exist as culturally distinctive groups." The Webb-Willard essay notwithstanding, in 1972 the National Center for Health Statistics reported that the three fastest-rising causes of death among Native Americans, in order of frequency, were cirrhosis of the liver, suicide and homicide, all of which could be traced to alcoholism. The same report estimated that the incidence of drinking among Indians was double that among the general population.

Moreover, from 1976 to 1978, the suicide rate for Native Americans age 15 to 24 was more than three times the national rate for that age group, and in 1977 the homicide rate for Native Americans age 24 to 34 was 3.3 times the national rate (Indian Health Service). It has been estimated that 30% of the male Native American population and 15% of the female Native American population may be alcoholic (Jones). There have been numerous attempts to explain why the problem of alcoholism is so great among Native Americans, and in these attempts, there has been a tendency to ignore the diversity of the population. Native Americans in North America comprise a large number of distinct peoples with unique cultures and world views (O'Brien and Chafetz).

The major cause of drinking problems and high rates of both homicide and suicide among Native Americans in the U.S. and Canada is probably socio-cultural stress. As O'Brien and Chafetz note, there is a lack of identification with the ways of white society and a rejection of its goals. Indian traditions have been weakened and family relations disturbed; the elderly no longer enjoy the same prestige and guiding role they once did. Native Americans today experience strong feelings of powerlessness and anxiety because of conflicts between their ways and the ways of the white man. They have been placed on reservations, their religions and cultures have been undermined, and their children have been placed in schools where non-Indian traditions are taught.

Urban Native Americans have their own set of special problems, living in a setting where they are generally disadvantaged, economically, educationally and socially, and where they do not have the support systems, such as families and familiar customs, found on reservations.

In late summer and early fall of 1985, a chain of suicides claimed the lives of nine young tribesmen on the Wind River (Wisconsin) Indian Reservation. Elders tried to form closer ties with their troubled youth by reviving traditions, such as a pipe ceremony last held in 1918.

Mental health experts believe the youths who killed themselves—all by hanging—probably suffered from a lack of cultural identity and low self-esteem. Denice Romersa-Kulia, director of the Shoshone-Arapahoe Indian Child Welfare Program, says, "That is a problem for all our youth. I think Native Americans as a whole suffer from a lack of self-esteem. But the (tribal) council has made a commitment to address the needs of these people." They have now formed a youth services committee, made up of representatives of both Arapahoe and Shoshone councils of elders to work as a clearinghouse for youth activities. Romersa-Kulia notes that recent research shows a strong feeling of tradition among adolescents makes them feel more secure. "That doesn't mean," she says, "that things have to be as strict as they were 100 years ago. This is a matter of sharing tradition. We now have a program where youths and the elders spend a couple of weeks together in the mountains. That is another way to let them see how their forefathers handled things."

The tribes also have formed a youth council designed to give young people a voice in tribal affairs. Officials see this as a way to develop leadership and instill pride among the remote reservation's younger residents. Plans are progressing for a basketball game to raise money for a Native American scholarship fund, plus a Native American art festival featuring noted Indian artists.

The strategy appears to be having a positive effect; there have been 10 suicide attempts since then, but no suicides. And the number of native American youths being referred to social workers for counseling is now down, say authorities. Dr. Brian Miracle, who has helped evaluate high-risk youths at the Pine Ridge Hospital in Lander, Wyoming, says "The kids all of a sudden recognized that they were not alone."

The two-million-acre reservation's barren plains and rolling hills normally appear inhospitable, but 6,000 people live there. It is located on a windswept expanse of central Wyoming, about 100 miles southeast of Yellowstone National Park.

The most promising methods of handling problems concerning alcoholism, suicide and homicide probably should include Native Americans in the planning and implementation of their own programs on a community (tribal) basis. It is important, as O'Brien and Chafetz point out, for therapists, social workers and counselors to be sensitive to tribal cultures and variations from tribe to tribe. Interestingly, some specifically-Indian ALCOHOLICS ANONYMOUS groups have integrated elements of their traditional cultures into the AA format and setting, and they have achieved more success than standard AA programs.

Robert O'Brien and Morris Chafetz, MD, *The Encyclopedia of Alcoholism* (New York: Facts On File, 1982).

Bruce Johansen, "The Tepees Are Empty and the Bars Are Full," *Alcoholism*, 1:2 (November/December 1980), 33-38.

Jim Angell, "Tribes Try to Counter a Series of Suicides," Associated Press, December 27, 1985; dateline: Fort Washakie, Wyoming.

Nazi concentration camps Despite the heroic defense mechanisms brought into play by those persons imprisoned in the infamous Nazi concentration camps—what Dr. Robert Jay Lifton has described as a "psychic closing-off"—many committed suicide. Thousands of Jews from Eastern Europe, for example, were sent to TREBLINKA to be exterminated. Most realized they were without hope and destined never to leave the camp alive. They were numb to everyone and everything around them. Then, one by one, people began committing suicide and, writes Francine Klagsbrun in *Too Young to Die*, "their deaths served as an affirmation of their freedom to control their own lives and deaths." These suicidal acts led to a solidarity of sorts, and those who chose to remain alive helped those who wanted to die quickly. "These flickerings of friendship," writes Klagsbrun in *Too Young to Die*, "marked the beginning of a rebellion that later took the form of open revolt, one of the few such revolts that occurred in a concentration camp."

There are no reliable statistics available that reveal just how many people opted for suicide while subjected to the monstrous brutalities of life in the Nazi camps.

negative (passive) euthanasia Where life-sustaining treatment for the individual, competent or incompetent, is removed or refused, allowing the person to die. This phenomenon was dramatized by the famous and controversial KAREN ANN QUINLAN case. Most doctors who have acknowledged patient needs have condoned passive euthanasia for the hopelessly ill who wished to be allowed to die. Roughly more than half the articles on euthanasia that appeared in the *Cumulative Index Medicus* were concerned with some aspect of passive euthanasia—in several cases, both passive and active means were addressed.

Efforts are currently underway to introduce the Humane and Dignified Death Act in California, which will, if passed, allow a physician not only to switch off life-support systems, but also to take the life of the dying patient upon a competent request.

Nero Roman emperor (37-68 A.D.), who fled Rome with enemies hard on his heels. He took refuge in a villa several miles outside the city, where four faithful servants insisted that he commit suicide honorably, rather than fall into the hands of those who had seized power in Rome. As he watched the men prepare his funeral pyre, he muttered through tears, "Qualis artifex pereo!" ("How great an artist dies here!") Nero actually had himself killed by an attendant. During his lifetime, he had caused several suicides, including those of his teacher SENECA, the poet Lucan, and Petronius, thought to be the author of the *Satyricon*. These were all compulsory suicides in lieu of execution.

Netherlands See HOLLAND.

New Jersey Among those states ranked by suicide rates per 100,000 population (1983), New Jersey, despite its dense population, was far below the national average that year, with a rate of 7.5 suicides per 100,000. The U.S. suicide rate in 1983 was 12.1 per 100,000. In terms of number of actual reported suicides, the state ranked 19th, with 564 suicides.

New Testament According to medical historian Dr. George Rosen, biblical suicides are rare. There is only one instance reported in the New Testament, that being the death of JUDAS ISCARIOT, reported simply and briefly in the Book of Matthew, 27:5—"he went and hanged himself."

New York City Psychiatrist Herbert Hendin's study of black suicide in New York

City (in the late 1960s) revealed that, among blacks of both sexes between the ages of 20 and 35, suicide was "more of a problem than it was among the white population of the same age." In fact, in New York City, young black men between the ages of 20 and 35 kill themselves at twice the rate of young white men. Similar trends have appeared in other urban centers. After age 45, the white suicide rate rises to a total level much higher than that of the black rate. The cause of so many young black suicides, says Hendin in *Black Suicide*, may be traced to rage, self-hatred, and the frustration of ghetto living. With a sense of hopelessness and despair that life holds little for them, young blacks—particularly males—kill themselves while still young. Incidentally, jumping as a suicide method is relatively high in New York City for whites as well as blacks; this because of the proximity of tall buildings in the city, perhaps.

In 1967, Paul Friedman's "Suicide among Police: A Study of 93 Suicides among New York City Policemen, 1934-1940," indicated that nine out of every 10 of the police in the study group killed themselves with revolvers.

news coverage (See MEDIA.) Discussed at length under the heading MEDIA, the ongoing debate is whether photographs, movies and television in particular strike responsive notes in suicidal people. While this may be so, generally speaking, the media noted above do not evoke responsive notes. The drama of TV, for instance, seems pretty much tailored to fit predispositions that are already extant in the national audience. Dr. Samuel C. Klagsbrun, medical director of Four Winds Hospital, Katonah, New York, and associate clinical professor in psychiatry at Columbia University College of Physicians and Surgeons, says the way in which the subject (of suicide) is handled "is the telling feature in figuring out outcomes—I don't think we encourage suicide by talking about it."

On January 22, 1987, R. Budd Dwyer, Pennsylvania state treasurer, convicted for bribery a month before, shot and killed himself at a news conference in his office in Harrisburg, the state capitol. Cameras provided a graphic record for newspapers and television, facing the news media with a decision of whether to use the images. A few affiliate TV stations used some, but not all, of the graphic footage. The major networks did not show the graphic footage, but did report the incident. The Associated Press transmitted a series of photographs of the suicide to its members with an alert as to their nature.

Nietzsche, Friedrich Wilhelm German philosopher (1844-1900), early influenced by Schopenhauer, then by a close friendship with Wagner, with whom he broke (1878), believing him tainted by a decadent morality. Profoundly moral and religious, Nietzsche was regarded in his own time as an Antichrist because of his rejection of time-honored values. He often contemplated suicide and wrote, "The thought of suicide is a strong consolation: it helps to get over many a bad night." He did not, however, advocate suicide as a solution to all life's problems, saying, "Suffering is no argument against life."

night (darkness), effect on suicide rate There are persistent myths that tell us that many suicides occur during nighttime. One California study reported that 14% of suicides occur between 9 A.M. and 10 A.M., while 13% occur between 1 P.M. and 2 P.M. EDWIN SHNEIDMAN and Norman L. Farberow, co-founders of the Los Angeles Suicide Prevention Center, found that significantly more suicides do occur between noon and 6 P.M. and significantly fewer between midnight and 6 A.M. It should be noted that it is often difficult to determine precisely when a suicide actually took place. Researchers admit they must sometimes discard cases from their samples because they cannot pinpoint when a suicide occurred. For instance, if a person ingests a lethal dose of drugs at 10 A.M., but doesn't "die" until 3 P.M., when did the person commit suicide?

Night, Mother Marsha Norman's Pulitzer prize-winning drama about a young woman, an epileptic, who tells her mother at the beginning of the play, "I'm going to kill myself." She then proceeds to get her mother's life in order before she commits the act. During the tense, controversial 90-minute work, the mother, Thelma, strongly but ineffectually tries to dissuade her daughter from using the gun. The daughter is a person who has never realized any of her dreams and finds herself in a vacuum. It is a two-character close-up of suicide—not the actual act, but the motivations behind Tessie's carefully-planned self-destruction.

nomia (morality) The French social philosopher EMILE DURKHEIM, exponent of the sociological perspective as it relates to suicide, said that an "integrated" social situation is one where people are strongly attached to society's governing rules by a sense of moral obligation or structural interdependence—or both—and it is characterized by strict sanctions for breaking the rules. As Ronald W. Maris writes in "Sociology," chapter 5 of Perlin's *A Handbook for the Study of Suicide*, "A state of morality (nomia) prevails when individual interests are subordinated to the common interest." Durkheim believed that "the suicide rate varies inversely with the integration of social groups of which the individual forms a part."

North Carolina In 1983, the state ranked 24th among states in suicide rates per 100,000 population, with a 12.3 rate. In ranking by number of suicides in 1983, North Carolina was ninth, with 748 suicides reported.

North Dakota The state in 1983 ranked 44th by suicide rates per 100,000 population, with a 9.8 rate; ranked by actual reported suicides that year, it was 48th, with a 67 total.

Northern Ireland See GREAT BRITAIN.

Norway On the basis of relatively high rates in Sweden and Denmark but low rates in Norway, Hendin investigated (see his *Suicide in Scandinavia*) and discovered different personality structures in persons in the three countries. Hendin describes Norway's suicides as "moral" (in contrast to Sweden's "performance" suicides and Denmark's "dependency loss" suicides), stemming from guilt aroused by aggressive antisocial behavior occurring in a puritanical setting. There appear to be true variations in suicide among countries; however, experts warn that different places often have very different methods of defining and reporting suicide and this presents problems when comparing rates among countries.

According to the World Health Organization (WHO) 1984 statistics, Norway has a suicide rate per 100,000 population of 14.5 (males 21.9 and females 7.2). The age group with the highest suicide rate per 100,000 population is 55 to 64; it had a 25.8 rate (males 36.8, females 15.3).

Notebooks The French journalist, dramatist, novelist Albert Camus wrote in his *Notebooks*: "There is only one liberty, to come to terms with death. After which, everything is possible." Camus was awarded the Nobel Prize for Literature in 1957. He died at age 47 in 1960, the result of an automobile accident near Sens, France.

notes, suicide EDWIN S. SHNEIDMAN and Norman L. Farberow, in a study to learn more about how suicidal persons relate to others at the final moments before death, had a select group of people compose suicide notes as though they were about to commit suicide. They compared contents and vocabulary of these fake notes with actual suicide notes taken from the Los Angeles County coroner. They discovered that the real notes contained more anger, more hostile feelings, and more desire for revenge than the false notes. The genuine notes also included more concrete instructions to survivors and used specific names of people, places and things. The notes, it seems, served as a means of reaching out to specific individuals, of trying to influence and even control them after the writers' deaths. Later Shneidman developed an extensive system for analysis of the psycho-logic of the notes.

Farberow and Shneidman coined the term "cry for help" to describe many suicidal acts. As Francine Klagsbrun points out in *Too Young to Die*, however, "the same concept of a cry, of a message being sent and an impact being made, often can extend to the death act itself." In such instances, suicide is a way of communicating with others after all other forms of communication have been blocked or cease to exist.

Research indicates that somewhere between 10 and 35% of suicide victims leave notes.

Nouvelle, Heloise, La Novel by the French philosopher Jean-Jacques Rousseau in which he emphasizes the natural right people have to end their lives—as long as they cause no harm to others by doing so. He did establish one condition: People who have responsibilities to others should not commit suicide. *La Nouvelle Heloise*, published in 1761, was highly successful.

"Now" generation and suicide Adolescents are often immature, impatient and impulsive. The adolescent has a "right now" mind-set. He or she may find it difficult to comprehend the fact, as psychiatrist Mary Giffin points out, that "three years is a short time in the scheme of things." The adolescent thinks about today, right now, and not next year in high school. As one youngster put it: "Time seemed so long to us—to get through a week, even a day!" In this context, young people are easily "stressed out" by social or academic failures, by divorce decisions decimating parents' marriages, by trying to compete successfully for the best schools, by the constant threat of nuclear war. Today's children live with the terrifying knowledge that their world can be annihilated within minutes—and at any time. They learn quickly that the world's resources are now limited and the environment is being despoiled. They see that terrorism, wars and government scandal are leading to adult disillusionment with the country's leaders, and it's all a part of their daily existence. The result is often disturbed attitudes toward relationships, school and the future.

There are some authorities who attribute the rising teen suicide rate, at least in significant part, to a loss of belief in the future, not just because of the bomb, but because of this country's monumental national debt, the troubling trade deficit and the uncertain status of the economy in general.

The adolescent and teen years are recognized by mental health authorities as a time of sharp and rapid emotional ups-and-downs. Shocking as it is, some young people often look on suicide as a way out of all the striving to cope, as the ultimate rebellion against a pervasive sense of chaos and disorder.

nuclear war, threat of Young people today often say that they "cannot imagine" what the future will bring. In truth, many children imagine only too well. But they do not deny the greatest issue of our time—the threat of nuclear annihilation. It is this literal, yet unresolved threat which underlies their daily lives and undermines their quality of life. It hovers in the background noise of today's generation; by ignoring nuclear war, they can only live life in the present, the "now." The hideous prospect of the nuclear threat affects everything they do and produces fears that cause the stifling dislocation, disconnection and loss of meaning that young people experience so much of the time.

As Edwin Shneidman says in *Definitions of Suicide*, "At the moment of committing suicide, the individual may feel he controls the world—and by his death can bring it down. At least he controls his own destiny, and realistically typically touches and influences the destinies of at least several others." And then he adds, significantly, "the great loss in suicide is the loss of self."

If we do not prevent global suicide, then, in Professor Shneidman's words, "all the other items on our life-saving agenda will not matter because the agenda itself, and the agenda makers along with it, will have disappeared."

nurses Data on the relation between occupation and suicide are very sparse and tend to be mixed. In general it seems that those engaged in work-giving nurturance and help to others (including nurses, social workers, physicians, policemen) tend to have higher suicide rates than most other professions or occupations.

As for their role as a key segment of the "gatekeeping" process, nurses, along with doctors, social workers, clergymen and others, have the unique opportunity of being in a position to identify and improve the potential suicide's dangerous behavior situation. The nurse, for instance, who works with a family physician is of central importance in both suicide treatment and reduction. She is often in a position to establish a meaningful relationship with the distraught person. Yet, too often many nurses, not unlike their doctor counterparts, are restricted by insufficient time and/or lack of suicide prevention-intervention knowledge. As Rabbi Earl A. Grollman notes in *Suicide*, more educational process is needed for "gatekeepers" (such as nurses)—more adequate training in the recognition and management of persons bent on killing themselves. "Such training," writes Rabbi Grollman, "would ensure the development of a cadre of understanding people who could later recognize suicidal threats, and thereby prevent the loss of precious life." (See OCCUPATIONS AND SUICIDE RELATIONSHIPS.)

Earl A. Grollman, *Suicide: Prevention, Intervention, Postvention (Boston: Beacon Press, 1971).*

O

obsession with death, as suicide clue Psychiatrist HERBERT HENDIN in *The Age of Sensation*, uses the expression "drawn to death as a way of life" to describe people (in this case, young students) who reveal this suicidal clue. Another psychiatrist, MARY GIFFIN, says, "indeed, the only love affair in a suicidal child's life may be his love affair with death." Poets SYLVIA PLATH and ANNE SEXTON, both of whom killed themselves, appeared to have a romance with death. Sexton, who committed suicide in 1974, wrote "Wanting to Die" (a poem published in 1966) in which she describes her desire to die as "the almost unnameable lust."

Newspaper columnist and author James Wechsler recalled that his son displayed suicidal gestures, such as almost walking into a moving car, driving his motor bike into a bus, and almost strangling himself on the strings of his guitar. In his book, *In a Darkness*, Wechsler says his son's deathwish remained strong—until Michael did kill himself. Wechsler wrote "... how often we failed to say or do some things that might (or might not) have mattered."

occupations and suicide relationships The relationship of occupation to suicide has received remarkably little attention. What has been done has resulted in sometimes opposite conclusions, which may not be surprising in the light of the complexity in both fields. One of the early contentions was that suicide occurred relatively more frequently among the higher-level occupations (as a result of more stress and greater impact of job loss) and less frequently among the lower-level occupations (accustomed to more frequent job change). In partial contradiction, one study in England reported high suicide rates in the professional group, but also reported high rates among the unskilled workers.

A thorough study of U.S. data by Karcher and Linden in 1982, using standardized mortality ratios (SMR, the number of observed deaths divided by the number of expected deaths in any group multiplied by 100) and 12 major occupational categories found that the professional group had the lowest suicide rate while business and repair services, construction, agriculture, forestry and fisheries, mining, and entertainment and recreation had the highest rates. A similar study of suicides in Sacramento County, California, reported the same findings, an inverse relationship between occupational class and suicide, that is, the higher the level of occupational class the fewer suicides.

Nevertheless, Karcher and Linden also reported that further analysis among the professional class of the suicides of subgroups yielded contradictory results. Thus, the medical personnel, legal and engineering subgroups indicated higher than average rates, while educational, welfare, religious and membership organizations reported very low rates. There is evidence, too, that the suicide rate among college students is higher than that among youths not in college.

Herbert Hendin writes in *Suicide in America*: "Demographic evidence suggests that a large birth cohort manifests increased stress throughout life and high suicide rates at every age level." It is a phenomenon affected by so many complex social and psychological forces that relation of suicide to occupation, profession, age, marital status, mental illness, whatever, still needs to be researched and studied in more detail and depth.

Charles J. Karcher and Leonard L. Linden, "Is Work Conducive to Self-destruction," *Suicide and Life-Threatening Behavior*, 12:3 (Fall 1982) 151-175.

Oklahoma Oklahoma ranks 15th among our states by suicide rates per 100,000 population, but is 25th in terms of total number of reported suicides (436). Figures are for year 1983.

old age and suicide In the United States, suicide rates remain highest (see figures in AGE) among the elderly. The rate for those 75 or older is almost two times the rate of that among the young (whose increased rate of self-destruction over the last three decades has received widespread attention). This disturbing rate increase has been receiving much attention (since 1980).

Among the many reasons why the suicide rate is so high for the elderly, say experts, is the isolation and loneliness that leads to despair, also boredom, depression, uselessness, loss of loved ones, economic hardships, general feeling of unhappiness with life, and persons who suffer from a psychological affliction, from loss of purpose and a sense of meaningfulness after retirement and separation from family and friends. But another important factor may be the acceptance by more and more people of the option of "rational suicide" for those in advanced terminal illness or serious incurable physical illness. In her thoughtful examination of this step, author DORIS PORTWOOD calls it *COMMON SENSE SUICIDE: THE FINAL RIGHT*. *DEREK HUMPHRY*, co-founder with his second wife, Ann, of the HEMLOCK SOCIETY, is author of *LET ME DIE BEFORE I WAKE*, an actual guide for "self-deliverance for the dying."

Many elderly people have indicated clearly that they no longer want to be burdens, according to Portwood, and wish to end their lives with a certain dignity and grace while they are still aware. "Today," writes Portwood, "the needs of the individual and those of the social community appear to merge, in an economic sense, on the question of old-age suicide. A planned departure that serves oneself, one's family, and also the state surely is worthy of decent consideration."

Among professionals in the field of suicide, both clinicians and researchers, older people have not received the attention their group deserves. DR. HERBERT HENDIN writes in *Suicide in America*: "This neglect stems in part from the mistaken assumption that little can be done to treat older people who are suicidal, an assumption that is related to and reflects our general neglect of the mental health of older people. In addition, since the suicide rate among older people, although high, has been relatively constant, it has not created the sudden alarm accompanying the dramatic increase in youthful suicide."

Hendin seems to believe that "culture and character" play even greater roles than economic circumstances in determining suicide in older people. One fact seems clear: The steady increase in the number of the aged who, as noted, contribute such a high percentage of suicides, will make it difficult to prevent a continued rise in the suicide rate in the U.S., and throughout the world. This is especially the case if the suicide rate among young persons resumes its climb.

Omaha, Nebraska (cluster suicides) Three students from the same high school in Omaha committed suicide within a five-day period in early February 1986. School official Rene Hlavac said, "It reflects an illness in our community." Students wore paper hearts that said "Choose Life" as they jammed the high school auditorium to discuss the tragedy. Psychologists and counselors visited the Bryan High School to talk to students and teachers. Counselors also visited the homes of students who teachers, classmates or counselors said showed signs of depression. Parents held a meeting to talk about suicide prevention.

The Omaha tragedy is an example of the suicide "cluster" phenomenon—chains of deaths among young people—that appears in recent years to be devastating more and more communities. (See also CLUSTER SUICIDES.)

Omega: Journal of Death and Dying Quarterly publication, published by Baywood Publishing Company, Inc., 120 Marine Street, P.O. Box D, Farmingdale, NY 11735. Editor is Robert J. Kastenbaum, PhD, Department of Communications, Stauffer Hall, Arizona State University, Tempe, AZ 85281.

On Suicide Essay written by DAVID HUME discussing the difficulties and contradictions in moral arguments for and against the act of suicide. The famed Scottish philosopher's essay was published following his death in 1776, but then was quickly suppressed. The short essay argues against the position of suicide as a crime. "The life of a man," wrote Hume, "is of no greater importance to the universe than that of an oyster." The man who commits suicide, according to Hume, does not disrupt the larger order of the universe. Hume adds, that person "does no harm to society; he only ceases to do good; which if it is an injury is of the lowest kind." Other 18th-century philosophers agreed with David Hume's stance that suicide is the individual's moral right.

Oppenheim, David E. In 1910 this prominent Viennese educator met, in Vienna, Austria, with members of the Vienna Psychoanalytical Society to try to discover the mysterious causes of suicide among that city's high school students. Luminaries in attendance included Alfred Adler, Wilhelm Stekel, and the "Founder of Psychoanalysis," Sigmund Freud. Freud later said of the April 27th meeting (formally called to discuss "Suicide in Children") that little was accomplished and indicated that much more work in this area needed to be done.

Ordinary People Novel, later made as a movie, by Judith Guest. It deals with the aftermath of a teenage suicide attempt after a 17-year-old had failed in trying to save his older brother in a boating accident. No one in the upper-middle-class family talks about the accident, but young Conrad is filled with "SURVIVOR GUILT." He feels that his parents, particularly his mother, blame him for not being able to save his brother, Buck. He feels his parents wish that he'd been the son to die, since his brother seemed to be the favored child.

The parents of this seemingly all-American family miss all the suicidal clues and signals. Conrad attempts suicide with a razor blade. The turning point comes only when Conrad realizes he wasn't guilty of causing his brother's death and that nobody, in fact, was guilty, and that he didn't have to be the perfect son. The novel gives readers realistic insights into the problems of the suicidal.

Origen of Alexandria As a youth, Origen (ca. 185-ca. 254 A.D.) experienced the martyrdom of his father in 202 A.D. and was possessed by a desire to suffer the same fate. His mother prevented him from self-destruction, but he still victimized himself through self-castration—to become a eunuch for the kingdom of heaven. As historian George Rosen notes: "Perhaps his self-castration . . . may be interpreted as a symbolic surrogate for voluntary death." After years of teaching in Caesarea in Palestine, he died as a result of tortures inflicted during the Decian persecution.

Osbourne, Ozzy Former leader of the rock group, Black Sabbath, that made the album "Speak to the Devil" and a macabre song called "Suicide Solution," which contains such lines as, "Suicide is the only way out; don't you know what it's really about?"

In October 1984, John McCollum, 19, a fan of Osbourne's, put on the album and shot himself in the head with his father's pistol. Osbourne and CBS Records were sued in Los Angeles Superior Court by the suicide's parents. Osbourne, 37, said his lyrics were misinterpreted, that "They're really anti-suicide, anti-drink and drugs." McCollum's father, Jack, charged that the music was an "invocation to the devil." On August 7, 1986, Judge John Cole dismissed the lawsuit saying that the McCollum attorney failed to show why Osbourne's songs should not be provided First Amendment protection. Judge Cole was quoted by the wire services as saying: "Trash can be given First Amendment protection, too."

Ostrow, Mortimer See SIDNEY FURST.

Otto, Emperor German emperor referred to by GOETHE as the one person who, in the writer's youth, he had so admired. Since the Emperor Otto had stabbed himself, Goethe decided that if he were not brave enough to die in such a manner, he wasn't brave enough to die at all. Goethe wrote: "By this conviction, I saved myself from the purpose, or indeed, more properly speaking, from the whim of suicide." Goethe, who authored the autobiographical novel *The Sorrows of Young Werther*—acclaimed all over Europe, with its themes of martyrdom, unrequited love and excessive sensibility—died at the age of 83, asking for more light.

outpatient treatment Many community psychiatry services in England and more recently across the U.S. are set up to provide competent, effective outpatient treatment. Such a service, performed properly, enhances the community psychiatry services' potential as a suicide prevention and intervention service. There are critics of such outpatient treatment and care, of course, but there is little evidence available to support such a criticism as: Patients are a danger to themselves or to the outside community. In such a service, it is not only possible, but desirable to have the cooperation of relatives and other members of the patient's household.

For an excellent discussion of this matter, read Peter Sainsbury's "Community Psychiatry," chapter 9 in Perlin's *A Handbook for the Study of Suicide*. Sainsbury is an MD, and director of research, Medical Research Council, Clinical Psychiatry Unit, Graylingwell Hospital, Chichester, England.

overprotection, "smothering" Overprotection or "smothering" often results in a lack of self-confidence and in feelings of uselessness. Overprotective parents instill in children a feeling of being unable to cope. Dr. MARY GIFFIN theorizes that "When trouble arises, they are not prepared to face it. They certainly can't talk about it. Frequently, suicide turns up as an answer."

Giffin believes that overprotective parents talk *at* their children rather than *to* them. She notes in *A Cry for Help* that "Parents like these often don't listen to their children or respond meaningfully because they are too preoccupied with telling them what to do and how to do it."

Being overly protective of children can prove just as disastrous to the young person's emotional and psychological stability as being extremely neglectful.

P

parasuicide Term introduced by Norman Kreitman, a psychiatrist of the Unit for Epidemiological Studies in Psychiatry, Royal Edinburgh Hospital, Edinburgh, Scotland in 1969 in an effort to supply a word which indicated a behavioral analogue and thus avoid the troubling problem of deciding whether intention, a psychological factor, was present. Kreitman, recent winner of the Dublin Award given by the AAS for outstanding services and contributions in the field of suicide prevention, defined parasuicide as a non-fatal act in which an individual deliberately causes self-injury or ingests a substance in excess of any prescribed or generally recognized therapeutic dosage. The term has been suggested as a replacement for the phrase "attempted suicide" which was often difficult to decide in terms of intention, consciousness, extent of injury, extent of effort to injure, differentiation from substance abuse, and other factors.

Norman Kreitman, *Parasuicide* (London: Wiley, 1977).

Parents Anonymous Founded in 1970 by Jolly K. and Leonard L. Lieber, then a young psychiatric social worker, Parents Anonymous offers help to parents who feel they are abusing or neglecting their children (physically, sexually, or emotionally). Members work in a mutual-aid environment to establish a healthy co-existence between themselves and their children. Over 600 chapters nationally hold meetings where membership is voluntary and fees are by donations. PA headquarters are at: 2810 Artesia Blvd., Redondo Beach, CA 90278; phone is (213) 371-3501. (See also CHILD ABUSE.)

parents of suicides, self-help for A suicide almost always concerns several other people. As the experts have noted, the parents feel most responsible. This is especially true when a teenager or young adult commits suicide; parents blame themselves regardless of what may have caused the tragic action. SURVIVOR GUILT, a major factor in the suffering of a young person after the suicide of a parent, is also usually strong in the case of surviving parents. While nobody can minimize the impact of a suicide, and nobody can wholly free survivor parents of the anger, guilt, remorse and pain they feel, there are today a number of self-help groups nationwide that are set up to help parents (as well as other survivors) do the mourning essential to getting on with their lives and saving both themselves and their families from further destruction.

EDWIN S. SHNEIDMAN coined the term "POSTVENTION" to describe this help. It means giving survivors the kind of support they need immediately after a suicide and, in time, assisting them in coming to terms with the tragedy that has struck them.

Aside from professional help provided by doctors, psychiatrists and psychologists, surviving parents need the sharing, caring and understanding of others who have been there. They need to be able to talk with other people who will not judge them, not patronize them, but through their own experiences know how to listen intelligently. Members of these self-help groups know what the other person is going through, have discovered the age-old principle of mutual aid—of sharing common problems and solving them together.

For information, write to: National Committee on Youth Suicide Prevention, 67 Irving Place South, New York, NY 10003 (they publish a *National Directory of Youth Suicide Prevention and Intervention Programs*); the National Self-Help Clearinghouse, 33 West 42nd Street, Room 1227, New York, NY 10036; or Youth Suicide National Center, 1825 Eye St., N.W., Suite 400, Washington, DC 20006; phone is (202) 429-2016.

partial suicide Term sometimes used for self-mutilation. This is, properly speaking, a "quasi-suicidal attempt," or as Edwin S. Shneidman notes most accurately, "non-suicidal attempts."

Peau de Chagrin, La Essay written by HONORE DE BALZAC in 1831 to support the Romantic dogma that the intense, true feeling of life does not survive into one's middle years. Balzac said the alternatives were "To kill the emotions and so live on to old age, or to accept the martyrdom of our passions and die young. . ." Interestingly, Balzac died in 1850 at age 51.

Penitentials Written by Egbert, archbishop of York, the *Penitentials* appeared in the mid-eighth century, and made of the insane an exception to the church position refusing burial in consecrated ground to suicides. There was, throughout the medieval period, a growing recognition that mental and emotional disorder may lead to suicide.

Peri parthenion Fragmentary Hippocratic work, *Peri parthenion* (*On the Diseases of Maidens*) comments on mental symptoms, including suicidal tendencies, to which young girls are prone if they suffer menstrual problems. These symptoms, particularly as related to suicidal behavior, have been interpreted, according to Dr. George Rosen, writing in Perlin's *A Handbook for the Study of Suicide*, as "an example of psychopathic collective behavior." (See also MILETUS, THE MAIDENS OF.)

Perlin, Seymour, MD Editor of the definitive collection, *A Handbook for the Study of Suicide*. Dr. Perlin is professor of psychiatry and behavioral science, Department of Psychiatry, George Washington University Medical Center in Washington, D.C. He is also senior research scholar, Center for Bioethics, the Joseph and Rose Kennedy Institute, Washington, D.C., and formerly professor of psychiatry, director, Suicidology Program, School of Medicine, The Johns Hopkins University, Baltimore, Maryland. He is a consulting editor to *Suicide and Life-Threatening Behavior*, the official publication of the AMERICAN ASSOCIATION OF SUICIDOLOGY and serves as chairman, the board of directors, YOUTH SUICIDE NATIONAL CENTER, in Washington, D.C.

personality A number of studies have shown that a large percentage of young suicidals—both attempters and completers—have come from disrupted or disturbed home environments, lacking in stability and support. For instance, parents may be divorced, constantly quarreling, or one or both parents absent because of death or desertion. Sometimes a parent is alcoholic, or a child abuser. Children who grow up in these kinds of unstable or broken homes can feel abandoned and lonely, filled with resentment and anger at both the parent(s) who have hurt them and at themselves.

Psychologists often stress that broken homes are the essential, underlying cause for many kinds of antisocial behavior in young people, including juvenile violence, vandalism, delinquency, drug and alcohol abuse and, it sometimes follows, suicide. As Francine Klagsbrun notes in *Too Young to Die*, "The degree to which a child becomes depressed, isolated and lonely within such an environment influences the extent to which that child becomes openly suicidal." She points out that these precursors to suicide do not, necessarily, plague youngsters from broken homes only. Nor does every broken home produce suicidal children. "The common denominator," says Klagsbrun, "that may lead a child to depression and possible suicide in any home is a lack of love and support."

It should be added that some personality disorders, resulting in serious mental illnesses, are traceable to chemical changes in the body or to brain damage. We are all born with different temperaments and different personality factors, as Klagsbrun notes, and certainly not all our actions, good or bad, can be blamed on our parents. One major danger signal of possible suicide in an individual is changes in personality or behavior, e.g., a tendency for a person to become uncommunicative and to isolate him- or herself. There is a noticeable loss of interest in friends, family and activities and decreased sexual desire.

Cynthia R. Pfeffer, MD, author of *The Suicidal Child*, and a past president of the American Association of Suicidology, writes that, "Studies show the presence of an affective disorder is one of the most important factors that promoted risk for suicidal behavior in adults and children."

philosophers Down through recorded history, suicide has been many things to many people. Certainly philosophers were no exception. They have greatly influenced peoples and societies in this regard. For example, Greek and Roman philosophers discussed suicide and usually endorsed it within specific limitations. The STOICS were perhaps staunchest of the pro-suicide group, led by their founder ZENO. The EPICUREANS considered that one's destiny was a personal choice. CATO, Pliny and SENECA all thought the choice of suicide was acceptable. However, there have been many dissenters among philosophers. PLATO, for one, strongly opposed suicide, as did Virgil, Ovid and Cicero.

In later times, new views of suicide came into play. John Donne, reacted against the existing attitudes of the church toward suicide and viewed the act as neither a violation of the law nor against reason (though he considered it contrary to the law of self-preservation). Other 17th-century philosophers and secular writers echoed Donne's position: Hume, Montesquieu, Voltaire and Rousseau defended suicide under certain conditions.

In more recent times, Kant said: "Suicide is an insult to humanity." Dietrich Bonhoeffer viewed suicide as a sin in that it represented a denial of God. Modern-day attitudes toward suicide are no less complex and controversial than those of earlier times. The arrival of sociology, psychology and psychiatry has cast some light on this dark subject. Varying attitudes toward suicide among philosophers have emerged down through the years and will, no doubt, continue to emerge with the passage of time.

Two safe things that may be said about philosophers' views on suicide are that: (1) they usually strongly impact the attitude of mind in their time . . . and (2) they have forcefully demonstrated that virtually any view of suicide is possible, from the rational-accepting attitude to the sin-and-crime viewpoint.

physical health, loss of It is not uncommon for someone victimized by loss of physical health to view him- or herself as being less than a complete person. This can often lead to serious depression and, ultimately, suicidal thoughts. Loss of physical health can be as psychologically damaging or devastating as a loss of identity. For instance, since the spread of AIDS in the past five years or so, there have been a number of suicides by hapless victims of this dread disease. It is not difficult to understand why loss of physical health can crush the individual's spirit and lead to the lonely nightmare of clinical depression, or dark and self-destructive thoughts. No data of reliability are available to indicate what percent of suicides result from loss of physical health. So many other psychological and social factors affect such suicides that no single causal force can be pinpointed.

physician-patient relationship In "Medical Sociology" a chapter of Perlin's *A Handbook for the Study of Suicide*, George J. Vlasak, PhD (assistant professor, Department of Behavioral Sciences, School of Hygiene and Public Health, the Johns Hopkins University) examines the complex interaction of the suicide with that of the helping physician—as well as other health practitioners. Dr. Vlasak points out the reciprocal nature of the physician-patient relationship and shows where both often fail. His is a grim analysis, and shows that this vital doctor-patient relationship leaves, in general, much to be desired. Dr. Vlasak concludes in his summary:

> But the competent helper, the health system, as a system of status-roles pertaining to the existing medical and allied occupations and callings, is far from being ready, able, or willing to present the suicide patient with an alternative and equally far-reaching solution, and confines its operations to its much more limited domain, resisting its redefinition by the claims of the suicide case.

Dr. Vlasak adds it "would seem important to investigate whether or not there are any patterns of organizational behavior (which permit the helpers to step outside of some of the expectations of their professional roles) clearly pertaining to suicides as such, but not to alcoholics, assailants in violent crimes, or known prostitutes."

physicians Medical doctors are in the high-risk suicide category and have one of the highest suicide rates of any professional group. The number of doctors who commit suicide in the U.S. each year—between 100 and 150—is greater than the size of an entire graduating class from an average-size medical school. More doctors die by suicide each year than from drownings, plane crashes, accidents and homicides combined.

Unlike the general population, medical doctors are much more likely to use drugs, not guns, to kill themselves. And they tend to do so during the most productive years (the mean age being about 48). The suicide rate for male physicians is estimated at 1.15 times greater than the expected rate of the general male population (some studies indicate the rate is double.) For female physicians, the rate is three times greater than the expected rate of the female population. In the 25 to 39 age group, 26% of all physicians' deaths are attributed to suicide (D. DeSole, S. Aronson, P. Singer: "Suicide and Role Strain Among Physicians," paper presented to APA, Detroit, May 1967). Stephen C. Scheiber and Brian B. Doyle, writing in their book *The Impaired Physician*, say: "The most common cause of physician suicide is the ignoring or failure to recognize depression." They add, "Suicide prevention is urgently needed among physicians."

As for other specialities among physicians, Craig and Pitts in 1968 in "Suicide by Physicians" suggested that psychiatrists had a higher suicide rate than did physicians in other specialties. A 1980 study, however, indicates that psychiatrists appear to be overrepresented in the percentage of physician deaths due to suicide (C.L. Rich, F.N. Pitts: "Suicide by Psychiatrists: A Study of Medical Specialists Among 18,730 Consecutive Physician Deaths During a Five-year Period, 1967-1972").

It has been suggested by one group of physicians that a national clearinghouse be developed under the AMA's auspices to facilitate the collection of more reliable data on physician suicide. In the early 1980s, the American Medical Association set up a Physician's Mortality Study in conjunction with the American Psychiatric Association that may provide insight and new approaches for dealing with physician suicide.

Stephen C. Scheiber & Brian B. Doyle, eds., *The Impaired Physician* (New York: Plenum, 1983).

pills, as suicide method According to the U.S. Centers for Disease Control, there was a shift between 1970 and 1980 in the most frequent method of suicide for females. In 1970, poisoning by solids or liquids was the method most often used by females (36.7%), followed by firearms (and explosives) (30.2%). But by 1980, firearms and explosives were the methods most frequently used by females (38.6%), followed by poisoning by solids, including pills, and liquids (26.9%). The male pattern of suicide by method changed little between 1970 and 1980; firearms (and explosives) remained the leading method employed (58.4% and 63.1% respectively). Poisoning by solids (including pills) or liquids as a male pattern of suicide by method was 9.2% in 1970, dropping in 1980 to 6.6%.

Historically, suicidal women seemed to prefer ingesting a lethal dose of drugs, swallowing pills or poison, or inhaling gas. The speculation was that women didn't want to shed their blood or disfigure themselves, thus they would choose a more passive means of self-destruction. Others theorized that women opted for using a passive method, such as pills, because they really didn't want death by suicide, rather they were "crying out for help," calling attention to an intolerable situation. However, say officials at the U.S. Centers for Disease Control, "The marked increase in the percent of suicide deaths by firearms (and explosives) is of considerable public health concern." This increase in firearms as a method among female suicides indicates a move toward more lethal methods, say authorities—that is, methods with less chance for intervention or rescue.

Plath, Sylvia American poet and novelist (1932-1963), whose best-known work is the novel *The Bell Jar*, first published pseudonymously in England in 1962. A semi-autobiographical work, the novel is about a woman caught up in a crisis so severe that she attempts suicide. It recounts its heroine's rebellion against the constricting forces of society and her emotional and psychological conflicts resulting largely from family tensions. Similar themes may be found in Sylvia Plath's poetry.

In 1959, after suffering one nervous breakdown and suicide attempt, from which Plath recovered, and after a brief teaching stint at Smith College (her alma mater), she and her husband and two children moved to England. Her marriage to English poet Ted Hughes subsequently ended. On February 11, 1963, she committed suicide in London—some say accidentally. An account of her last days and death is given in A. Alvarez's book on suicide, *The Savage God*. (See also "LADY LAZARUS.")

Plato Greek philosopher (ca. 428-ca. 348 B.C.), who founded the famous Academy at Athens. His writings include *The Apology, Phaedo* and *The Republic*. His great teacher, Socrates, was one of the most notable suicides of ancient times. Plato quoted Socrates as saying before his death (which was really a form of execution ordered by the rulers of Athens), "No man has the right to take his own life, but he must wait until God sends some necessity upon him, as he has now sent me."

Plato, and his own student, Aristotle, both disapproved of suicide. Plato looked upon people as the "chattels" of God, and, as such, they had no right to destroy themselves, Alvarez, in *The Savage God*, tells us that Plato used the simile of the soldier on guard duty who must not desert his post, and also that of man as the property of the gods, who are as angry at our suicide as we would be if our chattels destroyed themselves. Life itself was the discipline of the gods.

poets Throughout the years, there has been a seemingly endless number of poet-suicides, many of whom concluded that life itself was poisoning their poetry at its source, to use Alvarez's term. Toward the end of the 18th century, the Romantics made suicide a major theme and preoccupation, if not obsession. In the Middle Ages, Alvarez notes that the church's influence was so powerful and pervasive that suicide was simply not a possible subject. He says that only during the Renaissance and Reformation did the churchly taboos begin to lose their power and the "topic re-emerged from the shadows." John Donne wrote the first book in English on the subject, BIATHANATOS (not published, however, in his lifetime).

It was after the Rationalists, such as Voltaire and Hume, attacked the suicide taboos, superstitions and primitive punishments, that the laws were slowly changed; along with shifting emotional attitudes, the stage was set for the Romantic era with its sublime agony.

Since then the world has witnessed poet-suicides who include: Thomas Chatterton, Gerard de Nerval, Virginia Woolf, Hart Crane, Dylan Thomas (drank himself to death), Delmore Schwartz, Malcolm Lowry, John Berryman—the list goes on and on—Cesare Pavese, Randall Jarrell, Sylvia Plath, Anne Sexton, and the Russian poets,

Mayakovsky, Yesenin and Tsvetayeva. There have been countless others.

As Alfred Alvarez sees it, "Once suicide is admitted wholly into the arts, it begins to dominate them." He theorizes that "for more serious and creative figures, suicide becomes an integral element of their work as the reality mirrored in their work has become increasingly more volatile and violent." Perhaps he sums it up best by stating that poets and artists offer, not solutions to the problem of suicide and prevention of suicide, but understanding.

poison, as suicide method Among the five most popular or preferred methods used to commit suicide in the 1980s, poison ranks second, depending upon how and what one classifies to be "poison." The U.S. Centers for Disease Control uses the classifications "poisoning by solids or liquids," as well as "poisoning by gasses." The former category would include poisoning by drugs or pills. Poisoning by gases in 1980 for all races, both male and female, were: males, 8.2% of suicides; females, 11.7% of suicides. These percentages were lower for males since 1970 (from 10.7%), but higher for females (up from 11.2%). Poisoning by solids in 1980 were: males 6.6% of suicides; females, 26.9%. These have dropped since 1970 for both males and females—males down from 9.2%, females down from 36.7%.

Pokorny, Alex D. Author-psychiatrist, whose contributions to the literature of suicide includes "Suicide Rates in Various Psychiatric Disorders," *Journal of Nervous, Mental Disorders*, (1964) 139:499-506. He investigated the suicide rate among former patients of a psychiatric service of a Veteran's Hospital (in Texas) over a 15-year period and calculated the suicide rates on the basis of 100,000 such patients per year as follows: depression, 566; schizophrenia, 167; neurosis, 119; personality disorder, 130; alcoholism, 133; and organic brain syndrome, 78. He noted that, as a subgroup, manic-depressive patients had the highest rate.

police Policemen and policewomen are in a high-risk suicide occupation. It appears that, generally speaking, people whose work involves giving nurturance and help to others have a greater predisposition toward suicide. This propensity holds true for service workers such as policemen/women. Theirs is a tense, frustrating, dangerous job—which often leads to great anxiety and stress. The police of our country also have a high rate of alcoholism and drug abuse that appears related to their occupation. The use of their own firearms as the most popular method of suicide among the police is of considerable concern to law enforcement officials throughout the country, but especially in major metropolitan centers where the crime/violence rate is highest.

The magnitude of the police-suicide problem is not precisely known because of: (1) inadequate information on which to make a determination of suicide as the cause of death and (2) coroner bias or error. The exact number of suicides specified in the national vital statistics reflects the judgments and professional opinions of the physicians, coroners or medical examiners who certify the medical/legal cause of death on a victim's death certificate. Experts say that not only police, but also *all* suicide statistics based on death certificates probably understate the true number of suicides.

A February 1987 segment of "The Phil Donahue Show" addressed this problem before a live audience of concerned policemen and policewomen from various areas of the country. All said their departments had established special suicide intervention and prevention counseling programs to help deal with the mushrooming problem.

politics, elections There have been a number of studies on the relation, if any, of presidential elections to suicide. The various studies, while generally inconclusive in their results, do indicate that there is usually a slight reduction in deaths by suicide prior to U.S. presidential elections—and a slight increase in the number of deaths by suicide following such elections. There was a noticeable increase in suicides in the U.S. following the assassination of President John F. Kennedy in 1963. For further information, read: Biller, O.A., "Suicide Related to the Assassination of President John F. Kennedy"; Boor, M., "Effects of United States Presidential Elections on Suicide and Other Causes of Death"; and Lester, D., "National Homicide and Suicide Rates as a Function of Political Stability."

Pollock, Jackson American painter (1912-1956). Died August 11, 1956, in Southampton, New York, in auto accident believed to have been deliberate. Many authorities called the accident "autocide." Pollock was filled with self-doubt and anxiety and was alcoholic.

Pontifex Maximus In Rome, a suicide by hanging was refused an honorable burial according to that part of the civil law administered by the Pontifex Maximus. According to historian George Rosen, this practice was continued into the Imperial period, and was a vestige of earlier religious views. However, suicide was never a penal offense in Rome and in time there were, for all practical purposes, no penalties.

Portwood, Doris Author of two books for children on Chinese subjects and of the thoughtful and honest examination of suicide, *Common Sense Suicide: The Final Right*. In the latter work, Portwood addresses the audience of which she is a member: the aging. She urges a reappraisal of current attitudes toward suicide in the context of the elderly, writing: "today, the needs of the individual and those of the social community appear to merge, in an economic sense, on the question of old-age suicide. A planned departure that serves oneself, one's family, and also the state surely is worthy of decent consideration." Doris Portwood worked as an editor in the U.S. Office of War Information (OWI) in India during World War II.

postvention Term coined by Edwin S. Shneidman, charter director of the Center for the Study of Suicide Prevention at the National Institute of Mental Health (NIMH) in Bethesda, Maryland, to describe the help and intervention of others that is needed by *all* survivors of suicide (attempters, families of suicides, friends, associates, etc.). It means, simply, extending to suicide survivors the caring support they need immediately after a suicide and, in time, assisting them in their coming to terms with the tragedy that has struck them. As Eric Lindemann describes postvention (for all who face bereavement): "Grief work is emancipation from the bondage to the deceased, readjustment to the environment in which the deceased is missing, and the formation of new relationships." The goal in postvention for survivors is to "assimilate the grief experience," as Rabbi Earl A. Grollman notes, in his book *Suicide: Prevention, Intervention, Postvention*, "and grow because of and through it."

potential suicides Almost every type of person, young or old, poor or rich, white or black, educated or illiterate, Christian or Jew, commits suicide. But the potential suicide, the person most likely to attempt or commit suicide is one who has: previously tried or threatened suicide; experienced chronic illness and/or isolation; suffered extreme financial stress resulting from joblessness or bankruptcy (or both); suffered a recent death in the family; experienced acute domestic troubles (e.g., divorce, separation or a broken home); experienced severe depression; been psychotic and exhibited withdrawal and confusion; been an alcoholic (active) for a number of years; chronically abused or misused addictive drugs (e.g., barbiturates); or has had a history of suicide in the family.

Most potential suicides leave clues to their imminent action. Sometimes these warning signs are broad hints; sometimes only subtle changes in behavior. But one must realize that suicide is usually premeditated—a decision that has come only after long consideration. It might be done on impulse, and to some of us appear capricious, as Dr. Edwin Shneidman notes, but the arrived-at decision is *not* impulsive. It is possible, therefore, for others to spot a potential suicide if others know what to look for. (See also CLUES, WARNING SIGNS.)

poverty In Europe during the mid-19th century, numerous writers on the subject of suicide related the action to poverty and said that for this reason, suicide occurred more frequently among the laboring poor in urban settings. Medical historian Dr. George Rosen says that although these developments were most notable in France, especially Paris, a more or less similar pattern was discerned in Great Britain, the German-language area of Central Europe, and the U.S.

Today, while poverty is certainly a public problem that merits concern, as it affects potential suicides, it is only one of the many more serious psychosocial circumstances behind the overall rate increases in the U.S. Poverty would surely not explain the marked increase in the contribution of young male and female suicides to the country's suicide problem since the 1950s. Although the potential for the act of suicide is a cultural universal, there are many and complex cultural, economic and social experiences that affect and shape the overall dynamics of the suicide phenomenon. Poverty alone cannot adequately explain how suicide has grown to its present proportions in our modern society.

Praz, Mario Author of *The Romantic Agony* in which he shows how fatalism gradually came to mean fatal sex; the femme fatale replaced the death ideal as the supreme inspiration for writers and poets. As social, religious, and legal taboos against the concept of suicide lost their power, the sexual taboos intensified, according to Alfred Alvarez, author of *The Savage God*, "Fatal sex also had the added advantage of being safer and slower than suicide," says Alvarez, "an enhancement rather than the contradiction of a life dedicated to art." Praz was professor of English language and literature at the University of Rome.

pregnancy While there have been cases where pregnant adult and teenage women have committed suicide, there is no indication of pregnancy being a key motivator for self-destruction. Everybody gets depressed from time to time, and certainly pregnant women—especially those who did not want to have a child—are no exception. They may experience profound feelings of worthlessness and lack of self-esteem (which lie at the base of many severe depressions); they sometimes take a negative view of both themselves and their relation to the world around them; and in extreme cases depressed pregnant women have a negative view of the future. If their depression grows and becomes too deep, they may give up all hope. These painful feelings sometimes cause depressed persons to blame themselves for their condition, and they want to punish themselves in various ways for the personal failings they believe they have. Sometimes the punishment takes the form of suicide.

prevention (of suicide) Edwin Shneidman writes in *Definition of Suicide*, "The immediate antidote for suicide lies in reduction of perturbation," to lower the potential by learning what is causing the distress, the tension and anguish—and then work to bring down the level of concern within the suicidal person. Professor Shneidman lists practical measures for helping highly suicidal persons: reduce the pain; fill the frustrated needs; provide a viable answer to the question of life's worth; indicate alternatives in life; give transfusions of hope; play for time; increase the options; listen to the cry, involve others; block the exit (for action on the suicidal person's part); and, invoke precious positive patterns of successful coping.

Prevention resources are available in psychotherapy, counseling, outreach groups (e.g., self-help) and private as well as federal agencies. On a national level, the development of special educational programs—both in and out of schools—is needed to teach ways of preventing suicides. The Centers for Disease Control (as a division of the U.S. Department of Health and Human Services) has done studies aimed at identifying possible victims and preventing suicide. During 1986, HHS sponsored three separate national conferences on the problems inherent in youth suicide. Private organizations are doing the same; e.g., the YOUTH SUICIDE NATIONAL CENTER was established in 1985 out of concern for the problem of youth suicide. As the organization's president/executive director Charlotte P. Ross, says: "The Youth Suicide National Center will help to provide an information network that will allow local programs to become national answers." In June 1985, the YSNC cosponsored a national conference in Washington, D.C., on youth suicide (with the Department of Health and Human Services; Administration for Children, Youth and Families). That year, the United Nations proclaimed 1985 as International Youth Year around the world, and President Ronald Reagan proclaimed 1985 as International Youth Year in the U.S.

In addition, the National Committee on Youth Suicide Prevention (NCYSP) was formed in 1984 as a private nonprofit group to reduce the number of committed and attempted suicides among the nation's youth by establishing and supporting prevention programs and public awareness campaigns. Alfred B. DelBello, former lieutenant governor of New York State, is the organization's national chairman. Executive Director Linda Laventhall says the group's *National Directory of Youth Suicide Prevention and Intervention Programs* (a comprehensive listing of the community resources available for assistance in dealing with potentially suicidal young people) is being updated for publication in the Fall of 1987. For information about how to order (it costs $6 per copy), write or call: National Committee on Youth Suicide Prevention, 666 Fifth Avenue, 13th Floor, New York, NY 10103, Attn: Director Corrections.

Officials at the Centers for Disease Control in Atlanta note that it is also:

> critically important to design and evaluate programs targeted to high risk individuals as well as educational programs, programs designed to improve the identification and treatment of depression, and programs to reduce access to lethal means of suicide. Epidemiologic analyses will help to identify risk factors that might be compiled to effectively identify high risk individuals.

All of this, combined with biochemical advances toward eliminating depression, is aimed at reducing the suicide rate in the U.S.

primitive societies Suicide is an act whose primary aim is the intentional and deliberate taking of one's own life. Ruth S. Cavan, writing in *Suicide*, postulates that suicides are of two types: conventional and personal. Conventional suicide occurs as a result of tradition plus the force of public opinion. That is why, among some tradition-bound peoples, within certain situations, suicide is demanded. Notable examples include SEPPUKU, the ritualistic suicide of a Japanese man of rank faced with disgrace or humiliation; the SUTTEE of the Indian widow who was forced to self-immolation (by cremation) on her husband's funeral pyre; and in certain primitive tribes, exposure to the elements of the old and infirm and their abandonment—as among primitive Eskimos. "Such conventional suicides," wrote Cavan, "are typical of societies in which most problem situations are solved by strongly-held customs."

These types of suicides were also traditional among several widely scattered primitive tribes. Early records show that widows committed suicide in northwest Europe immediately after the husband's death. More recent anthropological studies of certain African tribes indicate that their frequency of suicide was comparable to that of European countries with relatively low suicide rates and that suicide among the tribes was considered evil. Erwin Stengel, author of *Suicide and Attempted Suicide*, explains:

> Physical contact with the body of a suicide is feared to have disastrous effects, such as illness or suicide among one's kin. The tree on which a person hanged himself is felled and burned. The ancestors have to be placated by sacrifices. The place where the suicide happened is believed to be a haunt of evil spirits. Suicide is dreaded in the community, and a threat of suicide is sometimes used to exert pressure on the family.

In Tikopia, a small island in the western Pacific where pagan ideology lingers, suicide is looked at with mild disapproval. The gods will receive the souls of the dead, it is believed, but not of suicides. Their souls are destined to wander aimlessly until their ancestral spirits find them. Yet the spirits have no objection to the man who commits suicide by going off to sea in a canoe, or the woman who swims out to sea. These suicide methods are admired. The Christian Tikopians believe that a suicide's soul goes not to paradise, but to Satan.

Among the Gisu of Uganda, suicides of the aged and infirm usually took place after all means of alleviating their condition had been tried and found ineffective. In some primitive societies, it seems, suicide was an act of last resort. The Joluo of Kenya, who hold attitudes toward suicide not unlike the Gisu, manage to keep knowledge of a suicide within the clan, to protect the community's prestige. The Tiv of Nigeria appear to have the lowest incidence of suicide yet recorded; so few, it seems, that one anthropologist-researcher was unable to document cases of Tiv suicide.

An excellent book that embodies results of research into both homicide and suicide in a number of African societies is *African Homicide and Suicide*, edited by P.J. Bohannan; also see D. de Catanzaro's *Suicide and Self-Damaging Behavior*.

Prinze, Freddie American comedian-actor (1954-1977) who killed himself in January, 1977, at the age of 23. Friends and business associates told authorities that Prinze was despondent about the breakup of his marriage, which may have been caused by a desire for too much love. The young comedian, co-star of the TV series "Chico and the Man," despite his early success in show business, seemed never to have developed an internal feeling of competence and self-confidence.

prisoners (institutional) While it is known that many incarcerated people kill themselves while in jails and state prisons, there are no reliable data on rates as compared to suicides in the general population. Among those prisoners of institutions who do commit suicide, the majority seem to hang themselves. Also, there appears to be a complexity of motivations along with a mix of conflicting tendencies underlying prisoners' suicidal acts. There is also the tendency, at times, on the part of prison or jail authorities to protect the particular institution's reputation and/or record by concealing the suicidal acts of prisoners. Some prisons put on a special "suicide watch" for prisoners convicted of especially heinous crimes.

This particular area of suicide research is in dire need of more concentrated and critical scrutiny. A lack of uniformity of search procedures and criteria of categorization, not to mention comparability of data, have made study to date unreliable.

prisoners of war In JOHN L. McINTOSH's comprehensive *Research on Suicide: A Bibliography*, only one article relates to suicide and prisoners of war. That sole entry is D. Lester's 1973 "Suicide in Released Prisoners of War" (*Journal of the American Medical Association*, 225 [1973]: 747). The literature and data on this particular suicide phenomenon is woefully lacking, especially since not a few hapless, hopeless POW's do commit suicide. In fact, it would seem that the various aspects and factors that suicide research has uncovered would place POW's in the high-risk group.

Protestants In the United States, Catholics appear to have suicide rates that are higher than rates for Jews, but lower than the rates for Protestants. This same relationship occurs in most countries (but not *all*) where the major religious groups are Jews, Catholics and Protestants. An exception is Austria, primarily a Catholic country, yet with a suicide rate that has consistently ranked as one of the highest in the world.

Generally speaking, the highest suicide rates—relating suicide to religious groups—are found among the multi-denominational, loosely-federated Protestants. Another disturbing trend is that suicide rates among Jews in the U.S., and in Israel, appear to be gradually increasing. Henry Morselli, an Italian professor of psychological medicine and Thomas Masaryk, philosopher, both felt that Protestantism contributed to suicide by favoring individualism, free thought and free inquiry, leading people more easily to doubt and despair.

It should be pointed out that there is a need for caution in the comparison and evaluation of rate differences relating religion and suicide. The World Health Organization warns: "The true incidence of suicide is hard to ascertain. Varying methods of certifying causes of death, different registration and coding procedures, and other factors affect the extent and completeness of coverage, making international comparisons impracticable."

It is perhaps safe to say that while the attitude of most Protestant factions remains one of general condemnation of suicide, the specific sanctions are not as equally severe as in the past—or in all denominations. The funeral rites accorded suicides still differ in many cases, more or less, from the rites of those who have died a natural death. Also, exemption from sanctions on the ground of mental instability or disturbance is usually more readily granted than in the past. Overall, there seems to be a greater willingness to understand rather than to condemn the suicide. However, the tendency to conceal suicidal acts still persists, but that may well be primarily out of a sense of guilt felt by those who feel they could have prevented the act.

psychedelic drugs Psychiatrist Herbert Hendin, for his book, *the Age of Sensation*, studied students abusing several kinds of drugs (as part of a larger psychoanalytic study of Columbia University students). Although many drug users and abusers mixed drugs, others favored use of one or another group or type of drugs to suit their particular emotional needs. For example, the LSD and psychedelic users wanted to "escape" beyond all emotions and feelings. Most admitted to having grown up feeling rejected or lonely, and didn't allow anyone to become close to them for fear they would be hurt if trouble resulted. So, they opted for psychedelic drugs to "blow their minds" and open up fantastic new worlds of sensation and experience. This only served to push further away their true emotions, to temporarily shelter them from the anger, despair and loneliness they might feel if they permitted themselves, to use Francine Klagsbrun's words from *Too Young to Die*, "to feel anything."

Drug abusers, notes Klagsbrun, learn all too soon that even such "mind-blowing" experiences do not block out the emotional hurts that plague them. The syndrome has been likened to a fast-moving merry-go-round that is impossible to dismount—and the victims may very well use the drug to kill themselves.

Psychedelic drugs, or hallucinogens, act on the central nervous system and produce mood changes and perceptual changes varying from sensory illusion to hallucination. Hallucinogens are classified as Schedule I drugs under the Controlled Substances Act, and include: LSD, mescaline, peyote, DMT, psilocybin (psilocin), marijuana, and tetrahydrocannabinols, among others. With some of the more powerful hallucinogens, a user may lose all sense of reality. Cases exist where individuals have become permanently psychotic either from the stress of the experience or from the precipitation of a schizophrenic reaction. Some of the hallucinogens are also known to produce convulsions on occasion. Chronic users of hallucinogens can become psychologically addicted, the mental state induced by the drug so much a part of the user's life that to be without it seems abnormal.

There are several recorded instances of people killing themselves while using the so-called psychedelic drugs. (See also DRUG ABUSE AND SUICIDE.)

psychodynamic theory The branch of psychology that investigates motivation and emotional processes—in this instance, how psychic, social and cultural factors are interwoven to produce suicidal behavior in individuals from very different backgrounds. It is the systematized knowledge and theory of human behaviors and motivation in which the role of emotions is of special significance. In HERBERT HENDIN's words, "The organizing issue of a psychosocial frame of reference must be the connection between psychic and social conditions." Psychodynamic theory describes psychoanalytic and related depth psychologies as they pertain to processes undergoing change or development. Psychodynamics incorporates the role of unconscious motivation, as well as conscious, and assumes that behavior is determined by past experience, genetic endowment and current reality.

psychological autopsy One of the most significant research tools to come along since the field of suicidology grew into recognition. The psychological autopsy, brainchild of psychologists Edwin S. Shneidman and Norman L. Farberow, cofounders in 1958 of the Los Angeles Suicide Prevention Center, is a method whereby coroners and medical examiners are helped in efforts to determine the cause of a death when cause is not clearly indicated.

In such cases, members of the L.A. Center's "death investigation team" will interview friends, relatives, associates, teachers and any significant other who might have played a role in the victim's life. Team members consider carefully the suicide's routine in the several days and hours before death, then attempt to paint an overall picture of the person's character, personality and state of mind. On the strength and significance of data gathered and put together, team members try to judge whether the person's death was suicide or non-suicide, i.e., any of the other four categories of death—natural, homicide, accident or undetermined. The team then reports its findings to the coroner or medical examiner, who includes this with his/her own postmortem investigation and determines whether to list the death as a suicide, homicide, accident, natural or undetermined.

psychosis A major mental disorder of organic or emotional origin involving a person's ability to think, respond emotionally, remember, communicate, interpret reality and behave appropriately, characterized by impairment sufficient enough to interfere grossly with the capacity to meet the ordinary demands of life. Disturbances may appear in the form of aggressive behavior and diminished impulse control, along with delusions and hallucinations.

psychosomatic Pertains to processes that are both somatic (bodily) and psychic (mental) in nature; thus psychosomatic pertains to the relation of mind and body.

psychotherapy Stated simply, the application of specialized techniques to the treatment of mental disorders or to the problems of everyday adjustments. In a more specific sense, the term includes only those techniques (such as psychoanalysis, nondirective or directive counseling, psychodrama) utilized by specialists.

Ultimately, the objective of any and all forms of psychotherapy is to relieve symptoms or to resolve problems in living or to seek personal growth.

psychotic suicide Most suicides do not suffer from psychotic illness, contrary to popular opinion. Usually, suicidal behavior stems from deep depression and, at times, from neurotic disturbances that are less severe or intense than psychotic ones. Some suicides, however, do result from psychotic illnesses. The victim suffers a break with reality, loses the ability to distinguish what is occurring and what is imagined. He or she acts out fantasies, not realizing his or her behavior seems weird and disorganized to other people. Some, in fact most, psychotics have periods of lucidness, and many are able to live relatively normal lives until something triggers a break with reality.

Authorities say some psychotic illnesses are organically caused, such as early-life brain damage. Some result from biochemical imbalances in the body that may be hereditary or may develop over a number of years. Still others have deep-seated psychological or emotional causes that result from unstable or disruptive family relationships. Psychotic illnesses are usually treated with drugs, often in tandem with psychotherapy, and with family therapy that involves parents, siblings and other relatives.

Psychotic illness may lead to suicidal thoughts and actions without family members or friends recognizing that the victim is deeply disturbed. Usually, this is because they won't allow themselves to acknowledge how sick the victim really is. They cannot bring themselves to admit that the psychotic person is mentally disturbed.

punishment, suicide as The first question asked by anyone who knew the person who committed suicide is: Why did he or she kill him- or herself? One cause for suicide is a wish to punish—either the self or someone else. The psychologists usually understand and explain suicide in terms of various levels of pressure on the individual, which may parlay into killing oneself.

SIGMUND FREUD implied that murder is aggression turned upon another; suicide is aggression turned upon the self. Suicide, in other words, becomes "murder in the 180th degree." Sometimes confused suicidal persons, especially the very young, view killing themselves as a way to "punish" others, to make someone close to them show more respect or love for them. Strangely, perhaps because they have a misguided attitude toward death, they view themselves as being present to enjoy the punishment their death has inflicted or the belated love it has generated. Or, the suicidal person feels he or she has "let someone down," disappointed a loved one or a close friend by not living up to their expectations. Then the punishment that is suicide is turned inward. Dr. Karl Menninger, in *Man Against Himself*, says everyone who attempts or completes suicide is driven—consciously and unconsciously—by three motives: the wish to kill, the wish to be killed, and the wish to die.

The fallacy of those suicides who fantasize about killing themselves as a form of punishment—whether someone else or the self—is that they, in Francine Klagsbrun's terms, "deny the one and only truth about death; that is, that it irrevocably ends life."

Q

Quinlan, Karen Ann Though she did not commit suicide, the name Karen Ann Quinlan will long be remembered because her case set a legal precedent for future court actions and laid the groundwork for passage of legislation granting terminally ill persons and their families the right to authorize withdrawal of life-sustaining procedures when death is believed imminent. The problem posed by the 21-year-old woman from Morris County, New Jersey, as she lay breathing mechanically day after day in a fixed death-in-life situation sparked new and enlightening discussions on the definition of death.

Quinlan's parents went to court and lost, then appealed to the New Jersey Supreme Court, which overturned the lower court ruling, a major concern being Karen's right to privacy, which was asserted in her behalf by her family.

As a result, she was weaned from the respirator. She did not die as expected, however, and was transferred from the hospital to a nursing home, where she remained in a coma, fed through tubes, until she died in July 1985, 10 years later. Before Karen Ann Quinlan's tragic case came to light, right-to-die legislation had been introduced in only five states. Shortly afterward, 50 bills were introduced in 38 states; in eight, they were signed into law. "The Quinlan case has had a strong effect on bringing this out in the open," said Alice Mehling, then executive director for the Society for the Right to Die (formerly the Euthanasia Society of America).

R

race (ethnic groups, minorities) Although there are reputedly a few isolated parts of the world where no suicides are committed—or at least none are reported (e.g., several small South Sea islands and the Hindu Kush Mountains of India)—no race or ethnic group is exempt from the potential. The Soviets explain that suicide is a "bourgeois activity" that does not occur in the Soviet Union. Thus, the actual suicide rate for that country is unknown. Among the world's nations, the countries usually high on the scale in terms of suicide rates per 100,000 population are: Hungary, Denmark, Finland, Austria, Czechoslovakia, West Germany, Sweden, Switzerland and Japan. In recent years, the U.S. has ranked around 21st. Countries on the low end of the suicide rate charts include: the Philippines, Angola, Jamaica, Mexico, the Bahamas, Kuwait, Jordan, Kenya and Egypt.

Within the U.S., the suicide rate for blacks is lower than the rate for whites. However, the figures for both groups are considerably closer in urban areas, and in certain metropolitan areas (e.g., Harlem in New York City), the rate for blacks is higher than it is for whites living in other sections of the city. Also, the rate is higher for *young* blacks than it is for whites. Ethnic groups with predominantly Catholic members appear to have suicide rates that are higher than the rate for Jews, but lower than the rates for ethnic members of predominantly Protestant faiths. A very high risk group in the U.S. is the American Indian (many believe such causal factors as isolation, alienation, poverty, hopelessness, and drugs and alcohol play a major role in the Indian suicide rate being as high as it is).

However, before you finish reading this page, someone in America will try to commit suicide. And that someone could be Irish or Indian, Christian or Jew, rich or poor, white or black, tall or short . . . it makes no difference. Suicide, it's obvious, is one of the few facets of life in the U.S. that remains wholly democratic.

Raskolniki In 17th-century Russia, the Great Schism (the Raskol) left the dissenting religious group (the Raskolniki) in such despair that many of its members sought death rather than wait for the end of the world, which they had predicted would occur before century's end. Between 1672 and 1691, some 37 mass immolations took place, with more than 20,000 Raskolniki voluntarily burned to death. By these mass suicides, they confirmed their belief that it was senseless to remain on Earth and risk contamination by heresy.

Isaac Asimov, ed., *Isaac Asimov's Book of Facts* (New York: Bell, 1979).

rates, suicide Information contained in the report, *Centers for Disease Control: Suicide Surveillance, 1970-1980*, issued in November 1986, employs two types of data: (1) numbers of deaths due to suicide and (2) population data for calculating suicide rates per 100,000 population. Suicide deaths are taken from national mortality computer files compiled by the National Center for Health Statistics (NCHS). Variables on each suicide included: age, race, sex, place of residence, place of occurrence, date of death, cause of death.

As for rates, special estimates (prepared by the U.S. Bureau of Census) were used to compute rates for the years 1970 to 1980. Unpublished population statistics of U.S. residents provided by NCHS were used to compute rates for 1979 and 1980. Updated population estimates for the intercensal years 1971 to 1979 are based on the 1980 U.S. Census. Because suicide varies by age, age-adjusted suicide rates are presented in some sections in this work to allow for comparison of rates between populations without concern for different age structures in the populations being compared.

Data on suicide deaths for various countries included in this work are absolute numbers and rates. Unfortunately, not all countries disclose such information and other countries lag behind in providing mortality data, so a listing by country is not exhaustive. Data for selected countries may be found under separate listings throughout this volume. These data were provided by Dr. Alan D. Lopez, statistician, Global Epidemiological Surveillance and Health Situation Assessment, World Health

Organization, Mondiale de la Sante, Geneva, Switzerland.

rational suicide Term coined by Manhattan artist and former social worker Jo Roman, who advocated choosing the time of one's own death—which she did at age 62 in 1979 before taking a fatal overdose of pills. She had been diagnosed as having a breast tumor that would have been treatable by mastectomy, but she rejected the operation. Roman called her friends in to say good-bye, had the group's conversation taped, then spent the evening with her husband and a close friend before ingesting the pills. Her videotapes on advocacy of self-termination were subsequently shown in an educational television documentary.

Rationalists, the During the early to mid-18th century, writers, philosophers and thinkers such as VOLTAIRE and HUME, who steadily hammered away at the suicide taboos, superstitions and the primitive punishments still being meted out. As a result, the strict laws were gradually changed, along with a corresponding shift in society's emotional attitudes.

razor blades, as suicide weapon Though razor blades are not a frequently used method of suicide (based on those deaths identified according to cause of death codes established by International Classification of Disease, or ICD), any person—family member, friend, acquaintance—who has doubts about a suicidal individual's intentions should check for any possible lethal weapon, including razor blades. Young people, especially, have used this method of suicide attempt or suicide.

reaction (to suicide attempt) Attempted suicide is a very serious matter, whatever the degree of physical harm accomplished; it is a self-destructive act which might have been lethal were it not for fortuitous circumstances beyond the person's control. An attempted suicide generally involves all elements of a completed suicide except that the person doesn't die. Experts estimate that there are roughly ten to 100 times as many attempts as there are completions (among adolescents).

As Giffin and Felsenthal note, every suicide attempt is a serious cry for help, and this cry must, and can, be heard, and suicide can be prevented with proper help being offered to the suicidal by established professionals and/or suicide prevention services. Many of those who have attempted will try again. The suicide attempter needs to be seen, evaluated, and usually treated by a professional therapist. But anyone can help by staying with the person until help arrives or a crisis passes, by listening intelligently and sympathizing with what the person says (showing that you care), and urging the person to seek help from a psychiatrist, psychologist, social worker or other qualified professional.

The fact that the suicide attempt rate is so much higher than the completed rate offers hope. Most people—particularly young people—who attempt suicide do not want to die. Suicide is called, with reason, the nation's number one *preventable* health problem. Several studies have shown that around 80% of people who commit suicide have given repeated warnings or CLUES. In fact, one of the MYTHS of suicide is that once a person decides to commit suicide, there's nothing we can do to prevent it. A suicide attempt that turns lethal is the last cry in a usually long series of cries for help.

reality, break with It is a break with reality that is the key aspect underlying all psychotic illnesses. The psychotic individual can no longer distinguish between what is actually happening and what he or she imagines is taking place. Such illnesses result from organic causes (e.g., brain damage in early childhood), from biochemical imbalances, and also from psychological or emotional causes that have developed from disturbed family relationships. The longer a psychotic condition is allowed to continue, that is, the longer the person's distortions of reality exist, the more difficult it usually is to treat.

Rebel Without a Cause A 1950s film starring actor JAMES DEAN who was killed on September 30, 1955, in a car accident in California (many experts called his death "AUTOCIDE"). Dean, who in real life appeared to live the characters he played on the screen, played the angry young *Rebel Without a Cause* who plays "chicken" with another teenager as their cars race toward each other along the edge of a high cliff. Tens of thousands of teenage fans identified with the complex actor's personal rebelliousness and his open defiance of the adult establishment.

reckless driving, as suicide clue Psychiatrist Norman Tabachnick, in "The Psychology of Fatal Accidents" (in Shneidman's *Essays in Self-Destruction*), explains results of a research project to learn more about how people who have been in serious auto accidents compare in personality and thinking with suicidal people. He and colleagues at the Los Angeles Suicide Prevention Center found that about 25% of the accident victims were depressed people with feelings of helplessness and a sense of loss typical of suicidal persons. Those studied had experienced fantasies, dreams of death and self-destruction, shortly before their accidents. Experts believe the serious accidents the victims suffered could well have resulted from underlying wishes to kill themselves.

Dr. Karl Menninger interpreted most accidents as the result of unconscious self-destructive drives. Dr. Alfred L. Moseley of the Harvard Medical School concludes that suicides are a "significant though unknown" proportion of the rising number of annual auto deaths in the U.S. As Earl A. Grollman observes, "The popular wisdom that says, when a car shoots past at ninety, 'Man, he's trying to kill himself,' may well be correct."

"Autocide" occurs when a car, an ideal instrument of self-destruction, is used as a method of self-imposed death.

recognition of suicide potential See CLUES, WARNING SIGNS.

Reformation A. Alvarez tells us in *The Savage God* that "It was only during the Renaissance and Reformation that the savage churchly taboos began gradually to lose their power and the topic [of suicide] re-emerged from the shadows. Sir Thomas More justified it as a form of euthanasia in his *Utopia*. Montaigne, later freer, more skeptical and more radical, defended the act strenuously."

The name "Reformation" is applied to the religious reform movements of the 1500s in Western Europe, which had as their object the correction of abuses that had arisen in the Western Catholic Church; those movements resulted in the disunity of that church and the foundation of Protestant churches. Martin Luther's teachings gave impetus to the Reformation, which began in Germany in 1515 with his thesis against the sale of indulgences.

rejection by parents Parents' attitudes, support, caring and love—along with the quality of family life—have an important and usually lasting impact on a child's development. In *Too Young to Die*, Francine Klagsbrun concludes that "More than anything else, family background and experiences during the early years of life play a major role in creating suicidal wishes among young people. Study after study has found that a large proportion of young suicide attempters and completers came from disturbed or disrupted homes lacking in stability and support."

Children who are rejected—for whatever reasons: divorce, drug abuse, alcoholism, abandonment—feel lonely and alienated, and are filled with rage at both the rejecting parent and themselves. Ironically and tragically, the more a child feels rejected and unloved by parents, the greater is the child's need for those parents, says psychiatrist James M. Toolan in "Depression in Children and Adolescents." Klagsbrun explains that as a child grows into the teen years, the reality of the child's predicament becomes clearer and more difficult to deny. It is at this time that they become filled with anger toward their parents, yet find themselves so consumed with guilt about their building rage that they sometimes turn the anger inward. This, then, is the vulnerable period when suicidal thoughts materialize and grow; and teen fantasies about death serve to nurture their thoughts. Klagsbrun concludes: "Almost anything can set off a suicide attempt at this time."

religion See CLERGY AND SUICIDE PREVENTION.

religion, decline in Among the many reasons put forth as affecting the patterns of family life in modern day America is a decline in the influence of institutional religions. Since World War II, when the family unit centered around religious beliefs, practices and activities, religion has been just one more institution that has suffered a decline. It has consistently lost its hold on many, if not most, people, and replacement institutions have not materialized to provide the support and stability religion once offered.

This, along with other socioeconomic changes, has surely helped to bring on feelings of uncertainty, anxiety and dislocation that affect young people most of all. Children grow up with divorce decimating their parents' marriages, within a framework of widespread economic and political instability, with religion characterized as having diminished influence, and the environment despoiled and polluted by years of careless waste. Add to that the always present nuclear threat and you can understand why so many young people are experiencing a pervasive sense of chaos, disorder and doom.

Ross, Klagsbrun, Giffen and others who have studied and written about suicide, especially among children, note that this sense of uncertainty and the rising pressures brought about by still more rapidly accelerating changes in the quality of life have contributed to the rise in suicides among the young, and especially to the growing suicide rates among today's college students.

Renaissance Time of the great revival of art, letters and learning in Europe from the 14th through the 16th centuries, marking the transition from the medieval to the modern world. With regard to suicide, new and less stringent attitudes toward suicide began to gradually emerge during the Renaissance. These more lenient, understanding attitudes finally came out into the open in the 18th century, as churchly taboos began, in A. Alvarez's words, "to lose their power."

research on suicide Suicide among young persons in particular is currently a priority concern of a number of federal and private sector agencies and organizations, especially the National Institute of Mental Health, the Division of Injury Epidemiology and Control, Center for Environmental Health, Centers for Disease Control (CDC). CDC, for instance, is studying youth suicide patterns to determine risk factors that can define subpopulations of teens and young adults at highest risk. Some factors, such as mental illness, hopelessness or a family history of suicide have already been associated with increased susceptibility to suicide. Experts at CDC believe additional research is needed to better characterize other possible risk factors, such as emotional stress, family structure, and drug and alcohol abuse.

Research continues but has not yet been completed to determine the effects of exposure to previous suicides on subsequent suicides. Direct exposure may occur through a friend or classmate's suicide; indirect exposure to suicide may also occur through news reports, books, movies or discussions. More research is needed as well to determine the effectiveness of suicide prevention centers, services such as 24-hour hot lines, walk-in counseling, self-help groups for suicidal persons and their families, or crisis center-sponsored outreach programs in the community. CDC officials believe that,

> It is also critically important to design and evaluate programs targeted to high-risk individuals as well as educational programs, programs designed to improve the identification and treatment of depression, and programs to reduce access to lethal means of suicide. Epidemiologic analyses will help to identify risk factors that might be compiled to effectively identify high-risk individuals.

In February 1987, first proof that mental illness can be inherited was found through research stemming from a 10-year study of manic-depression in three generations of an Old Order Amish family in Pennsylvania. The finding, reported by scientists in the British journal *Nature*, could revolutionize the diagnosis and treatment of mental disease. According to Dr. Darrel Regier of the National Institute of Mental Health (NIMH) in Bethesda, Maryland, "This is a landmark study, the findings are compelling." He called the findings "the start of an exciting new era in genetics." Dr. Regier says 85% of those diagnosed who had the gene for manic-depression developed the illness at some time during the 10-year period of the study.

The report says that a genetic defect that caused "strong predisposition to manic-depressive disease" was found near the tip of the short arm of chromosome II, one of 23 pairs of chromosomes that make up the human genetic archive. The specific segment of DNA that constitutes the defective gene has not yet been identified. DNA, or deoxyribonucleic acid, is the substance that provides the genetic blueprints for all living things.

Between one and two million American adults suffer depressive illness, says NIMH. Manic-depression is characterized by wide mood swings; it can be treated with drugs. The Amish, incidentally, were chosen for the study because their community is stable, homogeneous and noted for large families. There is virtually no violence, alcoholism or criminal behavior that can affect the outcome of the study, according to coauthors of the report, David Pauls of Yale University and David Houseman of Boston's Massachusetts Institute of Technology. Among the Amish, the incidence of the psychiatric disorder is the same as in the general population, 1.2%. Other authors of the new study include: Janice A. Egeland, James N. Sussex, Cleona R. Allen and Abram M. Hostette, all of Miami University's School of Medicine; Daniella S. Gerbard, also of M.I.T.; and Kenneth K. Kidd of Yale University's School of Medicine.

The landmark research development illustrates the growing power of molecular biology to expand scientists' understanding of disease. Early understanding of manic-depressive illness had emphasized environmental and social problems, but this new, highly significant research underlines the importance of the biological aspects as well.

Centers for Disease Control, Youth Suicide in the United States, 1970-1980 (Atlanta: Department of Health and Human Services, November 1986).

Harold M. Schmeck, Jr., "Defective Gene Tied to Form of Manic-Depressive Illness," *The New York Times* (February 26, 1987).

Research on Suicide: A Bibliography Comprehensive bibliography compiled by John L. McIntosh, assistant professor of psychology at Indiana University at South Bend, and published by the Greenwood Press, Westport, Connecticut, in 1985.

reserpine Drug commonly used for treatment of hypertension. Extensive clinical use revealed that it caused as many as 15% of patients to become depressed in a fashion indistinguishable from endogenous depression. Solomon H. Snyder, in "Biology," chapter six of Perlin's *A Handbook for the Study of Suicide,* writes that "Interestingly, reserpine depression was discovered by a cardiovascular researcher who noted an astoundingly high incidence of *suicide* in patients receiving this drug."

resources, natural Ross, Klagsbrun, Giffin and others who have studied and written about suicide, especially among children, feel that there is little in the overall quality of life today that encourages optimism and a sense of hope for continued progress. Young people grew up realizing that we are depleting irreplaceable natural resources, wasting our environment with callous disregard and becoming more and more dependent upon foreign sources for oil and other key commodities. Add to that the young people's knowledge that their world can be annihilated at any time, and one can understand why they see themselves as having inherited an unsatisfying condition . . . a condition of living life only in the present. All these things affect young people in negative ways.

revenge, suicide as L. Bender and P. Schilder studied suicide in a number of children under age 13 and found hardly an instance where spite was not the motivator. Notes left by some suicides indicate that the message behind the act is, "It's your fault" or "Now we're even!" as GIFFIN and Felsenthal note: "Whereas an adult who feels unloved might confront a spouse with his fears, suspicions and anger, a young person might make his point by killing himself."

The youngster's view of death usually includes the notion that after the act of suicide, he/she will remain behind, hovering invisibly over the funeral scene, taking diabolical pleasure in witnessing the parents' and friends' grief. One 17-year-old, who tried to kill herself twice, told the ABC "Nightline" program (April 24, 1981): "I had a long argument with my parents and everything. It was kind of to get back at 'em."

Grossman notes that "Death by suicide brings the greatest of all affronts to those who remain. As SHNEIDMAN said: 'The suicidal person places his psychological skeleton in the survivor's closet.'"

Edwin S. Shneidman and Norman L. Farberow, eds., *Clues to Suicide: An Investigation* (New York: McGraw-Hill, 1957), ch. 2.

"right to die" movement A complete discussion of this movement is to be found under the headings for both DEREK HUMPHRY and the HEMLOCK SOCIETY, of which he is cofounder with his wife Ann Wickett. The discussion covers both active and passive euthanasia, suicide, the medical and legal issues, as well as the moral and ethical questions involved.

"right to suicide" Every society throughout recorded history has had to contend with this complex issue. Each has had to determine when, if ever, suicide is justifiable, and when, if ever, it might be permitted. As Klagsbrun observes, "Obviously no society can survive if it allows widespread suicide among its members. And in most cultures and most times in history, people have feared, forbidden and condemned suicide. But at certain times, and under certain conditions, they have not only tolerated, but also encouraged it." (See also THE HISTORY OF SUICIDE, in the front of this work.)

Rimbaud, Jean Arthur French poet (1854-1891) who, at 19, abandoned poetry and left France for a life of adventure, traveling in Abyssinia and Arabia; contracted a disease from which he died at 37 in Marseilles. Rimbaud called himself a "litteraturicide" just before leaving France. He was one among many of the ROMANTICS, who helped to change the image of the poet radically.

ritual suicide Various cultures over the years have endorsed, even encouraged, ritual suicides. (See also SEPPUKU; SUTTEE; and GISU OF UGANDA.

Rollin, Betty Former television reporter for ABC and NBC, and author of the book, *Last Wish*, wherein Miss Rollin admits that she secretly helped her terminally ill mother, Ida, commit suicide in 1983. In the book, the author reveals that her mother expressed the desire to end her own life after months of torturous and apparently futile chemotherapy for inoperable ovarian cancer. Rollin maintains that her role in the drug overdose of 75-year-old Ida Rollin in her Manhattan apartment did not violate a New York State law against "promoting suicide."

"I did not directly help my mother to commit suicide," Rollin told reporters. "If I did, I would not have written a book about it." She said she "did research and gave my mother the information." Under New York state law, "promoting suicide" is a felony, punishable by up to four years in prison. Some legal authorities said such cases pose difficult problems. Miss Rollin was not indicted by the state for any wrongdoing. *Last Wish* went on to make several best-seller lists.

Roman Catholic Church By the end of the fourth century, ST. AUGUSTINE had established rules against suicide that would prove the basis for Christian doctrine down through the ages. He argued that suicide allowed no opportunity for repentance and branded all suicides as crimes. St. Augustine's teachings and those of other early church authorities were incorporated into the laws of the Roman Catholic Church and, later, the Anglican Church. Suicide was seen as an act inspired by the devil and was ruled to be a mortal sin. Bodies of suicides were denied Christian burial, and even attempters of suicide were excommunicated. Church laws did make an exception in the case of "insane" people, and also exempted young children from the severe penalties of law. These religious laws against suicide have remained in effect in the Roman Catholic Church (and in many Protestant churches, as well). Today, however, many priests and ministers appear inclined to find ways in which church laws can be altered toward leniency in special circumstances. As Anglican Bishop John Robinson suggests: "Truth finds expression in different ages. Times change and even Christians change with them."

For a more complete discussion of this matter, read Dr. Norman L. Farberow's "History of Suicide" in the front of this work.

romance, breakup of Some people, especially young people, suffer deep depression and feelings of worthlessness following the breakup of a romance. Such persons have been known to think and even talk about suicide—which is one clue to look for in persons who have been so affected by a romantic loss.

Francine Klagsbrun debunks the notion of romantic suicide, stating that "The myth of romanticizing suicide places it in the realm of artistry and beauty, and removes it from the grim realities of everyday life." She adds: "It is much easier to sympathize with the sorrows of Romeo and Juliet than to acknowledge the real-life suffering endured by parents of a young couple who shared a suicide pact."

While it is true that there is nothing romantic or beautiful about suicide, for some deeply distressed people, the breakup of a romance is impetus enough to consider committing suicide . . . and sometimes can precipitate an attempt at self-destruction. (See also ROMEO AND JULIET.)

Romans See "History of Suicide," the introduction to this book.

Romantic Agony, The Book written by MARIO PRAZ in which it is shown how fatalism gradually came to mean fatal sex. As ALFRED ALVAREZ notes, "the *femme fatale* replaced death as the supreme inspiration." He then adds that "Fatal sex also had the added advantage of being safer and slower than suicide, an enhancement rather than the contradiction of a life dedicated to art."

Romantics, the ALFRED ALVAREZ in *The Savage God*, explains how the Romantics—led by THOMAS CHATTERTON who killed himself in 1770 at the age of 17—thought of death as "the great inspirer" and "great consoler." It was they who made suicide fashionable, and during the epidemic in France in the 1830s, "practiced it as one of the most elegant of sports." Writes Alvarez: "For the young would-be poets, novelists, dramatists, painters, great lovers and members of countless suicide clubs, to die by one's own hand was a short and sure way to fame."

In England, though it started there with Chatterton's suicide, the epidemic never quite took hold. The suicide rate rose, but authorities thought the causes had little to do with literacy or artistic excesses. As the 19th century wore on, Romanticism gradually dissipated and along with it the idealization of death.

Romeo and Juliet Written ca. 1595, by William Shakespeare. This tragedy is based on a poem by Arthur Brooke which in turn was taken from a romance by Bendello. The Montagues and the Capulets, two powerful families in Verona, have an ancient grudge. A byzantine story line filled with twists and turns, plus one of the most beautiful love scenes in the English language, culminates in the deaths by suicide of both young lovers, Romeo and Juliet, he by poison and she by Romeo's dagger. The alarm is spread and the feuding Montagues and Capulets meet at the tomb. The families are reconciled by the tragedy their feud had caused.

ropes, as suicide weapon Hanging, strangulation and suffocation—closely related enough to be regarded as a single means of self-destruction—is today the second most common method of suicide in the 15 to 24 years of age group for all persons, male and female. The percentage of those who chose this method of suicide in the period from 1970 to 1980, according to the Centers for Disease Control, Atlanta, Georgia, was 15.8; it was second only to firearms and explosives, at 57.5%. Parents who suspect suicidal behavior or fear a suicidal act should clear their home of *all* lethal weapons, including ropes or lines.

Rothko, Mark Russian-born American painter (1903-1970), influenced by Max Weber, was originally a figurative painter but his later abstract works are his most famous. Rothko said he painted "tragedy, ecstasy, doom, and so on." Rothko committed suicide in New York City, February 25, 1970.

Rousseau, Jean-Jacques French philosopher, political thinker, and novelist

(1712-1778), who was born in Geneva, the son of a watchmaker. It was in his novel *La Nouvelle Heloise* (1769), a famous and influential work, that he emphasized people's natural right to end their lives as long as they cause no harm to others by doing so. Rousseau established one condition, however: People who have responsibilities to others should not commit suicide. His notion that the "natural," or primitive, man ("the noble savage") was inherently good, and that evil arose from the distortions of society, was enormously influential in the rise of romanticism in literature and music, and is still a powerful force, in education especially.

Russia The actual suicide rate in Russia or the Soviet Union, is not known, since they do not report data to the World Health Organization (WHO) in Geneva. They say that suicide is, after all, a "bourgeois activity" that does not occur in the Soviet Union. One could speculate that with their recent admitted problems with a high alcoholism rate, the suicide rate is keeping apace. But this is only speculation.

Ryder, Hugh Surgeon (fl. 1664-93) to King James II, who tells of "A young woman who had been at a Meetinghouse . . . in a great discontent went home and fell into such despair, that being melancholy by herself in her chamber, with a knife cut her throat . . ." The wound proved not to be lethal and under Ryder's care, the woman recovered. This account of a published case history served to reinforce the view of suicide being the result of a mental disorder.

Richard Hunter and Ida Macalpine, *Three Hundred Years of Psychiatry, 1535-1860* (London: Oxford University Press, 1963), pp. 226, 255.

S

St. Augustine of Hippo Born in North Africa (354-430 A.D.), the son of a Christian mother, St. Monica. After a dissolute youth, he was baptized at age 32 on Easter Sunday, 387, and in 391 was ordained a priest. He was consecrated a bishop in 394, at Hippo. A doctor of the church, he was one of the most prolific and influential doctrinal writers, with noted works to his credit such as *City of God* and *Confessions*. Until he denounced suicide as an unrepentable sin, there was no official church position against it. He considered suicide a form of homicide and thus a violation of the Decalogue Article, "Thou shalt not kill."

Saint-Exupéry, Antoine de French writer and aviator (1900-1944). Obsessed with aviation from an early age, he joined the French Army Air Force in 1921, then became a commercial pilot five years later. Throughout his career, he wrote popular books—many were fantasies for children—about flying. He celebrated his faith in man and life, his books being philosophical and mystical. Yet, all the while, he seemed preoccupied with thoughts of death. His father died when Saint-Exupéry was only four years old, and a brother died when he was 17.

His fantasy for young readers, *Le Petit Prince* (1943), romanticized suicide as a way of "going home," and depicted death as a painless process whereby one simply shed the body like "an old abandoned shell" after which the freed soul would soar into the skies. In 1944, while making a reconnaissance flight during World War II over Southern France, Saint-Exupéry disappeared. His *Citadelle* was published posthumously in 1948, with an English-language edition, *The Wisdom of the Sands*, in 1950.

Authorities never determined what happened to Saint-Exupéry's plane. Fellow pilots who saw him before he took off on his final mission said that he complained of a sleepless night and appeared restless and depressed. Also, the evening before the flight he had prepared a letter to serve as a last will. It is not known whether his death was a suicide or an accident.

Salvation Army In some areas of the U.S. and in Canada, the Salvation Army operates suicide prevention centers. For example, Syracuse, New York, runs the Salvation Army Barnabus and Booth House, complete with a hotline, referral and self-help group service. Check the front of the phone book or the white pages for such services in your area. You may also check the services listed in appendix 3 of this work.

Samaritans This organization was founded by the Reverend CHAD VARAH in London, in 1953, with the idea of befriending suicidal people. Today there are Samaritan suicide prevention and crisis centers in 26 countries, including the U.S. All of the workers are volunteers, themselves former suicide attempters, who work with suicidal people in much the same way ttat recovering alcoholics in ALCOHOLICS ANONYMOUS work with new members. Samaritan volunteers try to extend care and compassion, serving as substitute families or close friends. They do refer people to mental institutions, and will refer suicidals to professional therapists or psychiatrists.

There are two so-called suicide-prevention "chains" that operate worldwide: CONTACT (over 200 centers worldwide, 104 in the U.S.), and the Samaritans (approximately 220 worldwide, 6 in the U.S.). Check the white pages in your local phone book under "Contact" or "Samaritans."

The Samaritans gain their name from the parable of the Good Samaritan; their approach is always secular, practical and nonsectarian. Chad Varah edited *The Samaritans: To Help Those Tempted to Suicide or Despair.*

"Samsonic" suicides Samson's destruction of the Philistines in the Temple of Dagon was an act of vengeance, but, says historian George Rosen, "it was also suicidal." Dr. Rosen notes that "Recognizing that his desire for revenge could be achieved only at the cost of his life, Samson prayed, 'Let me die with the Philistines,' and his wish was granted" (Judges 16:23-31). This is probably the earliest historical description of a revenge type of suicide. Over the years, some have described revenge suicides as "Samsonic."

samurai The samurai, or members of the military class in feudal Japan, performed a ritualized suicide in the form of HARA-KIRI (described at length elsewhere in this work). It was an elaborate ceremonial death for the samurai warrior who had in some way humiliated or disgraced himself, and thus his family. Often, after a chieftain had died, the warrior would kill himself as a show of allegiance. And sometimes an emperor would order a samurai warrior to commit *hara kiri* to avoid the disgrace of a public execution. *Hara kiri* is an example of Durkheim's "altruistic" suicide, where the person is seemingly "boxed in," to use Shneidman's term, by the culture. Under such circumstances, self-infiicted death was considered honorable; to continue living would have been an act of ignominy. As Shneidman notes: "Society dictated their action and, as individuals, they were not strong enough to defy custom." (See also SEPPUKU.)

San Francisco Suicide Prevention Center One of the bigger centers in the U.S., it figures importantly in the education of individuals and groups in the vast Bay Area; it has a small paid staff, plus some 150 volunteer workers. One particular unique feature: Because the city has a high percentage of Chinese in its overall population, special staff members are hired to reach that minority group. Also, black consultants from the agency work with groups, churches or clubs in San Francisco to offer consultation and seminars about depression and self-destructive behavior. The center was started by Bernard Mayes, a former minister and British BBC correspondent in 1963, at a time when the city had the highest suicide rate in the U.S. First Executive director of San Francisco Suicide Prevention, Inc., was Roger Cornut. Jeanne Chadwick, MA, is the current director. The center's training period for volunteer workers lasts for eight weeks, with one three-hour meeting per week. The instruction is handled by a team that includes a psychiatrist, social workers, a drug specialist and other mental health professionals. The San Francisco Suicide Prevention Center is at 3940 Geary Boulevard, San Francisco, CA 94118; phone is (415) 221-1423.

Savage God, The: A Study of Suicide Non-fiction book by Alfred Alvarez, published in the U.S. by Random House in 1972. This excellent book is an account of poet Sylvia Plath's suicide and an investigation into motives for suicide, with particular emphasis on people in the arts—writers and poets, as well as philosophers. Alvarez, born in London in 1929, returns in the last section of the book to a very personal view of suicide as he chronicles, with candor, his own suicide attempt. The title comes from William Butler Yeats' "After Us the Savage God."

Scandinavia Among the three western Scandinavian countries (Denmark, Norway, Sweden) Denmark has the highest suicide rate per 100,000 population, according to World Health Organization (WHO) statistics, with a 1984 rate of 28% (all ages, both sexes). Sweden is in the middle with a 1983 (latest data) rate of 19.0%; Norway is third with a 1984 rate per 100,000 population of 14.5%. Denmark and Norway have both shown rate increases in the last decade, while Sweden's rate has shown a slight decline from 20.8% in 1975 to, the latest data available, 19.0%. Denmark's suicide rate in recent years has placed it in the top five countries for highest rates per 100,000 population.

Psychiatrist Herbert Hendin has written an informative book that will be of interest to many, entitled *Suicide and Scandinavia.*

schizophrenia General name for a group of psychotic reactions characterized by withdrawal, disturbances in emotional and affective life and, depending upon the type, the presence of hallucinations, delusions, negativistic behavior and progressive deterioration. Some types of schizophrenia are: disorganized, catatonic, paranoid and undifferentiated. The search for underlying causes has centered on both functional and organic factors. Because antipsychotic drugs have a marked effect on reducing the symptoms of the disorder, many authorities now believe that further research in the biochemistry of the brain is promising. (Investigators have searched for products in schizophrenics' blood that are not found in so-called normals and have tried to analyze disorders in the neurotransmitter substances in the brain.)

However, the cause or causes of schizophrenia are still obscure and may well be the result of the interaction of two or more factors. A better understanding of the complex disorder depends, of course, on the results of ongoing research.

Schizophrenia often strikes its victims during the early or mid-teen years and at first may be hardly noticeable. However, as the disorder progresses in severity, schizophrenics may develop strong suicidal tendencies. The break with reality, sometimes mixed with deep depression, occasionally leads to complex mixes of beliefs and fantasies that can bring about self-destruction. There have been cases, through relatively rare, where schizophrenics have attacked or killed others and then committed suicide.

Schopenhauer, Arthur German philosopher (1788-1860) who formulated a philosophy of pessimism: Discord or strife is the central feature of all existence, both within the individual and in the universe at large, with frustration and pain as the inevitable products, and resignation, or negation of the will, as by the saint or ascetic, as the only solution. In his basic work, *The World as Will and Idea* (1818), Schopenhauer postulates that the world is the expression of the individual's idea, and especially his will, which is, basically, an expression of a universal, blind impulse to exist. Art, he says, is both a means of understanding existence and of escape from the senseless strife.

Schopenhauer said that "It will generally be found that as soon as the terrors of life reach the point where they outweigh the terrors of death, a man will put an end to his life." He also said that suicide may be regarded as an experiment—but "a clumsy experiment to make, for it involves the destruction of the very consciousness which puts the question and awaits the answer." And the question is: What change will death produce in a person's existence and in his or her insight into the nature of things?

second attempts (among suicidal persons) Simply because a person shows improvement following a suicidal crisis doesn't mean that the suicidal risk is over. According to Shneidman and Farberow (in *Some Facts About Suicide*), most suicides occur within about three months following the beginning of "improvement," when the individual has the energy to put his morbid thoughts and feelings into effect. Many of the tens of thousands who attempt suicide will try again. Four out of five persons who commit suicide have attempted to kill themselves at least once previously.

self-destruction Many people, especially today's young people, seem bent on destroying themselves by alcohol and/or drug abuse, careless and fast driving, and other self-defeating actions. Freud said that all people have unconscious wishes to hurt themselves, punish themselves, or even destroy themselves in various ways. In his book *Man Against Himself*, Karl Menninger, an ardent follower of Freud, points out that people who do dangerously self-destructive things may unconsciously want to die without taking responsibility for killing themselves. He called such people "CHRONIC SUICIDES," people who destroy themselves gradually, usually on the pretext of "making life more bearable." He included the accident-prone as well as hypochondriacs in this category. The irony is, as noted by Klagsbrun in *Too Young to Die*, "In most of these situations nobody thinks to connect the destructive behavior to suicide."

Seneca, Lucius Annaeus Son of the rhetorician of the same name, Seneca (ca. 3 B.C.-65 A.D.) became entrusted with the education of Nero, later became consul, was charged with plotting against Nero and ultimately forced to commit suicide to avoid the emperor's vengeance. After he stabbed himself, Seneca's wife, Paulina, not wishing to be left behind, also killed herself in the same way. Seneca was a major representative of Roman Stoicism; his philosophy is contained in his *Moral Essays* and other works.

separations in marriage Marital separations and/or breakups strongly impact on children, and many experts are of the opinion that today's increased rate of young suicides reflects that impact. In recent years, John Bowlby's work on the contributions of psychoanalysis to understanding suicide has pinpointed the importance of separation, especially the *anxiety* aroused by separation and loss, and its impact on the family concomitant, suicide. Bowlby focused on the clear-cut connection between separation anxiety in children and marriage breakups and threats of suicide in parents.

Joseph Richman's book, *Family Therapy for Suicidal People*, discusses this issue at length. Dr. Richman writes that suicide is a form of "separation from a family that cannot separate without destructive consequences." He goes on to say that:

> Moreover, the actual occurrence of separation and loss experiences, and especially the amount of separation anxiety in the lives of families where suicide is a major issue, cannot be expressed in numbers . . . What has been overlooked . . . is that separation experiences occur in the entire family and not only in the suicidal individual. Overlooked, too, is that such separation experiences are handed down from one generation to the next.

Discussing characteristics of families with suicidal potential, Dr. Richman theorizes that children, therefore, may be "programmed or destined for success in the arts, sciences or politics; or for mental illness, or suicide, or a combination of these."

In summary, for suicidal families, the rites of passage so common in today's society—separation, divorce, abandonment, etc.—often prove fatal. The threat of separation or loss, role change or even function change, can lead to suicide within the family.

J. Bowlby, *Attachment and Loss*, Vol. I: "Attachment" (New York: Basic Books, 1969).

J. Bowlby, *Attachment and Loss*, Vol. II: "Loss" (New York: Basic Books, 1973).

J. Bowlby, *Maternal Care and Mental Health* (New York: Columbia University Press, 1951).

J. Richman, *Family Therapy for Suicidal People* (New York: Springer, 1986).

seppuku In Japan, when suicide was still an integral part of the Samurai warrior's moral code, the only honorable means for a disgraced warrior to redeem himself was to commit *seppuku* or hara-kiri, in which he disemboweled himself with his own sword. The elaborate procedure often took hours to complete; a second person ended the ceremonial death by cutting off the suicide's head.

Although Japan outlawed hara-kiri in 1868, the tradition of honorable suicide continues to influence Japanese practice. During World War II, for instance, more than 1,000 young Japanese soldiers served as kamikaze pilots who flew their planes at enemy warships and certain death. Near the end of the war and shortly before Japan's defeat, a number of military officers committed ritual seppuku rather than accept the humiliation of surrender. As recently as 1970, the internationally-famous author, YUKIO MISHIMA, committed seppuku as a plea to his countrymen for the return of old values and old traditions in Japan—one of which was the concept of dying with honor.

The word *seppuku* comes from the Japanese rendering of two Chinese characters meaning "cutting of the stomach." The same two characters in reverse order can also be pronounced *hara-kiri*, which became much more common in spoken Japanese. (See also JAPAN.)

sex differences, suicide rates Traditionally, women and young girls are the major suicide attempters in modern society; an estimated three to four times as many women as men attempt suicide every year, but roughly three times as many men as women complete suicide. Some experts estimate that, among young people, as many as nine times more girls than boys attempt suicide unsuccessfully.

In the 1980s, however, in several metropolitan centers (New York, Los Angeles and Chicago, among others), the ratio of lethal or completed suicides for young males and young females has been narrowing. In California, for example, the highest rise in suicide rates among any group of females during the decade has been among young urban black women (in their early to mid-twenties).

Suicide is still more prevalent among elderly males than among the female elderly (65 and over). In the U.S., in 1980, for instance, the suicide rate per 100,000 population for males 65 and over was 37.5 (white) and 11.4 (black); for their female counterparts—same age group—the rate was 6.5 (white) and only 1.4 (black).

There has not yet been sufficient, or intensive enough, research to determine why the apparent increase in completed suicides among young females in urban centers. Klagsbrun (1981) writes that it "may reflect a growing aggressiveness and violence on the part of women, as some authorities have suggested." There are, however, other complex and subtle influences at work in this situation, according to Klagsbrun: "As women have tried to change their roles and raise their aspirations, they have met increasing frustrations and pressures." It is true that too many doors are still closed to women, especially to young urban black females, trying to enter the job market or start professional careers. Add to that the fierce competition for jobs—for which many people simply aren't prepared—plus the pressure today to succeed, and many find the stresses and frustrations overwhelming. In desperation, they opt for suicide.

Still, again in Klagsbrun's words: "Suicide involves so many variables that no simple or definitive answers exist to how patterns change or why they differ among the sexes." It is a subject area that demands much more research by suicidologists and other experts.

Sexton, Anne Harvey American poet (1928-1974) and good friend of Sylvia Plath, both of whom killed themselves. Sexton wrote a poem titled, "Wanting to Die" (1966), in which she describes her desire as "the almost unnameable lust." She wrote in a memoir of her poet friend Plath, "We talked of death, and this was life to us." It is said that the two brilliant young poets spent many hours together going over details of their suicide attempts. And in the end both finally succeeded by completed suicides. Sexton is author of *Live or Die*, which includes the poem "Wanting to Die." The collection won the 1967 Pulitzer Prize for poetry.

Shneidman, Dr. Edwin S. One of the foremost authorities in the field of suicidology and currently professor of thanatology at the UCLA School of Medicine. Shneidman, author and editor of numerous books on suicide (including the recent *Definition of Suicide*), was cofounder and codirector—with Dr. Norman L. Farberow—of the famed Los Angeles Suicide Prevention Center. He was charter director of the Center for the Study of Suicide Prevention at the National Institute of Mental Health, Bethesda, Maryland. He has been a Public Health Service special research fellow and visiting professor at Harvard, visiting professor at the Ben Gurion University of the Negev, clinical associate at the Massachusetts General Hospital and the Karlinska (Stockholm) Hospital, and a fellow at the Center for Advanced Study in the Behavioral Sciences (at Stanford).

Dr. Shneidman has been president of the Clinical and Public Service Divisions of the American Psychological Association and founder-president of the American Association of Suicidology (Denver). His book, *Death of Man*, was nominated for a National Book Award. Dr. Shneidman has contributed chapters on suicide to a number of anthologies and other publications, including the *Encyclopaedia Britannica* (1973), *Comprehensive Textbook of Psychiatry* (1975) and *Encyclopaedia of Psychology* (1984).

Dr. Edwin S. Shneidman has devoted a lifetime of work to the field of suicidology and has made a major contribution to the thinking of members in all disciplines who are still trying to prevent suicides and help suicidal persons discover less drastic alternatives to life's problems.

shock treatment, and depression A form of somatic therapy consisting of application of weak electric currents to the head in order to produce convulsion and unconsciousness. Introduced some 40 years ago, about 10 years before antidepressant drugs. Few medical treatments have caused more controversy. Many consider ECT a kind of medieval torture, an inhumane procedure that should be banned.

ECT is still widely used in the treatment of depression, however. An estimated 60,000 to 100,000 persons undergo electroconvulsive (electroshock is the common name used for ECT) treatment every year. Obviously, then, many experts believe that ECT is an effective and viable treatment. It is almost always used with adults, most often with elderly patients who have enjoyed no relief from drugs or psychotherapy. ECT does have one side effect that gives it a particularly bad press: some memory loss of the hours and days that precede the treatment. But such loss is, generally speaking, transitory. (See also ELECTROCONVULSIVE THERAPY.)

siblings, grief after suicide The suicide of a brother or sister, whether older or younger, often produces not only grief but also fear, confusion and often guilt in surviving siblings. Dr. Mary Giffin observes that almost every youngster has wished during a time of anger, envy or jealousy for the death of a brother or sister. Then, when death occurs, the youngster is stricken with complex feelings of anguish that translate into: "Somehow I'm responsible." When the death is caused by suicide, the fear, confusion and guilt feelings sometimes become unbearable. Parents will often try to hide the facts of a suicide from surviving children in a family. This can only add to the child's fears and confused grief. Sibling guilt and desolation are only made worse by half-truths, conspiracies of silence, and implications of stigmatization, according to Dr. Giffin. Survivor brothers and sisters then suffer feelings of blame, wondering how they might have prevented the suicide, or in what ways they might unwittingly have contributed to their siblings' self-destructive decision.

sin, concept of While a few societies and religions have tolerated or even looked with favor on suicide, it has usually been regarded with repulsion. St. Augustine regarded suicide as a sin, and a number of Church councils denied the suicide religious rites. Jewish law and the Koran, the sacred text of Islam, denounced it, and medieval law decreed that a suicide's property be confiscated and the body desecrated by being dragged by the heels through the streets, face downward, or buried at a crossroads with a stake through its heart.

But it was St. Augustine's denouncement of suicide as a sin that effected an official Church position against an act, which, he asserted, "precluded the possibility of repentance." He called it a form of homicide and thus a violation of the Decalogue Article, "Thou shalt not kill." (See also "History of Suicide" at front of this book.)

sleeplessness Often one of the several symptoms of clinical depression. Severely depressed people may have trouble sleeping, and wake up in the middle of the night or the early morning hours. The opposite may be the case, as well; they often sleep all the time, dozing off in midday or early evening. Both types, the sleepless person and the constant dozer, will usually begin to lose their appetites, eat little or nothing, and become lifeless and gaunt.

People who cannot sleep are not all victims of clinical depression, of course. But if this is a reaction noticeable with a cluster of other symptoms, such as loss of appetite, loneliness, unusual silence and withdrawal from family and friends, then the individual may need real help in the form of professional treatment. If such symptoms go unnoticed or unattended, the depressed person sometimes retreats further into himself, and suicide may begin to seem a real alternative to a life of despair and misery. (See also DEPRESSION; INSOMNIA, AS SUICIDE CLUE.)

social workers The suicidal person has a very restrictive, limited focus, what some would call "tunnel vision." His troubled mind does not always grasp the complete picture of just how best to handle his serious, despairing problems. He usually has a need for professional help. Friends and family mean well but simply lack expertise and experience, and may be too emotionally involved.

One group of possible helpers is the social worker. Many are competent counselors, understanding and good listeners—and supportive. Even though they may be untrained in suicide crisis intervention, social workers are a good resource, with helpful information relating to both evaluation and referrals. By his or her acquired basic knowledge, skills and demeanor, a social worker has developed a capacity to listen, empathize, understand the suicidal person's innermost feelings, recognize dangerous symptoms, and direct that person toward constructive psychotherapeutic consultation.

Professional associations encourage the public to call for sources of recommendations and referrals. One such reputable organization in the U.S. is the National Association of Social Workers, 1425 H Street, N.W., Suite 600, Washington, DC, 20005; phone is (202) 628-6800. A social worker should be accredited by the Academy of Certified Social Workers.

society Suicide is still a whispered, almost unmentionable word in all too many segments of modern society. Some families and friends pretend not to hear the dread word which leaves such lasting scars. For suicide remains, as Rabbi Grollman notes, a taboo subject in the minds of many people, a subject which stigmatizes both victim and the survivors. Why? Because self-destruction is an act that violates the most basic and fundamental tenets of Western belief. After all, religions condemn it as a sin, legal systems throughout the world have promulgated laws which say it is a crime, and some courts have punished families of suicides while kings confiscated the property of a suicide.

Tragically, despite the fact that most of the cruel old laws are now no longer in effect, society's conscious as well as unconscious condemnation of suicide continues. Families of a suicide still are stigmatized by our society. We would rather our loved ones die of any other cause, no matter how painful or drawn out. As Shneidman says: "Suicide is never totally forgotten."

Probably society's present attitude stems from the fact that the very act itself contradicts the value of human life, an essentially democratic and social ethic. WILLIAM JAMES thought of suicide as a "religious disease," the cure for which is "religious faith." The following words, by the English essayist, novelist and poet G.K. Chesterton, express society's lingering perception of the seriousness of suicide.

> The man who kills a man kills a man.
> The man who kills himself kills all men.
> As far as he is concerned, he wipes out the world.

Chesterton's words suggest that no person ought to reject the great gift of life that has been bestowed. As a violation of one of the Ten Commandments, suicide has been called a crime against God, a horrendous offense punishable in hell.

Fortunately, while society is slow to change, scientists have come to take a more enlightened stand on the subject of suicide, particularly in the last 50 years or so. And, though the act of self-destruction is still socially taboo in the Western world, education and mental health advances have encouraged its study, and the effective treatment of the suicidal has not only begun but is progressing rapidly. As Shneidman notes, "In the wake of current professional studies and news articles about them, the public is beginning to realize that suicide can be prevented."

Socrates Greek philosopher (ca. 470-399 B.C.) who broke with earlier philosophical traditions and laid the foundations for the development of both ethics and logic. He wrote nothing himself, yet his ideas survive in the writings of Plato and Xenophon. Refusing to bow to tyranny, whether imposed by the mob or by oligarchs, Socrates was tried on the charge of corrupting the young people of Athens and sentenced to death by drinking HEMLOCK.

Sorrows of Young Werther, The Novel by JOHANN WOLFGANG VON GOETHE, German poet, dramatist and novelist. This romantic narrative (German title, *Die Leiden des jungen Werthers*, published in 1774) created a sensation throughout Europe. About a young man who kills himself, the novel had a startlingly strong influence on young people of the time. Men began to dress like Werther, speak like Goethe's protagonist and dream of killing themselves like Werther. The whole Werther phenomenon touched off a wave of romantic notions about suffering for one's genius, struggling for art and dying young while the world mourned its idealistic heroes.

South Carolina The state's rate per 100,000 population of suicide has declined since 1970, when it was 10.9%, and in 1980 stood at 9.5%. However, the actual number of suicides in South Carolina rose from 283 in 1970 to a total of 298 in 1980. The state's 9.5 rate per 100,000 population ranks it second only to Mississippi (9.2) rate of the 16 states classified as the "South" by the Centers for Disease Control, in Atlanta.

South Dakota South Dakota in 1980 had 88 suicides for a rate per 100,000 population of 12.7, highest of all 12 "North Central" states (as categorized by the Centers for Disease Control). This 1980 figure was an increase from the rate figure for 1970 of 9.0—a significant 3.7 rate jump. The state had 60 suicides in 1970, 88 in 1980.

Soviet Union See RUSSIA.

Soylent Green A 1973 movie starring Charlton Heston and Edward G. Robinson. Its theme was of an overpopulated world in which people are encouraged to go to special suicide centers to be assisted in dying. Similar to Kurt Vonnegut's short story, "Welcome to the Monkey House."

statistics In his explanatory remarks for chapter one of *Research on Suicide*, John L. McIntosh notes that certain specific aspects in the field of suicidology require resolution. One such aspect involves accuracy of official data. Writes Professor McIntosh: "While official data are readily available and frequently criticized, few have studied the extent of the data problems or have offered viable alternatives to them. At the minimum, clearer evidence as to the nature of the bias claimed for official figures is needed."

Erwin Stengel notes that:

> the validity of the statistical data concerning suicide and the comparability of national suicide rates have been questioned. A worldwide survey carried out with the help of a questionnaire revealed great differences in the methods and criteria of certification of suicide. For national suicide rates to be comparable, not only the methods of ascertainment ought to be equally reliable, but also the population census.

In any community, in any country, there are social pressures brought against categorizing death as suicide. Experts such as Stengel have long made clear the need for caution in the evaluation of national differences. The introduction to the suicide mortality statistics of the World Health Organization (WHO) for 1968 warns that: "The true incidence of suicide is hard to ascertain. Varying methods of certifying causes of death, different registration and coding procedures, and other factors affect the extent and completeness of coverage, making international comparisons impracticable."

However, as Stengel cautions,

> It would be a mistake to dismiss the statistical method in suicide research out of hand. But it is in need of critical scrutiny, and the comparability of data ought to be checked before conclusions about the significance of differences are drawn. Uniformity of search procedures and of criteria of categorization will not be easy to achieve, but they are worth striving for.

Indeed, the very definition of what precisely constitutes a suicidal act is essential to reliable suicide statistics. Statistical data based on varying concepts and/or different definitions of suicide are not strictly comparable, as Dr. Stengel has explained.

status loss and suicide In an age where image is so important (often it appears to be everything), loss of status or identity can prove devastating. This is especially true for young people and even children. Identity, after all, gives one a sense of self, of security, direction, of knowing who you are and what you should strive for in life.

If youngsters do (at long last) find an identity, and that identity is suddenly stripped from them, for whatever reason, before they feel secure and worthwhile, "suicide," says Dr. Mary Giffin, a Chicago psychiatrist, "may be the means they choose for coping with the loss."

When people are suicidal, there is no single trait by which all of them can be categorized. However, they are always disturbed, and often they are depressed. Loss of status or identity may be, in certain cases, the crucial indicator of imminent suicide.

stock market crash, 1929, and suicides On October 29, 1929, there was a startling end to postwar (World War I) prosperity as stock prices plummeted. Stock losses for the period from 1929 to 1931 were estimated at $50 billion, and the result was the worst depression in U.S. history. A number of businessmen lost everything in the precipitous crash and killed themselves, some by jumping from tall office buildings in Manhattan. No accurate data exist as to how many suicides were committed as a direct result of the crash.

Stoic philosophy The Roman Stoic who determined that he had had enough of life had his veins severed by trained technicians of the day. SENECA, one of the leaders of the Roman Stoics, wrote that, "If life please you, live. If not, you have a right to return whence you came." He and his fellow Stoics did not, however, advocate suicide merely to escape from everyday life. They were concerned with people living good and rational lives, free of serious sickness, debilitating disease or political oppression. They urged people to think very carefully before committing suicide, and to allow themselves to suffer before impulsively destroying themselves.

The Stoic philosophy started in Greece, where advocates adopted a lenient view of suicide, which was a result of their opinion that death is a release from the sufferings of life. Suicide to them was not so much a matter of right and wrong as it was determining the most logical way to act in a given situation. Legend says that ZENO, founder of the Stoic philosophy, killed himself after breaking his toe. He decided that God had sent his broken toe as a sign that he had lived long enough—he was 98 years old at the time. Zeno's successor, CLEANTHES, is thought to have committed suicide, too. He had developed a boil on his gum and was advised by a doctor to abstain from eating for a couple of days, thus allowing time for the boil to heal. Instead, Cleanthes continued to starve himself after the sore had healed. He argued that having gone so far on the path to death, he might as well complete the act.

"Stoicism," incidentally, is so called from the Stoa (porch) in Athens where Zeno taught.

"Stormy Monday" According to questionable suicide statistics, the so-called "Stormy Monday" is the favored day for self-destruction. For example, in 1979 (an "average" year), about 82 suicides occurred nationwide, every Monday. By contrast, Saturday statistics showed an average of 71 suicides, the lowest rate among days of the week. Interestingly, Saturday saw the most deaths by auto accident and homicide that particular year.

stress as suicide clue Suicide has become the tragic solution for a growing number of young people, including adolescents, who experience problems that may seem unresolvable. For many and diverse reasons, it has become increasingly difficult to be a young person in our society. A number of forces—cultural, social, biological, psychological—can and do join to create unbearable stress. The pressure to succeed, e.g., in school, is one major source of stressful friction between teenagers, college students and parents. Unrealistic expectations of both young people and parents in this regard can lead to extreme anxiety, communication problems and friction. School problems are now considered by experts as being leading suicide "at risk" factors in young people.

Dr. Jarad H. Kashani, a professor of psychiatry, believes that as many as one-quarter of all college freshmen will either consider or act out suicidal feelings. A quote from one student (from the 1970 White House Conference on Children) reads: "If I ever commit suicide, I'll leave my school schedule behind as a suicide note."

The unbelievable stress placed on Japanese teenagers during examinations is one of the factors that is contributing to the high teen suicide rate—one of the highest in the world—in Japan. The examination system is referred to as "Examination Hell."

Stressful behavior—where the person acts nervously, irrationally, peculiarly, "differently"—is one clue, or crucial indicator, of possible suicidal thoughts and/or intentions. Coupled or clustered with other verbal or behavioral clues, this often signals imminent suicide. (See also CLUES, WARNING SIGNS; plus individual entries, INSOMNIA, etc.)

suicidal crisis, acute See ACUTE SUICIDES.

suicidal crisis, how to help in Suicidal crises usually concern two people: the suicidal person and the "significant other." The latter may be a parent, lover, associate, friend, whoever. This "significant other" must be advised immediately of the situation, and, where possible, become involved in the life-saving efforts.

Edwin Shneidman says,

> Sometimes, really only a little help is needed during the period of the suicidal crisis. A person who verges on suicide also clings to life. All of his problems cannot be erased in a telephone call during the middle of the night to a staffman at a suicide prevention service. Should the posture of the "significant other" momentarily shift in this crucial relationship, there is no guarantee that the story will have a happy ending. But the suicide, for the moment, has been averted.

How quickly others intervene in a suicidal crisis is crucial. If you suspect suicidal behavior in a person, act on your judgment. Tell others immediately—parents, friends, doctor, teacher, minister, any key people in the person's life. Don't let others put you off by playing down your notion of how serious you think the situation is. Insist that others pay attention. As Klagsbrun says, "The worst you can do is be wrong, and feel foolish for stirring up a suicide scare where none exists. But you do far better to err in the direction of overcaution than to ignore the signals and take a chance on losing a life."

Trained professional or volunteer staff members of any accredited suicide prevention and crisis center can predict a suicide with more than chance accuracy. As Shneidman notes: "Active, increasingly effective suicide prevention services offer the suicidal person a fresh grasp on life."

Francine Klagsbrun, *Too Young to Die: Youth and Suicide* (New York: Pocket Books, 1981).

Edwin S. Shneidman, PhD, and Philip Mandelkorn, *Suicide: It Doesn't Have to Happen* (West Point, Pennsylvania: Merck, Sharp & Dohme-Health Information Services, in cooperation with the American Association of Suicidology).

suicidal ideation Having thoughts about killing oneself. Authorities say it is not abnormal to have such thoughts at one time or another during the course of a lifetime. A healthy, well-integrated personality, however, quickly dismisses such destructive thoughts as representing an unacceptable alternative to life, with its endless burdens.

suicide, definition of See DEFINITION OF SUICIDE.

suicide, "how-to" manuals Several controversial suicide "how-to" manuals have been published in Europe. In a *Time* magazine article by P. Blake, entitled "Going Gentle into That Good Night: Do Suicide Manuals Create a Bias Toward Death?" the writer discusses manuals from Britain and France, as well as publications of the U.S.-based HEMLOCK SOCIETY which support "the option of active voluntary euthanasia for the terminally ill." The "how-to" manuals and Hemlock publications include:

Guillon, C., and Y. Le Bonniec, *Suicide mode d'emploi: Histoire, technique, actualite* ("Suicide: Operating Instructions") (Paris: Editions Alain Moreau, 1982).

Humphry, D. *Let Me Die Before I Wake: Hemlock's Book of Self-Deliverance for the Dying* (Los Angeles: Hemlock Society, 1983). A third edition was published in 1984 by the society and distributed by the Grove Press, New York. First editions, 1981, were sold only to Hemlock Society members. The book addresses the option of "rational suicide" only for a person in advance terminal illness or serious incurable physical illness.

Humphry, D. and A. Wickett, *Jean's Way* (New York: Quartet Books, 1978; Fontana, 1981). The "Jean" in the book's title was Derek Humphry's first wife. It is considered a classic account of what the authors call, "rational voluntary euthanasia."

Koestler, A. *Exit: A Guide to Self-Deliverance* (London: EXIT, 1981). Book available only to EXIT members (British Voluntary Euthanasia Society) over 25 and distributed to over 8,000 members.

Suicide, Le First scientific study of suicide, by Emile Durkheim, noted French sociologist. Originally published in 1897 and published in this country in 1951 as *Suicide*, translated by J.A. Spaulding and G. Simpson. The historical, groundbreaking work, important in and of itself, has had a continuing and pervasive impact on subsequent work in the field of suicidology.

suicide, pre-teen The very young—children as young as two—are also trying to commit suicide in increasing numbers. Suicide, it would appear, is following the same pattern as drug use, that is, moving down the age scale from college students through high schoolers and then to elementary school young people. In 1986, on Long Island, a girl only 11 years old hanged herself. *Time* reported an eight-year-old boy attempted suicide by hanging but failed because he couldn't tie a strong enough knot. Dr. Mohammad Shafii, a professor of psychiatry, University of Louisville, says, "In the clinic, we have seen five- or six-year-olds who have attempted suicide by hanging or jumping out of a window." Dr. Mary Giffin reports that at the 1982 convention of the American Psychiatric Association, psychiatrist Perihan Rosenthal described encounters with six suicidal children, all under five years old. One boy, Benji, was only two and a half years old. He was upset over his parents' divorce.

Yet the National Center for Health Statistics still does not compute suicide data for children under age 10. There is a belief—in recent years shown to be erroneous—that suicide in children under 10 is so rare as to be unmeasurable. Thus, no reliable data exist for suicides of youngsters under 10. Psychologist Maria Kovacs surveyed 127 Pittsburgh elementary school children and found that 41% admitted to having suicidal thoughts. The tragic phenomenon of suicide in modern America is not the exclusive act of only the teenager and the elderly.

Suicide Education Institute of Boston, The (SEI) Nonprofit group actively engaged in the education of mental health clinicians on the issue of suicide and advances in the treatment of severely depressed and suicidal individuals. The institute's director is Dr. Douglas Jacobs, who has also developed and directed Harvard Medical School's annual suicide symposium for seven years. Address: Suicide Education Institute of Boston, 437 Newtonville Avenue, Newton, MA 02160; phone is (617) 332-5165; administrative director is Denise Brouillette, RN, MBA.

Suicide in America Book by psychiatrist-author Dr. Herbert Hendin, internationally known authority on the subject of suicide. The book examines the personal and social factors contributing to suicide among different groups of people, including the young, in America; published in 1982 by W.W. Norton. In 1982, Dr. Hendin received the Louis I. Dublin award of the American Association of Suicidology. His other books include: *The Age of Sensation; Black Suicide*; and *Suicide and Scandinavia.*

Suicide Information and Crisis Center (SIEC) Established in 1982, SIEC operates under the auspices of the Canadian

Mental Health Association. Its aim is to collect all the literature regarding suicidal behaviors published in the English language since 1955 and to make this data available to all interested persons. For address, see Appendix 3, Canada, under Provincial and Territorial Agencies.

"Suicide Is Painless" Also known as "Song from M*A*S*H." It was the theme song of the long-running television series starring Alan Alda, and was taken from the 1970 Twentieth Century-Fox motion picture of the same name. Words by Mike Altman, music by Johnny Mandell, the tune is copyrighted 1970 by Twentieth Century Music Corporation, Los Angeles, California, and Twentieth Century Music Corporation, Ltd., London, England.

Suicide and Life Threatening Behavior Official publication of the American Association of Suicidology, edited by Ronald Maris, PhD, Center for the Study of Suicide, University of South Carolina. Address orders and inquiries about the professional journal (currently in its 16th year) to: The Guilford Press, Journals Department, 200 Park Avenue South, New York, NY 10003.

suicide notes Research indicates that between 12 and 42% of suicide victims leave notes. The average figure shows that approximately one-third of all suicides leave a note. Many notes are destroyed by families who fear stigmatization. One study by psychologists Edwin Shneidman and Norman L. Farberow found that it is possible to distinguish between genuine and simulated (fake) notes—and that the genuine notes included more angry feelings and more expressions of revenge than the simulated notes (which were composed by carefully selected people asked to think as if they were about to kill themselves). Most genuine suicide notes are specific as to instructions to survivors, very decisive; they give little evidence of thinking about suicide *per se*, and more evidence of self-blame and hostility.

suicide pacts There have been a number of instances involving suicide pacts among various suicidal persons or parties. In the *Indian Journal of Social Work*, K. Sathyarathi, in 1975, wrote about "Usual and Unusual Suicide Pacts in Bangalore." Marvin Miller, PhD, compiled a non-annotated bibliography, *Suicide Pacts*, which is listed as Bibliography R-37 in the 1984 catalogue of his San Diego, CA, The Information Center.

One highly publicized suicide pact between two teenagers resulted in the book *Craig and Joan*. In 1969, Joan Fox and Craig Badiali, both 17, killed themselves by asphyxiation. The two New Jersey teens left 24 suicide notes between them protesting the Vietnam War.

On March 10, 1987, four Bergenfield, New Jersey, teenagers—two boys and two girls—decided to commit suicide together by sitting in a car with the motor running and inside a locked garage. Thomas Rizzo, 19; Thomas Olton, 18; and sisters Lisa and Cheryl Burress, 16 and 17, were discovered dead in the locked car on the morning of March 11, victims of carbon monoxide poisoning; estimated time of death was between 3:30 and 4:00 A.M. The four young people were reportedly distraught over the death of a friend, Joe Major, who had lost his life in a fall from the Palisades in Fort Lee, New Jersey, in September 1986.

Two days after the Bergenfield tragedy, another suicide pact cost the lives of teenagers Karen Logan, 17, and Nancy Grannan, in Alsip, Illinois. They had apparently killed themselves in a garage full of auto exhaust, and police said they had probably been influenced by the news of the joint suicides of the four New Jersey young people.

suicide prevention-crisis centers See listing of AAS accredited centers in Appendix 3.

suicide register See DATA BANKS, BASES.

suicide threats Any and all suicide threats, those said seriously or jokingly, should be taken seriously. It is a myth and misconception that people who talk about suicide don't do it. Sometimes they do. All threats must be taken as a serious warning. The slightest thing can sometimes turn the thought into reality. For instance, refusing to take a suicide threat seriously can be the triggering factor. To the suicidal, it confirms that "nobody cares" or understands, and may serve as the catalyst to attempt suicide.

A suicide or suicide attempt has often been recognized by experts as a "cry for help." Most suicides are ambivalent; there's an urge to die as expressed in the threat, but there's also an urge to live. If the cry for help is heard—for example, in the form of a threat—a life can be saved.

superstition Superstition concerning the act of suicide grew during the hundreds of years of the Middle Ages, when suicides were relatively rare (as a result of strict church rules). The suicide's body was degraded and often was dragged through the streets and spat on or hung on public gallows. Suicides were sometimes buried on the spot where the act took place; at other times, the body was left unburied in an area set aside for public executions. Often a suicide's corpse was superstitiously buried at a crossroads with a stake driven through its heart and a heavy stone placed on its face to prevent the dead person's spirit from rising.

In England, as late as 1823, the body of a suicide—a man known only as Mr. Griffiths—was dragged through London's streets and buried at a crossroads. His was the last such suicide to be treated in that manner.

There have always been myths, misconceptions, half-truths and fallacies about suicide. Not surprising, when you consider the taboos, fears and stigma that today still surround the subject.

survivor guilt With suicide, the emotions of the survivors are as intensified and unbearable as were those of the person who killed himself or herself. Those left behind experience the pain of sudden loss, but they also have exaggerated feelings of shame, guilt and self-blame. The act itself immediately raises obvious questions, such as "Why?" and "What could I have done to prevent it?" As Rabbi Earl A. Grollman writes in *Suicide: Prevention, Intervention, Postvention*: "Death is a robber. Death by suicide brings the greatest of all affronts to those who remain. As Shneidman said: 'The suicidal person places his psychological skeleton in the survivor's closet.'"

Survivors who have experienced the loss of a loved one through suicide need meaningful support. Today that support comes through what experts call "postvention," in the form of self-help groups and other organizations from neighborhood supports to the clergy to mental health professionals. What is vital is that everyone involved, relatives, friends and professionals, must realize that the survivor family is at "high risk" until proven otherwise. As psychiatrist Mary Giffin says, "Often in psychiatry, we wait and see. With the survivors of suicide, we must act and support, backing off only when the family is clearly making it on its own." Most communities today have mental health centers where active, effective survivor assistance services offer the victims of a loved one's self-destruction a fresh grasp on life.

George Santayana once said: "That life is worth living is the most necessary of assumptions, and were it not assumed, the most impossible of conclusions."

suttee In ancient India, widows practiced *suttee*, motivated by the pressure from the existing society's scheme of thinking. These women threw themselves upon their dead husband's funeral pyre or drowned themselves in the holy Ganges River. They were encouraged to this action by Hindu priests and their own relatives. The widows were taught that a faithful wife could atone for her husband's sins on earth and open to him the gates of paradise. Women who practiced *suttee* were venerated by the populace. Those who refused were not only condemned but also often threatened with harsh physical punishment.

The ancient practice continued in India for hundreds of years. Even after *suttee* was outlawed in 1829 by the British rulers of the country, slow-changing customs kept it going well into the 1900s.

Switzerland Tiny, peace-loving, beautiful Switzerland has one of the highest suicide rates per 100,000 population in the world. In 1984, World Health Organization statistics revealed that the total suicide rate for all ages was 24.8; the male rate was 36.1, that for females, 14.1. This rate (latest available) was down slightly from that of five years earlier, when the total rate per 100,000 population was 25.6 (males, 36.6; and females, 15.2).

Among age groups, highest rates among males was from ages 75 and up, with a rate of 66.3. For females, those 65 to 74 had the highest rate per 100,000 population, with 24.9. For the past decade, Switzerland has ranked among the top 10 countries having the highest suicide rates.

Synod of Nimes Voluntary martyrdom among Christians was discouraged by church leaders as Christianity spread and became tolerated as a recognized state religion in the Roman Empire. However, it was not until the Council of Braga in 563 A.D. that voluntary martyrdom and suicide as an act were condemned by the church. This position was confirmed by the Councils of Auxerre (578) and Antisidor (590) and remained the canon law until 1284 when the Synod of Nimes refused burial in consecrated ground to suicides. (See Dr. Norman L. Farberow's "The History of Suicide" in the front section of this work.)

Szasz, Dr. Thomas Psychiatrist and author, also a strong advocate of the "right to suicide." Considered by many of his peers to be a maverick, Dr. Szasz argues that physicians hold too much power over mentally ill patients. He believes a person should be allowed to commit suicide without intervention from others, unless the person asks for help. In his book, *Law, Liberty and Psychiatry*, Szasz writes: "In a free society, a person must have the right to injure or kill himself . . . there is no moral justification for depriving a person of his liberty in order to treat him." Causing one's own death, Dr. Szasz goes on, "should be called 'suicide' only by those who disapprove of it; and should be called 'death control' by those who approve of it." (The latter quote is from Szasz's book, *The Second Sin.*)

T

Tabachnick, Norman Psychiatrist who, with colleagues at the Los Angeles Suicide Prevention Center, studied the psychology of fatal accidents. The researchers learned that roughly 25% of accident victims among those studied during the project were depressed and had feelings of helplessness and a sense of loss similar to that in suicidal people. The victims admitted to fantasies and dreams of death and self-destruction just prior to their accidents. Researchers concluded that the serious accidents may have resulted from unconscious desires to destroy themselves.

Opposite traits characterized the remaining 75% of accident cases studied. These people were self-reliant and thought of themselves as strong and forceful. Under pressure, they reacted to difficulty quickly and impulsively, and gave little or no thought to the consequences of their actions.

Other studies into teenagers' driving habits have confirmed the combined role of personality traits and emotions in influencing serious accidents. Dr. Karl Menninger also interpreted most accidents as the result of unconscious self-destructive drives.

taboos It is because suicide is still such a taboo topic—one that stigmatizes not only the suicidal victim but the survivors as well—that so many people have difficulty discussing it openly and honestly. As Grossman said: "Death by suicide brings the greatest of all affronts to those who remain." Why? Because the very word 'suicide' describes "an act that violates the most basic tenets of Western belief," explains Francine Klagsbrun in *Too Young to Die*. "Religions condemn it as a sin, and for years law books of many lands listed it as a crime." Long ago, courts actually punished the families of suicides, and rulers of nations confiscated all the suicide's property. Churches denied suicides burial in consecrated sites.

Today, for the most part, such arcane laws and church practices have disappeared. But society's condemnation is still with us in many ways, especially in the West. It is this attitude of the whispered word, of stigmatized secrecy, that is the basic reason behind misleading inaccuracies in suicide data.

Fortunately, there is evidence in recent years that the dread curtain of silence is gradually being lifted, and ancient myths and misconceptions are slowly being removed as our knowledge expands of suicide as a disease of modern civilization.

Tacitus, Publius Cornelius Roman historian and a distinguished lawyer (A.D. ca. 55-120?). Best known for such historical works as the *Historiae*, in which he gives an account of Otho's death and how some soldiers killed themselves near his pyre, prompted by a desire to imitate his "glorious example and moved by affection for their emperor." Tacitus explains that after this many of every rank chose suicide at Bedriacum, Placentia and other camps as well.

It was Tacitus who reported, also, the ancient practice of bog burials—of pinning down the body of suicides. The practice antedates Christianity among the Germanic peoples of Europe. This was done to prevent the spirits of the dead from returning to haunt or do harm to the living.

Taiwan No suicide rate figures are available from the Geneva-based World Health Organization (WHO). In Norman L. Farberow's *Suicide in Different Cultures*, H. Rin has a chapter entitled "Suicide in Taiwan."

teachers, role in suicide prevention Dr. Mary Giffin calls teachers the "most untapped of suicide-prevention resources." Because they usually spend more hours with the child than do most parents, they are in a position to observe and be aware of what the individual child's life is really like. They can spot drug users, loners, depressed students, mood swings, and those who cut classes or are disruptive. All these are possible red flags that should alert teachers that something could be wrong.

In some communities across the U.S. today, teachers undergo training on how to recognize early warning signs, how to approach the suicidal child, and how to assess his/her potential to commit suicide. School counselors and nurses are usually included in the training courses. Teachers, properly trained to the clues of suicide, can be a valuable pipeline to students because young people reveal their despair and anguish in their school work.

Teenage Rebellion Book by co-authors the Reverend Truman E. Dollar and psychiatrist Grace H. Ketterman. The authors surveyed 100 teens and found 34% said they had "seriously considered" suicide; 14% said they had actually attempted suicide. In replying to the question, "If you could change one thing about your father, what would it be?" the most common answer was that the father "would not become so angry."

"Teenage Suicide: Don't Try It" Nationally-syndicated television show produced by Alan Landsburg Productions in 1981. The show, which included interviews with suicide attempters, created quite a stir nationally—and not a little criticism from those who feared that the imitative factor among young people might prevail. The critics were wrong. As most suicidologists agree, you don't give a suicidal person ideas about suicide. The ideas already exist. Dr. Michael Peck, at that time a staff member of the LOS ANGELES SUICIDE PREVENTION CENTER, served as consultant for the film.

teenagers Suicide is second only to accidents as the leading cause of death in the U.S. among those aged 15 to 24, according to the most recent figures. Every day, somewhere in America, 18 teenagers take their own lives. Every hour, 57 children and adolescents in our country attempt suicide—well over 1,000 attempts every day. A relatively recent phenomenon has been the so-called "cluster" suicides, surges of copycat self-destruction. Since 1982, clusters of suicides among teens have occurred in Omaha, Nebraska; Cheyenne, Wyoming; three cities in Texas—Plano, Clear Lake City and Richardson; and Westchester County, New York. In Bergenfield, New Jersey, a middle-class suburb 10 miles west of New York City, two teenage boys and two teenage sisters sat together in an idling car while it filled a garage with lethal carbon monoxide. The day after the quartet's suicide pact, two depressed teenage girls in Alsip, Illinois, killed themselves in much the same way, their bodies recovered in an exhaust-filled garage.

There is, however, a glimmer of good news: Teenage suicide totals have leveled off in the early to mid-1980s. But the suicide rate per 100,000 is still more than twice that of 1960, and authorities agree that a great many teen deaths that are recorded as accidents or homicides are really suicides.

Why so many teen suicides? Among other things, psychologists and others in the field cite drug and alcohol problems and alienation caused by working parents; divorce; low self-esteem; pressures at home, in school or among peers; and frequent moves. But, as a March 13, 1987, editorial in *The New York Times* states: "Clear answers are less obvious than the need for careful research." (See also CHILDREN AND SUICIDE.)

Tele-Care The suicide-prevention "chain," Contact, operates worldwide and has almost 200 centers where people can call. In Canada the organization is called Tele-Care. Check the front of the phonebook or the white pages under the name in Canada. (See also CONTACT USA.)

telephone, intervention, prevention As Edwin Shneidman says, "When a person calls to say that he or she is contemplating suicide, the voice of the suicide prevention worker on the other end can become the caller's lifeline." There have been instances when callers have shot themselves to death while talking to a suicide prevention worker. That first phone interview is crucial and often spells the difference between life and death. The caller *must* be made to feel he is being interviewed by an empathetic, knowledgeable authority who not only wants to but *can* help.

The AMERICAN ASSOCIATION OF SUICIDOLOGY and the NATIONAL COMMITTEE ON YOUTH SUICIDE PREVENTION both publish suicide prevention and crisis center listings of hotlines and counseling services. (See Appendix 3 for a listing of suicide prevention and crisis intervention centers in the U.S.)

television, effect on suicide Many experts hold the view that TV watching may, in some situations, be a catalyst for suicide on the part of impressionable young people who see news stories concerning teenage suicides. Others believe that incidents directly linked to TV are isolated cases. Dr. Mary Giffin writes in *A Cry for Help*: "The link between television and suicide is less direct, but there is a link. Television creates a limited frustration tolerance. The viewer lives a lifetime in a half hour. A struggle that, in reality, would take three years to resolve, in TV land takes three minutes . . .Life just doesn't work that way." The well-known psychiatrist adds that TV "leads to a decline in rational thought, analysis, reflection and patience." In real life, with no 60-minute script, day-to-day problems call for a lot of patience and hard work to solve.

The medium of television is often accused of exacerbating the problem and effects of teen suicide by publicizing and sometimes sensationalizing the facts. While this may be true in certain cases, someone doesn't become suicidal just by watching TV and seeing that someone else has done it. Experts such as Shneidman and Farberow agree that the suicide decision is not impulsive; it is, in fact, usually premeditated. While it might be done on impulse, generally suicide is an action that is given long consideration.

A far greater danger than television—or any of the other media—lies in *preventing* discussion of the subject of suicide. In fact, the element of candid discussion—educational, factual, informational—is the best weapon available to combat teenage self-destruction. Television, properly done, provides that vital, valuable forum. There was one incident where, as a result of the TV show, "The Facts of Life," a teenage girl wrote to the cast members and said, "watching the show made her think twice about suicide as a solution to her problems." As Kim Fields, a star of the show put it: "To know that you saved a life through a TV show is a wonderful feeling."

A common reaction among many, says Charlotte P. Ross, executive director of the YOUTH SUICIDE NATIONAL CENTER in Washington, D.C., is that addressing the issue of youth suicide "may make it happen. For a long time, we figured if we didn't tell the kids about sex, they would never figure it out and fool around with it. That's the same idea we've had about suicide."

Dr. Samuel Klagsbrun, medical director of Four Winds Hospital, Katonah, New York, and associate clinical professor in psychiatry at Columbia University College of Physicians and Surgeons, says the way in which the subject is handled "is the telling feature in figuring out outcomes. I don't think we encourage suicide by talking about it." (See also MEDIA, EFFECTS OF SUICIDE COVERAGE.)

temporal factors, time, season and relation to suicide One California study showed that about 14% of suicides occur between 9 A.M. and 10 A.M., while 13% take place from 1 P.M. to 2 P.M.

Shneidman and Farberow found that more suicides occur between noon and 6 P.M. and that fewer happened between midnight and 6 A.M. However, researchers are careful to point out that studies concerning this are hampered by incomplete samples because it's difficult to determine precisely when a particular suicide occurred.

As for the relation of suicide to seasons, spring is traditionally the most suicidal time of year. Some authorities think that because spring is a time of "rebirth" and most people feel happier, the suicidal person may regress and feel more depressed *because* he sees others being more cheerful—and such feelings may lead to suicide. Loren Coleman, author of *Suicide Clusters* and editor, *The Network News*—the Runaway Suicide Prevention Network Newsletter, published by the Human Services Development Institute, University of Southern Maine—found that while May is the peak month for suicides generally, February is the month when suicide clusters (suicides copycatting previous suicides in a brief time period) peak. Coleman poses the question, Is this "because it follows the depressing and stressful time for some teens of family holidays, and unfulfilled vacation hopes?"

The suicide rate among the general population reaches a low point in December, although researcher Kenneth Bollen found that for the age group from 15 to 29, November was the peak and January, the trough.

Monday appears to be the day on which most suicides occur. In 1979 (an average year), an estimated 82 suicides took place nationwide every Monday. Saturday statistics, by contrast, showed an average of 71 suicides, the lowest rate among days of the week.

Weather, holidays, phases of the moon and the occurrence of sunspots seem not to have all that much bearing on people's suicidal tendencies. While the word "lunacy" derives from the Latin word for "moon," no reliable evidence exists to indicate that more suicides than usual occur during a full moon. Also, some believe there is a global geographical correlation: Northerly places, such as Scandinavia, show higher suicide rates than do more tropical countries. In the U.S., the Rocky Mountain region has the highest suicide rate (16.2 in 1980), while New England was the region with the lowest rate per 100,000 population, 9.5, for the year 1980.

There simply isn't accurate enough authentication to support the majority of beliefs that crop up concerning suicide and geographical and weather correlations.

terminal illness Much has been written and discussed in recent years about making a case for euthanasia and suicide, that is, for "the right to die," particularly where terminal illness is the key factor. The subject is discussed at length elsewhere in this work under such listings as HEMLOCK SOCIETY, DEREK HUMPHRY, *COMMON SENSE SUICIDE* (a book by Doris Portwood), *LET ME DIE BEFORE I WAKE* (book by Humphry and his wife, Ann Wickett), KAREN ANN QUINLAN, and BETTY ROLLIN (dealing with her book *Last Wish*, about her terminally ill mother). Another good reading source regarding this topic is Dr. CHRISTIAAN BARNARD's book, *Good Life, Good Death*.

More and more, on the question of the terminally ill and the right to die, the needs of the patient and those of the surviving family and social community appear to be merging, if for no other reasons than compassion and economics. In fact, a March 1987 poll by Gallup published in *USA Today* indicates how willing adults would be to have their life support system disconnected should they lapse into a non-reversible coma: 70% very willing; 12% somewhat willing; 6% very unwilling; 4% somewhat unwilling; 8% either didn't know or had no opinion.

thanatology Study of death and dying. Thanatos is the Greek name for a mythical personification of death, borrowed by Freud to represent the death instinct. By the mid-1970s in the U.S., some 200 regular courses were being offered in universities and colleges by a new group of scholars calling themselves "thanatologists." In New York City, there is a Foundation of Thanatology.

Thanatos Greek name for a mythical personification of death. In his paper, "MOURNING AND MELANCHOLIA," FREUD presents his theory of suicide. There are two kinds of drives: one is the life instinct, or *Eros*; the other, the death, destructive and aggressive drive, or *Thanatos*. For Dr. Freud, death is willed, there being a constant shifting of the balance of power of the two popular instincts. Eros ages, he theorized, while ageless Thanatos may assert itself "until it, at length, succeeds in doing the individual to death." (See also THANATOLOGY.)

Thebes In ancient Greece, capital of Boeotia, and scene of many legends, such as those of Cadmus and Oedipus. People in Thebes openly condemned a person who committed suicide, and refused to allow that person funeral rites.

theological views on suicide See listings dealing with specific major religions, also SAINT AUGUSTINE and others.

theory (of suicide) Over the years, scores of theories of suicide have been propounded; hundreds of books and articles have been written; thousands upon thousands of words have been spoken at meetings, seminars and lectures. Some theories fault society for suicides of our fellow humans. Some blame parents for their children's self-destruction. Still others place the blame on heredity or body chemistry. Yet, as Francine Klagsbrun notes, all the scholarly weight in support of each theory notwithstanding, no single cause fully explains all suicides. Writes Klagsbrun: "Suicide is such a complex matter that it involves every aspect of life, from the society in which a person lives to family background to psychological make up and childhood history. All need to be considered in any attempt to unravel the mystery of suicide."

That is what the authors of this work have attempted to do—"unravel the mystery of suicide" by presenting a comprehensive and honest examination of the last taboo in our society.

therapy, in-home In Giffin's opinion, "Nobody is more important in determining therapy's success or failure than the parent." The psychiatrist-medical director of a mental health clinic in Illinois says, however, that time and again, consciously or unconsciously, parents sabotage their suicidal child's treatment. Many doubt that therapy can ever help and/or lack confidence in the therapist. Others adopt a "hands-off" attitude, telling the suicidal person, "That's your problem, handle it yourself."

Parents, says Dr. Giffin,

> should assure the child that therapy is nothing to be ashamed of, that, on the contrary, it is an opportunity to get in touch with one's feelings, to become happier and more sensitive. They should allow the child privacy but be available to talk and listen when the child is ready. During the course of therapy, they should be accepting of the new behaviors and attitudes that the child will undoubtedly want to try out.

Experts seem to agree that the best home-therapy advice is old advice: Be available to talk with your potentially suicidal child as often as he or she wants to discuss their problems. As Shneidman says, "Fortunately, people are not permanently suicidal. Even for those whose daily lives are as gloomy as the black despair inside their minds, the suicidal mood ebbs and flows like the tides."

Thomas, Dylan British poet and prose writer (1914-1953), born in Swansea, South Wales, he drank himself to death before his fortieth birthday. He exhibited death-oriented behavior much of his life by engaging in what many experts deemed "life-shortening activities." Thomas' compulsive drinking, his entire lifestyle, appeared to involve an inexorable movement, whether intentioned or subintentioned, toward the brink of self-destruction.

One of his most famous works, *Do Not Go Gentle Into That Good Night* (1952) was written for his father. Thomas died in New York while directing the final production of *Under Milk Wood*, which he described as a "play for voices." He is generally considered one of the finest English-speaking poets of the 20th century.

Thracians, the Herodotus describes a custom of the Thracians, who practiced polygamy, wherein following the man's death, his wives vied for the honor of being judged the one he loved most. The wife accorded this honor was slain over the grave and buried with her husband. This is a form of what experts call "institutional suicide," analagous to the Hindu custom of SUTTEE, in which the widow immolated herself with the corpse of her husband.

"Throwaway Society" The term "throwaways" comes from this country's social workers. That is what they call troublesome children literally thrown out of their homes by parents. Social workers say these victims of our "throwaway society" comprise a large and growing percentage of their caseload. Sister Dolores Gertenutti of New York's Noah's Ark Shelter calls this "the Kleenex mentality," according to Lynn Langway in *Newsweek*. "We live in a society where we use things and just throw them away. I swear, a lot of people have this attitude toward kids."

Psychiatrist Derek Miller, chief of the Adolescent Program, Northwestern University's Institute of Psychiatry, has remarked that for adolescents, this is the worst time to be growing up since the Middle Ages when the bubonic plague created chaos.

time of day See TEMPORAL FACTORS, TIME, SEASON AND RELATION TO SUICIDE.

Tiv of Nigeria In his *African Homicide and Suicide*, editor P.J. Bohannon describes how these people appear to have the lowest incidence of suicide yet recorded. So few, in fact, that Bohannon was unable to document cases of Tiv suicide. Yet they realize that it is something that does sometimes happen and they discussed the means by which it is typically accomplished.

Tojo, General Hideki Japanese general and prime minister from 1941 to 1944. Attempted suicide prior to his execution as a war criminal. Tojo (1885-1948) was instrumental in planning the December 7, 1941, attack on Pearl Harbor.

Tom Sawyer Mark Twain's (real name Samuel Langhorne Clemens) famous novel (1876) in which he showed a clear understanding of the childhood fantasy of making his point by killing himself. Frustrated by his Aunt Polly, Tom found comfort in the fantasy of drowning himself in the nearby Mississippi. He imagined with relish his limp body being brought to his aunt and her saying, "Oh, if I had only loved him more. How differently I would have treated him if we had only known." The vision brought tears of self-pity to his eyes.

Too Young to Die: Youth and Suicide One of the truly important works dealing with the subject of adolescent and teenage suicide, by Francine Klagsbrun. The latest Pocket Books edition, published in paperback in 1985, has an excellent introduction by Harold S. Kushner, author of the bestseller *When Bad Things Happen to Good People*. Elisabeth Kubler-Ross, MD, calls Klagsbrun's book "an important work . . . Let us hope that parents and counselors, teachers and ministers will read this book in order to understand the cry for help that so many children send out, before their despair exceeds their wish to live." Mrs. Klagsbrun's husband, Dr. Samuel C. Klagsbrun, serves in an advisory capacity for the National Committee on Youth Suicide Prevention.

Toronto Distress Centre One of several key centers in Canada's nationwide network of suicide prevention and crisis hotlines that service large population areas. The address: Toronto Distress Centre, 10 Trinity Square, Toronto, Ontario; phone is (416) 598-1121. Other centers include ones in Montreal, Quebec, and Vancouver, British Columbia. For complete details of Canada's many suicide hotlines and prevention agencies, contact the Suicide Information and Education Centre (SIEC), Suite 201, 1615 10th Avenue S.W., Calgary, Alberta T3C OJ7; phone is (403) 245-3900.

traffic accidents Authorities say that many deaths recorded by medical examiners as accidents are actually suicides in disguise. In fact, many coroners routinely list the death as an accident when the cause of death is not known. The Federal Center for Studies of Suicide Prevention, Bethesda, Maryland, states that many reckless, speeding drivers are playing unconscious roles in hastening their own deaths. Some experts believe that fully 25% of the drivers who die in auto accidents cause them subintentionally by careless, excessive risk-taking. Drs. Norman Tabachnik, Robert Litman et al. of the Los Angeles Suicide Prevention Center, studied the personalities and life situations of 30 drivers who died in one-car crashes and suggests that about 5% of such accidents were deliberate.

For further discussion on this topic, read additional information under the listings AUTOCIDE and that for psychiatrist NORMAN TABACHNICK. (See also JAMES DEAN.)

tranquilizers A group of depressant drugs that act selectively on the brain and spinal cord (central nervous system). They are not unlike BARBITURATES in many ways, especially in their sedative effect, but in normal doses they do not induce sleep or cause drowsiness. Tranquilizers are divided into two classes—major and minor. The major tranquilizers, also called neuroleptics, are haloperidol and chlorpromazine. They are used to treat serious mental illness. Minor tranquilizers, which include meprobamate (Miltown), chlordiazepoxide (Librium) and diazepam (Valium), can produce euphoria and, unfortunately, are all too often abused or misused—not only for their own effects, but also to offset the effects of alcohol, amphetamines and other drugs.

The minor tranquilizers have been used in a number of suicide attempts, especially by females—both adult and teenager—but fatalities are rare when used alone. Successful suicides are generally the result of a synergistic effect between the tranquilizer and another drug such as alcohol. Combining tranquilizers with alcohol or other depressant drugs is dangerous since each drug increases the effect of the other so that the combined effect is more powerful than the effect of either alone. Also, tolerance can develop with regular prolonged use and increased doses may be needed to produce the original tranquilizng effects. Long-term heavy use can result in psychological and even physical dependence, although physical dependence is infrequent when one considers the large number of people who use tranquilizers. They are legally available only on prescription.

Robert O'Brien and Sidney Cohen, MD, *The Encyclopedia of Drug Abuse* (New York: Facts On File, 1984).

treatment See THERAPY, IN-HOME; COUNSELING; POSTVENTION.

Treblinka One of the most notorious World War II Nazi concentration camps, located in Poland. Thousands of Jews, mostly from Eastern Europe, were exterminated there. Many chose to kill themselves as an affirmation of the freedom to control their own destiny. These suicidal acts, closely paralleling the situation at MASADA in A.D. 73, sparked the start of a rebellion that ultimately became an open revolt, one of the few such revolts that took place in a Nazi concentration camp. The courageous action was in keeping with the theme of death with honor to preserve one's beliefs prevalent throughout the long history of the Jewish people.

tricyclic antidepressants Drugs used to treat depression by increasing the supply of these chemicals at the synapses. Tricyclics partially inhibit the amount of chemical neurotransmitters that are reabsorbed, thus leaving more available for use in neurotransmission. Usually takes two to three weeks to take effect. If, after a few weeks on one or more of the tricyclics at maximum dosage, there is no response by the patient, doctors sometimes try a MAO INHIBITOR—another type of drug used to relieve depression.

Asendin, the newest tricyclic, appears to be an improvement over the older tricyclics in two key ways: It works faster (often within four to five days) and it seems to be virtually side effects free (not true of the older tricyclics and the MAO inhibitors).

LITHIUM, a third type of antidepressant, is used to treat bipolar or manic depression, which accounts for an estimated 5% of all depressions. Like all antidepressants, lithium has potentially toxic side effects.

Trosse, George British clergyman (1631-1713), who suffered a psychotic breakdown in the mid-17th century. His autobiography, published after his death, contains a vivid account of his experiences, including strong suicidal impulses. Trosse's experiences are recorded by Richard Hunter and Ida Macalpine in *Three Hundred Years of Psychiatry, 1535-1860* (pps. 113-115).

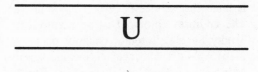

U

Ulysses See JAMES JOYCE.

unemployment and suicide Suicide rates increase when unemployment is high. Psychologists have postulated possible reasons for such increases. They include: depression among those unable to get work; tendency toward abuse of family members; dissolution of the family; increased abusive drinking and drug use; increased anguish and anxiety; and cultural frustration described generally as loss—loss of family love, loss of control over one's own destiny, loss of identity (alienation), loss of self-esteem and, in general, loss of meaning in life. Perhaps ST. THOMAS AQUINAS was right when he opined that "Unusual irritability, which leads to quarrels, shortens life."

While social disorganization, which greatly impressed French sociologist EMILE

DURKHEIM, surely has an important bearing on suicide rates, largely through detaching the individual from society, psychic aspects must also be considered. Unfortunately, the manner in which these processes operate is not all that clear. What is clear is that suicide is such a complex of causes—social, psychological, family interactions—that no single theory is sufficient to account for the intricacies of the suicide act. As Herbert Hendin writes in *Suicide in America*, "The differences in ways of coping with love and loss, life and death, make clear that suicide has much to tell us about how we live."

Unfinished Business Nonfiction book by noted American writer Maggie Scarf, a study of women and depression. The full title is *Unfinished Business: Pressure Points in the Lives of Women*. Scarf won a Niéman Fellowship at Harvard University and was twice a Fellow at the Center for Advanced Study in the Behavioral Sciences at Stanford University.

unintentional death Francine Klagsbrun notes in *Too Young to Die* that "the possibilities of unintentional deaths and the ambivalent feelings most suicidal persons share emphasize the potential for death in almost every suicide attempt and the unanswered appeal to life in almost every completed suicide." Exceptions to this scenario, of course, include individuals suffering from severe mental disorders, or who behave in irrational and bizarre ways, whose suicidal acts result from losing touch with reality.

The poet SYLVIA PLATH is a well-known example of an unfortunate and tragic death that many experts think resulted accidentally—unintentionally—from a suicide attempt. Until he or she dies, a suicide is pleading to be saved. As Shneidman and Farberow say, "Every suicide attempt is a serious cry for help."

United Kingdom See GREAT BRITAIN.

unmarried, singles See MARITAL STATUS AND SUICIDE.

urban suicide The state with the highest suicide rate is a western state, relatively low in population density: Nevada (1980 rate was 22.9 per 100,000 while the U.S. rate that year was 11.9 per 100,000). And Nevada's cities, e.g., Las Vegas and Reno, had higher suicide rates than did the state's rural areas. Other states that have high suicide rates are: Alaska, Arizona, California, Colorado, Florida, Montana, New Mexico, Oregon, Washington and Wyoming. In 1980, the state with the lowest suicide rate was America's most densely populated, New Jersey, at only 7.4 per 100,000.

Highest U.S. regional rates are those of the West Coast and the Rocky Mountain areas. The region with the lowest rate is the South (Florida being the exception).

It was felt for several decades in the 20th century that the rural suicide rate was much lower than that of urban areas. In recent years, since the decline of the nation's small- and medium-sized farms and the rise of corporate agribusinesses, it appears that the rural suicide rate in the U.S. is now on a level with the urban rate.

Additionally, however, the suicide rates have been found to be positively correlated with these factors: male sex, increasing age, widowhood, single and divorced status, childlessness, high density of population, residence in big towns, a high standard of living, economic crisis, drug and alcohol consumption, history of a broken home in childhood, mental disorder and physical illness. Again, many authorities say the validity of statistical data concerning suicide and the correlation of suicide rates to geographical area and other related factors are questionable and ought not to be generalized.

U.S. law See LAW AND THE LEGAL ASPECTS OF SUICIDE.

U.S. suicide statistics The most up-to-date and reliable suicide statistics available to researchers and others interested in the field of suicidology come from the Centers for Disease Control (CDC) in Atlanta. They analyze vital statistics from the National Center for Health Statistics for use by clinicians, health planners and evaluators, and other public health professionals interested in the number and characteristics of suicide, both among youths and adults. Two of CDC's most recent reports are: *Centers for Disease Control: Youth Suicide in the United States, 1970-1980* (issued November 1986) and *Centers for Disease Control: Suicide Surveillance, 1970-1980* (issued April 1985).

Address requests for information to: U.S. Department of Health and Human Services, Public Health Service, Centers for Disease Control, Center for Health Promotion and Education, Atlanta, GA 30333.

The suicide data specified in the national vital statistics reflects the judgments and professional opinions of the physicians, coroners or medical examiners who certify the medical/legal cause of death on the death certificate. Most authorities are of the opinion that suicide statistics based on death certificates probably *understate* the true number of suicides for several reasons:

1. Inadequate information on which to make a determination of suicide as the cause of death.
2. Certifier bias or error.
3. No death certificate filed on the victim.

Uses of Enchantment, The Nonfiction work by BRUNO BETTELHEIM in which he explains the unbridled power that fairy tales and myths have over children. Bettelheim's contention: that children love them so because the stories embody their strongest hopes and fears. One almost universal fear in fairy tales is the fear of being separated from one's parents. "Psychoanalysis has named this—man's greatest fear—separation anxiety; and the younger we are, the more excruciating is our anxiety when we feel deserted, for the young child actually perishes when not adequately protected and taken care of," writes Bettelheim.

Experts say, in describing the "typical" suicidal adolescent, that he is likely to be a teenager who quite early in his life was literally separated from vital relationships or who never experienced a real trusting relationship. "Thus," writes Dr. MARY GIFFIN, "he remained alone to cope with the stress and strain of growing up."

Bruno Bettleheim, *The Uses of Enchantment: The Meaning and Importance of Fairy Tales* (New York: Alfred Knopf, 1976).

Mary Giffin & Carol Felsenthal, *A Cry for Help: Exploring and Exploding the Myths About Teenage Suicide: A Guide for All Parents of Adolescents* (Garden City: Doubleday, 1983).

Utopia Written by English author and statesman Sir Thomas More (1478-1535), Lord Chancellor, 1529-32. More, who was beheaded in 1535 by command of Henry VIII for refusing to take an oath impugning the authority of the Pope (for which martyrdom he was canonized in 1935), is celebrated as author of *Utopia* (written in Latin, 1515-16; translated into English, 1551), depicting an ideal commonwealth. In the work, More justified suicide as a form of euthanasia.

V

Valium A trade name for diazepam, a tranquilizer and sedative hypnotic. Diazepam, a benzodiazepine derivative, is used in the treatment of tension and anxiety and for alcohol withdrawal. Users can develop tolerance along with a potential for physical and psychological dependence. Valium, or diazepam, is one of the most widely prescribed drugs in the U.S., and has a significant potential for abuse when taken with alcohol or other central nervous system depressants.

values, disappearance of Many authorities—sociologists, theologists, psychologists, etc.—have recently been asking, "Where have all the values gone?" Modern parents have been charged with not giving enough love, understanding and acceptance of their children as real persons. Experts say you can add lack of communication to the list. As Dr. Mary Giffin writes: "Children from families that appear completely normal groped for words to describe what they felt was a void in their lives—the lack of anything to stand for, of an altruistic goal, of a push to improve the community, the country, the world, of in two words, 'meaningful values.'"

In 1981, Jane Norman and Myron Harris, for their book *The Private Life of the American Teenager*, published the results of a poll of 160,000 teenagers. When asked, "What do you want most in life?" only 9% said they wanted to "do something worthwhile for the world."

As Giffin and Felsenthal report,

> Similarly, in a survey of nearly 300,000 college freshmen conducted in 1982 (by UCLA and the American Council on Education), 63.3 percent said that being well off was very important. In 1967, when the same question was asked, 43.5 percent said being well off was very important. In 1967, 82.9 percent chose the goal of 'developing a meaningful philosophy of life,' but in 1982 only 49 percent chose that goal.

Today there is an increasing stress on getting what your parents have, or more. Young people are more self-involved, self-indulgent and opt to go into corporations, law firms, their own businesses. Changing the world no longer seems as important as it was to the rebellious youth of the 1960s. Significantly, the teen suicide rate was lower in the turbulent 1960s, some believe because of the sense of community generated by the antiwar, antiestablishment movement. Today's teenagers have no common cause, no particular idealistic purpose to preoccupy them. As Giffin notes: "There's simply nothing left to distract today's teen . . . leaving him to brood over deficiencies in himself and his relationships."

Van Gogh, Vincent Dutch painter (1853-1890). One of the world's great premodernists, Van Gogh killed himself at the age of 37. Despite being a prolific painter, he sold only four pieces in his life. His tortured inner life led him to cut off an ear in a rage with Gauguin; and it found expression in his painting—but also brought him finally to suicide.

Vancouver Crisis Centre One of Canada's established centers—they call them "distress centres"—that service large population areas with suicide prevention hotlines. The address: Vancouver Crisis Intervention and Suicide Prevention Centre, 1946 W. Broadway, Vancouver, British Columbia; phone is (604) 733-4111.

Varah, Chad British clergyman (1911-). In 1953 he founded the SAMAR-

ITANS, a telephone service for the suicidal and despairing. The organization, which started with a single telephone, now has over 215 centers worldwide, six in the U.S. If there is a center near you, it will be listed in the phone book's white pages under "Samaritans." Canada also has branches of this organization. Helpers are on duty 24-hours-a-day.

Vatel Madame de Sévigné wrote in 1671 of Vatel (?1622-1671), the *maitre d'hotel* of the Prince de Conde, who killed himself out of shame when a dinner and entertainment for Louis XIV apparently turned out a fiasco. It seems Vatel misunderstood a fishmonger concerning the quantity of fish available for his use. "I cannot endure the disgrace," he cried. Going to his room, he fixed his sword to the door and ran upon the point. Mme. de Sévigné said Vatel was highly praised for his courage and resolution, even though the praise was mingled somewhat with reproach.

Verstehen Sociologist Max Weber, in *The Theory of Social and Economic Organization*, distinguishes between empirical (observational) understanding of social behavior and motivational (subjective) understanding. The former, Weber calls *Begreifen*; the latter *Verstehen*. He explains that *Verstehen* gives rise to "meaningfully adequate" understanding. RONALD MARIS, in his "Sociology," chapter five of Perlin's *A Handbook for the Study of Suicide*, says that concepts of Max Weber—as well as those of George Herbert Mead—are brought to bear on the sociological study of suicide by Jack D. Douglas in his *The Social Meanings of Suicide*. Maris writes: "Contrary to Durkheim, Douglas argues that there is need to consider the *internal meanings* of the external associations of suicide and abstract social characteristics like anomie and egoism. That is, a plea is being made for what Weber called *Verstehen*."

"victim-precipitated" murders When the victims, often young black males, appear to deliberately provoke others into killing them, sometimes flashing knives or wielding guns or goading others with threats of violence. The theory, say some psychologists, is that many black men consider suicide as a weak, cowardly way out of their problems. Rather than self-inflicted destruction, these young blacks aggressively create violence, hurt others in the process, but manage to get themselves killed—dying as heroes, preserving their definition of masculinity. According to psychologist Richard Seiden, author of "We're Driving Young Blacks to Suicide," suicide rates among the country's young blacks are probably higher than known because "victim-precipitated" murders are not included in suicide statistics.

Vienna Psychoanalytical Society Members of this group met on April 27, 1910, in Vienna, Austria, to try to learn more about the mysterious causes of suicide among that famed city's high school students. Leading psychoanalysts, such as Adler, Stekel and Freud, met with educator David E. Oppenheim, among others. It was Sigmund Freud, the father of psychoanalysis, who came away from the historic meeting admitting that they had accomplished very little, and that much more work was necessary in this area of concern. He said too little was known about suicide, but that perhaps the act was a repudiation of life because of the craving for death. This observation foreshadowed Freud's ultimate belief in a death instinct—a theory of suicide still accepted by many scholars—as set forth in his later paper, *Mourning and Melancholia*.

"Vincent" A song which tells the story of Vincent Van Gogh's alienation and suicide. Giffin writes of one 21-year-old, John Woytowitz, who hanged himself. He retreated to his room for hours at a time to listen to the songs "Vincent," and "Suicide Is Painless" (the theme song from *M*A*S*H*).

violence, TV-bred See listings under MEDIA and TELEVISION. Some authorities believe that tension may be caused by TV itself. According to ongoing studies by George Gerbner, dean of the University of Pennsylvania's Annenberg School of Communications, television can lead frequent viewers to regard the world as violent and fearsome.

On October 21, 1981, Dr. Thomas Radecki, an Illinois psychiatrist and crusader against TV violence, told a special congressional committee investigating television violence: "I can comfortably estimate that 25-50 percent of the violence in our society is coming from the culture of violence being taught by our entertainment media, most strongly by the television and movie industries. This estimate is based on solid research findings."

On the other hand, Dr. Mary Giffin says, "The most insidious effect of television is that it inhibits children from flowering individually. It's what they don't get to because of television that should concern us greatly. There's no reading out loud, no book heroes or plots to worry over all week long, no characters to grow up with as cherished companions, as projections of one's own fantasies."

While TV violence isn't exactly a catalyst for solid childhood development, it doesn't make it a homicidal (or suicidal) killer either. Studies have shown that children who are inveterate TV watchers, bombarded by video violence, learn to accept violence matter-of-factly, generally speaking. The end result is more likely to be one of numbness, rather than overt violence, as a solution to problems, because violence—except to the very susceptible or impressionable—has become a part of the child's everyday world. (See also MEDIA, EFFECTS OF SUICIDE COVERAGE; TELEVISION, EFFECT ON SUICIDE.)

Vivienne: The Life and Suicide of an Adolescent Girl Book by authors John E. Mack and Holly Hickler that describes in detail the months leading to Vivienne's suicide by hanging. While the signals and clues to her suicidal thinking and behavior were evident, nobody noticed or did anything to help the young girl. She was crying out for help—but her cries proved to be in vain.

Voltaire, Francois Marie Arouet de French philosopher, writer and wit (1694-1778). His inquiring mind and skeptical views, particularly on matters of religion, epitomize the French Enlightenment. One of the leaders of the Enlightenment—along with d'Holbach, Hume, Rousseau, Beaccaria—Voltaire condemned the existing conventional treatment of suicides. He steadily attacked the taboos, superstitions, and primitive punishments still being imposed for suicide victims. As a result, he and others laid the foundation for a secular approach to the problem of suicide; saw laws slowly changed; and were instrumental in a gradual shift in society's emotional attitudes.

Voluntary Euthanasia Bill Proposed by the Voluntary Euthanasia Society of Britain in 1936, defended in an address that later appeared in the *Medico-Legal and Criminal Review* (Great Britain) by Judge W.C. Earengey. The bill's full title was the Voluntary Euthanasia Legalization Bill. Protestant theologian R.F. Rattray also supported the controversial bill, more recently considered by the House of Lords in 1969. Introduced by Lord Raglan, the newly drafted and revised version of the 1936 bill was passed without debate on its first reading. Opposition came from right-wing conservatives, led by St. John-Stevas, the British

Medical Association, the Roman Catholic Auxiliary Bishop of Westminster, and a rabbi who said: "We cannot agree to purchasing the relief of pain at the cost of life itself . . ." Dr. Cicely Saunders, noted medical director of St. Christopher's Hospice in London, was also opposed to the bill. On the second reading in the House of Lords, the bill was rejected by a vote of 61 to 40. The bill's drafters are now rethinking their position and are considering amendments in their plans to resubmit the bill.

Voluntary Euthanasia Society In 1935, the British Voluntary Euthanasia Society was formed, followed in 1938 by the founding of the Euthanasia Society of America. Today, a number of countries have such societies, including Australia, South Africa and the Netherlands. Episcopal minister and leading Protestant ethicist Joseph Fletcher, author of *Morals and Medicine* (considered the classic modern defense of euthanasia), is the current head of the Euthanasia Society of America.

volunteers (at suicide prevention-crisis centers) Ideally, suicide prevention and crisis centers will be staffed with at least one, or perhaps two, professionals, such as psychiatrists, psychologists or psychiatric social workers. The remainder of the staff is usually non-professional volunteers. Shneidman writes that,

> Experience has shown that lay volunteers can be very effective staff members *if* they are *carefully selected* and *rigorously trained.* Generally, housewives who are mature, usually over 40, and have weathered psychological storms within their own lives, are potentially good members. For example, women who have lost children through accident or disease and have since adjusted to these personal tragedies often are compassionate, resilient, and unafraid staff members.

Professor Shneidman, founder and past-president, the American Association of Suicidology, adds that: "As a rule, it may be a good idea not to select people who have suffered psychotic breakdowns or who themselves at one time attempted suicide, or who appear overzealously interested in suicide."

An efficient suicide prevention service relies heavily on these lay volunteer staff members who offer consultation, training and seminars to high schools, universities, hospitals and mental health agencies. Their direct, person-to-person services are the foundation for suicide intervention and prevention programs available at centers across the country. They provide a ready contact between the community's disturbed, suicidal persons and the many helping agencies that are available to them. And they often spell the difference between life and death.

Vonnegut, Kurt, Jr. Author of numerous novels, who wrote in *God Bless You, Mr. Rosewater*, "Sons of suicides seldom do well." He could have made that "Children of suicides . . . ," since both sons and daughters of suicides have a higher than average rate of suicide. This is not due to any genetic inheritance factors, but because they grow up in an environment of guilt, anger and with a sense of low self-esteem. It was Vonnegut who also wrote, "How nice—to feel nothing, and still get full credit for being alive."

vulnerability See CLUES, WARNING SIGNS OF SUICIDE.

Vulteius Lucan, in *The Civil War*, describes how the Roman tribune Vulteius and his cohorts, in their attempt to cross the Adriatic, found themselves surrounded by Pompeian troops. They had defended themselves courageously, but realized that escape was impossible. Vulteius thus called upon his men to die by their own hands rather than to fall alive into the enemy's hands. Not one soldier survived to become a prisoner of Pompey. As Lucan noted, "How simple a feat it is to escape slavery by suicide."

W

Wales The World Health Center (WHO) statistics combine suicide rate numbers for England and Wales. The suicide rate per 100,000 totals for the two United Kingdom countries in 1982 (latest figures) was 8.9; among males, the rate was 11.4; for females, 6.5. The 45 to 54 and 55 to 64 age groups had the highest total suicide rates, both at 14.0. Among males, the highest rate was in the 74-plus age group, with a 22.5 rate; for females, the 65 to 74 age group was highest at an 11.7 rate per 100,000 (See also GREAT BRITAIN.)

Wallace, Samuel E. In his book, *After Suicide*, sociologist Samuel Wallace explains the vital need suicide survivors have for the sympathetic understanding of friends, associates and relatives. "Listening to someone else talk. How simple," says Wallace, "and how few do it." He conducted in-depth interviews with 12 widows of suicides over a one-year period after their spouses' deaths. The interviewers taped the widows' words, saying little themselves. After the study, the survivor women agreed that just being able to talk out their feelings had helped them enormously. One woman observed that, "It saves your life, really."

As Klagsbrun notes: "Dealing with it (a suicide) openly can help preserve . . . other lives."

"Wanting to Die" See SEXTON, ANNE.

war, effect on suicide rate It is an irony that suicide rates tend to drop in time of war. During World War I, for example, suicide rates dropped in Europe both in the countries involved (e.g., France, Germany, Belgium) and in countries that were neutral (e.g., Switzerland). Following the armistice, the suicide rates began to return to pre-war levels. As noted British clergyman and author William Ralph Inge observed: "The statistics of suicide show that, for non-combatants at least, life is more interesting in war than in peace."

warning signs, suicidal See CLUES, WARNING SIGNS (OF SUICIDE).

Washington (state) One of nine states where attempted suicide is still regarded as a felony. Attempters, however, are almost never prosecuted. According to Centers for Disease Control (CDC) statistics, Washington's suicide rate per 100,000 dropped from 15.0 in 1970 to 13.3 in 1980. The actual number of suicides rose, however, from 511 in 1970 to 550 in 1980 (latest figures available). The 1980 suicide rate for the state was higher than the U.S. rate of 11.9 per 100,000.

weather Studies have shown that oppressive weather has little to do with causing suicide. The same studies do indicate that suicide rates tend to rise during the spring months, reaching a peak in April and May, then falling back during winter months, with low points during December and January. Klagsbrun speculates that, "Perhaps the sense of rebirth and joy that abounds at springtime makes depressed people more aware of their own inner gloom and despondency." Interestingly, though, suicide "clusters" (where several persons, usually teens, kill themselves in a relatively short time frame) tend to peak in February. Lauren Coleman, in his book *Suicide Clusters*, asks why and wonders, "Is it because it follows the depressing and stressful time for some teens of family holidays and unfulfilled vacation hopes?"

It is thought that the notion of dull, dismal, inclement weather causing suicides goes back to the superstition that suicide is a dark and mysterious, devil-inspired act. (See also GEOGRAPHIC FACTORS; TEMPORAL FACTORS, TIME, SEASON AND RELATION TO SUICIDE.)

Weber, Max See *VERSTEHEN*.

Wechsler, James and Michael James A. Wechsler, a noted writer for *The New York Post*, discussed the effect of his son Michael's suicide in a column dated May 17, 1977. He and his wife had collaborated on a book concerning the dread episode—*In a Darkness*—the primary message being ". . . how often we failed to say or do some things that might (or might not) have mattered . . ."

Wechsler also discussed candidly in his newspaper column the attitude of stigmatization and shamed secrecy still prevalent among some survivors. "Even in the numbness of those hours," he wrote, "we were astonished at the prevalence of the view that suicide was a dishonorable or at least disreputable matter, to be charitably covered up to protect Michael's good name and the sensibilities of the family." (Note: The local police had actually offered to "hide" the circumstances of Michael Wechsler's death.)

Wells, H.G. British novelist (1866-1946). One night, while sitting with friend and fellow writer C.P. Snow, Wells suddenly asked, "Ever thought of suicide, Snow?" Snow reflected, then said, "Yes, H.G., I have." Wells replied, "So have I. But not till I was past seventy." The famed writer of futuristic fantasies was then 72. Snow remembers, "We drank some more whisky and looked somberly at the palms."

Clifton Fadiman, ed., *The Little, Brown Book of Anecdotes* (Boston/Toronto: Little, Brown, 1985).

West Germany World Health Organization (WHO) statistics for 1984 (latest available) show a total rate per 100,000 of 20.5 (male rate total 28.5; female, 13.2). The suicide rates were highest in the 75-plus age group; with total rates 43.2; males, 76.0; and females, 27.9 (in that particular age category). West Berlin has the highest city suicide rate in the world, 40.9 per 100,000 (the rate is almost twice that of the country as a whole). The alcoholism and drug abuse rate is high in West Berlin, too.

widows/widowers An excellent book for widows and widowers is Wallace's *After Suicide*. (See also SURVIVOR GUILT and SAMUEL E. WALLACE.)

will, loss of as suicide clue One of several distress signals or warning signs is a sudden loss or lack of the will or desire to do anything, such as go to school or work, be with friends or family, any activity. Suicidal people often suffer that dragged-down, do-nothing feeling. Life becomes a useless struggle, they can't get moving, feel everything is too much trouble, and there's not that much worth doing anyway.

withdrawal, as suicide clue Another warning signal that something is wrong. Usually follows periods of uncharacteristic irritability, fighting, then depression. Along with withdrawal come other suicidal telltales, such as loss of will, sudden lack of interest in appearance, irregular sleeping habits. "If these things seem different or deeper than the usual mood changes, ask about them," says Charlotte P. Ross, executive director, the

Youth Suicide National Center in Washington, D.C.

women Women attempt suicide about three times as often as men; however, men complete suicide about three times as often as do women. This has been the case ever since suicide records have been kept. In 1980, the *highest* percent of suicide for women was in the age group 30 to 34 (16.3%); the suicide rate for the same year (1980) was 10.3 in the age group 50 to 54. The suicide rate per 100,000 dropped for women from 6.5 in 1979 to 5.9 in 1980, lowest in the past decade. Males in the U.S. have a markedly higher risk of suicide than do females, and the differential between male and female rates is widening even more. Between 1970 and 1980 almost three-fourths (72.8%) of suicide deaths occurred to males.

Centers for Disease Control, Suicide Surveillance, 1970-1980 (Atlanta: Department of Health & Human Services, April 1985).

Woolf, Virginia English writer (1882-1941). She and her husband, Leonard, founded the famous Hogarth Press in 1917. Woolf wrote several extraordinary novels, the fantasy *Orlando: A Biography* (1928), volumes of short stories and literary criticism. She suffered a mental breakdown during World War I. Threatened by its return in 1941, she drowned herself—by placing stones in her coat pockets—in the River Over, near her home in Rodmell, near Lewes, Sussex.

World Health Organization (WHO) The organization is headquartered in Geneva, Switzerland. Many of the statistics on suicide deaths (absolute numbers and rates) for this work—particularly those on various WHO member nations—were furnished by WHO's Dr. Alan D. Lopez, statistician, Global Epidemiological Surveillance and Health Situation Assessment. Address: 1211 Geneva 27, Switzerland. Full title is: World Health Organization, Mondiale de la Sante. Phone: Central Exchange 91-21-11.

wrist-slashing, as suicide method Both males and females who attempt suicide without fatal results usually do not use such lethal (violent) methods as guns and hanging. Most, it appears, will take pills or poisons, or slash their wrists with ordinary razor blades—all methods, incidentally, that generally allow time for rescue. In fact, the Centers for Disease Control includes this method in the classification "all other means" in its surveillance methods (from those deaths identified as having cause-of-death codes E950-E959 from International Classification of Diseases [ICD], eighth revision [2], and ninth revision [3]).

X

Xenophon Athenian soldier, historian and wealthy disciple of Socrates (ca. 430-ca. 355 B.C.). Principal historical work, the *Anabasis*. His other writings included *Memorabilia*, a defense of Socrates, and *Hellenica*, a history of Greece. According to Xenophon, hemlock—the poison drunk by Socrates—was introduced in 403 B.C.

Xerxes I Son of Darius I and King of Persia, 486-465 B.C., he conquered Egypt and invaded Greece over a bridge of boats at the Hellespont. Victorious at Thermopylae, Xerxes (ca. 519-465 B.C.) pillaged Athens, but retired to Asia when his fleet was destroyed at Salamis, in 480 B.C. His army, under Mardonius, was defeated at Plataea, 479 B.C. On his retreat from Greece, a number of his men threw themselves overboard to lighten the overloaded vessel and the ship came safely to harbor.

After he landed, Xerxes ordered that a golden crown be presented to the pilot for saving the king's life. He also commanded that the man's head be cut off, as he had caused the loss of so many Persian lives.

Y

Yeats, William Butler Irish poet (1865-1939), one of the great writers of modern times, he won the Nobel Prize for Literature in 1923. It was Yeats who penned the line, "After us the Savage God"—from whence A. Alvarez got the title for his well-known book, *The Savage God: A Study of Suicide*. Yeats meant that the ultimate concern of art was, inevitably, the end of self-death. Said Alvarez: "I think Yeats prophesied correctly. In a sense, the whole of twentieth-century art has been dedicated to the service of this earthbound Savage God who, like the rest of his kind, has thrived on blood-sacrifice."

Youth Suicide, National Conference on The task Force on Youth Suicide, sponsored by the U.S. Department of Health and Human Services, sponsored three national conferences during 1986: on May 8-9, in Bethesda, Maryland, Conference on Risk Factors for Youth Suicide; June 11-13, in Oakland, California, Conferences on Prevention and Interventions in Youth Suicide; and November 18, in Bethesda, a National Conference on Strategies for the Prevention of Youth Suicide. All three conferences were attended by practitioners and theoreticians in suicidology, mental health, medicine, education, social work, and community-based service programs; concerned citizens were also in attendance. (See also YOUTH SUICIDE NATIONAL CENTER.)

Youth Suicide National Center Established in 1985 as a nonprofit organization, headquartered in the nation's capital. Its purpose is to facilitate effective action on both the local and national level by:

- serving as an information clearinghouse;
- developing and distributing educational materials;
- providing educational programs and related services;
- reviewing current youth suicide prevention programs and developing models which can be responsive to the needs of diverse groups and settings in communities across the country;
- providing a national toll-free hotline to respond to depressed and suicidal youths and their families;
- coordinating and supporting efforts to reduce youth suicide in America.

The YSNC's chairman is Seymour Perlin, MD; president/executive director is Charlotte P. Ross. Norman L. Farberow, PhD, coauthor of this work, is a member of the board of directors. Address is: 1825 Eye Street, N.W., Suite 400, Washington, DC 20006; phone is (202) 429-2016.

In June 1985, the YSNC cosponsored with the U.S. Department of Health and Human Services, a two-day National Conference on Youth Suicide in Washington, D.C. That year President Ronald Reagan proclaimed June as Youth Suicide Prevention Month, 1985.

youth and the very young According to the Centers for Disease Control (CDC) in Atlanta, in the period from 1970 to 1980, one out of every six suicides reported in the U.S. was of a young person 15 to 24 years of age. The suicide rate for this age group increased 40% from 1970 to 1980, while the rate for the remainder of the population remained stable. Rates for males increased by 49.6% compared to a 2.4% increase for females, so that by 1980, the ratio of suicides committed by young males to those committed by young females was almost five to one. Most (89.5%) male suicide victims were white.

Young adults (20 to 24 years old) consistently had about twice the number and rate of suicides as adolescents 15 to 19 years old. Although in 1980 suicide rates for persons 15 to 24 years old (12.3) were still lower than rates for persons 65 years of age and older (17.8), a greater number of suicides occurred among persons 15 to 24 years old (5,239) than among persons 65 years of age and older (4,537). Thus, suicides among young persons represent a very large part of the total suicide burden borne by society.

Among all persons 15 to 24 years of age, white males 20 to 24 years old have the highest suicide risk. In 1978, the base year for the 1990 objectives, suicides to white males 20 to 24 years of age accounted for almost half (47.8%) of all suicides to the 15- to 24-year-old population. The 1978 suicide rate for white males 20 to 24 (28.1) was more than twice the rate of the overall target population as stated by the objectives (12.4). Statistically, if by 1990 there were a 25% reduction in the suicide rate for white males 20 to 24 years of age (from 28.1 to 21.1), and even if the rates for other age, race and sex groups remained unchanged from their 1978 rates, the overall 1990 objective (a rate of 11.0 for all persons 15 to 24) could be achieved. Research is needed, says the CDC, to explain the high rate of suicide among young males and to characterize their deaths more precisely.

Although suicide rates are lower for young males of black and other races than for white males, the rates for blacks and other males 15 to 24 years of age more than doubled between 1950 and 1980. Furthermore, a greater proportion of all suicides to black and other males were among the young. In 1980, 28.4% of all suicides among males of black and other races were to persons 15 to 24 years of age; for whites, the percent was 20.5.

Studies show that the very young—as young as two years old—are killing themselves as well, although there are no reliable figures for those under 10 because the National Center for Health Statistics does not even compute suicide figures for children in that age category. Figures for 10- to 14-year-olds show that rates for that group have risen by 32% in the decade between 1968 and 1978.

Between 1955 and 1975, the rate of teen suicide very nearly tripled—from 4.1 per 100,000 in 1955 to 11.8 per 100,000 in 1975. Between 1965 and 1975, the rate almost doubled. Just between 1974 and 1975, the suicide rate mushroomed by 10%.

Studies have shown that as many as 41% of high school children surveyed admitted having thoughts about suicide and up to 10% may be considered at risk for suicide.

Teenage suicides peaked in 1977 with 13.3 deaths per 100,000. The rate dropped to 11.9 in 1983, but rose to 12.5 per 100,000 in 1984, the most recent years for available statistics.

The result of all this? Suicide is second only to accidents as the leading cause of death in the U.S. among those young people aged 15 to 24. There is, however, a glimmer of good news. Teen suicide totals appear to be leveling off in the 1980s. But the rate per 100,000 is still more than twice that of 1960. (See also ADOLESCENTS AND SUICIDE; CHILDREN AND SUICIDE.)

Yugoslavia World Health Organization figures for 1982 (latest available) show a total suicide rate per 100,000 of 16.1 (males 22.3, females 10.0). This is up from a 14.7 total in

1980, when the male rate per 100,000 was 20.8, the female rate 8.7. Highest rates for both genders is found in the 75-plus age group: 54.2 total, 85.8 males and 33.2 females.

Yuit Eskimos Anthropologists A.H. Leighton and C.C. Hughes, writing in "Notes on Eskimo Patterns of Suicide," describe how among the Yuit Eskimos, an individual may decide to die in order for his spirit to be able to save the life of a close relative—or to earn the prestige that this society affords the person who "honorably" ends his life while still at the peak of his powers. His death is a public ceremonial with the actual act being performed by his closest kinsman, who is ritually purified afterwards.

According to anthropologist Jean La Fontaine, "In this society the decision to die and its implementation are separate acts, but the man who deals the death blow is an agent of his victim, which makes a public performance essential to demonstrate this." Dr. LaFontaine explains: "The Eskimo case thus comes under the definition of suicide that is usually recognized by anthropologists: a death for which responsibility is socially attributed to the dead person."

Jean LaFontaine, "Anthropology," ch. 4 in *A Handbook for the Study of Suicide*, Seymour Perlin, ed. (New York: Oxford University Press, 1975).

Z

Zealots See JAIR, ELEAZAR BEN and MASADA.

Zeno (of Citium) Greek philosopher (ca. 363-264 B.C.), born at Citium, Cyprus. He trained at Athens under Cynic teachers and later founded the school of Stoicism around 300 B.C. Legend has it that Zeno committed suicide after breaking his toe. He was 98 years old at the time and decided that God had sent the broken toe as a sign that he had lived long enough.

Zilboorg, Dr. Gregory The late Dr. Gregory Zilboorg (1890-1959) was psychiatrist-in-chief of the United Nations. He stated that every suicidal case, in Shneidman's words, "contained not only unconscious hostility, but also an unusual lack of capacity to love others." This is a refinement of Karl Menninger's assertion that the drives in suicide are made up of: (a) the wish to kill; (b) the wish to be killed; and (c) the wish to die.

Dr. Zilboorg once said that "Statistical data on suicides as compiled today deserve little credence. All too many suicides are not reported as such."

Zimri Usurped the throne of Israel in 876 B.C. After the capture of the city of Tirzah, Zimri realized the hopelessness of his situation and this led him to seek death. "He went into the citadel of the king's house and burned the king's house over him with fire, and died" (I Kings 16:18).

APPENDIXES

Appendix 1

Youth Suicide Statistics, 1950-1980, Figures, Tables

Appendix 2

Suicide in the United States, 1970-1980, Figures, Tables

Appendix 3

Sources of Information

Appendix I

Youth Suicide Statistics for Selected Years, 1950-1980

Figure 1
Suicide rates for all persons 15 to 24 years of age by age group, United States, 1970-1980

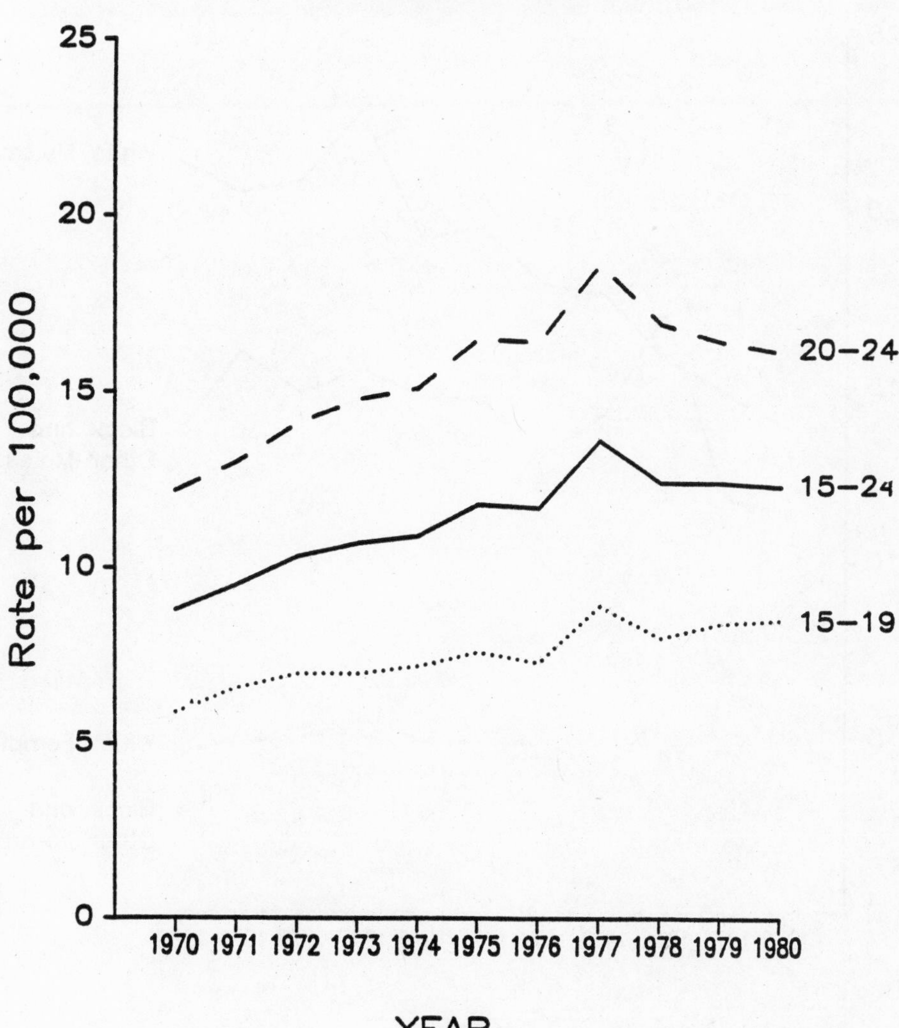

Figure 2
Suicide rates for all persons 15 to 24 years of age by race and sex, United States, 1970-1980

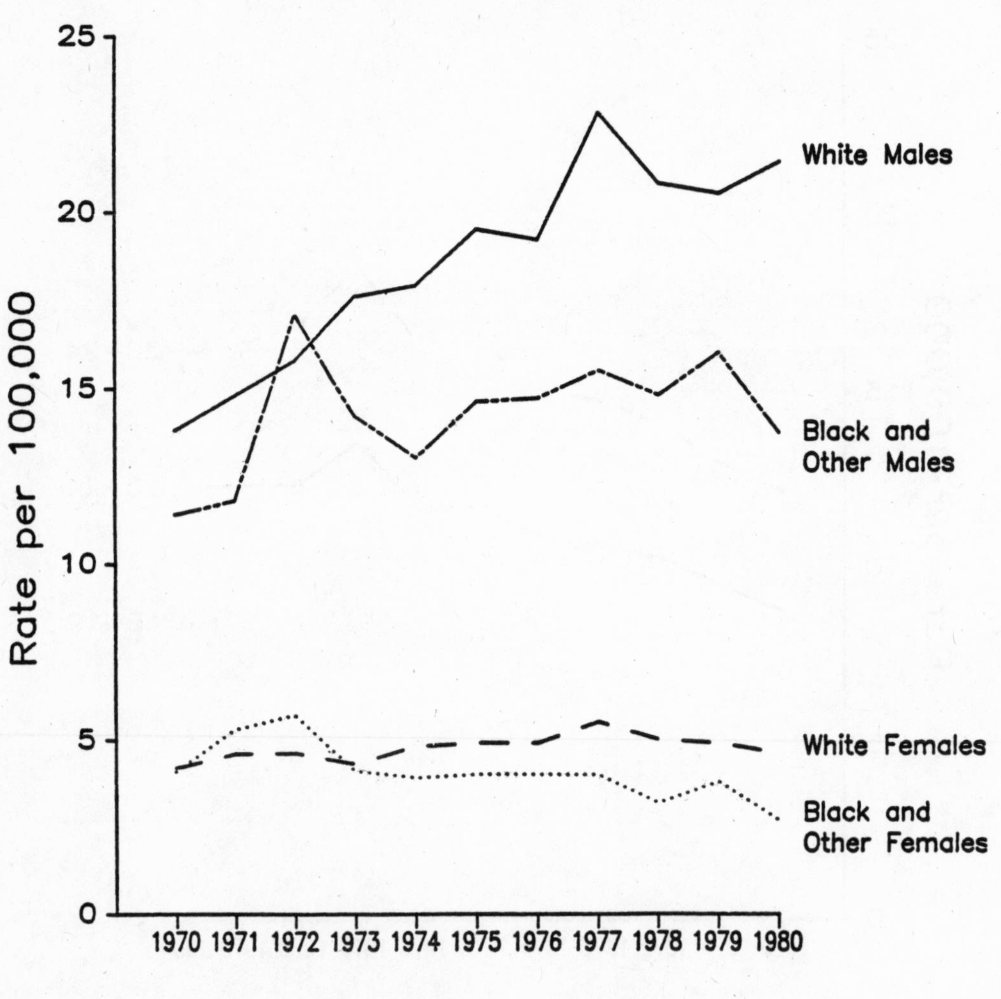

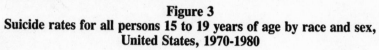

Figure 3
Suicide rates for all persons 15 to 19 years of age by race and sex, United States, 1970-1980

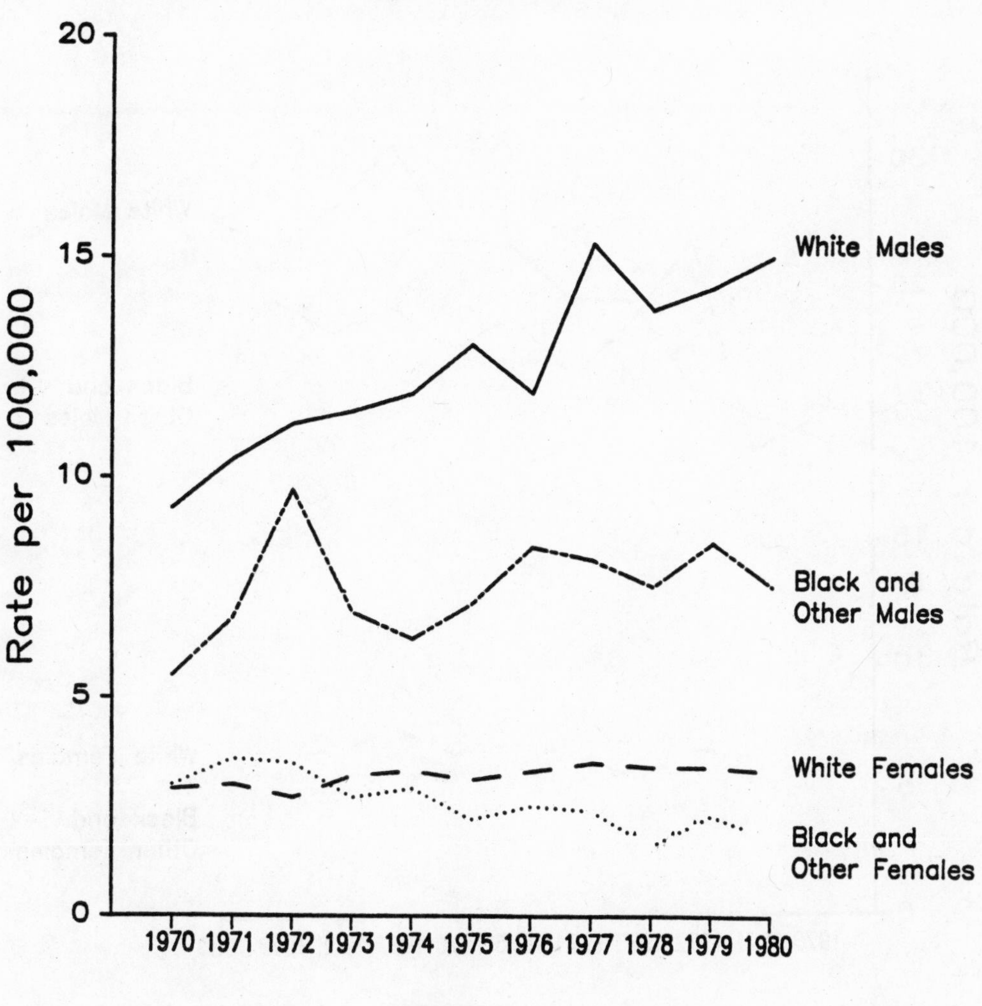

Figure 4
Suicide rates for all persons 20 to 24 years of age by race and sex, United States, 1970-1980

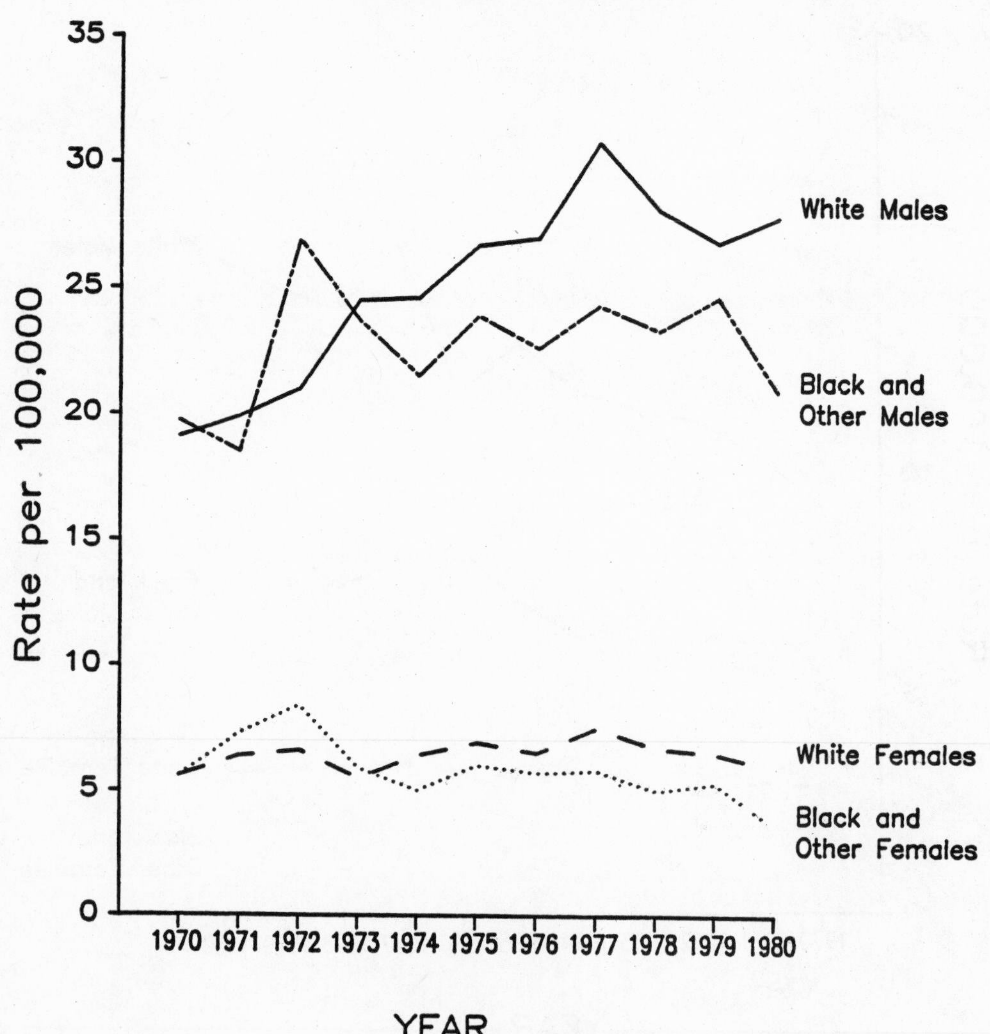

Figure 5
Suicide rates for all persons 15 to 24 years of age by geographic region, United States, 1970-1980

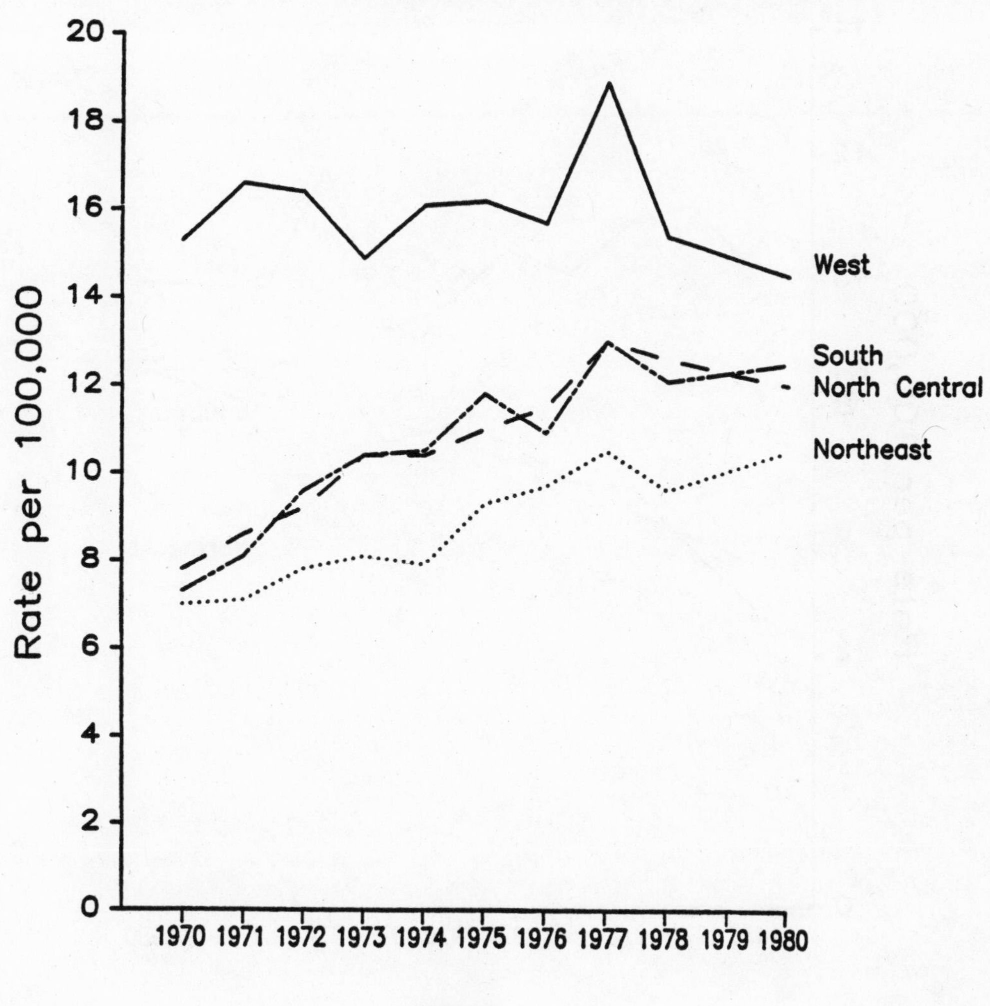

Figure 6
Suicide rates for all persons 15 to 19 years of age by geographic region, United States, 1970-1980

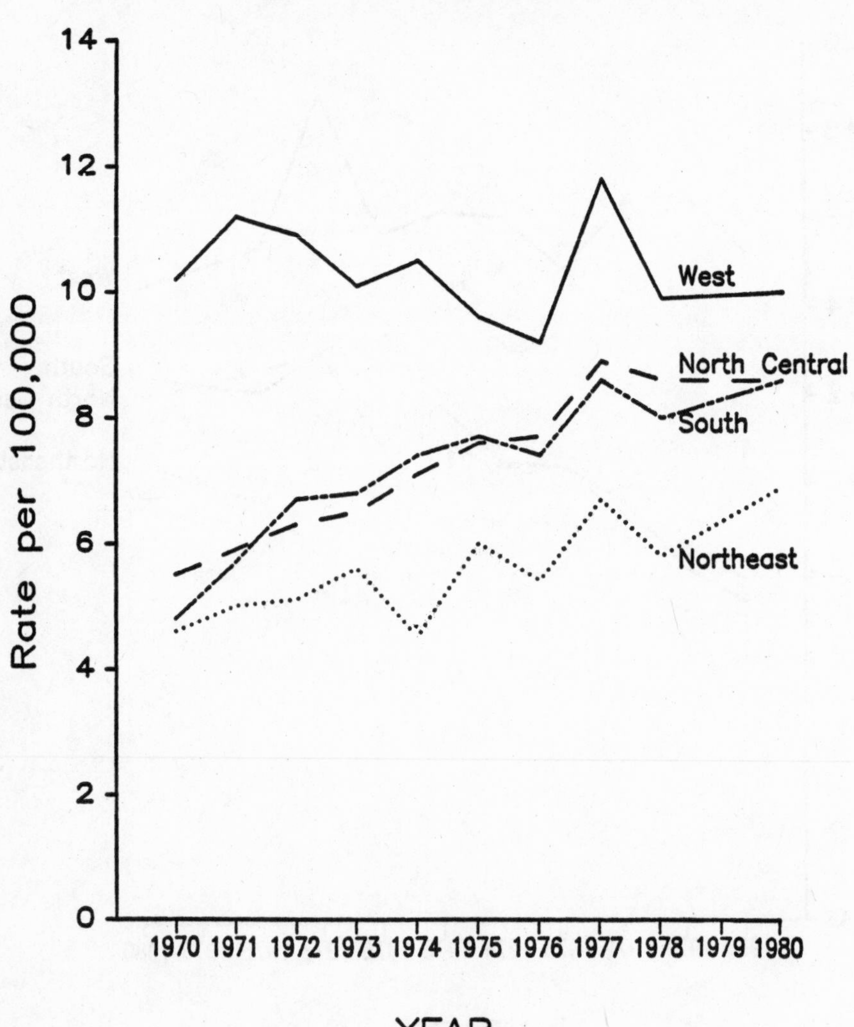

Figure 7
Suicide rates for all persons 20 to 24 years of age by geographic region, United States, 1970-1980

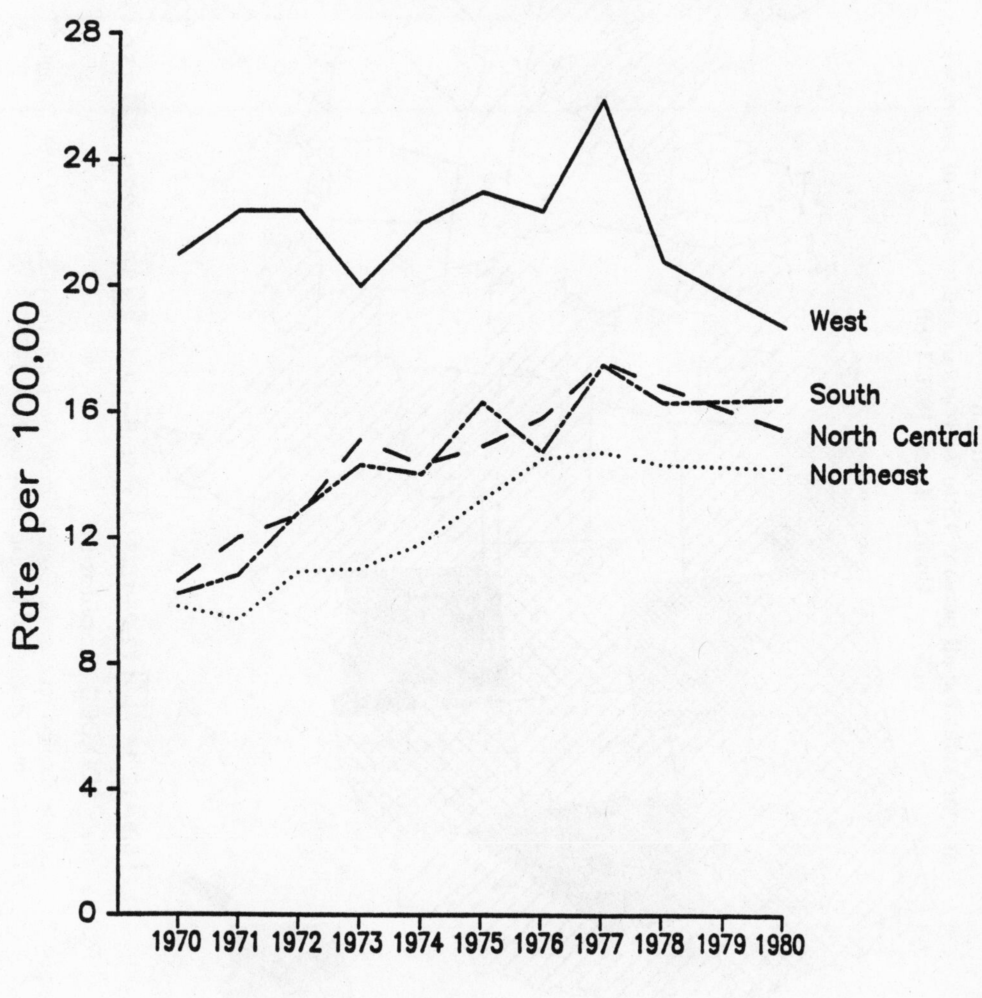

Figure 8
Suicide rates for all persons 15 to 24 years of age by state of residence, United States, 1970-1980

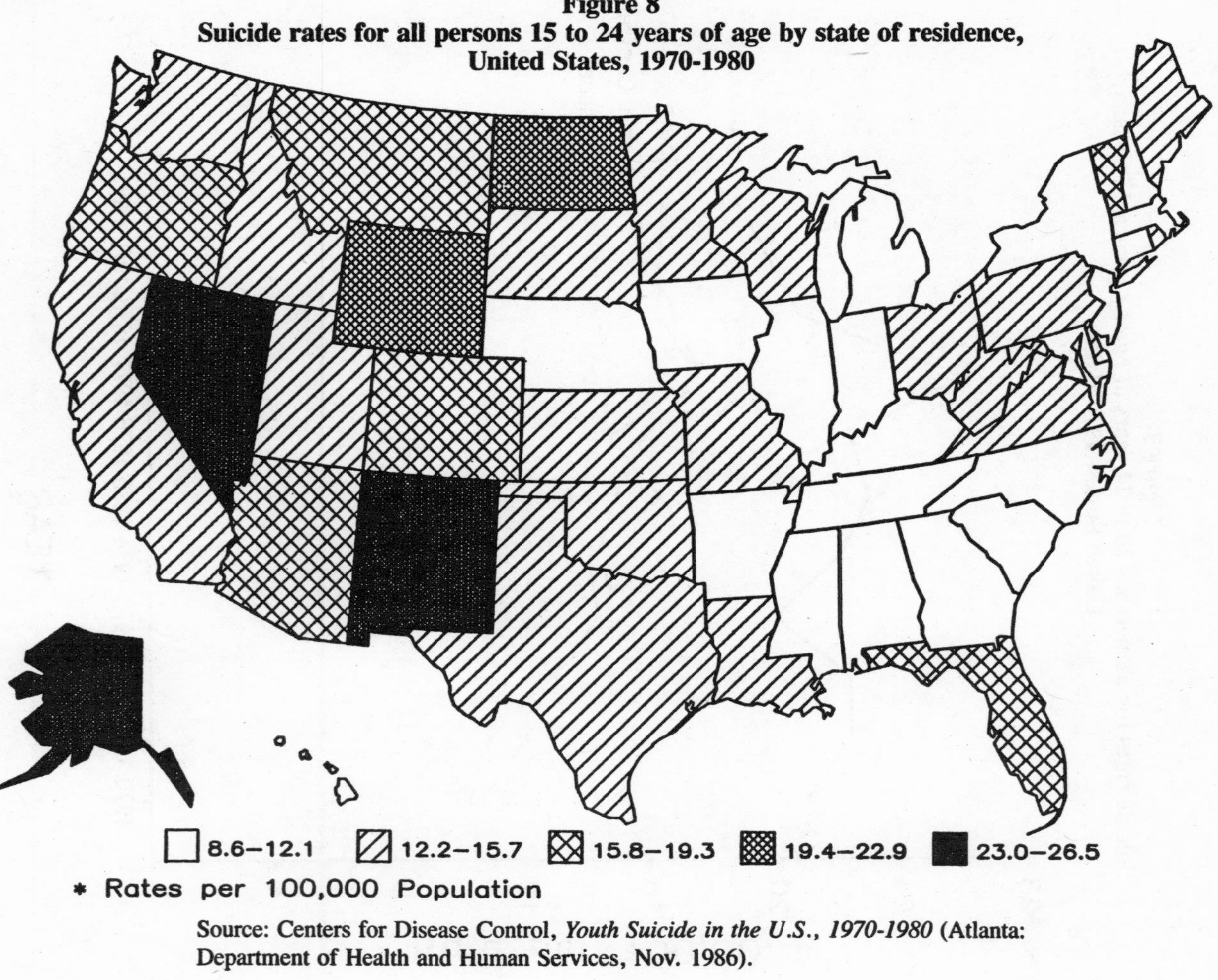

Source: Centers for Disease Control, *Youth Suicide in the U.S., 1970-1980* (Atlanta: Department of Health and Human Services, Nov. 1986).

Figure 9
Suicide rates for all persons 15 to 24 years of age by SMSA status, United States, 1970-1978

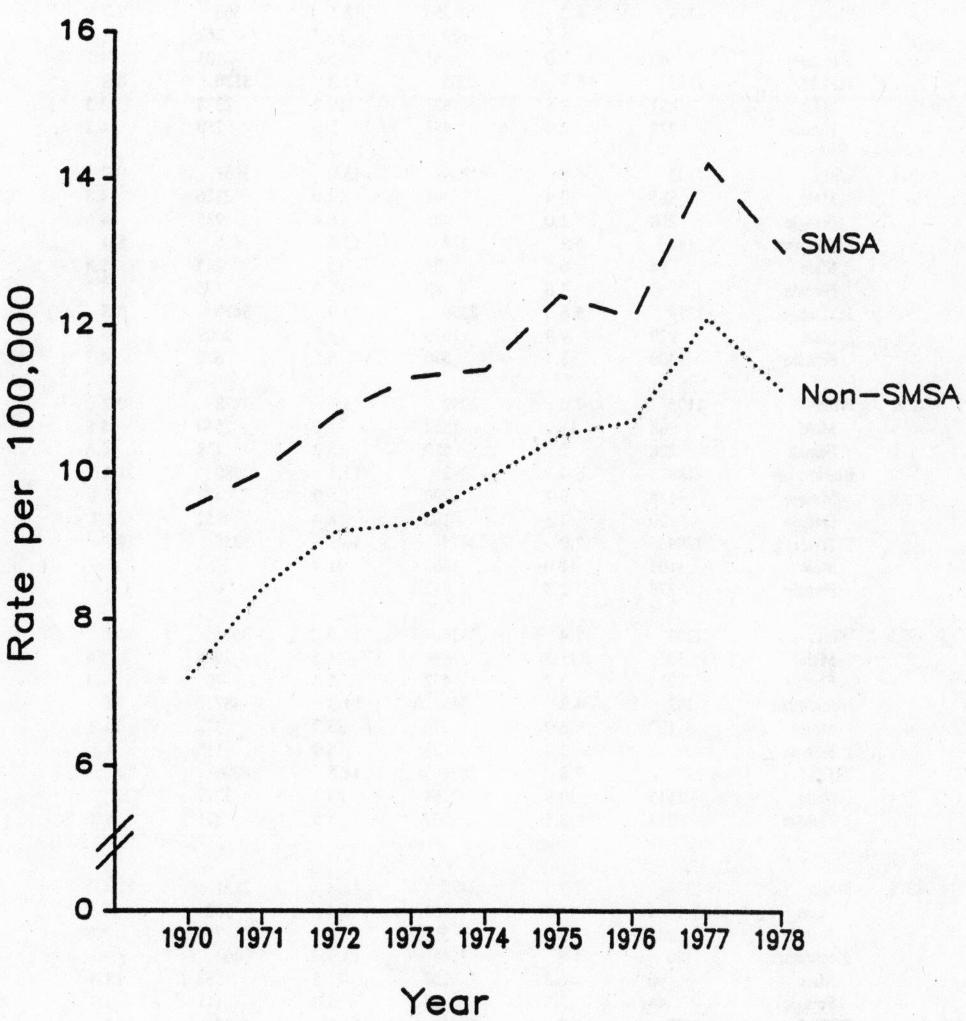

Table 1
Number of suicides and suicide rates for all persons 15 to 24 years of age by age group, race, sex and year, United States, 1970-1980

		Age Group				Total	
		15-19		20-24		15-24	
Year	Race and Sex	No.	Rate	No.	Rate	No.	Rate
1970	White	1010	6.1	1755	12.2	2765	9.0
	Male	778	9.3	1338	19.1	2116	13.8
	Female	232	2.9	417	5.6	649	4.2
	Black/other	113	4.2	250	12.1	363	7.7
	Male	73	5.5	189	19.7	262	11.4
	Female	40	3.0	61	5.6	101	4.1
	TOTAL	**1123**	**5.9**	**2005**	**12.2**	**3128**	**8.8**
	Male	851	8.8	1527	19.2	2378	13.5
	Female	272	2.9	478	5.6	750	4.2
1971	White	1135	6.8	1926	13.0	3061	9.7
	Male	885	10.4	1441	19.9	2326	14.8
	Female	250	3.0	485	6.4	735	4.6
	Black/other	144	5.2	274	12.6	418	8.4
	Male	94	6.8	189	18.5	283	11.8
	Female	50	3.6	85	7.3	135	5.3
	TOTAL	**1279**	**6.6**	**2200**	**13.0**	**3479**	**9.5**
	Male	979	9.9	1630	19.8	2609	14.4
	Female	300	3.1	570	6.5	870	4.7
1972	White	1196	7.0	2082	13.7	3278	10.2
	Male	968	11.2	1572	21.0	2540	15.8
	Female	228	2.7	510	6.6	738	4.6
	Black/other	188	6.4	392	17.1	580	11.2
	Male	138	9.7	290	26.9	428	17.1
	Female	50	3.5	102	8.4	152	5.7
	TOTAL	**1384**	**7.0**	**2474**	**14.1**	**3858**	**10.3**
	Male	1106	11.0	1862	21.8	2968	15.9
	Female	278	2.8	612	6.9	890	4.7
1973	White	1285	7.4	2326	14.9	3611	11.0
	Male	1011	11.5	1894	24.5	2905	17.6
	Female	274	3.2	432	5.5	706	4.3
	Black/other	142	4.8	345	14.3	487	9.0
	Male	102	6.9	270	23.7	372	14.2
	Female	40	2.7	75	5.9	115	4.1
	TOTAL	**1427**	**7.0**	**2671**	**14.8**	**4098**	**10.7**
	Male	1113	10.9	2164	24.4	3277	17.2
	Female	314	3.1	507	5.5	821	4.3
1974	White	1349	7.7	2472	15.4	3821	11.4
	Male	1064	11.9	1961	24.6	3025	17.9
	Female	285	3.3	511	6.4	796	4.8
	Black/other	140	4.6	324	12.9	464	8.3
	Male	96	6.3	257	21.5	353	13.0
	Female	44	2.9	67	5.0	111	3.9
	TOTAL	**1489**	**7.2**	**2796**	**15.1**	**4285**	**10.9**
	Male	1160	11.1	2218	24.2	3378	17.2
	Female	329	3.2	578	6.2	907	4.6

*Rates per 100,000 population

Sources: National Center for Health Statistics Annual Mortality Data Files: U.S. Bureau of Census Population Estimates

Table 1
Number of suicides and suicide rates for all persons 15 to 24 years of age by age group, race, sex and year, United States, 1970-1980 (continued)

		Age Group				Total	
		15-19		20-24		15-24	
Year	Race and Sex	No.	Rate	No.	Rate	No.	Rate
1975	White	1449	8.1	2761	16.8	4210	12.3
	Male	1178	13.0	2200	26.7	3378	19.5
	Female	271	3.1	561	6.9	832	4.9
	Black/other	145	4.6	381	14.5	526	9.1
	Male	111	7.1	298	23.9	409	14.4
	Female	34	2.2	83	6.0	117	4.0
	TOTAL	**1594**	**7.6**	**3142**	**16.5**	**4736**	**11.8**
	Male	1289	12.1	2498	26.3	3787	18.8
	Female	305	2.9	644	6.7	949	4.8
1976	White	1381	7.7	2812	16.8	4193	12.1
	Male	1086	11.9	2268	27.0	3354	19.2
	Female	295	3.3	544	6.5	839	4.9
	Black/other	175	5.4	379	13.8	554	9.3
	Male	135	8.4	297	22.6	432	14.7
	Female	40	2.5	82	5.7	122	4.0
	TOTAL	**1556**	**7.3**	**3191**	**16.4**	**4747**	**11.7**
	Male	1221	11.4	2565	26.4	3786	18.5
	Female	335	3.2	626	6.4	961	4.8
1977	White	1700	9.5	3275	19.2	4975	14.3
	Male	1389	15.3	2638	30.8	4027	22.8
	Female	311	3.5	637	7.5	948	5.5
	Black/other	171	5.2	419	14.6	590	9.6
	Male	132	8.1	333	24.3	465	15.5
	Female	39	2.4	86	5.8	125	4.0
	TOTAL	**1871**	**8.9**	**3694**	**18.6**	**5565**	**13.6**
	Male	1521	14.2	2971	29.9	4492	21.8
	Female	350	3.4	723	7.3	1073	5.3
1978	White	1537	8.7	3021	17.5	4558	13.0
	Male	1244	13.8	2445	28.1	3689	20.8
	Female	293	3.4	576	6.7	869	5.0
	Black/other	149	4.5	408	13.8	557	8.9
	Male	123	7.5	331	23.3	454	14.8
	Female	26	1.6	77	5.0	103	3.2
	TOTAL	**1686**	**8.0**	**3429**	**16.9**	**5115**	**12.4**
	Male	1367	12.8	2776	27.4	4143	19.9
	Female	319	3.1	653	6.4	972	4.7
1979	White	1602	8.9	3000	16.7	4602	12.8
	Male	1305	14.3	2422	26.8	3727	20.5
	Female	297	3.4	578	6.5	875	4.9
	Black/other	186	5.4	458	14.6	644	9.8
	Male	147	8.5	371	24.6	518	16.0
	Female	39	2.3	87	5.3	126	3.8
	TOTAL	**1788**	**8.4**	**3458**	**16.4**	**5246**	**12.4**
	Male	1452	13.4	2793	26.5	4245	19.8
	Female	336	3.2	665	6.3	1001	4.8

Table 1
Number of suicides and suicide rates for all persons 15 to 24 years of age by age group, race, sex and year, United States, 1970-1980 (continued)

		Age Group				Total	
		15-19		20-24		15-24	
Year	Race and Sex	No.	Rate	No.	Rate	No.	Rate
1980	White	1635	9.2	3057	16.9	4692	13.1
	Male	1352	15.0	2529	27.8	3881	21.4
	Female	283	3.3	528	5.9	811	4.6
	Black/other	162	4.7	385	11.9	547	8.1
	Male	131	7.5	324	20.9	455	13.7
	Female	31	1.8	61	3.6	92	2.7
	TOTAL	**1797**	**8.5**	**3442**	**16.1**	**5239**	**12.3**
	Male	1483	13.8	2853	26.8	4336	20.2
	Female	314	3.0	589	5.5	903	4.3

Table 2
Number of suicides and suicide rates for all persons 15 to 24 years of age by age group, geographic region, state, and year, United States, 1970-1980

		Age Group				Total	
		15-19		20-24		15-24	
Year	Geographic Region	No.	Rate	No.	Rate	No.	Rate
1970	Northeast	197	4.6	362	9.8	559	7.0
	North Central	297	5.5	467	10.6	764	7.8
	South	294	4.8	539	10.2	833	7.3
	West	335	10.2	637	21.0	972	15.3
	TOTAL	**1,123**	**5.9**	**2,005**	**12.2**	**3,128**	**8.8**
1970	Northeast						
	Connecticut	17	6.4	20	8.7	37	7.5
	Maine	7	7.4	7	9.2	14	8.2
	Massachusetts	21	4.1	51	11.0	72	7.3
	New Hampshire	2	3.0	6	10.2	8	6.3
	New Jersey	22	3.6	41	8.0	63	5.6
	New York	62	4.0	117	8.5	179	6.1
	Pennsylvania	60	5.6	109	12.8	169	8.7
	Rhode Island	2	2.3	6	6.8	8	4.6
	Vermont	4	9.0	5	13.8	9	11.1
	Total	**197**	**4.6**	**362**	**9.8**	**559**	**7.0**
1970	North Central						
	Illinois	49	4.8	84	9.9	133	7.2
	Indiana	28	5.6	48	11.5	76	8.3
	Iowa	11	4.0	16	7.8	27	5.6
	Kansas	11	5.1	23	12.2	34	8.4
	Michigan	59	6.7	84	11.9	143	9.1
	Minnesota	17	4.5	31	10.6	48	7.2
	Missouri	36	8.4	28	7.9	64	8.1
	Nebraska	1	0.7	10	8.7	11	4.2
	North Dakota	5	7.7	2	4.1	7	6.1
	Ohio	52	5.1	104	12.5	156	8.4
	South Dakota	5	7.1	3	6.1	8	6.7
	Wisconsin	23	5.3	34	10.1	57	7.4
	Total	**297**	**5.5**	**467**	**10.6**	**764**	**7.8**
1970	South						
	Alabama	10	2.9	18	6.5	28	4.5
	Arkansas	14	7.6	11	7.7	25	7.6
	Delaware	2	3.9	9	20.5	11	11.5
	Dist. of Columbia	1	1.5	8	10.1	9	6.2
	Florida	45	7.7	59	11.8	104	9.6
	Georgia	21	4.7	42	10.0	63	7.3
	Kentucky	6	1.9	22	8.3	28	4.8
	Louisiana	14	3.7	28	9.3	42	6.2
	Maryland	13	3.6	44	13.5	57	8.3
	Mississippi	9	3.8	11	6.3	20	4.9
	North Carolina	25	4.8	31	6.7	56	5.7
	Oklahoma	10	4.1	17	8.2	27	6.0
	South Carolina	9	3.2	22	9.2	31	5.9
	Tennessee	17	4.5	30	9.3	47	6.7
	Texas	63	5.7	124	12.9	187	9.1
	Virginia	29	6.5	57	12.9	86	9.7
	West Virginia	6	3.5	6	4.7	12	4.0
	Total	**294**	**4.8**	**539**	**10.2**	**833**	**7.3**

*Rates per 100,000 population

Table 2
Number of suicides and suicide rates for all persons 15 to 24 years of age by age group, geographic region, state, and year, United States, 1970-1980 (continued)

		Age Group				Total	
		15-19		20-24		15-24	
Year	Geographic Region	No.	Rate	No.	Rate	No.	Rate
1970	West						
	Alaska	2	7.3	9	24.3	11	17.1
	Arizona	14	8.0	33	22.2	47	14.5
	California	222	12.2	410	23.4	632	17.7
	Colorado	19	8.6	34	16.5	53	12.4
	Hawaii	2	2.8	6	7.3	8	5.2
	Idaho	7	9.4	12	22.3	19	14.8
	Montana	6	8.5	7	13.5	13	10.6
	Nevada	2	4.9	8	20.3	10	12.5
	New Mexico	11	10.4	22	26.4	33	17.4
	Oregon	11	5.4	24	14.7	35	9.5
	Utah	15	12.8	18	18.3	33	15.3
	Washington	18	5.4	48	16.2	66	10.5
	Wyoming	6	18.0	6	24.1	12	20.6
	Total	**335**	**10.2**	**637**	**21.0**	**972**	**15.3**
1971	Northeast	220	5.0	358	9.4	578	7.1
	North Central	325	5.9	542	12.0	867	8.6
	South	357	5.7	595	10.8	952	8.1
	West	377	11.2	705	22.4	1,082	16.6
	TOTAL	**1,279**	**6.6**	**2,200**	**13.0**	**3,479**	**9.5**
1971	Northeast						
	Connecticut	10	3.7	29	12.3	39	7.7
	Maine	8	8.3	14	17.4	22	12.4
	Massachusetts	24	4.6	38	7.9	62	6.2
	New Hampshire	8	11.4	12	19.4	20	15.1
	New Jersey	33	5.3	39	7.5	72	6.3
	New York	75	4.7	118	8.4	193	6.4
	Pennsylvania	49	4.5	95	10.8	144	7.3
	Rhode Island	6	6.8	8	8.9	14	7.9
	Vermont	7	15.3	5	13.3	12	14.4
	Total	**220**	**5.0**	**358**	**9.4**	**578**	**7.1**
1971	North Central						
	Illinois	53	5.1	85	9.8	138	7.3
	Indiana	28	5.5	50	11.7	78	8.3
	Iowa	15	5.4	23	10.9	38	7.8
	Kansas	8	3.6	15	7.7	23	5.6
	Michigan	51	5.7	119	16.4	170	10.5
	Minnesota	24	6.3	47	15.5	71	10.4
	Missouri	26	5.9	37	10.2	63	7.9
	Nebraska	10	6.9	12	9.9	22	8.2
	North Dakota	5	7.6	6	11.5	11	9.3
	Ohio	74	7.2	96	11.2	170	9.0
	South Dakota	8	11.3	7	13.5	15	12.2
	Wisconsin	23	5.2	45	12.8	68	8.6
	Total	**325**	**5.9**	**542**	**12.0**	**867**	**8.6**

Table 2
Number of suicides and suicide rates for all persons 15 to 24 years of age by age group, geographic region, state, and year, United States, 1970-1980 (continued)

		Age Group				Total	
		15-19		20-24		15-24	
Year	Geographic Region	No.	Rate	No.	Rate	No.	Rate
1971	South						
	Alabama	15	4.3	27	9.5	42	6.6
	Arkansas	10	5.3	12	7.9	22	6.5
	Delaware	3	5.6	4	8.7	7	7.0
	Dist. of Columbia	3	4.6	7	8.8	10	6.9
	Florida	37	6.0	76	14.1	113	9.8
	Georgia	23	5.1	50	11.7	73	8.3
	Kentucky	23	7.1	33	12.0	56	9.3
	Louisiana	15	3.9	28	9.0	43	6.2
	Maryland	27	7.3	36	10.7	63	9.0
	Mississippi	15	6.3	15	8.1	30	7.1
	North Carolina	23	4.4	47	9.8	70	6.9
	Oklahoma	15	6.1	22	10.3	37	8.0
	South Carolina	9	3.2	19	7.7	28	5.2
	Tennessee	19	4.9	34	10.2	53	7.4
	Texas	82	7.3	124	12.3	206	9.7
	Virginia	32	7.1	47	10.4	79	8.7
	West Virginia	6	3.5	14	10.4	20	6.5
	Total	**357**	**5.7**	**595**	**10.8**	**952**	**8.1**
1971	West						
	Alaska	4	13.9	8	21.1	12	18.0
	Arizona	29	15.7	43	26.5	72	20.7
	California	222	11.9	442	24.6	664	18.2
	Colorado	29	12.6	40	18.2	69	15.3
	Hawaii	8	10.7	11	12.8	19	11.8
	Idaho	15	19.5	16	27.7	31	23.0
	Montana	8	11.1	14	25.5	22	17.3
	Nevada	4	9.3	12	28.6	16	18.8
	New Mexico	13	11.8	22	24.7	35	17.6
	Oregon	10	4.8	30	17.5	40	10.5
	Utah	9	7.5	17	16.3	26	11.6
	Washington	24	7.2	43	14.4	67	10.6
	Wyoming	2	5.8	7	26.1	9	14.7
	Total	**377**	**11.2**	**705**	**22.4**	**1,082**	**16.6**
1972	Northeast	230	5.1	422	10.9	652	7.8
	North Central	352	6.3	592	12.7	944	9.2
	South	426	6.7	732	12.8	1,158	9.6
	West	376	10.9	728	22.4	1,104	16.4
	TOTAL	**1,384**	**7.0**	**2,474**	**14.1**	**3,858**	**10.3**
1972	Northeast						
	Connecticut	6	2.2	20	8.3	26	5.0
	Maine	14	14.1	4	4.7	18	9.8
	Massachusetts	20	3.7	62	12.6	82	8.0
	New Hampshire	8	11.0	4	6.2	12	8.7
	New Jersey	14	2.2	78	14.7	92	7.8
	New York	74	4.6	120	8.4	194	6.4
	Pennsylvania	82	7.4	122	13.5	204	10.2
	Rhode Island	8	8.9	6	6.6	14	7.8
	Vermont	4	8.6	6	15.4	10	11.7
	Total	**230**	**5.1**	**422**	**10.9**	**652**	**7.8**

Table 2
Number of suicides and suicide rates for all persons 15 to 24 years of age by age group, geographic region, state, and year, United States, 1970-1980 (continued)

		Age Group				Total	
		15-19		20-24		15-24	
Year	**Geographic Region**	**No.**	**Rate**	**No.**	**Rate**	**No.**	**Rate**
1972	North Central						
	Illinois	64	6.1	106	12.0	170	8.8
	Indiana	12	2.3	32	7.3	44	4.6
	Iowa	20	7.1	14	6.4	34	6.8
	Kansas	18	8.1	32	16.0	50	11.9
	Michigan	68	7.5	138	18.4	206	12.4
	Minnesota	24	6.2	36	11.5	60	8.5
	Missouri	34	7.6	38	10.2	72	8.8
	Nebraska	8	5.4	8	6.3	16	5.8
	North Dakota	8	12.0	2	3.6	10	8.2
	Ohio	64	6.1	122	14.0	186	9.7
	South Dakota	2	2.8	14	25.6	16	12.6
	Wisconsin	30	6.7	50	13.7	80	9.8
	Total	**352**	**6.3**	**592**	**12.7**	**944**	**9.2**
1972	South						
	Alabama	16	4.5	24	8.1	40	6.2
	Arkansas	12	6.3	8	5.1	20	5.7
	Delaware	0	—	6	12.5	6	5.8
	Dist. of Columbia	4	6.1	10	12.7	14	9.7
	Florida	62	9.6	70	12.2	132	10.8
	Georgia	34	7.3	68	15.5	102	11.3
	Kentucky	22	6.7	22	7.8	44	7.2
	Louisiana	20	5.1	34	10.5	54	7.6
	Maryland	24	6.3	50	14.6	74	10.2
	Mississippi	18	7.4	26	13.4	44	10.1
	North Carolina	24	4.5	56	11.3	80	7.8
	Oklahoma	14	5.6	32	14.5	46	9.8
	South Carolina	18	6.2	38	14.8	56	10.3
	Tennessee	26	6.6	36	10.4	62	8.4
	Texas	76	6.6	178	17.0	254	11.5
	Virginia	52	11.2	66	14.2	118	12.7
	West Virginia	4	2.3	8	5.7	12	3.8
	Total	**426**	**6.7**	**732**	**12.8**	**1,158**	**9.6**
1972	West						
	Alaska	6	19.7	16	41.1	22	31.7
	Arizona	20	10.2	50	28.5	70	18.9
	California	238	12.5	420	22.8	658	17.6
	Colorado	28	11.7	64	27.5	92	19.4
	Hawaii	4	5.2	12	13.5	16	9.6
	Idaho	4	5.1	12	19.5	16	11.4
	Montana	2	2.7	18	30.9	20	15.1
	Nevada	10	21.9	18	40.5	28	31.1
	New Mexico	16	14.0	20	21.1	36	17.3
	Oregon	20	9.4	24	13.4	44	11.2
	Utah	8	6.5	14	12.7	22	9.4
	Washington	14	4.2	48	16.0	62	9.7
	Wyoming	6	17.1	12	41.7	18	28.2
	Total	**376**	**10.9**	**728**	**22.4**	**1,104**	**16.4**

Table 2
Number of suicides and suicide rates for all persons 15 to 24 years of age by age group, geographic region, state, and year, United States, 1970-1980 (continued)

		Age Group				Total	
		15-19		20-24		15-24	
Year	Geographic Region	No.	Rate	No.	Rate	No.	Rate
1973	Northeast	255	5.6	437	11.0	692	8.1
	North Central	369	6.5	721	15.1	1,090	10.4
	South	445	6.8	842	14.3	1,287	10.4
	West	358	10.1	671	20.0	1,029	14.9
	TOTAL	**1,427**	**7.0**	**2,671**	**14.8**	**4,098**	**10.7**
1973	Northeast						
	Connecticut	10	3.6	23	9.4	33	6.3
	Maine	10	9.8	16	18.1	26	13.7
	Massachusetts	34	6.2	63	12.5	97	9.2
	New Hampshire	10	13.2	9	13.3	19	13.3
	New Jersey	37	5.6	41	7.5	78	6.5
	New York	67	4.1	149	10.2	216	7.0
	Pennsylvania	78	7.0	116	12.5	194	9.5
	Rhode Island	4	4.4	13	14.1	17	9.3
	Vermont	5	10.5	7	17.3	12	13.6
	Total	**255**	**5.6**	**437**	**11.0**	**692**	**8.1**
1973	North Central						
	Illinois	63	5.9	108	12.0	171	8.7
	Indiana	32	6.1	70	15.5	102	10.5
	Iowa	12	4.2	30	13.2	42	8.2
	Kansas	16	7.2	22	10.7	38	8.9
	Michigan	80	8.6	147	19.0	227	13.4
	Minnesota	33	8.4	61	18.8	94	13.1
	Missouri	29	6.4	53	13.9	82	9.8
	Nebraska	9	6.0	8	6.0	17	6.0
	North Dakota	7	10.3	9	15.3	16	12.6
	Ohio	59	5.6	143	16.0	202	10.3
	South Dakota	4	5.5	4	6.9	8	6.1
	Wisconsin	25	5.5	66	17.4	91	10.9
	Total	**369**	**6.5**	**721**	**15.1**	**1,090**	**10.4**
1973	South						
	Alabama	21	5.9	29	9.5	50	7.5
	Arkansas	10	5.1	14	8.4	24	6.6
	Delaware	7	12.2	13	25.9	20	18.6
	Dist. of Columbia	1	1.5	13	16.5	14	9.7
	Florida	53	7.8	111	18.2	164	12.7
	Georgia	30	6.3	67	15.0	97	10.5
	Kentucky	12	3.6	41	14.1	53	8.5
	Louisiana	25	6.3	43	12.9	68	9.3
	Maryland	22	5.6	54	15.4	76	10.2
	Mississippi	15	6.1	19	9.3	34	7.5
	North Carolina	43	7.9	55	10.8	98	9.3
	Oklahoma	22	8.6	30	13.2	52	10.8
	South Carolina	21	7.2	29	10.9	50	9.0
	Tennessee	24	6.0	47	13.2	71	9.4
	Texas	91	7.7	190	17.4	281	12.4
	Virginia	42	8.8	66	13.9	108	11.4
	West Virginia	6	3.4	21	14.5	27	8.4
	Total	**445**	**6.8**	**842**	**14.3**	**1,287**	**10.4**

Table 2
Number of suicides and suicide rates for all persons 15 to 24 years of age by age group, geographic region, state, and year, United States, 1970-1980 (continued)

		Age Group				Total	
		15-19		20-24		15-24	
Year	Geographic Region	No.	Rate	No.	Rate	No.	Rate
1973	West						
	Alaska	7	21.9	16	40.2	23	32.0
	Arizona	16	7.8	46	24.4	62	15.7
	California	205	10.6	384	20.4	589	15.4
	Colorado	24	9.6	58	23.5	82	16.5
	Hawaii	6	7.5	11	11.9	17	9.8
	Idaho	8	9.8	5	7.6	13	8.8
	Montana	10	13.2	11	17.9	21	15.3
	Nevada	7	14.5	10	21.3	17	17.9
	New Mexico	20	17.0	28	27.9	48	22.0
	Oregon	21	9.7	32	17.2	53	13.2
	Utah	5	3.9	11	9.5	16	6.6
	Washington	25	7.4	54	17.9	79	12.3
	Wyoming	4	11.2	5	16.3	9	13.5
	Total	**358**	**10.1**	**671**	**20.0**	**1,029**	**14.9**
1974	Northeast	209	4.5	476	11.8	685	7.9
	North Central	408	7.1	700	14.3	1,108	10.4
	South	490	7.4	856	14.0	1,346	10.5
	West	382	10.5	764	22.0	1,146	16.1
	TOTAL	**1,489**	**7.2**	**2,796**	**15.1**	**4,285**	**10.9**
1974	Northeast						
	Connecticut	16	5.6	30	12.0	46	8.6
	Maine	3	2.9	11	12.0	14	7.1
	Massachusetts	27	4.8	64	12.4	91	8.5
	New Hampshire	7	9.1	12	17.2	19	12.9
	New Jersey	28	4.2	60	10.9	88	7.2
	New York	69	4.2	134	9.1	203	6.5
	Pennsylvania	53	4.7	144	15.1	197	9.5
	Rhode Island	3	3.3	12	13.7	15	8.4
	Vermont	3	6.2	9	21.7	12	13.4
	Total	**209**	**4.5**	**476**	**11.8**	**685**	**7.9**
1974	North Central						
	Illinois	40	3.7	93	10.1	133	6.6
	Indiana	24	4.5	52	11.3	76	7.7
	Iowa	22	7.7	32	13.7	54	10.4
	Kansas	12	5.3	26	12.4	38	8.7
	Michigan	80	8.5	143	18.1	223	12.9
	Minnesota	47	11.7	56	16.7	103	14.0
	Missouri	33	7.2	63	16.1	96	11.3
	Nebraska	16	10.5	26	19.0	42	14.5
	North Dakota	6	8.7	13	21.1	19	14.5
	Ohio	81	7.6	134	14.7	215	10.9
	South Dakota	6	8.2	9	14.9	15	11.2
	Wisconsin	41	8.8	53	13.6	94	11.0
	Total	**408**	**7.1**	**700**	**14.3**	**1,108**	**10.4**

Table 2
Number of suicides and suicide rates for all persons 15 to 24 years of age by age group, geographic region, state, and year, United States, 1970-1980 (continued)

		Age Group				Total	
		15-19		20-24		15-24	
Year	Geographic Region	No.	Rate	No.	Rate	No.	Rate
1974	South						
	Alabama	12	3.3	29	9.2	41	6.0
	Arkansas	17	8.5	14	8.0	31	8.3
	Delaware	4	6.8	3	5.8	7	6.3
	Dist. of Columbia	5	7.7	7	9.0	12	8.4
	Florida	63	8.9	132	20.4	195	14.4
	Georgia	47	9.7	67	14.6	114	12.1
	Kentucky	17	5.0	22	7.3	39	6.1
	Louisiana	24	6.0	43	12.4	67	8.9
	Maryland	33	8.3	61	17.0	94	12.4
	Mississippi	12	4.8	19	8.9	31	6.7
	North Carolina	30	5.5	67	12.7	97	9.0
	Oklahoma	26	10.0	43	18.4	69	14.0
	South Carolina	25	8.4	25	9.0	50	8.7
	Tennessee	32	7.9	50	13.6	82	10.6
	Texas	97	8.0	194	17.1	291	12.4
	Virginia	37	7.6	63	12.9	100	10.3
	West Virginia	9	5.1	17	11.3	26	8.0
	Total	**490**	**7.4**	**856**	**14.0**	**1,346**	**10.5**
1974	West						
	Alaska	6	17.6	15	36.1	21	27.7
	Arizona	32	14.9	57	28.5	89	21.5
	California	195	9.9	422	21.8	617	15.8
	Colorado	33	12.9	53	20.9	86	16.9
	Hawaii	6	7.4	15	15.8	21	11.9
	Idaho	8	9.5	12	17.2	20	13.0
	Montana	9	11.6	21	32.5	30	21.1
	Nevada	8	15.8	19	38.4	27	27.0
	New Mexico	24	19.7	24	22.7	48	21.1
	Oregon	24	10.9	44	22.7	68	16.4
	Utah	7	5.4	15	12.4	22	8.8
	Washington	28	8.1	59	18.9	87	13.2
	Wyoming	2	5.4	8	24.2	10	14.2
	Total	**382**	**10.5**	**764**	**22.0**	**1,146**	**16.1**
1975	Northeast	277	6.0	539	13.2	816	9.3
	North Central	440	7.6	748	14.9	1,188	11.0
	South	521	7.7	1,029	16.3	1,550	11.8
	West	356	9.6	826	23.0	1,182	16.2
	TOTAL	**1,594**	**7.6**	**3,142**	**16.5**	**4,736**	**11.8**
1975	Northeast						
	Connecticut	18	6.2	37	14.5	55	10.1
	Maine	9	8.4	16	16.7	25	12.4
	Massachusetts	29	5.1	65	12.4	94	8.6
	New Hampshire	4	5.1	20	28.0	24	16.0
	New Jersey	38	5.6	70	12.5	108	8.7
	New York	78	4.7	154	10.4	232	7.4
	Pennsylvania	86	7.6	160	16.4	246	11.7
	Rhode Island	10	11.3	8	9.6	18	10.5
	Vermont	5	10.2	9	21.1	14	15.3
	Total	**277**	**6.0**	**539**	**13.2**	**816**	**9.3**

Table 2
Number of suicides and suicide rates for all persons 15 to 24 years of age by age group, geographic region, state, and year, United States, 1970-1980 (continued)

		Age Group				Total	
		15-19		20-24		15-24	
Year	Geographic Region	No.	Rate	No.	Rate	No.	Rate
1975	North Central						
	Illinois	54	4.9	109	11.6	163	8.0
	Indiana	30	5.6	63	13.5	93	9.3
	Iowa	16	5.5	30	12.4	46	8.7
	Kansas	19	8.3	25	11.6	44	9.9
	Michigan	90	9.4	156	19.2	246	13.9
	Minnesota	36	8.9	67	19.4	103	13.7
	Missouri	34	7.3	44	11.0	78	9.0
	Nebraska	14	9.1	17	12.0	31	10.5
	North Dakota	6	8.5	8	12.4	14	10.4
	Ohio	88	8.1	157	17.0	245	12.2
	South Dakota	8	10.8	5	8.0	13	9.5
	Wisconsin	45	9.6	67	16.6	112	12.8
	Total	**440**	**7.6**	**748**	**14.9**	**1,188**	**11.0**
1975	South						
	Alabama	27	7.3	35	10.7	62	8.9
	Arkansas	15	7.3	22	12.1	37	9.6
	Delaware	3	5.0	5	9.3	8	7.1
	Dist. of Columbia	5	7.8	13	17.0	18	12.8
	Florida	68	9.2	143	21.0	211	14.9
	Georgia	42	8.5	92	19.5	134	13.9
	Kentucky	27	7.8	45	14.5	72	11.0
	Louisiana	22	5.4	69	19.1	91	11.8
	Maryland	20	4.9	58	15.9	78	10.1
	Mississippi	10	4.0	19	8.6	29	6.1
	North Carolina	49	8.8	72	13.3	121	11.0
	Oklahoma	29	11.1	54	22.5	83	16.5
	South Carolina	18	5.9	42	14.6	60	10.2
	Tennessee	32	7.8	47	12.4	79	10.0
	Texas	106	8.6	200	17.0	306	12.7
	Virginia	40	8.1	96	19.1	136	13.6
	West Virginia	8	4.5	17	11.0	25	7.5
	Total	**521**	**7.7**	**1,029**	**16.3**	**1,550**	**11.8**
1975	West						
	Alaska	10	27.6	22	50.8	32	40.2
	Arizona	34	15.3	57	27.0	91	21.0
	California*	174	8.6	467	23.4	641	16.0
	Colorado	20	7.7	60	22.9	80	15.3
	Hawaii	5	6.0	10	10.3	15	8.3
	Idaho	10	11.6	19	25.8	29	18.1
	Montana	11	13.9	10	14.8	21	14.3
	Nevada	6	11.3	18	34.6	24	22.8
	New Mexico	22	17.5	27	24.4	49	20.7
	Oregon	18	8.1	43	21.4	61	14.4
	Utah	20	15.1	20	15.8	40	15.5
	Washington	21	5.9	61	19.0	82	12.1
	Wyoming	5	13.0	12	34.1	17	23.0
	Total	**356**	**9.6**	**826**	**23.0**	**1,182**	**16.2**

Table 2
Number of suicides and suicide rates for all persons 15 to 24 years of age by age group, geographic region, state, and year, United States, 1970-1980 (continued)

		Age Group				Total	
		15-19		20-24		15-24	
Year	Geographic Region	No.	Rate	No.	Rate	No.	Rate
1976	Northeast	250	5.4	603	14.5	853	9.7
	North Central	449	7.7	807	15.8	1,256	11.5
	South	509	7.4	952	14.7	1,461	10.9
	West	348	9.2	829	22.4	1,177	15.7
	TOTAL	**1,556**	**7.3**	**3,191**	**16.4**	**4,747**	**11.7**
1976	Northeast						
	Connecticut	17	5.8	36	13.9	53	9.6
	Maine	6	5.6	19	19.5	25	12.2
	Massachusetts	25	4.4	77	14.6	102	9.3
	New Hampshire	4	4.9	10	13.5	14	9.0
	New Jersey	37	5.4	67	11.7	104	8.3
	New York	84	5.0	203	13.4	287	9.0
	Pennsylvania	66	5.8	160	16.3	226	10.7
	Rhode Island	6	6.7	19	22.3	25	14.3
	Vermont	5	10.0	12	27.5	17	18.2
	Total	**250**	**5.4**	**603**	**14.5**	**853**	**9.7**
1976	North Central						
	Illinois	64	5.8	131	13.7	195	9.5
	Indiana	32	6.0	50	10.5	82	8.1
	Iowa	19	6.5	47	19.0	66	12.3
	Kansas	20	8.7	32	14.5	52	11.5
	Michigan	90	9.4	174	21.2	264	14.9
	Minnesota	36	8.8	50	14.1	86	11.2
	Missouri	43	9.1	52	12.7	95	10.8
	Nebraska	10	6.5	20	13.9	30	10.0
	North Dakota	6	8.6	8	12.1	14	10.3
	Ohio	79	7.3	158	16.9	237	11.8
	South Dakota	5	6.7	13	20.2	18	13.0
	Wisconsin	45	9.4	72	17.4	117	13.1
	Total	**449**	**7.7**	**807**	**15.8**	**1,256**	**11.5**
1976	South						
	Alabama	20	5.3	35	10.4	55	7.7
	Arkansas	21	10.2	19	10.3	40	10.2
	Delaware	4	6.7	10	18.3	14	12.2
	Dist. of Columbia	3	4.7	15	19.7	18	12.9
	Florida	48	6.5	138	20.0	186	13.0
	Georgia	39	7.8	70	14.4	109	11.1
	Kentucky	24	6.8	42	13.1	66	9.8
	Louisiana	24	5.8	52	14.1	76	9.7
	Maryland	44	10.8	47	12.7	91	11.7
	Mississippi	16	6.3	27	12.0	43	9.0
	North Carolina	42	7.5	69	12.6	111	10.1
	Oklahoma	17	6.3	41	16.2	58	11.1
	South Carolina	13	4.2	32	10.9	45	7.5
	Tennessee	31	7.4	59	15.2	90	11.1
	Texas	115	9.1	205	16.7	320	12.8
	Virginia	40	7.9	82	16.0	122	12.0
	West Virginia	8	4.5	9	5.6	17	5.0
	Total	**509**	**7.4**	**952**	**14.7**	**1,461**	**10.9**

Table 2
Number of suicides and suicide rates for all persons 15 to 24 years of age by age group, geographic region, state, and year, United States, 1970-1980 (continued)

		Age Group				Total	
		15-19		20-24		15-24	
Year	Geographic Region	No.	Rate	No.	Rate	No.	Rate
1976	West						
	Alaska	7	17.1	22	45.5	29	32.5
	Arizona	20	8.9	51	23.8	71	16.2
	California	180	8.8	451	22.0	631	15.4
	Colorado	29	11.0	63	23.6	92	17.3
	Hawaii	6	7.1	11	11.2	17	9.3
	Idaho	12	13.6	22	28.8	34	20.7
	Montana	10	12.5	20	28.7	30	20.0
	Nevada	12	21.7	23	41.7	35	31.7
	New Mexico	16	12.4	42	36.5	58	23.8
	Oregon	13	5.7	38	18.3	51	11.7
	Utah	11	8.2	15	11.4	26	9.8
	Washington	25	6.9	63	19.0	88	12.7
	Wyoming	7	17.5	8	21.5	15	19.5
	Total	**348**	**9.2**	**829**	**22.4**	**1,177**	**15.7**
1977	Northeast	312	6.7	617	14.7	929	10.5
	North Central	518	8.9	919	17.6	1,437	13.0
	South	590	8.6	1,165	17.5	1,755	13.0
	West	451	11.8	993	25.9	1,444	18.9
	TOTAL	**1,871**	**8.9**	**3,694**	**18.6**	**5,565**	**13.6**
1977	Northeast						
	Connecticut	12	4.1	39	14.8	51	9.2
	Maine	11	10.1	18	18.0	29	13.9
	Massachusetts	38	6.8	75	14.1	113	10.3
	New Hampshire	7	8.4	16	20.6	23	14.3
	New Jersey	35	5.2	73	12.6	108	8.6
	New York	99	6.0	184	12.1	283	8.9
	Pennsylvania	89	8.0	189	19.0	278	13.2
	Rhode Island	16	17.9	14	16.1	30	17.0
	Vermont	5	10.0	9	20.2	14	14.8
	Total	**312**	**6.7**	**617**	**14.7**	**929**	**10.5**
1977	North Central						
	Illinois	77	7.0	147	15.0	224	10.8
	Indiana	38	7.1	79	16.3	117	11.5
	Iowa	30	10.3	46	18.2	76	14.0
	Kansas	16	7.0	48	21.1	64	14.0
	Michigan	100	10.6	159	19.0	259	14.5
	Minnesota	44	10.7	77	21.0	121	15.6
	Missouri	34	7.3	78	18.6	112	12.6
	Nebraska	11	7.2	20	13.7	31	10.3
	North Dakota	9	12.9	16	23.6	25	18.2
	Ohio	98	9.2	160	16.8	258	12.8
	South Dakota	5	6.8	7	10.7	12	8.6
	Wisconsin	56	11.7	82	19.4	138	15.3
	Total	**518**	**8.9**	**919**	**17.6**	**1,437**	**13.0**

Table 2
Number of suicides and suicide rates for all persons 15 to 24 years of age by age group, geographic region, state, and year, United States, 1970-1980 (continued)

		Age Group				Total	
		15-19		20-24		15-24	
Year	Geographic Region	No.	Rate	No.	Rate	No.	Rate
1977	South						
	Alabama	30	8.0	35	10.1	65	9.0
	Arkansas	17	8.2	34	17.8	51	12.8
	Delaware	8	13.4	7	12.7	15	13.0
	Dist. of Columbia	3	4.9	13	17.3	16	11.7
	Florida	67	9.1	161	22.9	228	15.8
	Georgia	50	10.0	78	15.7	128	12.9
	Kentucky	21	6.0	46	14.0	67	9.9
	Louisiana	28	6.7	73	19.0	101	12.6
	Maryland	39	9.6	79	21.2	118	15.1
	Mississippi	15	5.9	21	9.2	36	7.5
	North Carolina	46	8.3	85	15.4	131	11.8
	Oklahoma	30	11.1	49	18.8	79	14.9
	South Carolina	18	5.9	57	19.3	75	12.5
	Tennessee	27	6.4	64	16.0	91	11.1
	Texas	131	10.3	249	19.6	380	15.0
	Virginia	47	9.3	92	17.6	139	13.5
	West Virginia	13	7.3	22	13.3	35	10.2
	Total	**590**	**8.6**	**1,165**	**17.5**	**1,755**	**13.0**
1977	West						
	Alaska	10	24.3	18	35.8	28	30.6
	Arizona	44	19.4	68	30.9	112	25.1
	California	229	11.1	562	26.4	791	18.9
	Colorado	26	9.8	65	23.8	91	16.9
	Hawaii	5	6.0	18	18.2	23	12.6
	Idaho	11	12.3	23	28.8	34	20.1
	Montana	14	17.5	17	23.7	31	20.4
	Nevada	14	24.6	28	47.9	42	36.4
	New Mexico	29	22.4	45	37.4	74	29.6
	Oregon	21	9.2	45	20.9	66	14.8
	Utah	14	10.3	24	17.3	38	13.8
	Washington	31	8.5	73	21.1	104	14.7
	Wyoming	3	7.3	7	17.7	10	12.4
	Total	**451**	**11.8**	**993**	**25.9**	**1,444**	**18.9**
1978	Northeast	264	5.8	602	14.3	866	9.9
	North Central	496	8.6	896	16.8	1,392	12.6
	South	547	8.0	1,106	16.3	1,653	12.1
	West	379	9.9	825	20.8	1,204	15.4
	TOTAL	**1,686**	**8.0**	**3,429**	**16.9**	**5,115**	**12.4**
1978	Northeast						
	Connecticut	15	5.2	49	18.4	64	11.6
	Maine	9	8.3	8	7.9	17	8.1
	Massachusetts	23	4.1	70	13.1	93	8.5
	New Hampshire	9	10.7	14	17.2	23	13.9
	New Jersey	30	4.5	63	10.8	93	7.4
	New York	93	5.7	203	13.4	296	9.4
	Pennsylvania	78	7.1	169	17.0	247	11.8
	Rhode Island	2	2.3	16	18.3	18	10.2
	Vermont	5	10.0	10	22.0	15	15.7
	Total	**264**	**5.8**	**602**	**14.3**	**866**	**9.9**

Table 2
Number of suicides and suicide rates for all persons 15 to 24 years of age by age group, geographic region, state, and year, United States, 1970-1980 (continued)

		Age Group				Total	
		15-19		20-24		15-24	
Year	Geographic Region	No.	Rate	No.	Rate	No.	Rate
1978	North Central						
	Illinois	75	6.9	146	14.7	221	10.7
	Indiana	45	8.5	77	15.6	122	11.9
	Iowa	24	8.3	32	12.4	56	10.2
	Kansas	14	6.1	43	18.4	57	12.3
	Michigan	94	10.0	175	20.6	269	15.1
	Minnesota	31	7.6	64	17.0	95	12.1
	Missouri	44	9.5	67	15.5	111	12.4
	Nebraska	10	6.5	16	10.8	26	8.6
	North Dakota	4	5.8	9	13.1	13	9.5
	Ohio	91	8.6	175	18.0	266	13.1
	South Dakota	6	8.3	12	18.0	18	13.0
	Wisconsin	58	12.1	80	18.4	138	15.1
	Total	**496**	**8.6**	**896**	**16.8**	**1,392**	**12.6**
1978	South						
	Alabama	22	5.9	45	12.7	67	9.2
	Arkansas	13	6.2	29	14.8	42	10.4
	Delaware	8	13.6	10	17.9	18	15.7
	Dist. of Columbia	0	—	7	9.5	7	5.2
	Florida	65	8.9	140	19.8	205	14.2
	Georgia	34	6.8	80	15.9	114	11.4
	Kentucky	29	8.3	48	14.4	77	11.3
	Louisiana	38	9.1	69	17.5	107	13.2
	Maryland	34	8.4	74	19.7	108	13.8
	Mississippi	20	7.9	30	13.0	50	10.3
	North Carolina	38	6.9	61	10.9	99	8.9
	Oklahoma	25	9.2	76	28.0	101	18.6
	South Carolina	27	8.8	49	16.4	76	12.6
	Tennessee	31	7.4	50	12.2	81	9.7
	Texas	115	9.0	238	18.2	353	13.7
	Virginia	36	7.2	82	15.3	118	11.4
	West Virginia	12	6.8	18	10.8	30	8.8
	Total	**547**	**8.0**	**1,106**	**16.3**	**1,653**	**12.1**
1978	West						
	Alaska	10	25.2	12	24.6	22	24.8
	Arizona	34	15.0	70	31.2	104	23.0
	California	178	8.6	429	19.5	607	14.2
	Colorado	19	7.1	69	24.8	88	16.2
	Hawaii	15	18.0	15	15.1	30	16.4
	Idaho	13	14.5	13	15.6	26	15.0
	Montana	11	13.6	21	28.0	32	20.5
	Nevada	14	23.9	17	27.5	31	25.7
	New Mexico	15	11.6	38	30.8	53	21.0
	Oregon	21	9.1	42	18.7	63	13.8
	Utah	12	8.8	28	19.4	40	14.2
	Washington	33	9.0	61	16.8	94	12.9
	Wyoming	4	9.6	10	23.6	14	16.6
	Total	**379**	**9.9**	**825**	**20.8**	**1,204**	**15.4**

Table 2
Number of suicides and suicide rates for all persons 15 to 24 years of age by age group, geographic region, state, and year, United States, 1970-1980 (continued)

		Age Group				Total	
		15-19		20-24		15-24	
Year	Geographic Region	No.	Rate**	No.	Rate**	No.	Rate**
1979	Northeast	293		586		879	
	North Central	490		883		1,373	
	South	589		1,146		1,735	
	West	416		843		1,259	
	TOTAL	**1,788**		**3,458**		**5,246**	
1979	Northeast						
	Connecticut	20		31		51	
	Maine	11		15		26	
	Massachusetts	30		70		100	
	New Hampshire	4		16		20	
	New Jersey	37		62		99	
	New York	95		197		292	
	Pennsylvania	82		166		248	
	Rhode Island	7		19		26	
	Vermont	7		10		17	
	Total	**293**		**586**		**879**	
1979	North Central						
	Illinois	74		139		213	
	Indiana	43		80		123	
	Iowa	19		33		52	
	Kansas	18		35		53	
	Michigan	84		172		256	
	Minnesota	42		60		102	
	Missouri	39		67		106	
	Nebraska	16		21		37	
	North Dakota	7		17		24	
	Ohio	77		168		245	
	South Dakota	9		10		19	
	Wisconsin	62		81		143	
	Total	**490**		**883**		**1,373**	
1979	South						
	Alabama	22		48		70	
	Arkansas	12		30		42	
	Delaware	7		11		18	
	Dist. of Columbia	0		8		8	
	Florida	64		162		226	
	Georgia	38		80		118	
	Kentucky	42		38		80	
	Louisiana	43		78		121	
	Maryland	33		67		100	
	Mississippi	13		28		41	
	North Carolina	51		67		118	
	Oklahoma	36		56		92	
	South Carolina	19		38		57	
	Tennessee	37		70		107	
	Texas	119		241		360	
	Virginia	37		107		144	
	West Virginia	16		17		33	
	Total	**589**		**1,146**		**1,735**	

*Rates for 1979 by geographic region were not calculated because population estimates were not available.

Table 2
Number of suicides and suicide rates for all persons 15 to 24 years of age by age group, geographic region, state, and year, United States, 1970-1980 (continued)

		Age Group				Total	
		15-19		20-24		15-24	
Year	Geographic Region	No.	Rate	No.	Rate	No.	Rate
1979	West						
	Alaska	6		6		12	
	Arizona	29		65		94	
	California	196		426		622	
	Colorado	30		67		97	
	Hawaii	17		26		43	
	Idaho	5		19		24	
	Montana	10		14		24	
	Nevada	16		19		35	
	New Mexico	25		43		68	
	Oregon	22		46		68	
	Utah	15		28		43	
	Washington	38		72		110	
	Wyoming	7		12		19	
	Total	**416**		**843**		**1,259**	
1980	Northeast	313	6.9	615	14.2	928	10.5
	North Central	483	8.6	857	15.4	1,340	12.0
	South	611	8.6	1,169	16.4	1,780	12.5
	West	390	10.0	801	18.7	1,191	14.5
	TOTAL	**1,797**	**8.5**	**3,442**	**16.1**	**5,239**	**12.3**
1980	Northeast						
	Connecticut	18	6.2	32	11.7	50	8.9
	Maine	10	9.3	16	16.3	26	12.6
	Massachusetts	31	5.7	73	13.2	104	9.4
	New Hampshire	6	6.8	14	16.7	20	11.7
	New Jersey	42	6.3	83	13.5	125	9.7
	New York	103	6.4	196	12.7	299	9.6
	Pennsylvania	90	8.3	175	16.5	265	12.4
	Rhode Island	6	6.7	16	17.7	22	12.2
	Vermont	7	13.6	10	20.6	17	17.0
	Total	**313**	**6.9**	**615**	**14.2**	**928**	**10.5**
1980	North Central						
	Illinois	84	7.9	156	14.5	240	11.2
	Indiana	38	7.2	57	11.0	95	9.1
	Iowa	17	6.1	36	13.2	53	9.6
	Kansas	19	8.7	46	19.8	65	14.4
	Michigan	76	8.4	140	15.7	216	12.0
	Minnesota	33	8.3	69	17.5	102	12.9
	Missouri	43	9.3	71	15.9	114	12.6
	Nebraska	10	6.8	18	12.1	28	9.5
	North Dakota	10	15.6	16	23.1	26	19.5
	Ohio	91	9.0	162	16.1	253	12.6
	South Dakota	9	13.1	11	16.5	20	14.8
	Wisconsin	53	11.4	75	16.7	128	14.0
	Total	**483**	**8.6**	**857**	**15.4**	**1,340**	**12.0**

Table 2

Number of suicides and suicide rates for all persons 15 to 24 years of age by age group, geographic region, state, and year, United States, 1970-1980 (continued)

		Age Group				Total	
		15-19		20-24		15-24	
Year	Geographic Region	No.	Rate	No.	Rate	No.	Rate
1980	South						
	Alabama	19	5.0	55	15.2	74	10.0
	Arkansas	22	10.3	23	11.9	45	11.0
	Delaware	6	10.0	10	17.2	16	13.6
	Dist. of Columbia	4	6.9	7	10.1	11	8.6
	Florida	81	10.0	177	21.8	258	15.9
	Georgia	42	7.9	79	15.3	121	11.6
	Kentucky	32	9.0	50	14.4	82	11.7
	Louisiana	47	11.0	73	17.4	120	14.2
	Maryland	27	6.7	64	16.3	91	11.4
	Mississippi	15	5.8	40	17.1	55	11.2
	North Carolina	46	8.1	83	14.3	129	11.3
	Oklahoma	27	9.7	51	17.9	78	13.8
	South Carolina	22	6.9	35	11.2	57	9.0
	Tennessee	27	6.3	58	13.7	85	10.0
	Texas	136	10.1	246	17.3	382	13.8
	Virginia	44	8.7	88	16.6	132	12.7
	West Virginia	14	8.0	30	17.4	44	12.7
	Total	**611**	**8.6**	**1,169**	**16.4**	**1,780**	**12.5**
1980	West						
	Alaska	6	16.1	15	33.3	21	25.5
	Arizona	33	13.1	62	23.5	95	18.4
	California	191	9.0	357	15.2	548	12.0
	Colorado	30	11.2	60	19.8	90	15.8
	Hawaii	4	4.6	19	18.0	23	12.0
	Idaho	9	10.2	18	20.9	27	15.5
	Montana	12	16.1	16	21.6	28	18.8
	Nevada	11	15.7	28	36.2	39	26.4
	New Mexico	15	11.3	49	39.1	64	24.8
	Oregon	31	13.7	45	18.9	76	16.4
	Utah	11	7.9	30	19.3	41	13.9
	Washington	33	8.9	87	21.7	120	15.6
	Wyoming	4	9.4	15	29.6	19	20.4
	Total	**390**	**10.0**	**801**	**18.7**	**1,191**	**14.5**

Source: National Center for Health Statistics annual mortality data files
U.S. Bureau of the Census population estimates data file

Table 3
Number and percent of suicides for all persons 15 to 24 years of age by sex, method of suicide, and year, United States, 1970-1980

		15-24 AGE GROUP					
		Male		Female		Total	
YEAR	METHOD OF SUICIDE	NO.	%	NO.	%	NO.	%
1970							
	Firearms and explosives	1,233	51.9	242	32.3	1,475	47.2
	Hanging, strangulation and suffocation	404	17.0	66	8.8	470	15.0
	Poisoning by solid or liquid substances	336	14.1	318	42.4	654	20.9
	Poisoning by gases	218	9.2	44	5.9	262	8.4
	Other means	187	7.9	80	10.7	267	8.5
	TOTAL	**2,378**	**100.0**	**750**	**100.0**	**3,128**	**100.0**
1971							
	Firearms and explosives	1,413	54.2	332	38.2	1,745	50.2
	Hanging, strangulation and suffocation	472	18.1	66	7.5	538	15.5
	Poisoning by solid or liquid substances	319	12.2	343	39.4	662	19.0
	Poisoning by gases	209	8.0	47	5.4	256	7.4
	Other means	196	7.5	82	9.4	278	8.0
	TOTAL	**2,609**	**100.0**	**870**	**100.0**	**3,479**	**100.0**
1972							
	Firearms and explosives	1,768	59.6	378	42.5	2,146	55.6
	Hanging, strangulation and suffocation	448	15.1	76	8.5	524	13.6
	Poisoning by solid or liquid substances	314	10.6	314	35.3	628	16.3
	Poisoning by gases	246	8.3	38	4.3	284	7.4
	Other means	192	6.5	84	9.4	276	7.2
	TOTAL	**2,968**	**100.0**	**890**	**100.0**	**3,858**	**100.0**
1973							
	Firearms and explosives	1,923	58.7	333	40.6	2,256	55.1
	Hanging, strangulation and suffocation	611	18.6	82	10.0	693	16.9
	Poisoning by solid or liquid substances	253	7.7	294	35.8	547	13.3
	Poisoning by gases	266	8.1	39	4.8	305	7.4
	Other means	224	6.8	73	8.9	297	7.2
	TOTAL	**3,277**	**100.0**	**821**	**100.0**	**4,098**	**100.0**
1974							
	Firearms and explosives	2,111	62.5	426	47.0	2,537	59.2
	Hanging, strangulation and suffocation	585	17.3	68	7.5	653	15.2
	Poisoning by solid or liquid substances	217	6.4	266	29.3	483	11.3
	Poisoning by gases	251	7.4	70	7.7	321	7.5
	Other means	214	6.3	77	8.5	291	6.8
	TOTAL	**3,378**	**100.0**	**907**	**100.0**	**4,285**	**100.0**
1975							
	Firearms and explosives	2,294	60.6	450	47.4	2,744	57.9
	Hanging, strangulation and suffocation	706	18.6	91	9.5	797	16.8
	Poisoning by solid or liquid substances	282	7.4	261	27.5	543	11.5
	Poisoning by gases	290	7.7	60	6.3	350	7.4
	Other means	215	5.7	87	9.2	302	6.4
	TOTAL	**3,787**	**100.0**	**949**	**100.0**	**4,736**	**100.0**

Table 3
Number and percent of suicides for all persons 15 to 24 years of age by sex, method of suicide, and year, United States, 1970-1980 (continued)

		15-24 AGE GROUP					
		Male		Female		Total	
YEAR	METHOD OF SUICIDE	NO.	%	NO.	%	NO.	%
1976							
	Firearms and explosives	2,255	59.6	432	45.0	2,687	56.6
	Hanging, strangulation and suffocation	692	18.3	113	11.3	805	17.0
	Poisoning by solid or liquid substances	285	7.5	265	27.6	550	11.6
	Poisoning by gases	289	7.6	53	5.5	342	7.2
	Other means	265	7.0	98	10.2	363	7.6
	TOTAL	**3,786**	**100.0**	**961**	**100.0**	**4,747**	**100.0**
1977							
	Firearms and explosives	2,813	62.6	519	48.4	3,332	59.9
	Hanging, strangulation and suffocation	757	16.9	96	8.9	853	15.3
	Poisoning by solid or liquid substances	305	6.8	310	28.9	615	11.1
	Poisoning by gases	331	7.4	55	5.1	386	6.9
	Other means	286	6.4	93	8.7	379	6.8
	TOTAL	**4,492**	**100.0**	**1,073**	**100.0**	**5,565**	**100.0**
1978							
	Firearms and explosives	2,592	62.6	481	49.5	3,073	60.1
	Hanging, strangulation and suffocation	722	17.4	75	7.7	797	15.6
	Poisoning by solid or liquid substances	254	6.1	234	24.1	488	9.5
	Poisoning by gases	296	7.1	63	6.5	359	7.0
	Other means	279	6.7	119	12.2	398	7.8
	TOTAL	**4,143**	**100.0**	**972**	**100.0**	**5,115**	**100.0**
1979							
	Firearms and explosives	2,709	63.8	512	51.1	3,221	61.4
	Hanging, strangulation and suffocation	713	16.8	93	9.3	806	15.4
	Poisoning by solid or liquid substances	225	5.3	232	23.2	457	8.7
	Poisoning by gases	275	6.5	62	6.2	337	6.4
	Other means	323	7.6	102	10.2	425	8.1
	TOTAL	**4,245**	**100.0**	**1,001**	**100.0**	**5,246**	**100.0**
1980							
	Firearms and explosives	2,787	64.3	474	52.5	3,261	62.2
	Hanging, strangulation and suffocation	792	18.3	91	10.1	883	16.9
	Poisoning by solid or liquid substances	216	5.0	181	20.0	397	7.6
	Poisoning by gases	263	6.1	71	7.9	334	6.4
	Other means	278	6.4	86	9.5	364	6.9
	TOTAL	**4,336**	**100.0**	**903**	**100.0**	**5,239**	**100.0**
1970-80							
	Firearms and explosives	23,898	60.7	4,579	45.4	28,477	57.5
	Hanging, strangulation and suffocation	6,902	17.5	917	9.1	7,819	15.8
	Poisoning by solid or liquid substances	3,006	7.6	3,018	29.9	6,024	12.2
	Poisoning by gases	2,934	7.4	602	6.0	3,536	7.1
	Other means	2,659	6.7	981	9.7	3,640	7.4
	TOTAL	**39,399**	**100.0**	**10,097**	**100.0**	**49,496**	**100.0**

Source: National Center for Health Statistics Annual Mortality Data Files

Note: Method of Suicide—1970-78: 8th Revision of the International Classification of Diseases Adapted for Use in the U.S. 1979-80: 9th Revision of the International Classification of Diseases

Table 3A
Number and percent of suicides for all persons 15 to 19 years of age by sex, method of suicide, and year, United States, 1970-1980

		15-19 AGE GROUP					
		Male		Female		Total	
YEAR	METHOD OF SUICIDE	NO.	%	NO.	%	NO.	%
1970							
	Firearms and explosives	445	52.3	93	34.2	538	47.9
	Hanging, strangulation and suffocation	182	21.4	23	8.5	205	18.3
	Poisoning by solid or liquid substances	85	10.0	113	41.5	198	17.6
	Poisoning by gases	80	9.4	20	7.4	100	8.9
	Other means	59	6.9	23	8.5	82	7.3
	TOTAL	851	100.0	272	100.0	1,123	100.0
1971							
	Firearms and explosives	542	55.4	110	36.7	652	51.0
	Hanging, strangulation and suffocation	196	20.0	24	8.0	220	17.2
	Poisoning by solid or liquid substances	105	10.7	127	42.3	232	18.1
	Poisoning by gases	79	8.1	18	6.0	97	7.6
	Other means	57	5.8	21	7.0	78	6.1
	TOTAL	979	100.0	300	100.0	1,279	100.0
1972							
	Firearms and explosives	644	58.2	114	41.0	758	54.8
	Hanging, strangulation and suffocation	214	19.3	20	7.2	234	16.9
	Poisoning by solid or liquid substances	78	7.1	100	36.0	178	12.9
	Poisoning by gases	90	8.1	14	5.0	104	7.5
	Other means	80	7.2	30	10.8	110	7.9
	TOTAL	1,106	100.0	278	100.0	1,384	100.0
1973							
	Firearms and explosives	670	60.2	120	38.2	790	55.4
	Hanging, strangulation and suffocation	236	21.2	29	9.2	265	18.6
	Poisoning by solid or liquid substances	72	6.5	122	38.9	194	13.6
	Poisoning by gases	79	7.1	17	5.4	96	6.7
	Other means	56	5.0	26	8.3	82	5.7
	TOTAL	1,113	100.0	314	100.0	1,427	100.0
1974							
	Firearms and explosives	716	61.7	176	53.5	892	59.9
	Hanging, strangulation and suffocation	226	19.5	22	6.7	248	16.7
	Poisoning by solid or liquid substances	66	5.7	82	24.9	148	9.9
	Poisoning by gases	82	7.1	24	7.3	106	7.1
	Other means	70	6.0	25	7.6	95	6.4
	TOTAL	1,160	100.0	329	100.0	1,489	100.0
1975							
	Firearms and explosives	792	61.4	165	54.1	957	60.0
	Hanging, strangulation and suffocation	284	22.0	38	12.5	322	20.2
	Poisoning by solid or liquid substances	70	5.4	72	23.6	142	8.9
	Poisoning by gases	85	6.6	10	3.3	95	6.0
	Other means	58	4.5	20	6.5	78	4.9
	TOTAL	1,289	100.0	305	100.0	1,594	100.0

Table 3A
Number and percent of suicides for all persons 15 to 19 years of age by sex, method of suicide, and year, United States, 1970-1980 (continued)

		15-19 AGE GROUP					
		Male		Female		Total	
YEAR	METHOD OF SUICIDE	NO.	%	NO.	%	NO.	%
1976							
	Firearms and explosives	739	60.5	172	51.3	911	58.5
	Hanging, strangulation and suffocation	263	21.5	33	9.9	296	19.0
	Poisoning by solid or liquid substances	70	5.7	89	26.6	159	10.2
	Poisoning by gases	79	6.5	8	2.4	87	5.6
	Other means	70	5.7	33	9.9	103	6.6
	TOTAL	**1,221**	**100.0**	**335**	**100.0**	**1,556**	**100.0**
1977							
	Firearms and explosives	979	64.4	192	54.9	1,171	62.6
	Hanging, strangulation and suffocation	282	18.6	34	9.7	317	16.9
	Poisoning by solid or liquid substances	66	4.3	84	24.0	150	8.0
	Poisoning by gases	112	7.4	16	4.5	128	6.8
	Other means	81	5.3	24	6.9	105	5.6
	TOTAL	**1,521**	**100.0**	**350**	**100.0**	**1,871**	**100.0**
1978							
	Firearms and explosives	885	64.7	175	54.9	1,060	62.9
	Hanging, strangulation and suffocation	271	19.8	30	9.4	301	17.9
	Poisoning by solid or liquid substances	55	4.0	60	18.8	115	6.8
	Poisoning by gases	76	5.6	16	5.0	92	5.5
	Other means	80	5.9	38	11.9	118	7.0
	TOTAL	**1,367**	**100.0**	**319**	**100.0**	**1,636**	**100.0**
1979							
	Firearms and explosives	966	66.5	171	50.9	1,137	63.6
	Hanging, strangulation and suffocation	255	17.6	39	11.6	294	16.4
	Poisoning by solid or liquid substances	56	3.9	78	23.2	134	7.5
	Poisoning by gases	90	6.2	16	4.8	106	5.9
	Other means	85	5.9	32	9.5	117	6.5
	TOTAL	**1,452**	**100.0**	**336**	**100.0**	**1,788**	**100.0**
1980							
	Firearms and explosives	962	64.9	175	55.7	1,137	63.3
	Hanging, strangulation and suffocation	324	21.8	35	11.1	359	20.0
	Poisoning by solid or liquid substances	58	3.9	54	17.2	112	6.2
	Poisoning by gases	73	4.9	23	7.3	96	5.3
	Other means	66	4.5	27	8.6	93	5.2
	TOTAL	**1,483**	**100.0**	**314**	**100.0**	**1,797**	**100.0**
1970-80							
	Firearms and explosives	8,340	61.6	1,663	48.2	10,003	58.9
	Hanging, strangulation and suffocation	2,734	20.2	327	9.5	3,061	18.0
	Poisoning by solid or liquid substances	781	5.8	981	28.4	11,762	10.4
	Poisoning by gases	925	6.8	182	5.3	1,107	6.5
	Other means	762	5.6	299	8.7	1,061	6.2
	TOTAL	**13,542**	**100.0**	**3,452**	**100.0**	**16,994**	**100.0**

Source: National Center for Health Statistics Annual Mortality Data Files

Note: Method of Suicide—1970-78: 8th Revision of the International Classification of Diseases Adapted for Use in the U.S. 1979-80: 9th Revision of the International Classification of Diseases

Table 3B
Number and percent of suicides for all persons 20 to 24 years of age by sex, method of suicide, and year, United States, 1970-1980

		20-24 AGE GROUP					
		Male		Female		Total	
YEAR	METHOD OF SUICIDE	NO.	%	NO.	%	NO.	%
1970							
	Firearms and explosives	788	51.6	149	31.2	937	46.7
	Hanging, strangulation and suffocation	222	14.5	43	9.0	265	13.2
	Poisoning by solid or liquid substances	251	16.4	205	42.9	456	22.7
	Poisoning by gases	138	9.0	24	5.0	162	8.1
	Other means	128	8.4	57	11.9	185	9.2
	TOTAL	**1,527**	**100.0**	**487**	**100.0**	**2,005**	**100.0**
1971							
	Firearms and explosives	871	53.4	222	38.9	1,093	49.7
	Hanging, strangulation and suffocation	276	16.9	42	7.4	318	14.5
	Poisoning by solid or liquid substances	214	13.1	216	37.9	430	19.5
	Poisoning by gases	130	8.0	29	5.1	159	7.2
	Other means	139	8.5	61	10.7	200	9.1
	TOTAL	**1,630**	**100.0**	**570**	**100.0**	**2,200**	**100.0**
1972							
	Firearms and explosives	1,124	60.4	264	43.1	1,388	56.1
	Hanging, strangulation and suffocation	234	12.6	56	9.2	290	11.7
	Poisoning by solid or liquid substances	236	12.7	214	35.0	450	18.2
	Poisoning by gases	156	8.4	24	3.9	180	7.3
	Other means	112	6.0	54	8.3	166	6.7
	TOTAL	**1,862**	**100.0**	**612**	**100.0**	**2,474**	**100.0**
1973							
	Firearms and explosives	1,253	57.9	213	42.0	1,466	54.9
	Hanging, strangulation and suffocation	375	17.3	53	10.5	428	16.0
	Poisoning by solid or liquid substances	181	8.4	172	33.9	353	13.2
	Poisoning by gases	187	8.6	22	4.3	209	7.8
	Other means	168	7.8	47	9.3	215	8.0
	TOTAL	**2,164**	**100.0**	**507**	**100.0**	**2,671**	**100.0**
1974							
	Firearms and explosives	1,395	62.9	250	43.3	1,645	58.8
	Hanging, strangulation and suffocation	359	16.2	46	8.0	405	14.5
	Poisoning by solid or liquid substances	151	6.8	184	31.8	335	12.0
	Poisoning by gases	169	7.6	46	8.0	215	7.7
	Other means	144	6.5	52	9.0	196	7.0
	TOTAL	**2,218**	**100.0**	**578**	**100.0**	**2,796**	**100.0**
1975							
	Firearms and explosives	1,502	60.1	285	44.3	1,787	56.9
	Hanging, strangulation and suffocation	422	16.9	53	8.2	475	15.1
	Poisoning by solid or liquid substances	212	8.5	189	29.3	401	12.8
	Poisoning by gases	205	8.2	50	7.8	255	8.1
	Other means	157	6.3	67	10.4	224	7.1
	TOTAL	**2,498**	**100.0**	**644**	**100.0**	**3,142**	**100.0**

Source: Centers for Disease Control, *Youth Suicide in the U.S., 1970-1980* (Atlanta: Department of Health and Human Services, Nov. 1986).

Table 3B
Number and percent of suicides for all persons 20 to 24 years of age by sex, method of suicide, and year, United States, 1970-1980 (continued)

		20-24 AGE GROUP					
		Male		Female		Total	
YEAR	METHOD OF SUICIDE	NO.	%	NO.	%	NO.	%
1976							
	Firearms and explosives	1,516	59.1	260	41.5	1,776	55.7
	Hanging, strangulation and suffocation	429	16.7	80	12.3	509	16.0
	Poisoning by solid or liquid substances	215	8.4	176	28.1	391	12.3
	Poisoning by gases	210	8.2	45	7.2	255	8.0
	Other means	195	7.6	65	10.4	260	8.1
	TOTAL	**2,565**	**100.0**	**626**	**100.0**	**3,191**	**100.0**
1977							
	Firearms and explosives	1,834	61.7	327	45.2	2,161	58.5
	Hanging, strangulation and suffocation	474	16.0	62	8.6	536	14.5
	Poisoning by solid or liquid substances	239	8.0	226	31.3	465	12.6
	Poisoning by gases	219	7.4	39	5.4	258	7.0
	Other means	205	6.9	69	9.5	274	7.4
	TOTAL	**2,971**	**100.0**	**723**	**100.0**	**3,694**	**100.0**
1978							
	Firearms and explosives	1,707	61.5	306	46.9	2,013	58.7
	Hanging, strangulation and suffocation	451	16.2	45	6.9	496	14.5
	Poisoning by solid or liquid substances	199	7.2	174	26.5	373	10.9
	Poisoning by gases	220	7.9	47	7.2	267	7.8
	Other means	199	7.2	81	12.4	280	8.2
	TOTAL	**2,776**	**100.0**	**653**	**100.0**	**3,429**	**100.0**
1979							
	Firearms and explosives	1,743	62.4	341	51.3	2,084	60.3
	Hanging, strangulation and suffocation	458	16.4	54	8.1	512	14.8
	Poisoning by solid or liquid substances	169	6.1	154	23.2	323	9.3
	Poisoning by gases	185	6.6	46	6.9	231	6.7
	Other means	238	8.5	70	10.5	308	8.9
	TOTAL	**2,793**	**100.0**	**665**	**100.0**	**3,458**	**100.0**
1980							
	Firearms and explosives	1,825	64.0	299	50.8	2,124	61.7
	Hanging, strangulation and suffocation	468	16.4	56	9.5	524	15.2
	Poisoning by solid or liquid substances	158	5.5	127	21.6	285	8.3
	Poisoning by gases	190	6.7	48	8.1	238	6.9
	Other means	212	7.4	59	10.0	271	7.9
	TOTAL	**2,853**	**100.0**	**589**	**100.0**	**3,442**	**100.0**
1970-80							
	Firearms and explosives	1,558	6.0	2,916	43.9	18,474	56.8
	Hanging, strangulation and suffocation	4,168	16.1	590	8.9	4,758	14.6
	Poisoning by solid or liquid substances	2,225	8.6	2,037	30.7	4,262	13.1
	Poisoning by gases	2,009	7.8	420	6.3	2,429	7.5
	Other means	1,897	7.3	682	10.3	2,579	7.9
	TOTAL	**25,857**	**100.0**	**6,645**	**100.0**	**32,502**	**100.0**

Source: National Center for Health Statistics Annual Mortality Data Files

Note: Method of Suicide—1970-78: 8th Revision of the International Classification of Diseases Adapted for Use in the U.S. 1979-80: 9th Revision of the International Classification of Diseases

Appendix 2

Suicide in the United States, 1970-1980

Table 1
Suicide as a leading cause of death by age group, United States, 1980

Rank	1-14	15-24	25-34	35-44	45-54	55-64	65+	Total*
1	Accidents 8.537	Accidents 26.206	Accidents 17.161	Malignant Neoplasms 12.470	Heart Diseases 41.078	Heart Diseases 107.244	Heart Diseases 595.406	Heart Diseases 760.132
2	Malignant Neoplasms 2.070	Homicide 6.647	Homicide 7.267	Heart Diseases 11.433	Malignant Neoplasms 41.030	Malignant Neoplasms 94.645	Malignant Neoplasms 258.389	Malignant Neoplasms 416.368
3	Congenital Anomalies 1.587	Suicide 5.239	Suicide 5.920	Accidents 9.561	Accidents 8.887	Cerebrovascular Diseases 14.159	Cerebrovascular Diseases 146.417	Cerebrovascular Diseases 170.052
4	Homicide 734	Malignant Neoplasms 2.683	Malignant Neoplasms 5.081	Suicide 3.935	Liver Diseases and Cirrhosis 7.050	Bronchitis, Asthma and Emphysema 9.277	Pneumonia and Influenza 45.512	Accidents 104.449
5	Heart Diseases 668	Heart Diseases 1.223	Heart Diseases 3.080	Homicide 3.869	Cerebrovascular Diseases 5.750	Accidents 9.253	Bronchitis, Asthma and Emphysema 43.587	Bronchitis, Asthma and Emphysema 55.987
6	Pneumonia and Influenza 461	Congenital Anomalies 600	Liver Diseases and Cirrhosis 1.292	Liver Diseases and Cirrhosis 3.490	Suicide 3.623	Liver Diseases and Cirrhosis 9.039	Atherosclerosis 28.081	Pneumonia and Influenza 53.592
7	Meningitis 274	Cerebrovascular Diseases 418	Cerebrovascular Diseases 965	Cerebrovascular Diseases 2.189	Homicide 2.530	Diabetes 5.789	Diabetes 25.216	Diabetes 34.842
8	Cerebrovascular Diseases 154	Pneumonia and Influenza 348	Diabetes 572	Pneumonia and Influenza 904	Bronchitis, Asthma and Emphysema 2.237	Pneumonia and Influenza 4.044	Accidents 24.844	Liver Diseases and Cirrhosis 30.535
9	Meningococcal Infection 144	Bronchitis, Asthma and Emphysema 141	Pneumonia and Influenza 563	Diabetes 900	Diabetes 2.188	Suicide 3.456	Nephritis and Nephrosis 12.968	Atherosclerosis 29.441
10	Suicide 142	Anemias 133	Congenital Anomalies 482	Bronchitis, Asthma and Emphysema 411	Pneumonia and Influenza 1.760	Nephritis and Nephrosis 1.957	Liver Diseases and Cirrhosis 9.519	Suicide 26.852
11	Anemias 142	Benign Neoplasms 130	Nephritis and Nephrosis 246	Nephritis and Nephrosis 362	Nephritis and Nephrosis 824	Homicide 1.527	Septicemia 6.843	Homicide 23.992
12	Benign Neoplasms 142	Diabetes 128	Bronchitis, Asthma and Emphysema 202	Congenital Anomalies 335	Benign Neoplasms 541	Septicemia 1.261	Hypertension 6.241	Nephritis and Nephrosis 16.525
13	Bronchitis, Asthma and Emphysema 132	Liver Diseases and Cirrhosis 122	Benign Neoplasms 195	Benign Neoplasms 264	Septicemia 530	Benign Neoplasms 1.057	Stomach Ulcers 4.612	Septicemia 9.193
14	Septicemia 109	Complications of Pregnancy 114	Complications of Pregnancy 160	Septicemia 232	Hypertension 408	Atherosclerosis 1.035	Suicide 4.537	Hypertension 7.8[illegible]1
15	Perinatal Conditions 96	Nephritis and Nephrosis 111	Anemias 157	Hypertension 151	Congenital Anomalies 390	Hypertension 931	Hernias 4.332	Benign Neoplasms 6.126
Residual**	3.484	4.784	6.897	7.912	14.331	27.507	125.344	197.840
Total Deaths	18.876	49.027	50.240	58.418	133.157	292.181	1.341.848	1.943.747

*Excludes persons < 1 year of age and persons of unknown age.
**Deaths from all other causes

Source:
See end of Appendix 2 for a complete listing of sources.
Source 1.

Table 2
Number of suicides by race, sex and year, United States, 1970-1980

Year	White			Black and Other			All Races		
	Male	Female	Total	Male	Female	Total	Male	Female	Total
1970	15,591	6,468	22,059	1,038	383	1,421	16,629	6,851	23,480
1971	15,802	6,775	22,577	1,058	457	1,515	16,860	7,232	24,092
1972	16,476	6,788	23,264	1,292	448	1,740	17,768	7,236	25,004
1973	16,823	6,589	23,412	1,285	421	1,706	18,108	7,010	25,118
1974	17,263	6,660	23,923	1,332	428	1,760	18,595	7,088	25,683
1975	18,206	6,967	25,173	1,416	474	1,890	19,622	7,441	27,063
1976	17,996	6,858	24,854	1,497	481	1,978	19,493	7,339	26,832
1977	19,531	7,048	26,579	1,578	524	2,102	21,109	7,572	28,681
1978	18,619	6,631	25,250	1,569	475	2,044	20,188	7,106	27,294
1979	18,504	6,441	24,945	1,752	509	2,261	20,256	6,950	27,206
1980	18,901	5,928	24,829	1,604	436	2,040	20,505	6,364	26,869
1970-80	193,712	73,153	266,865	15,421	5,036	20,457	209,133	78,189	287,322

SOURCES:

See end of Appendix 2 for a complete listing of sources

Sources 2 - 10 (Table 1-26)

Source 11 (Table 11)

Source 12 (Table 5)

Table 3
Age-adjusted suicide rates by race, sex and year, United States, 1970-1980

Year	White			Black and Other			All Races			Unadjusted
	Male	Female	Total	Male	Female	Total	Male	Female	Total	Rate
1970	18.2	7.2	12.4	10.3	3.3	6.5	17.3	6.8	11.8	11.6
1971	18.0	7.4	12.4	10.1	3.8	6.7	17.2	7.0	11.8	11.6
1972	18.4	7.3	12.6	11.8	3.6	7.4	17.8	6.9	12.1	11.9
1973	18.6	7.0	12.5	11.5	3.3	7.1	17.8	6.6	11.9	11.9
1974	18.9	7.0	12.7	11.6	3.2	7.1	18.1	6.6	12.1	12.0
1975	19.6	7.3	13.2	11.9	3.5	7.4	18.8	6.8	12.5	12.6
1976	19.0	7.0	12.7	12.1	3.4	7.4	18.3	6.6	12.1	12.3
1977	20.3	7.1	13.5	12.2	3.6	7.6	19.4	6.7	12.8	13.1
1978	19.0	6.6	12.5	11.9	3.2	7.2	18.2	6.1	11.9	12.3
1979	18.6	6.3	12.2	12.7	3.3	7.7	17.9	5.9	11.7	12.1
1980	18.9	5.7	12.1	11.3	2.8	6.7	18.0	5.4	11.4	11.9

SOURCES:

See end of Appendix 2 for a complete listing of sources

Source 12 (Table 4)

Source 13

*Age-adjusted rates per 100,000 population computed by the direct method of standardization using the total population for 1940 as the standard population

Table 4
Number and percent of suicides by race, sex and 5-year age group, United States, 1970 and 1980

All Races

Age Group	Males 1970 No.	Males 1970 %	Males 1980 No.	Males 1980 %	Females 1970 No.	Females 1970 %	Females 1980 No.	Females 1980 %	Total 1970 No.	Total 1970 %	Total 1980 No.	Total 1980 %
<15	102	0.6	116	0.6	30	0.4	26	0.4	132	0.6	142	0.5
15-19	851	5.1	1,483	7.2	272	4.0	314	4.9	1,123	4.8	1,797	6.7
20-24	1,527	9.2	2,853	13.9	478	7.0	589	9.3	2,005	8.5	3,442	12.8
25-29	1,312	7.9	2,589	12.6	568	8.3	639	10.0	1,880	8.0	3,228	12.0
30-34	1,113	6.7	2,009	9.8	523	7.6	683	10.7	1,636	7.0	2,692	10.0
35-39	1,133	6.8	1,572	7.7	635	9.3	578	9.1	1,768	7.5	2,150	8.0
40-44	1,349	8.1	1,252	6.1	780	11.4	533	8.4	2,129	9.1	1,785	6.6
45-49	1,579	9.5	1,180	5.8	780	11.4	521	8.2	2,359	10.0	1,701	6.3
50-54	1,550	9.3	1,340	6.5	729	10.6	582	9.1	2,279	9.7	1,922	7.2
55-59	1,562	9.4	1,367	6.7	624	9.1	526	8.3	2,186	9.3	1,893	7.0
60-64	1,309	7.9	1,118	5.5	489	7.1	445	7.0	1,798	7.7	1,563	5.8
65-69	1,086	6.5	1,098	5.4	341	5.0	324	5.1	1,427	6.1	1,422	5.3
70-74	869	5.2	955	4.7	289	4.2	253	4.0	1,158	4.9	1,208	4.5
75-79	613	3.7	766	3.7	159	2.3	175	2.7	772	3.3	941	3.5
80-84	430	2.6	446	2.2	97	1.4	90	1.4	527	2.2	536	2.0
85+	230	1.4	345	1.7	57	0.8	85	1.3	287	1.2	430	1.6
Age Not Stated	14	0.1	16	0.1	0	0.0	1	<0.1	14	0.1	17	0.1
All Ages	16,629	100.0	20,505	100.0	6,851	100.0	6,364	100.0	23,480	100.0	26,869	100.0
Median Age	47.9		38.8		45.9		43.3		47.2		39.9	

SOURCES:

See end of Appendix 2 for a complete listing of sources

Source 1

Source 2 (Table 1-26)

Table 4
Number and percent of suicides by race, sex and 5-year age group, United States, 1970 and 1980 (continued)

White

Age	Males				Females				Total			
	1970		1980		1970		1980		1979		1980	
Group	No.	%	No.	%	No.	%	No.	%	No.	%	No.	%
<15	97	0.6	108	0.6	24	0.4	24	0.4	121	0.5	132	0.5
15-19	778	5.0	1,352	7.2	232	3.6	283	4.8	1,010	4.6	1,635	6.6
20-24	1,338	8.6	2,529	13.4	417	6.4	528	8.9	1,755	8.0	3,057	12.3
25-29	1,157	7.4	2,303	12.2	514	7.9	573	9.7	1,671	7.6	2,876	11.6
30-34	983	6.3	1,779	9.4	479	7.4	612	10.3	1,462	6.6	2,391	9.6
35-39	1,046	6.7	1,444	7.6	601	9.3	535	9.0	1,647	7.5	1,979	8.0
40-44	1,278	8.2	1,147	6.1	749	11.6	492	8.3	2,027	9.2	1,639	6.6
45-49	1,481	9.5	1,103	5.8	753	11.6	493	8.3	2,234	10.1	1,596	6.4
50-54	1,492	9.6	1,267	6.7	699	10.8	553	9.3	2,191	9.9	1,820	7.3
55-59	1,506	9.7	1,293	6.8	615	9.5	507	8.6	2,121	9.6	1,800	7.2
60-64	1,277	8.2	1,071	5.7	477	7.4	431	7.3	1,754	8.0	1,502	6.0
65-69	1,050	6.7	1,055	5.6	329	5.1	314	5.3	1,379	6.3	1,369	5.5
70-74	852	5.5	925	4.9	279	4.3	245	4.1	1,131	5.1	1,170	4.7
75-79	606	3.9	749	4.0	154	2.4	167	2.8	760	3.4	916	3.7
80-84	414	2.7	433	2.3	94	1.5	87	1.5	508	2.3	520	2.1
85+	223	1.4	328	1.7	52	0.8	83	1.4	275	1.2	411	1.7
Age Not Stated	13	0.1	15	0.1	0	0.0	1	<0.1	13	0.1	16	0.1
All Ages	15,591	100.0	18,901	100.0	6,468	100.0	5,928	100.0	22,059	100.0	24,829	100.0
Median Age	48.8		39.8		46.5		44.2		48.0		41.0	

Table 4
Number and percent of suicides by race, sex and 5-year age group, United States, 1970 and 1980 (continued)

Black and Other

Age	Males				Females				Total			
	1970		1980		1970		1980		1970		1980	
Group	No.	%	No.	%	No.	%	No.	%	No.	%	No.	%
<15	5	0.5	8	0.5	6	1.6	2	0.5	11	0.8	10	0.5
15–19	73	7.0	131	8.2	40	10.4	31	7.1	113	8.0	162	7.9
20–24	189	18.2	324	20.2	61	15.9	61	14.0	250	17.6	385	18.9
25–29	155	14.9	286	17.8	54	14.1	66	15.1	209	14.7	352	17.3
30–34	130	12.5	230	14.3	44	11.5	71	16.3	174	12.2	301	14.8
35–39	87	8.4	128	8.0	34	8.9	43	9.9	121	8.5	171	8.4
40–44	71	6.8	105	6.5	31	8.1	41	9.4	102	7.2	146	7.2
45–49	98	9.4	77	4.8	27	7.0	28	6.4	125	8.8	105	5.1
50–54	58	5.6	73	4.6	30	7.8	29	6.7	88	6.2	102	5.0
55–59	56	5.4	74	4.6	9	2.3	19	4.4	65	4.6	93	4.6
60–64	32	3.1	47	2.9	12	3.1	14	3.2	44	3.1	61	3.0
65–69	36	3.5	43	2.7	12	3.1	10	2.3	48	3.4	53	2.6
70–74	17	1.6	30	1.9	10	2.6	8	1.8	27	1.9	38	1.9
75–79	7	0.7	17	1.1	5	1.3	8	1.8	12	0.8	25	1.2
80–84	16	1.5	13	0.8	3	0.8	3	0.7	19	1.3	16	0.8
85+	7	0.7	17	1.1	5	1.3	2	0.5	12	0.8	19	0.9
Age Not Stated	1	0.1	1	0.1	0	0.0	0	0.0	1	0.1	1	<0.1
All Ages	1,038	100.0	1,604	100.0	383	100.0	436	100.0	1,421	100.0	2,040	100.1
Median Age	33.7		31.2		33.5		34.1		33.7		31.9	

Table 5
Suicide rates by race, sex and 5-year age group, United States, 1970-1980

Total

Age Group	Year 1970	1971	1972	1973	1974	1975	1976	1977	1978	1979	1980
<15	0.2	0.2	0.2	0.3	0.3	0.3	0.3	0.4	0.3	0.3	0.3
15-19	5.9	6.5	6.8	6.9	7.1	7.5	7.2	8.7	7.9	8.4	8.5
20-24	12.2	12.4	13.8	14.6	14.9	16.3	16.1	18.2	16.5	16.4	16.1
25-29	13.9	13.9	14.7	14.8	15.6	16.2	15.4	18.0	17.0	17.1	16.5
30-34	14.3	13.5	14.6	14.6	15.4	16.0	15.7	16.3	15.4	15.2	15.3
35-39	15.9	15.8	16.1	15.7	16.3	16.2	15.9	16.6	15.6	15.4	15.4
40-44	17.8	18.2	17.4	17.1	17.3	18.6	16.7	17.1	16.0	15.5	15.3
45-49	19.5	19.3	20.6	19.4	19.3	19.9	19.1	18.8	16.7	16.0	15.3
50-54	20.5	20.4	19.2	19.6	19.8	20.2	19.3	19.0	17.6	17.0	16.4
55-59	21.9	22.7	21.2	20.9	20.3	20.4	20.2	19.1	17.5	16.3	16.3
60-64	20.9	20.0	21.4	19.4	18.6	19.1	19.0	19.0	18.1	17.0	15.5
65-69	20.4	20.9	20.8	19.4	18.1	19.2	19.0	19.0	17.9	17.5	16.2
70-74	21.3	20.9	19.9	20.2	19.7	20.2	20.2	21.4	19.9	18.2	17.8
75-79	20.1	20.5	20.1	21.4	20.4	20.0	19.5	20.7	21.0	20.9	19.6
80-84	23.1	22.5	24.4	19.8	19.8	19.1	20.0	19.6	21.1	20.6	18.3
85+	19.0	19.1	20.8	20.2	17.9	18.6	19.6	18.1	19.6	17.9	19.2
All Ages	11.6	11.6	11.9	11.9	12.0	12.6	12.3	13.1	12.3	12.1	11.9

*Rate per 100,000 population

Source:

See end of Appendix 2 for a complete listing of sources

Source 14

Table 5
Suicide rates by race, sex and 5-year age group, United States, 1970-1980 (continued)

White – Male

Age Group	Year 1970	1971	1972	1973	1974	1975	1976	1977	1978	1979	1980
<15	0.4	0.4	0.3	0.5	0.6	0.5	0.5	0.7	0.5	0.4	0.5
15-19	9.4	10.3	11.0	11.3	11.7	12.9	11.8	15.1	13.6	14.3	15.0
20-24	19.3	18.9	20.4	24.0	24.2	26.3	26.5	30.2	27.4	26.8	27.8
25-29	19.8	20.0	20.8	21.8	23.4	24.6	23.5	28.0	26.7	27.5	27.5
30-34	20.0	18.4	20.6	21.2	22.6	23.2	22.8	23.9	23.3	23.0	23.5
35-39	21.9	21.0	21.3	21.6	24.0	22.8	23.1	25.3	22.6	22.3	24.0
40-44	24.6	25.1	24.5	23.9	23.5	26.1	24.0	24.0	22.3	22.6	23.0
45-49	28.2	27.7	29.8	27.6	27.7	29.1	27.3	26.9	23.6	23.0	23.2
50-54	30.9	29.5	29.6	29.3	28.9	30.3	28.1	27.8	25.9	25.0	25.3
55-59	34.9	36.1	32.0	32.0	32.3	31.9	31.2	29.6	27.0	25.3	26.2
60-64	35.0	32.7	35.1	32.6	31.5	32.0	31.6	31.8	31.5	27.5	25.4
65-69	37.4	36.6	37.9	35.4	32.1	34.8	34.2	34.1	32.1	31.5	30.0
70-74	40.4	39.4	39.1	39.1	38.8	37.7	38.8	42.0	39.8	35.9	35.9
75-79	42.2	43.1	41.4	45.2	43.0	43.0	42.2	46.2	45.8	46.4	44.9
80-84	51.4	52.8	57.4	45.5	47.5	43.6	46.5	46.3	52.5	51.0	46.5
85+	45.8	52.1	54.7	54.9	48.9	51.1	50.8	51.0	54.5	50.2	52.8
All ages	18.0	17.9	18.4	18.7	19.0	19.9	19.5	21.0	19.9	19.6	19.9

*Rate per 100,000 population

Table 5
Suicide rates by race, sex and 5-year age group, United States, 1970-1980 (continued)

Black and Other - Male

Age Group	Year 1970	1971	1972	1973	1974	1975	1976	1977	1978	1979	1980
<15	0.1	0.3	0.0	0.2	0.3	0.1	0.2	0.3	0.2	0.2	0.2
15-19	5.4	6.7	9.5	6.7	6.1	6.9	8.2	7.9	7.2	8.5	7.5
20-24	19.4	17.7	25.7	22.9	20.9	23.1	22.0	23.6	22.6	24.6	20.9
25-29	20.1	18.1	22.6	25.1	23.2	26.5	23.1	27.3	24.9	25.8	21.4
30-34	19.4	16.6	18.2	18.6	21.1	20.4	20.1	20.7	19.4	22.2	20.8
35-39	13.9	17.0	18.3	17.9	15.7	16.8	18.1	16.3	19.0	18.7	15.2
40-44	11.4	12.7	13.0	10.4	15.0	14.5	14.7	14.8	13.7	14.9	14.7
45-49	16.5	10.6	14.8	14.5	10.5	14.4	15.1	13.2	15.1	14.2	12.2
50-54	11.3	10.0	11.7	12.6	13.9	11.8	12.7	10.9	12.2	12.9	12.1
55-59	12.3	13.6	11.0	12.5	13.7	12.8	11.1	13.5	9.2	12.0	13.4
60-64	8.4	9.8	12.7	11.5	10.9	9.5	13.3	12.3	11.5	12.4	10.5
65-69	11.5	13.3	10.7	11.3	15.7	9.3	13.6	10.8	11.5	12.1	11.2
70-74	8.2	17.6	13.1	12.4	13.1	14.9	13.8	13.9	12.8	15.5	10.9
75-79	5.7	9.0	11.5	12.8	17.9	15.5	12.0	12.5	11.9	11.5	9.5
80-84	22.9	5.4	12.8	12.0	13.1	6.9	12.1	10.8	13.3	15.1	14.9
85+	12.6	17.0	8.5	10.4	18.0	13.0	34.5	16.1	13.8	20.3	28.0
All ages	8.5	8.5	10.2	9.9	10.1	10.5	10.9	11.2	10.9	12.0	10.6

*Rate per 100,000 population

Table 5
Suicide rates by race, sex and 5-year age group, United States, 1970-1980 (continued)

White - Female

Age Group	Year 1970	1971	1972	1973	1974	1975	1976	1977	1978	1979	1980
<15	0.1	0.1	0.1	0.1	0.2	0.2	0.1	0.1	0.1	0.2	0.1
15–19	2.9	3.0	2.7	3.2	3.2	3.1	3.3	3.5	3.3	3.4	3.3
20–24	5.7	6.2	6.6	5.5	6.3	6.8	6.4	7.4	6.6	6.5	5.9
25–29	8.6	8.3	8.7	7.9	8.3	7.9	7.6	8.5	8.0	7.4	6.9
30–34	9.5	9.4	9.8	9.1	8.9	9.8	9.5	9.8	8.5	8.1	8.1
35–39	12.2	12.2	12.3	11.2	10.7	11.4	10.5	10.1	9.9	10.0	8.8
40–44	13.8	13.8	12.8	13.2	13.5	13.9	11.7	12.5	12.2	10.4	9.6
45–49	13.5	14.3	14.6	14.2	14.4	14.0	13.7	13.5	12.2	11.3	10.0
50–54	13.5	14.8	12.2	13.2	13.9	13.6	13.8	13.5	12.0	11.9	10.3
55–59	13.1	13.2	13.9	13.1	11.9	12.6	13.1	11.8	11.4	10.1	9.3
60–64	11.5	11.7	12.4	10.5	9.8	10.4	10.4	10.0	8.6	9.7	8.9
65–69	9.4	10.9	10.0	9.3	8.9	9.5	9.1	9.7	8.8	8.3	7.2
70–74	9.7	9.5	8.2	8.7	8.0	9.3	8.5	8.8	7.8	7.2	6.9
75–79	7.3	7.4	7.9	8.0	7.8	7.4	7.6	7.2	8.1	7.2	6.2
80–84	7.2	6.8	7.1	6.8	5.8	7.5	7.2	6.9	6.1	5.9	4.9
85+	5.8	3.7	5.9	4.4	4.1	4.8	6.0	4.5	5.4	5.0	5.8
All ages	7.1	7.3	7.3	7.0	7.0	7.3	7.1	7.2	6.7	6.5	5.9

*Rate per 100,000 population

Table 5
Suicide rates by race, sex and 5-year age group, United States, 1970-1980 (continued)

Black and Other - Female

Age Group	Year 1970	1971	1972	1973	1974	1975	1976	1977	1978	1979	1980
<15	0.1	0.1	0.1	0.1	0.2	0.1	0.3	0.2	0.2	0.1	<0.1
15–19	2.9	3.5	3.4	2.6	2.8	2.1	2.4	2.3	1.5	2.3	1.8
20–24	5.5	7.1	8.2	5.8	5.0	5.9	5.6	5.6	4.9	5.3	3.6
25–29	6.0	6.7	6.8	6.0	5.7	6.6	6.1	6.9	5.5	5.5	4.4
30–34	5.6	6.6	4.2	4.4	6.8	5.9	6.6	6.3	5.4	5.6	5.5
35–39	4.5	5.7	5.8	6.4	4.0	5.5	4.0	4.4	5.6	4.6	4.3
40–44	4.1	6.2	4.5	4.5	5.1	4.4	5.4	5.7	3.6	4.0	4.9
45–49	4.0	4.1	5.2	2.9	4.1	4.0	5.0	6.0	3.7	4.1	3.7
50–54	5.1	4.1	2.2	3.5	3.9	5.0	3.6	4.3	5.5	3.3	3.9
55–59	1.8	3.4	4.3	5.1	3.4	3.7	3.1	3.9	3.6	4.1	2.9
60–64	2.8	2.6	3.0	3.5	3.2	4.2	2.2	4.5	3.7	4.9	2.5
65–69	3.2	2.9	1.5	2.0	2.1	2.7	3.6	1.6	2.6	4.0	2.0
70–74	3.9	1.5	1.5	3.0	3.0	4.4	4.7	2.3	2.8	2.6	2.2
75–79	3.1	4.5	4.3	3.6	2.0	2.3	1.7	2.9	3.2	4.7	3.0
80–84	3.2	3.8	5.3	3.3	2.4	2.3	2.2	2.8	2.9	5.8	2.1
85+	6.4	2.7	0.0	7.6	1.2	2.2	1.0	2.9	5.5	0.9	1.7
All ages	2.9	3.4	3.2	3.0	3.0	3.2	3.2	3.4	3.0	3.1	2.6

*Rate per 100,000 population

Table 6
Number and percent of suicides by race, sex and method of suicide, United States, 1970 and 1980

Method of Suicide	White				Black and Other				All Races			
	Male		Female		Male		Female		Male		Female	
	No.	%	No.	%	No.	%	No.	%	No.	%	No.	%
1970												
Firearms and Explosives	9,127	58.5	1,944	30.1	577	55.6	124	32.4	9,704	58.4	2,068	30.2
Poisoning by Solids or Liquids	1,439	9.2	2,378	36.8	88	8.5	137	35.8	1,527	9.2	2,515	36.7
Poisoning by Gases	1,742	11.2	765	11.8	30	2.9	5	1.3	1,772	10.7	770	11.2
Hanging, Strangulation, and Suffocation	2,235	14.3	772	11.9	187	18.0	59	15.4	2,422	14.6	831	12.1
All Other Means	1,048	6.7	609	9.4	156	15.0	58	15.1	1,204	7.2	667	9.7
Total	15,591	100.0	6,468	100.0	1,038	100.0	383	100.0	16,629	100.0	6,851	100.0
1980												
Firearms and Explosives*	11,997	63.5	2,295	38.7	948	59.1	164	37.6	12,945	63.1	2,459	38.6
Poisoning by Solids or Liquids	1,249	6.6	1,617	27.3	76	4.7	93	21.3	1,325	6.5	1,710	26.9
Poisoning by Gases	1,642	8.7	733	12.4	30	1.9	13	3.0	1,672	8.2	746	11.7
Hanging, Strangulation, and Suffocation	2,666	14.1	622	10.5	331	20.6	72	16.5	2,997	14.6	694	10.9
All Other Means	1,347	7.1	661	11.2	219	13.7	94	21.6	1,566	7.6	755	11.9
Total	18,901	100.0	5,928	100.0	1,604	100.0	436	100.0	20,505	100.0	6,364	100.0

Sources:
See end of Appendix 2 for a complete listing of sources
Source 1
Source 2 (Table 1-27)
*In 1980, eight suicides were classified under explosives (E955.5) or unspecified (E955.9)

Table 7
Number and rate of suicides for each geographic region and state of residence, United States, 1970 and 1980

Area	1970		1980	
	Number	Rate*	Number	Rate*
United States	23,480	11.6	26,869	11.9
Northeast:	4,280	8.7	4,712	9.6
Connecticut	304	10.0	276	8.9
Maine	127	12.8	141	12.5
Massachusetts	478	8.4	473	8.2
New Hampshire	82	11.1	101	11.0
New Jersey	460	6.4	547	7.4
New York	1,419	7.8	1,675	9.5
Pennsylvania	1,286	10.9	1,318	11.1
Rhode Island	72	7.6	106	11.2
Vermont	52	12.6	75	14.7
North Central:	6,098	10.8	6,464	11.0
Illinois	1,012	9.1	1,067	9.3
Indiana	557	10.7	572	10.4
Iowa	329	11.6	321	11.0
Kansas	253	11.3	258	10.9
Michigan	974	11.0	1,063	11.5
Minnesota	382	10.0	441	10.8
Missouri	524	11.2	585	11.9
Nebraska	168	11.3	158	10.1
North Dakota	74	12.0	72	11.0
Ohio	1,275	12.0	1,288	11.9
South Dakota	60	9.0	88	12.7
Wisconsin	490	11.1	551	11.7

Area	1970		1980	
	Number	Rate	Number	Rate
South:	7,139	11.4	9,310	12.4
Alabama	309	9.0	435	11.2
Arkansas	198	10.3	266	11.6
Washington DC	68	9.0	63	9.9
Delaware	67	12.2	71	11.9
Florida	1,046	15.4	1,501	15.4
Georgia	543	11.8	688	12.6
Kentucky	378	11.7	470	12.8
Louisiana	336	9.2	511	12.1
Maryland	427	10.9	454	10.8
Mississippi	152	6.9	231	9.2
North Carolina	540	10.6	657	11.2
Oklahoma	253	9.9	395	13.1
South Carolina	283	10.9	298	9.5
Tennessee	496	12.6	560	12.2
Texas	1,288	11.5	1,752	12.3
Virginia	561	12.1	715	13.4
West Virginia	194	11.1	243	12.5
West:	5,959	17.1	6,383	14.8
Alaska	37	12.3	68	16.9
Arizona	257	14.5	460	16.9
California	3,707	18.6	3,425	14.5
Colorado	383	17.4	470	16.3
Hawaii	79	10.3	110	11.4
Idaho	112	15.7	124	13.1
Montana	75	10.8	114	14.5
Nevada	113	23.1	183	22.9
New Mexico	166	16.3	227	17.4
Oregon	301	14.4	384	14.6
Utah	153	14.4	193	13.2
Washington	511	15.0	550	13.3
Wyoming	65	19.6	75	16.0

Source:

See end of Appendix 2 for a complete listing of sources

Source 2 (1-14)

Source 1

Source 15

*Rates per 100,000 population

Table 8
Number of suicides by month of occurrence, United States, 1970-1980

Month	1970	1971	1972	1973	1974	1975	1976	1977	1978	1979	1980	Total	%
January	1,867	2,102	2,124	1,988	2,127	2,346	2,171	2,236	2,261	2,185	2,141	23,548	8.
February	1,789	1,852	1,972	1,919	1,840	2,130	2,061	2,315	1,995	1,929	2,055	21,857	7.
March	1,944	2,098	2,130	2,152	2,275	2,382	2,256	2,585	2,354	2,433	2,294	24,903	8.
April	2,094	2,165	2,176	2,097	2,119	2,354	2,267	2,466	2,354	2,311	2,332	24,735	8.
May	2,097	2,102	2,270	2,173	2,132	2,399	2,409	2,513	2,507	2,498	2,314	25,414	8.
June	1,981	2,003	2,136	2,083	2,065	2,239	2,299	2,346	2,264	2,346	2,266	24,028	8.
July	1,887	1,926	2,090	2,196	2,102	2,272	2,325	2,494	2,304	2,277	2,279	24,152	8.
August	2,024	1,999	2,092	2,231	2,172	2,249	2,351	2,499	2,355	2,270	2,318	24,560	8.
September	1,928	2,021	2,042	2,094	2,214	2,263	2,250	2,401	2,173	2,279	2,254	23,919	8.
October	2,032	1,964	2,062	2,174	2,354	2,221	2,179	2,493	2,370	2,258	2,156	24,263	8.
November	1,978	2,016	1,908	2,018	2,075	2,104	2,084	2,212	2,177	2,249	2,209	23,030	8.
December	1,859	1,844	2,002	1,993	2,208	2,104	2,180	2,121	2,180	2,171	2,251	22,913	8
Total	23,480	24,092	25,004	25,118	25,683	27,063	26,832	28,681	27,294	27,206	26,869	287,322	100

Sources:
See end of Appendix 2 for a complete listing of sources
Source 1
Sources 2-10 (Table 1-24)

Figure 1
Age-adjusted death rates for selected causes of death, United States, 1950-1980

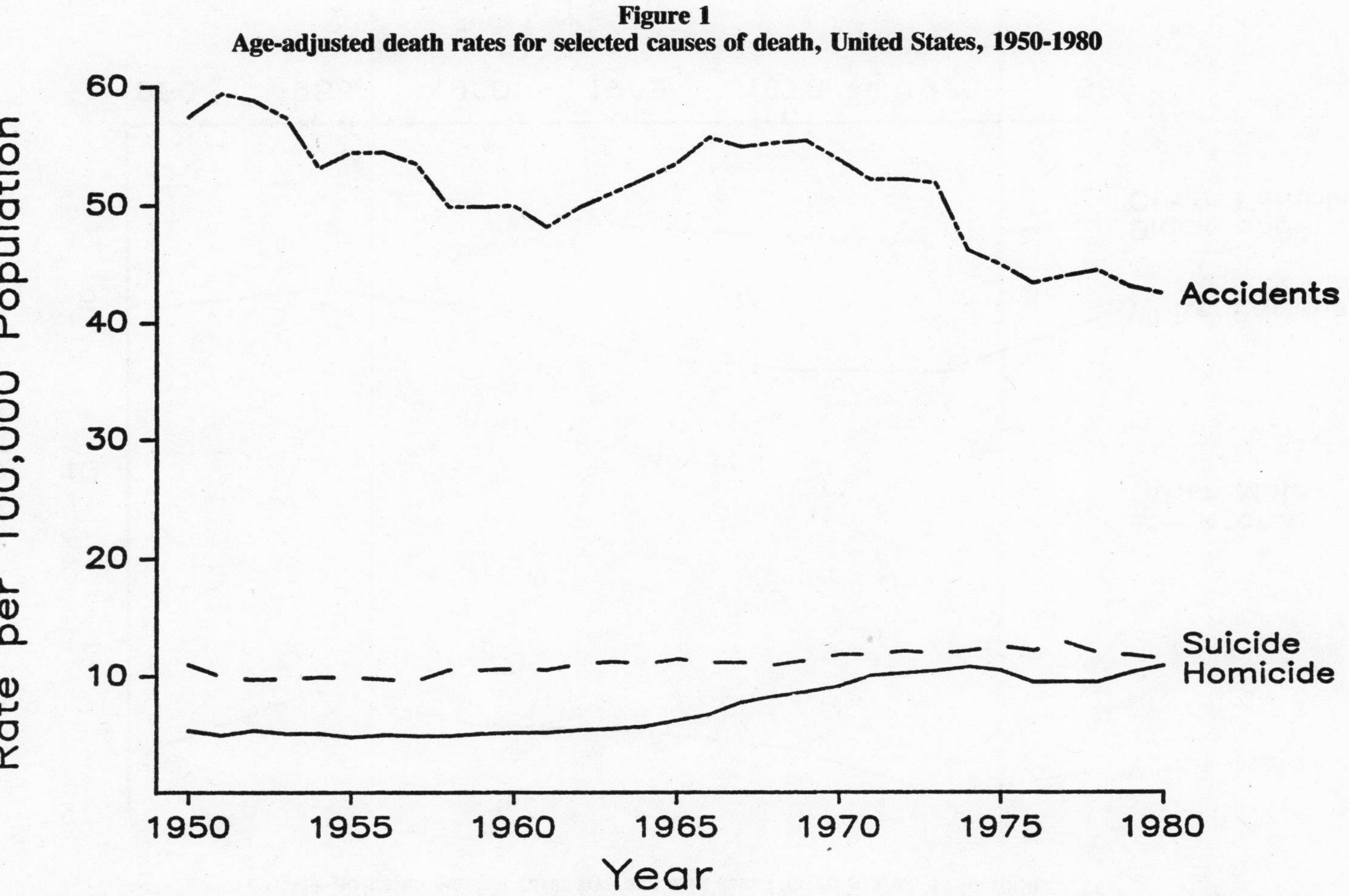

Source: Centers for Disease Control, *Suicide Surveillance, 1970-1980* (Atlanta: Department of Health and Human Services, April 1985).

Figure 2
Age-adjusted suicide rates by race and sex, United States, 1950-1980

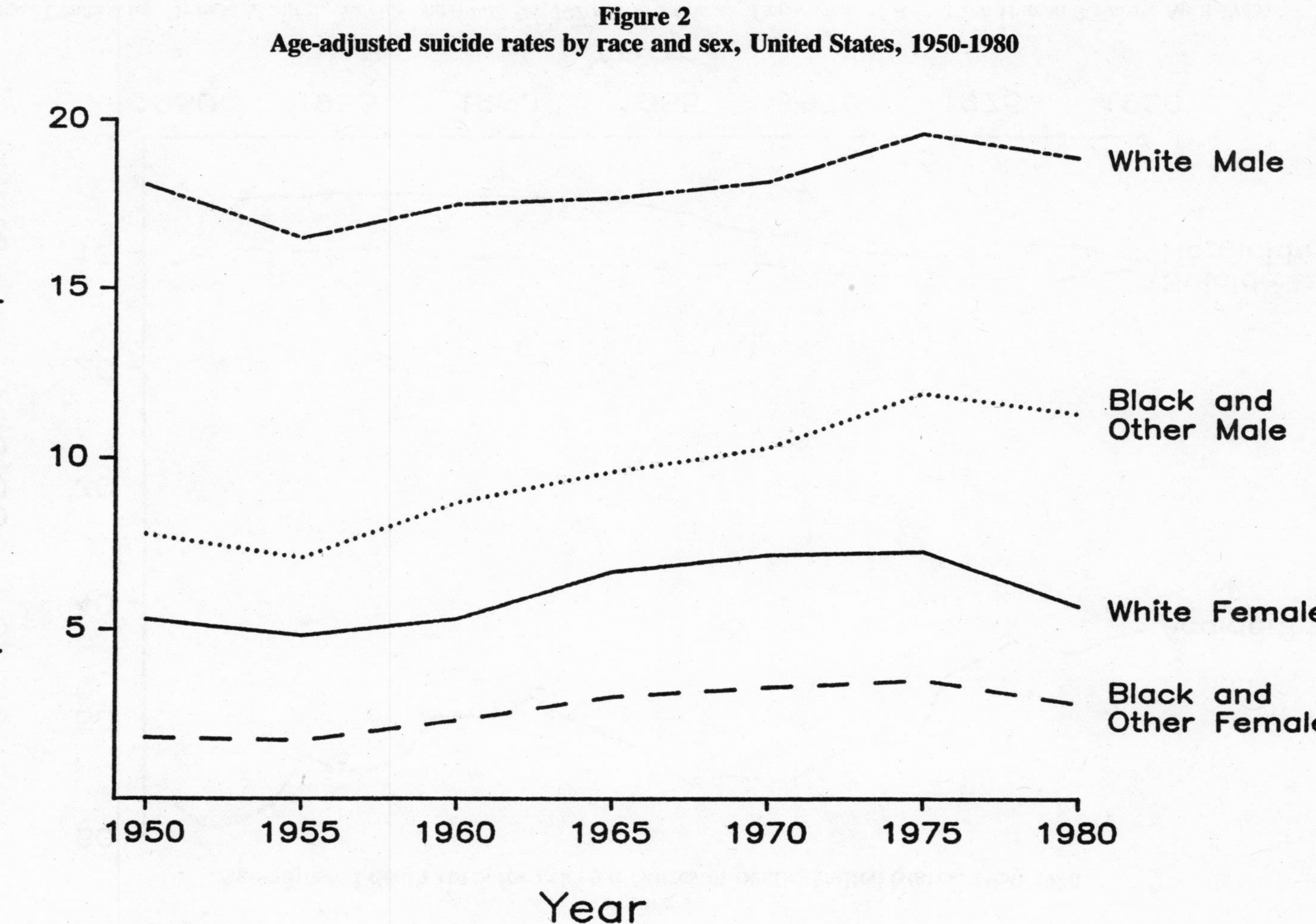

Figure 3
Suicide rates by age group and sex for selected years, United States

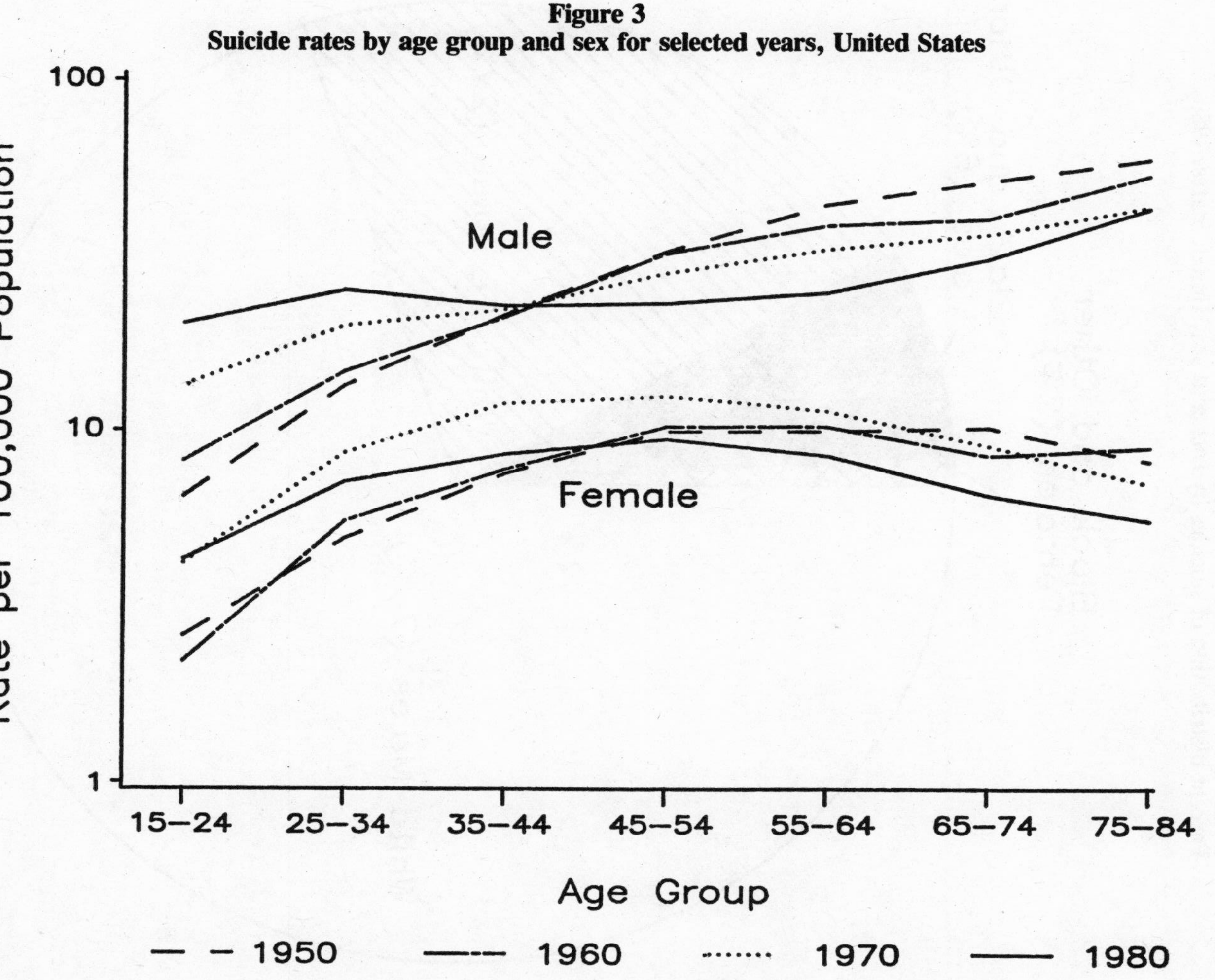

Figure 4
Percent distribution of suicides by race and sex, United States, 1980

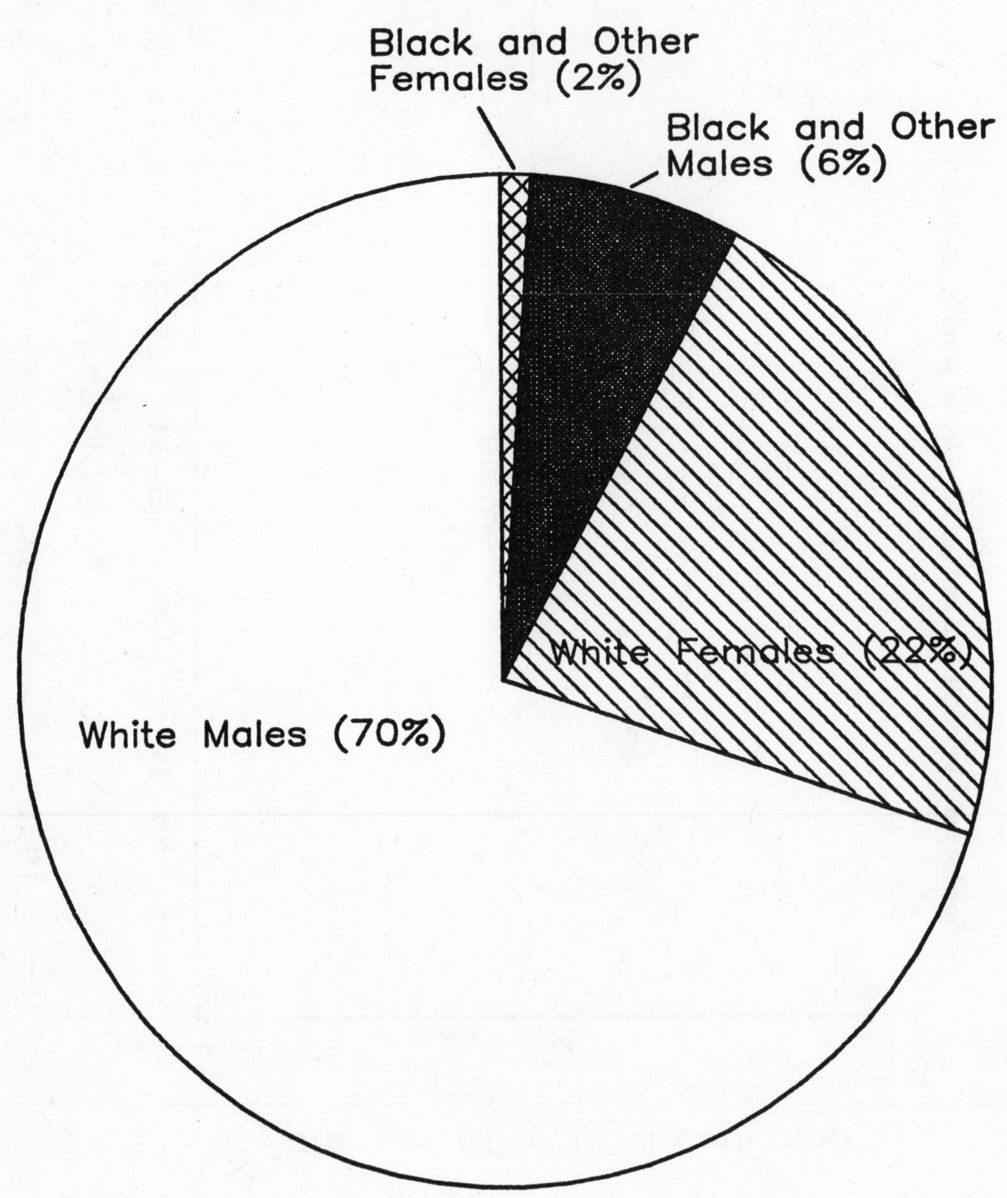

Figure 5
Ratio of the suicide rate for males to the suicide rate for females by race and year, United States, 1970-1980

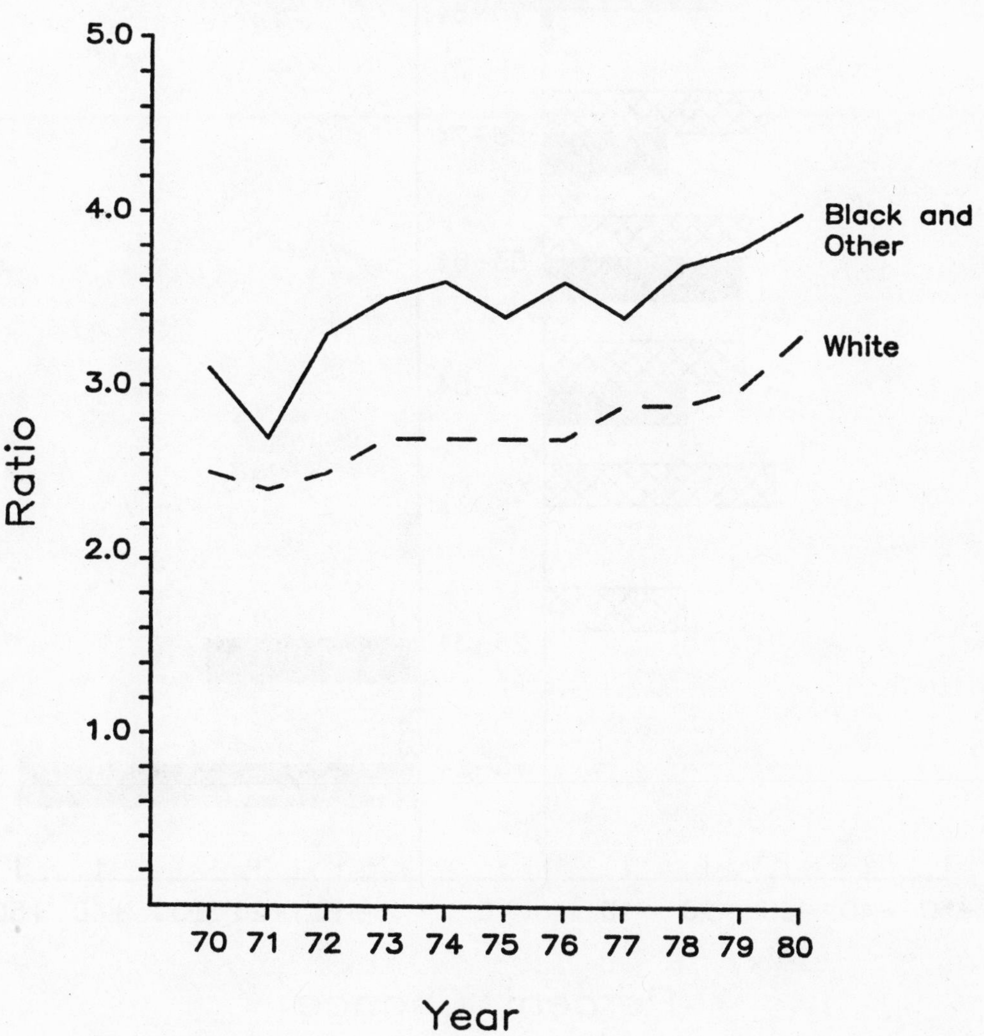

Figure 6
Percent change in suicide rates by age group and sex, United States, 1970 and 1980

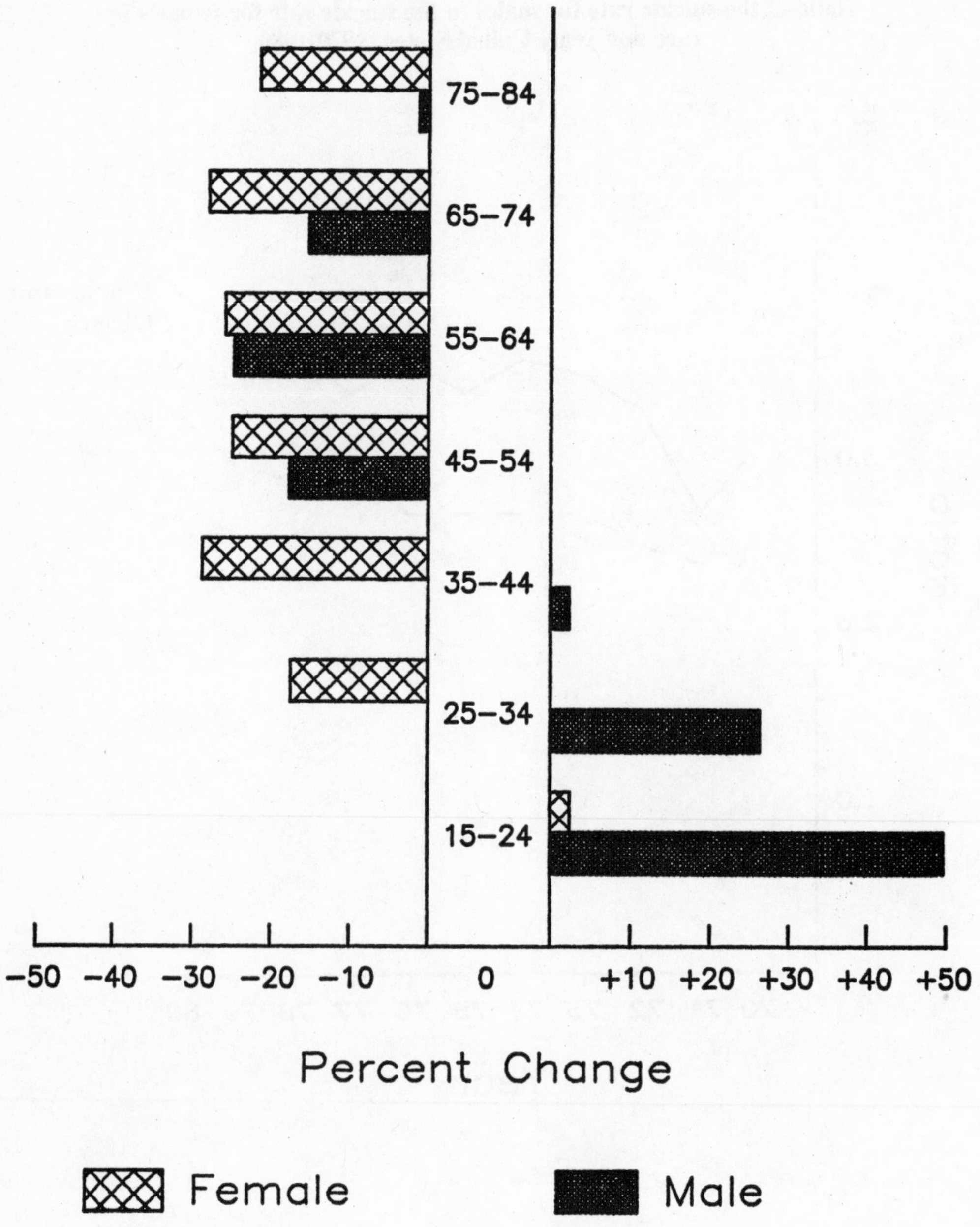

75–84
65–74
55–64
45–54
35–44
25–34
15–24

−50 −40 −30 −20 −10 0 +10 +20 +30 +40 +50

Percent Change

Female  Male

Figure 7
Suicide rates by state, United States, 1980

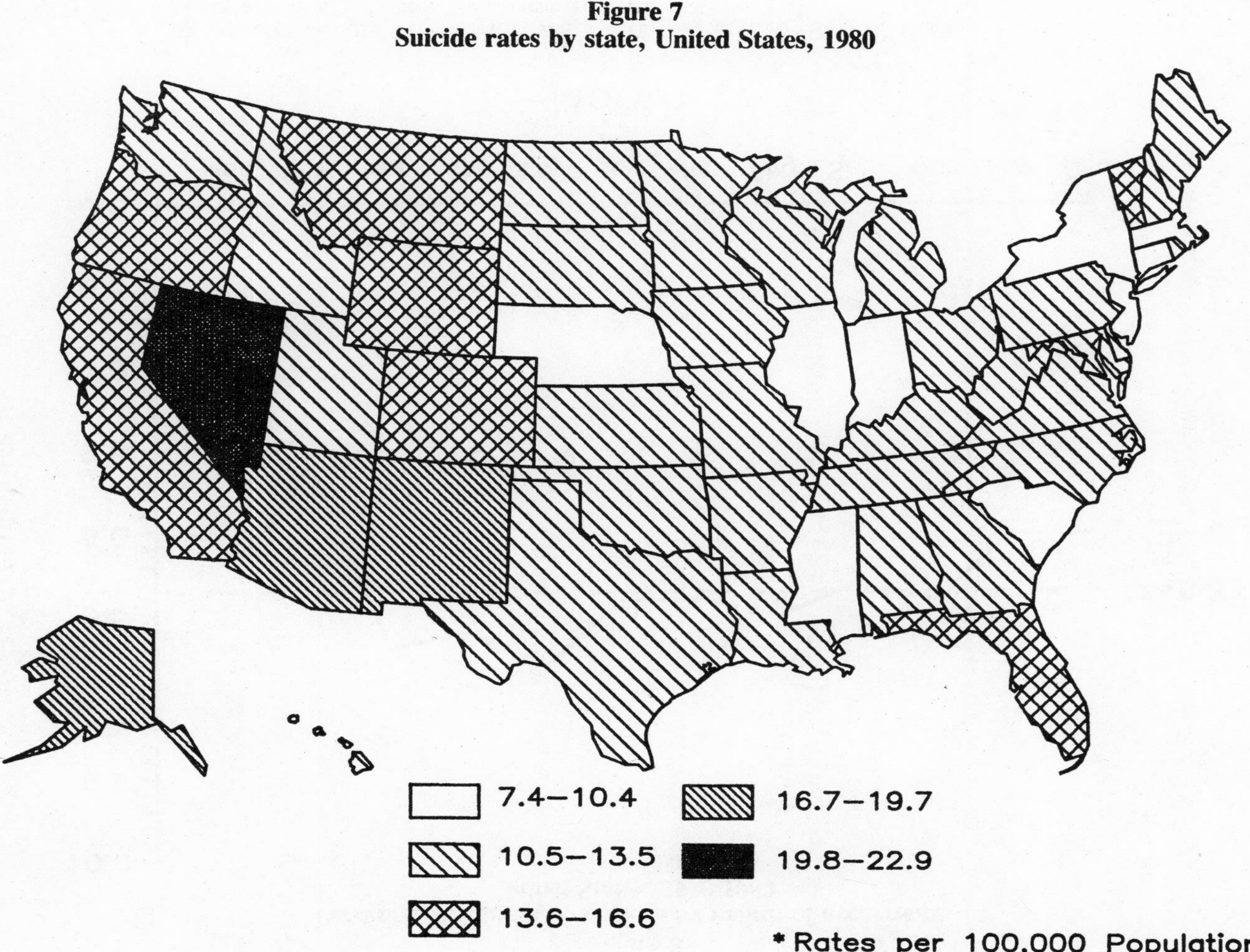

Figure 8
Percent distribution of suicides by month of occurrence, United States, 1970-1980

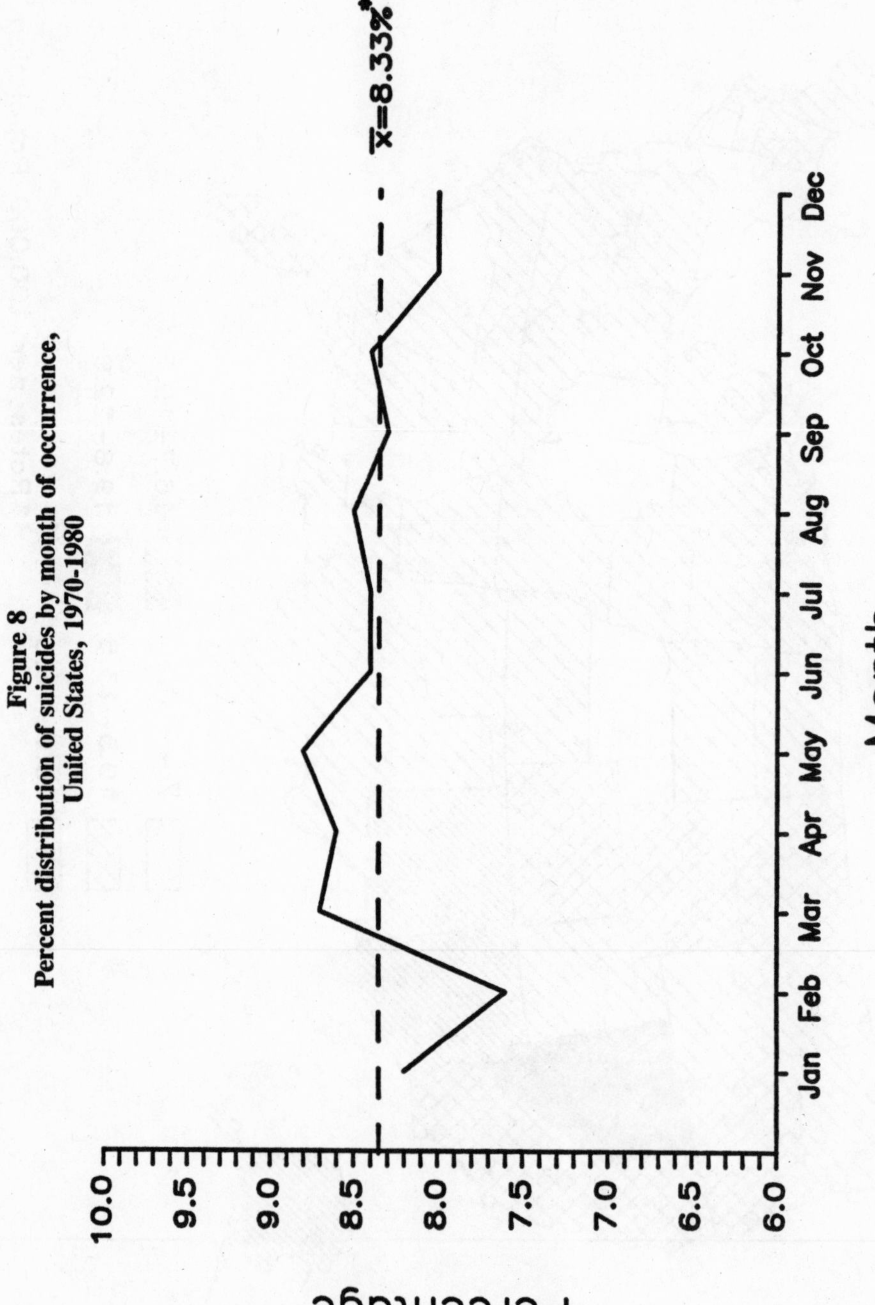

*Percent of suicide deaths which would occur per month if suicide deaths were evenly distributed throughout the year.

Figure 9
Age-adjusted suicide rates by marital status, race and sex, United States, 1979

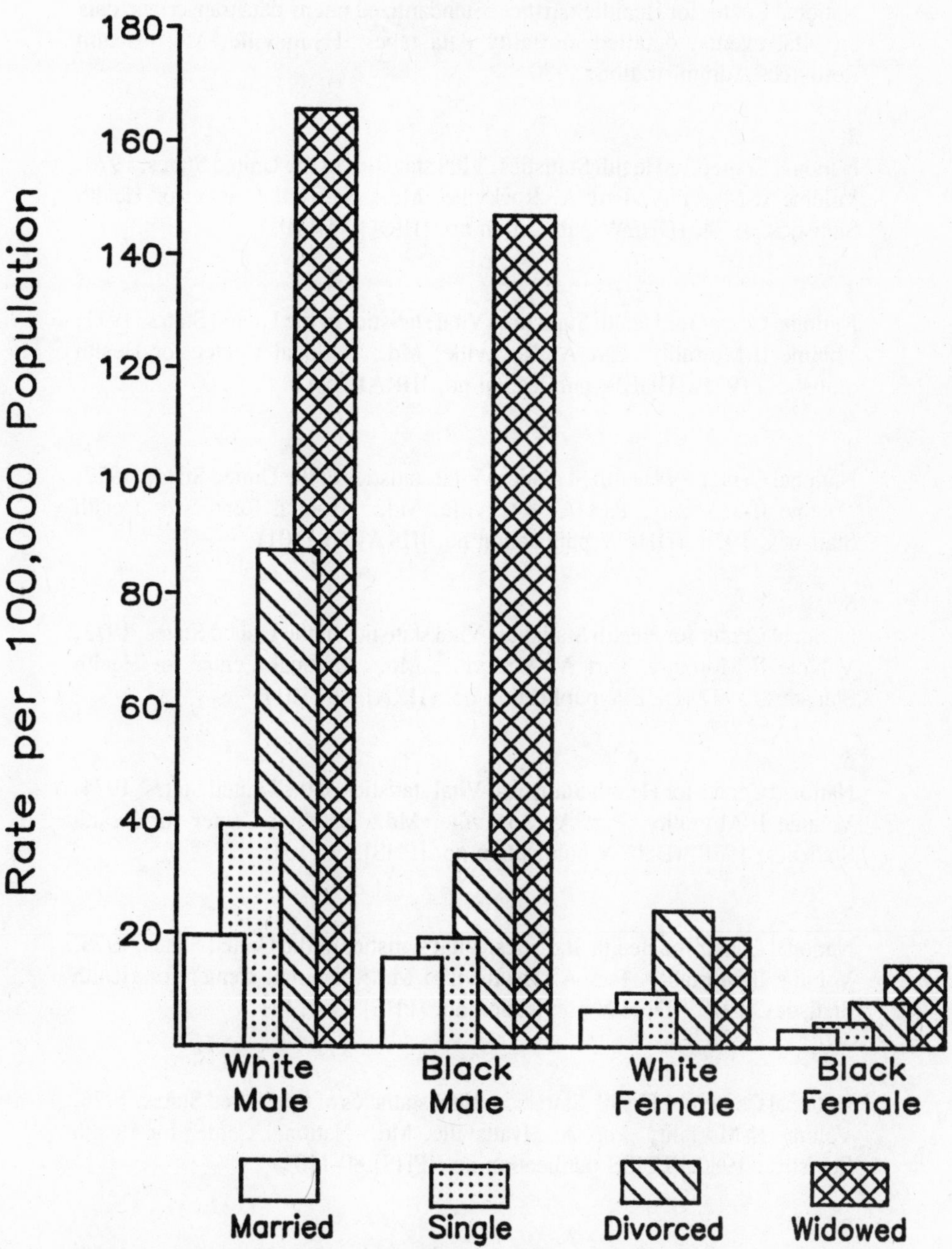

Source: Centers for Disease Control, *Suicide Surveillance, 1970-1980* (Atlanta: Department of Health and Human Services, April 1985).

Sources of Table and Figure Data

1.
National Center for Health Statistics. Standardized micro-data transcripts, data on vital events, detailed mortality data tapes. Hyattsville, Md.: Health Resources Administration, 1980.

2.
National Center for Health Statistics. Vital statistics of the United States, 1970, Volume II-Mortality, Part A. Rockville, Md.: National Center for Health Statistics, 1974. (DHEW publication no. [HRA] 75-1101)

3.
National Center for Health Statistics. Vital statistics of the United States, 1971, Volume II-Mortality, Part A. Rockville, Md.: National Center for Health Statistics, 1975. (DHEW publication no. [HRA] 75-1114)

4.
National Center for Health Statistics. Vital statistics of the United States, 1972, Volume II-Mortality, Part A. Rockville, Md.: National Center for Health Statistics, 1976. (DHEW publication no. [HRA] 76-1101)

5.
National Center for Health Statistics. Vital statistics of the United States, 1973, Volume II-Mortality, Part A. Rockville, Md.: National Center for Health Statistics, 1977 (DHEW publication no. [HRA] 77-1101)

6.
National Center for Health Statistics. Vital statistics of the United States, 1974, Volume II-Mortality, Part A. Rockville, Md.: National Center for Health Statistics, 1978. (DHEW publication no. [PHS] 79-1101)

7.
National Center for Health Statistics. Vital statistics of the United States, 1975, Volume II-Mortality, Part A. Hyattsville, Md.: National Center for Health Statistics, 1979. (DHEW publication no. [PHS] 79-1114)

8.
National Center for Health Statistics. Vital statistics of the United States, 1976, Volume II-Mortality, Part A. Hyattsville, Md.: National Center for Health Statistics, 1980. (DHSS publication no. [PHS] 80-1101)

9.
National Center for Health Statistics. Vital statistics of the United States, 1977, Volume II-Mortality, Part A. Hyattsville, Md.: National Center for Health Statistics, 1981. (DHSS publication no. [PHS] 81-1101)

10.
National Center for Health Statistics. Vital statistics of the United States, 1978, Volume II-Mortality, Part A. Hyattsville, Md.: National Center for Health Statistics, 1982. (DHSS publication no. [PHS] 83-1101)

11.
National Center for Health Statistics. Monthly Vital Statistics Report of Final Mortality Statistics, 1979. Hyattsville, Md.: National Center for Health Statistics, Sept. 1982. (Vol. 31, No. 6, Supplement; DHHS publication no. [PHS] 82-1120)

12.
National Center for Health Statistics. Monthly Vital Statistics Report, Advance Report of Final Mortality Statistics, 1980. Hyattsville, Md.: National Center for Health Statistics, August 1983. (Vol 32, No. 4, Supplement; DHSS publication no. [PHS])

13.
National Center for Health Statistics. Unpublished data: crude and age-adjusted suicide rates, U.S., 1900-1980.

14.
National Center for Health Statistics. Unpublished data: death rates for suicide (E950-959) by 5-year age groups, color and sex, U.S., 1968-1980.

15.
U.S. Bureau of the Census, General Population Characteristics, U.S. Summary, PC80-1, B1.

APPENDIX 3

SOURCES OF INFORMATION

This section lists selected major sources of information on suicide, including some organizations which provide assistance with, and information on, prevention, intervention and postvention. Additional information on such suicide programs is usually available from regional and local agencies—both private and governmental. However, it was not possible to provide information sources for every foreign country, since many nations do not choose to provide such data.

CONTENTS

UNITED STATES
NATIONAL ASSOCIATIONS, INSTITUTES, ORGANIZATIONS AND GOVERNMENT AGENCIES

A.A. World Services, Inc.
470 Park Avenue South
New York, NY 10016

Adam Walsh Child Resource Center
4200 Wisconsin Avenue
Washington, DC 20016
Tel: (202) 686-1791

Administration for Children, Youth & Families
400 Sixth Street, S.W.
Washington, DC 20201
Tel: (202) 755-7762

Al-Anon Family Group Headquarters
P.O. Box 182
Madison Square Station
New York, NY 10010

Alcohol and Drug Problems Association of North America
1101 Fifteenth Street, N.W., #204
Washington, DC 20005

Alcoholics Anonymous
General Service Office
470 Park Avenue South
New York, NY 10016
(212) 686-1100

Alcohol, Drug Abuse and Mental Health Administration
Department of Health and Human Services
5600 Fishers Lane, Room 6615
Rockville, MD 10857

American Academy of Child Psychiatry
3615 Wisconsin Avenue, N.W.
Washington, DC 20016
Tel: (202) 966-7300

American Academy of Clinical Psychiatrists
P.O. Box 3212
San Diego, CA 92103
Tel: (619) 460-2675

American Academy of Family Physicians
1740 West 92nd Street
Kansas City, MO 64114
Tel: (800) 821-2512

American Academy of Physicians Assistants
2341 Jefferson Davis Highway, Suite 700
Arlington, VA 22202
Tel: (703) 920-5730

American Association Against Addiction
1668 Bush Street
San Francisco, CA 94109

American Association for Advancement of Health Education
1900 Association Drive
Reston, VA 22091
Tel: (703) 476-3440

American Association for Counseling and Development
5999 Stevenson Avenue
Alexandria, VA 22304

American Association of Suicidology
2459 South Ash Street
Denver, CO 80222
Tel: (303) 692-0985

American Bar Association
1155 East 60th Street
Chicago, IL 60637

American Board of Family Practice
2228 Young Drive
Lexington, KY 40505
Tel: (606) 269-5626

American Council on Alcohol Problems
119 Constitution Avenue, N.E.
Washington, DC 20002

American Council of Life Insurance
1270 Avenue of the Americas
New York, NY 10020

American Council on Marijuana and Other Psychoactive Drugs
6193 Executive Boulevard
Rockville, MD 20852

American Dental Association
211 East Chicago Avenue
Chicago, IL 60611

American Institute of Family Relations
5287 Sunset Boulevard
Los Angeles, CA 90027

American Medical Association Department of Mental Health
535 North Dearborn Street
Chicago, IL 60610
Tel: (312) 645-5076

American Association for Marriage and Family Therapy
924 West Ninth Street
Upland, CA 91786
Tel: (714) 981-0888

American Medical Student Association
1910 Association Drive
Reston, VA 22091
Tel: (703) 620-6600

American Psychiatric Association
1700 18th Street, N.W.
Washington, DC 20009
Tel: (202) 797-4900

American Psychological Association
1200 17th Street, N.W.
Washington, DC 20036

American Association of Psychiatric Services for Children (AAPSC)
1133 Fifteenth Street, N.W., Suite 1000
Washington, DC 20005
Tel: (202) 429-9440

American Sociological Association
1722 North Street, N.W.
Washington, DC 20036

Association of Halfway House Alcoholism Programs of North America
786 East 7th Street
St. Paul, MN 55106

BASH Treatment and Research Center for Eating and Mood Disorders
6125 Clayton Avenue, Suite 215
St. Louis, MO 63139
Tel: (314) 567-4080

Center of Alcohol Studies
Rutgers, The State University of New Jersey
New Brunswick, NJ 08903

Centers for Disease Control
Department of Health and Human Services
Violence Epidemiology Branch
1600 Clifton Road, N.E.
Atlanta, GA 30333

Center for Multicultural Awareness
2924 Columbia Pike
Arlington, VA 22204

Center for the Study of Drug Policy
530 Eighth Street, S.E.
Washington, DC 20003

Center for the Study of Responsive Law
P.O. Box 19367
Washington, DC 20036

Center for Suicide Research and Prevention
Rush-Presbyterian-St. Luke's Medical Center
1753 West Congress Parkway
Chicago, IL 60612
Tel: (312) 942-7208

Commission for the Advancement of Public Interest Organizations
1875 Connecticut Avenue, N.W.
Washington, DC 20009

Committee on Problems of Drug Dependence
4105 Dunnel Lane
Kensington, MD 20795

Drug Enforcement Administration
1405 I Street, N.W.
Washington, DC 20537

Families in Action
3845 N. Druid Hills Road
Decatur, GA 30333
Tel: (404) 325-5799

Families Anonymous
P.O. Box 344
Torrance, CA 90501
Tel: (213) 775-3211

Family Life Publications
Box 427
Saluda, NC 28773

Family Service Association of America
44 East 23rd Street
New York, NY 10010
Tel: (212) 674-6100

Food and Drug Administration (FDA)
Consumer Inquiries HFG-10
5600 Fishers Lane
Rockville, MD 20857

Hazelden Foundation, Inc.
Box 11
Center City, MN 55012

House Select Committee on Narcotics Abuse and Control
3287 House Office Building - Annex 2
Second and D Streets, N.W.
Washington, DC 20515

Institute for Studies of Destructive Behavior/Suicide Prevention Center
1041 South Menlo Avenue
Los Angeles, CA 90006
Tel: (213) 386-5111

Indian Health Service
5600 Fishers Lane, Room 5A-55
Rockville, MD 20857
Tel: (301) 443-1083

Mental Health Material Center
20 East 29th Street
New York, NY 10016

Narcotics Anonymous
Box 622
Sun Valley, CA 93352

Narcotics Educational Foundation of America
5055 Sunset Boulevard
Los Angeles, CA 90027
Tel: (213) 663-5171

Narcotics Education
6830 Laurel Avenue, N.W.
Washington, DC 20012
Tel: (202) 723-4774

National Academy of Sciences
2101 Constitution Avenue, N.W.
Room JH-751
Washington, DC 20418

National Anti-Drug Coalition
304 West 58th Street, 5th Floor
New York, NY 10019
Tel: (212) 247-8820

National Association for City Drug and Alcohol Coordination
House Offices Building, Suite 711
818 Harrison Avenue
Boston, MA 02118
Tel: (617) 424-4757

National Association on Drug Abuse Problems
355 Lexington Avenue
New York, NY 10017
Tel: (212) 986-1170

National Association of County Health Officials
440 First Street, N.W., Fourth Floor
Washington, DC 20001
Tel: (202) 783-5550

National Association of Social Workers
7981 Eastern Avenue
Silver Spring, MD 20910
Tel: (301) 565-0333

National Association of State Alcohol and Drug Abuse Directors
918 F Street, N.W., Suite 400
Washington, DC 20004

National Center for Health Statistics
3700 East-West Highway, Room 1-57
Hyattsville, MD 20782
Tel: (301) 436-8500

National Center for Juvenile Justice
701 Forbes Avenue
Pittsburgh, PA 15219
Tel: (412) 227-6950

National Center for Voluntary Action
1785 Massachusetts Avenue, N.W.
Washington, DC 20036

National Child Safety Council
P.O. Box 1368
Jackson, MI 49204
Tel: (517) 764-6070

National Clearinghouse for Alcohol Information
P.O. Box 2345
Rockville, MD 20852

National Clearinghouse for Drug Abuse Information
Department of Health and Human Services
5600 Fishers Lane, Room 10A53
Rockville, MD 20857
Tel: (301) 443-6500

National Committee for the Prevention of Alcoholism and Drug Dependency
6830 Laurel Street, N.W.
Washington, DC 20012

National Committee for Prevention of Child Abuse
111 East Wacker, Suite 510
Chicago, IL 60601
Tel: (312) 565-1100

National Committee on Youth Suicide Prevention
67 Irving Place South
New York, NY 10003

National Council on Alcoholism
12 West 23rd Street
New York, NY 10010
(212) 737-6770

National Council on Alcoholism, Inc.
1511 K Street, N.W.
Washington, DC 20005
(202) 737-8122

Natonal Education Association
1201 16th Street, N.W.
Washington, DC 20036
Tel: (202) 822-7253

National Federation of Parents for Drug-Free Youth
8730 Georgia Avenue, Suite 200
Silver Spring, MD 20910

National Indian Social Workers Association
410 N.W. 18th Street, No. 101
Portland, OR 97209
Tel: (503) 221-2026

National Institute of Alcohol Abuse and Alcoholism (NIAAA)
P.O. Box 2345
Rockville, MD 20852

National Institute on Drug Abuse (NIDA)
5600 Fishers Lane
Rockville, MD 20857

National Institute of Mental Health (NIMH)
5600 Fishers Lane, Room 17-99
Rockville, MD 20857
Tel: (301) 443-3673

National Save-A-Life League
815 Second Avenue, Suite 409
New York, NY 10017
Tel: (212) 736-6191

National Self-Help Clearinghouse
Graduate School and University Center
City University of New York (CUNY)

33 West 42nd Street, Room 1227
New York, NY 10036
Tel: (212) 840-1259

National PTA
700 North Rush Street
Chicago, IL 60611
Tel: (312) 787-0977

New York City Affiliate, Inc.
National Council on Alcoholism
133 East 62nd Street
New York, NY 10021

Odyssey Institute
656 Avenue of the Americas
New York, NY 10010
Tel: (212) 691-8510

Phoenix House Foundation
164 West 74th Street
New York, NY 10023
Tel: (212) 595-5810

Pil-Anon Family Program
P.O. Box 120
Gracie Square Station
New York, NY 10028
Tel: (212) 744-2020

Pills Anonymous
P.O. Box 473
Ansonia Station
New York, NY 10023

Potsmokers Anonymous
316 East 3rd Street
New York, NY 10009
Tel: (212) 254-1777

Project Hope Center for Health Affairs
Millwood, VA 22646
Tel: (703) 837-2100

Public Affairs Pamphlets
381 Park Avenue South
New York, NY 10016

Public Citizen, Inc.
Health Research Group
2000 P Street, N.W.
Washington, DC 20036

Runaway Suicide Prevention Network
Human Services Development Institute
University of Southern Maine
246 Deering Avenue
Portland, ME 04102
Tel: (207) 780-4430

The Samaritans
500 Commonwealth Avenue
Kenmore Square
Boston, MA 02215
Tel: (617) 536-2460

Suicide Education Institution of Boston
437 Newtonville Avenue
Newton, MA 02160

Teenage Suicide Center
Western Psychiatric Institute and Clinic, University of Pittsburgh
3811 O'Hara Street
Pittsburgh, PA 15213
Tel: (412) 624-0719

U.S. Department of Health and Human Services (Office of the Secretary)
Hubert Humphrey Building, Room 615-F
200 Independence Avenue, S.W.
Washington, DC 20201
Tel: (202) 245-7000

U.S. Department of Health and Human Services (Office of Education)
400 Maryland Avenue, S.W.
Washington, DC 20202

U.S. Public Health Service
5600 Fishers Lane, Room 17-05
Rockville, MD 20857
Tel: (301) 443-6660

Valium Anonymous
P.O. Box 404
Altoona, PA 50009
Tel: (515) 967-6781

Women for Sobriety
P.O. Box 618
Quakertown, PA 18951
Tel: (215) 536-8026

Youth Suicide National Center
1825 Eye Street, N.W.
Washington, D.C. 20006
Tel: (202) 429-2016

SUICIDE PREVENTION AND CRISIS INTERVENTION AGENCIES IN THE UNITED STATES

* Member, American Association of Suicidology
#AAS Certified

ALABAMA

Andalusia
* South Central Mental Health Board Helpline
P.O. Box 1028
Andalusia, AL 36420
Crisis Phone 1: (205) 222-7794
Business Phone: (205) 222-2523

Auburn
* Crisis Center of E. Alabama, Inc.
P.O Box 1949
Auburn, AL 36830
Crisis Phone 1: (205) 821-8600
Business Phone: (205) 821-8600
Hrs Avail: 24

Birmingham
*# Crisis Center of Jefferson County
3600 8th Ave. S.
Birmingham, AL 35222
Crisis Center: (205) 323-7777
Business Phone: (205) 323-7782
Hrs Avail: 24

Decatur
Crisis Call Center
North Central Alabama MH Center
P.O. Box 637
Decatur, AL 35601
Crisis Phone 1: (205) 355-6091
Business Phone: (205) 355-6091

Florence
Riverbend Center for Mental Health
P.O. Box 941
Florence, AL 35630
Crisis Phone 1: (205) 764-3431
Business Phone: (205) 764-3431

Foley
Contact South Baldwin Co.
P.O. Box 481
Foley, AL 36535
Crisis Phone 1: (205) 943-5675
Business Phone: (205) 943-5675

Huntsville
Huntsville, Helpline
P.O. Box 92
Huntsville, AL 35804
Crisis Phone 1: (205) 539-3424
Business Phone: (205) 534-1779
Hrs Avail: 24

Mobile
* Contact Mobile
3224 Executive Park Circle
Mobile, AL 36606
Crisis Phone 1: (205) 342-3333
Business Phone: (205) 473-5330
Hrs Avail: 24

Mobile
Mobile Mental Health Center
Crisis Intervention Services
2400 Gordon Smith Drive

Mobile, AL 36617
Crisis Phone 1: (205) 473-4423
Business Phone: (205) 473-4423
Hrs Avail: 24

Montgomery
Help A Crisis
101 Collisium Boulevard
Montgomery, AL 36109
Crisis Phone 1: (205) 279-7837
Business Phone: (205) 279-7830
Hrs Avail: 24

Tuscaloosa
Indian Rivers Mental Health Center
Tuscaloosa Crisis Line
P.O. Box 2190
Tuscaloosa, AL 35403
Crisis Phone 1: (205) 345-1600
Business Phone: (205) 345-1600
Hrs Avail: 24

ALASKA

Anchorage
* Anchorage Comm. Mental Health Services, Inc.
4020 Folker
Anchorage, AK 99508
Crisis Phone 1: (907) 563-1000
Business Phone: (907) 563-1000
Hrs Avail: 24

Anchorage
*# Suicide Prevention and Crisis Center
2611 Fairbanks St.
Anchorage, AK 99503
Crisis Phone 1: (907) 276-1600
Business Phone: (907) 272-2496
Hrs Avail: 24

Fairbanks
* Fairbanks Crisis Clinic Foundation
P.O. Box 832
Fairbanks, AK 99707
Crisis Phone: 1: (907) 452-4403
Business Phone: (907) 479-0166
Hrs Avail: 24

Juneau
Juneau Mental Health Clinic
210 Admiral Way
Juneau, AK 99801
Crisis Phone 1: (907) 586-5280
Crisis Phone 2: (907) 789-4889
Business Phone: (907) 586-5280
Hrs Avail: 08:00AM-04:30PM

Kenai
Central Peninsula MH Center
11355 Kenai Spur Rd., Ste. 228
Kenai, AK 99611
Crisis Phone 1: (907) 283-7501
Business Phone: (907) 283-7501
Hrs Avail: 24

Ketchikan
Gateway Mental Health
3134 Tongass
Ketchikan, AK 99901
Crisis Phone 1: (907) 225-4135
Business Phone: (907) 225-4135
Hrs Avail: 24

Wasilla
Mat-su Crisis Line
P.O. Box 873388
Wasilla, AK 99687
Crisis Phone 1: (907) 376-3706
Business Phone: (907)376-3356
Hrs Avail: 24

ARIZONA

Clifton
Graham-Greenlee Comm. Service Center
169 Frisco Ave.
P.O. Box 987
Clifton, AZ 85533
Crisis Phone 1: (602) 865-4531
Business Phone: (602) 865-4531
Hrs Avail: 24

Phoenix
Phoenix Crisis Intervention Program
1250 S. 7th Ave.

Phoenix, AZ 85007
Crisis Phone 1: (602) 258-8011
Business Phone: (602) 258-8011
Hrs Avail: 24

Phoenix
Psychiatric Crisis Center
Maricopa County Hospital
2601 E. Roosevelt
Phoenix, AZ 85008
Crisis Phone 1: (602) 267-5881
Business Phone: (602) 267-5881
Hrs Avail: 24

Safford
Safford Crisis Line
P.O. Box 956
Safford, AZ 85546
Crisis Phone 1: (602) 428-4550
Business Phone: (602) 428-4550
Hrs Avail: 24

Tucson
Tucson Help On Call
Information and Referral Service
2555 E. First St., Suite 107
Tucson, AZ 85716
Crisis Phone 1: (602) 323-9373
Business Phone: (602) 323-1303
Hrs Avail: 24

ARKANSAS

Hot Springs
Contact Hot Springs
705 Malvern Ave.
Hot Springs, AR 71901
Crisis Phone 1: (501) 623-2515
Business Phone: (501) 623-4048
Hrs Avail: 24

Little Rock
Contact Little Rock
P.O. Box 2572
Little Rock, AR 72203
Crisis Phone 1: (501) 666-0234
Business Phone: (501) 666-0235
Hrs Avail: 24

Little Rock
Crisis Center of Arkansas, Inc.
1616 W. 14th St.
Little Rock, AR 72202
Crisis Phone 1: (501) 375-5151
Business Phone: (501) 664-8834
Hrs Avail: 12:00PM-12:00AM

Pine Bluff
Contact Pine Bluff
P.O. Box 8734
Pine Bluff, AR 71601
Crisis Phone 1: (501) 536-4226
Business Phone: (501) 536-4228
Hrs Avail: 24

CALIFORNIA

Anaheim
* Hotline Help Center
P.O. Box 999
Anaheim, CA 92805
Crisis Phone 1: (714) 778-1000
Business Phone: (714) 778-1000
Hrs Avail: 24

Arcata
Arcata Contact Center
Warren House #53 HSU
Arcata, CA 95521
Crisis Phone 1: (707) 826-4400
Business Phone: (707) 826-4373
Hrs Avail: 24

Berkeley
* Suicide Prev/Crisis Interv. of Alameda County
P.O. Box 9102
Berkeley, CA 94709
Crisis Phone 1: (415) 849-2212
Crisis Phone 2: (415) 889-1333
Crisis Phone 3: (415) 794-5211
Crisis Phone 4: (415) 449-5566
Business Phone: (415) 848-1515
Hrs Avail: 24

Davis
* Suicide Prevention of Yolo County
P.O. Box 622
Davis, CA 95617
Crisis Phone 1: (916) 756-5000
Crisis Phone 2: (916) 666-7778
Crisis Phone 3: (916) 372-6565
Business Phone: (916) 756-7542
Hrs Avail: 24

El Cajon
Crisis House/Crisis Interv. Center
144 S. Orange
El Cajon, CA 92020
Crisis Phone 1: (714) 444-1194
Business Phone: (714) 444-6506
Hrs Avail: 24

Fort Bragg
Crisis Line Care Project
461 N. Franklin St.
P.O. Box 764
Fort Bragg, CA 95437
Crisis Phone 1: (707) 964-4357
Business Phone: (707) 964-4055
Hrs Avail: 24

Fresno
Contact Fresno
7172 N. Cedar
Fresno, CA 93710
Crisis Phone 1: (209) 298-2022
Business Phone: (209) 298-8001
Hrs Avail: 24

Fresno
* Help In Emotional Trouble
P.O. Box 4282
Fresno, CA 93744
Crisis Phone 1: (209) 485-1432
Business Phone: (209) 486-4703
Hrs Avail: 24

Garden Grove
New Hope Counseling Center
12141 Lewis St.
Garden Grove, CA 92640
Crisis Phone 1: (714) 639-4673
Business Phone: (714) 971-4123
Hrs Avail: 24

Hemet
Valley Hotline
602 E. Florida
Hemet, CA 92343
Crisis Phone 1: (714) 676-5800
Business Phone: (714) 658-7227
Hrs Avail: 24

Lafayette
Contact Care Center
P.O. Box 901
Lafayette, CA 94549
Crisis Phone 1: (415) 284-2273
Business Phone: (415) 284-2273
Hrs Avail: 24

Lake Arrowhead
The Help Line
P.O. Box 1263
Lake Arrowhead, CA 92352
Crisis Phone 1: (714) 337-4300
Business Phone: (714) 337-4300
Hrs Avail: 24

Lakeport
Lake Co. Mental Health Emerg. Serv.
922 Bevins Court
Lakeport, CA 95453
Crisis Phone 1: (707) 263-0160
Business Phone: (707) 263-2258
Hrs Avail: 24

Los Alamitos
West Orange County Hotline
P.O. Box 32
Los Alamitos, CA 90720
Crisis Phone 1: (213) 596-5548
Business Phone: (213) 594-0969
Hrs Avail: 24

Los Angeles
*# Los Angeles SPC
1041 S. Menlo
Los Angeles, CA 90006
Crisis Phone 1: (213) 381-5111
Business Phone: (213) 386-5111
Hrs Avail: 24

Napa
* North Bay Suicide Prevention, Inc.
P.O. Box 2444
Napa, CA 94558
Fairfield: (707) 422-2555
Napa: (707) 255-2555
Vallejo: (707) 643-2555
Business Phone: (707) 257-3470
Hrs Avail: 24

Newark
Second Chance, Inc.
P.O. Box 643
Newark, CA 94560
Crisis Phone 1: (415) 792-4357
Business Phone: (415) 792-4357
Hrs Avail: 24

Pacific Grove
* Suicide Preven. Cent./Monterey Co.
P.O. Box 52078
Pacific Grove, CA 93950-7078
Crisis Phone 1: (408) 649-8008
Salinas: (408) 424-1485
Business Phone: (408) 375-6966
Hrs Avail: 24

Pasadena
Contact Pasadena
73 N. Hill Ave.
Pasadena, CA 91106
Crisis Phone 1: (818) 449-4500
Business Phone: (818) 449-4502
Hrs Avail: 24

Pasadena
Pasadena Mental Health Center
1495 N. Lake
Pasadena, CA 91104
Crisis Phone 1: (213) 798-0907
Business Phone: (213) 681-1381
Hrs Avail: 9A.M-12A.M.

Pleasanton
* The Center
Counseling, Education, Crisis Service
4361 Railroad Ave., Suite B
Pleasanton, CA 94566
Crisis Phone 1: (415) 828-help
Business Phone: (415) 462-544
Hrs Avail: 24

Redding
* Help, Inc.
P.O. Box 2498
Redding, CA 96099
Crisis Phone 1: (916) 246-2711
Business Phone: (916) 225-5255
Hrs Avail: 9A.M-12A.M.

Riverside
Riverside Crisis & Outpatient Serv.
9707 Magnolia St.
Riverside, CA 92503
Crisis Phone 1: (714) 351-7853
Business Phone: (714) 351-7861
Hrs Avail: M-Th 8 A.M.-9 P.M.; F 8 A.M.-5 P.M.

Sacramento
* Suicide Prev. Serv. of Sacramento
P.O. Box 449
Sacramento, CA 95802
Crisis Phone 1: (916) 441-1135
Business Phone: (916) 441-1138
Hrs Avail: 24

San Anselmo
Marin Suicide Prevention Center
P.O. Box 792
San Anselmo, CA 94960
Crisis Phone 1: (415) 454-4524
Business Phone: (415) 454-4566
Hrs Avail: 24

San Bernardino
* Suicide & Crisis Interv. Service
1669 N. "E" St.
San Bernardino, CA 92405
Crisis Phone 1: (714) 886-4889
Business Phone: (714) 886-6730
Hrs Avail: 24

San Diego
*# The Crisis Team
P.O. Box 85524
San Diego, CA 92138

Crisis Phone 1: (619) 236-3339
Crisis Phone 2: (800) 351-0757
Business Phone: (619) 236-4576
Hrs Avail: 24

San Diego
San Diego Help Center
5059 College Ave.
San Diego, CA 92115
Crisis Phone 1: (714)582-4357
Business Phone: (714) 582-1288
Hrs Avail: 2 P.M.-10 P.M.

San Diego
* Suicide Hotline
Harbor View Med. Cent.
120 Elm St.
San Diego, CA 92101
Crisis Phone 1: (619) 232-7070
TTY: (619) 232-7078
Business Phone: (619) 232-4331, x624
Hrs Avail: 24

San Francisco
* San Francisco Suicide Prevention
3940 Geary Blvd.
San Francisco, CA 94118
Crisis Phone 1: (415) 221-1423
Crisis Phone 2: (415) 221-1424
Crisis Phone 3: (415) 221-1428
Business Phone: (415) 752-4866
Hrs Avail: 24

San Jose
Contact Santa Clara Co.
P.O. Box 24978
San Jose, CA 95154
Crisis Phone 1: (408) 266-8228
Business Phone: (408) 266-1020
Hrs Avail: 24

San Jose
* Santa Clara Suicide & Crisis Service
2220 Moorpark
San Jose, CA 95128
Crisis Phone 1: (408) 279-3312
Business Phone: (408) 279-6250
Hrs Avail: 24

San Luis Obispo
San Luis Obispo County Hotline, Inc.
P.O. Box 654
San Luis Obispo, CA 93406
Crisis Phone 1: (805) 544-6162
Business Phone: (805) 544-6164
Hrs Avail: 24

San Mateo County
*# Suicide Prev./CC of San Mateo County
1811 Trousdale Dr.
Burlingame, CA 94010
Crisis Phone 1: (415) 877-5600
Crisis Phone 2: (415) 367-8000
Crisis Phone 3: (415) 726-5228
Business Phone: (415) 877-5604
Hrs Avail: 24

Santa Barbara
* Call-Line
P.O. Box 14567
Sant Barbara, CA 93107
Crisis Phone 1: (805) 569-2255
Business Phone: (805) 961-4114
Hrs Avail: 24

Santa Barbara
Santa Barbara Crisis Intervention
Psychiatric Emergency Team
4444 Calle Real
Santa Barbara, CA 93110
Daytime Hrs. Ext.: (805) 964-6713
Business Phone: (805) 964-6713
Hrs Avail: 24

Santa Cruz
Crisis Interven. Service
Santa Cruz Mental Health Services
1060 Emeline Ave.
Santa Cruz, CA 95060
North County: (408) 425-2237
South County: (408) 722-3577
Business Phone: (408) 425-2237

Santa Cruz County
* SPS of Santa Cruz County
P.O. Box 734
Capitola, CA 95010

Crisis Phone 1: (408) 426-2342
Crisis Phone 2: (408) 688-6581
Business Phone: (408) 426-2342
Hrs Avail: 24

Santa Monica
Newstart
1455 19th St.
Santa Monica, CA 90404
Crisis Phone 1: (213) 828-5561
Business Phone: (213) 828-5561
Hrs Avail: 24

Sonoma
Family Center Crisis Interv. Prog.
Sonoma Valley Family Center Crisis
Intervention Program
P.O. Box 128
Sonoma, CA 95476
Crisis Phone 1: (707) 938-help
Business Phone: (707) 996-7877
Hrs Avail: 24

St. Helena
* Crisis-Help of Napa Valley, Inc.
1360 Adams St.
St. Helena, CA 94574
Crisis Phone 1: (707) 963-2555
Crisis Phone 2: (707) 944-2212
Business Phone: (707) 942-4319
Hrs Avail: 24

Stockton
San Joaquin Co. Mental Health
1212 N. California
Stockton, CA 95202
Crisis Phone 1: (209) 948-4484
Hrs Avail: 24
Business Phone: (209) 982-1818

Ventura
Crisis Evaluation Unit
Ventura Co. Mental Health Dept.
300 Hillmont Ave.
Ventura, CA 93003
Crisis Phone 1: (805) 652-6727
Business Phone: (805) 652-6727
Hrs Avail: 24

Vista
Lifeline Community Services
200 Jefferson St.
Vista, CA 92083
Crisis Phone 1: (619) 726-4900
Business Phone: (714) 726-6396
Hrs Avail: M-F 8 A.M.-8 P.M.;
Sat 11 A.M.-3 P.M.

Walnut Creek
* Contra Costa Crisis/Suicide Interv.
P.O. Box 4852
Walnut Creek, CA 94596
Crisis Phone 1: (415) 939-3232
Business Phone: (415) 939-1916
Hrs Avail: 24

Yuba City
Sutter-Yuba MH Crisis Clinic
1965 Live Oak Blvd.
Yuba City, CA 95991
Crisis Phone 1: (916) 673-8255
Business Phone: (916) 674-8500
Hrs Avail: 24

COLORADO

Arvada
Contact Life Line of Denver
5742 Field Street
Arvada, CO 80002
Crisis Phone 1: (303) 458-7777
Business Phone: (303) 421-6453
Hrs Avail: 24

Aurora
Comitis Crisis Center
9840 E. 17th Ave.
P.O. Box 913
Aurora, CO 80040
Crisis Phone 1: (303) 343-9890
Business Phone: (303) 341-9160
Hrs Avail: 24

Boulder
Emerg. Psych. Services
1333 Iris Ave.

Boulder, CO 80302
Crisis Phone 1: (303) 447-1665
Business Phone: (303) 443-8500
Hrs Avail: 24

Colorado Springs
Colorado Springs Crisis Services
Pikes Peak Mental Health
875 W. Moreno
Colorado Springs, CO 80903
Crisis Phone 1: (303) 471-8300
Business Phone: (303) 471-3343
Hrs Avail: 24

Colorado Springs
Helpline of Colorado Springs
12 N. Meade Ave.
Colorado Springs, CO 80909
Crisis Phone 1: (303) 417-4357
Business Phone: (303) 633-4601
Hrs Avail: 24

Colorado Springs
Terros
P.O. Box 2642
Colorado Springs, CO 80901
Crisis Phone 1: (303) 471-4127
Business Phone: (303) 471-4128
Hrs Avail: 24

Denver
* Suicide and Crisis Control
2459 South Ash
Denver, CO 80222
Crisis Phone 1: (303) 757-0988
Crisis Phone 2: (303) 789-3073
Business Phone: (303) 756-8485
Hrs Avail: 24

Ft. Collins
* Crisis/Info. Helpline of Larimer Co.
700 W. Mountain Ave.
Ft. Collins, CO 80521-2506
Crisis Phone 1: (303) 493-3888
Business Phone: (303) 493-3896
Hrs Avail: 24

Ft. Morgan
Ft. Morgan Helpline
330 Meaker Street
Ft. Morgan, CO 80701
Crisis Phone 1: (303) 867-3411
Crisis Phone 2: (303) 867-2451
Business Phone: (303) 867-3411
Hrs Avail: 24

Grand Junction
Grand Junction Helpline
P.O. Box 3302
Grand Junction, CO 81502
Crisis Phone 1: (303) 242-help
Business Phone: (303) 245-3270
Hrs Avail: 24

Pueblo
*# Pueblo Suicide Prevention, Inc.
229 Colorado Ave.
Pueblo, CO 81004
Crisis Phone 1: (303) 544-1133
Business Phone: (303) 545-2477
Hrs Avail: 24

CONNECTICUT

Greenwich
* Hotline of Greenwich, Inc.
189 Mason St.
Greenwich, CT 06830
Crisis Phone 1: (203) 661-help
Business Phone: (203) 661-4378
Hrs Avail: 24

Norwalk
Info Line of Southwestern CT
7 Academy St.
Norwalk, CT 06850
Bridgeport: (203) 333-7555
Norwalk: (203) 853-2525
Stamford: (203) 324-1010
Business Phone: (203) 333-7555
Hrs Avail: 24

Plainville
*# The Wheeler Clinic, Inc.
Emergency Services
91 Northwest Dr.
Plainville, CT 06062
Crisis Phone 1: (203) 747-3434
Crisis Phone 2: (203) 524-1182
Business Phone: (203) 747-6801
Hrs Avail: 24

Uncasville
* Contact of SE Connecticut, Inc.
P.O. Box 277
Uncasville, CT 06382
Crisis Phone 1: (203) 848-1281
Business Phone: (203) 848-1655
Hrs Avail: 24

Westport
Open Line, Ltd.
245 Post Road East
Westport, CT 06880
Crisis Phone 1: (203) 226-3546
Business Phone: (203) 226-3546
Hrs Avail: 12 P.M.-12 A.M.

DELAWARE

Georgetown
Georgetown Helpline
Sussex County Community MHC
Georgetown, DE 19947
Crisis Phone 1: (302) 856-6626
Business Phone: (302) 856-2151
Hrs Avail: 24

New Castle
Psychiatric Emergency Services
S. New Castle County Community MH
14 Central Ave.
New Castle, DE 19720
Crisis Phone 1: (302) 421-6711
Business Phone: (302) 421-6711
Hrs Avail: 8 A.M.-12 A.M.

Wilmington
Contact Wilmington, Inc.
Washington St. at Lea Blvd.
Wilmington, DE 19802
Crisis Phone 1: (302) 575-1112
Deaf Contact: (302) 656-6660
Business Phone: (302) 762-4989
Hrs Avail: 24

WASHINGTON, DC

D.C. Hotline
P.O. Box 12044
Washington, DC 20005
Crisis Phone 1: (202) 223-2255
Business Phone: (202) 223-0020
Hrs Avail: 1 P.M.-1 A.M.

D.C. Suicide Prevention
Crisis Resolution Branch
D.C. Dept. of Human Serv.
1905 E. St., S.E.
Washington, DC 20005
Crisis Phone 1: (202) 727-3622
Business Phone: (202) 727-3622
Hrs Avail: 24

* Fact Hotline
(Families and Children in Trouble)
Family Stress Services of DC/NCPCA
2001 "O" St., N.W. Suite G-1200
Washington, DC 20036
Crisis Phone 1: (202) 628-3228
Business Phone: (202) 965-1900
Hrs Avail: 24

* St. Francis Center
2633-15th St. N.W., Ste. 11
Washington, DC 20009
Crisis Phone 1: (202) 234-5613
Business Phone: (202) 234-5613
Hrs Avail: 24

FLORIDA

Bartow
* Crisis Interv. Services
Peace River Center
1745 Highway 17 South

Bartow, FL 33830
Crisis Phone 1: (813) 533-4323
Crisis Phone 2: (800) 282-6342
Business Phone: (813) 533-3141
Hrs Avail: 24

Bradenton
Manatee Mental Health Center
Crisis Services
P.O. Box 9478
Bradenton, FL 33506
Crisis Phone 1: (813) 748-8648
Business Phone: (813) 747-8648
Hrs Avail: 24

De Funiak Springs
Cope Center
Hwy. 90
De Funiak Springs, FL 32433
Crisis Phone 1: (904) 892-2167
Business Phone: (904) 892-2167
Hrs Avail: 24

Fort Lauderdale
Crisis Interv. Center of Broward Co.
P.O. Box 7537
Fort Lauderdale, FL 33338
Crisis Phone 1: (305) 323-8553
Business Phone: (305)763-1213
Hrs Avail: 24

Ft. Myers
Ft. Myers Crisis Intervention Center
Lee Mental Health Center
P.O. Box 06137
Ft. Myers, FL 33906
Crisis Phone 1: (813) 332-1477
Business Phone: (813) 334-3537
Hrs Avail: 24

Ft. Pierce
Indian River Comm. MHC
800 Ave. H
Ft. Pierce, FL 33450
Crisis Phone 1: (305) 464-8111
Business Phone: (305) 464-8111
Hrs Avail: 24

Ft. Walton Beach
Crisis Line
205 Shell Ave.
Ft. Walton Beach, FL 32548
Crisis Phone 1: (904) 244-9191
Crestview, Toll Free: (904) 682-0101
Business Phone: (904) 244-0151 x35
Hrs Avail: 24

Gainesville
*# Alachua County Crisis Center
730 N. Waldo Rd., Suite 100
Gainesville, FL 32601
Crisis Phone 1: (904) 376-4444
Crisis Phone 2: (904) 376-4445
Business Phone: (904) 372-3659
Hrs Avail: 24

Jacksonville
* Suicide Prevention Service
2218 Park St.
Jacksonville, FL 32204
Crisis Phone 1: (904) 384-2234
Business Phone: (904) 387-5641
Hrs Avail: 24

Key West/Monroe County
* Helpline, Inc.
Fla. Keys Memorial Hosp.
5900 Junior College Rd.
Key West, FL 33040
Crisis Phone 1: (305) 296-Help
Crisis Phone 2: (305) 294-line
Middle & Upper Keys: (800) 341-4343
Business Phone: (305) 294-5531, x3412
Hrs Avail: 24

Kissimmee
Help Now in Osceola, Inc.
917 Emmett St.
Kissimmee, FL 32741
Crisis Phone 1: (305) 847-8811
Business Phone: (305) 847-8811
Hrs Avail: 24

Lake City
Columbia Counseling Center
P.O. Box 2818

Lake City, FL 32056
Crisis Phone 1: (904) 752-1045
After 5:00 P.M: (904) 752-2140
Business Phone: (904) 752-1045
Hrs Avail: 24

Lakeland
Contact Help Line
P.O. Box 2021
Lakeland, FL 33803
Crisis Phone 1: (813) 688-1977
Business Phone: (813) 688-9114
Hrs Avail: 24

Miami
* Switchboard of Miami, Inc.
35 S.W. 8th St.
Miami, FL 33130
Crisis Phone 1: (305) 358-4357
Business Phone: (305) 358-1640
Hrs Avail: 24

Milton
Santa Rosa MH Crisis Line
705 Stewart St. SW
Milton, FL 32570
Crisis Phone 1: (904) 623-6363
Business Phone: (904) 626-0616
Hrs Avail: 24

Orlando
* Mental Health Services of Orange
2520 North Orange Ave.
Orlando, FL 32804
Crisis Phone 1: (305) 896-9306
Business Phone: (305) 896-9306
Hrs Avail: 24

Orlando
We Care, Inc.
112 Pasadena Place
Orlando, FL 32803
Crisis Phone 1: (305) 628-1227
Teen/Kid: (305) 644-2027
Business Phone: (305) 425-2624
Hrs Avail: 24

Osprey
Lifeline
Suncoast Mental Health Center
873 S. Tamiami Trail
Osprey, FL 33559
Crisis Phone 1: (813) 957-5003
Business Phone: (813) 966-7471
Hrs Avail: 24

Panama City
Panama City Crisis Line
Northwest Mental Health Center
615 N. McArthur Ave.
Panama City, FL 32401
Crisis Phone 1: (904) 769-9481
Business Phone: (904) 769-9481
Hrs Avail: 24

Pensacola
Pensacola Help Line
Lakeview Center, Inc.
1221 W. Lakeview St.
Pensacola, FL 32501
Crisis Phone 1: (904) 438-1617
Business Phone: (904) 432-1222, x300
Hrs Avail: 24

Rockledge
Suicide/Crisis Hotline
Brevard County Mental Health Center
566 Barton Blvd., #304
Rockledge, FL 32955
Crisis Phone 1: (305) 631-8944
Business Phone: (305) 631-9790
Hrs. Avail: 24

Rockledge
Teen & Parent Stress Line
1770 Cedar St.
P.O. Box 69
Rockledge, FL 32955
Crisis Phone 1: (305) 631-8944
Business Phone: (305) 631-9290
Hrs. Avail: 24

St. Petersburg
Hotline/Information and Referral
P.O. Box 13087

St. Petersburg, FL 33733
Crisis Phone 1: (813) 531-4664
Business Phone: (813) 536-9464
Hrs Avail: 24

Tallahassee
* Telephone Counsel. & Referral Serv.
P.O. Box 20169
Tallahassee, FL 32316
Crisis Phone 1: (904) 224-6333
Business Phone: (904) 224-6333
Hrs Avail: 24

Tampa
Contact Tampa Help Line
P.O. Box 10117
Tampa, FL 33679
Crisis Phone 1: (813) 251-4000
Business Phone: (813) 251-4040
Hrs Avail: 24

Tampa
*# Suicide & Crisis Center of Hillsborough County
2214 E. Henry Ave.
Tampa, FL 33610
Crisis Phone 1: (813) 238-8821
Business Phone: (813) 238-8411
Hrs Avail: 24

West Palm Beach
* Crisis Line Info. & Referral Service
P.O. Box 15522
West Palm Beach, FL 33416
North and Central: (305) 686-4000
South: (305) 278-1121
West (Glades): (305) 996-1121
Business Phone: (305) 689-3334
Hrs Avail: 24

Winter Haven
Polk Co. Help & Resource Line
Community Mental Health Center
Winter Haven Hospital
Winter Haven, FL 33880
Crisis Phone 1: (813) 299-5858
Business Phone: (813) 293-1121, x1158
Hrs Avail: 24

GEORGIA

Atlanta
De Kalb Emerg./Crisis Interv. Serv.
Georgia Mental Health Institute
1256 Briarcliff Rd., N.E.
Atlanta, GA 30306
Crisis Phone 1: (404) 892-4646
Business Phone: (404) 892-4646
Hrs Avail: 24

Atlanta
Emergency Mental Health Service
99 Butler S.E.
Atlanta, GA 30311
Crisis Phone 1: (404) 522-9222
Business Phone: (404) 522-9222
Hrs Avail: 24

Augusta
Help Line
P.O. Box 1724
Augusta, GA 30903
Crisis Phone 1: (404) 724-4357
Business Phone: (404) 724-4357
Hrs Avail: 24

Columbus
Contact Chattahoochee Valley
P.O. Box 12002
Columbus, GA 31907
Crisis Phone 1: (404) 327-3999
Business Phone: (404) 327-0199
Hrs Avail: 24

Gainesville
Contact Hall County
P.O. Box 1616
Gainesville, GA 30503
Crisis Phone 1: (404) 534-0617
Business Phone: (404) 536-7145
Hrs Avail: 24

Lawrenceville
Lawrenceville Emergency Services
Gwinnett County Mental Health
100 Clayton St., S.E.
Lawrenceville, GA 30245

Crisis Phone 1: (404) 963-8141
Evening, Week-ends: (404) 963-3223
Business Phone: (404) 963-8141
Hrs Avail: 24

Macon
Crisis Line of Macon and Bibb Co.
Mercer University
P.O. Box 56
Macon, GA 31207
Crisis Phone 1: (912) 745-9292
Business Phone: (912) 745-9292
Hrs Avail: 24

Marietta
Marietta Emergency Services
Cobb-Douglas Mental Health
Community Services Building
737 Church St., Suite 420
Marietta, GA 30060
Crisis Phone 1: (404) 422-0202
Business Phone: (404) 424-0870
Hrs Avail: 24

Riverdale
Clayton Crisis Line
Clayton General Hospital
11 S.W. Upper Riverdale Rd.
Riverdale, GA 30274
Crisis Phone 1: (404) 996-4357
Business Phone: (404) 996-4361
Hrs Avail: 24

Savannah
First Call For Help
P.O. Box 9119
Savannah, GA 31412
Crisis Phone 1: (912) 232-3383
Business Phone: (912) 232-3383
Hrs Avail: 24

HAWAII

Honolulu/Oahu
* Suicide and Crisis Center
200 N. Vineyard Blvd. Rm. 603
Honolulu, HI 96817
Crisis Phone 1: (808) 521-4555
Business Phone: (808) 536-7234
Hrs Avail: 24

Kailua-Kona
Kona Crisis Center, Inc.
P.O. Box 4363
Kailua-Kona, HI 96740
Crisis Phone 1: (808) 329-9111
Business Phone: (808) 329-6744
Hrs Avail: 24

Lihue
Helpline Kauai
P.O. Box 3541
Lihue, HI 96766
Crisis Phone 1: (808) 822-4114
Business Phone: (808) 822-7435
Hrs Avail: 24

Wailuku
* Helpline/Suicide & Crisis Center
Maui Kokua Services, Inc.
95 Mahalani St.
Wailuku, HI 96793
Crisis Phone 1: (808) 244-7407
Business Phone: (808) 244-7405
Hrs Avail: 24

IDAHO

Boise
Emergency Line
Region IV Services/Mental Health
1105 S. Orchard
Boise, ID 83705
Crisis Phone 1: (208) 338-7044
Business Phone: (208) 338-7020
Hrs Avail: 24

Coeur d'Alene
Coeur d'Alene Emergency Line
W. George Moody Health Center
2195 Ironwood Court
Coeur d'Alene, ID 83814
Crisis Phone 1: (208) 667-6406

Business Phone: (208) 667-6406
Hrs Avail: 24

Idaho Falls
Idaho Falls Emergency Services
Region VII Mental Health
150 Shoup
Idaho Falls, ID 83402
Crisis Phone 1: (208) 525-7129
Business Phone: (208) 525-7129
Hrs Avail: 24

Kellogg
Kellogg Emergency Line
Health and Welfare Service Center
313 W. Cameron
Kellogg, ID 83837
Crisis Phone 1: (208) 667-6406
Crisis Phone 2: (208) 773-2906
Business Phone: (208) 784-1351
Hrs Avail: 24

Lewiston
YWCA Crisis Services
300 Main St.
Lewiston, ID 83501
Crisis Phone 1: (208) 746-9655
Business Phone: (208) 746-9655
Hrs Avail: 24

St. Maries
St. Maries Emergency Line
Health and Welfare Service Center
128 S. 7th St.
St. Maries, ID 83861
Crisis Phone 1: (208)245-2527
Business Phone: (208)245-2541
Hrs Avail: 8 A.M.-5 P.M.

Twin Falls
Twin Falls Emergency Services
Region 5 Mental Health
823 Harrison
Twin Falls, ID 83301
Crisis Phone 1: (208) 734-4000
Business Phone: (208) 734-9770
Hrs Avail: 24

ILLINOIS

Alton
Madison Co. Mental Health Center
1625 Edwards St.
P.O. Box 1054
Alton, IL 62002
Crisis Phone 1: (618) 462-3505
Evenings, Week-ends: (618) 463-1058
Business Phone: (618) 462-3505
Hrs Avail: 24

Anna
Union County Counseling Service
204 South St.
Anna, IL 62906
Crisis Phone 1: (618) 833-8551
Business Phone: (618) 833-8551
Hrs Avail: 24

Aurora
Crisis Line of the Fox Valley
309 W. New Indian Trail Ct.
Aurora, IL 60506
Crisis Phone 1: (312) 897-5522
Business Phone: (312) 897-5531

Beardstown
Cass County Mental Health Center
101 W. 15th St.
Beardstown, IL 62618
Crisis Phone 1: (217) 323-2980
Business Phone: (217) 323-2980
Hrs Avail: 24

Belleville
*# Call For Help
Suicide & Crisis Interv. Service
500 Wilshire Dr.
Belleville, IL 62223
Crisis Phone 1: (618) 397-0963
Business Phone: (618) 397-0968
Hrs Avail: 24

Bloomington
* Emergency Crisis Intervention Team
McLean Co. Center For Human Serv.
108 W. Market

Bloomington, IL 61701
Crisis Phone 1: (309) 827-4005
Business Phone: (309) 827-5351
Hrs Avail: 24

Bloomington
PATH
(Personal Assistance Telephone Help)
427 N. Main
Bloomington, IL 61701
Crisis Phone 1: (309) 827-4005
Toll Free Number: (800) 322-5015
Business Phone: (309) 828-1922
Hrs Avail: 24

Cairo
Cairo Crisis Line
Mental Health Center
218 10th St.
Cairo, IL 62914
Crisis Phone 1: (618) 734-2665
Business Phone: (618) 734-2665
Hrs Avail: 24

Champaign
Champaign Emergency Service
Champaign Mental Health Clinic
600 E. Park
Champaign, IL 61820
Crisis Phone 1: (217) 359-4141
Business Phone: (217) 398-8080
Hrs Avail: 24

Chicago
Chicago Crisis Intervention
City of Chicago Dept. of Human Serv.
640 N. La Salle
Chicago, IL 60610
Crisis Phone 1: (312) 947-8300
Business Phone: (312) 744-4045
Hrs Avail: 24

Chicago
In Touch Helpline
Student Counseling Service
University of Illinois
P.O. Box 4348
Chicago, IL 60680
Crisis Phone 1: (312) 996-5535
Business Phone: (312) 996-5535

Chicago
* Society of Samaritans—Chicago
5638 S. Woodlawn Ave.
Chicago, IL 60637
Crisis Phone 1: (312) 947-8300
Business Phone: (312) 947-8844
Hrs Avail: 24

Clinton
Dewitt County Human Resource Center
109 W. Jefferson
Clinton, IL 61727
Crisis Phone 1: (217) 935-9496
Business Phone: (217) 935-9496
Hrs Avail: 24

Collingsville
Community Counseling Services
1315 Vandalia
Collingsville, IL 62234
Crisis Phone 1: (618) 877-4420
Business Phone: (618) 344-0393
Hrs Avail 24

Danville
Contact Danville
504 N. Vermilion
Danville, IL 61832
Crisis Phone 1: (217) 443-2273
Business Phone: (217) 446-8212
Hrs Avail 24

Du Quoin
Perry County Help Line
R.R. #1
P.O. Box 106
Du Quoin IL 62832
Crisis Phone 1: (618) 542-4357
Business Phone: (618) 542-4357
Hrs Avail: 24

Edwardsville
Edwardsville Comm. Counseling Serv.
1507 Troy Rd., Suite 3
Edwardsville, IL 62025
Crisis Phone 1: (618) 877-4420

Business Phone: (618) 656-8721
Hrs Avail: 24

Elgin
* Community Crisis Center
P.O. Box 1390
Elgin, IL 60121
Crisis Phone 1: (312) 697-2380
Business Phone: (312) 742-4031
Hrs Avail: 24

Elk Grove
Talk Line/Kids Line, Inc.
P.O. Box 1321
Elk Grove, IL 60007
Talk Line: (312) 228-6400
Kids Line: (312) 228-KIDS
Business Phone: (312) 981-1271

Evanston
Evanston Hospital Crisis Interv.
2650 Ridge Ave.
Evanston, IL 60201
Crisis Phone 1: (312) 492-6500
Business Phone: (312) 492-6500
Hrs Avail: 24

Freeport
Contact Stephenson Co.
P.O. Box 83
Freeport, IL 61032
Crisis Phone 1: (815) 233-4357
Business Phone: (815) 233-4357
Hrs Avail: 24

Galesburg
* Spoon River Community MHC
302 E. Main St., Suite 530
Galesburg, IL 61401
Crisis Phone 1: (800) 322-7143
Business Phone: (309) 343-5155
Hrs Avail: 24

Granite City
Mental Health Center
2024 State St.
Granite City, IL 62040
Crisis Phone 1: (618) 877-4420
Business Phone: (618) 877-4420
Hrs Avail: 24

Highland
Highland Comm. Counseling Services
508 Broadway
Highland, IL 62249
Crisis Phone 1: (618) 877-4420
Business Phone: (618) 654-7232
Hrs Avail: 24

Hillsboro
Hillsboro Helpline
Montgomery Co. Counseling Center
200 S. Main St.
Hillsboro, IL 62049
Crisis Phone 1: (217) 532-9581
Crisis Phone 2: (217) 523-6191
Business Phone: (217) 532-9581
Hrs Avail: 24

Joliet
Crisis Line of Will County
P.O. Box 2354
Joliet, IL 60435
Crisis Phone 1: (815) 722-3344
Frankfort: (815) 469-6166
Wilmington: (815) 476-6969
Business Phone: (815) 744-5280
Hrs Avail: 24

Libertyville
Connection Telephone Counseling
& Referral Service
P.O. Box 906
Libertyville, IL 60048
Crisis Phone 1: (312) 367-1080
Business Phone: (312) 362-3381
Hrs Avail: 24

Lincoln
Lincoln Crisis Clinic
A. Lincoln Mental Health Center
315 8th
Lincoln, IL 62656
Crisis Phone 1: (217) 732-3500
Business Phone: (217) 732-2161
Hrs Avail: 24

Mt. Vernon
Mt. Vernon Crisis Line
Comprehensive Services
601 N. 18th
P.O. Box 428
Mt. Vernon, IL 62864
Crisis Phone 1: (618) 242-1512
Business Phone: (618) 242-1510
Hrs Avail: 24

Northfield
Irene Josselyn Clinic
405 Central
Northfield, IL 60093
Crisis Phone 1: (312) 441-5600
Business Phone: (312) 441-5600
Hrs Avail: 8 A.M.-5 P.M.

Paris
Human Resources Center
P.O. Box 302
Paris, IL 61944
Days: (217) 465-4118
Evenings, Weekends: (217) 465-4141
Business Phone: (217) 465-4118
Hrs Avail: 24

Peoria
Peoria Call For Help
5407 N. University
Peoria, IL 61614
Crisis Phone 1: (309) 673-7373
Business Phone: (309) 692-1766
Hrs Avail: 24

Quincy
Quincy Suicide Prev. & Crisis Serv.
4409 Maine
Quincy, IL 62301
Crisis Phone 1: (217) 222-1166
Business Phone: (217) 223-0413
Hrs Avail: 24

Rockford
* Contact Rockford
P.O. Box 1976
Rockford, IL 61110
Crisis Phone 1: (815) 964-4044
Business Phone: (815) 964-0400
Hrs Avail: 24

Sullivan
Sullivan Crisis Line
Moultree Co. Counseling Center
2 W. Adams
Sullivan, IL 61951
Crisis Phone 1: (217) 728-7611
Business Phone: (217) 728-4358
Hrs Avail: 24

Taylorville
Taylorville Helpline
Christian Co. Mental Health Center
301 S. Webster
Taylorville, IL 62568
Days: (217) 824-4905
Evening, Weekends: (217) 824-3335
Business Phone: (217) 824-4905
Hrs Avail: 24

Wood River
* Crisis Services of Madison County
P.O. Box 570
Wood River, IL 62095
Crisis Phone 1: (618) 877-4420
Crisis Phone 2: (618) 463-1058
Business Phone: (618) 251-4073
Hrs Avail: 24

INDIANA

Anderson
Contact/Help
P.O. Box 303
Anderson, IN 46015
Crisis Phone 1: (317) 649-5211
Business Phone: (317) 649-4939
Hrs Avail: 24

Evansville
* Southwestern Indiana MHC, Inc.
415 Mulberry
Evansville, IN 47713
Crisis Phone 1: (812)423-7791

Business Phone: (812) 423-7791
Hrs Avail: 24

Ft. Wayne
Switchboard, Inc.
316 W. Creighton
Ft. Wayne, IN 46807
Crisis Phone 1: (219) 456-4561
Business Phone: (219) 745-7914
Hrs Avail: 24

Gary
Rap Line—Crisis Center
215 N. Grand Blvd.
Gary, IN 46403
Crisis Phone 1: (219) 980-9243
Business Phone: (219) 980-4207
Hrs Avail: 24

Greencastle
Contact Putnam County
P.O. Box 15
Greencastle, IN 46135
Crisis Phone 1: (317) 653-2645
Business Phone: (317) 653-5040
Hrs Avail: 24

Indianapolis
* Mental Health Assoc. in Marion Co.
Crisis & Suicide Intervention Service
1433 N. Meridian St., Rm. 202
Indianapolis, IN 46202
Crisis Phone 1: (317) 632-7575
Business Phone: (317) 269-1569
Hrs Avail: 24

Lafayette
Lafayette Crisis Center
803 N. 8th St.
Lafayette, IN 47904
Crisis Phone 1: (317) 742-0244
Business Phone: (317) 742-0244
Hrs Avail: 24

Lawrenceburg
Lawrenceburg Crisis Line
Community Mental Health Center
285 Bielby Rd.
Lawrenceburg, IN 47025
Crisis Phone 1: (812) 537-1302
Toll Free Number: (800) 832-5378
Business Phone: (812) 537-1302
Hrs Avail: 24

Lebanon
Project Help
Crisis Intervention Service
St. Peter's Episcopal Church
950 E. Washington St.
Lebanon, IN 46052
Crisis Phone 1: (317) 482-1599
Business Phone: (317) 482-1599
Hrs Avail: 24

Maryville
Contact Tele. of Blount Co.
P.O. Box 0382
Maryville, IN 37803
Crisis Phone 1: (615) 984-7689
Business Phone: (615) 984-7690
Hrs Avail: 24

Merrillville
Contact—Cares of NW Indiana
P.O. Box 8143
Merrillville, IN 46410
Crisis Phone 1: (219) 769-3141
Business Phone: (219) 769-3278
Hrs Avail: 24

Monticello
Twin Lakes Contact—Help
P.O. Box 67
Monticello, IN 47960
Crisis Phone 1: (219) 583-4357
Business Phone: (219) 583-4357
Hrs Avail: 24

IOWA

Ames
Open Line
Welch Ave. Station
P.O. Box 1138
Ames, IA 50010

Crisis Phone 1: (515)292-7000
Business Phone: (515) 292-4983
Hrs Avail: 18

Cedar Rapids
* Foundation 2, Inc.
1251 Third Ave. SE
Cedar Rapids, IA 52403
Crisis Phone 1: (319) 362-2174
Business Phone: (319) 362-2176
Hrs Avail: 24

Clearlake
Suicide Help-Line of Iowa
P.O. Box 711
Clearlake, IA 50428
Iowa Toll Free: (800) 638-help
Business Phone: (515) 357-4357
Hrs Avail: 24

Des Moines
* Community Telephone Counseling/Crisis Line
Service of the Amer. Red Cross
P.O. Box 7067
Des Moines, IA 50309
Crisis: (515) 244-1000
Counseling: (515) 244-1010
Business Phone: (515) 244-6700
Hrs Avail: M-Th 3 P.M.-8 A.M.; All other: 24

Dubuque
Phone A Friend Crisis Line
Suite 420
Nesler Center
Dubuque, IA 52001
Crisis Phone 1: (319) 588-4016
Business Phone: (319) 557-8331
Hrs Avail: 24

Iowa City
Iowa City Crisis Intervention Center
26 East Market
Iowa City, IA 52240
Crisis Phone 1: (319)351-0140
Business Phone: (319) 351-2726
Hrs Avail: 24

Sioux City
Aid Center
406 5th St.
Sioux City, IA 51101
Crisis Phone 1: (712) 252-1861
Business Phone: (712) 252-1861
Hrs Avail: 24

Waterloo
Integrated Crisis Service
2530 University Ave.
Waterloo, IA 50701
Crisis Phone 1: (319) 233-8484
Business Phone: (319) 233-8484
Hrs Avail: 24

KANSAS

Dodge City
Area Mental Health Center
W. Highway 50 Bypass
Dodge City, KS 67801
Crisis Phone 1: (316) 227-8566
Business Phone: (316) 227-8566
Hrs Avail: 24

Emporia
Emporia Emergency Services
MH Center of E. Central Kansas
705 S. Commercial
Emporia, KS 66801
Crisis Phone 1: (316) 343-2626
Business Phone: (316) 342-6116
Hrs Avail: 24

Ft. Scott
Ft. Scott Helpline
Mental Health Association
1st and Scott Ave.
Ft. Scott, KS 66701
Crisis Phone 1: (316) 223-2420
Business Phone: (316) 223-5030
Hrs Avail: 24

Garden City
Garden City Area MHC
156 Gardendale

Garden City, KS 67846
Crisis Phone 1: (316) 276-7689
Business Phone: (316) 276-7689
Hrs Avail: 24

Kansas City
Wyandotte Mental Health Center
Wyandotte County Crisis Line
36th and Eaton
Kansas City, KS 66103
Crisis Phone 1: (913) 831-1773
Business Phone: (913) 831-9500
Hrs Avail: 24

Lawrence
Headquarters, Inc.
1419 Massachusetts
P.O. Box 999
Lawrence, KS 66044
Crisis Phone 1: (913) 841-2345
Business Phone: (913) 841-2345
Hrs Avail: 24

Manhattan
Regional Crisis Center
P.O. Box 164
Manhattan, KS 66502
Crisis Phone 1: (913) 539-2785
Business Phone: (913) 539-2785
Hrs Avail: 24

Salina
Hotline Crisis Info. & Referral
P.O. Box 1982
Salina, KS 67402-1878
Crisis Phone 1: (913) 827-4747
Business Phone: (913) 827-4803
Hrs Avail: 24

Scott City
Scott City Area Mental Health Center
Scott Co. Courthouse
Scott City, KS 67871
Crisis Phone 1: (316) 872-5338
Business Phone: (316) 872-5338
Hrs Avail: 24

Topeka
* Shawnee Comm. MHC Emergency Service
2401 W. 6th
Topeka, KS 66606
Crisis Phone 1: (913) 233-1730
Business Phone: (913) 233-1370
Hrs Avail: 24

Ulysses
Ulysses Area Mental Health Center
102 W. Flower
Ulysses, KS 76880
Crisis Phone 1: (316) 356-3198
Business Phone: (316) 356-3198
Hrs Avail: 24

Wichita
* Sedgwick Co. Dept. of Mental Health
1801 E. Tenth St.
Wichita, KS 67214-3197
Crisis Phone 1: (316) 686-7465
Business Phone: (316) 268-8251
Hrs Avail: 24

KENTUCKY

Ashland
Ashland Crisis Service
Landsdowne Mental Health Center
P.O. Box 790
Ashland, KY 41101
Crisis Phone 1: (606) 324-1141
Business Phone: (606) 324-1141
Hrs Avail: 24

Bowling Green
Bowling Green Helpline
Barren River Mental Health
822 Woodway Dr.
Bowling Green, KY 42101
Crisis Phone 1: (502) 842-5642
Business Phone: (502) 843-4382
Hrs Avail: 24

Corbin
Corbin Emergency Services
Cumberland River Compreh. Care Ctr.

American Greeting Rd.
P.O. Box 568
Corbin, KY 40701
Crisis Phone 1: (606) 528-7010
Business Phone: (606) 528-7010
Hrs Avail: 24

Covington
Covington Emergency Line
Northern Ky. Comprehensive Care Center
503 Farrell Dr.
Covington, KY 41012
Crisis Phone 1: (606) 331-1900
Business Phone: (606) 331-6505
Hrs Avail: 24

Elizabethtown
Elizabethtown Crisis Line
N. Central Comprehensive Care Ctr.
907 N. Dixie Ave.
Elizabethtown, KY 42701
Crisis Phone 1: (502) 769-1304
Business Phone: (502) 769-1304
Hrs Avail: 24

Hopkinsville
Hopkinsville Crisis Line
Pennyroyal Regional Mental Health
735 North Drive
Hopkinsville, KY 42240
Crisis Phone 1: (502) 886-5163
Business Phone: (502) 886-5163
Hrs Avail: 24

Jackson
Hazard/Jackson Crisis Line
Kentucky River Community Care
P.O. Box 603
Jackson, KY 41339
Toll Free Number: (800) 262-7491
Business Phone: (606) 666-4904
Hrs Avail: 24

Lexington
Crisis Intervention Mental Health
201 Mechanic St.
Lexington, KY 40507
Crisis Phone 1: (606) 254-3844
Business Phone: (606) 254-3844
Hrs Avail: 24

Louisville
*# Seven Counties Services
Crisis & Information Center
600 S. Preston St.
Louisville, KY 40202
Crisis Phone 1: (502) 589-4313
Business Phone: (502) 583-3951 x284
Hrs Avail: 24

Maysville
Maysville Crisis Line
Comprehend, Inc. District MH
P.O. Box G
Maysville, KY 51056
Crisis Phone 1: (606) 564-4016
Business Phone: (606) 564-4016
Hrs Avail: 24

Morehead
Morehead Crisis Center
Cave Run Comprehensive Care Center
325 E. Main St.
Morehead, KY 40351
Crisis Phone 1: (800) 262-74-70
Business Phone: (606) 784-4161
Hrs Avail: 24

Owensboro
Owensboro Crisis Line
Green River Compreh. Care Ctr.
1001 Fredericka St.
Owensboro, KY 42301
Crisis Phone 1: (502) 684-9466
Business Phone: (502) 683-0277
Hrs Avail: 24

Paducah
Paducah Crisis Line
Western Kentucky Regional MH/MR Bd.
1530 Lone Oak Rd.
Paducah, KY 42001
Crisis Phone 1: (800) 592-3980
Business Phone: (502) 442-7121
Hrs Avail: 24

Prestonsburg
Prestonburg Helpline
Mountain Comprehensive Care Center
18 S. Front Ave.
Prestonsburg, KY 41653
Crisis Phone 1: (800) 422-1060
Business Phone: (606) 886-8572
Hrs Avail: 24

Somerset
Somerset Emergency Services
Community Mental Health Services
324 Cundiff Sq.
Somerset, KY 42501
Crisis Phone 1: (800) 632-8581
Business Phone: (606) 679-7348
Hrs Avail: 24

LOUISIANA

Alexandria
ALexandria Helpline
P.O. Box 749
Alexandria, LA 71301
Crisis Phone 1: (318) 445-4357
Business Phone: (318) 445-4357
Hrs Avail: 24

Baton Rouge
*# Baton Rouge Crisis Interv. Center
P.O. Box 80738
Baton Rouge, LA 70898
Crisis Phone 1: (504) 924-3900
Business Phone: (504) 924-1595
Hrs. Avail: 24

De Ridder
* Beauregard De Ridder Comm. Help-line
P.O. Box 815
De Ridder, LA 70634
Crisis Phone 1: (318) 462-0609
Crisis Phone 2: (318) 239-6196
Business Phone: (318) 462-1452
Hrs Avail: 8 A.M.-5 P.M.; 7-10 P.M.

Hammond
* Tangipahoa Crisis Phone, Inc.
P.O. Box 153
Hammond, LA 70404
Crisis Phone 1: (504) 345-6120
Business Phone: (504) 345-5335
Hrs Avail: 24

Houma
Houma-Terrebonne Crisis Line
341 Levron
Houma, LA 70360
Crisis Phone: (504) 872-1111
Business Phone: (504) 851-5950
Hrs Avail: 24

Lafayette
SW Louisiana Educ. & Referral Center
P.O. Box 3844
Lafayette, LA 70502
Crisis Phone: (318) 232-help
Business Phone: (318) 232-4357
Hrs Avail: 24

Lake Charles
* ETC Counseling Center
1146 Hodges
Lake Charles, LA 70601
Crisis Phone 1: (318) 439-2273
Business Phone: (318) 433-1062
Hrs Avail: 24

Monroe
Main Line
P.O. Box 1322
Monroe, LA 71201
Crisis Phone 1: (318) 387-5690
Business Phone: (318) 387-5683
Hrs Avail: 24

New Orleans
*# Mental Health Assoc. of New Orleans
Crisis Line Program
2515 Canal St., STE-200
New Orleans, LA 70119
Crisis Phone 1: (504) 523-2673
Business Phone: (504) 821-1024
Hrs Avail: 24

New Orleans
* River Oaks Crisis Center
1525 River Oaks Rd. W.
New Orleans, LA 70123
Crisis Phone 1: (504) 733-2273
Business Phone: (504) 734-1740
Hrs Avail: 24

Shreveport
Open Ear
Centenary College
P.O. Box 247
Shreveport, LA 71106
Crisis Phone 1: (318) 869-1228
Business Phone: (318) 869-1228
Hrs Avail: 8 P.M.-12 A.M.

Slidell
Slidell Crisis Line, Inc.
360 Robert Rd.
Slidell, LA 70458
Crisis Phone 1: (504) 643-6832
Business Phone: (504) 643-6832

Ville Platte
Ville Platte M.H.C.I.C.
520 De Moncherveaux Blvd.
Ville Platte, LA 70586
Crisis Phone 1: (318) 363-5579
Business Phone: (313) 363-5525
Hrs Avail: 24

MAINE

Bangor
Dial Help
43 Illinois Ave.
Bangor, ME 04401
Crisis Phone 1: (207) 947-6143
Toll Free Number: (800) 431-7810
Business Phone: (207) 947-6143
Hrs Avail: 24

Portland
* Ingraham Volunteers, Inc.
142 High St.
Portland, ME 04101
Crisis Phone 1: (207) 774-HELP
TTY/TTD: (207) 773-7321
Business Phone: (207) 773-4830
Hrs Avail: 24

Skowhegan
* Crisis Stabilization Unit
147 Water St.
Skowhegan, ME 04976
Augusta: (207) 623-4511
Waterville: (207) 872-2276
Skowhegan: (800) 452-1933
Business Phone: (207) 474-2506
Hrs Avail: 24

MARYLAND

Baltimore
Baltimore Crisis Center
Walter P. Carter MHC
630 W. Fayette St.
Baltimore, MD 21201
Crisis Phone 1: (301) 528-2200
Business Phone: (301) 528-2200

Baltimore
Baltimore Crisis Line
Sinai Hospital
Belvedere and Greenspring Ave.
Baltimore, MD 21215
Weekdays: (301) 578-5457
Evenings & Weekends: (301) 578-5000
Business Phone: (301) 578-5457
Hrs Avail: 24

Baltimore
Contact Baltimore
710 N. Charles St.
Baltimore, MD 21201
Crisis Phone 1: (301) 332-1114
Business Phone: (301) 332-0567
Hrs Avail: 24

Bowie
Bowie Hotline
P.O. Box 535
Bowie, MD 20715

Crisis Phone 1: (301) 262-2433
Business Phone: (301) 262-2433
Hrs Avail: 4 P.M.-12 A.M.

Columbia
Grass Roots
8045 Rt. 32
Columbia, MD 21044
Crisis Phone 1: (301) 531-6677
Business Phone: (301) 351-6006 or -6080
Hrs Avail: 24

Kensington
*# Montgomery County Hotline
10920 Connecticut Ave.
Kensington, MD 20795
Crisis Phone 1: (301) 949-6603
Business Phone: (301) 949-1255
Hrs Avail: 24

Riverdale
* Prince George's County Hotline
6607 Riverdale Rd.
Riverdale, MD 20737
Crisis Phone 1: (301) 441-8384
Business Phone: (301) 577-3140
Hrs Avail: 4 P.M.-Midnight, 7 days

MASSACHUSETTS

Acton
Code Hotline
481 Great Rd.
Acton, MA 01720
Crisis Phone 1: (617) 263-8777
Crisis Phone 2: (617) 486-3130
Business Phone: (617) 263-8777
Hrs Avail: 24

Attleboro
New Hope/Attleboro
P.O. Box 48
Attleboro, MA 02703
Crisis Phone 1: (617) 695-2113
Crisis Phone 2: (617) 226-4015
Crisis Phone 3: (617) 762-1350
Business Phone: (617) 824-4757
Hrs Avail: 24

Beverly
Project Rap, Inc.
9 Highland Ave.
Beverly, MA 01915
Crisis Phone 1: (617) 922-0000
Business Phone: (617) 927-4506
Hrs Avail: 24

Boston
*# The Samaritans
500 Commonwealth Ave.
Boston, MA 02215
Crisis Phone 1: (617) 247-0220
Business Phone: (617) 536-2460
Hrs Avail: 24

Brockton
Brockton, Canton Helpline
837 N. Main St.
Brockton, MA 02401
Crisis Phone 1: (617) 828-6666
Business Phone: (617) 584-4357
Hrs Avail: 24

Fall River
* Samaritans of Fall River-New Bedford, Inc.
386 Stanley St.
Fall River, MA 02720
Crisis Phone 1: (617) 636-6111
Business Phone: (617) 636-6111
Hrs Avail: 24

Falmouth
* Samaritans on Cape Cod
P.O. Box 65
Falmouth, MA 02540
Crisis Phone 1: (617) 548-8900
Crisis Phone 2: (617) 548-8901
Business Phone: (617) 548-8900
Hrs Avail: 24

Fitchburg
LUK Crisis Center, Inc.
9 Day St.
Fitchburg, MA 01420
Crisis Phone 1: (617) 345-7353
Crisis Phone 2: (617) 632-7374
Crisis Phone 3: (617) 772-2203

Crisis Phone 4: (617) 365-6750
Business Phone: (617) 345-0685
Hrs Avail: 24

Framingham
* Samaritans of South Middlesex, Inc.
73 Union Ave.
Framingham, MA 01701
Crisis Phone 1: (617) 875-4500
Business Phone: (617) 875-4500
Hrs Avail: 24

Greenfield
Greenfield Emergency Services
196 Federal St.
Greenfield, MA 01030
Crisis Phone 1: (413) 774-2758
Business Phone: (413) 774-2758
Hrs Avail: 24

Lawrence
* Greater Lawrence MHC
351 Essex St.
Lawrence, MA 01840
Crisis Phone 1: (617) 683-3128
Business Phone: (617) 683-6303
Hrs Avail: 24

Lawrence
* Psychiatric Associates of Lawrence
42 Franklin St.
Lawrence, MA 01840
Crisis Phone 1: (617) 682-7442
Business Phone: (617) 682-7442
Hrs Avail: 24

Lawrence
* Samaritans of the Merrimack Valley
55 Jackson St.
Lawrence, MA 01840
Crisis Phone 1: (617) 688-6607
Crisis Phone 2: (617) 452-6733
Crisis Phone 3: (617) 372-7200
Business Phone: (617) 688-6607
Hrs Avail: 24

Melrose
Eastern Middlesex CIS
150 Green St.
Melrose, MA 01880
Crisis Phone 1: (617) 662-6623
Business Phone: (617) 662-6623
Hrs Avail: 24

Newburyport
Turning Point Hot Line
5 Middle St.
Newburyport, MA 01950
Crisis Phone 1: (617) 465-8800
Business Phone: (617) 462-8251
Hrs Avail: 24

Newtonville/Boston Area
Contact Boston
P.O. Box 287
Newtonville, MA 02160
Crisis Phone 1: (617) 244-4350
Business Phone: (617) 244-4353
Hrs Avail: 24

North Adams
Help Line, Inc.
111 Main St.
North Adams, MA 01247
Crisis Phone 1: (413) 664-6391
Business Phone: (413) 663-5244
Hrs Avail: 24

Northampton
Northampton Emergency Services
48 Pleasant St.
Northampton, MA 01060
Crisis Phone 1: (413) 586-5555
Business Phone: (413) 586-5555
Hrs Avail: 24

Norwood
Pulse Hotline
P.O. Box 273
Norwood, MA 02062
Crisis Phone 1: (617) 762-5144
Business Phone: (617) 762-5144
Hrs Avail: 7 P.M.-11 P.M.

Norwood
*# So. Norfolk Screening & Emerg. Team
91 Central St.
Norwood, MA 02062

Crisis Phone 1: (617) 769-6060
Business Phone: (617) 769-6060
Hrs Avail: 24

Salem
Samaritans of Salem
P.O. Box 8133
Salem, MA 01970
Crisis Phone 1: (617) 744-5000
Business Phone: (617) 744-5000
Hrs Avail: 5:30 P.M.-10:30 P.M.

Saugus
Listen, Inc.
28 Taylor St.
Saugus, MA 01906
Crisis Phone 1: (617) 233-8911
Business Phone: (617) 233-8911
Hrs Avail: 24

Ware
Ware Helpline
Valley Human Services
96 South St.
Ware, MA 01082
Crisis Phone 1: (413) 283-3473
Business Phone: (413) 967-6241
Hrs Avail: 24

Worcester
* Crisis Center, Inc.
P.O. Box 652
Worcester, MA 01602
Crisis Phone 1: (617) 791-6762
Business Phone: (617) 791-7205
Hrs Avail: 24

MICHIGAN

Adrian
Call Someone Concerned
227 N. Winter, #215
Adrian, MI 49221
Crisis Phone 1: (517) 263-6737
Toll Free Number: (800) 322-0044
Business Phone: (517) 263-6739
Hrs Avail: 24

Ann Arbor
Washtenaw County Community MHC
2929 Plymouth Rd.
Ann Arbor, MI 48105
Crisis Phone 1: (313) 996-4747
Business Phone: (313) 994-2285
Hrs Avail: 24

Birmingham
Common Ground
1090 S. Adams
Birmingham, MI 48011
Crisis Phone 1: (313) 645-9676
Business Phone: (313) 645-1173
Hrs Avail: 24

Detroit
Contact Life Line
7430 2nd St., Rm. 428
Detroit, MI 48202
Crisis Phone 1: (313) 894-5555
Business Phone: (313) 875-0426
Hrs Avail: 24

Detroit
*# Suicide Prevention Center/Detroit
220 Bagley, Suite 626
Detroit, MI 48226
Crisis Phone 1: (313) 224-7000
Business Phone: (313) 963-7890

East Lansing
Listening Ear of East Lansing
547 1/2 E. Grand River
East Lansing, MI 48823
Crisis Phone 1: (517) 337-1717
Business Phone: (517) 337-1717
Hrs Avail: 24

Flint
Flint Emergency Service
Genesee Co. Mental Health
420 W. 5th Ave.
Flint, MI 48503
Crisis Phone 1: (313) 257-3740
Business Phone: (313) 257-3742
Hrs Avail: 24

Grand Haven
Grand Haven Helpline
Ottawa County Mental Health Center
1111 Fulton St.
Grand Haven, MI 49417
Crisis Phone 1: (616) 842-4357
Business Phone: (616) 842-5350
Hrs Avail: 24

Hart
* Oceana Co. Community Mental Health
P.O. Box 127
Hart, MI 49420
Crisis Phone 1: (616) 873-2108
Business Phone: (616) 873-2108
Hrs Avail: 24

Holland
Holland Helpline
12265 James St.
Holland, MI 49423
Crisis Phone 1: (616) 396-4357
Business Phone: (616) 392-1873
Hrs Avail: 24

Jackson
Help Line/Jackson
P.O. Box 1526
Jackson, MI 49204
Crisis Phone 1: (517) 783-2671
Business Phone: (517) 783-2861
Hrs Avail: 24

Kalamazoo
* Gryphon Place
1104 S. Westnedge
Kalamazoo, MI 49008
Crisis Phone 1: (616) 381-4357
Business Phone: (616) 381-1510
Hrs Avail: 24

Lapeer
* Lapeer Co. Comm. MHC
1575 Suncrest Dr.
Lapeer, MI 48446
Crisis Phone 1: (313) 667-0500
Business Phone: (313) 667-0500
Hrs Avail: 24

Livonia
Telephone Listening Center
P.O. Box 9391
Livonia, MI 48150
Crisis Phone 1: (313) 422-4852
Business Phone: (313) 422-4854
Hrs Avail: 24

Mt. Clemens
Macomb County Crisis Center
5th Floor, County Building
Mt. Clemens, MI 48043
Crisis Phone 1: (313) 578-8700
Business Phone: (313) 578-8700
Hrs Avail: 24

Mt. Pleasant
Listening Ear Crisis Center, Inc.
P.O. Box 65
Mt. Pleasant, MI 48858
Crisis Phone 1: (517) 772-2918
Business Phone: (517) 772-2918
Hrs Avail: 24

Muskegon
* Comm. MH Services of Muskegon Co.
125 E. Southern
Muskegon, MI 49442
Crisis Phone 1: (616) 722-4357
Business Phone: (616) 726-5266
Hrs Avail: 24

Plymouth
Turning Point Crisis Center
P.O. Box 115
Plymouth, MI 48170
Crisis Phone 1: (313) 455-4900
Business Phone: (313) 455-4902
Hrs Avail: 6:30 P.M.-10:30 P.M.

Port Huron
* Blue Water MH & Child Guidance Clinic
1501 Krafft Rd.
Port Huron, MI 48060
Crisis Phone 1: (313) 985-5125
Business Phone: (313) 985-5125
Hrs Avail: 24

Port Huron
* Center for Human Resources
1113 Military St.
Port Huron, MI 48060
Crisis Phone 1: (313) 985-7161
Business Phone: (313) 985-5168
Hrs Avail: 24

Port Huron
* St. Clair Co. Comm MH Services
3415 28th St.
Port Huron, MI 48060
Crisis Phone 1: (313) 985-7161
Crisis Phone 2: (800) 462-5350
Business Phone: (313) 985-9618
Hrs Avail: 24

St. Joseph
St. Joseph Helpline
Riverwood Community MHC
Memorial Hospital
2681 Morton Ave.
St. Joseph, MI 49085
Crisis Phone 1:(616) 927-4447
Toll Free Number: (800) 422-0757
Business Phone: (616) 983-7781
Hrs Avail: 24

Traverse City
Third Level Crisis Interv. Center
908 W. Front St.
Traverse City, MI 49684
Crisis Phone 1: (616) 941-2280
Toll Free Number: (800) 442-7315
Business Phone: (616) 941-2282
Hrs Avail: 24

Ypsilanti
SOS Crisis Center
114 North River St.
Ypsilanti, MI 48198
Crisis Phone 1: (313) 485-3222
Business Phone: (313) 485-8730
Hrs Avail: 24

MINNESOTA

Alexandria
Listening Ear Crisis Center
111 17th Ave. East
Alexandria, MN 56308
Crisis Phone 1: (612) 763-6638
Business Phone: (612) 762-1511, x283
Hrs Avail: 24

Austin
Victims Crisis Center
908 N.W. 1st Dr.
Austin, MN 55912
Crisis Phone 1: (507) 437-6680
Business Phone: (507) 437-6680
Hrs Avail: 24

Grand Rapids
Nightingale Help Phone
Information and Referral Service
P.O. Box 113
Grand Rapids, MN 55744
Crisis Phone 1: (218) 326-8565
Business Phone: (218) 326-8565
Hrs Avail: 24

Minneapolis
Contact Twin Cities
83 S. 12th St.
Minneapolis, MN 55403
Crisis Phone 1: (612) 341-2896
Business Phone: (612) 341-2212
Hrs Avail: 24

Minneapolis
*# Crisis Interv. Center
Hennepin County Medical Center
701 Park Ave. South
Minneapolis, MN 55415
Crisis: (612) 347-3161
Suicide: (612) 347-2222
Crisis Home Program: (612) 347-3170
Sexual Assault Serv.: (612) 347-5838
Business Phone: (612) 347-3164
Hrs Avail: 24

Owatonna
Owatonna—Steele Co. Contact
P.O. Box 524
Owatonna, MN 55060
Crisis Phone 1: (507) 451-9100
Business Phone: (507) 451-1897
Hrs Avail: 24

Worthington/Luverne/Pipestone/Windom
* 24 Hour Crisis Hotline
Southwestern Mental Health Center
1224 Fourth Ave.
Worthington, MN 56187
Crisis Phone 1: (800) 642-1525
Business Phone: (507) 372-7671
Hrs Avail: 24

MISSISSIPPI

Columbus
Golden Triangle Contact
P.O. Box 1304
Columbus, MS 39703-1304
Crisis Phone 1: (601) 328-0200
Business Phone: (601) 328-0200
Hrs Avail: 24

Hattiesburg
Hattiesburg Help Line, Inc.
P.O. Box 183
Hattiesburg, MS 39401
Crisis Phone 1: (601) 545-help
Business Phone: (601) 545-help
Hrs Avail: 24

Jackson
Contact Jackson
P.O. Box 5192
Jackson, MS 39216
Crisis Phone 1: (601) 969-2077
Business Phone: (601) 969-2077
Hrs Avail: 24

Meridian
Weems Mental Health Center
P.O. Box 4376 WS
Meridian, MS 39301
Crisis Phone 1: (601) 483-4821
Business Phone: (601) 483-4821
Hrs Avail: 24

MISSOURI

Joplin
Joplin Crisis Intervention, Inc.
P.O. Box 582
Joplin, MO 64801
Crisis Phone 1: (417) 781-2255
Business Phone: (417) 781-2255
Hrs Avail: 24

Kansas City
K.C. Suicide Prevention Line
Western Mo. Mental Health Center
600 E. 22nd St.
Kansas City, MO 64108
Crisis Phone 1: (816) 471-3939
Crisis Phone 2: (816) 471-3940
Business Phone: (816) 471-3000
Hrs Avail: 24

St. Joseph
St. Joseph Crisis Service
St. Joseph State Hospital
St. Joseph, MO 64506
Crisis Phone 1: (816) 232-8431
Business Phone: (816) 232-8431
Hrs Avail: 24

St. Louis
Contact St. Louis
P.O. Box 160070
St. Louis, MO 36116
Crisis Phone 1: (314) 771-8181
Business Phone: (314) 771-0404
Hrs Avail: 24

St. Louis
*# Life Crisis Services, Inc.
1423 S. Big Bend Blvd.
St. Louis, MO 63117
Crisis Phone 1: (314) 647-4357
Business Phone: (314) 647-3100
Hrs Avail: 24

MONTANA

Billings
Billings Helpline
Yellowstone Co. Welfare
3021 3rd Ave. N
Billings, MT 59191
Crisis Phone 1: (406) 248-1691
Business Phone: (406) 248-1691
Hrs Avail: 24

Bozeman
Bozeman Help Center
323 S. Wallace
Bozeman, MT 59715
Crisis Phone 1: (406) 248-1691
Business Phone: (406) 248-1691
Hrs Avail: 24

Great Falls
Great Falls Crisis Center
P.O. Box 124
Great Falls, MT 59403
Crisis Phone 1: (406) 453-6512
Business Phone: (406) 453-6512
Hrs Avail: 24

Helena
Southwest Montana MHC
572 Logan
Helena, MT 59601
Crisis Phone 1: (406) 443-9667
Business Phone: (406) 443-9667
Hrs Avail: 24

Missoula
Missoula Crisis Center, Inc.
P.O. Box 9345
Missoula, MT 59807
Crisis Phone 1: (406) 543-4555
Business Phone: (406) 543-4555

NEBRASKA

Lincoln
Personal Crisis Service
P.O. Box 80083
Lincoln, NE 68506
Crisis Phone 1: (402) 475-5171
Business Phone: (402) 475-5171
Hrs Avail: 24

Norfolk
24 Hour Hotline
Northern Nebraska Comp. MHC
201 Miller Ave.
Norfolk, NE 68701
Crisis Phone 1: (800) 672-8323
Business Phone: (402) 371-7530
Hrs Avail: 24

North Platte
North Platte Emergency Services
Great Plains Mental Health Center
P.O. Box 1209
North Platte, NE 69103
Crisis Phone 1: (308) 532-9332
Business Phone: (308) 532-4050
Hrs Avail: 24

Omaha
Omaha Personal Crisis Service, Inc.
4102 Woolworth Ave.
Omaha, NE 68105
Crisis Phone 1: (402) 444-7335
Business Phone: (402) 444-7335
Hrs Avail: 24

NEVADA

Las Vegas
Las Vegas Suicide Prevention Center
2408 Santa Clara Dr.
Las Vegas, NV 89104
Crisis Phone 1: (702) 732-1622
Business Phone: (702) 732-1622
Hrs Avail: 24

Reno
* Suicide Prev. & Crisis Call Center
P.O. Box 8016
Reno, NV 89507
Crisis Phone 1: (702) 323-6111
Business Phone: (702) 323-4533
Hrs Avail: 24

NEW HAMPSHIRE

Claremont
*# Intake/Crisis/Evaluation Unit
Counseling Center of Sullivan Co.
18 Bailey Ave.
Claremont, NH 03743
Crisis Phone 1: (603) 542-2578
Business Phone: (603) 542-2578
Hrs Avail: 24

Concord
*# Emergency Services/Concord
CNHCMS, Inc.
P.O. Box 2032
Concord, NH 03301
Crisis Phone 1: (603) 228-1551
Business Phone: (603) 228-1551
Hrs Avail: 24

Dover
* Strafford Guidance Center, Inc.
Emergency Crisis Team
180 Washington St.
Dover, NH 03820
Crisis Phone 1: (603) 742-0630
Crisis Phone 2: (603) 332-8090
Business Phone: (603) 742-0630
Hrs Avail: 24

Keene
The Samaritans of Keene
25 Lamson St.
Keene, NH 03431
Crisis Phone 1: (603) 357-5505
Business Phone: (603) 357-5505
Hrs Avail: 24

Lebanon
* Headrest, Inc.
14 Church St.
P.O. Box 221
Lebanon, NH 03766
Crisis Phone 1: (603) 448-4400
Business Phone: (603) 448-4872
Hrs Avail: 24

Manchester
*# Greater Manchester MHC
401 Cypress St.
Manchester, NH 03103
Crisis Phone 1: (603) 668-4111
Business Phone: (603) 668-4111
Hrs Avail: 24

Portsmouth
* Seacoast Mental Health Center
1145 Sagamore Ave.
Portsmouth, NH 03801
Crisis Phone 1: (603) 431-6703
Business Phone: (603) 431-6703
Hrs Avail: 24

Salem
*# Center For Life Management
Salem Prof Park
44 Stiles Rd.
Salem, NH 03079
Crisis Phone 1: (603) 432-2253
Business Phone: (603) 893-3548
Hrs Avail: 24

NEW JERSEY

Atlantic City
Crisis Intervention Program/AC
Atlantic City Medical Center
1925 Pacific Ave.
Atlantic City, NJ 08401
Crisis Phone 1: (609) 344-1118
Business Phone: (609) 344-1118
Hrs Avail: 24

Bridgewater
Guideline
500 N. Bridge
Bridgewater, NJ 08807
Crisis Phone 1: (201) 526-4100
Business Phone: (201) 725-2800
Hrs Avail: 24

Camden
* Emergency and Advocacy Services
Guidance Center of Camden Co., Inc

1600 Haddon Ave.
Camden, NJ 08103
Crisis Phone 1: (609) 428-4357
Crisis Phone 2: (609) 541-2222
Business Phone: (609) 428-1300
Hrs Avail: 24

Cherry Hill
Contact "609"
1050 N. Kings Highway
Cherry Hill, NJ 08034
Crisis Phone 1: (609) 667-3000
Crisis Phone 2: (609) 428-2900
Business Phone: (609) 667-0285
Hrs Avail: 24

Flemington
Hunterdon Helpline
Rt. 31, Box 36
Flemington, NJ 08822
Crisis Phone 1: (201) 782-4357
Business Phone: (201) 782-4357
Hrs Avail: 24

Glassboro
Together, Inc.
7 State St.
Glassboro, NJ 08028
Crisis Phone 1: (609) 881-4040
Business Phone: (609) 881-7045
Hrs Avail: 24

Hackensack
* So. Bergen Mental Health Center
Bergen Regional Couns. Center
395 Main St.
Hackensack, NJ 07601
Crisis Phone 1: (201) 460-0160
Business Phone: (201) 460-0160
Hrs Avail: 24

Linwood
Contact Atlantic City
P.O. Box 181
Linwood, NJ 08221
Crisis Phone 1: (609) 646-6616
Business Phone: (609) 646-2101
Hrs Avail: 24

Manchester
Greater Manchester MHC
401 Cypress St.
Manchester, NJ 03103
Crisis Phone 1: (603) 688-4111
Business Phone: (603) 688-4111
Hrs Avail: 24

Millville
Cumberland Co. Guidance Center
RD 1, Carmel Rd.
P.O. Box 808
Millville, NJ 08332
Crisis Phone 1: (609) 327-2222
Business Phone: (609) 825-6810
Hrs Avail: 24

Montclair
North Essex Help Line
Mental Health Resource Center
60 S. Fullerton Ave.
Montclair, NJ 07042
Crisis Phone 1: (201) 744-1954
Business Phone: (201) 744-6522
Hrs Avail: 24

Moorestown
Contact Burlington Co.
P.O. Box 333
Moorestown, NJ 08057
Crisis Phone 1: (609) 234-8888
Business Phone: (609) 234-5484
Hrs Avail: 24

Morristown
Memo Helpline
100 Madison Ave.
Morristown, NJ 07960
Crisis Phone 1: (201) 540-5045
Business Phone: (201) 540-5168
Hrs Avail: 24

Mt. Holly
Screening and Crisis Interv. Program
Co. Memorial Hospital
175 Madison Ave.
Mt. Holly, NJ 08060
Crisis Phone 1: (609) 261-8000

Business Phone: (609) 267-0700, x609
Hrs Avail: 24

Newark
Newark Emergency Services
Mt. Carmel Guild Community MHC
17 Mulberry St.
Newark, NJ 07102
Crisis Phone 1: (201) 596-4100
Business Phone: (201) 596-4100
Hrs Avail: 24

Pequannock
Contact Morris-Passaic
P.O. Box 219
Pequannock, NJ 07440
Crisis Phone 1: (201) 831-1870
Business Phone: (201) 831-1870
Hrs Avail: 24

Red Bank
Helpline - Crisis Unit
Riverview Medical Center
Children's Psych. Center
35 Union St.
Red Bank, NJ 07701
Crisis Phone 1: (201) 671-5250
Business Phone: (201) 530-2438
Hrs Avail: 24

Richwood
Contact Gloucester Co.
P.O. Box 222
Richwood, NJ 08074
Crisis Phone 1: (609) 881-6200
Business Phone: (609) 881-6200
Hrs Avail: 24

Roselle
Contact Union-Essex
P.O. Box 225
Roselle, NJ 07203
Crisis Phone 1: (201) 527-0555
Business Phone: (201) 241-9350
Hrs Avail: 24

Salem
Contact Help of Salem Co.
P.O. Box 36
Salem, NJ 08079
Crisis Phone 1: (609) 935-4357
Business Phone: (609) 935-4484
Hrs Avail: 24

Toms River
Contact of Ocean County
P.O. Box 1121
Toms River, NJ 08753
Crisis Phone 1: (201) 240-6100
Business Phone: (201) 240-6104
Hrs Avail: 24

Union
Communication-Help Center
Kean College of New Jersey
Morris Avenue
Union, NJ 07083
Crisis Phone 1: (201) 527-2360
Crisis Phone 2: (201) 527-2330
Crisis Phone 3: (201) 289-2101
Business Phone: (201) 289-2100
Hrs Avail: 9 A.M.-1 A.M.

West Trenton
Contact of Mercer County, NJ, Inc.
Katzenbach School for the Deaf
310 Sullivan Way
W. Trenton, NJ 08628
Crisis Phone 1: (609) 883-2880
TTY: (609) 587-3050
TTY: (609) 452-1919
Business Phone: (609) 883-2880
Hrs Avail: 24

Westfield
Contact-We Care
P.O. Box 37
Westfield, NJ 07090
Crisis Phone 1: (201) 232-2880
Crisis Phone 2: (201) 132-3333
Business Phone: (201) 232-2936
Hrs Avail: 24

NEW MEXICO

Albuquerque
Crisis Unit

Bernalillo Co. Mental Health Center
2600 Marble N.E.
Albuquerque, NM 87106
Crisis Phone 1: (505) 843-2800
Business Phone: (505) 843-2800
Hrs Avail: 24

Albuquerque
Agora
The Univ. of New Mexico Crisis Ctr.
Student Union
P.O. Box 29
Albuquerque, NM 87131
Crisis Phone 1: (505) 277-3013
Business Phone: (505) 277-3013
Hrs Avail: 24

NEW YORK

Albany
Capitol Dist. Psychiatric Center
75 New Scotland Ave.
Albany, NY 12208
Crisis Phone 1: (518) 447-9650
Business Phone: (518) 844-7965
Hrs Avail: 24

Albany
Refer Switchboard
Project Equinox
70 Central Ave.
Albany, NY 12210
Crisis Phone 1: (518) 434-1200
Business Phone: (518) 434-1200
Hrs Avail: 24

Albany
Samaritans of Capitol Dist.
200 Central Ave.
Albany, NY 12206
Crisis Phone 1: (518) 463-2323
Business Phone: (518) 463-0861
Hrs Avail: 24

Bellmore
Middle Earth Crisis Counseling & Referral Center
2740 Martin Ave.
Bellmore, NY 11710
Crisis Phone 1: (516) 826-0600
Business Phone: (516) 826-0244
Hrs Avail: 24

Berlin
Berlin Emergency Services
Androscoggin Valley MH Clinic
Pageville Rd.
Berlin, NY 03570
Crisis Phone 1: (603) 752-7404
Business Phone: (603) 752-7404
Hrs Avail: 24

Buffalo
Buffalo Suicide Prev. & Crisis Serv
3258 Main St.
Buffalo, NY 14214
Crisis Phone 1: (716) 834-3131
Business Phone: (716) 834-3131
Hrs Avail: 24

Ellenville
Family of Woodstock, Inc.
Ellenville, NY 12428
Crisis Phone 1: (914) 626-8109
Business Phone: (914) 626-8109
Hrs Avail: 24

Goshen
Orange County Help Line
Mental Health Association
255 Greenwich Ave
Goshen, NY 10924
Crisis Phone 1: (914) 343-6906
Crisis Phone 2: (914) 294-9355
Crisis Phone 3: (914) 294-9445
Crisis Phone 4: (914) 342-5871
Crisis Phone 5: (914) 565-6381
Business Phone: (914) 294-7411
Hrs Avail: 24

Islip
Islip Hotline
Town Hall
Islip, NY 11751
Crisis Phone 1: (516) 277-4700

Business Phone: (516) 277-4700
Hrs Avail: 9 A.M.-12 A.M.

Ithaca
*# Suicide Prevention & Crisis Service
P.O. Box 312
Ithaca, NY 14850
Crisis Phone 1: (607) 272-1616
Business Phone: (607) 272-1505
Hrs Avail: 24

Jamestown
Jamestown Crisis Line
Jamestown General Hospital
Jamestown, NY 14701
Crisis Phone 1: (716) 484-1314
Business Phone: (716) 484-1161, x321
Hrs Avail: 24

Lincroft
Contact Monmouth County
P.O. Box 137
Lincroft, NY 07738
Crisis Phone 1: (201) 544-1444
Business Phone: (201) 544-1444
Hrs Avail: 24

New Paltz
Family of New Paltz
2 Church St.
New Paltz, NY 12561
Crisis Phone 1: (914) 255-8801
Business Phone: (914) 255-8801
Hrs Avail: 24

New Paltz
Oasis
Counseling Center
State Univ. College
New Paltz, NY 12561
Crisis Phone 1: (914) 257-2141
Business Phone: (914) 257-2250
Hrs Avail: 24

New York
Help-Line Telephone Services
3 W. 19th St., Suite 1010
New York, NY 10001
Crisis Phone 1: (212) 532-2400
TTY: (212) 532-0942
Business Phone: (212) 684-4480
Hrs Avail: 24

Niagara Falls
Niagara Hotline/Crisis Interv. Serv.
775 3rd St.
Niagara Falls, NY 14302
Crisis Phone 1: (716) 285-3515
Business Phone: (716) 285-9636
Hrs Avail: 24

Oneonta
Project 85
259 Chestnut St.
Oneonta, NY 14302
Crisis Phone 1: (607) 432-2111
Business Phone: (607) 432-2111
Hrs Avail: 24

Peekskill
Peekskill Crisis Intervention
1137 Main St.
Peekskill, NY 10566
Crisis Phone 1: (914) 739-6403
Business Phone: (914) 739-6403
Hrs Avail: 24

Plattsburgh
Plattsburgh Comm. Crisis Center
29 Protection Ave.
Plattsburgh, NY 12901
Crisis Phone 1: (518) 561-2330
Business Phone: (518) 561-2331
Hrs Avail: 24

Queens Village
Dial-For-Help
Creedmor Psychiatric Center
80-45 Winchester Blvd.
Queens Village, NY 11427
Crisis Phone 1: (212) 464-7515
Business Phone: (212) 464-7500, x3111
Hrs Avail: 24

Rochester
* Life Line/Health Assn. of Rochester
973 East Ave.
Rochester, NY 14607

Crisis Phone 1: (716) 275-5151
Business Phone: (716) 271-3540
Hrs Avail: 24

Stony Brook
* Response of Suffolk Co., Inc.
P.O. Box 300
Stony Brook, NY 11790
Crisis Phone 1: (516) 751-7500
Business Phone: (516) 751-7620
Hrs Avail: 24

Syracuse
Contact Syracuse
958 Salt Springs Rd.
Syracuse, NY 13224
Crisis Phone 1: (315) 445-1500
Business Phone: (315) 446-2610
Hrs Avail: 24

Syracuse
Suicide Prev/Crisis Counsel. Serv.
St. Joseph's Hospital Health Center
301 Prospect Ave.
Syracuse, NY 13203
Crisis Phone 1: (315) 474-1333
Business Phone: (315) 474-1333
Hrs Avail: 24

Utica
Utica Crisis Intervention
1213 Court St., Cottage 46
Utica, NY 13502
Crisis Phone 1: (315) 736-0883
Rome: (315) 337-7299
Herkimer: (315) 866-0123
Business Phone: (315) 797-6800, x4210
Hrs Avail: 24

Valhalla
Crisis Intervention Unit
Westchester County Medical Center
Grasslands Rd.
Valhalla, NY 10595
Crisis Phone 1: (914) 347-7075
Business Phone: (914) 347-7075
Hrs Avail: 24

White Plains
Suicide Preven./Crisis Interv. Serv.
MHA of Westchester Co., Inc.
29 Sterling Ave.
White Plains, NY 10606
Suicide Prev. Serv: (914) 946-0121
Crisis Interv. Serv.: (914) 949-6741
Business Phone: (914) 949-6741
Hrs Avail: 24

Woodstock
Family of Woodstock
16 Rock City Rd.
Woodstock, NY 12498
Crisis Phone 1: (914) 338-2370
Business Phone: (914) 338-2370
Hrs Avail: 24

NORTH CAROLINA

Asheville
Contact-Asheville/Buncombe
P.O. Box 6747
Asheville, NC 28816
Crisis Phone 1: (704) 253-4357
Business Phone: (704) 252-7703
Hrs Avail: 24

Burlington
*# Suicide & Crisis Serv/Alamance Co.
P.O. Box 2573
Burlington, NC 27215
Crisis Phone 1: (919) 227-6220
Business Phone: (919) 228-1720
Hrs Avail: 24

Chapel Hill
Chapel Hill Helpline
333 McMasters St.
Chapel Hill, NC 27514
Crisis Phone 1: (919) 929-0479
Business Phone: (919) 929-0479
Hrs Avail: 24

Charlotte
Contact Tele. Counseling
501 N. Tryon St.

Charlotte, NC 28202
Crisis Phone 1: (704) 333-6121
Business Phone: (704) 333-6121
Hrs Avail: 24

Charlotte
The Relatives, Inc.
1000 E. Boulevard
Charlotte, NC 28203
Crisis Phone 1: (704) 377-0602
Business Phone: (704) 377-0602
Hrs Avail: 24

Durham
Contact Durham
806 A Clarendon St.
Durham, NC 27705
Crisis Phone 1: (919) 683-1595
Business Phone: (919) 286-4175
Hrs Avail: 24

Durham
* Helpline of Durham
414 E. Main St.
Durham, NC 27701
Crisis Phone 1: (919) 683-8628
Business Phone: (919) 683-2392
Hrs Avail: 24

Fayetteville
Contact of Fayetteville, Inc
P.O. Box 456
Fayetteville, NC 28302
Crisis Phone 1: (919) 485-4134
Business Phone: (919) 483-8970
Hrs Avail: 24

Franklin
Respect, Inc.
431 Wide Horizon Dr
Franklin, NC 28734
Crisis Phone 1: (704) 369-6143
Business Phone: (704) 369-7333
Hrs Avail: 24

Goldsboro
Wayne Co. MHC Hotline
301 N. Herman St.
Goldsboro, NC 27514
Crisis Phone 1: (919) 735-4357
Business Phone: (919) 736-7330
Hrs Avail: 24

Greensboro
Crisis Control Center, Inc.
P.O. Box 735
Greensboro, NC 27402
Crisis Phone 1: (919) 852-4444
Business Phone: (919) 852-6366
Hrs Avail: 24

Greensboro
Switchboard Crisis Center
330 S. Greene
Greensboro, NC 27402
Crisis Phone 1: (919) 275-0896
Business Phone: (919) 275-9341
Hrs Avail: 24

Greenville
Real Crisis Interv., Inc
312 E. 10th St.
Greenville, NC 28203
Crisis Phone 1: (919) 758-HELP
Crisis Phone 2: (919) 758-0787
Business Phone: (704) 377-0602
Hrs Avail: 24

Harrellsville
Roanoke-Chowan
Human Services Center
Wiccacon Center
P.O. Box 407
Harrellsville, NC 27942
Crisis Phone 1: (919) 332-4442
Business Phone: (919) 356-2938
Hrs Avail: 24

High Point
Contact High Point
462 S. Main St.
High Point, NC 27260
Crisis Phone 1: (919) 882-8121
Business Phone: (919) 885-0191
Hrs Avail: 24

Lexington
Contact Lexington

P.O. Box 924
Lexington, NC 27292
Crisis Phone 1: (704) 249-8974
Business Phone: (704) 249-8824
Hrs Avail: 24

Manteo
Outer Banks Hotline
P.O. Box 1417
Manteo, NC 27954
Crisis Phone 1: (919) 473-3366
Crisis Phone 2: (919) 995-5104
Crisis Phone 3: (919) 338-2829
Business Phone: (919) 437-5121
Hrs Avail: 24

Morehead
Helpline of Morehead
P.O. Box 3537
Morehead, NC 28557
Crisis Phone 1: (919) 247-3023
Business Phone: (919) 247-3023
Hrs Avail: 24

Raleigh
Hopeline, Inc.
P.O. Box 6036
Raleigh, NC 27628
Crisis Phone 1: (919) 755-6555
Business Phone: (919) 755-6555
Hrs Avail: 24

Roanoke Rapids
Roanoke Rapids Crisis Line
Halifax Co. Mental Health
P.O. Box 1199
Roanoke Rapids, NC 27870
Crisis Phone 1: (919) 537-2909
Business Phone: (919) 537-2909
Hrs Avail: 24

Salisbury
Salisbury Dial Help
156 Mahaley
Salisbury, NC 28144
Crisis Phone 1: (704) 636-9222
Business Phone: (704) 633-3616
Hrs Avail: 24

Sanford
Lee County MH Crisis Line
130 Carbonton Rd.
Sanford, NC 27330
Crisis Phone 1: (919) 774-4520
Business Phone: (919) 774-6521
Hrs Avail: 24

Smithfield
Contact Johnston Co.
140 Market St.
Smithfield, NC 27577
Crisis Phone 1: (919) 934-6161
Business Phone: (919) 934-6979
Hrs Avail: 24

Statesville
The Cup of Water, Inc.
125 W. Bell St.
Statesville, NC 28677
Crisis Phone 1: (704) 872-7638
Business Phone: (704) 872-7638
Hrs Avail: 24

Wilmington
Crisis Line/Open House
419 Chestnut St.
Wilmington, NC 28401
Crisis Phone 1: (919) 763-3695
Business Phone: (919) 343-0145
Hrs Avail: 24

Wilson
Wilson Crisis Center
P.O. Box 593
Wilson, NC 27893
Crisis Phone 1: (919) 237-5156
Business Phone: (919) 237-5156
Hrs Avail: 24

Winston-Salem
Contact: Winston-Salem
1111 W. First St.
Winston-Salem, NC 27101
Crisis Phone 1: (919) 722-5153
Business Phone: (919) 723-4338
Hrs Avail: 24

NORTH DAKOTA

Beulah
* Mercer County Women's Resource Center
Hillside Office Complex
Highway 49 NW
Beulah, ND 58523
Crisis Phone 1: (701) 748-2274
Business Phone: (701) 873-2274
Hrs Avail: 24

Bismarck
Crisis and Emergency Services
West Central Human Service Center
600 S. 2nd St.
Bismarck, ND 58501
Crisis Phone 1: (701) 255-3090
Business Phone: (701) 255-3090
Hrs Avail: 24

Fargo
Fargo Hotline
P.O. Box 447
Fargo, ND 58107
Crisis Phone 1: (701) 235-7335
Crisis Phone 2: (701) 232-4357
Business Phone: (701) 293-6462
Hrs Avail: 24

Grand Forks
Grand Forks MH Crisis Line
1407 24th Ave. S.
Grand Forks, ND 58201
Crisis Phone 1: (701) 775-0525
Business Phone: (701) 746-9411
Hrs Avail: 24

Minot
Minot Suicide Prevention Service
St. Joseph's Hospital
Minot, ND 58701
Crisis Phone 1: (701) 839-2222
Business Phone: (701) 857-2000
Hrs Avail: 24

OHIO

Akron
*# Support, Inc.
1361 W. Market St.
Akron, OH 44313
Crisis Phone 1: (216) 434-9144
Business Phone: (216) 864-7743
Hrs Avail: 24

Ashtabula
Contact Ashtabula
P.O. Box 674
Ashtabula, OH 44004
Crisis Phone 1: (216) 998-2607
Business Phone: (216) 998-2609
Hrs Avail: 24

Athens
Care Line, Inc.
28 W. Stimson
Athens, OH 45701
Crisis Phone 1: (614) 593-3344
Business Phone: (614) 593-3346
Hrs Avail: 24

Bucyrus
Contact Crawford Co.
P.O. Box 631
Bucyrus, OH 44820
Crisis Phone 1: (419) 562-9010
Enterprise: (419) 468-9081
Business Phone: (419) 562-9099
Hrs Avail: 24

Canton
*# Crisis Interv. Center of Stark Co.
2421 13th St., N.W.
Canton, OH 44708
Crisis Phone 1: (216) 452-6000
Business Phone: (216) 452-9812
Hrs Avail: 24

Chillicothe
Chillicothe Crisis Center
Scioto-Paint Valley MH Center

425 Chestnut St.
Chillicothe, OH 45601
Crisis Phone 1: (614) 773-4357
Business Phone: (614) 773-0760
Hrs Avail: 24

Cincinnati
* 281-Care/Talbert House
3891 Reading Rd.
Cincinnati, OH 45206
Crisis Phone 1: (513) 281-2273
Business Phone: (513) 281-2866
Hrs Avail: 24

Cincinnati
Contact Queen City
P.O. Box 42071
Cincinnati, OH 45242
Crisis Phone 1: (513) 791-4673
Business Phone: (513) 791-5673
Hrs Avail: 24

Columbus
Suicide Prevention Services
1301 High
Columbus, OH 43201
Crisis Phone 1: (614) 221-5445
Business Phone: (614) 299-6600
Hrs Avail: 24

Dayton
Contact Dayton
P.O. Box 125
Dayton, OH 45459
Crisis Phone 1: (513) 434-6684
Business Phone: (513) 434-1798
Hrs Avail: 24

Dayton
*# Suicide Prevention Center, Inc.
184 Salem Ave.
Dayton, OH 45406
Crisis Phone 1: (513) 223-4777
Business Phone: (513) 223-9096
Hrs Avail: 24

Delaware
* Help Anonymous, Inc.
11 E. Central Ave.
Delaware, OH 43015
Crisis Phone 1: (614) 369-3316
Crisis Phone 2: (614) 548-7324
Business Phone: (614) 363-1835
Hrs Avail: 24

Dover
Crisis Help Line
201 Hospital Dr.
Dover, OH 44622
Crisis Phone 1: (216) 343-1811
Business Phone: (216) 343-6631
Hrs Avail: 24

Eaton
Preble Counseling Center Hotline
101 North Barron St.
Eaton, OH 45320
Crisis Phone 1: (513) 456-1166
Business Phone: (513) 456-1166
Hrs Avail: 24

Fostoria
Bureau of Concern
716 N. County Line St.
Fostoria, OH 44830
Crisis Phone 1: (419) 435-4357
Business Phone: (419) 435-4357
Hrs Avail: 8:30 A.M.-5 P.M., M-F

Greenville
Crisis Hotline
Drake County Mental Health Clinic
212 E. Main
Greenville, OH 45331
Crisis Phone 1: (513) 548-1635
Business Phone: (513) 548-1635
Hrs Avail: 24

Kent
Townhall II Helpline
225 E. College St.
Kent, OH 44240
Crisis Phone 1: (216) 678-4357
Business Phone: (216) 678-3006
Hrs Avail: 24

Lancaster
Info. & Crisis Serv./Fairfield Co.

P.O. Box 1054
Lancaster, OH 43130
Crisis Phone 1: (614) 687-0500
Business Phone: (614) 687-0500
Hrs Avail: 24

Mansfield
Help Line/Adapt
741 Sholl Rd.
Mansfield, OH 44907
Crisis Phone 1: (419) 522-4357
Business Phone: (419) 526-4332
Hrs Avail: 24

Marion
Care Line
320 Executive Dr.
Marion, OH 43302
Crisis Phone 1: (614) 387-7200
Business Phone: (614) 387-7200
Hrs Avail: 24

Marysville
Marysville Crisis Hotline
Charles B. Mills Center
715 Plum St.
Marysville, OH 43040
Crisis Phone 1: (513) 644-6363
Plain City: (614) 873-8610
Richwood: (614) 943-2916
Business Phone: (513) 644-9192
Hrs Avail: 24

Medina
Medina Crisis Intervention Help Line
Catholic Social Services
246 Northland Dr.
Medina, OH 44256
Crisis Phone 1: (216) 725-4357
Crisis Phone 2: (216) 225-4357
Crisis Phone 3: (216) 336-4357
Business Phone: (216) 725-4923
Hrs Avail: 24

Mt. Gilead
* Hope Line, Inc.
P.O. Box 142
Mt. Gilead, OH 43338
Crisis Phone 1: (419) 947-2520
Business Phone: (419) 947-2520
Hrs Avail: 24

Oxford
Oxford Crisis & Referral Center
111 E. Walnut St.
Oxford, OH 45056
Crisis Phone 1: (513) 523-4146
Business Phone: (513) 523-4148
Hrs Avail: 24

Shelby
Shelby Helpline
60 1/2 West Main St.
Shelby, OH 44875
Crisis Phone 1: (419) 347-6307
Business Phone: (419) 347-6307
Hrs Avail: 7 A.M.-7 P.M.

Springfield
Suicide Prev. Center Life-Line
1101 East High St.
Springfield, OH 45505
Crisis Phone 1: (513) 322-5433
Business Phone: (513) 328-5300
Hrs Avail: 24

Toledo
* The New Rescue Crisis Service
3314 Collingwood Ave.
Toledo, OH 43610
Crisis Phone 1: (419) 255-5500
Business Phone: (419) 255-5500
Hrs Avail: 24

Toledo
Toledo First Call For Help
1 Stranahan Sq. #141
Toledo, OH 43604
Crisis Phone 1: (419) 244-3728
Business Phone: (419) 244-3728
Hrs Avail: 24

Warren
* Contact Community Connection
P.O. Box 1403
Warren, OH 44482
Crisis Phone 1: (216) 393-1565

Crisis Phone 2: (216) 545-4371
Business Phone: (216) 395-5255
Hrs Avail: 24

Wooster
Dial A Friend
P.O. Box 303
Wooster, OH 44691
Crisis Phone 1: (216) 262-9999
Business Phone: (216) 262-9499
Hrs Avail: 2 P.M. to 12 P.M.

Xenia
Greene County Crisis Center
452 W. Market
Xenia, OH 45385
Crisis Phone 1: (513) 429-0679
Crisis Phone 2: (513) 429-0933
Business Phone: (513) 376-8700
Hrs Avail: 24

Youngstown
*# Help Hotline, Inc.
P.O. Box 46
Youngstown, OH 44501
Crisis Phone 1: (216) 747-2696
Crisis Phone 2: (216) 424-7767
Crisis Phone 3: (216) 426-9355
TTY: (216) 744-0579
Business Phone: (216) 747-5111
Hrs Avail: 24

Zanesville
* Six County, Inc. Crisis Hotline
2845 Bell St.
Zanesville, OH 43701
Crisis Phone 1: (614) 452-8403
Business Phone: (614) 454-9766
Hrs Avail: 24

OKLAHOMA

Clinton
Contact Western Oklahoma
P.O. Box 572
Clinton, OK 73601
Crisis Phone 1: (405) 323-1064
Business Phone: (405) 323-1064
Hrs Avail: 24

Enid
Contact Northwest Oklahoma
P.O. Box 3165
Enid, OK 73702
Crisis Phone 1: (405) 234-1111
Business Phone: (405) 237-8400
Hrs Avail: 11 A.M.-11 P.M.

Lawton
Crisis Telephone Service
P.O. Box 2011
Lawton, OK 73502
Crisis Phone 1: (405) 355-7575
Business Phone: (405) 355-7575
Hrs Avail: 24

Norman
United Way Helpline
319 W. Main St.
Norman, OK 73069
Crisis Phone 1: (405) 364-3800
Business Phone: (405) 364-3800
Hrs Avail: 8 A.M.-5 P.M.

Oklahoma City
* Contact of Metro. Oklahoma City
P.O. Box 12832
Oklahoma City, OK 73157
Crisis Phone 1: (405) 848-2273
Business Phone: (405) 840-9396
Hrs Avail: 24

Ponca City
Helpline/Ponca City
P.O. Box 375
Ponca City, OK 74602
Crisis Phone 1: (405) 765-5551
Business Phone: (405) 765-5551
Hrs Avail: 24

Tulsa
Tulsa Helpline
P.O. Box 52847
Tulsa, OK 74152
Crisis Phone 1: (918) 583-4357
Business Phone: (918) 585-1144
Hrs Avail: 24

OREGON

Albany
Linn County Mental Health
P.O. Box 100
Albany, OR 97321
Crisis Phone 1: (503) 757-2299
Business Phone: (503) 967-3866
Hrs Avail: 24

Corvallis
Benton County Mental Health
530 N.W. 27th
Corvallis, OR 97330
Crisis Phone 1: (503) 757-2299
Business Phone: (503) 757-6846
Hrs Avail: 24

Eugene
Mental Health Emergency Center/CIRT
151 W. 5th St.
Eugene, OR 97401
Crisis Phone 1: (503) 687-4000
Business Phone: (503) 687-3608
Hrs Avail: 24

Eugene
Whitebird Clinic Med. Aid Station
341 E. 12th
Eugene, OR 97401
Crisis Phone 1: (503) 342-8255
Business Phone: (503) 342-8255
Hrs Avail: 24

Grants Pass
Josephine County Info & Ref Serv.-H.L.
P.O. Box 670
Grants Pass, OR 97526
Crisis Phone 1: (503) 479-help
Business Phone: (503) 479-2349
Hrs Avail: 24

Klamath Falls
Hope In Crisis
P.O. Box 951
Klamath Falls, OR 97601
Crisis Phone 1: (503) 884-0636
Business Phone: (503) 882-8974
Hrs Avail: 24

Medford
Crisis Intervention Services
P.O. Box 819
Medford, OR 97501
Crisis Phone 1: (503) 779-4357
Business Phone: (503) 779-4490
Hrs Avail: 24

Portland
* Metro Crisis Intervention Service
P.O. Box 637
Portlant, OR 97207
Crisis Phone 1: (503) 223-6161
Business Phone: (503) 226-3099
Hrs Avail: 24

Salem
Northwest Human Services, Inc.
674 Church St. N.
Salem, OR 97303
Crisis Phone 1: (503) 581-5535
Business Phone: (503) 588-5828
Hrs Avail: 24

PENNSYLVANIA

Allentown
Lehigh Valley
Lifeline-Valley Wide Help
1244 Hamilton St.
Allentown, PA 18102
Crisis Phone 1: (215) 435-7111
Business Phone: (215) 435-7111
Hrs Avail: 24

Allentown
Crisis Intervention Team
Lehigh County
512 Hamilton St., Suite 300
Allentown, PA 18101
Crisis Phone 1: (215) 820-3127
Business Phone: (215) 820-3127
Hrs Avail: 24

Altoona
Contact Altoona
P.O. Box 11

Altoona, PA 16603
Crisis Phone 1: (814) 946-9050
Business Phone: (814) 946-0531
Hrs Avail: 24

Bethlehem
Crisis Intervention Team (MH/MR)
Northampton County
Broad & New Streets
Bethlehem, PA 18018
Crisis Phone 1: (215) 865-0944
Business Phone: (215) 865-0944
Hrs Avail: 24

Chambersburg
Contact Chambersburg
221 N. Main St.
Chambersburg, PA 17201
Crisis Phone 1: (717) 264-7799
Business Phone: (717) 263-8007
Hrs Avail: 24

Darby
* Psych. Crisis Center
Fitzgerald Mercy Hospital
Darby, PA 19023
Crisis Phone 1: (215) 565-4300
Business Phone: (215) 565-2041
Hrs Avail: 24

Erie
Info. & Referral Division
United Way of Erie County
110 W. 10th St.
Erie, PA 16501-1466
Erie Hotline: (814) 453-5656
Business Phone: (814) 456-2937
Hrs Avail: 24

Gettysburg
Adams/Hanover Counseling Service
37 West St.
Gettysburg, PA 17325
Crisis Phone 1: (717) 334-9111
Business Phone: (717) 334-9111
Hrs Avail: 24

Harrisburg
Contact Harrisburg
P.O. Box 6270
Harrisburg, PA 17112
Crisis Phone 1: (717) 652-4400
Business Phone: (717) 652-4987
Hrs Avail: 24

Indiana
The Open Door
1008 Philadelphia St.
Indiana, PA 15701
Crisis Phone 1: (412) 465-2605
Business Phone: (412) 456-2605
Hrs Avail: 24

Lancaster
Contact Lancaster
447 E. King St.
Lancaster, PA 17602
Crisis Phone 1: (717) 299-4855
Business Phone: (717) 291-2261
Hrs Avail: 24

Media
Delaware Co. Crisis Intervention/SPS
600 N. Olive St.
Media, PA 19063
Crisis Phone 1: (215) 565-4300
Business Phone: (215) 565-2041
Hrs Avail: 24

Nanticoke
Hazelton-Nanticoke Crisis Services
Hazelton-Nanticoke MHC
W. Washington, St.
Nanticoke, PA 18634
Crisis Phone 1: (717) 735-7590
Business Phone: (717) 735-7590
Hrs Avail: 24

New Bloomfield
Perry County Hotline
Perry Human Services
Courthouse Annex
New Bloomfield, PA 17068
Crisis Phone 1: (717) 582-8052
Business Phone: (717) 582-8703
Hrs Avail: 24

New Brighton
Contact Beaver Valley
P.O. Box 75
New Brighton, PA 15066
Crisis Phone 1: (412) 728-3650
Business Phone: (412) 728-3650
Hrs Avail: 24

New Castle
Contact E.A.R.S.
P.O. Box 7804
New Castle, PA 16107
Crisis Phone 1: (412) 658-5529
Business Phone: (412) 652-0333
Hrs Avail: 24

Newtown
Contact Lower Bucks
P.O. Box 376
Newtown, PA 18940
Crisis Phone 1: (215) 752-1850
Business Phone: (215) 860-1803
Hrs Avail: 24

Norristown
Montgomery Co. MH/MR Emerg. Serv.
Bldg 16, Stangridge & Sterigere
Norristown, PA 19401
Crisis Phone 1: (215) 279-6100
Business Phone: (215) 277-6225
Hrs Avail: 24

Philadelphia
Contact Philadelphia
P.O. Box 12586
Philadelphia, PA 19151
Crisis Phone 1: (215) 879-4402
Business Phone: (215) 877-9099
Hrs Avail: 24

Philadelphia
Philadelphia Suicide & C.I. Center
1101 Market, 7th Floor
Philadelphia, PA 19107
Crisis Phone 1: (215) 686-4420
Business Phone: (215) 592-5565
Hrs Avail: 24

Pittsburgh
see Glenshaw

Pittsburgh
* Helpline/Pittsburgh
200 Ross St.
Pittsburgh, PA 15219
Crisis Phone 1: (412) 255-1155
Business Phone: (412) 255-1133
Hrs Avail: 24

Scranton
Free Info & Referral System Teleph.
200 Adams Ave.
Scranton, PA 18503
Crisis Phone 1: (717) 961-1234
Business Phone: (717) 961-1234
Hrs Avail: 24

Shamokin Dam
S.U.N. Contact
P.O. Box 442
Shamokin Dam, PA 17862
Snyder, Union: (717) 743-4357
Northumberland: (717) 286-2800
Business Phone: (717) 743-5534
Hrs Avail: 24

Sharpsville
Contact Penn-Ohio
P.O. Box 91
Sharpsville, PA 16150
Crisis Phone 1: (412) 962-5777
Business Phone: (412) 962-5777
Hrs Avail: 8 A.M.-Midnight

Wilkes Barre
Luzerne/Wyoming Co. MH/MR Center 1
103 S. Main St.
Wilkes Barre, PA 18702
Crisis Phone 1: (717) 823-2155
Business Phone: (717) 823-2155
Hrs Avail: 24

Williamsport
Williamsport Helpline
815 W. 4th St.
Williamsport, PA 17701
Crisis Phone 1: (717) 323-8555

Crisis Phone 2: (800) 624-4636
Business Phone: (717) 323-8555
Hrs Avail: 24

York
Contact York
145 S. Duke St.
York, PA 17403
Crisis Phone 1: (717) 845-3656
Business Phone: (717) 845-9125
Hrs Avail: 24

RHODE ISLAND

Providence
* The Samaritans of Providence
33 Chestnut St.
Providence, RI 02903
Crisis Phone 1: (401) 272-4044
Business Phone: (401) 272-4044
Hrs Avail: 24

Wakefield
Sympatico
29 Columbia St.
Wakefield, RI 02879
Crisis Phone 1: (401) 783-0650
Business Phone: (401) 783-0782
Hrs Avail: 24

SOUTH CAROLINA

Aiken
Aiken County Crisis Line
P.O. Box 2712
Aiken, SC 29801
Crisis Phone 1: (803) 648-9900
Business Phone: (803) 648-0000
Hrs Avail: 24

Charleston Hts.
P.O. Box 71583
Charleston Hts., SC 29415-1583
Crisis Phone 1: (803) 744-4357
Business Phone: (803) 747-3007
Hrs Avail: 24

Chesnee
Heartline, Inc.
Rt. 3 Box 442
Chesnee, SC 29323
Crisis Phone 1: (803) 461-7301
Business Phone: (803) 461-7301
Hrs Avail: 24

Columbia
* Helpline of Midland, Inc.
P.O. Box 6336
Columbia, SC 29260
Crisis Phone 1: (803) 771-4357
Business Phone: (803) 799-6329
Hrs Avail: 24

Greenville
Help-Line/Greenville
P.O. Box 1085
Greenville, SC 29602
Crisis Phone 1: (803) 233-HELP
Business Phone: (803) 242-0955
Hrs Avail: 24

SOUTH DAKOTA

Aberdeen
New Beginnings Center
1206 North Third
Aberdeen, SD 57401
Crisis Phone 1: (605) 229-1239
Business Phone: (605) 229-1239
Hrs Avail: 24

Huron
Our Home, Inc.
510 Nebraska
Huron, SD 57350
Crisis Phone 1: (605) 352-9449
Business Phone: (605) 352-9098
Hrs Avail: 24

Sioux Falls
Community Crisis Line
313 S. 1st Ave.
Sioux Falls, SD 57102

Crisis Phone 1: (605) 334-7022
Business Phone: (605) 334-7022
Hrs Avail: 24

TENNESSEE

Athens
McMinn/Meigs Contact
P.O. Box 69
Athens, TN 37303
Crisis Phone 1: (615) 745-9111
Business Phone: (615) 745-1042
Hrs Avail: 24

Chattanooga
Contact of Chattanooga
1202 Duncan
Chattanooga, TN 37404
Crisis Phone 1: (615) 266-8228
Crisis Phone 2: (615) 622-5193
Business Phone: (615) 629-0039
Hrs Avail: 24

Cleveland
Contact of Cleveland
P.O. Box 962
Cleveland, TN 37311
Crisis Phone 1: (615) 479-9666
Business Phone: (615) 472-1916
Hrs Avail: 24

Johnson City
Contact Ministries
P.O. Box 1403
Johnson City, TN 37601
Crisis Phone 1: (615) 926-0144
Business Phone: (615) 926-0140
Hrs Avail: 24

Kingsport
Contact-Concern
P.O. Box 798
Kingsport, TN 37662
Crisis Phone 1: (615) 246-2273
Business Phone: (615) 247-7761
Hrs Avail: 24

Knoxville
Contact Tele. of Knoxville
P.O. Box 11234
Knoxville, TN 37939-1234
Crisis Phone 1: (615) 523-9124
Business Phone: (615) 523-9108
Hrs Avail: 24

Knoxville
Kelen Ross McNabb Center
1520 Cherokee Trail
Knoxville, TN 37920
Crisis Phone 1: (615) 637-9711
Business Phone: (615) 637-9711
Hrs Avail: 24

Maryville
Contact of Blount County
P.O. Box 0382
Maryville, TN 37803
Crisis Phone 1: (615) 984-7689
Business Phone: (615) 984-7690
Hrs Avail: 24

Memphis
* Suicide/Crisis Interv. Serv./Memphis
P.O. Box 40068
Memphis, TN 38104
Crisis Phone 1: (901) 274-7477
Business Phone: (901) 276-1111
Hrs Avail: 24

Nashville
*# Crisis Intervention Center, Inc.
P.O. Box 120934
Nashville, TN 37212
Crisis Phone 1: (615) 244-7444
Business Phone: (615) 298-3359
Hrs Avail: 24

Oak Ridge
Contact of Oak Ridge
P.O. Box 641
Oak Ridge, TN 37830
Crisis Phone 1: (615) 482-4949
Business Phone: (615) 482-4940
Hrs Avail: 24

Tullahoma
Tullahoma Contact-Life Line
P.O. Box 1614
Tullahoma, TN 37388
Coffee County: (615) 455-7133
Franklin Co.: (615) 967-7133
Bedford Co.: (615) 684-7133
Moore Co.: (615) 759-7133
Business Phone: (615) 967-7133
Hrs Avail: 24

TEXAS

Amarillo
* Suicide Prev/Crisis Int. Center
P.O. Box 3250
Amarillo, TX 79106
Crisis Phone 1: (806) 376-4251
Toll Free In-State: (800) 692-4039
Business Phone: (806) 353-7235
Hrs Avail: 24

Arlington
Contact Tarrant County
P.O. Box 1431
Arlington, TX 76010
Crisis Phone 1: (817) 277-2233
Business Phone: (817) 277-0071
Hrs Avail: 24

Austin
Information Hotline & Crisis Center
102 Neches
Austin, TX 78705
Crisis Phone 1: (512) 472-help
Business Phone: (512) 475-5695
Hrs Avail: 24

Beaumont
* Rape & Suicide Crisis of SE Texas
P.O. Box 5011
Beaumont, TX 77706
Crisis Phone 1: (409) 835-3355
Business Phone: (409) 832-6530
Hrs Avail: 24

Beaumont
Suicide Rescue, Inc.
2750 I-10E
Beaumont, TX 77703
Crisis Phone 1: (713) 833-2311
Business Phone: (713) 833-2311
Hrs Avail: 24

Corpus Christi
* Crisis Services/Corpus Christi
4906-B Everhart
Corpus Christi, TX 78411
Crisis Phone 1: (512) 993-7410
Business Phone: (512) 993-7416
Hrs Avail: 24

Dallas
Contact-Dallas/Teleph. Counsel.
P.O. Box 742224
Dallas, TX 75374
Crisis Phone 1: (214) 233-2233
Business Phone: (214) 233-0866
Hrs Avail: 24

Dallas
*# Suicide & Crisis Center
2808 Swiss Ave.
Dallas, TX 75204
Crisis Phone 1: (214) 828-1000
Business Phone: (214) 824-7020
Hrs Avail: 24

Del Rio
Del Rio Crisis Line
Youth Counseling Center
609 Griner St.
Del Rio, TX 78840
Crisis Phone 1: (512) 775-0571
Business Phone: (512) 774-2585
Hrs Avail: 24

Edinburgh
Edinburgh Help Line
P.O. Box 1108
Edinburgh, TX 78539
Crisis Phone 1: (512) 383-0121
Business Phone: (512) 383-5341
Hrs Avail: 24

El Paso
El Paso Crisis Intervention Services
5308 El Paso Dr.
El Paso, TX 79905
Crisis Phone 1: (915) 779-1800
Business Phone: (915) 779-7383
Hrs Avail: 24

Ft. Worth
*# Tarrant County Crisis Intervention
C/o Family Service, Inc.
716 Magnolia
Ft. Worth, TX 76104
Crisis Phone 1: (817) 336-3355
Business Phone: (817) 336-0108
Hrs Avail: 24

Houston
*# Crisis Intervention of Houston, Inc.
P.O. Box 13066
Houston, TX 77219
Central: (713) 228-1505
Bay Area: (713) 333-5111
Business Phone: (713) 527-9426
Hrs Avail: 24

Houston
Houston-Bay Area Crisis Helpline
16811 El Camino Real #126
Houston, TX 77058
Crisis Phone 1: (713) 488-7222
Business Phone: (713) 486-9683
Hrs Avail: 24

Lubbock
Contact Lubbock
P.O. Box 6377
Lubbock, TX 79493-6477
Crisis Phone 1: (806) 765-8393
Teen Line: (806) 765-7272
Business Phone: (806) 765-7272
Hrs Avail: Sun-Th: 6 A.M.-10 P.M.; F-S: 6 P.M.-Mid

Orange
Suicide Rescue
P.O. Box 891
Orange, TX 77630
Crisis Phone 1: (713) 883-5521
Business Phone: (713) 883-5521
Hrs Avail: 24

Plano
Plano Crisis Center
P.O. Box 1808
Plano, TX 75074
Crisis Phone 1: (214) 881-0088
Business Phone: (214) 881-0081
Hrs Avail: 9 A.M.-Midnight

Richardson
Richardson Crisis Center
P.O. Box 877
Richardson, TX 75080
Crisis Phone 1: (214) 783-0008
Business Phone: (214) 783-0008
Hrs Avail: 24

San Angelo
* Concho Valley Ctr. For Human Advance
244 N. Magdalen
San Angelo, TX 76903
Crisis Phone 1: (915) 653-5933
Business Phone: (915) 655-8965
Hrs Avail: 24

San Antonio
Contact San Antonio
P.O. Box 5217
San Antonio, TX 78201
Crisis Phone 1: (512) 736-1876
Business Phone: (512) 732-2216
Hrs Avail: 24

San Antonio
* United Way Help Line
P.O. Box 898
San Antonio, TX 78293-0898
Crisis Phone 1: (512) 227-4357
Business Phone: (512) 224-5000
Hrs Avail: 24

Wichita Falls
Concern, Inc.
P.O. Box 1945
Wichita Falls, TX 76307

Crisis Phone 1: (817) 723-0821
Business Phone: (817) 723-8231
Hrs Avail: 24

UTAH

Logan
Logan Helpline
121 A UMC Utah State Univ
Logan, UT 84322
Crisis Phone 1: (801) 752-3964
Business Phone: (801) 752-1702
Hrs Avail: 24

Midvale
Salt Lake Co. Div. of MH
6856 South 700 East
Midvale, UT 84047
Crisis Phone 1: (801) 566-2455
Business Phone: (801) 566-2455
Hrs Avail: 24

Ogden
Ogden Emergency Services
Weber Co. MHC
2510 Washington Blvd, 5th Fl.
Ogden, UT 84401
Crisis Phone 1: (801) 626-9270
Business Phone: (801) 626-9100
Hrs Avail: 24

Salt Lake City
Salt Lake City Crisis Intervention
50 N. Medical Dr.
Salt Lake City, UT 84132
Crisis Phone 1: (801) 581-2296
Business Phone: (801) 581-2296
Hrs Avail: 24

Salt Lake City
Salt Lake Co. Div. of Mental Health
54 S. 700 East
Salt Lake City, UT 84102
Crisis Phone 1: (801) 531-8909
Business Phone: (801) 531-8909
Hrs Avail: 24

VERMONT

Brattleboro
Hotline for Help, Inc
17 Elliot St.
Brattleboro, VT 05301
Crisis Phone 1: (802) 257-7989
Business Phone: (802) 257-7980
Hrs Avail: 24

Randolph
Orange Co. MH Service Emer. Service
P.O. Box G
Randolph, VT 05060
Crisis Phone 1: (802) 728-9641
Business Phone: (802) 728-3230
Hrs Avail: 24

St. Albans
St. Albans Emer. & Crisis Service
Franklin Grand Isle MH Service, Inc
8 Ferris Street
St. Albans, VT 05478
Crisis Phone 1: (802) 524-6554
Business Phone: (802) 524-6554
Hrs Avail: 24

VIRGINIA

Alexandria
Alexandria C.A.I.R. Hotline
418 S. Washington St. Suite 101
Alexandria, VA 22314
Crisis Phone 1: (703) 548-3810
Business Phone: (703) 548-0010
Hrs Avail: Noon to Midnight

Alexandria
Alexandria Comm MH Center
206 N. Washington St., 5th Fl.
Alexandria, VA 22314
Crisis Phone 1: (703) 836-5751
Business Phone: (703) 836-5751
Hrs Avail: 24

Arlington
*# Northern Virginia Hotline

P.O. Box 187
Arlington, VA 22210
Crisis Phone 1: (703) 527-4077
Business Phone: (703) 522-4460
Hrs Avail: 24

Blacksburg
RAFT
201 Main St.
Blacksburg, VA 24060
Crisis Phone 1: (703) 951-3434
Business Phone: (703) 951-4283
Hrs Avail: 24

Bristol
Bristol Crisis Center
P.O. Box 642
Bristol, VA 24203-0642
Crisis Phone 1: (703) 466-2312
Crisis Phone 2: (703) 628-7731
Business Phone: (703) 466-2312
Hrs Avail: 24

Danville
Danville Helpline
382 Taylor Dr.
Danville, VA 24541
Danville: (804) 799-1414
Chatham: (804) 432-0639
Gretna: (804) 656-1231
Business Phone: (804) 799-1414
Hrs Avail: 24

Fredericksburg
Fredericksburg Hotline
P.O. Box 7132
Fredericksburg, VA 22404
Crisis Phone 1: (703) 321-1212
Business Phone: (703) 373-6608
Hrs Avail: 24

Harrisonburg
Listening Ear Services
Harrisonburg, VA 22801
Crisis Phone 1: (703) 434-2538
Business Phone: (703) 434-2539
Hrs Avail: 24

Lynchburg
Crisis Line of Central Virginia
P.O. Box 2376
Lynchburg, VA 24501
Crisis Phone 1: (804) 528-help
Business Phone: (804) 384-0231
Hrs Avail: 6P.M.-12 A.M.

Martinsville
Contact Martinsville-Henry Co.
P.O. Box 1287
Martinsville, VA 24112
Crisis Phone 1: (703) 632-7295
Business Phone: (703) 638-8980
Hrs Avail: 24

Newport News
Contact Peninsula
211 32nd St.
Newport News, VA 23607
Crisis Phone 1: (804) 245-0041
Business Phone: (804) 861-0330
Hrs Avail: 24

Petersburg
Contact Tri- City Area
P.O. Box 942
Petersburg, VA 23803
Crisis Phone 1: (804) 733-1100
Business Phone: (804) 861-0330
Hrs Avail: 24

Portsmouth
* Suicide-Crisis Center, Inc.
P.O. Box 1493
POrtsmouth, VA 23705
Crisis Phone 1: (804) 399-6393
Business Phone: (804) 393-0502
Hrs Avail: 24

Richmond
Emergency Service/Richmond Co. MHC
501 N. 9th St., Rm 205
Richmond, VA 23218
Crisis Phone 1: (804) 780-8003
Business Phone: (804) 643-5301
Hrs Avail: 24

Roanoke
Trust: Roanoke Valley Trouble Center
360 Washington Ave.
Roanoke, VA 24016
Crisis Phone 1: (703) 563-0311
Business Phone: (703) 345-8859
Hrs Avail: 24

Virginia Beach
Contact Tidewater
P.O. Box 23
Virginia Beach, VA 23458
Crisis Phone 1: (804) 428-2211
Business Phone: (804) 425-1647
Hrs Avail: 24

Winchester
Concern Hotline, Inc.
P.O. Box 2032
Winchester, VA 22601
Winchester: (703) 667-0145
Front Royal: (703) 635-4357
Woodstock: (703) 459-4742
Business Phone: (703) 667-8208
Hrs Avail: 24

WASHINGTON

Bainbridge Island
Helpline House
282 Knechtel Way NE
Bainbridge Island, WA 98110
Crisis Phone 1: (206) 842-HELP
Business Phone: (206) 842-7621
Hrs Avail: 24

Bellingham
The Crisis Line
Whatcom Co. Crisis Services
124 E. Holly St. #201
Bellingham, WA 98225
Crisis Phone 1: (206) 734-7271
Whatcom Co.: (206) 384-1485
Business Phone: (206) 671-5754
Hrs Avail: 24

Bremerton
Bremerton Crisis Clinic
500 Union
Bremerton, WA 98312
Crisis Phone 1: (206) 479-3033
Business Phone: (206) 373-5031
Hrs Avail: 24

Chehalis
Lewis Co. Info. & Referral/Hotline
P.O. Box 337
Chehalis, WA 98532
Crisis Phone 1: (206) 748-6601
In Washington: (800) 562-6160
Business Phone: (206) 748-6601
Hrs Avail: 24

Ellensburg
Ellensburg Crisis Line
507 Nanum
Ellensburg, WA 98926
Crisis Phone 1: (509) 925-4168
Business Phone: (509) 925-2166
Hrs Avail: 24

Everett
Care-Crisis Line
2801 Lombard Ave.
Everett, WA 98201
Crisis Phone 1: (206) 258-4357
Business Phone: (206) 258-4357
Hrs Avail: 24

Moses Lake
Grant County Crisis Line
Mental Health & Family Service
P.O. Box 1057
Moses Lake, WA 98837
Crisis Phone 1: (509) 765-1717
Business Phone: (509) 765-9239
Hrs Avail: 24

Olympia
Crisis Clinic/Thurston & Macon Co.
P.O. Box 2463
Olympia, WA 98507
Crisis Phone 1: (206) 352-2211
Business Phone: (206) 754-3888
Hrs Avail: 24

Pullman
Whitman County Crisis Line/Latah County Nightline
P.O. Box 2615 CS
Pullman, WA 99163
Crisis Phone 1: (509) 332-1505
Business Phone: (509) 332-1505
Hrs Avail: 24

Richland
Contact Tri-Cities Area
P.O. Box 684
Richland, WA 99352
Crisis Phone 1: (509) 943-6606
Business Phone: (509) 943-9017
Hrs Avail: 24

Richland
* Mid Columbia Psych. Hosp. & MHC
Dial Help
1175 Gribble
Richland, WA 99352
Crisis Phone 1: (509) 943-9104
Business Phone: (509) 943-9104
Hrs Avail: 24

Seattle
*# Crisis Clinic
1530 Eastlake East
Seattle, WA 98102
Crisis Phone 1: (206) 447-3222
Business Phone: (206) 447-3210
Hrs Avail: 24

Spokane
Spokane Crisis Services
Spokane City Comm. MH
S. 107 Division
Spokane, WA 99202
Crisis Phone 1: (509) 838-4428
Business Phone: (509) 838-4651
Hrs Avail: 24

Tacoma
Tacoma Crisis Clinic
P.O. Box 5007
Tacoma, WA 98405
Crisis Phone 1: (206) 759-6700
Business Phone: (206) 756-5250
Hrs Avail: 24

Yakima
Open Line/Yakima
Central Washington Comprehensive MH
P.O. Box 959
Yakima, WA 98907
Crisis Phone 1: (509) 575-4200
Statewide Toll Free: (800) 572-8122
Business Phone: (509) 575-4084
Hrs Avail: 24

WEST VIRGINIA

Charleston
Contact Kanawha Valley
Christ Church United Methodist
Quarrier & Morris Sts.
Charleston, WV 25301
Crisis Phone 1: (304) 346-0826
Business Phone: (304) 346-0828
Hrs Avail: 24

Huntington
Contact Huntington
520 11th St.
Huntington, WV 25701
Crisis Phone 1: (304) 523-3448
Business Phone: (304) 523-3447
Hrs Avail: 24

Huntington
Prestera Center for MH Services
3375 U.S. Rt. 60 East
P.O. Box 8069
Huntington, WV 25705
Crisis Phone 1: (304) 525-7851
Business Phone: (304) 525-7851
Hrs Avail: 24

Lewisburg
Greenbriar Valley MH Clinic
100 Church St.
Lewisburg, WV 24901
Crisis Phone 1: (304) 647-5587

Business Phone: (304) 645-3319
Hrs Avail: 24

Oak Hill
Contact-Care of Southern WV
P.O. Box 581
Oak Hill, WV 25901
Crisis Phone 1: (304) 877-3535
Business Phone: (304) 877-3535
Hrs Avail: 24

Princeton
Southern Highlands Comm MHC
12th St. Extension
Princeton, WV 24740
Crisis Phone 1: (304) 425-9541
Business Phone: (304) 425-9541
Hrs Avail: 24

Wheeling
Upper Ohio Valley Crisis Hotline
P.O. Box 653
Wheeling, WV 26003
Crisis Phone 1: (304) 234-8161
Business Phone: (304) 234-1848
Hrs Avail: 24

WISCONSIN

Appleton
Appleton Crisis Intervention Center
3365 West Brewster
Appleton, WI 54914
Crisis Phone 1: (414) 731-3211
Business Phone: (414) 735-5354
Hrs Avail: 24

Beloit
Beloit Hotline
P.O. Box 1293
Beloit, WI 53511
Crisis Phone 1: (608) 365-4436
Business Phone: (608) 364-4436
Hrs Avail: 24

Boscobel
Suicide Prevention Group
401 E. Bluff St.
Boscobel, WI 53805
Crisis Phone 1: (608) 365-4436
Business Phone: (608) 365-4436
Hrs Avail: 24

Eau Claire
* Suicide Prevention Center
1221 Whipple St.
Eau Claire, WI 54701
Crisis Phone 1: (715) 834-6040
Business Phone: (715) 839-3274
Hrs Avail: 24

Elkhorn
Lakeland Community Center
P.O. Box 1005
Elkhorn, WI 53121
Crisis Phone 1: (414) 723-5400
Business Phone: (414) 723-5400
Hrs Avail: 24

Elkhorn
* Lakeland Counseling Center
Hwy Inn
P.O. Box 1005
Elkhorn, WI 53121
Crisis Phone 1: (414) 741-3200
Business Phone: (414) 741-3200
Hrs Avail: 24

Fond Du Lac
CIC/Fond Du Lac
459 E. 1st St.
Fond Du Lac, WI 54935
Crisis Phone 1: (414) 929-3535
Business Phone: (414) 929-3500
Hrs Avail: 24

Green Bay
C.I.C./Manitowoc Area
131 So. Madison St.
Green Bay, WI 54301
Crisis Phone 1: (414) 682-9172
Business Phone: (414) 432-7855
Hrs Avail: 24

La Crosse
First Call For Help
P.O. Box 2373

La Crosse, WI 54602-2373
First Call For Help: (608) 782-8010
First Call WI: (800) 326-8255
First Call MN & IA: (800) 356-9588
Business Phone: (608) 782-8010
Hrs Avail: 24

La Crosse
Harbor House
1608 Market St.
La Crosse, WI 54601
Crisis Phone 1: (608) 785-0530
Business Phone: (608) 785-0530 x3516
Hrs Avail: 24

Madison
* Dane Co. MHC Emergency Services
31 S. Henry
Madison, WI 53703
Crisis Phone 1: (608) 251-2345
Business Phone: (608) 251-2341
Hrs Avail: 24

Milwaukee
* Milwaukee County CI Service
Mental Health Emerg. Serv.
8700 W. Wisconsin Ave.K Rd.
Milwaukee, WI 53226
Crisis Phone 1: (414) 257-7222
Business Phone: (414) 257-7222
Hrs Avail: 24

Milwaukee
Underground Switchboard
P.O. Box 92455
Milwaukee, WI 53202
Crisis Phone 1: (414) 271-3123
Business Phone: (414) 271-2810
Hrs Avail: 24

Oshkosh
Crisis Interv. Center/Oshkosh
P.O. Box 1411
Oshkosh, WI 54902
Crisis Phone 1: (414) 722-7707
Crisis Phone 2: (414) 233-7707
Business Phone: (414) 233-7709
Hrs Avail: 24

Sturgeon Bay
Door County Helpline
P.O. Box F
Sturgeon Bay, WI 54235
Crisis Phone 1: (414) 743-8818
Business Phone: (414) 743-8818
Hrs Avail: 24

Thiensville
COPE
Ozaukee County Hotline
P.O. Box 493
Thiensville, WI 53092
Crisis Phone 1: (414) 242-6578
Business Phone: (414) 242-6578
Hrs Avail: 24

Wisconsin Rapids
Wood Co. Unified Services
Crisis Interv. & Referral
310 Dewey St.
Wisconsin Rapids, WI 54494
Wisconsin Rapids: (715) 421-2345
Marshfield: (715) 384-5555
Business Phone: (715) 421-2345
Hrs Avail: 24

WYOMING

Casper
* Casper Suicide Prevention
Family Support Group Assoc., Inc.
611 Thelm Dr.
Casper, WY 82609
Crisis Phone 1: (307) 234-5061
Business Phone: (307) 234-5061
Hrs Avail: 24

Cheyenne
Cheyenne Helpline
P.O. Box 404
Cheyenne, WY 82001
Crisis Phone 1: (307) 634-4469
Business Phone: (307) 632-4132
Hrs Avail: 6 P.M. to 7 A.M.

Rock Springs
* Crisis Intervention Program
731 C.
Rock Springs, WY 82901
Crisis Phone 1: (307) 382-6060
Business Phone: (307) 382-6060
Hrs Avail: 24

Worland
Community Crisis Service, Inc.
P.O. Box 872
Worland, WY 82401
Crisis Phone 1: (307) 347-4991
Business Phone: (307) 347-4992
Hrs Avail: 24

CANADA

PROVINCIAL AND TERRITORIAL AGENCIES

ALBERTA

Suicide Information and Education Centre
1615 10th Avenue, S.W., #201
Calgary, Alberta T3C 057
Tel: (403) 245-3900

Suicide Prevention Training Program
1515 10th Avenue, S.W., #201
Calgary, Alberta T3C 057
Tel: (403) 245-3900

Canadian Mental Health Association (CMHA)
9707 110th Street
Edmonton, Alberta T5K 2L9

Canadian Mental Health Association (CMHA) and Providing Assistance, Counselling and Education (PACE)
9917 101st Avenue #301
Grand Prairie, Alberta T80 0X7
Tel: (403) 539-6660

Suicide Prevention Program
9909 Franklin Avenue
Fort McMurray, Alberta T9H 2K4
Tel: (403) 743-7894

Canadian Mental Health Association (CMHA)
631 Prospect Drive
Medicine Hat, Alberta T1A 4C2
Tel: (403) 572-7781

Canadian Mental Health Association (CMHA)
412 St. Michael's Building
1412 9th Avenue South
Lathbridge, Alberta T1J 4C5
Tel: (403) 329-4775

Family Service Association of Edmonton
Family Service Building
9919 106th Street
Edmonton, Alberta T5K 1E2
Tel: (403) 423-2831

BRITISH COLUMBIA

The Alcohol and Drug Commission of British Columbia
805 West Broadway, 8th Floor
Vancouver, British Columbia V5Y 1P9
Tel: (604) 731-9121

Family Services of Greater Vancouver
1616 Seventh Avenue
Vancouver, B.C. V6J 1S5
Tel: (604) 731-4951

MANITOBA

Alcoholism Foundation of Manitoba
1580 Dublin Avenue
Winnipeg, Manitoba R3E O24
Tel: (204) 775-8601

Department of Health and Social Development
139 Tuxedo Boulevard
Building 21, Box 17
Winnipeg, Manitoba

Family Services of Winnipeg
287 Broadway Avenue, 4th Floor
Winnipeg, Manitoba R3C OR9
Tel: (204) 947-1401

NEW BRUNSWICK

Alcoholism and Drug Dependency Commission
103 Church Street
P.O. Box 6000
Fredericton, New Brunswick E3B 5H1
Tel: (506) 453-2136

Department of Health
P.O. Box 6000
348 King Street
Fredericton, New Brunswick E3B 5H1
No tel. listed

NEWFOUNDLAND

Department of Health
Confederation Building
St. John's, Newfoundland A1C 5T7
Tel: (709) 737-2300

Alcohol and Drug Addiction Foundation of Newfoundland
3 Blackmarsh Road
St. John's, Newfoundland A1E 1S2
Tel: (709) 579-4041

NOVA SCOTIA

Nova Scotia Commission on Drug Dependency
5668 South Street
Halifax, Nova Scotia B3J 1A6
Tel: (902) 424-4270

ONTARIO

Alcoholism and Drug Addiction Foundation
33 Russell Street
Totonto, Ontario M5S 2S1
Tel: (416) 595-6000

Canadian Medical Association
Box 8650
Ottawa, Ontario K1G 0G8
Tel: (613) 731-9331

Ministry of Health
9th Floor, Hepburn Block
Queen's Pane
Toronto, Ontario M7A 1S2
Tel: (416) 865-5167

Suicide Prevention/Awareness Committee
Department of Psychology, University of Windsor
401 Sunset Avenue
Windsor, Ontario N9B 3P4
Tel: (519) 253-4232

Ontario Association of Distress Centres
811 A Queen Street East
Toronto, Ontario M4M 1H8
Tel: (416) 463-6606

Drug Advisory Bureau
Department of National Health and Welfare
Tunney's Pasture
Ottawa, Ontario K1A 0K9
No tel. listed

Family Service Association of Metro Toronto
22 Wellesley Street East
Toronto, Ontario M4Y 1G3
Tel: (416) 922-3126

PRINCE EDWARD ISLAND

Addiction Foundation of Prince Edward Island

Box 37
Charlottestown, Prince Edward Island CIA 7K2
Tel: (902) 892-4265

QUEBEC

Department of Social Affairs
Information Centre on Alcoholism and Other Addictions
1075 Chemin Ste. Foy
Quebec, P.Q. G15 2M1
Tel: (418) 643-9621

Ville Marie Social Service Centre
4018 Catharine Street W.
Montreal, Quebec H32 1P2
Tel: (514) 989-1885

SASKATCHEWAN

Alcoholism Commission of Saskatchewan
3475 Albert Street
Regina, Saskatchewan S45 6X6
Tel: (306) 565-4085

Catholic Family Services
635 Main Street
Saskatoon, Saskatchewan S7H 0J8
Tel: (306) 244-7773

Family Service Bureau
200-245 Third Avenue S.
Saskatoon, Saskatchewan S7K 1M4
Tel: (306) 244-0127

National Native Association of Treatment Directors
P.O. Box 1882
Saskatoon, Saskatchewan S7K 3S2
Tel: (306) 934-1646

NORTHWEST TERRITORIES

Alcohol and Drug Program
Department of Social Services
Government of the Northwest Territories
Yellowknife, N.W.T. X1A 2L9
Tel: (403) 873-7155

Alcohol and Drug Coordinating Council
Box 1769
Yellowknife, N.W.T. X0E 1H0
Tel: (403) 873-7155

YUKON

Alcohol and Drug Services
Box 2703
Whitehorse, Y.T. X1A 2C6
Tel: (403) 667-5777

INTERNATIONAL AND FOREIGN AGENCIES AND ORGANIZATIONS

SPECIALIZED AGENCIES OF THE UNITED NATIONS

Association Medica Pan Americana
222 Kent Terrace
West Palm Beach, FL 33407

United Nations
Division of Narcotic Drugs (DND)
P.O. Box 500
A-1400 Vienna, Austria

United Nations Educational, Scientific and Cultural Organization (UNESCO)
7, Place de Fontenoy
F-7500 Paris, France

United Nations Social Defence
Research Institute
Via Giulia 52
I-00186 Rome, Italy

World Health Organization (WHO)
Regional Office for the Western Pacific
P.O. Box 2932
12115 Manila, Philippines

World Health Organization (WHO)
Regional Office for Europe
Scherfigsvej, 8
DK-2100 Copenhagen, Denmark

World Health Organization (WHO)
20, Avenue Appia
CH-1211 Geneva, Switzerland

OTHER INTERNATIONAL ORGANIZATIONS

Centre for Social Development and Humanitarian Affairs (CSDHA)
P.O. Box 500
A-1400 Vienna, Austria

International Association for Suicide Prevention
Central Administrative Office
Psychiatric University Clinic
Spitalgasse 23
A-1090 Vienna, Austria

International Commission for the Prevention of Alcoholism
6830 Laurel Street, N.W.
Washington, DC 20012

International Council on Alcohol and Addictions
Case Postale 140
CH-1001 Lausanne, Switzerland

International Council of Volunteer Agencies
17, Avenue de la Paix
CH-1202 Geneva, Switzerland

International Narcotics Control Board (IHCB)
P.O. Box 500
A-1400 Vienna, Austria

International Council on Social Welfare
Berggasse None
A-1090 Vienna, Austria

MAJOR ENGLISH-LANGUAGE JOURNALS, NEWSPAPERS AND PERIODICALS

Alcohol Health and Research World
P.O. Box 2345
Rockville, Maryland 20852

Alcoholism: The National Magazine
P.O. Box C19051
Queen Anne Station
Seattle, Washington 98109

The Alcoholism Report
744 National Press Building
Washington, DC 20045

American Journal of Drug and Alcohol Abuse
Marcel Dekker Journals, Inc.
270 Madison Avenue
New York, New York 10016

American Journal of Epidemiology
Johns Hopkins University
School of Hygiene and Health
615 N. Wolfe Street
Baltimore, Maryland 21205

American Journal of Pharmacy and the Sciences Supporting Public Health

Philadelphia College of Pharmacy and Science
43rd Street and King Sessing Hall
Philadelphia, Pennsylvania 19104

American Journal of Psychiatry
American Psychiatric Association
1700 18th Street N.W.
Washington, DC 20009

American Journal of Psychology
University of Illinois Press
Urbana, Illinois 61801

American Journal of Public Health
American Public Health Association
1015 18th Street, N.W.
Washington, DC 20036

American Journal of Sociology
University of Chicago Press
5801 South Ellis Avenue
Chicago, Illinois 60637

Annals of Internal Medicine
American College of Physicians
4200 Pine Street
Philadelphia, Pennsylvania 19104

Annals of the New York Academy of Sciences
The New York Academy of Sciences
2 East 63rd Street
New York, New York 10021

Archives of General Psychiatry
American Medical Association
535 N. Dearborn Street
Chicago, Illinois 60610

British Journal of Addiction
Longman Group, Ltd.
Journals Division
43-45 Annandale Street
Edinburgh EH7 4AT, Scotland
United Kingdom

British Journal on Alcohol and Alcoholism
3 Grosvenor Crescent
London SWIX 7EE, England
United Kingdom

British Journal of Psychiatry
Headley Bros., Ltd.
Ashford
Kent TN 24 8HH, England
United Kingdom

British Medical Journal
British Medical Association
B.M.A. House, Tavistock Square
London WCI, England
United Kingdom

Canadian Medical Association Journal
Canadian Medical Association
Box 8650
Ottawa K1G 068, Ontario
Canada

Clinical Pharmacology and Therapeutics
C.V. Mosby Co.
11830 Westline Industrial Drive
St. Louis, Missouri 63141

Clinical Toxicology
Marcel Dekker Journals
270 Madison Avenue
New York, New York 10016

Contempory Drug Problems
Federal Legal Publications, Inc.
95 Morton Street
New York, New York 10014

Crime and Delinquency
National Council on Crime and Delinquency
411 Continental Plaza
Hackensack, New Jersey 07601

Criminology
Sage Publications, Inc.
275 S. Beverly Drive
Beverly Hills, California 90212

Crisis: International Journal of Suicide and Crisis Studies
C.J. Hogrefe, Inc.
525 Eglinton Avenue East
Toronto, Ontario M4P 1N5
Canada

Digest of Alcoholism Theory and Application (DATA)
10700 Olson Memorial Highway
Minneapolis, Minnesota 55441

Diseases of the Nervous System
Physicians Post Graduate Press
Box 38293
Memphis, Tennessee 38138

Drug Abuse and Alcoholism Newsletter
Vista Hill Foundation
3420 Camino del Rio North, Suite 100
San Diego, California 92108

Drugs and Alcohol Dependence
Elsevier Sequoia S.A.
Box 851
CH-1001 Lausanne 1, Switzerland

Drug Forum
Baywood Publishing Co., Inc.
120 Marine Street
Farmingdale, New York 11735

Essence: Issues in the Study of Aging, Dying and Death
Atkinson College Press
4700 Keele Street
Downview, Ontario M3J 2R7
Canada

The Grapevine
The Alcoholics Anonymous Grapevine, Inc.
468 Park Avenue South
New York, New York 10016

Human Pathology
Saunders Co.
West Washington Square
Philadelphia, Pennsylvania 19105

International Journal of the Addictions
Marcel Dekker Journals
270 Madison Avenue
New York, New York 10016

The Journal
Addiction Research Foundation
33 Russell Street
Toronto, Ontario M5S 2S1
Canada

Journal of Abnormal Psychology
American Psychological Association
1200 17th Street, N.W.
Washington, DC 20036

Journal on Alcohol and Drug Education
1120 East Oakland
P.O. Box 10212
Lansing, Michigan 48901

Journal of the American Medical Association (JAMA)
535 North Dearborn Street
Chicago, Illinois 60610

Journal of Clinical Psychology
Clinical Psychology Publishing Co., Inc.
4 Conant Square
Brandon, Vermont 05733

Journal of Consulting and Clinical Psychology
American Psychological Association
1200 17th Street, N.W.
Washington, DC 20036

Journal of Criminal Law and Criminology
Williams and Wilkins Co.
428 East Preston Street
Baltimore, Maryland 21202

Journal of Drug Education
Baywood Publishing Co., Inc.
120 Marine Street
Farmingdale, New York 11735

Journal of Drug Issues
Box 4021
Tallahassee Florida 32303

Journal of General Psychology
Journal Press
2 Commercial Street
Provincetown, Massachusetts 02657

Journal of Health and Social Behavior
American Sociological Association
1722 North Street, N.W.
Washington, DC 20036

Journal of Nervous and Mental Diseases
Williams and Wilkins Co.
428 East Preston Street
Baltimore, Maryland 21202

Journal of Personality
Duke University Press
6697 College Station
Durham, North Carolina 27708

Journal of Personality and Social Psychology
American Psychological Association
1200 17th Street, N.W.
Washington, DC 20036

Journal of Pharmacy and Pharmacology
Pharmaceutical Society of Great Britain
One Lambeth High Street
London SE1 7JN, England
United Kingdom

Journal of Pharmacology and Experimental Therapeutics
Williams and Wilkins Co.
428 East Preston Street
Baltimore, Maryland 21202

Journal of Psychoactive Drugs
Transaction Periodicals Consortium, Department 2000
Rutgers, The State University
New Brunswick, New Jersey 08903

Journal of General Psychology
Journal Press
2 Commercial Street
Provincetown, Massachusetts 02657

Journal of Studies on Alcohol
Rutgers Center of Alcohol Studies
Publication Division
New Brunswick, New Jersey 08903

New England Journal of Medicine
Massachusetts Medical Society
10 Shattuck Street
Boston, Massachusetts 02115

New York State Journal of Medicine
Medical Society of the State of New York
420 Lakeville Road
Lake Success, New York 11040

Newslink
American Association of Suicidology
2459 South Ash Street
Denver, Colorado 80222

Omega: Journal of Death and Dying
Baywood Publishing Co., Inc.
120 Marine Street
P.O. Box D
Farmingdale, New York 11735

Psychiatry
William Alanson White Psychiatric Foundation, Inc.
1610 New Hampshire Avenue, N.W.
Washington, DC 20009

Psychological Reports
Box 9229
Missoula, Montana 59801

Psychology
Box 6495, Station C
Savannah, Georgia 31405

Psychopharmacology
Springer-Verlag
174 Fifth Avenue
New York, New York 10010

Social Problems
Society for the Study of Social Problems
114 Rockwell Hall
State University College
Buffalo, New York 14222

Sociology Quarterly
Midwest Sociological Society
Department of Sociology
Southern Illinois University
Carbondale, Illinois 62901

Suicide and Life-Threatening Behavior
Guilford Publications, Inc.
200 Park Avenue South
New York, New York 10003

U.S. Journal of Drug and Alcohol Dependence
2119-A Hollywood Boulevard
Hollywood, Florida 33020

BIBLIOGRAPHY

Abram, H.S., G.L. Moore and F.B. Westervalt, Jr., "Suicidal Behavior in Chronic Dialysis Patients," *American Journal of Psychiatry*, 127 (1971):1199-1204.

Adler, A., "Selbstmord," *Internationale Zeitschrift für Individual Psychologie*, 15(1937):49-56; reprinted in *Journal of Individual Psychology*, 14(1958):57-61.

Allen, Nancy H., MPH, and Michael L. Peck, PhD, *Suicide in Young People*. Denver: American Association of Suicidology.

Alvarez, A., *The Savage God: A Study of Suicide*. New York: Random House, 1972.

Angell, Jim, "Tribes Try to Counter a Series of Suicides," Associated Press, December 27, 1985; dateline, Fort Washakie, Wyoming.

Aponte, R., "Epidemiological Aspects of Suicide in Latin America," *Crisis*, 1:35-41

Aristotle, *The Ethics of Aristotle*. Harmondsworth, England: Penguin, 1953.

Armour, David J., J. Michael Polich and Harriet B. Stanbul, *Alcoholism and Treatment*. New York: John Wiley, 1978.

Asimov, Isaac, *Isaac Asimov's Book of Facts*. New York: Bell Publishing Co., 1979.

Asinof, Eliot, *Craig and Joan*. New York: Viking Press, 1971.

Attwater, Donald, *The Penguin Dictionary of Saints*. New York: Penguin, 1965.

Augustinus, St., *The City of God*, Books I-VII (Fathers of the Church Series, Vol. 8). Washington, D.C.: Catholic University Press, 1950.

Baechler, J., *Suicides*. New York: Basic Books, 1979· first published in 1975 as *Les Suicides*.

Barnard , Christiaan, *Good Life, Good Death*. Englewood Cliffs, New Jersey: Prentice-Hall, 1980.

Bartel, J., "Über Obduktionsbefunde bei Selbstmordfällen," *Deutsche Zschr. f.d. ges. gerichtl. Med.*, 1(1922):389.

Bartel, J., "Zur Pathologischen Anatomie des Selbstmordes," *Wein. Klin. Wschr.*, 23(1910):495.

Battin, M.P., *Ethical Issues in Suicides*: Englewood Cliffs, New Jersey: Prentice-Hall, 1982.

Battin, M.P. and D.J. Mayo, Eds., *Suicide: The Philosophical Issues*. New York: St Martin's Press, 1980.

Beck, Aaron T., *Depression*. Philadelphia: University of Pennsylvania Press, 1970.

Beitzke, H., "Pathologisch-anatomische Untersuchungen an Selbstmördern," *Wien. Klin. Wschr.*, 51(1938):625-628.

Berne, Eric, *Games People Play*. New York: Grove Press, 1964.

Bettelheim, Bruno, *The Uses of Enchantment: The Meaning and Importance of Fairy Tales*. New York: Knopf, 1976.

Biller, O.A., "Suicide Related to the Assassination of President John F. Kennedy," *Suicide and Life-Threatening Behavior*, 7(1977):40-44.

Birtchnell, J. and S. Floyd, "Attempted Suicide and the Menstrual Cycle—A Negative Conclusion," *Journal of Psychosomatic Research*, 18(1974):361-369.

Blachly, P.H., H.T. Osterud and R. Josslin, "Suicide in Professional Groups," *New England Journal of Medicine* (1963).

Blake, P., "Going Gentle into That Good Night: Do Suicide Manuals Create a Bias Toward Death?" *Time*, March 21, 1983, p. 85.

Bohannan, P., ed., *African Homicide and Suicide*. Princeton, New Jersey: Princeton University Press, 1970.

Bolton, Iris, *My Son, My Son: A Guide to Healing After Death*. Atlanta: Boston Press, 1983.

Boor, M., "Effects of United States Presidential Elections on Suicide and Other Causes of Death," *American Sociological Review*, 46(1981):616-618.

Bowlby, John, *Attachment and Loss*, 2 vols. New York: Basic Books, 1969, 1973.

Bowlby, John, *Maternal Care and Mental Health*. New York: Columbia University Press, 1951.

Brierre de Boismont, A., *Du Suicide et de la Folie Suicide, Considérés dans leurs Rapport avec la Statistique, la Médicin et la Philosophie*, 2nd ed. Paris: Germer Baillière, 1856.

Bronfenbrenner, Urie, "Nobody Home: The Erosion of the American Family," *Psychology Today* (May 1977).

Bronfenbrenner, Urie, "Origins of Alienation," *Scientific American*, 231:53-57.

Burton, Robert, *The Anatomy of Melancholy*. New York: AMS Press, 1983; reprint of 1893 ed., first pub. 1621.

Camus, Albert, *The Myth of Sisyphus and Other Essays*. New York: Alfred A. Knopf, 1975.

Cantor, Pamela, "The Effects of Youthful Suicide on the Family," *Psychiatric Opinion*, 12:6(1975).

Casper, J.L., *Über den selbstmord unde seine Zunahme in unserer Zeit*. Berlin, 1825.

Cavan, R., *Suicide*. New York: Russell and Russell, 1965; first published by University of Chicago Press, 1928.

CDC, *Suicide Surveillance. 1910-1980*. Atlanta: Department of Health and Human Services, April 1985.

CDC Youth Suicide Surveillance, *Youth Suicide in the U.S., 1970-1980*. Atlanta: Department of Health and Human Services, November 1986.

Cheyne, G., *The English Malady.* Delmar, New York: Scholars' Facsimiles and Reprints, 1976; first published 1733.

Choron, Jacques, *Suicide*. New York: Scribners, 1972.

Coleman, Loren, *Suicide Clusters*. Boston/London: Faber and Faber, 1987.

Craig, A.G. and F.N. Pitts, "Suicide by Physicians," *Dis Nerv System*, 29(1968):763-772.

Crocker, Lester G., "The Discussion of Suicide in the Eighteenth Century," *Journal of the History of Ideas*, 13(1952):47-52.

Cutter, F., *Art and the Wish to Die*. Chicago: Nelson-Hall, 1983.

Dahlgren, K.G., *On Suicide and Attempted Suicide: A Psychiatrical and Statistical Investigation*. Lund: Lindstedts, 1945.

de Bracton, Henry, *De legibus et consuetudinibus Angliae*, 2 vols., (ed.) George E. Woodbine. New Haven: Yale University Press, 1915.

de Cantanzaro, D., *Suicide and Self-Damaging Behavior*. New York: Academic Press, 1981.

DeSole, D., S. Aronson and P. Singer, "Suicide and Role Strain Among Physicians," paper presented to APA, Detroit, May 1967.

Devereux, G., *Mohave Ethnopsychiatry and Suicide: The Psychiatric Knowledge and the Psychic Disturbances of an Indian Tribe*. Washington, D.C.: Smithsonian Institution, 1961.

Diogenes Laertius, *Lives of Eminent Philosophers*, 2 vols., tr. R.R. Hicks. London: Loeb Classical Library/Heinemann, 1930; 2:235.

Doan, Michael and Sarah Peterson, "As Cluster Suicides Take Toll of Teenagers," *U.S. News & World Report*, November 12, 1984.

Dollar, Truman E. and Grace H. Ketterman, *Teenage Rebellion*. Old Tappan, New Jersey: Revell, 1979.

Donne, J., *Biathanatos*. New York: Arno, 1977; first published, 1644.

Dorpat, T. and H. Ripley, "The Relationship between Attempted Suicide and Committed Suicide," *Comprehensive Psychiatry*, 8(1967):74-77.

Dostoevsky, Feodor, *The Diary of a Writer*, 2 vols., tr. Boris Brasol. New York: Octagon, 1973; reprint of 1949 ed.

Doughty, Oswald, "The English Malady of the Eighteenth Century," *Review of English Studies*, 2(1926):257-69.

Douglas, Jack D., *The Social Meanings of Suicide*. Princeton, New Jersey: Princeton University Press, 1967.

Dublin, Louis I., *The Facts of Life from Birth to Death*. New York: Macmillan, 1951.

Dublin, L.I., *Suicide: A Sociological and Statistical Study*. New York: Ronald Press, 1963.

Dublin, L. and B. Bunzel, *To Be or Not to Be: A Study of Suicide*. New York: Smith and Haas, 1933.

Duncan, Robert, *Only the Good Die Young*. New York: Harmony Books, 1986.

Durkheim, Emile, *Suicide*, tr. J.A. Spaulding and G. Simpson. Glencoe, Illinois: The Free Press, 1951; first published in 1897 as *Le Suicide*.

East, W.N., "On Attempted Suicide, with an Analysis of 1,000 Consecutive Cases," *Journal of Mental Science*, 59(1913):428.

Eby, Mary Sheila, "How Publicity Affects Violent Behavior," *Psychology Today* (January 1981).

Eickhoff, C., "Ein Beitrag zum sogenannton Status thymico-lymfaticus bei Selbstmördern," *Deutsche Zschr. f. d. ges. gerichtl. Med.*, 7(1926):561.

Elkind, David, "Growing Up Faster," *Psychology Today* (February 1974).

Elo, Ol, "Über Selbstmord und Selbstmorder in Finnland," *Deutsche Zschr. f. d. ges. gerichtl. Med.*, 17(1931):348-406.

Elwin, V., *Maria Murder and Suicide*. London: Oxford University Press, 1943.

Epectetus, *The Discourses as Reported by Arrian. The Manual and Fragments*, 2 vols., tr. W.A. Oldfather. Cambridge, Massachusetts: Loeb Classical Library/Harvard, 1954-64; 2:10-11, 28-29, 288-89.

Erasmus, D., *In Praise of Folly*. London: George Allen and Unwin, 1937; first published, 1509.

Esquirol, J.E., *Des Maladies Mentales, Considerés sous les Rapports Médicaux, Hygieniques et Medico-legaux*, 2 vols. Paris: J.B. Bailliere, 1838.

Etoc-Demazy, G.F. *Recherches Statistiques sur le Suicide*. Paris, 1844.

Eusebius, *The Ecclesiastical History*, 2 vols., tr. J.E.L. Oulton. Cambridge, Massachusetts: Loeb Classical Library/Harvard University Press, 1959-64.

Fadiman, Clifton (ed.), *The Little, Brown Book of Anecdotes*. Boston: Little, Brown, 1985.

Falret, J.P., *De l'Hypochondrie et du Suicide*. Paris, 1822.

Farber, Maurice, L., *Theory of Suicide*. New York: Funk & Wagnalls, 1968.

Farberow, Norman L., *Bibliography on Suicide and Suicide Prevention*, P.H.S. Pub. No. 1979. Washington, D.C.: USGPO, 1969.

Farberow, Norman L., *Bibliography on Suicide and Suicide Prevention, 1897-1970*. Washington, D.C.: HEW, 1972.

Farberow, Norman L., "Cultural History of Suicide," in Skandia International Symposium, *Suicide and Attempted Suicide*. Stockholm: Nordiska Bokhandelns Forlag, 1972.

Farberow, Norman L., *Suicide in Different Cultures*. Baltimore: University Park Press, 1975.

Farberow, N.L., (ed.), *The Many Faces of Suicide: Indirect Self-Destructive Behavior*. New York: McGraw-Hill, 1980.

Farberow, N. and E. Shneidman, "Attempted, Threatened and Completed Suicide," *Journal of Abnormal Social Psychiatry*, 50(1955):230.

Farberow, N.L. and E.S. Shneidman (eds.), *The Cry for Help*. New York: McGraw-Hill, 1961.

Fawcett, J.A., M. Leff and William G. Bonney, Jr., "Suicide: Clues from Interpersonal Communication," *Arch. Gen. Psychiatry*, 21:2(1969):129-37.

Fawcett, Jan, *Before It's Too Late*. Denver: The American Association of Suicidology (pamphlet).

Fedden, H.R., *Suicide: A Social and Historical Study*. London: Peter Davies, 1938.

Feldman, Sylvia, Dr., *Choices in Childbirth*. New York: Grosset & Dunlap, 1978.

Firth, R.W., "Suicide and risk-taking in Tikopia society," *Psychiatry*, 24(1961):1-17.

Firth, Raymond W., *Tikopia Ritual and Belief*. Boston: Beacon Press, 1967.

Flood, R.A. and C.P. Seager, "A Retrospective Examination of Psychiatric Case Records of Patients Who Subsequently Committed Suicide," *British Journal of Psychiatry*, 114:509(1968):433-50.

Folk, E.F., "Psychological Continuities: From Dissociative States to Alcohol Use and Suicide in Arctic Populations," *Journal of Operational Psychiatry*, 11(1980):156-161.

Freud, Sigmund, *Beyond the Pleasure Principle*. London: Hogarth Press, 1950; first published, 1922.

Freud, Sigmund, "Mourning and Melancholia," in *Collected Papers*, vol. 4. London: Hogarth Press, 1949.

Friedman, Myra, *Buried Alive: The Biography of Janis Joplin*. New York: William Morrow, 1973.

Gardner, Sandra and Gary Rosenberg, *Teenage Suicide*. New York, J. Messner, 1986.

Garfinkel, Harold, *Studies in Ethnomethodology*. Englewood Cliffs, New Jersey: Prentice-Hall, 1967.

Gaupt, R., *Über den Selbstmord*, 2nd ed. Munich, 1910.

Gerber, K.E., A.M. Nehemkis, N.L. Farberow and J. Williams, "Indirect Self-Destructive Behavior in Chronic Hemodialysis Patients," *Suicide and Life-Threatening Behavior*, 11(1981):31-42.

Gharagozlov, H. and M. Hadjmohammadi, "Report on a Three-Year Follow-Up of 100 Cases of Suicidal Attempts in Shiraz, Iran," *International Journal of Social Psychiatry*, 23(1977):209-210.

Giffin, Mary and Carol Felsenthal, *A Cry for Help: Exploring and Exploding the Myths about Teenage Suicide—A Guide for All Parents of Adolescents*. Garden City: Doubleday, 1983.

Glass, F.L., Mortality of New England Dentists, U.S. Public Health Service Publication, November 999-RH-18. Washington, D.C.: HEW, 1966.

Goethe, Johann Wolfgang von, *The Sorrows of Young Werther*. New York: Random House/ Vintage, 1971; first published, 1774.

Grollman, Earl A., *Suicide: Prevention, Intervention, Postvention*. Boston: Beacon Press, 1971.

Gruhle, H.W., *Selbstmord*. Leipzig: Thieme, 1940.

Guest, Judith, *Ordinary People*. New York: Viking, 1976.

Guillon, C. and Y. Le Bonniec, *Suicide mode d'emploi: Histoire, technique, actualite* (''Suicide: Operating Instructions"). Paris: Editions Alan Moreau, 1982.

Gunther, John, *Death Be Not Proud: A Memoir*. New York: Modern Library, 1953.

Halbwachs, M., *Les Causes du Suicide*. Paris: Alcan, 1930.

Hankoff, L.D. and B. Einsidler, *Suicide: Theory and Clinical Aspects*. Littleton, Massachusetts: PSG Publishing Co., 1979.

Headley, Lee A., Dr., *Suicide in Asia and the Near East*. Berkeley: University of California Press, 1983.

Heller, A., ''Lehre von Selbstmord nach 300 Sektionen," *Münch. Med. Wschr.*, 47(1900):1653.

Hendin, Herbert, *The Age of Sensation*. New York: W.W. Norton, 1975.

Hendin, Herbert, ''Black Suicide," *Arch. of Gen. Psychiatry*, 21(1969):407-22.

Hendin, Herbert, *Black Suicide*. New York: Basic Books, 1969.

Hendin, Herbert, *Suicide in America*. New York: W.W. Norton, 1982.

Hendin, Herbert, *Suicide and Scandinavia*. New York: Grune and Stratton, 1964.

Henry, Andrew and James Short, *Suicide and Homicide: Some Economic, Sociologial and Psychological Aspects of Aggression*. Glencoe, Illinois: Free Press, 1954.

Hewitt, J.H., *After Suicide*. Philadelphia: Westminster Press. 1980.

Huffine, Carol L., PhD, *Social and Cultural Risk Factors for Youth Suicide*. Berkeley: California School of Professional Psychology, 1986.

Hume, D., *An Essay on Suicide*. Yellow Springs, Ohio: Kahoe and Co., 1929; first published, 1783.

Humphry, Derek, *Let Me Die Before I Wake*. Los Angeles: Hemlock Society, 1984.

Humphry, Derek and Ann Wickett, *Jean's Way*. New York: Quartet Books.

Humphry, Derek and Ann Wickett, The Right to Die: Understanding Euthanasia. New York: Harper & Row, 1986.

Hunter, Richard and Ida Mecalpine, *Three Hundred Years of Psychiatry, 1535-1860*. London: Oxford U. Press, 1963

Hyde, Margaret G., *Hot Line!* New York: McGraw-Hill, 1974.

Hyde, Margaret O. and Elizabeth Held Forsyth, MD, *Suicide: The Hidden Epidemic*. New York: Franklin Watts, 1978.

Irfani, S., "Personality Correlates of Suicidal Tendency Among Iranian and Turkish Students," *Journal of Psychology*, 99(1978):151-153.

Jakab, I. and M.D. Howard, *Psychotherapy and Psychosomatics*, 17:5-6(1969), 309-324.

James, William, "Is Life Worth Living?" in *The Will to Believe*. Cambridge, Massachusetts: Harvard University Press, 1979; first published, 1897.

James, William, *Principles of Psychology*. New York: Henry Holt & Co., 1890.

Johansen, Bruce, "The Tepees Are Empty and the Bars Are Full," *Alcoholism*, 1:2(Nov./Dec. 1980), 33-38.

Johnson, Barclay D., "Durkheim's One Cause of Suicide," *American Sociological Review*, 30(December 1965):875-86.

Johnston, Jerry, *Why Suicide?* Nashville: Oliver Nelson, 1987.

Joyce, James, *Ulysses*, 2 vols. Hamburg: Odyssey Press, 1932.

Kant, I., *The Metaphysics of Ethics*, tr. J.W. Semple and T. and T. Clark. Edinburgh, 1971.

Karcher, Charles J. and Leonard L. Linden, "Is Work Conducive to Self-Destruction?" *Suicide and Life-Threatening Behavior*, 12:3(Fall 1982), 151-195.

Kiev, Ari, *The Courage to Live*. New York: Crowell, 1979.

Killinger, John, *The Loneliness of Children*. New York: Vanguard, 1980.

Klagsbrun, Francine, *Too Young to Die: Youth and Suicide*. New York: Pocket Books, 1985; originally published by Houghton-Mifflin, 1976.

Kleist, J., "Age, Depression, Drugs Linked to Suicide," *Science News*, 130:15(October 11, 1986).

Koestler, A., *Exit: A Guide to Self-Deliverance*. London: EXIT, 1981. (Available only to over-25 members of British Voluntary Euthanasia Society [EXIT].)

Koestler, Arthur and Cynthia Koestler, *Stranger on the Square*, with Preface by Harold Harris. New York: Random House, 1984.

Kolata, G., "Manic-Depression: Is It Inherited?" *Science*, 232(May 2, 1986):575.

Kraepelin, Emil, *Lectures on Clinical Psychiatry*. New York: Hafner, 1968; reprint of 1904 ed.

Kreitman, Norman, *Parasuicide*. London: Wiley, 1977.

Kubler-Ross, Elizabeth, *Death: The Final Stage of Growth*. Englewood Cliffs, New Jersey: Prentice-Hall, 1975.

Kubler-Ross, Elizabeth, *On Death and Dying*. New York: Macmillan, 1969.

Kubler-Ross, Elizabeth, *Questions and Answers on Death and Dying*. New York: Macmillan, 1974.

Kubler-Ross, Elizabeth, *To Live Until We Say Goodbye*. Englewood Cliffs, New Jersey: Prentice-Hall, 1978.

Landsberg, P.L., *The Moral Problem of Suicide: The Experience of Death*. New York: Philosophical Library, 1953.

Langone, John, *Death Is a Noun: A View of the End of Life*. Boston: Little, Brown, 1972.

Langway, Lynn, "A Nation of Runaway Kids," *Newsweek* (October 18, 1982).

Leighton, A.H. and C.C. Hughes, "Notes on Eskimo Patterns of Suicide," *Southwestern Journal of Anthropology*, 11(Winter 1955):327-338.

Lester, D., "National Homicide and Suicide Rates as a Function of Political Stability," *Psychological Reports*, 33(1973):298.

Lester, D., B.H. Sell and K.D. Sell, *Suicide: A Guide to Information Sources*. Detroit: Yale Research Co., 1980.

Lester, David, *Why People Kill Themselves*. Springfield, Illinois: C.C. Thomas, 1982.

Levy, J., "Navajo Suicide," *Human Organization*, 24(1965).

Levy, J.E. and S. Kunitz, "Indian Reservations, Anomic and Social Pathologies," *Southwestern Journal of Anthropology* (1971).

Lifton, R.J., *The Broken Connection*. New York: Simon and Schuster, 1979.

Lifton, Robert J., *Death in Life: Survivors of Hiroshima*. New York: Random House, 1967.

Linzer, N. (ed.), *Suicide: The Will to Live vs. the Will to Die*. New York: Human Sciences Press, 1984.

Lisle, E., *Du Suicide Statistique, Histoire et Legislation*. Paris: J.B. Bailliere, 1856.

Long, Kim and Terry Reim, *Kicking the Bucket*. New York: William Morrow/Quill, 1985.

Loo, Robert, "Suicide Among Police in a Federal Force," *Suicide and Life-Threatening Behavior*, 16:3(Fall 1986).

Lopez, Alan D., Dr. (compiled), *Suicide and Self-Inflicted Injury*. Geneva: World Health Organization, 1986.

Lum, D., *Responding to the Suicidal Crisis*. Grand Rapids, Michigan: William B. Eerdmans Publishing Co., 1974.

Mack, John E. and Holly Hickler, *Vivienne: The Life and Suicide of an Adolescent Girl*. Boston: Little, Brown, 1981.

Madison, Arnold, *Suicide and Young People*. New York: Houghton-Mifflin/Clarion, 1978.

Maguire, Daniel C., *Death by Choice*. Garden City: Doubleday, 1973.

Malinowski, B., *Crime and Custom in Savage Society*. London: Routledge and Kegan Paul, 1926.

Malinowski, B., "Suicide: A Chapter in Comparative Ethics," *Sociology Review*, 1(1908):14.

Marcus Aurelius Antoninus, *Meditations of the Emperor Marcus Aurelius*, 2 vols., ed. and tr. A.S.L. Farquarson. New York: Oxford University Press, 1944.

Maris, Ronald, *Biology of Suicide*. New York: Guilford Press, 1986.

Maris, Ronald,*Pathways to Suicide*. Baltimore: The Johns Hopkins University Press, 1981.

Martin, C.E., *Readings in Suicide for Law Enforcement Officers*, Public Administration Series Bibliography P-635. Monticello, Illinois: Vance Bibliographies, 1980.

Masaryk, T.G., *Suicide and the Meaning of Civilization*. Chicago: University of Chicago Press, 1970; first published, 1831.

May, John (ed.), *Curious Facts*. New York: Holt, Rinehart & Winston, 1980.

McCormick, D., *The Unseen Killer*. London: Frederick Muller, Ltd., 1964.

McCoy, Kathleen, *Coping with Teenage Depression: A Parents' Guide*. New York: New American Library, 1982.

McIntosh, John L., *Research on Suicide: A Bibliography*. Westport, Connecticut: Greenwood Press, 1985.

McIntosh, J.L., *Suicide Among U.S. Racial Minorities: A Comprehensive Bibliography*, Public Administration Series Bibliography No. P684. Monticello, Illinois: Vance Bibliographies, 1981.

Mead, George Herbert, *Mind, Self and Society*. Chicago: University of Chicago Press, 1934.

Meerlo, Joost A.M., *Suicide and Mass Suicide*. New York: Grune and Stratton, 1962.

Menninger, Karl A., *Man Against Himself*. New York: Harcourt, Brace and Co., 1938.

Merian, "Sur la crainte de la mort, sur la mépris de la mort, sur le suicide, memoire," vol. 19 of *Histoire de l'Academie Royale des Sciences et Belles-Lettres de Berlin*. 1763.

Meyers, S., "The Child Slayer: A 25 Year Survey of Homicides Involving Preadolescent Victims," *Arch. Gen. Psychiatry*, 17 (1967):211-13.

Meynard, L., *Le Suicide, Étude Morale et Metaphysique*. Paris: Pr. Universitaires de France, 1954.

Miller, Marvin, *Suicide Pacts*, Bibliography R-37. San Diego: Information Center, n.d.

Miller, S.S., J.A. Miller and D.E. Miller, *Life Span Plus*. New York: Macmillan, 1986.

Montaigne, M.E.M., *Essais*, ed. A. Thibaudet. Paris: Gallinard, 1958.

Moore, C., *A Full Inquiry Into the Subject of Suicide*. London: Rivington, 1790.

More, Thomas, *Utopia*. New York: Penguin, 1965; first published, 1551.

Morgan, H.G., *Death Wishes? The Understanding and Management of Deliberate Self-Harm*. New York: John Wiley, 1979.

Morselli, H., *Suicide, an Essay on Comparative Moral Statistics*. New York: D. Appleton and Co., 1881; Arno, 1975.

Mosdzien, K., "Beitrag zur Lösung des Selbstmord-probleme. Ein Vergleich von Motiven mit pathol.-anat. Befunden," *Deutsche Zschr. f. d. ges. gerichtl. Med.*, 6(1925):53-63.

Motto, J., "Suicide Attempts: A Longitudinal View," *Archives of General Psychiatry*, 13(1965):516-20.

Motto, Jerome, "Newspaper Influence on Suicide: A Controlled Study," *Archives of General Psychiatry*, 23(1970):143-48.

Motto, Jerome A. et al., *Standards for Suicide Prevention and Crisis Centers*. New York: Behavioral Publications, 1974.

Myers, S., "The Child Slayer A 25-Year Survey of Homicides Involving Preadolescent Victims," *Arch. Gen. Psychiatry*, 17(1967):211-13.

Neser, J., *Drei Christliche Predigten*. Witterbers: Wolffgang Meissner, 1613.

Neste, E., "Die Beziehungen des Status thymico-lymphaticus zum Selbstmord von Soldaten," *Arch. f. Psychiatrie un Nervenkrankheiten*, 60(1919):43-61.

Newsweek, Editors of, "Chico's Last Act," *Newsweek*, February 7, 1977.

Norman, Jane and Myron Harris, *The Private Life of the American Teenager*. New York: Rawson, Wade, 1981.

O'Brien, Robert and Morris Chafetz, MD, *The Encyclopedia of Alcoholism*. New York: Facts On File, 1982.

O'Brien, Robert and Sidney Cohen, MD, *The Encyclopedia of Drug Abuse*. New York: Facts On File, 1984.

Orner, G. and R.D. Mumma, "Mortality Study of Dentists," Temple University School of Dentistry, 1976.

Osiander, F.B., *Über den Selbstmord, seine Ursachen, Arten, madizinisch-gerichtliche und den Mittel gegen denselben*. Hanover, 1813.

Peck, M., *Youth Suicide*. New York: Springer, 1984.

Perlin, Seymour (ed.), *A Handbook for the Study of Suicide*. New York: Oxford University Press, 1975.

Pfeffer, Cynthia R., *The Suicidal Child*. New York: Guilford Press, 1986.

Pfeiffer, H., *Über den Selbstmord*. Jena: Fischer, 1912.

Philips, E., *New World of Words*. 1662.

Phillips, David, "The Influence of Suggestions on Suicide: Substantive and Theoretical Implications of the Werther Effect," *American Sociological Review*, 39(1974):340-54.

Pierce, Albert, "The Economic Cycle and the Social Suicide Rate," *American Sociological Review*, 32(June 1967):427-62.

Plath, Sylvia, *The Collected Poems: Sylvia Plath*. New York: Harper & Row, 1981.

Pokorny, Alex D., "A Follow-Up Study of 618 Suicidal Patients," *American Journal of Psychiatry*, 122(1966):1109-1116.

Pokorny, Alex D., "Suicide Rates in Various Psychiatric Disorders," *Journal of Nervous, Mental Disorders*, 139(1964):499-506.

Portwood, Doris, *Common Sense Suicide: The Final Right*. New York: Dodd, Mead and Co., 1978.

Post, Hans, *Bibliographie des Selbst Mordes*. Augsburg, 1927.

Praz, Mario, *The Romantic Agony*. New York: Oxford University Press, 1970; first published, 1951.

Prentice, Ann E., *Suicide*. Metuchen, New Jersey: Scarecrow Press, 1974.

Rabkin, Brenda, *Growing Up Dead: A Hard Look at Why Adolescents Commit Suicide*. Nashville, Tennessee: Abingdon, 1979.

Rachels, James, *The End of Life: Euthanasia and Mortality*. New York: Oxford University Press, 1986.

Rasmussen, K., *The Netsilik Eskimos*. New York: AMS Press, 1976; first published, 1931. (Report of the Fifth Thule Expedition, vol. 8.)

Rauscher, William V., *The Case Against Suicide*. New York: St. Martin's Press, 1981.

Rehfisch, E., *Der Selbstmord*. Berlin, 1893.

Rich, C.L. and F.N. Pitts, "Suicide by Psychiatrists: A Study of Medical Specialists Among 18,730 Consecutive Physician Deaths During a Five-Year Period, 1967-1972," *Journal of Clinical Psychiatry*, 41(1980):261-263.

Richman, Joseph, *Family Therapy for Suicidal People*. New York: Springer, 1986.

Robins, E. et al., "The Communications of Suicidal Intent: A Study of 134 Consecutive Cases of Successful (Completed) Suicides," *American Journal of Psychiatry*, 115(1959):724-33.

Rollin, Betty, *Last Wish*. New York: Linden Press/Simon and Schuster, 1985.

Roman, Jo, *Exit House: Choosing Suicide as an Alternative*. New York: Seaview Books, 1980.

Rosen, George, "History in the Study of Suicide," *Psychological Medicine: A Journal for Research in Psychiatry and the Allied Sciences*, 1(1971):4.

Ross, Charlotte P., "The Relationship of Crisis Intervention to Suicide Prevention." Paper delivered at the International Association for Suicide Prevention Conference, Jerusalem, October 1975.

Ross, Charlotte P., *Youth Suicide: and What You Can Do About It*. Washington, D.C.: National Committee for Youth Suicide Prevention, 1984. (Produced and distributed in connection with CBS's "Silence of the Heart," televised on October 30, 1984.)

Rousseau, J.J., *Le Nouvelle Héloise*. Paris, 1761; letters 21 and 22.

Russell, Bertrand, *Autobiobraphy*, vol. 1. Boston: Little, Brown, 1967.

Sainsbury, Peter, *Suicide in London*, Maudsley Monograph No. 1. London: Chapman & Hall, 1955.

Saint-Exupéry, Antoine de, *The Little Prince*. New York: Harcourt, Brace and World, 1943.

Sathyarathi, K., "Usual and Unusual Suicide in Bangalore," *Indian Journal of Social Work*, 36(1975):173-80.

Scarf, Maggie, *Unfinished Business: Pressure Points in the Lives of Women*. Garden City: Doubleday, 1980.

Scheiber, Stephen C. and Brian B. Doyle (eds.), *The Impaired Physician*. New York: Plenum, 1983.

Schmeck, Harold M., Jr., "Defective Gene Tied to Form of Manic-Depressive Illness," *The New York Times* (February 26, 1987).

Schneider, K., *Psychiatrische Vorlesungen für Arzte*. Leipzig, 1934.

Schneider, K., "Selbstmordversuche," *Deutsche Med. Wschr.*, 59(1932):1389.

Schopenhauer, A., "On Suicide," in *Complete Essays of Schopenhauer*, tr. T.B. Saunders. New York: Wiley; first published, 1851.

Seiden, Richard H., "Campus Tragedy: A Study of Student Suicides," *Journal of Abnormal Psychology*, 3(1966):285-289; also in *Contemporary Research in Personality*, (ed.) I.G. Sarason.

Seiden, Richard H., *Suicide Among Youths*, Public Health Service Publ. No. 1971. Chevy Chase, Maryland: USGPO, 1969.

Seiden, Richard H., "We're Driving Young Blacks to Suicide," *Psychology Today* (August 1970).

Serin, S., *Les cases du suicide d'après une enquête médico-sociale dans la Ville de Paris*. Presse médic, 1926.

Serin, S., "Une enquête médico-sociale sur le suicide á Paris," *Ann. medico-psychologie*, 84(1926):356

Seward, Jack, *Hara-Kiri: Japanese Ritual Suicide*. Rutland, Vermont: Charles F. Tuttle, 1968.

Sexton, Anne, *Live or Die*. Boston: Houghton-Mifflin, 1966.

Shneidman, Edwin S., *Death of Man*. New York: Jason Aronson, 1983; first published, 1973.

Shneidman, Edwin S., *Definition of Suicide*. New York: John Wiley & Sons, 1985.

Shneidman, E., *Voices of Death*. New York: Harper & Row, 1980; Bantam, 1982.

Shneidman, E.S. (ed.), *Essays in Self-Destruction*. New York: J.Aronson, 1967.

Shneidman, Edwin S. (ed.), *Suicidology: Contemporary Developments*. New York: Grune and Stratton, 1976.

Shneidman, E.S. and N.L. Farberow, *Clues to Suicide*. New York: McGraw-Hill, 1957.

Shneidman, E.S., N.L. Farberow and R.E. Lifman (eds.), *The Psychology of Suicide*. New York: Science House, 1970.

Shneidman, Edwin S. and Philip Mandelkorn, *Suicide—It Doesn't Have to Happen*. West Point, Pennsylvania: MSD-Health Information Services, in cooperation with the American Association of Suicidology.

Sieveking, E.H., H. Koopman and A. Bottiger, "Die Selbstmorde im Hamburg wahrend der letzen drei Jahrfünte (1909-23)," *Deutsche Med. Wschr.*, 51(1925):694-698.

Siljeström, "Om mord och sjelfmord i Sverige under tidsskifen, 1750-1870," *Statistisk. Tidskr.*, 145(1875).

Smart, William E., "When Parting's Not Such Sweet Sorrow," *The Washington Post*, November 18, 1986.

Sobell, M.B. and L.C. Sobell, *Behavioral Treatment of Alcohol Problems*. New York: Plenum Press, 1978.

Stack, Steven, "A Leveling Off in Young Suicides," *The Wall Street Journal*, May 28, 1986.

Steinmetz, S.R., "Suicide Among Primitive Peoples," *American Anthropologist*, 7(1894):53-60.

Stelzner, H., *Analyse von 200 Selbstmordfällen*. Berlin: S. Karger, 1906.

Stengel, E., *Suicide and Attempted Suicide*, rev. ed. New York: Jason Aronson, 1974; first published, 1964.

Stevens, William K., "Official Calls In Press and Kills Himself," *The New York Times*, January 23, 1987.

St. John-Stevas, Norman, *The Right to Life*. New York: Holt, Rinehart and Winston, 1964.

Sym, J., *Life's Preservation Against Self-Killing*. London: Dawlman and Fawne, 1637.

Szasz, Thomas, *Law, Liberty and Psychiatry: An Inquiry into the Social Uses of Mental Health Practices*. New York: Collier, 1968.

Szasz, Thomas, *The Second Sin*. Garden City: Anchor, 1974.

Tayal, SS., "The Communication of Suicidal Ideation in Art Therapy," *Psychiatry and Art*, 2:205-209.

Time, Editors of, "Freddie Prinze: Too Much Too Soon," *Time*, 190:37(February 7, 1977).

Toolan, James M., "Depression in Children and Adolescents," *American Journal of Orthopsychiatry*, 32(1962):405-415.

Traufman, J. and C. Pollard, *Literature and Medicine: An Annotated Bibliography*. Pittsburgh: University of Pittsburgh Press, 1982.

Varah, Chad, *The Samaritans: To Help Those Tempted to Suicide or Despair*. New York: Macmillan, 1966.

Voltaire, F.M.A., *De Caton, du suicide, et du livre de l'abbe de Saint-Cyran qui legitime le Suicide*. 1766.

Wagner, A., *Die Gesetzmassingkeit in den Scheinbar Willkurlichen Menschlichen Handlungen vom Standpunkt der Statistik*. Hamburg, 1864.

Wallace, Samuel E., *After Suicide*. New York: John Wiley & Sons, 1973.

Wassermeyer, "Über den Selbstmord," *Arch. fur Psychiatrie und Nervenkrankheiten*, 50(1913):255-284.

Weber, Max, *The Theory of Social and Economic Organization*. New York: Macmillan/Free Press of Glencoe, 1947.

Wechsler, James A., *In a Darkness*. New York: W.W. Norton, 1972.

Weisman, Avery and Robert Kastenbaum, *The Psychological Autopsy: A Study of the Terminal Phase of Life*. New York: Behavioral Publications, 1968.

Wenzel, Siegfried, *The Sin of Sloth, Acedia in Medieval Thought and Literature*. Chapel Hill: University of North Carolina, 1967.

West, Jessamyn, *The Woman Said Yes*. New York: Harcourt Brace Jovanovich, 1976.

Westermarck, E., "Suicide: A Chapter in Comparative Ethics," *Sociological Review*, 1(1908):12-33.

Weyer, E.C., *The Eskimos*. New Haven, Connecticut: Yale University Press, 1932.

Williams, G., *The Sanctity of Life and the Criminal Law*. New York: Alfred A. Knopf, 1957.

Winslow, Forbes, *The Anatomy of Suicide*. London, 1840.

Wofgang, Marvin, "An Analysis of Homicide-Suicide," *Journal of Clinical and Experimental Psychopathology*, 19(1958):208-18.

Wolman, Benjamin and H.H. Krauss (eds.), *Between Survuval and Suicide*. New York: Halsted Press, 1976.

Yourcenar, Marguerite, *Mishima: A Vision of the Void*. New York: Farrar, Straus & Giroux, 1986.

Zilboorg, G., "Considerations on Suicide," *American Journal of Orthopsychiatry*, 15:31.

Zilboorg, G., "Suicide Among Civilized and Primitive Roles," *American Journal of Psychiatry*, 92(1936):1347-1369.

INDEX